HAKIM'S ODYSSEY

FABIEN TOULMÉ

HAKIM'S ODYSSEY

Book 1: From Syria to Turkey

graphic mundi

To all those who, like Hakim and his family, have had to flee their countries.

PREFACE

Using a spoken account as the basis for transcribing a life—or a part of one—as a book is a particularly delicate undertaking, since it involves presenting an experience that is not the author's own.

Before I set about writing this graphic novel, I spent a lot of time considering the question of respecting the original story that I was being told, and I was very concerned about the idea of betraying, in one way or another, what was being given to me.

I quickly realized that I couldn't stick to reality perfectly: I wasn't there to see the things Hakim had seen, or hear what he'd heard…

And of course there's the old Italian saying: "Traduttore, traditore" (to translate is to betray).

Hakim and his wife don't speak French, so all the interviews that took place over the course of the book's development were conducted in the presence of an interpreter (whom I've chosen, for purely narrative reasons, not to show in the book).

In the creation of this book, these "betrayals," which I was so worried about, were therefore many: the translation of my questions for Hakim, then of his answers, then their transcription into written words and finally art…

Not to mention the changing of certain details and names to preserve the main character's anonymity, and thus his and his family's safety.

Even so, I've done my best to remain true to nature and, to the extent that I could, to the words that were entrusted to me.

I daresay my "betrayals" have changed nothing of the substance of the narrative, which is a true story.

Fabien Toulmé

Prologue

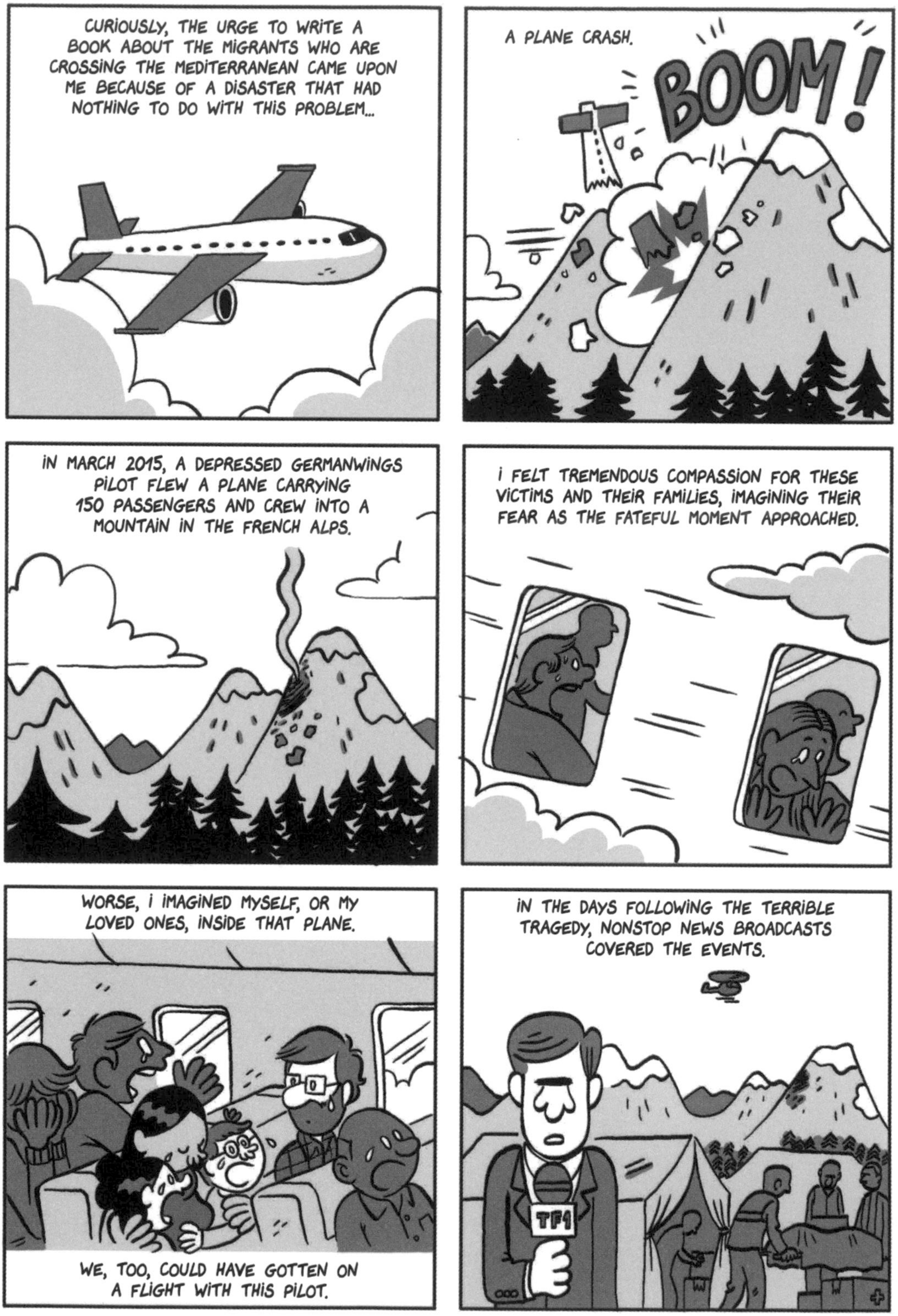
CURIOUSLY, THE URGE TO WRITE A BOOK ABOUT THE MIGRANTS WHO ARE CROSSING THE MEDITERRANEAN CAME UPON ME BECAUSE OF A DISASTER THAT HAD NOTHING TO DO WITH THIS PROBLEM...
A PLANE CRASH.
BOOM!
IN MARCH 2015, A DEPRESSED GERMANWINGS PILOT FLEW A PLANE CARRYING 150 PASSENGERS AND CREW INTO A MOUNTAIN IN THE FRENCH ALPS.
I FELT TREMENDOUS COMPASSION FOR THESE VICTIMS AND THEIR FAMILIES, IMAGINING THEIR FEAR AS THE FATEFUL MOMENT APPROACHED.
WORSE, I IMAGINED MYSELF, OR MY LOVED ONES, INSIDE THAT PLANE.
WE, TOO, COULD HAVE GOTTEN ON A FLIGHT WITH THIS PILOT.
IN THE DAYS FOLLOWING THE TERRIBLE TRAGEDY, NONSTOP NEWS BROADCASTS COVERED THE EVENTS.
TF1

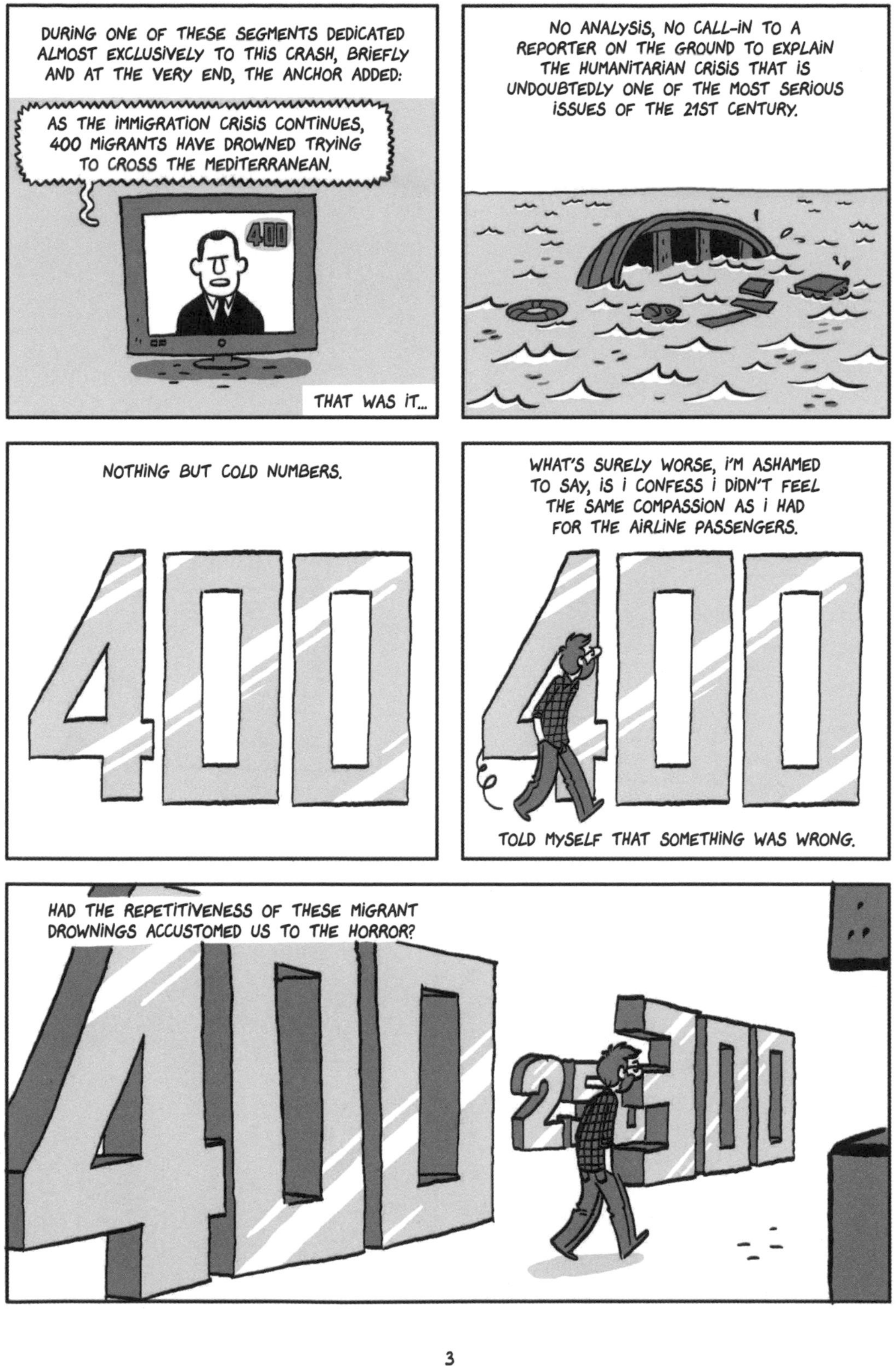
DURING ONE OF THESE SEGMENTS DEDICATED ALMOST EXCLUSIVELY TO THIS CRASH, BRIEFLY AND AT THE VERY END, THE ANCHOR ADDED:
AS THE IMMIGRATION CRISIS CONTINUES, 400 MIGRANTS HAVE DROWNED TRYING TO CROSS THE MEDITERRANEAN.
400
THAT WAS IT...
NO ANALYSIS, NO CALL-IN TO A REPORTER ON THE GROUND TO EXPLAIN THE HUMANITARIAN CRISIS THAT IS UNDOUBTEDLY ONE OF THE MOST SERIOUS ISSUES OF THE 21ST CENTURY.
NOTHING BUT COLD NUMBERS.
400
WHAT'S SURELY WORSE, I'M ASHAMED TO SAY, IS I CONFESS I DIDN'T FEEL THE SAME COMPASSION AS I HAD FOR THE AIRLINE PASSENGERS.
400
TOLD MYSELF THAT SOMETHING WAS WRONG.
HAD THE REPETITIVENESS OF THESE MIGRANT DROWNINGS ACCUSTOMED US TO THE HORROR?
400

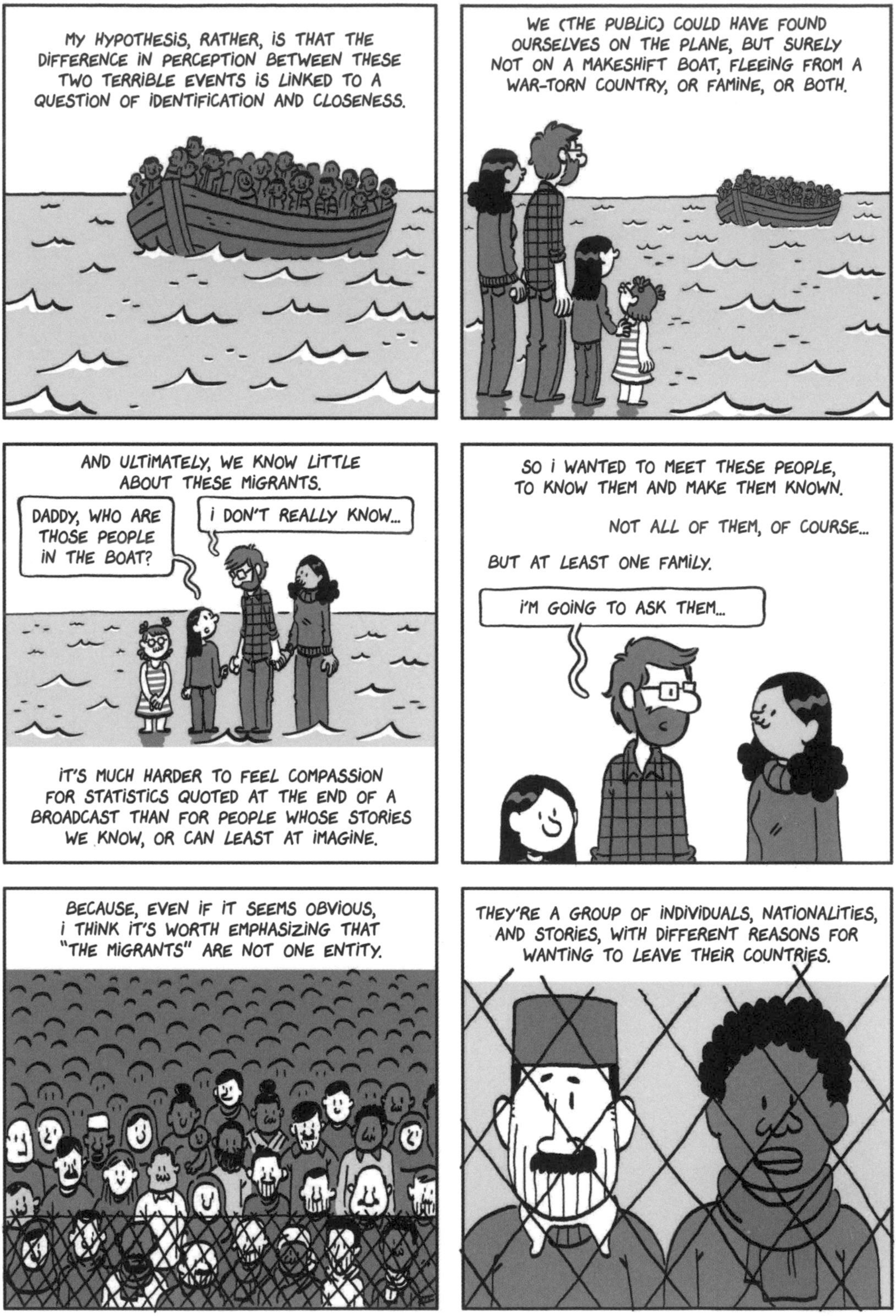
MY HYPOTHESIS, RATHER, IS THAT THE DIFFERENCE IN PERCEPTION BETWEEN THESE TWO TERRIBLE EVENTS IS LINKED TO A QUESTION OF IDENTIFICATION AND CLOSENESS.
WE (THE PUBLIC) COULD HAVE FOUND OURSELVES ON THE PLANE, BUT SURELY NOT ON A MAKESHIFT BOAT, FLEEING FROM A WAR-TORN COUNTRY, OR FAMINE, OR BOTH.
AND ULTIMATELY, WE KNOW LITTLE ABOUT THESE MIGRANTS.
DADDY, WHO ARE THOSE PEOPLE IN THE BOAT?
I DON'T REALLY KNOW...
IT'S MUCH HARDER TO FEEL COMPASSION FOR STATISTICS QUOTED AT THE END OF A BROADCAST THAN FOR PEOPLE WHOSE STORIES WE KNOW, OR CAN LEAST AT IMAGINE.
SO I WANTED TO MEET THESE PEOPLE, TO KNOW THEM AND MAKE THEM KNOWN.
NOT ALL OF THEM, OF COURSE...
BUT AT LEAST ONE FAMILY.
I'M GOING TO ASK THEM...
BECAUSE, EVEN IF IT SEEMS OBVIOUS, I THINK IT'S WORTH EMPHASIZING THAT "THE MIGRANTS" ARE NOT ONE ENTITY.
THEY'RE A GROUP OF INDIVIDUALS, NATIONALITIES, AND STORIES, WITH DIFFERENT REASONS FOR WANTING TO LEAVE THEIR COUNTRIES.

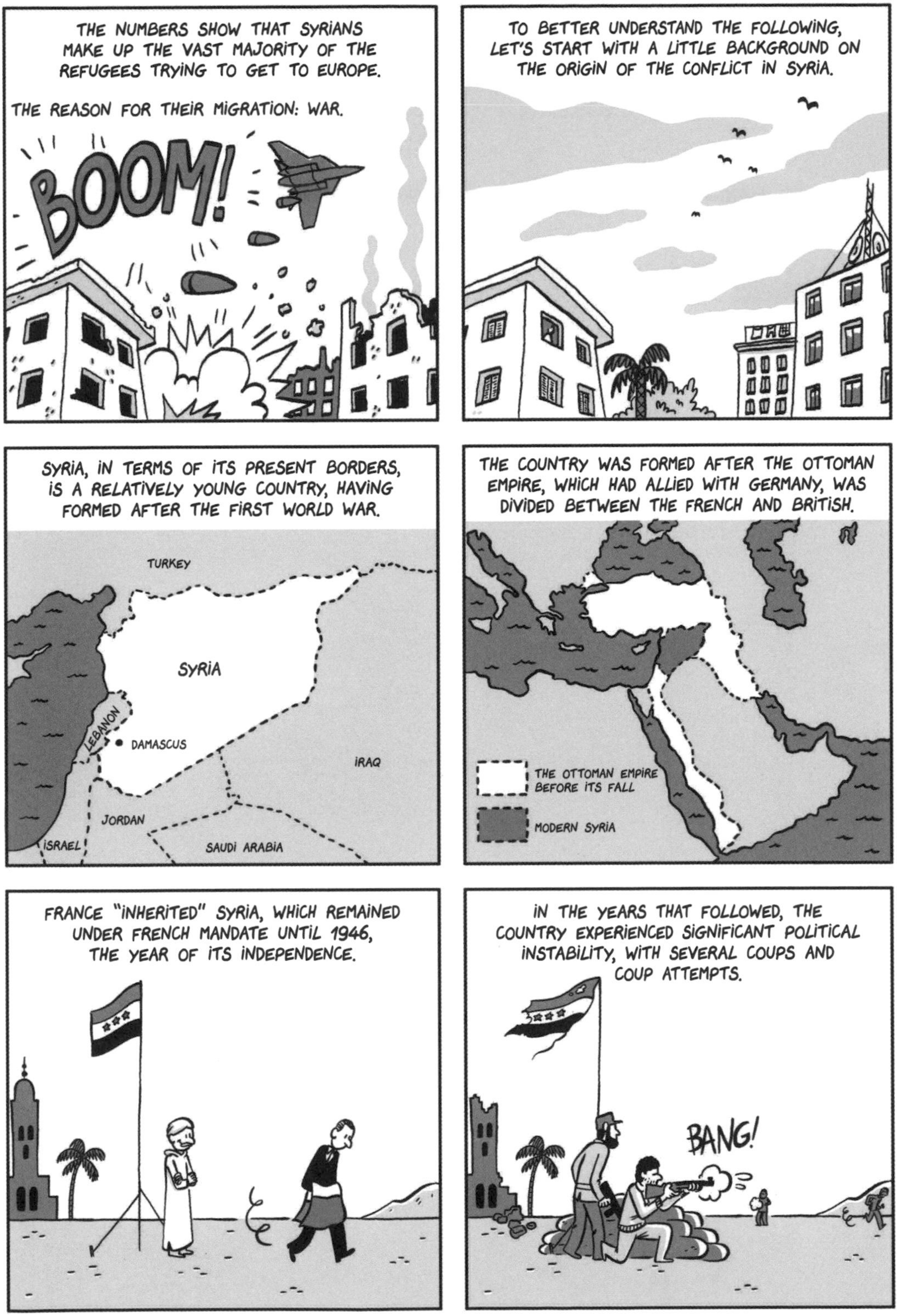
THE NUMBERS SHOW THAT SYRIANS MAKE UP THE VAST MAJORITY OF THE REFUGEES TRYING TO GET TO EUROPE.
THE REASON FOR THEIR MIGRATION: WAR.
BOOM!
TO BETTER UNDERSTAND THE FOLLOWING, LET'S START WITH A LITTLE BACKGROUND ON THE ORIGIN OF THE CONFLICT IN SYRIA.
SYRIA, IN TERMS OF ITS PRESENT BORDERS, IS A RELATIVELY YOUNG COUNTRY, HAVING FORMED AFTER THE FIRST WORLD WAR.
TURKEY
SYRIA
LEBANON
DAMASCUS
IRAQ
JORDAN
ISRAEL
SAUDI ARABIA
THE COUNTRY WAS FORMED AFTER THE OTTOMAN EMPIRE, WHICH HAD ALLIED WITH GERMANY, WAS DIVIDED BETWEEN THE FRENCH AND BRITISH.
THE OTTOMAN EMPIRE BEFORE ITS FALL
MODERN SYRIA
FRANCE "INHERITED" SYRIA, WHICH REMAINED UNDER FRENCH MANDATE UNTIL 1946, THE YEAR OF ITS INDEPENDENCE.
IN THE YEARS THAT FOLLOWED, THE COUNTRY EXPERIENCED SIGNIFICANT POLITICAL INSTABILITY, WITH SEVERAL COUPS AND COUP ATTEMPTS.
BANG!

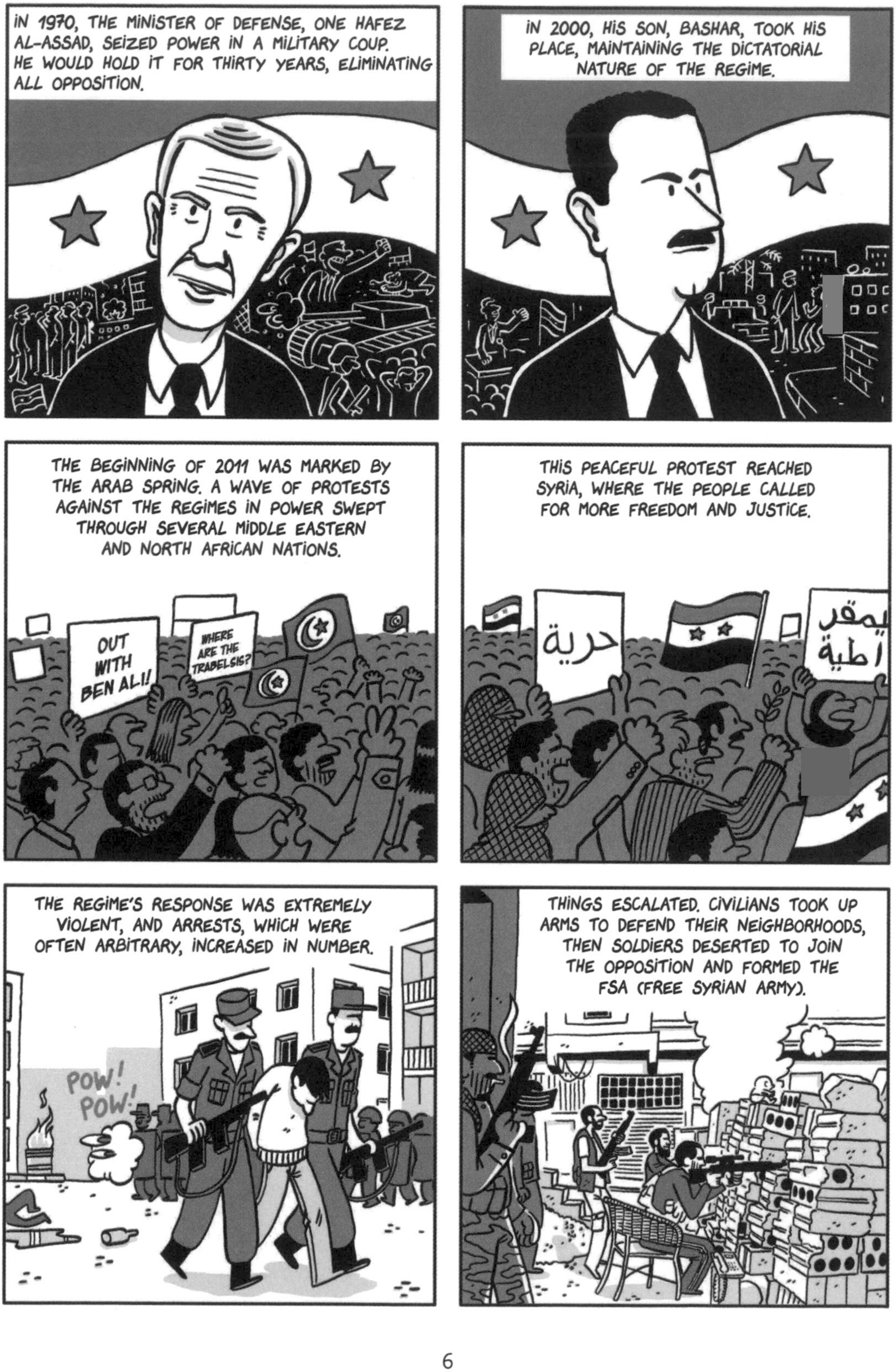
IN 1970, THE MINISTER OF DEFENSE, ONE HAFEZ AL-ASSAD, SEIZED POWER IN A MILITARY COUP. HE WOULD HOLD IT FOR THIRTY YEARS, ELIMINATING ALL OPPOSITION.
IN 2000, HIS SON, BASHAR, TOOK HIS PLACE, MAINTAINING THE DICTATORIAL NATURE OF THE REGIME.
THE BEGINNING OF 2011 WAS MARKED BY THE ARAB SPRING. A WAVE OF PROTESTS AGAINST THE REGIMES IN POWER SWEPT THROUGH SEVERAL MIDDLE EASTERN AND NORTH AFRICAN NATIONS.
OUT WITH BEN ALI!
WHERE ARE THE TRABELSIS?
THIS PEACEFUL PROTEST REACHED SYRIA, WHERE THE PEOPLE CALLED FOR MORE FREEDOM AND JUSTICE.
حرية
THE REGIME'S RESPONSE WAS EXTREMELY VIOLENT, AND ARRESTS, WHICH WERE OFTEN ARBITRARY, INCREASED IN NUMBER.
POW! POW!
THINGS ESCALATED. CIVILIANS TOOK UP ARMS TO DEFEND THEIR NEIGHBORHOODS, THEN SOLDIERS DESERTED TO JOIN THE OPPOSITION AND FORMED THE FSA (FREE SYRIAN ARMY).

LITTLE BY LITTLE, THE FSA GREW STRONGER AND GAINED GROUND. MOST NOTABLY, IT SEIZED SEVERAL AREAS IN ALEPPO, THE SECOND-LARGEST CITY IN THE COUNTRY.

AREAS WHERE THE FSA WAS PRESENT AS OF JULY 2012.

ALEPPO

THE REGIME RESPONDED BY BOMBING THE ZONES WHERE CIVILIANS STILL LIVED, ON AN ALMOST DAILY BASIS.

THESE TWO PLAYERS IN THE CONFLICT WERE JOINED BY TWO OTHER FORCES THAT TOOK ADVANTAGE OF THE REGIME'S FRAGILITY:

DAESH, MADE UP OF 80% NON-SYRIANS, WHICH WAS TRYING TO EXPAND ITS CALIPHATE.

THE YPG (SYRIAN KURDISH FORCES), FIGHTING FOR THEIR AUTONOMY IN THE NORTHWESTERN PART OF THE COUNTRY.

THIS ALREADY VERY COMPLEX SITUATION HAS GOTTEN EVEN MORE COMPLICATED AS THE CONFLICT HAS DRAWN GLOBAL ATTENTION. EACH OF THE CAMPS IS SUPPORTED BY COUNTRIES THAT HAVE AN INTEREST IN ONE OR THE OTHER BEING VICTORIOUS (OR, FOR THAT MATTER, DEFEATED).

	ASSAD REGIME	ANTI-ASSAD REBELS	KURDISH FORCES	
FORCES PRESENT IN SYRIA	ASSAD REGIME	ANTI-ASSAD REBELS	KURDISH FORCES	
REGIONAL SUPPORT	LEBANESE HEZBOLLAH, IRAQ, IRAN	TURKEY, QATAR, JORDAN, SAUDI ARABIA	TURKISH KURDS (PKK), IRAQI KURDS (PDK)	
GLOBAL SUPPORT	RUSSIA	UNITED STATES, CANADA, FRANCE	THE UK, AUSTRALIA	

(CHART MAY HAVE CHANGED BY THE TIME YOU READ THIS)

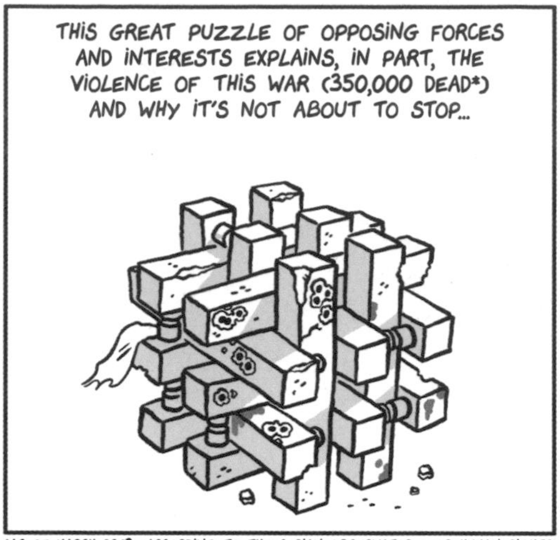
THIS GREAT PUZZLE OF OPPOSING FORCES AND INTERESTS EXPLAINS, IN PART, THE VIOLENCE OF THIS WAR (350,000 DEAD*) AND WHY IT'S NOT ABOUT TO STOP...

*AS OF MARCH 2018 (ACCORDING TO THE SYRIAN OBSERVATORY FOR HUMAN RIGHTS)

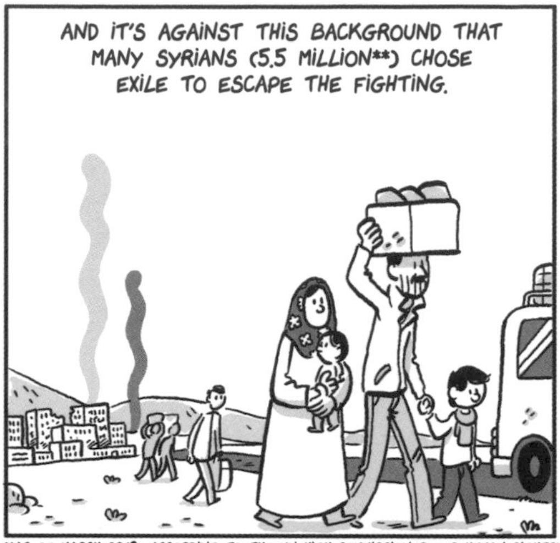
AND IT'S AGAINST THIS BACKGROUND THAT MANY SYRIANS (5.5 MILLION**) CHOSE EXILE TO ESCAPE THE FIGHTING.

**AS OF MARCH 2018 (ACCORDING TO THE UN HIGH COMMISSIONER FOR HUMAN RIGHTS)

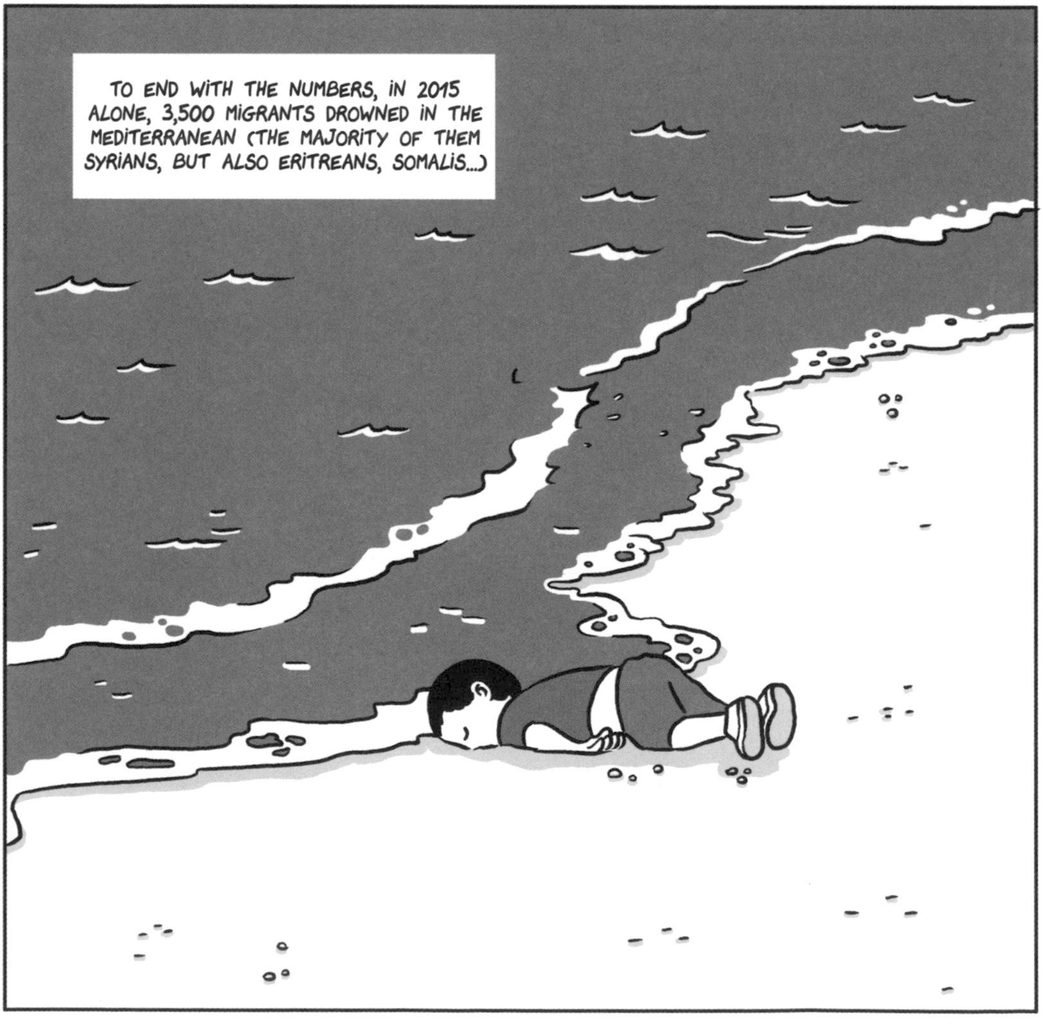
TO END WITH THE NUMBERS, IN 2015 ALONE, 3,500 MIGRANTS DROWNED IN THE MEDITERRANEAN (THE MAJORITY OF THEM SYRIANS, BUT ALSO ERITREANS, SOMALIS...)

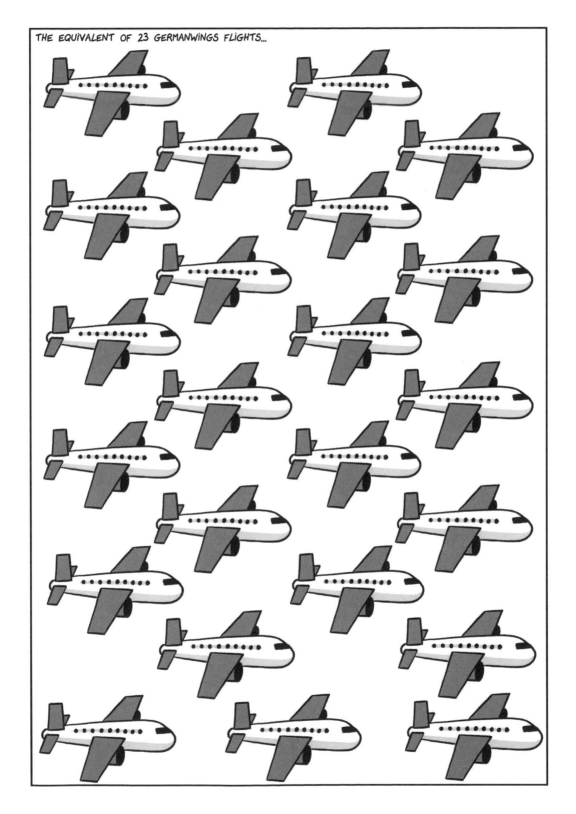

THE EQUIVALENT OF 23 GERMANWINGS FLIGHTS...

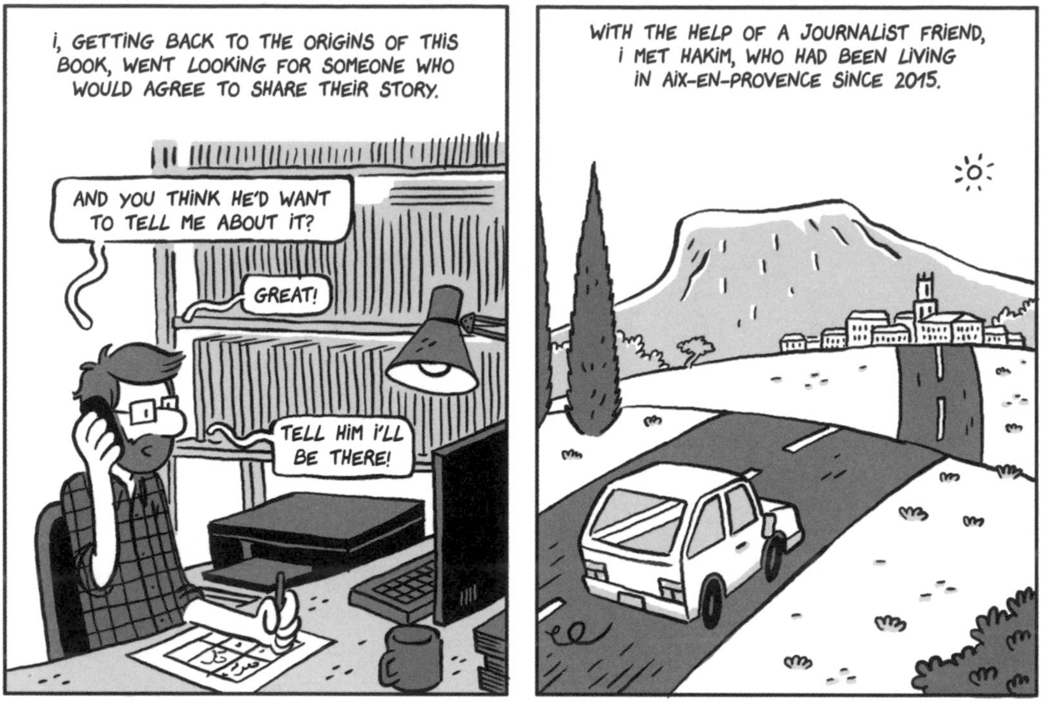
I, GETTING BACK TO THE ORIGINS OF THIS BOOK, WENT LOOKING FOR SOMEONE WHO WOULD AGREE TO SHARE THEIR STORY.
AND YOU THINK HE'D WANT TO TELL ME ABOUT IT?
GREAT!
TELL HIM I'LL BE THERE!
WITH THE HELP OF A JOURNALIST FRIEND, I MET HAKIM, WHO HAD BEEN LIVING IN AIX-EN-PROVENCE SINCE 2015.

I REALLY WANTED TO LISTEN AND THEN TELL THE STORY OF HIS JOURNEY FROM SYRIA.

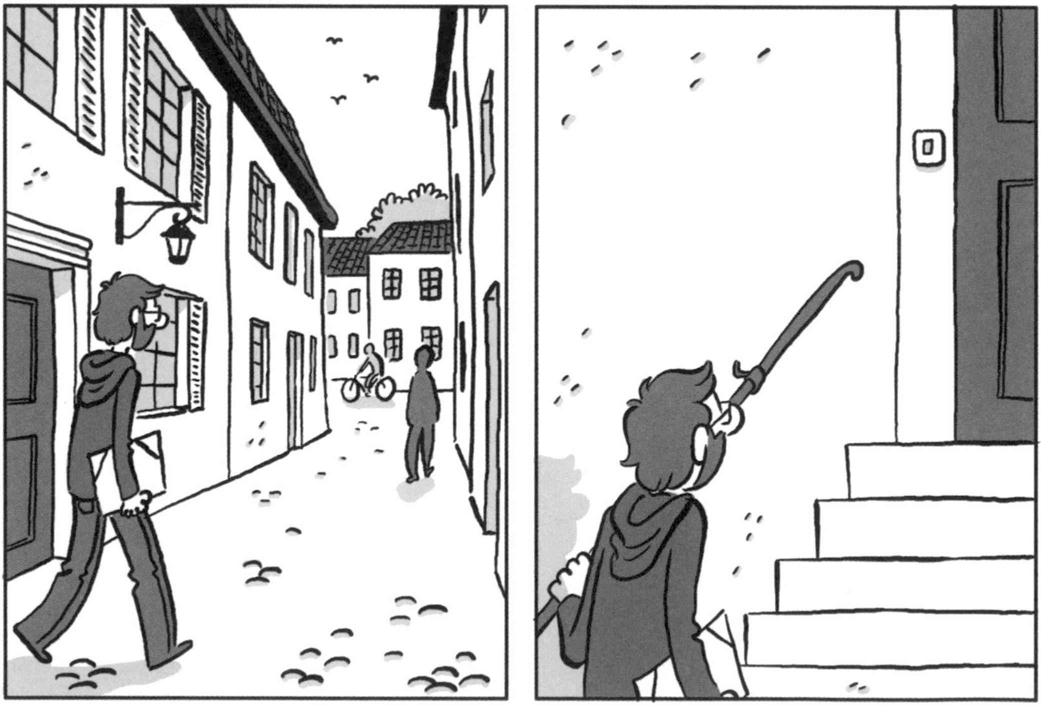

SO IT'S HIS STORY, AND HIS FAMILY'S, THAT YOU'LL READ IN THE PAGES THAT FOLLOW.

Chapter 1:
Hakim and Syria
(Before 2011)

"GARDENER? YOU WANT TO BE A GARDENER LIKE ME?"

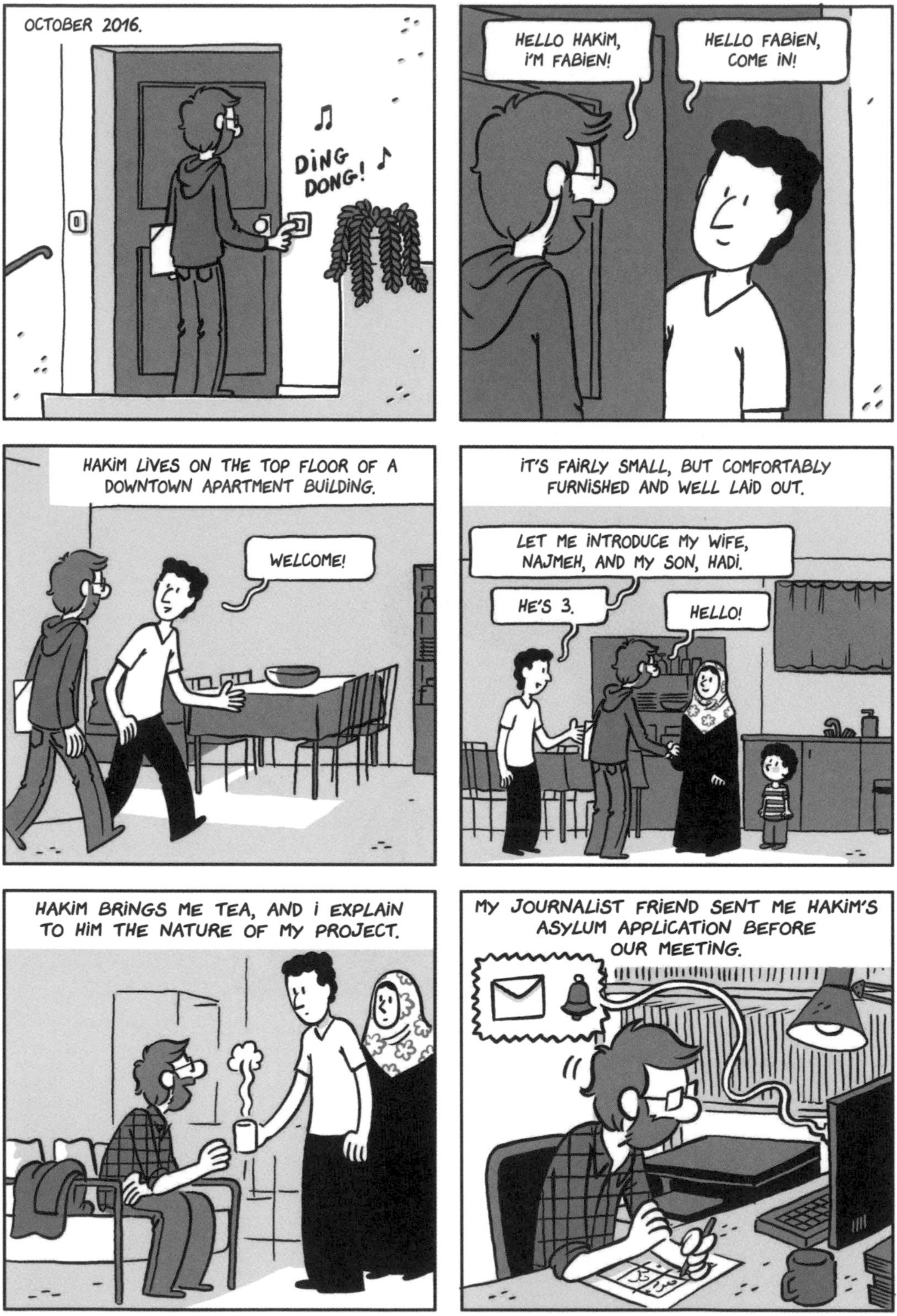
OCTOBER 2016.
DING DONG!
HELLO HAKIM, I'M FABIEN!
HELLO FABIEN, COME IN!
HAKIM LIVES ON THE TOP FLOOR OF A DOWNTOWN APARTMENT BUILDING.
WELCOME!
IT'S FAIRLY SMALL, BUT COMFORTABLY FURNISHED AND WELL LAID OUT.
LET ME INTRODUCE MY WIFE, NAJMEH, AND MY SON, HADI.
HE'S 3.
HELLO!
HAKIM BRINGS ME TEA, AND I EXPLAIN TO HIM THE NATURE OF MY PROJECT.
MY JOURNALIST FRIEND SENT ME HAKIM'S ASYLUM APPLICATION BEFORE OUR MEETING.

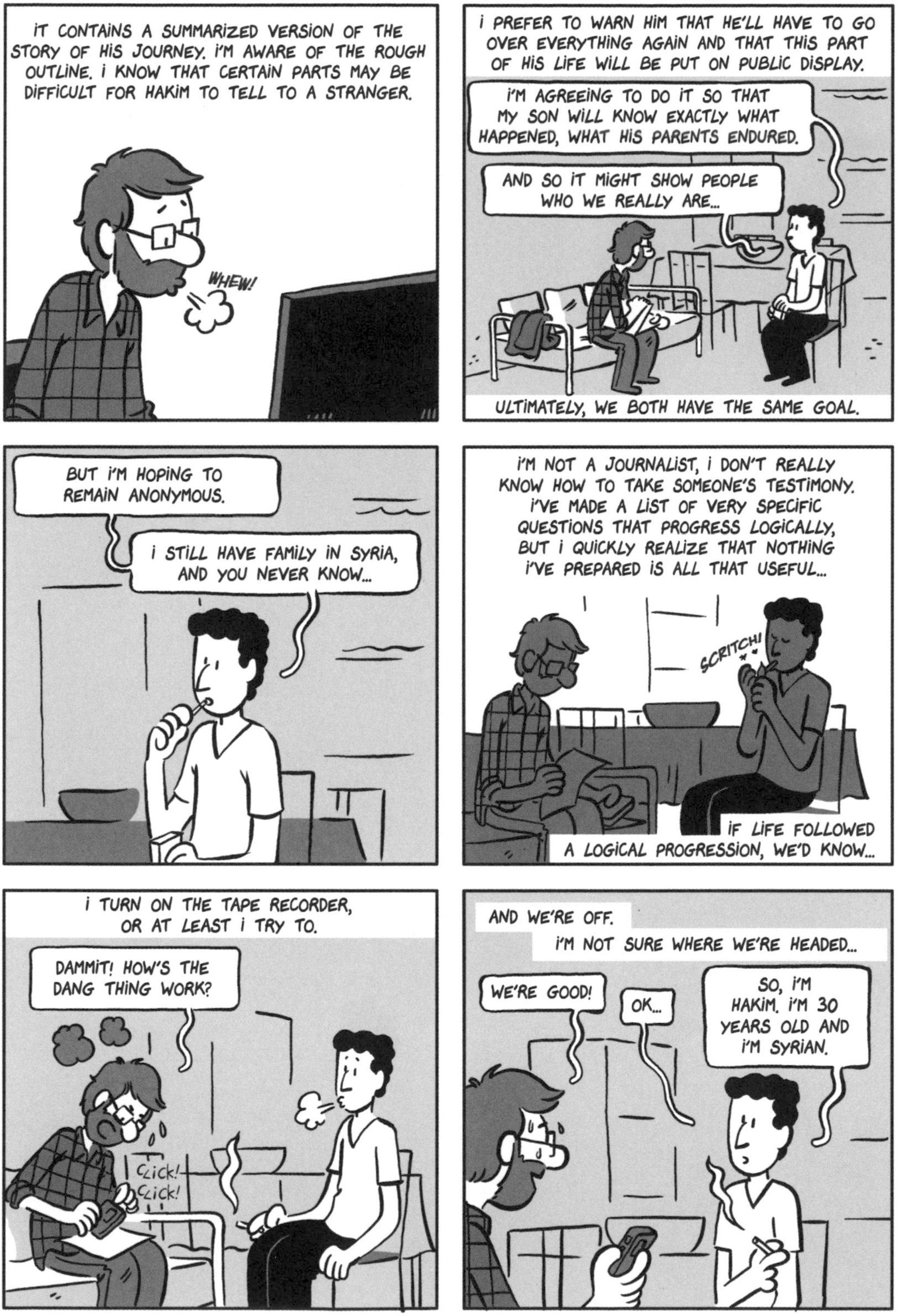
IT CONTAINS A SUMMARIZED VERSION OF THE STORY OF HIS JOURNEY. I'M AWARE OF THE ROUGH OUTLINE. I KNOW THAT CERTAIN PARTS MAY BE DIFFICULT FOR HAKIM TO TELL TO A STRANGER.
WHEW!
I PREFER TO WARN HIM THAT HE'LL HAVE TO GO OVER EVERYTHING AGAIN AND THAT THIS PART OF HIS LIFE WILL BE PUT ON PUBLIC DISPLAY.
I'M AGREEING TO DO IT SO THAT MY SON WILL KNOW EXACTLY WHAT HAPPENED, WHAT HIS PARENTS ENDURED.
AND SO IT MIGHT SHOW PEOPLE WHO WE REALLY ARE...
ULTIMATELY, WE BOTH HAVE THE SAME GOAL.
BUT I'M HOPING TO REMAIN ANONYMOUS.
I STILL HAVE FAMILY IN SYRIA, AND YOU NEVER KNOW...
I'M NOT A JOURNALIST, I DON'T REALLY KNOW HOW TO TAKE SOMEONE'S TESTIMONY. I'VE MADE A LIST OF VERY SPECIFIC QUESTIONS THAT PROGRESS LOGICALLY, BUT I QUICKLY REALIZE THAT NOTHING I'VE PREPARED IS ALL THAT USEFUL...
SCRITCH!
IF LIFE FOLLOWED A LOGICAL PROGRESSION, WE'D KNOW...
I TURN ON THE TAPE RECORDER, OR AT LEAST I TRY TO.
DAMMIT! HOW'S THE DANG THING WORK?
CLICK! CLICK!
AND WE'RE OFF.
I'M NOT SURE WHERE WE'RE HEADED...
WE'RE GOOD!
OK...
SO, I'M HAKIM. I'M 30 YEARS OLD AND I'M SYRIAN.

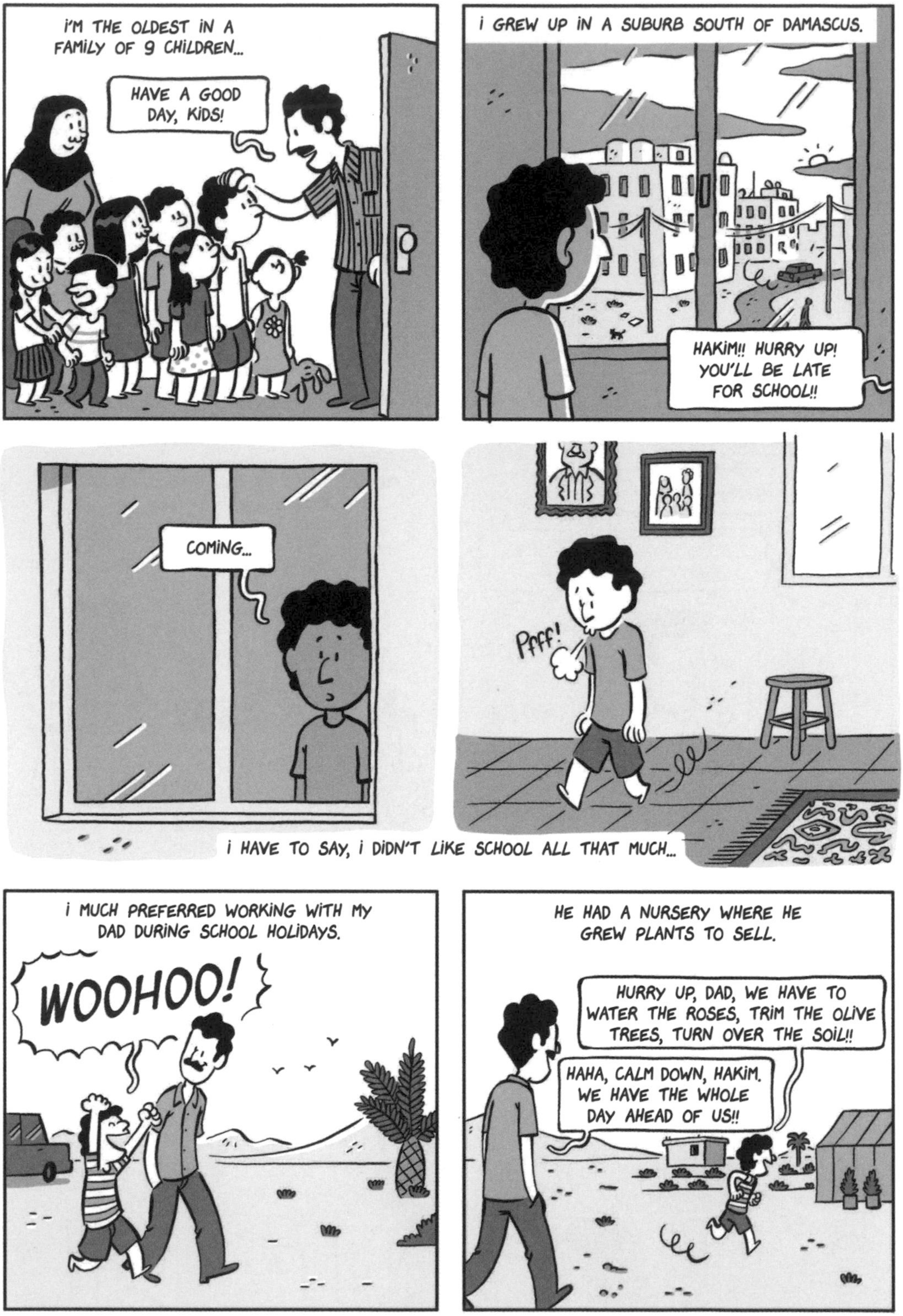
I'M THE OLDEST IN A FAMILY OF 9 CHILDREN...
HAVE A GOOD DAY, KIDS!
I GREW UP IN A SUBURB SOUTH OF DAMASCUS.
HAKIM!! HURRY UP! YOU'LL BE LATE FOR SCHOOL!!
COMING...
Pfff!
I HAVE TO SAY, I DIDN'T LIKE SCHOOL ALL THAT MUCH...
I MUCH PREFERRED WORKING WITH MY DAD DURING SCHOOL HOLIDAYS.
WOOHOO!
HE HAD A NURSERY WHERE HE GREW PLANTS TO SELL.
HURRY UP, DAD, WE HAVE TO WATER THE ROSES, TRIM THE OLIVE TREES, TURN OVER THE SOIL!!
HAHA, CALM DOWN, HAKIM. WE HAVE THE WHOLE DAY AHEAD OF US!!

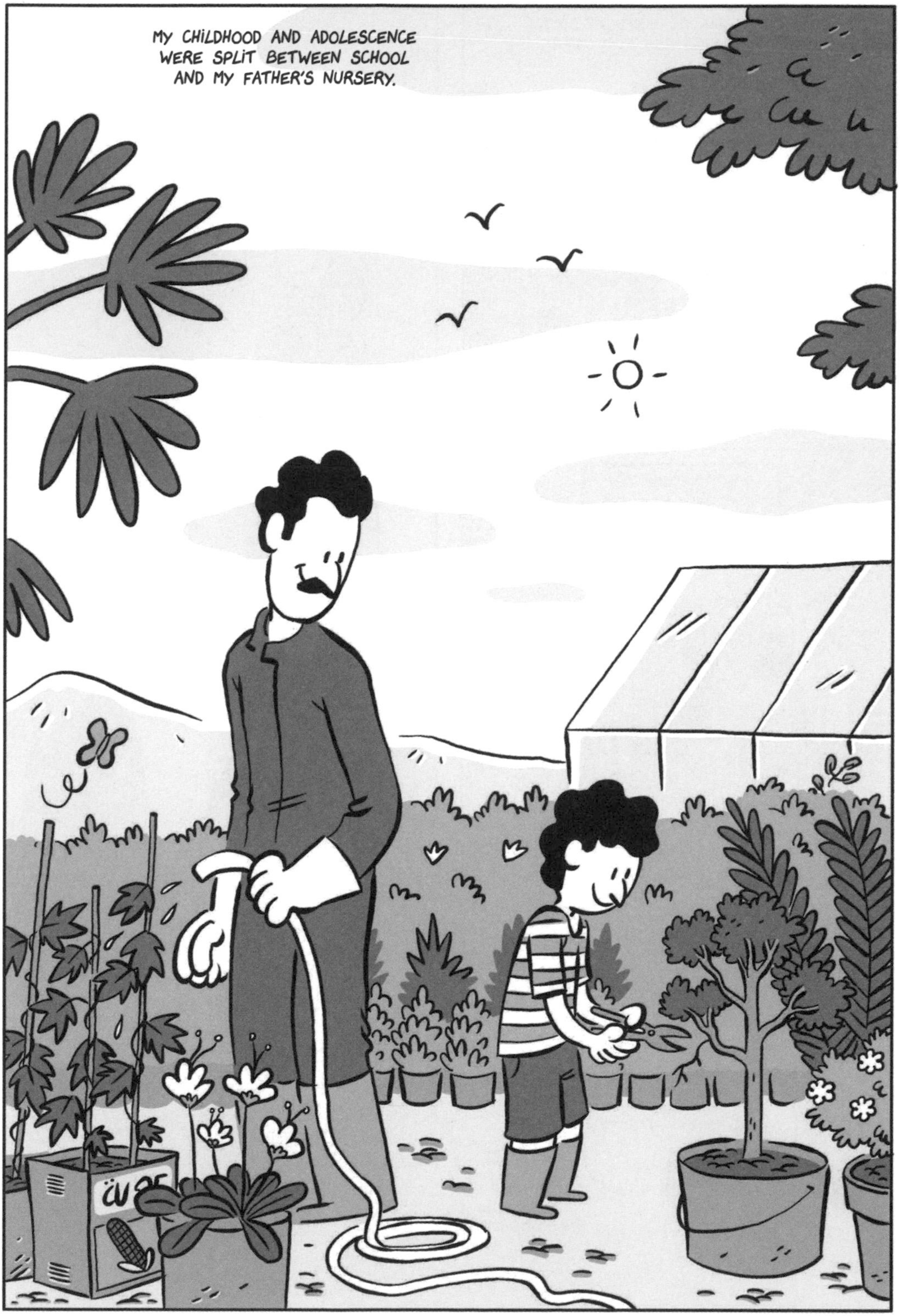
MY CHILDHOOD AND ADOLESCENCE WERE SPLIT BETWEEN SCHOOL AND MY FATHER'S NURSERY.

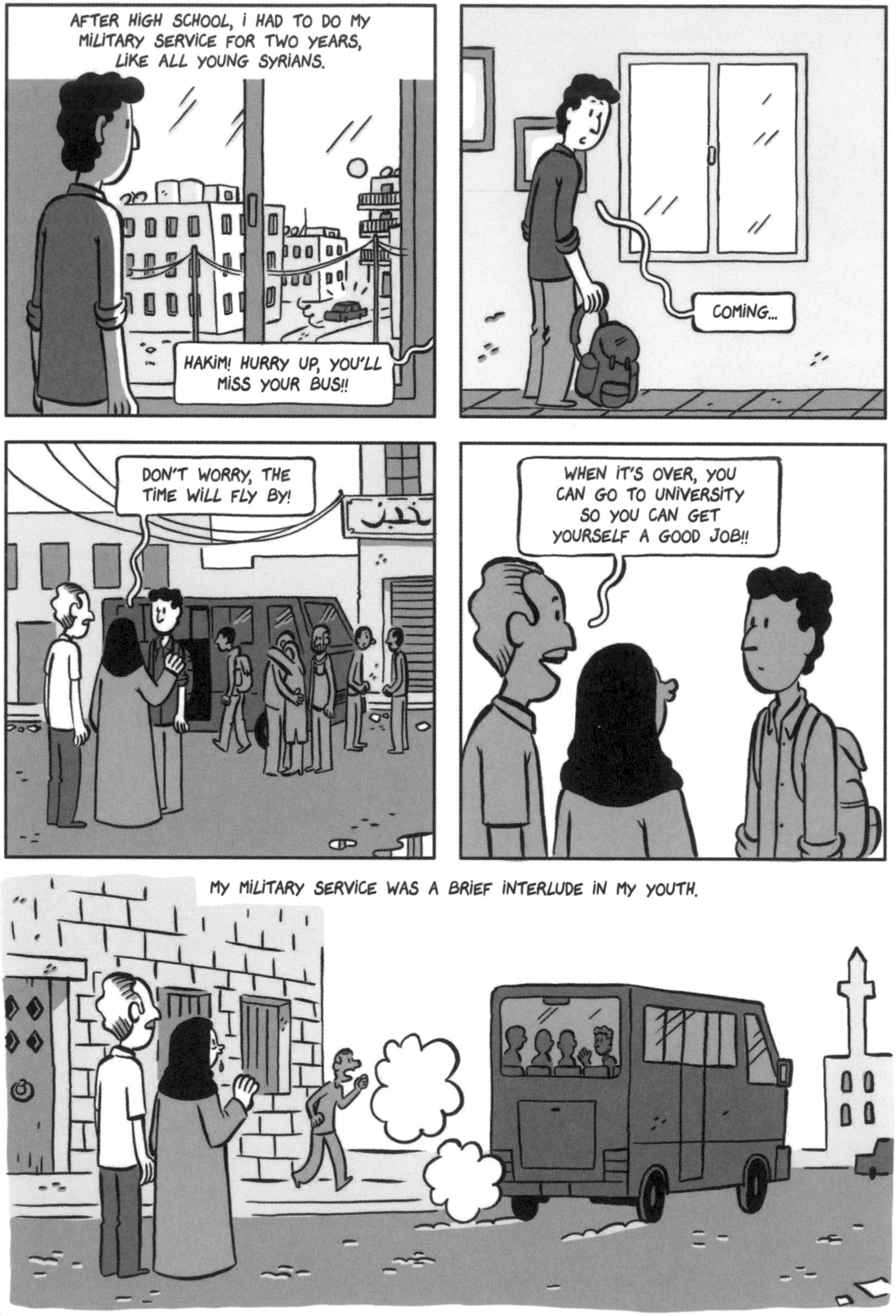
AFTER HIGH SCHOOL, I HAD TO DO MY MILITARY SERVICE FOR TWO YEARS, LIKE ALL YOUNG SYRIANS.
HAKIM! HURRY UP, YOU'LL MISS YOUR BUS!!
COMING...
DON'T WORRY, THE TIME WILL FLY BY!
WHEN IT'S OVER, YOU CAN GO TO UNIVERSITY SO YOU CAN GET YOURSELF A GOOD JOB!!
MY MILITARY SERVICE WAS A BRIEF INTERLUDE IN MY YOUTH.

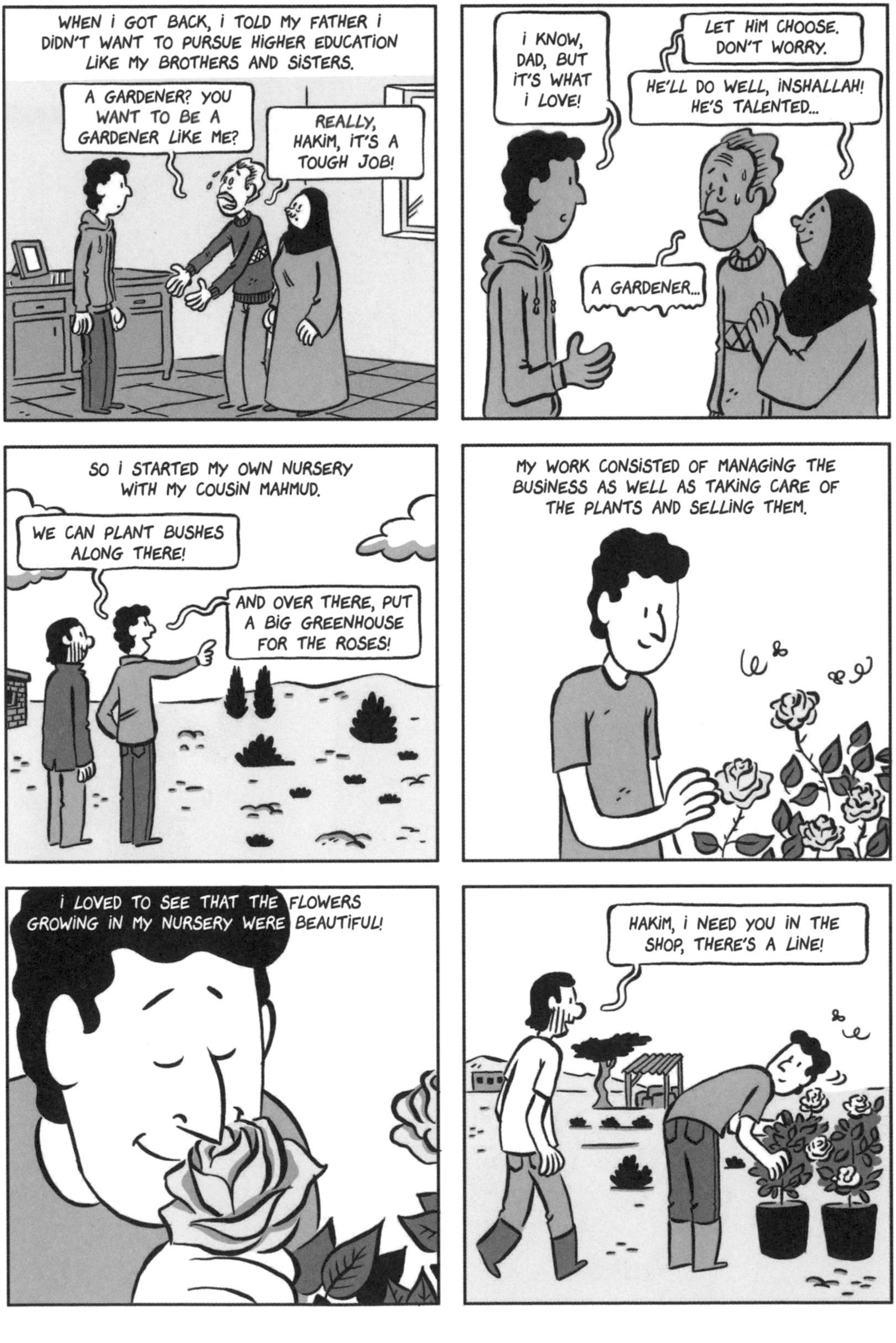
WHEN I GOT BACK, I TOLD MY FATHER I DIDN'T WANT TO PURSUE HIGHER EDUCATION LIKE MY BROTHERS AND SISTERS.
A GARDENER? YOU WANT TO BE A GARDENER LIKE ME?
REALLY, HAKIM, IT'S A TOUGH JOB!
I KNOW, DAD, BUT IT'S WHAT I LOVE!
LET HIM CHOOSE. DON'T WORRY.
HE'LL DO WELL, INSHALLAH! HE'S TALENTED...
A GARDENER...
SO I STARTED MY OWN NURSERY WITH MY COUSIN MAHMUD.
WE CAN PLANT BUSHES ALONG THERE!
AND OVER THERE, PUT A BIG GREENHOUSE FOR THE ROSES!
MY WORK CONSISTED OF MANAGING THE BUSINESS AS WELL AS TAKING CARE OF THE PLANTS AND SELLING THEM.
I LOVED TO SEE THAT THE FLOWERS GROWING IN MY NURSERY WERE BEAUTIFUL!
HAKIM, I NEED YOU IN THE SHOP, THERE'S A LINE!

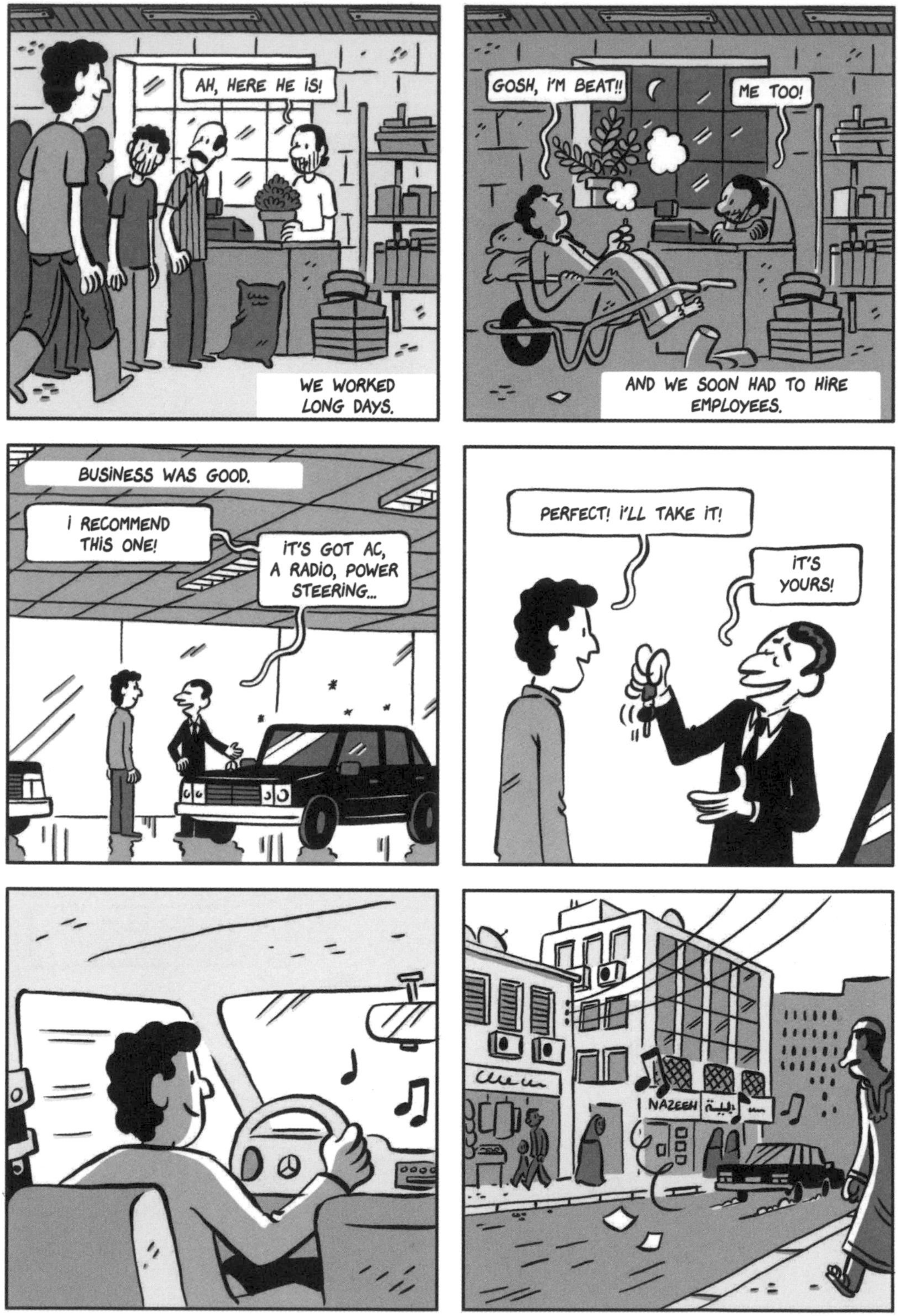
AH, HERE HE IS!
WE WORKED LONG DAYS.
GOSH, I'M BEAT!!
ME TOO!
AND WE SOON HAD TO HIRE EMPLOYEES.
BUSINESS WAS GOOD.
I RECOMMEND THIS ONE!
IT'S GOT AC, A RADIO, POWER STEERING...
PERFECT! I'LL TAKE IT!
IT'S YOURS!
NAZEEH

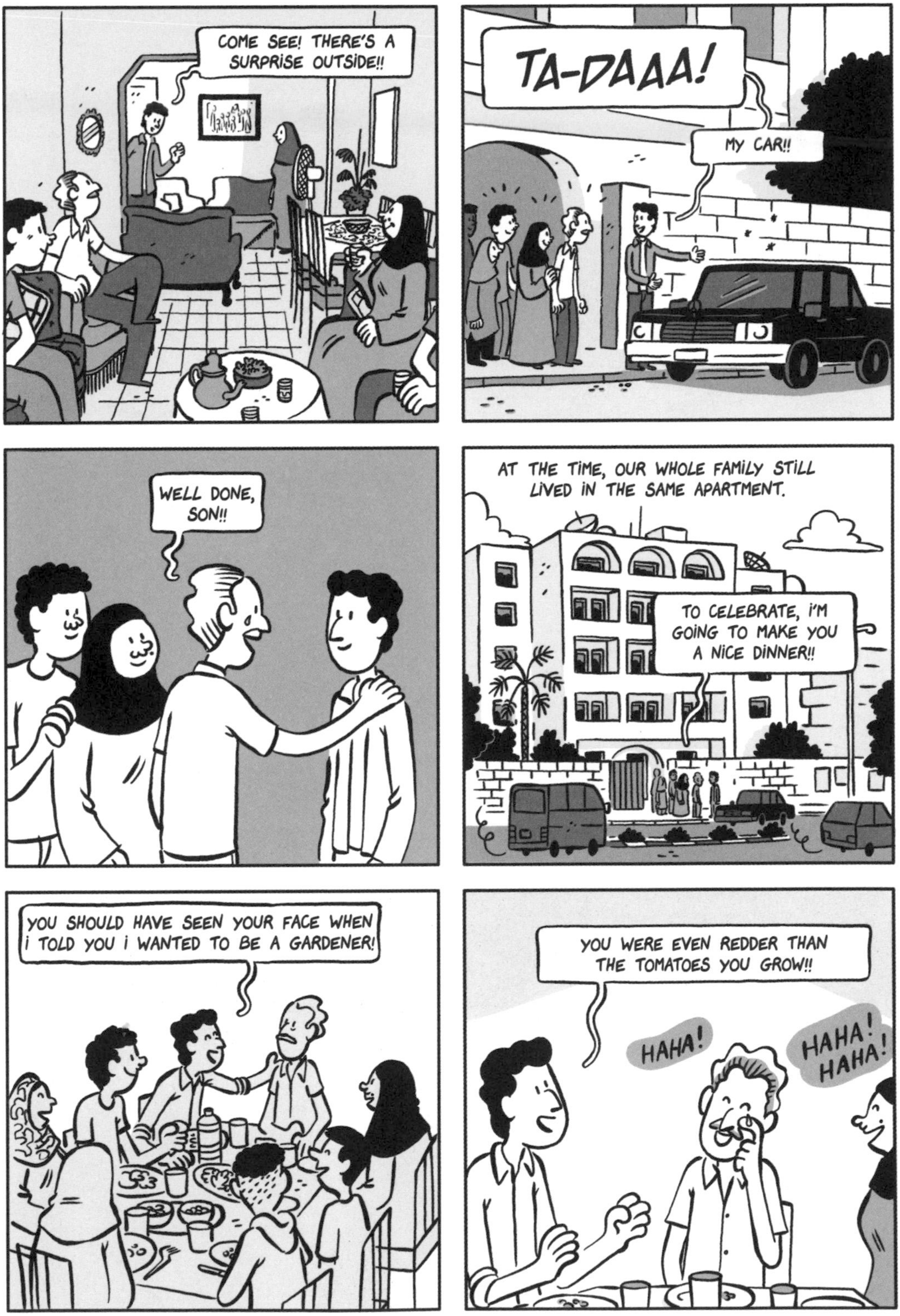
COME SEE! THERE'S A SURPRISE OUTSIDE!!
TA-DAAA!
MY CAR!!
WELL DONE, SON!!
AT THE TIME, OUR WHOLE FAMILY STILL LIVED IN THE SAME APARTMENT.
TO CELEBRATE, I'M GOING TO MAKE YOU A NICE DINNER!!
YOU SHOULD HAVE SEEN YOUR FACE WHEN I TOLD YOU I WANTED TO BE A GARDENER!
YOU WERE EVEN REDDER THAN THE TOMATOES YOU GROW!!
HAHA!
HAHA! HAHA!

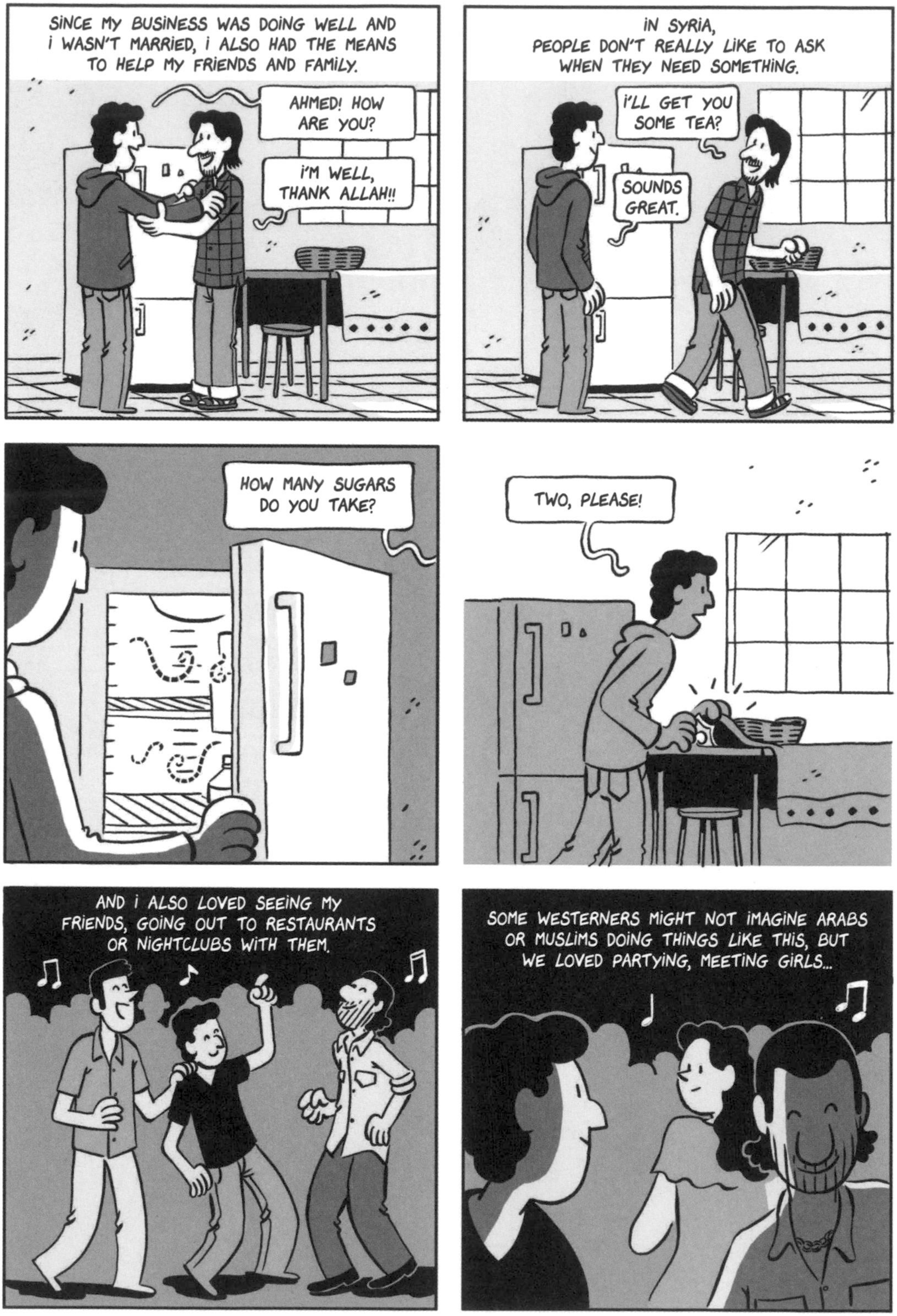
SINCE MY BUSINESS WAS DOING WELL AND I WASN'T MARRIED, I ALSO HAD THE MEANS TO HELP MY FRIENDS AND FAMILY.
AHMED! HOW ARE YOU?
I'M WELL, THANK ALLAH!!
IN SYRIA, PEOPLE DON'T REALLY LIKE TO ASK WHEN THEY NEED SOMETHING.
I'LL GET YOU SOME TEA?
SOUNDS GREAT.
HOW MANY SUGARS DO YOU TAKE?
TWO, PLEASE!
AND I ALSO LOVED SEEING MY FRIENDS, GOING OUT TO RESTAURANTS OR NIGHTCLUBS WITH THEM.
SOME WESTERNERS MIGHT NOT IMAGINE ARABS OR MUSLIMS DOING THINGS LIKE THIS, BUT WE LOVED PARTYING, MEETING GIRLS...

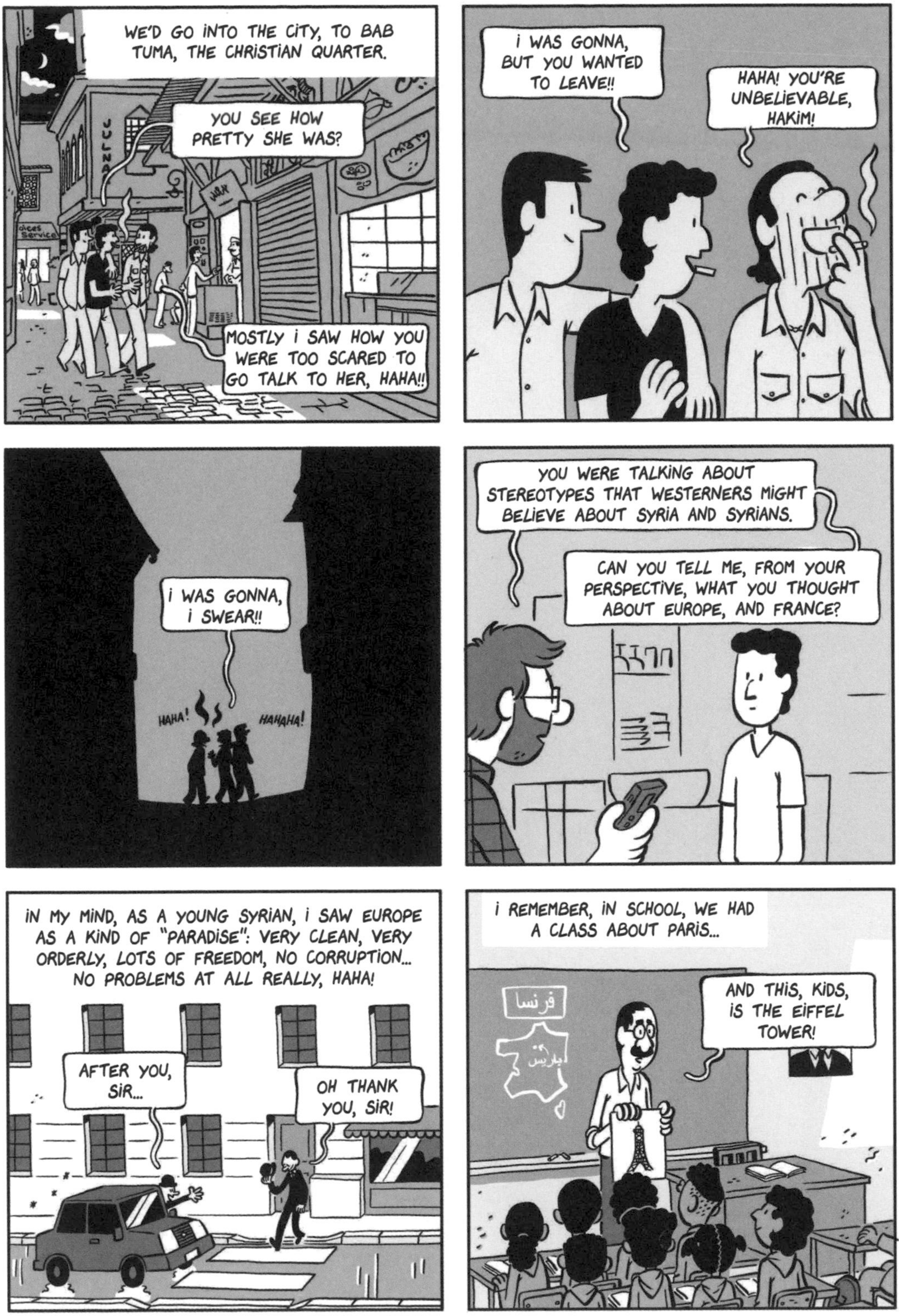
WE'D GO INTO THE CITY, TO BAB TUMA, THE CHRISTIAN QUARTER.
YOU SEE HOW PRETTY SHE WAS?
MOSTLY I SAW HOW YOU WERE TOO SCARED TO GO TALK TO HER, HAHA!!
I WAS GONNA, BUT YOU WANTED TO LEAVE!!
HAHA! YOU'RE UNBELIEVABLE, HAKIM!
I WAS GONNA, I SWEAR!!
HAHA!
HAHAHA!
YOU WERE TALKING ABOUT STEREOTYPES THAT WESTERNERS MIGHT BELIEVE ABOUT SYRIA AND SYRIANS.
CAN YOU TELL ME, FROM YOUR PERSPECTIVE, WHAT YOU THOUGHT ABOUT EUROPE, AND FRANCE?
IN MY MIND, AS A YOUNG SYRIAN, I SAW EUROPE AS A KIND OF "PARADISE": VERY CLEAN, VERY ORDERLY, LOTS OF FREEDOM, NO CORRUPTION... NO PROBLEMS AT ALL REALLY, HAHA!
AFTER YOU, SIR...
OH THANK YOU, SIR!
I REMEMBER, IN SCHOOL, WE HAD A CLASS ABOUT PARIS...
فرنسا
باريس
AND THIS, KIDS, IS THE EIFFEL TOWER!

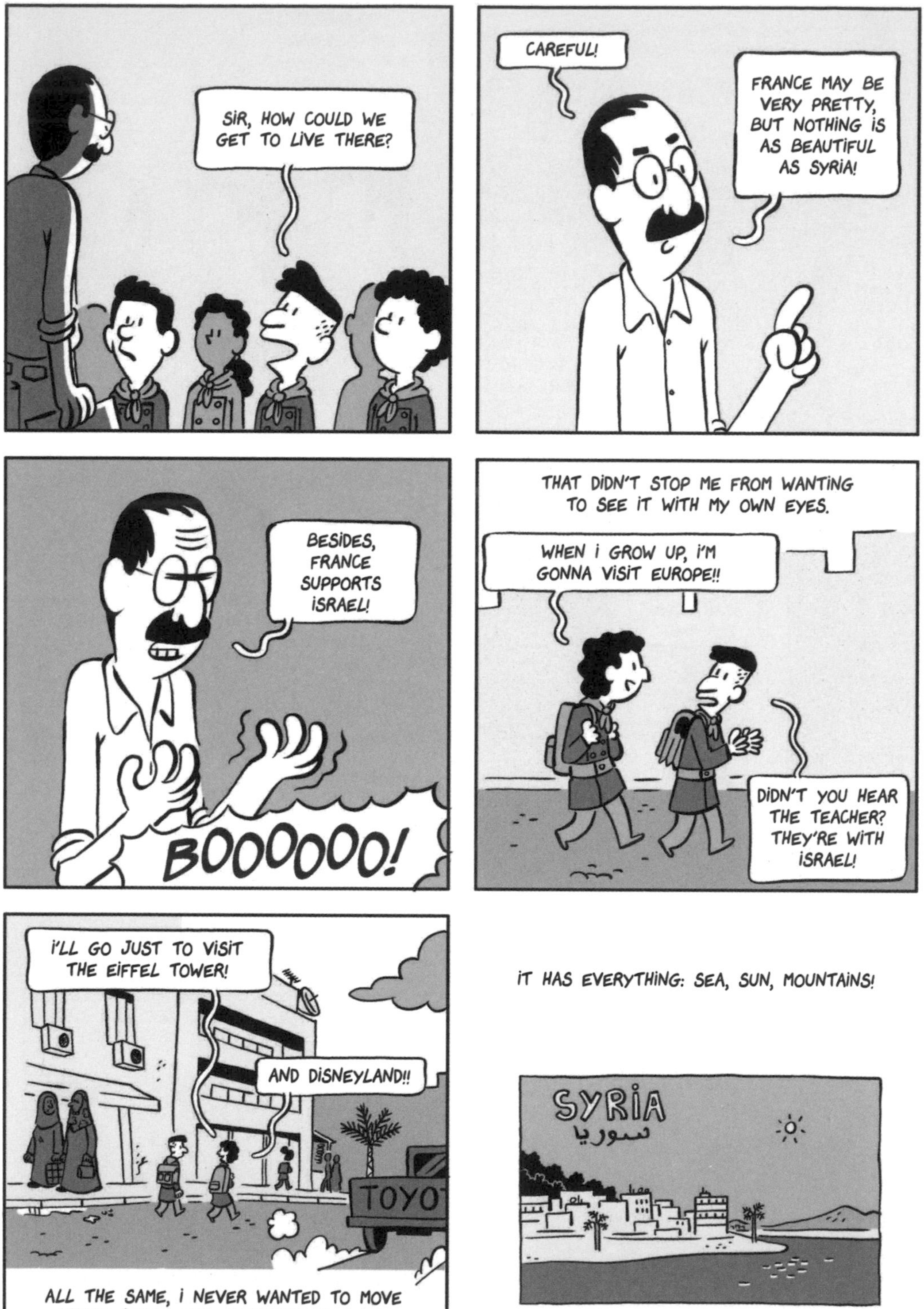
SIR, HOW COULD WE GET TO LIVE THERE?
CAREFUL!
FRANCE MAY BE VERY PRETTY, BUT NOTHING IS AS BEAUTIFUL AS SYRIA!
BESIDES, FRANCE SUPPORTS ISRAEL!
BOOOOOO!
THAT DIDN'T STOP ME FROM WANTING TO SEE IT WITH MY OWN EYES.
WHEN I GROW UP, I'M GONNA VISIT EUROPE!!
DIDN'T YOU HEAR THE TEACHER? THEY'RE WITH ISRAEL!
I'LL GO JUST TO VISIT THE EIFFEL TOWER!
AND DISNEYLAND!!
TOYO
ALL THE SAME, I NEVER WANTED TO MOVE THERE. I WAS TOO ATTACHED TO SYRIA.
IT HAS EVERYTHING: SEA, SUN, MOUNTAINS!
SYRIA
سوريا

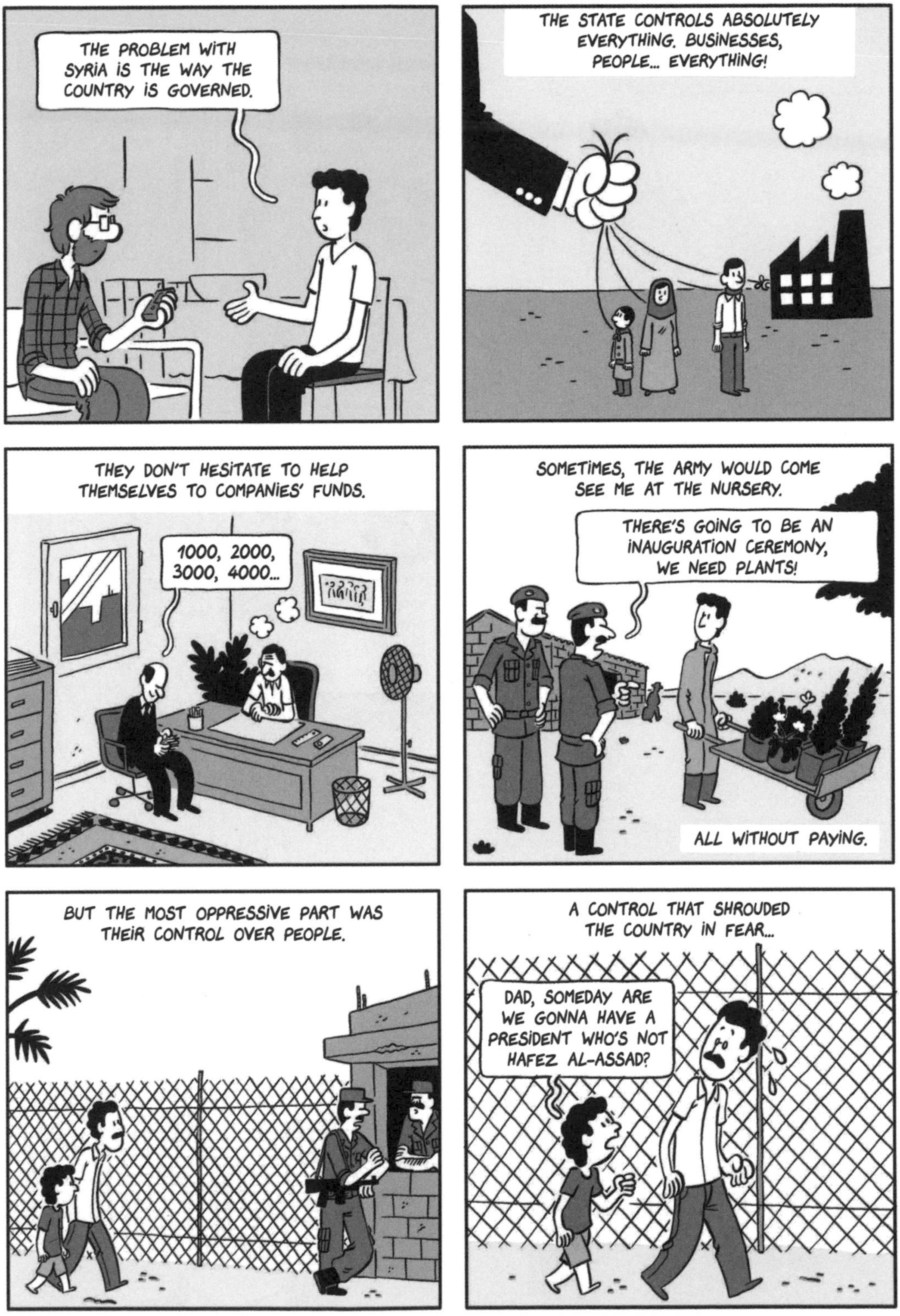
THE PROBLEM WITH SYRIA IS THE WAY THE COUNTRY IS GOVERNED.
THE STATE CONTROLS ABSOLUTELY EVERYTHING. BUSINESSES, PEOPLE... EVERYTHING!
THEY DON'T HESITATE TO HELP THEMSELVES TO COMPANIES' FUNDS.
1000, 2000, 3000, 4000...
SOMETIMES, THE ARMY WOULD COME SEE ME AT THE NURSERY.
THERE'S GOING TO BE AN INAUGURATION CEREMONY, WE NEED PLANTS!
ALL WITHOUT PAYING.
BUT THE MOST OPPRESSIVE PART WAS THEIR CONTROL OVER PEOPLE.
A CONTROL THAT SHROUDED THE COUNTRY IN FEAR...
DAD, SOMEDAY ARE WE GONNA HAVE A PRESIDENT WHO'S NOT HAFEZ AL-ASSAD?

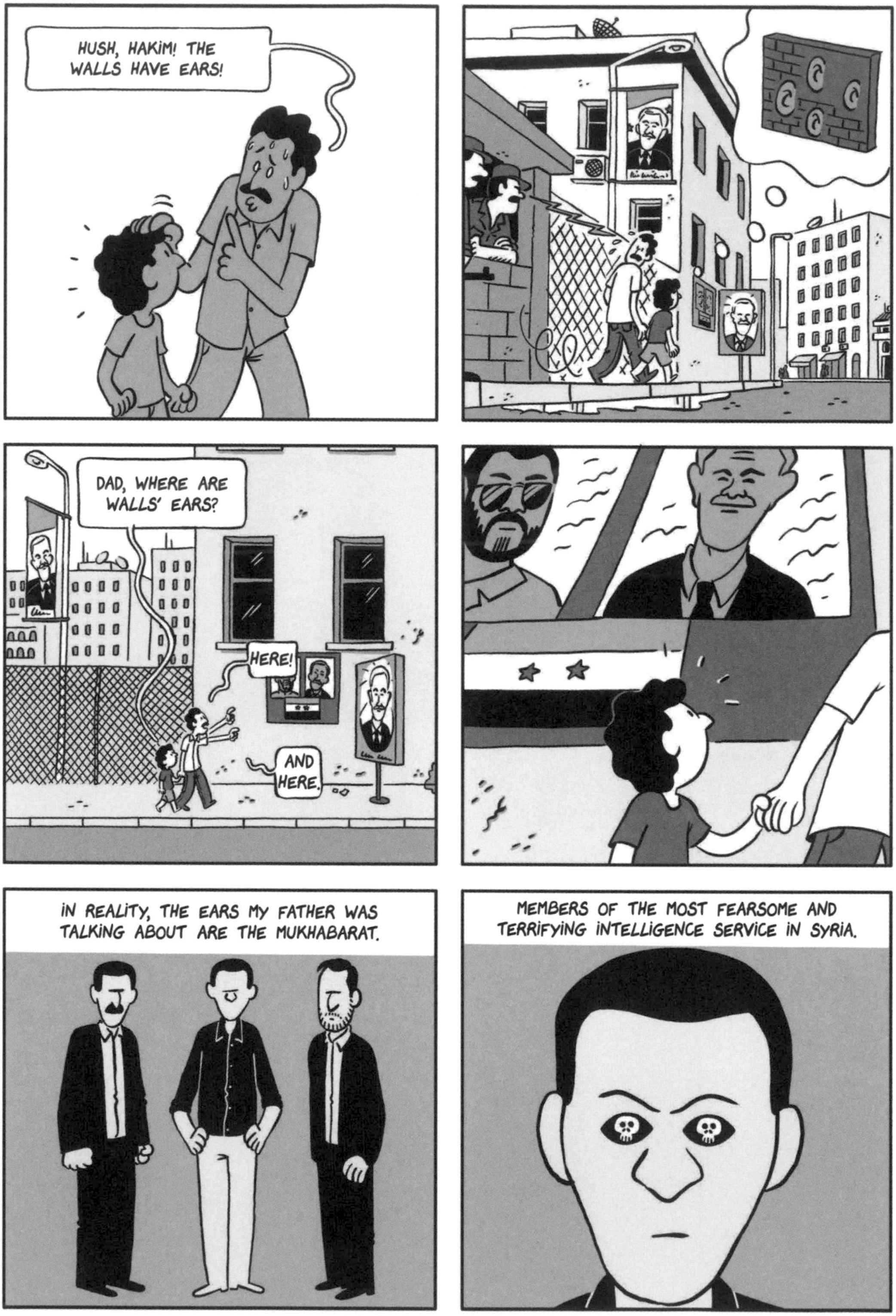
HUSH, HAKIM! THE WALLS HAVE EARS!
DAD, WHERE ARE WALLS' EARS?
HERE!
AND HERE.
IN REALITY, THE EARS MY FATHER WAS TALKING ABOUT ARE THE MUKHABARAT.
MEMBERS OF THE MOST FEARSOME AND TERRIFYING INTELLIGENCE SERVICE IN SYRIA.

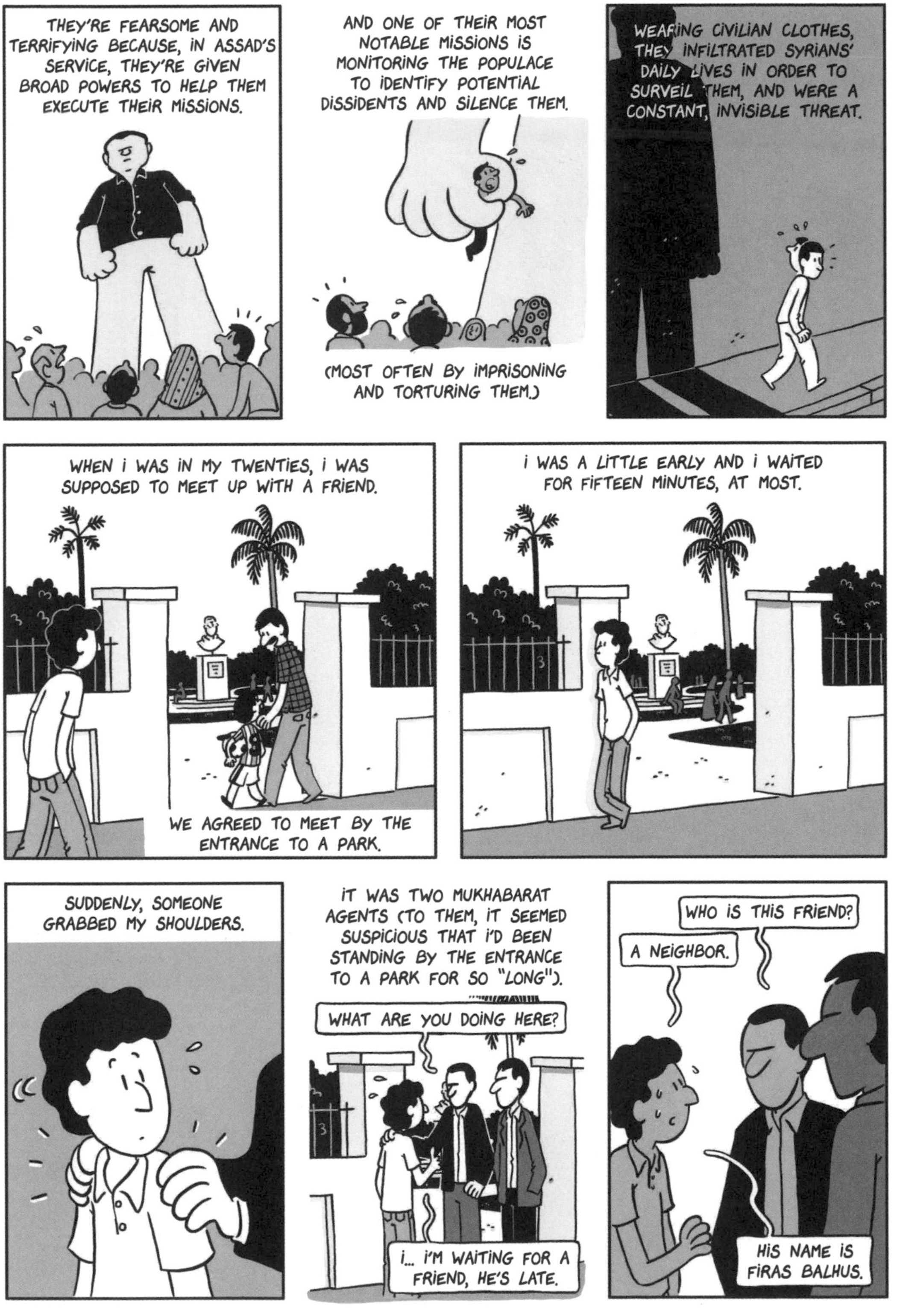
THEY'RE FEARSOME AND TERRIFYING BECAUSE, IN ASSAD'S SERVICE, THEY'RE GIVEN BROAD POWERS TO HELP THEM EXECUTE THEIR MISSIONS.
AND ONE OF THEIR MOST NOTABLE MISSIONS IS MONITORING THE POPULACE TO IDENTIFY POTENTIAL DISSIDENTS AND SILENCE THEM.
(MOST OFTEN BY IMPRISONING AND TORTURING THEM.)
WEARING CIVILIAN CLOTHES, THEY INFILTRATED SYRIANS' DAILY LIVES IN ORDER TO SURVEIL THEM, AND WERE A CONSTANT, INVISIBLE THREAT.
WHEN I WAS IN MY TWENTIES, I WAS SUPPOSED TO MEET UP WITH A FRIEND.
WE AGREED TO MEET BY THE ENTRANCE TO A PARK.
I WAS A LITTLE EARLY AND I WAITED FOR FIFTEEN MINUTES, AT MOST.
SUDDENLY, SOMEONE GRABBED MY SHOULDERS.
IT WAS TWO MUKHABARAT AGENTS (TO THEM, IT SEEMED SUSPICIOUS THAT I'D BEEN STANDING BY THE ENTRANCE TO A PARK FOR SO "LONG").
WHAT ARE YOU DOING HERE?
I... I'M WAITING FOR A FRIEND, HE'S LATE.
WHO IS THIS FRIEND?
A NEIGHBOR.
HIS NAME IS FIRAS BALHUS.

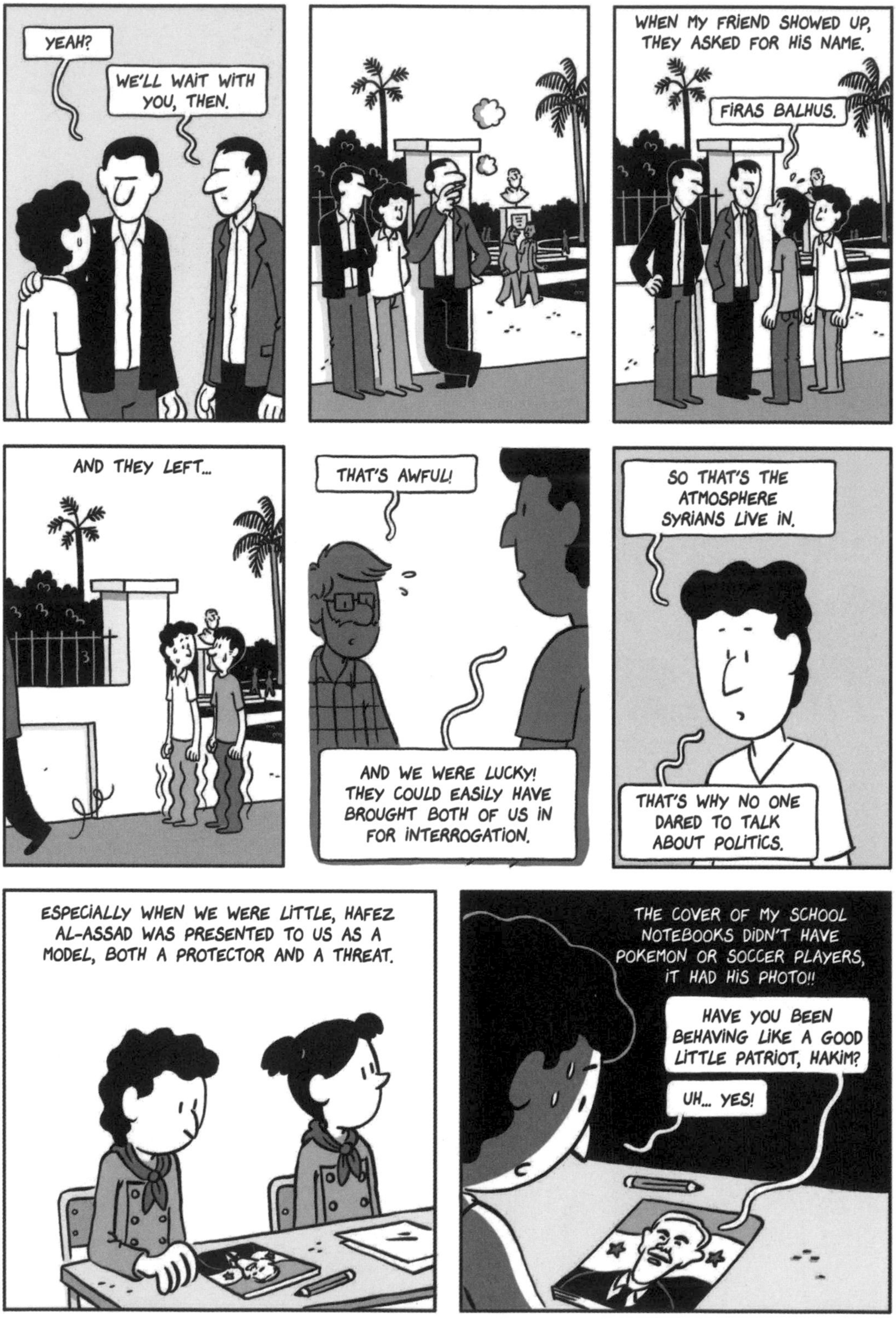
YEAH?
WE'LL WAIT WITH YOU, THEN.
WHEN MY FRIEND SHOWED UP, THEY ASKED FOR HIS NAME.
FIRAS BALHUS.
AND THEY LEFT...
THAT'S AWFUL!
AND WE WERE LUCKY! THEY COULD EASILY HAVE BROUGHT BOTH OF US IN FOR INTERROGATION.
SO THAT'S THE ATMOSPHERE SYRIANS LIVE IN.
THAT'S WHY NO ONE DARED TO TALK ABOUT POLITICS.
ESPECIALLY WHEN WE WERE LITTLE, HAFEZ AL-ASSAD WAS PRESENTED TO US AS A MODEL, BOTH A PROTECTOR AND A THREAT.
THE COVER OF MY SCHOOL NOTEBOOKS DIDN'T HAVE POKEMON OR SOCCER PLAYERS, IT HAD HIS PHOTO!!
HAVE YOU BEEN BEHAVING LIKE A GOOD LITTLE PATRIOT, HAKIM?
UH... YES!

EVEN HIS FAMILY MEMBERS WERE PRESENTED IN THIS ALMOST SUPERNATURAL LIGHT:

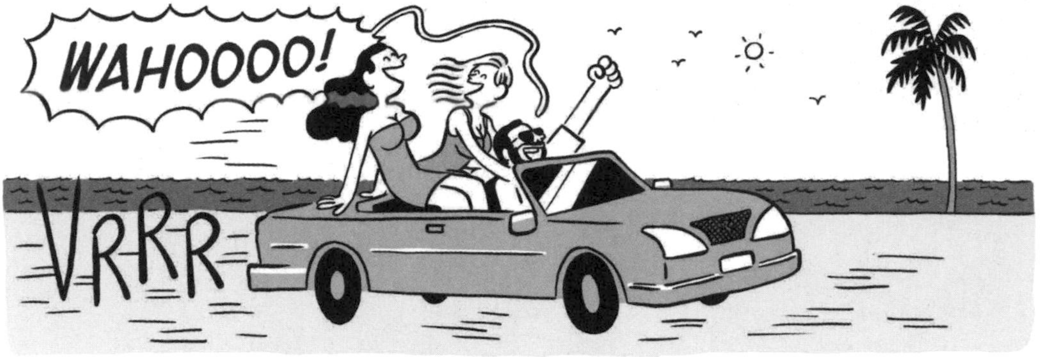
WAHOOOO!
VRRR

HAFEZ AL-ASSAD'S OLDEST SON, BASSEL, WHO WAS SUPPOSED TO SUCCEED HIS FATHER AS PRESIDENT, DIED IN A CAR ACCIDENT IN 1994. HE LOVED DRUGS, AND WOMEN...

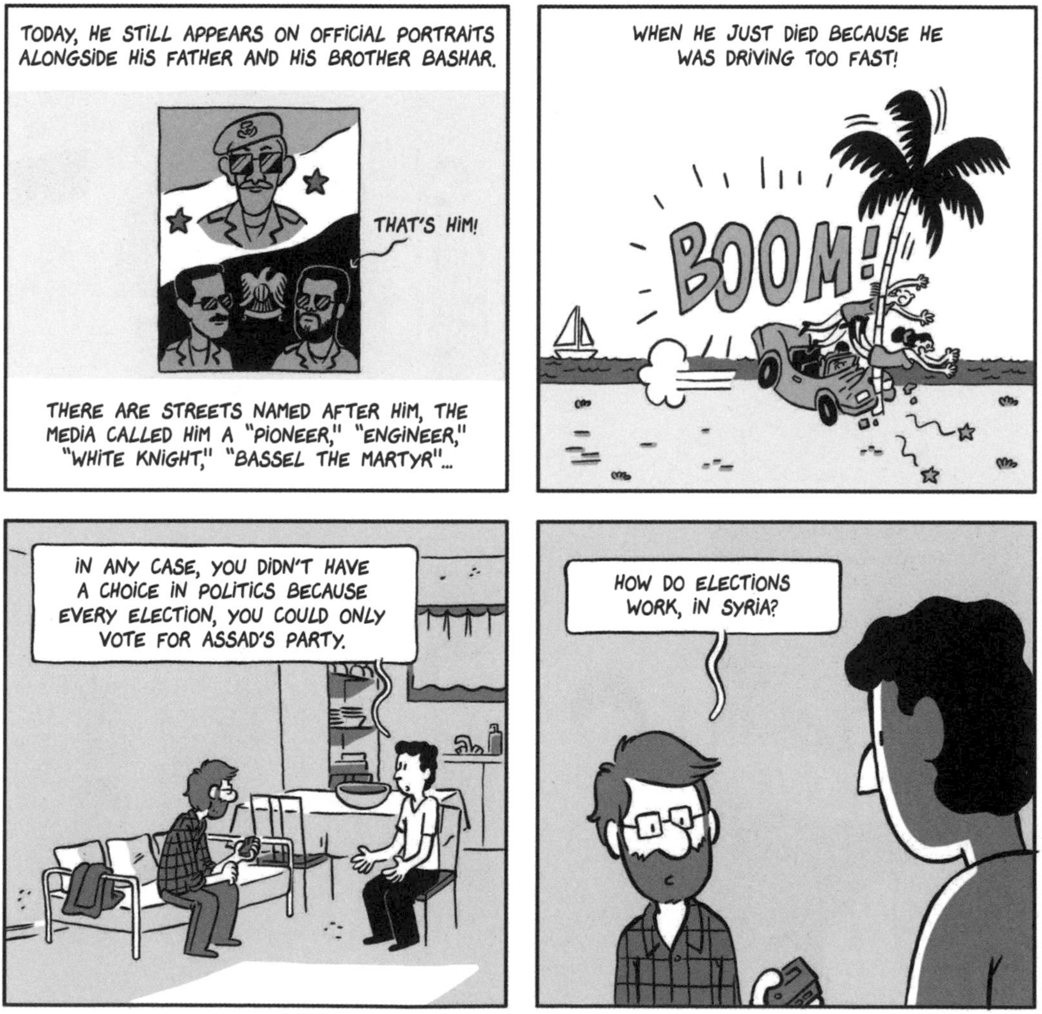
TODAY, HE STILL APPEARS ON OFFICIAL PORTRAITS ALONGSIDE HIS FATHER AND HIS BROTHER BASHAR.
THAT'S HIM!
THERE ARE STREETS NAMED AFTER HIM, THE MEDIA CALLED HIM A "PIONEER," "ENGINEER," "WHITE KNIGHT," "BASSEL THE MARTYR"...
WHEN HE JUST DIED BECAUSE HE WAS DRIVING TOO FAST!
BOOM!
IN ANY CASE, YOU DIDN'T HAVE A CHOICE IN POLITICS BECAUSE EVERY ELECTION, YOU COULD ONLY VOTE FOR ASSAD'S PARTY.
HOW DO ELECTIONS WORK, IN SYRIA?

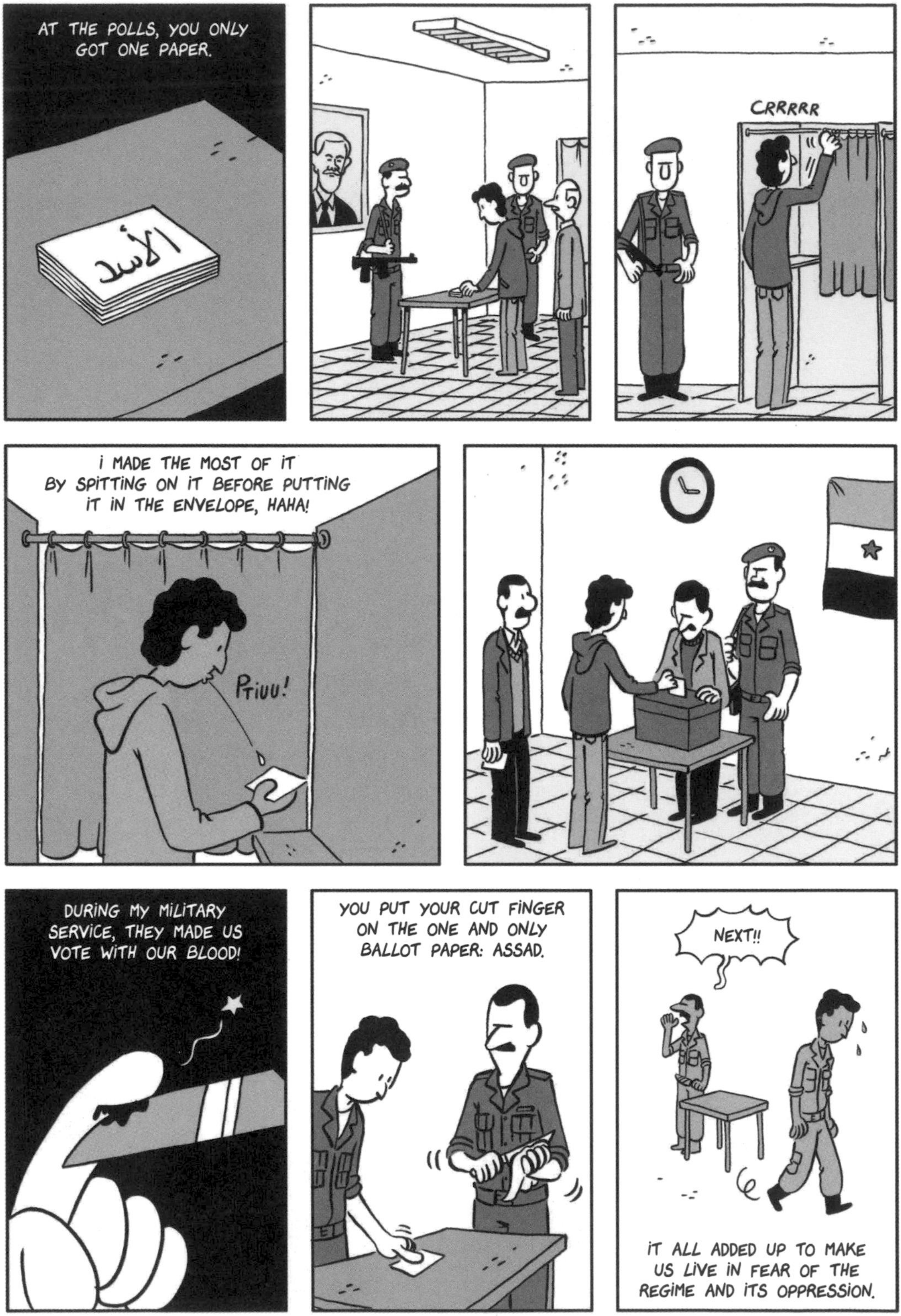
AT THE POLLS, YOU ONLY GOT ONE PAPER.
الأسد
CRRRRR
I MADE THE MOST OF IT BY SPITTING ON IT BEFORE PUTTING IT IN THE ENVELOPE, HAHA!
PTIUU!
DURING MY MILITARY SERVICE, THEY MADE US VOTE WITH OUR BLOOD!
YOU PUT YOUR CUT FINGER ON THE ONE AND ONLY BALLOT PAPER: ASSAD.
NEXT!!
IT ALL ADDED UP TO MAKE US LIVE IN FEAR OF THE REGIME AND ITS OPPRESSION.

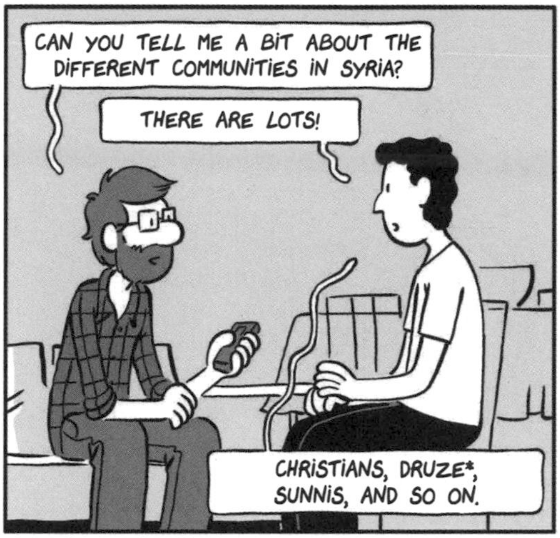
CAN YOU TELL ME A BIT ABOUT THE DIFFERENT COMMUNITIES IN SYRIA?
THERE ARE LOTS!
CHRISTIANS, DRUZE*, SUNNIS, AND SO ON.

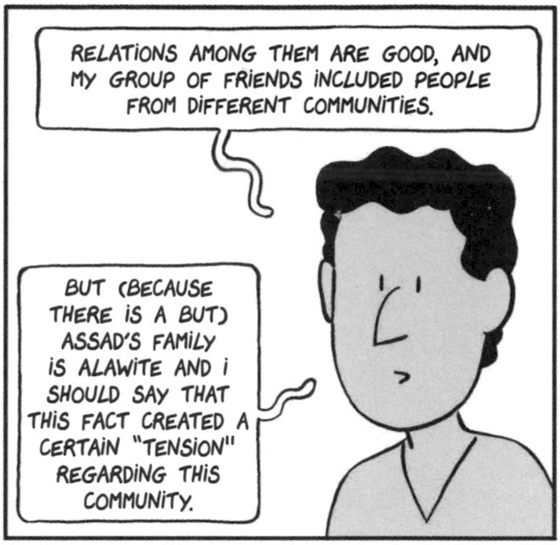
RELATIONS AMONG THEM ARE GOOD, AND MY GROUP OF FRIENDS INCLUDED PEOPLE FROM DIFFERENT COMMUNITIES.
BUT (BECAUSE THERE IS A BUT) ASSAD'S FAMILY IS ALAWITE AND I SHOULD SAY THAT THIS FACT CREATED A CERTAIN "TENSION" REGARDING THIS COMMUNITY.

*A COMMUNITY ESTABLISHED IN SEVERAL MIDDLE EASTERN COUNTRIES (SYRIA, LEBANON, ISRAEL) THAT PRACTICES THE DRUZE RELIGION, WHICH IS DERIVED FROM ISMAILI SHIA ISLAM.

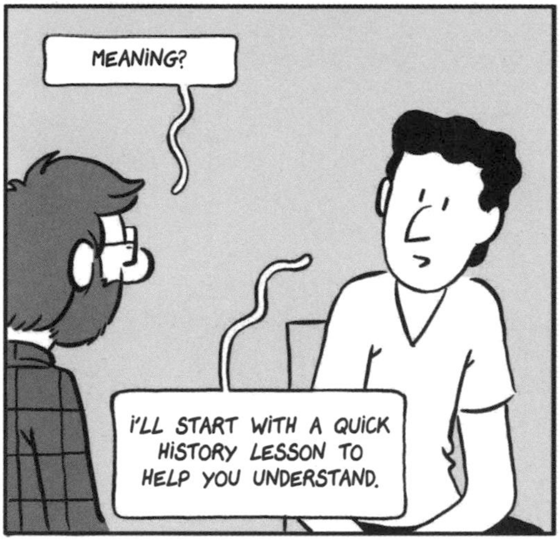
MEANING?
I'LL START WITH A QUICK HISTORY LESSON TO HELP YOU UNDERSTAND.

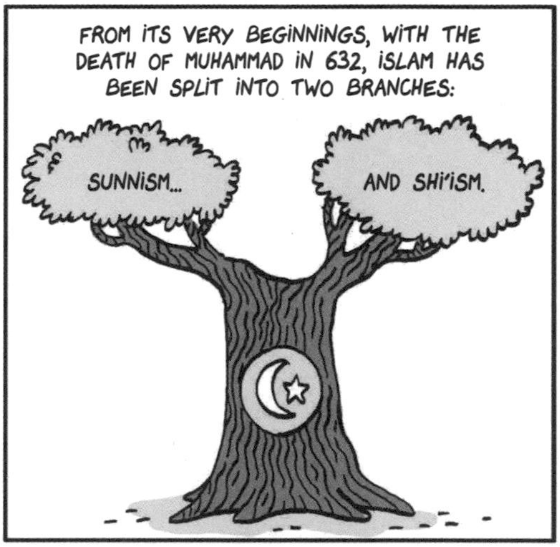
FROM ITS VERY BEGINNINGS, WITH THE DEATH OF MUHAMMAD IN 632, ISLAM HAS BEEN SPLIT INTO TWO BRANCHES:
SUNNISM...
AND SHI'ISM.

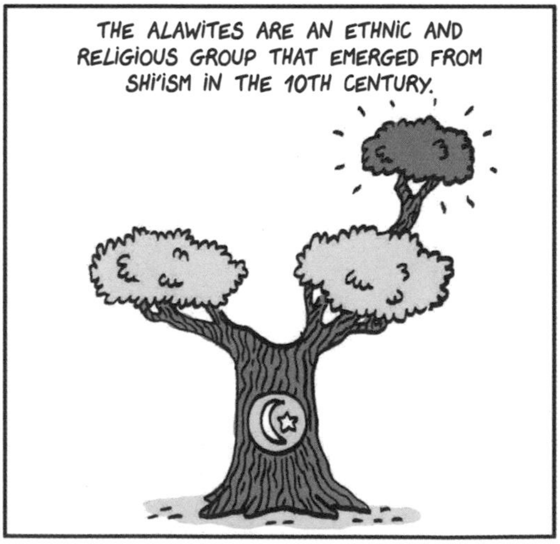
THE ALAWITES ARE AN ETHNIC AND RELIGIOUS GROUP THAT EMERGED FROM SHI'ISM IN THE 10TH CENTURY.

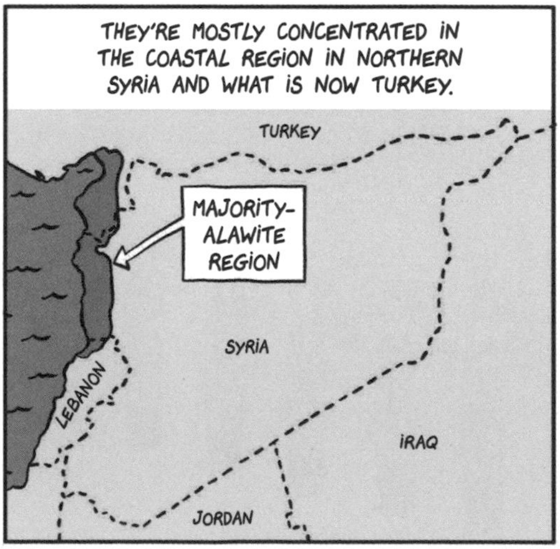
THEY'RE MOSTLY CONCENTRATED IN THE COASTAL REGION IN NORTHERN SYRIA AND WHAT IS NOW TURKEY.
TURKEY
MAJORITY-ALAWITE REGION
SYRIA
LEBANON
IRAQ
JORDAN

AT THE END OF THE 19TH CENTURY, THE ALAWITES IN THE OTTOMAN EMPIRE FACED POLITICAL AND RELIGIOUS PRESSURE (FOR EXAMPLE, THEY WERE PUSHED TO CONVERT TO SUNNI ISLAM).

WHEN THE OTTOMAN EMPIRE WAS DISMANTLED AFTER THE FIRST WORLD WAR, AND SYRIA FOUND ITSELF UNDER FRENCH MANDATE, THE FRENCH SUPPORTED THE CREATION OF AN ALAWITE TERRITORY.

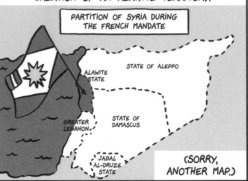

PARTITION OF SYRIA DURING THE FRENCH MANDATE

ALAWITE STATE

STATE OF ALEPPO

GREATER LEBANON

STATE OF DAMASCUS

JABAL AL-DRUZE STATE

(SORRY, ANOTHER MAP.)

THE ATTEMPT TO CREATE A FULL-FLEDGED ALAWITE STATE WOULD FAIL AFTER SYRIA GAINED INDEPENDENCE IN 1946 AND THE CHARISMATIC LEADER OF THE ALAWITES, SULEIMAN AL-MURSHID, WAS HANGED IN THE PUBLIC SQUARE.

THE ALAWITE COMMUNITY, A MINORITY IN SYRIA (AT AROUND 10% OF THE POPULATION), WAS GENERALLY OF MODEST MEANS AND OFTEN EMPLOYED IN LOW-LEVEL JOBS. THEY WOULD PROGRESSIVELY INTEGRATE INTO THE SYRIAN ARMY, SEEING IT AS A MEANS OF SOCIAL ADVANCEMENT.

AT THE TIME, THE BA'ATH PARTY, WHICH WAS FOUNDED IN SYRIA, WAS FINDING SUPPORT AMONG MINORITIES (ISMAILIS, DRUZE, AND ALAWITES) WHO WERE SEDUCED BY ITS NOTIONS OF SOCIALISM AND SECULARISM.

AND IT WAS MAINLY BECAUSE OF THIS INFILTRATION BY THE BA'ATH PARTY (THE INTERMEDIARY FOR THE ALAWITES) THAT HAFEZ AL-ASSAD, WHO CAME FROM THIS COMMUNITY, WAS ABLE TO SUCCEED IN HIS COUP IN 1970.

THIS EVENT MARKED A RADICAL CHANGE IN THE ALAWITES' CONDITIONS SINCE, IN THEIR DETERMINATION TO CONTROL STATE AGENCIES, THEY RESERVED TOP GOVERNMENTAL POSITIONS, ESPECIALLY IN THE ARMY, FOR THEMSELVES.

I SHOULD POINT OUT, TO AVOID STEREOTYPING, THAT NOT ALL ALAWITES BENEFITED FROM THE REGIME.

SOME MEMBERS OF THIS COMMUNITY ARE VERY POOR AND HAVE NO LINKS TO THOSE IN POWER.

BUT THIS "COMMUNITY FAVORITISM" WOULD CREATE A CERTAIN FEELING OF INJUSTICE AMONG SYRIANS. AND ABOVE ALL, GIVEN THE REGIME'S HIGHLY OPPRESSIVE CHARACTER, IT WOULD INSTILL FEAR AROUND THIS PART OF THE POPULATION.

LET ME TELL YOU A QUICK STORY ABOUT SOMETHING THAT HAPPENED TO ME, TO SHOW YOU HOW ALL OF THIS AFFECTS OUR EVERYDAY LIVES...

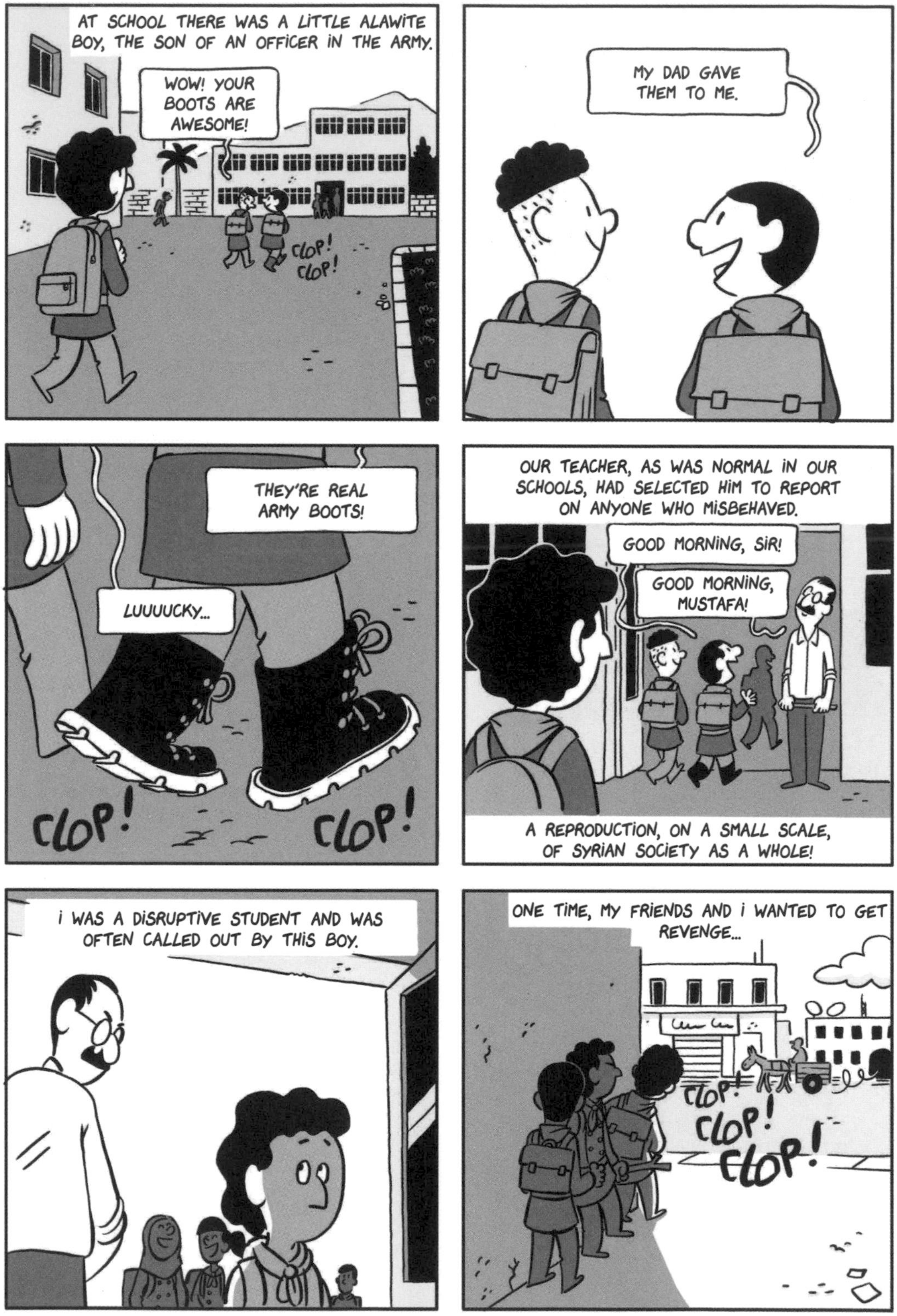
AT SCHOOL THERE WAS A LITTLE ALAWITE BOY, THE SON OF AN OFFICER IN THE ARMY.
WOW! YOUR BOOTS ARE AWESOME!
CLOP! CLOP!
MY DAD GAVE THEM TO ME.
THEY'RE REAL ARMY BOOTS!
LUUUUCKY...
CLOP!
CLOP!
OUR TEACHER, AS WAS NORMAL IN OUR SCHOOLS, HAD SELECTED HIM TO REPORT ON ANYONE WHO MISBEHAVED.
GOOD MORNING, SIR!
GOOD MORNING, MUSTAFA!
A REPRODUCTION, ON A SMALL SCALE, OF SYRIAN SOCIETY AS A WHOLE!
I WAS A DISRUPTIVE STUDENT AND WAS OFTEN CALLED OUT BY THIS BOY.
ONE TIME, MY FRIENDS AND I WANTED TO GET REVENGE...
CLOP!
CLOP!
CLOP!

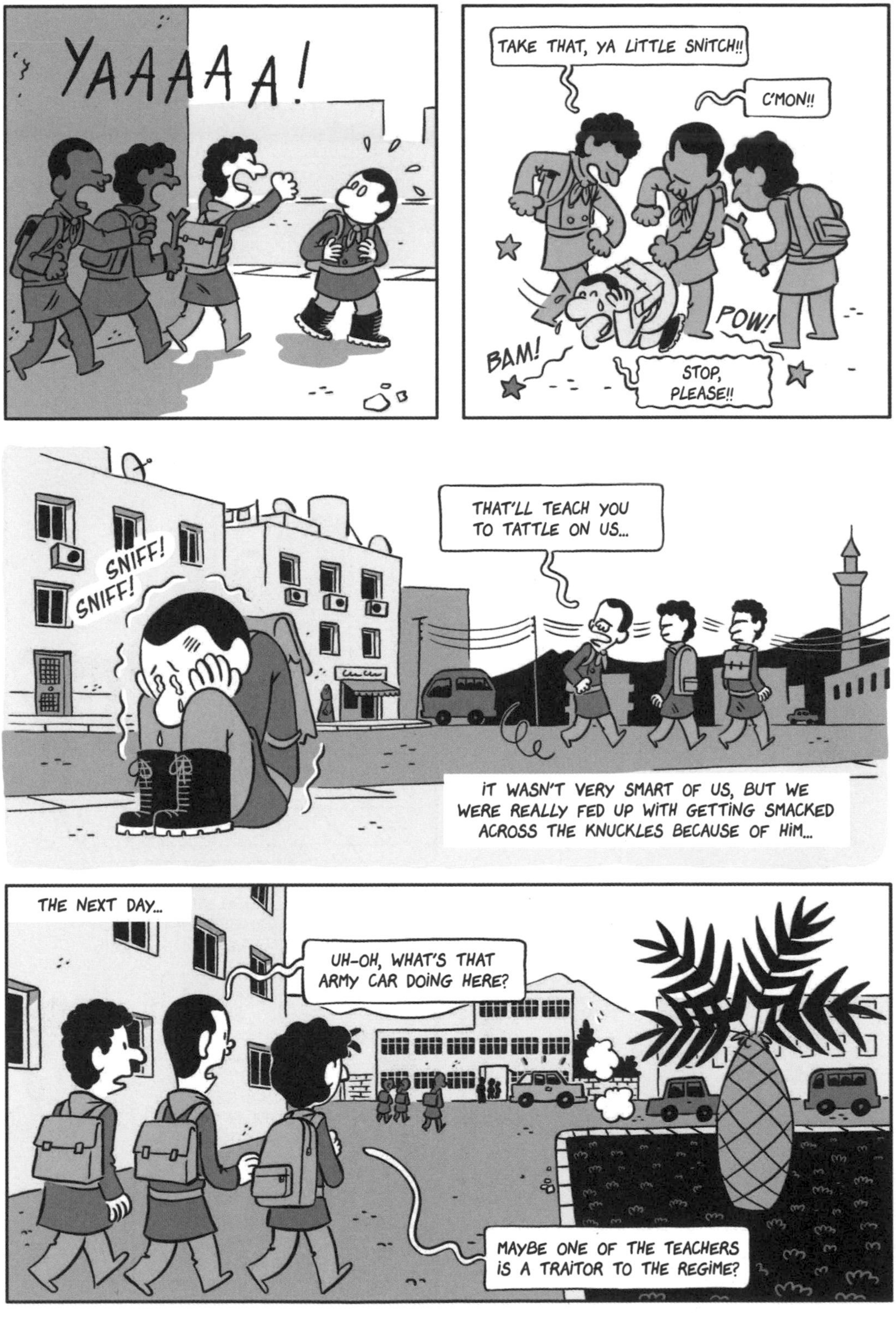
YAAAAA!
TAKE THAT, YA LITTLE SNITCH!!
C'MON!!
BAM!
POW!
STOP, PLEASE!!
SNIFF! SNIFF!
THAT'LL TEACH YOU TO TATTLE ON US...
IT WASN'T VERY SMART OF US, BUT WE WERE REALLY FED UP WITH GETTING SMACKED ACROSS THE KNUCKLES BECAUSE OF HIM...
THE NEXT DAY...
UH-OH, WHAT'S THAT ARMY CAR DOING HERE?
MAYBE ONE OF THE TEACHERS IS A TRAITOR TO THE REGIME?

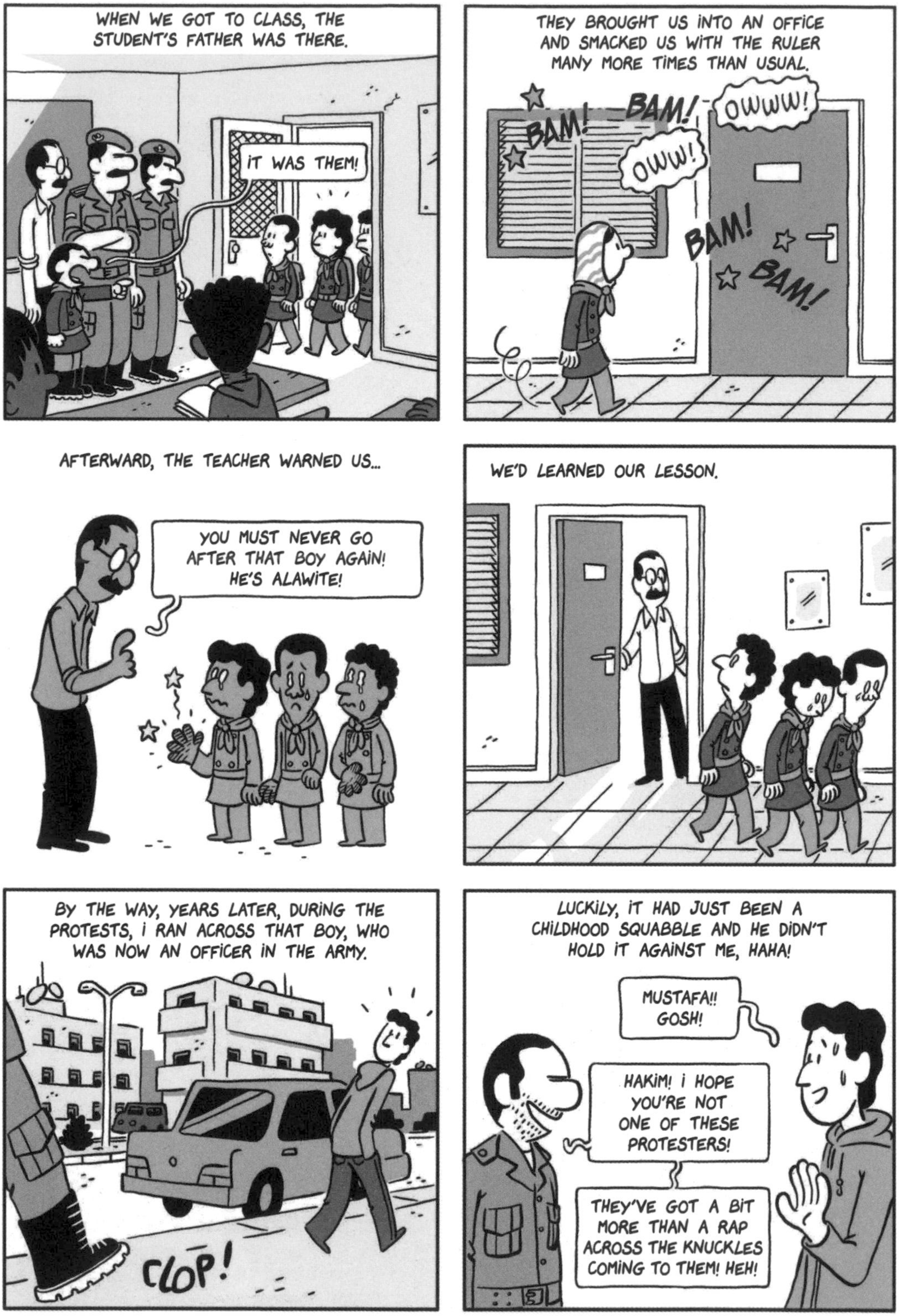
WHEN WE GOT TO CLASS, THE STUDENT'S FATHER WAS THERE.
IT WAS THEM!
THEY BROUGHT US INTO AN OFFICE AND SMACKED US WITH THE RULER MANY MORE TIMES THAN USUAL.
BAM!
BAM!
OWWW!
OWW!
BAM!
BAM!
AFTERWARD, THE TEACHER WARNED US...
YOU MUST NEVER GO AFTER THAT BOY AGAIN! HE'S ALAWITE!
WE'D LEARNED OUR LESSON.
BY THE WAY, YEARS LATER, DURING THE PROTESTS, I RAN ACROSS THAT BOY, WHO WAS NOW AN OFFICER IN THE ARMY.
CLOP!
LUCKILY, IT HAD JUST BEEN A CHILDHOOD SQUABBLE AND HE DIDN'T HOLD IT AGAINST ME, HAHA!
MUSTAFA!! GOSH!
HAKIM! I HOPE YOU'RE NOT ONE OF THESE PROTESTERS!
THEY'VE GOT A BIT MORE THAN A RAP ACROSS THE KNUCKLES COMING TO THEM! HEH!

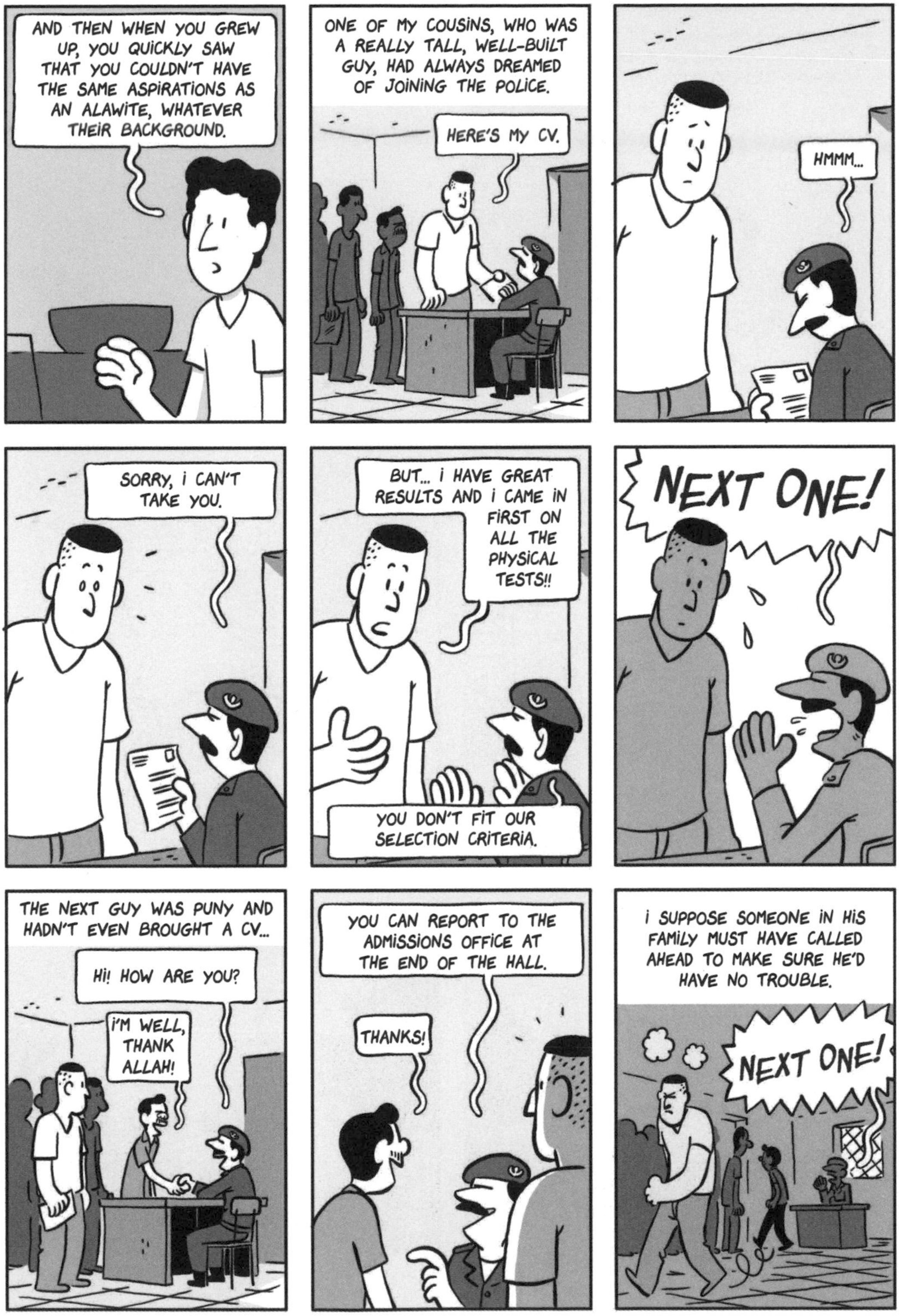
AND THEN WHEN YOU GREW UP, YOU QUICKLY SAW THAT YOU COULDN'T HAVE THE SAME ASPIRATIONS AS AN ALAWITE, WHATEVER THEIR BACKGROUND.
ONE OF MY COUSINS, WHO WAS A REALLY TALL, WELL-BUILT GUY, HAD ALWAYS DREAMED OF JOINING THE POLICE.
HERE'S MY CV.
HMMM...
SORRY, I CAN'T TAKE YOU.
BUT... I HAVE GREAT RESULTS AND I CAME IN FIRST ON ALL THE PHYSICAL TESTS!!
YOU DON'T FIT OUR SELECTION CRITERIA.
NEXT ONE!
THE NEXT GUY WAS PUNY AND HADN'T EVEN BROUGHT A CV...
HI! HOW ARE YOU?
I'M WELL, THANK ALLAH!
YOU CAN REPORT TO THE ADMISSIONS OFFICE AT THE END OF THE HALL.
THANKS!
I SUPPOSE SOMEONE IN HIS FAMILY MUST HAVE CALLED AHEAD TO MAKE SURE HE'D HAVE NO TROUBLE.
NEXT ONE!

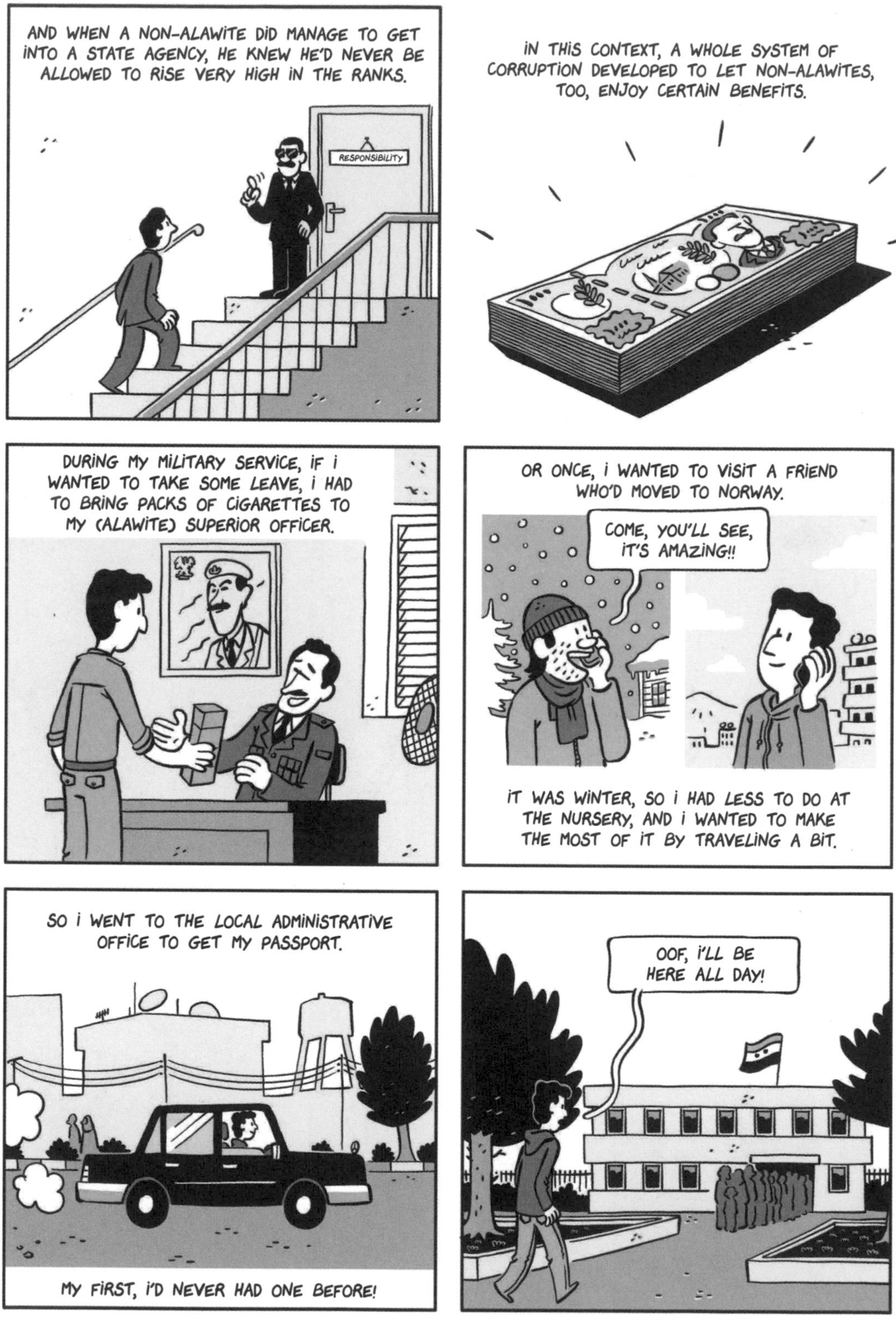
AND WHEN A NON-ALAWITE DID MANAGE TO GET INTO A STATE AGENCY, HE KNEW HE'D NEVER BE ALLOWED TO RISE VERY HIGH IN THE RANKS.
RESPONSIBILITY
IN THIS CONTEXT, A WHOLE SYSTEM OF CORRUPTION DEVELOPED TO LET NON-ALAWITES, TOO, ENJOY CERTAIN BENEFITS.
DURING MY MILITARY SERVICE, IF I WANTED TO TAKE SOME LEAVE, I HAD TO BRING PACKS OF CIGARETTES TO MY (ALAWITE) SUPERIOR OFFICER.
OR ONCE, I WANTED TO VISIT A FRIEND WHO'D MOVED TO NORWAY.
COME, YOU'LL SEE, IT'S AMAZING!!
IT WAS WINTER, SO I HAD LESS TO DO AT THE NURSERY, AND I WANTED TO MAKE THE MOST OF IT BY TRAVELING A BIT.
SO I WENT TO THE LOCAL ADMINISTRATIVE OFFICE TO GET MY PASSPORT.
MY FIRST, I'D NEVER HAD ONE BEFORE!
OOF, I'LL BE HERE ALL DAY!

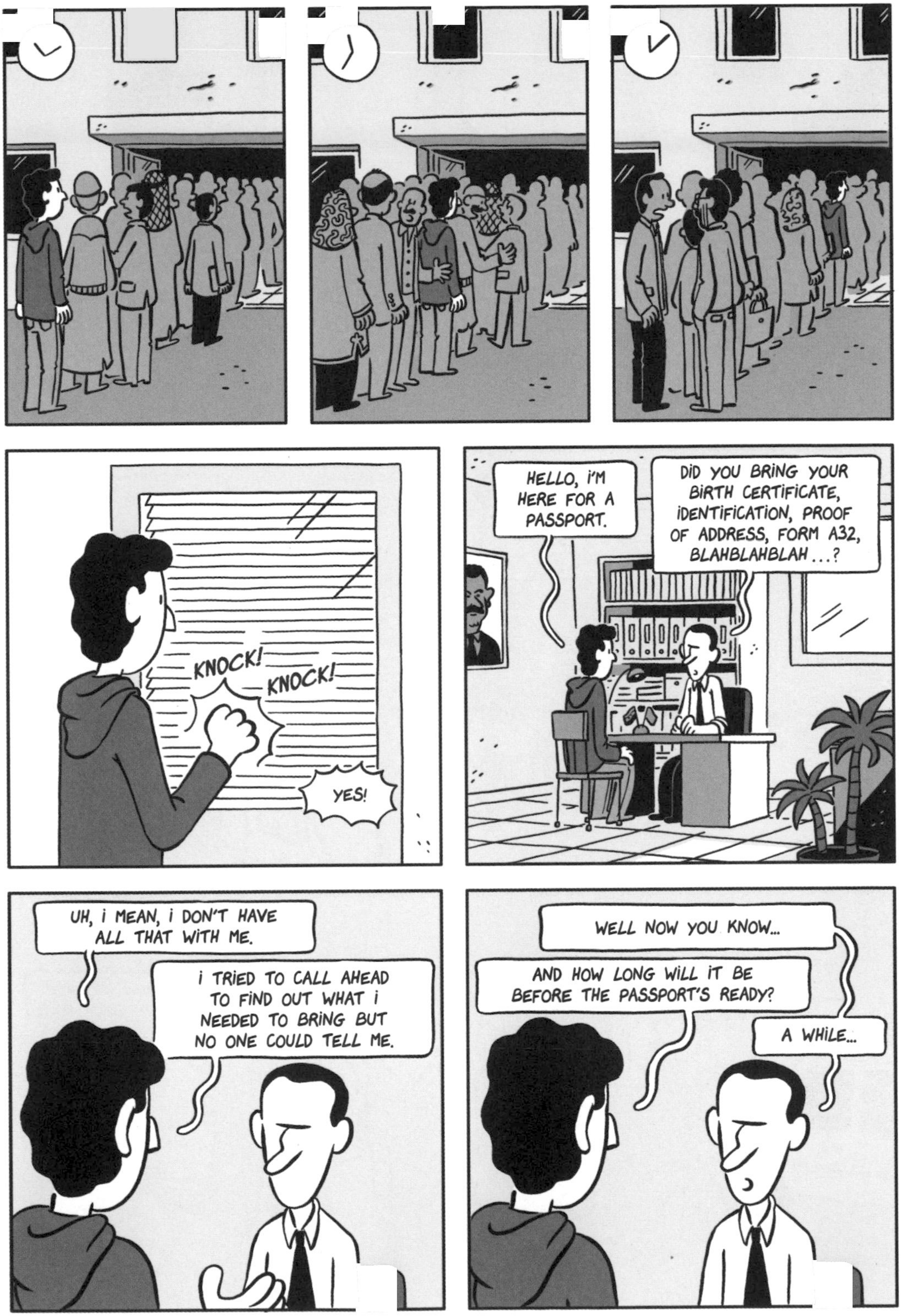
KNOCK!
KNOCK!
YES!
HELLO, I'M HERE FOR A PASSPORT.
DID YOU BRING YOUR BIRTH CERTIFICATE, IDENTIFICATION, PROOF OF ADDRESS, FORM A32, BLAHBLAHBLAH ...?
UH, I MEAN, I DON'T HAVE ALL THAT WITH ME.
I TRIED TO CALL AHEAD TO FIND OUT WHAT I NEEDED TO BRING BUT NO ONE COULD TELL ME.
WELL NOW YOU KNOW...
AND HOW LONG WILL IT BE BEFORE THE PASSPORT'S READY?
A WHILE...

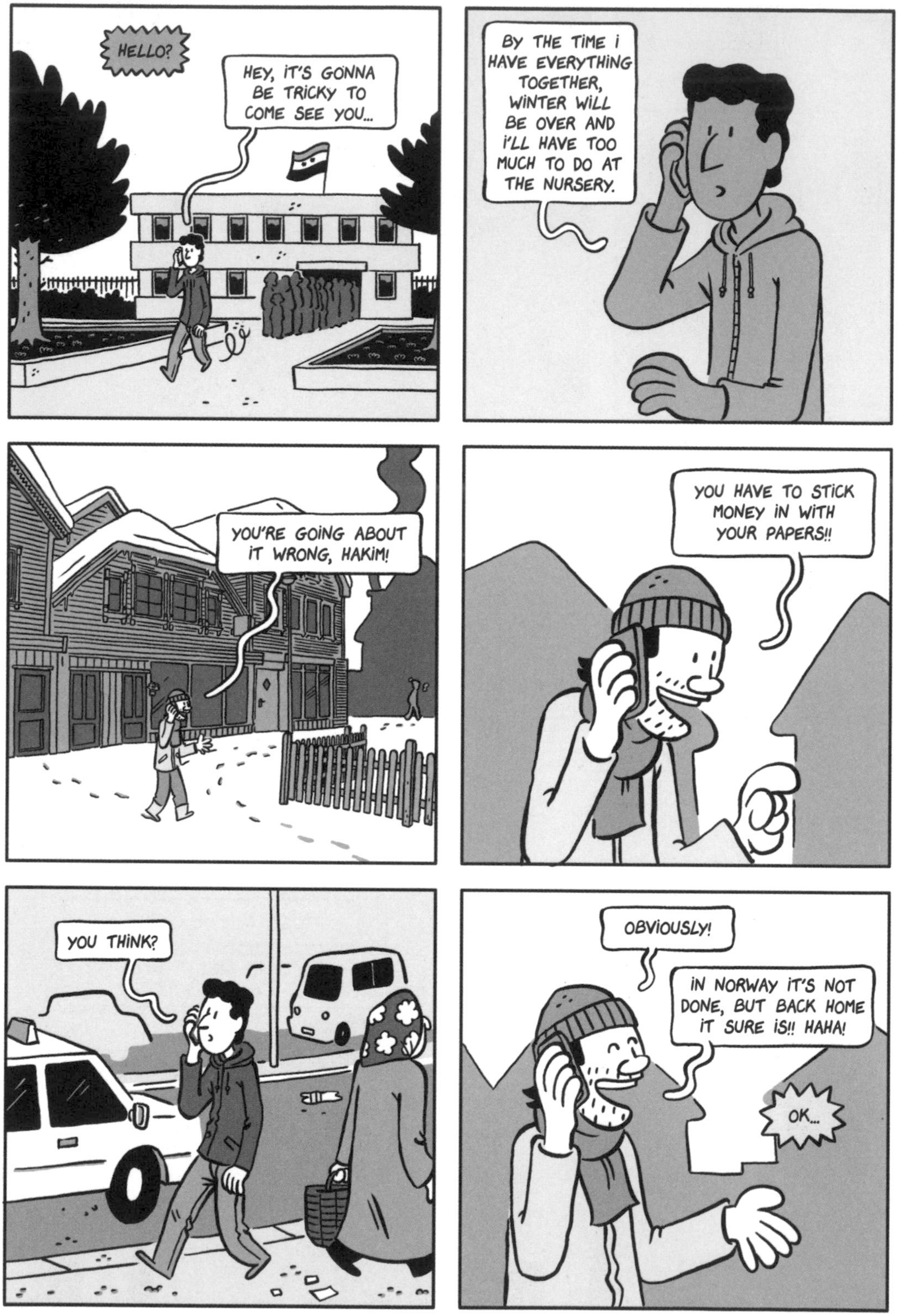
HELLO?
HEY, IT'S GONNA BE TRICKY TO COME SEE YOU...
BY THE TIME I HAVE EVERYTHING TOGETHER, WINTER WILL BE OVER AND I'LL HAVE TOO MUCH TO DO AT THE NURSERY.
YOU'RE GOING ABOUT IT WRONG, HAKIM!
YOU HAVE TO STICK MONEY IN WITH YOUR PAPERS!!
YOU THINK?
OBVIOUSLY!
IN NORWAY IT'S NOT DONE, BUT BACK HOME IT SURE IS!! HAHA!
OK...

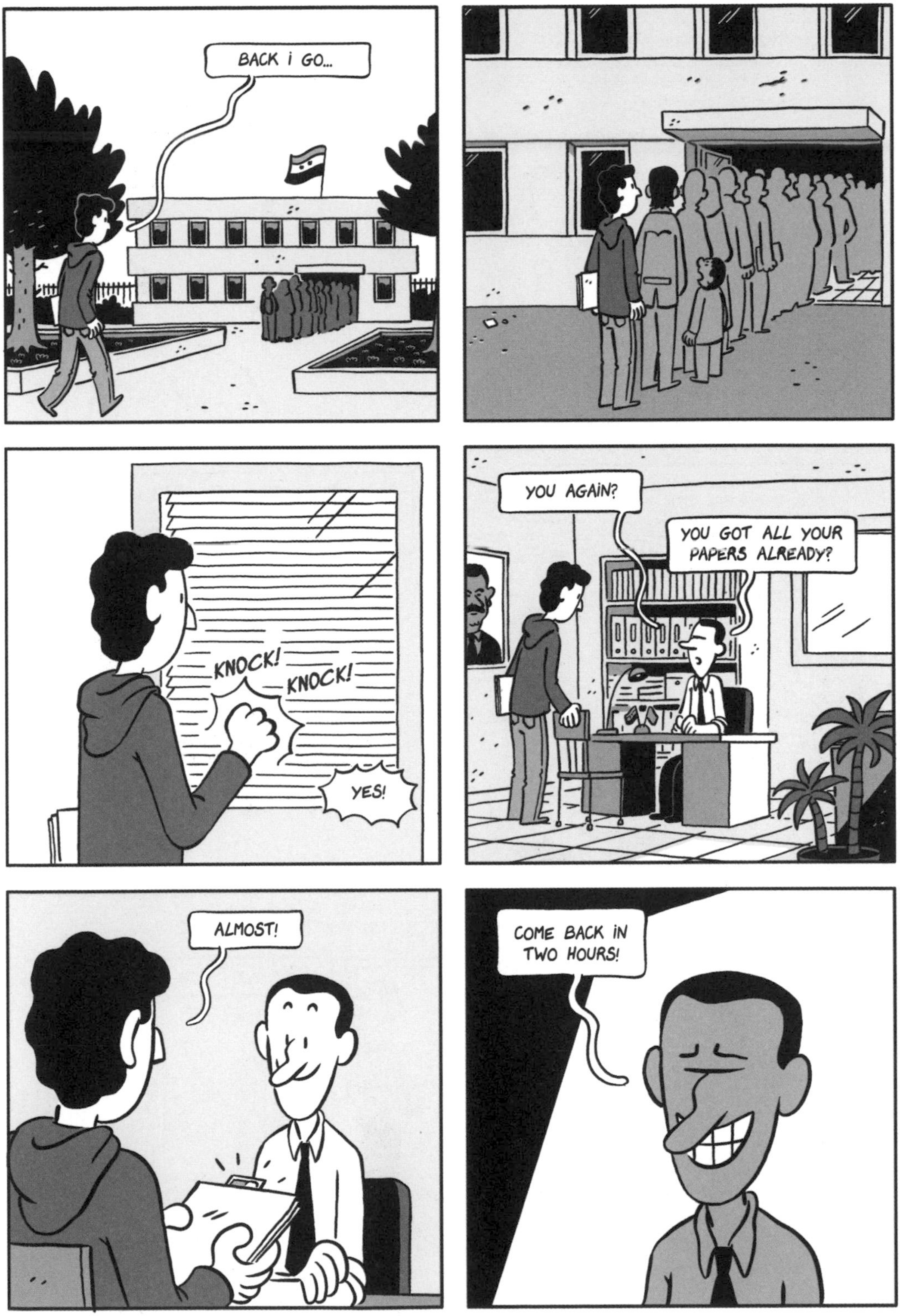
BACK i GO...
YOU AGAIN?
YOU GOT ALL YOUR PAPERS ALREADY?
KNOCK!
KNOCK!
YES!
ALMOST!
COME BACK iN TWO HOURS!

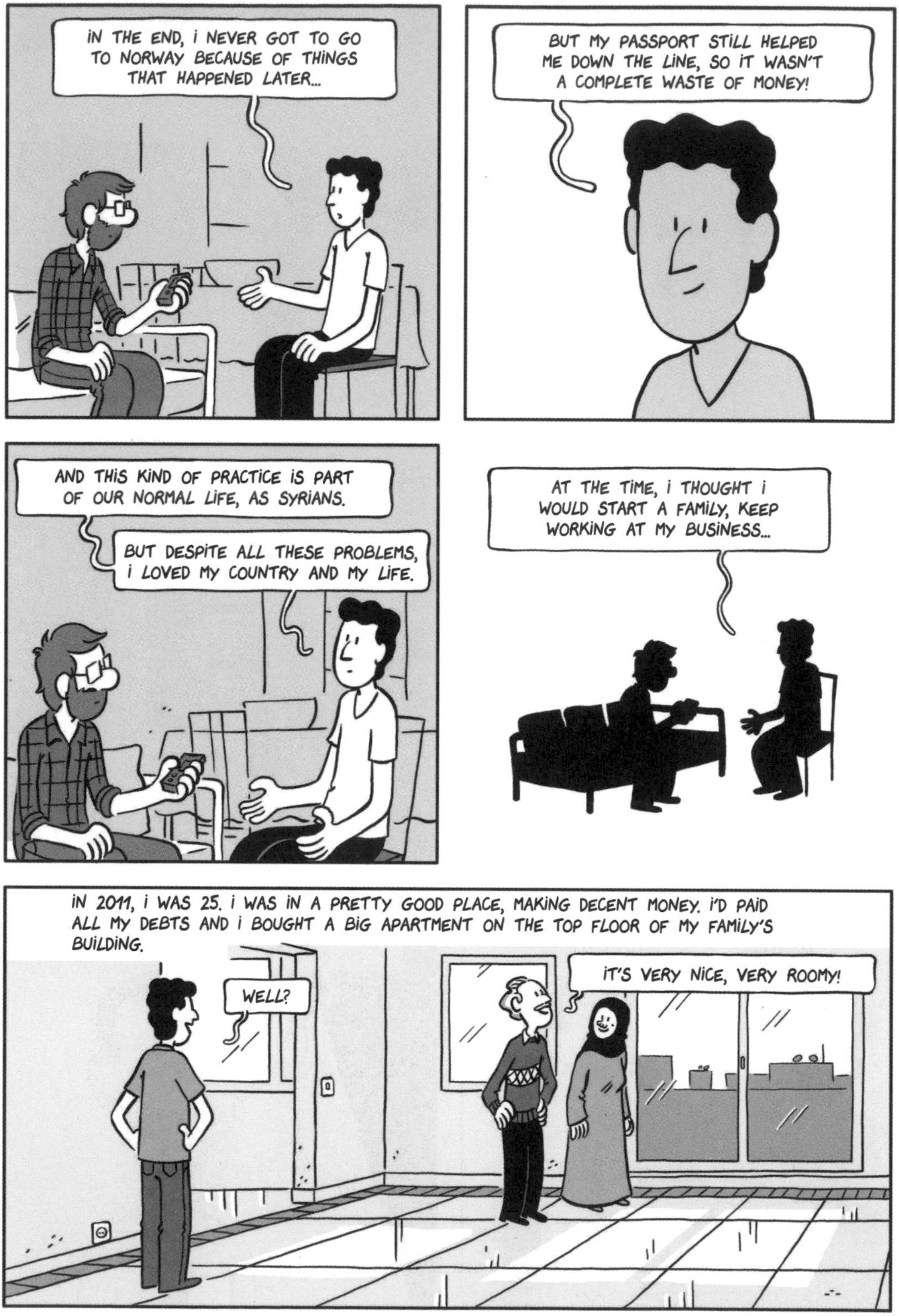
IN THE END, I NEVER GOT TO GO TO NORWAY BECAUSE OF THINGS THAT HAPPENED LATER...
BUT MY PASSPORT STILL HELPED ME DOWN THE LINE, SO IT WASN'T A COMPLETE WASTE OF MONEY!
AND THIS KIND OF PRACTICE IS PART OF OUR NORMAL LIFE, AS SYRIANS.
BUT DESPITE ALL THESE PROBLEMS, I LOVED MY COUNTRY AND MY LIFE.
AT THE TIME, I THOUGHT I WOULD START A FAMILY, KEEP WORKING AT MY BUSINESS...
IN 2011, I WAS 25. I WAS IN A PRETTY GOOD PLACE, MAKING DECENT MONEY. I'D PAID ALL MY DEBTS AND I BOUGHT A BIG APARTMENT ON THE TOP FLOOR OF MY FAMILY'S BUILDING.
WELL?
IT'S VERY NICE, VERY ROOMY!

UP TO THAT POINT, I'D ALWAYS LIVED WITH MY PARENTS AND YOUNGER SIBLINGS.

BUT YOUR LIVING ROOM IS ABOVE OUR BEDROOM, SO YOU'LL HAVE TO KEEP THE NOISE DOWN! HAHA!

I STARTED HAVING WORK DONE, BUYING FURNITURE, DECORATING.

IT WAS MY DREAM APARTMENT AND I WANTED TO MOVE IN ONCE I FOUND A WIFE.

I REMEMBER, ONE THURSDAY IT WAS ALL READY...

THE EVENTS BEGAN THE NEXT DAY...

CLICK!

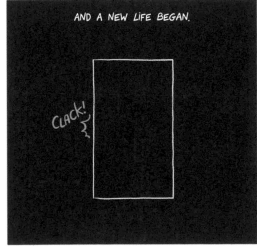

AND A NEW LIFE BEGAN.

CLACK!

41

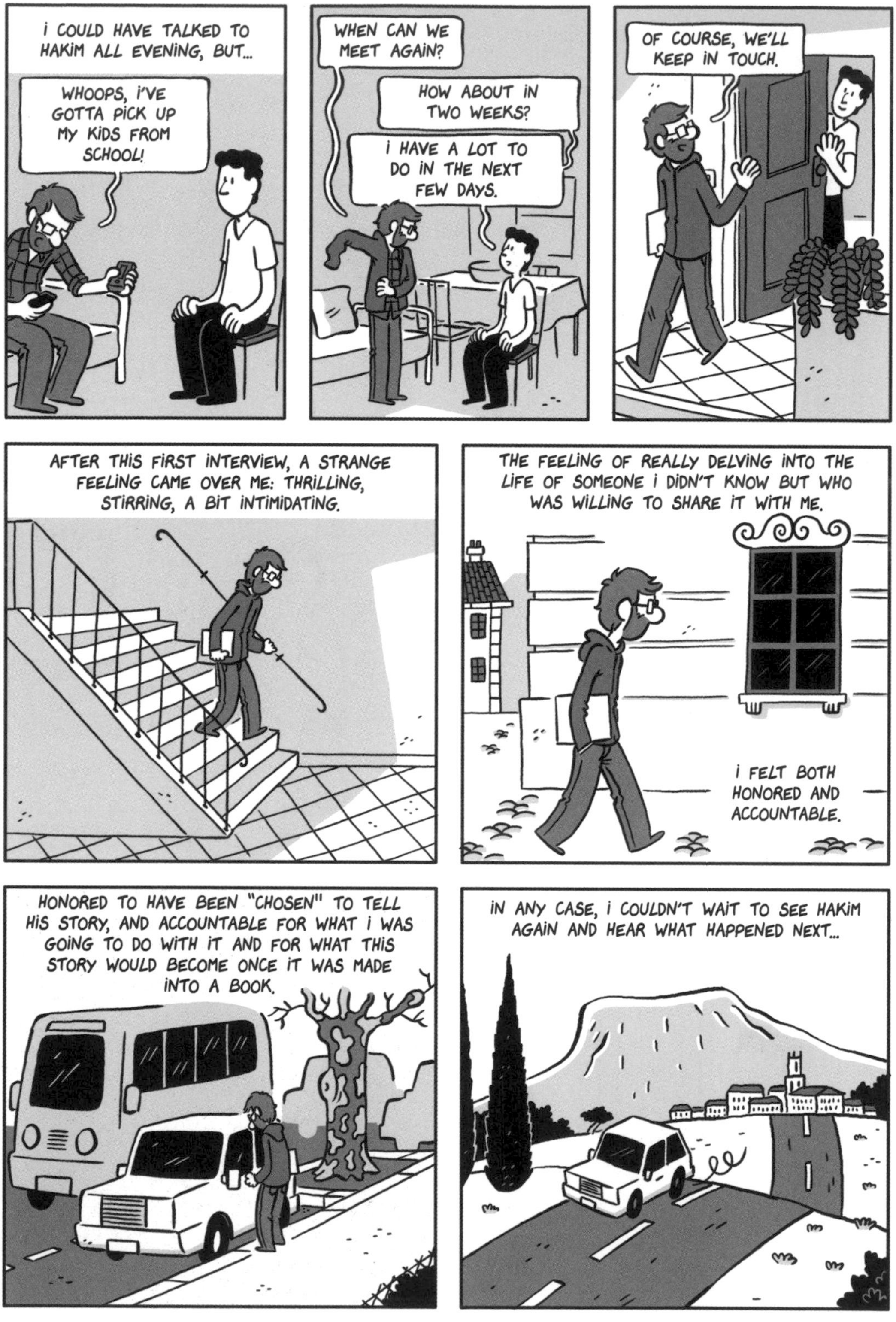
I COULD HAVE TALKED TO HAKIM ALL EVENING, BUT...
WHOOPS, I'VE GOTTA PICK UP MY KIDS FROM SCHOOL!
WHEN CAN WE MEET AGAIN?
HOW ABOUT IN TWO WEEKS?
I HAVE A LOT TO DO IN THE NEXT FEW DAYS.
OF COURSE, WE'LL KEEP IN TOUCH.
AFTER THIS FIRST INTERVIEW, A STRANGE FEELING CAME OVER ME: THRILLING, STIRRING, A BIT INTIMIDATING.
THE FEELING OF REALLY DELVING INTO THE LIFE OF SOMEONE I DIDN'T KNOW BUT WHO WAS WILLING TO SHARE IT WITH ME.
I FELT BOTH HONORED AND ACCOUNTABLE.
HONORED TO HAVE BEEN "CHOSEN" TO TELL HIS STORY, AND ACCOUNTABLE FOR WHAT I WAS GOING TO DO WITH IT AND FOR WHAT THIS STORY WOULD BECOME ONCE IT WAS MADE INTO A BOOK.
IN ANY CASE, I COULDN'T WAIT TO SEE HAKIM AGAIN AND HEAR WHAT HAPPENED NEXT...

Chapter 2: The Events (2011)

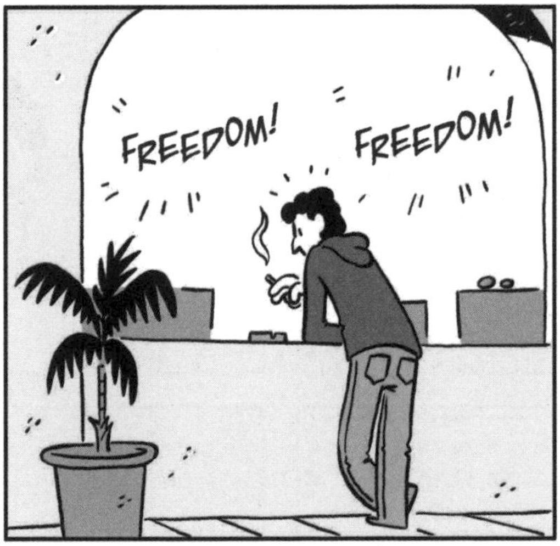
FREEDOM!
FREEDOM!

"CAN YOU IMAGINE? WE MARCHED!!"

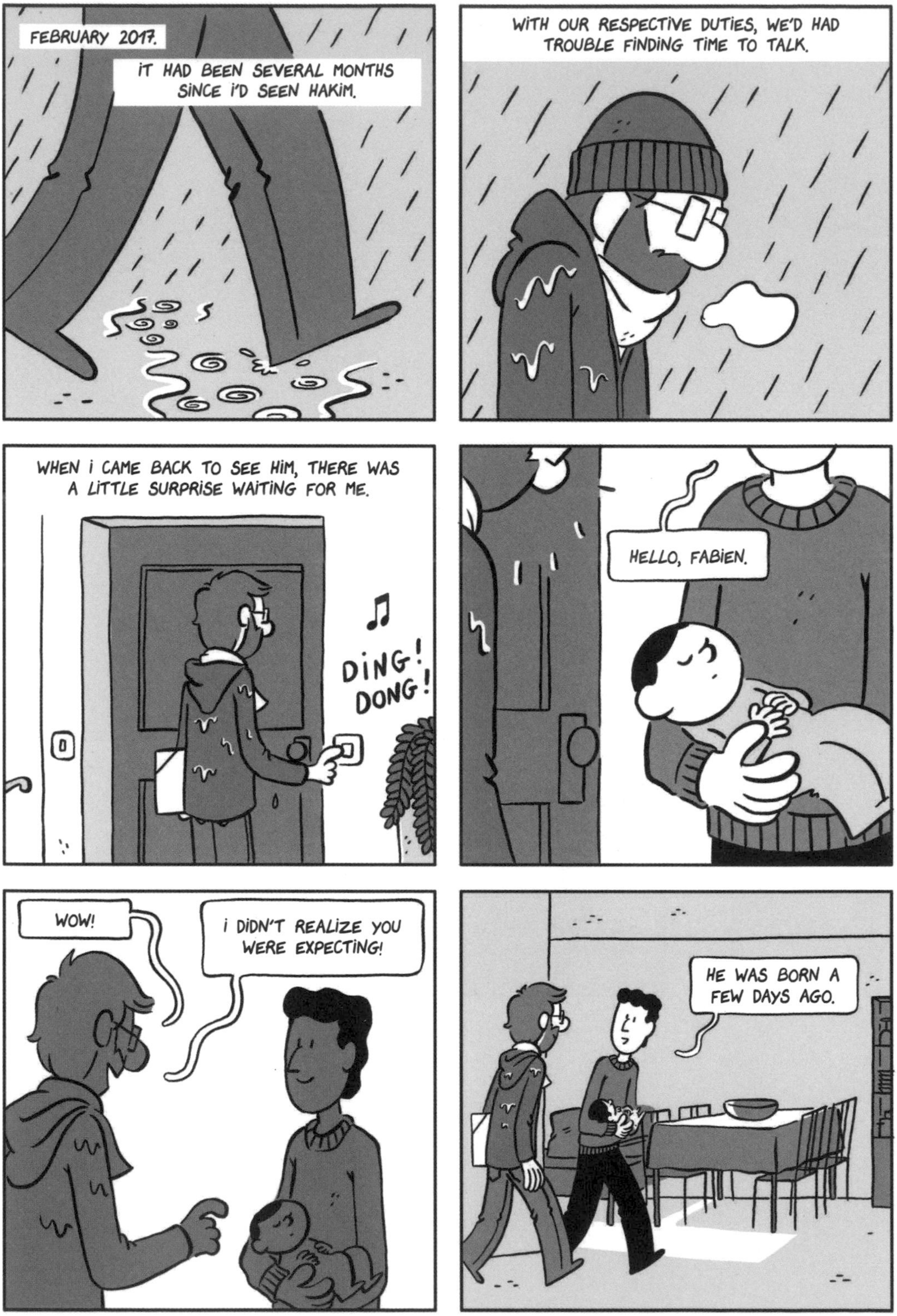
FEBRUARY 2017.
IT HAD BEEN SEVERAL MONTHS SINCE I'D SEEN HAKIM.
WITH OUR RESPECTIVE DUTIES, WE'D HAD TROUBLE FINDING TIME TO TALK.
WHEN I CAME BACK TO SEE HIM, THERE WAS A LITTLE SURPRISE WAITING FOR ME.
DING! DONG!
HELLO, FABIEN.
WOW!
I DIDN'T REALIZE YOU WERE EXPECTING!
HE WAS BORN A FEW DAYS AGO.

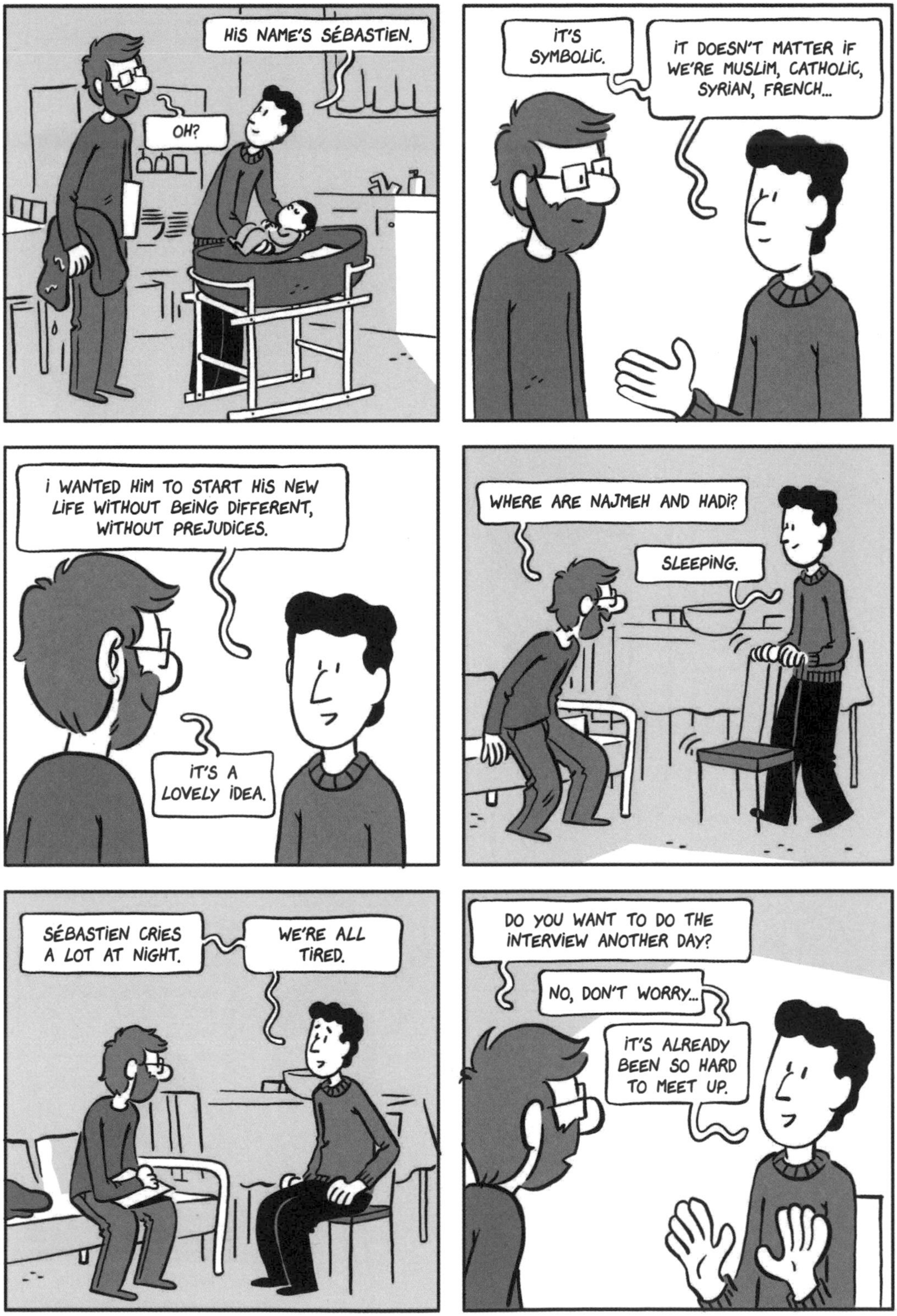
HIS NAME'S SÉBASTIEN.
OH?
IT'S SYMBOLIC.
IT DOESN'T MATTER IF WE'RE MUSLIM, CATHOLIC, SYRIAN, FRENCH...
I WANTED HIM TO START HIS NEW LIFE WITHOUT BEING DIFFERENT, WITHOUT PREJUDICES.
IT'S A LOVELY IDEA.
WHERE ARE NAJMEH AND HADI?
SLEEPING.
SÉBASTIEN CRIES A LOT AT NIGHT.
WE'RE ALL TIRED.
DO YOU WANT TO DO THE INTERVIEW ANOTHER DAY?
NO, DON'T WORRY...
IT'S ALREADY BEEN SO HARD TO MEET UP.

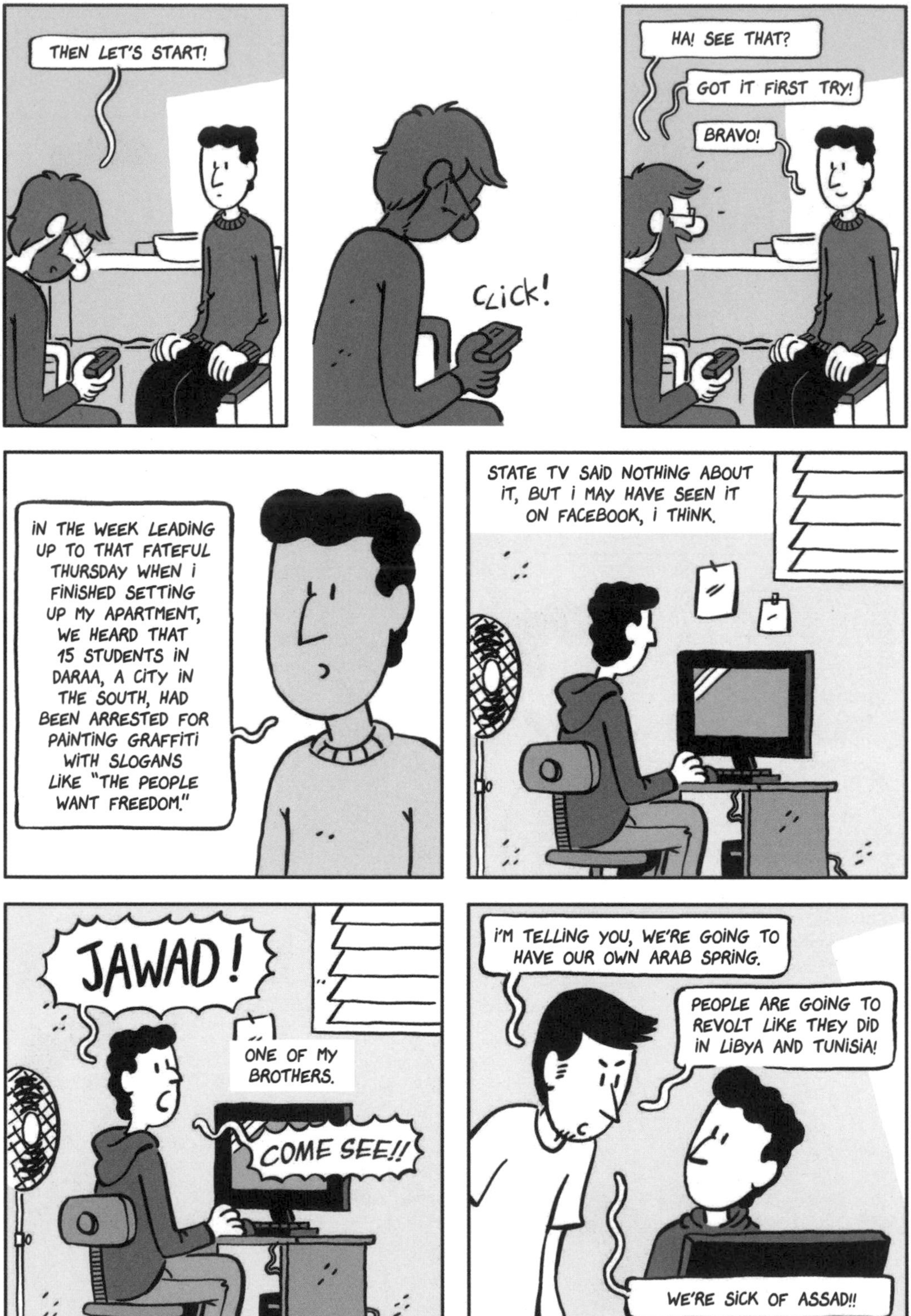
THEN LET'S START!
CLICK!
HA! SEE THAT?
GOT IT FIRST TRY!
BRAVO!
IN THE WEEK LEADING UP TO THAT FATEFUL THURSDAY WHEN I FINISHED SETTING UP MY APARTMENT, WE HEARD THAT 15 STUDENTS IN DARAA, A CITY IN THE SOUTH, HAD BEEN ARRESTED FOR PAINTING GRAFFITI WITH SLOGANS LIKE "THE PEOPLE WANT FREEDOM."
STATE TV SAID NOTHING ABOUT IT, BUT I MAY HAVE SEEN IT ON FACEBOOK, I THINK.
JAWAD!
ONE OF MY BROTHERS.
COME SEE!!
I'M TELLING YOU, WE'RE GOING TO HAVE OUR OWN ARAB SPRING.
PEOPLE ARE GOING TO REVOLT LIKE THEY DID IN LIBYA AND TUNISIA!
WE'RE SICK OF ASSAD!!

DEEDALEE...

HELLO?

YEAH, OK!

I'LL BE RIGHT UP!

THEY'VE JUST FINISHED SETTING UP MY FURNITURE.

I'LL GO SEE.

WOW GUYS, YOU DID A GREAT JOB!

SO I FINISHED SETTING UP MY APARTMENT ON THURSDAY...

CLICK!

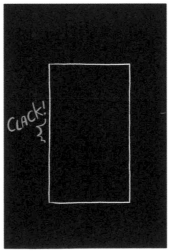

CLACK!

AND ON FRIDAY, I LEFT FOR WORK REALLY EARLY.

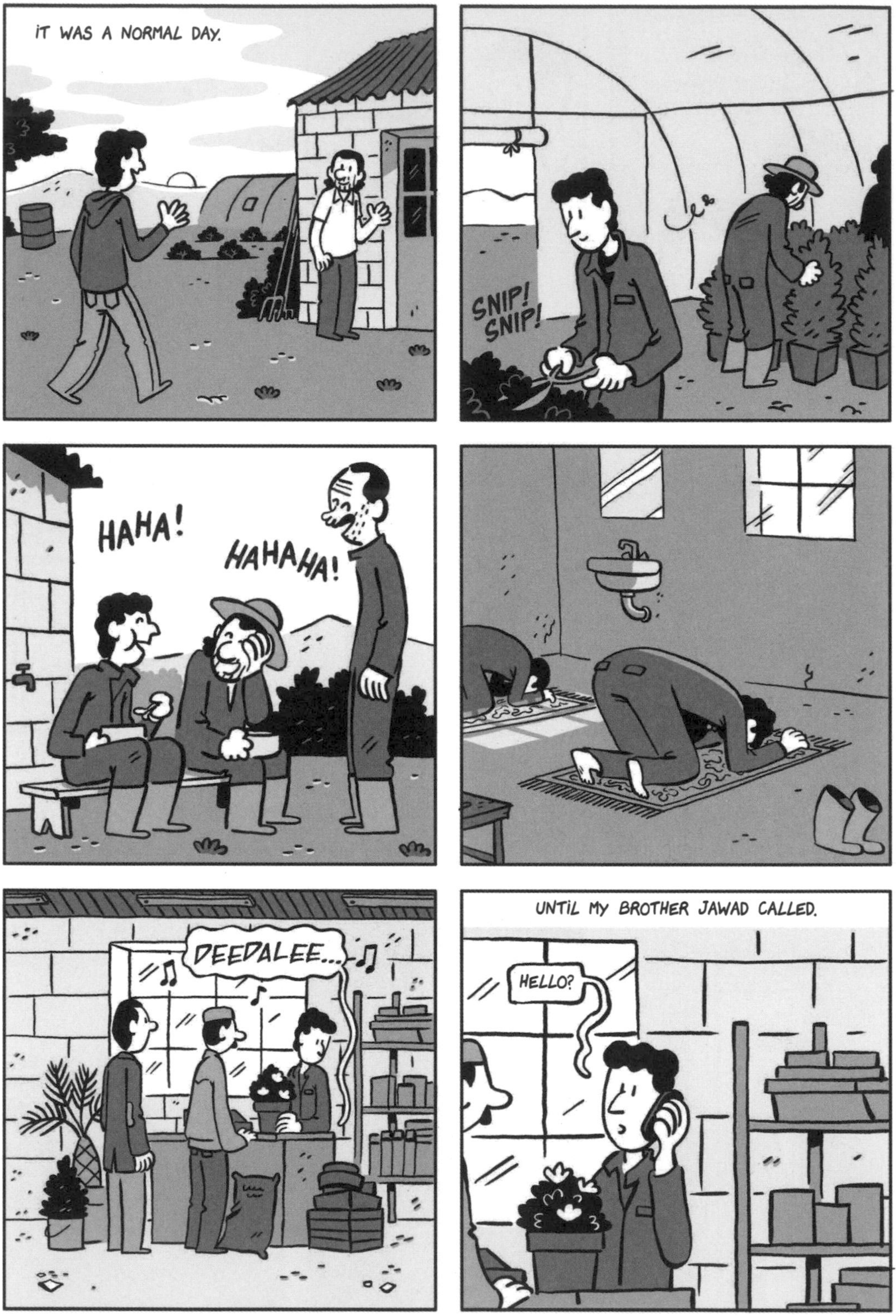
IT WAS A NORMAL DAY.
SNIP! SNIP!
HAHA!
HAHAHA!
DEEDALEE...
UNTIL MY BROTHER JAWAD CALLED.
HELLO?

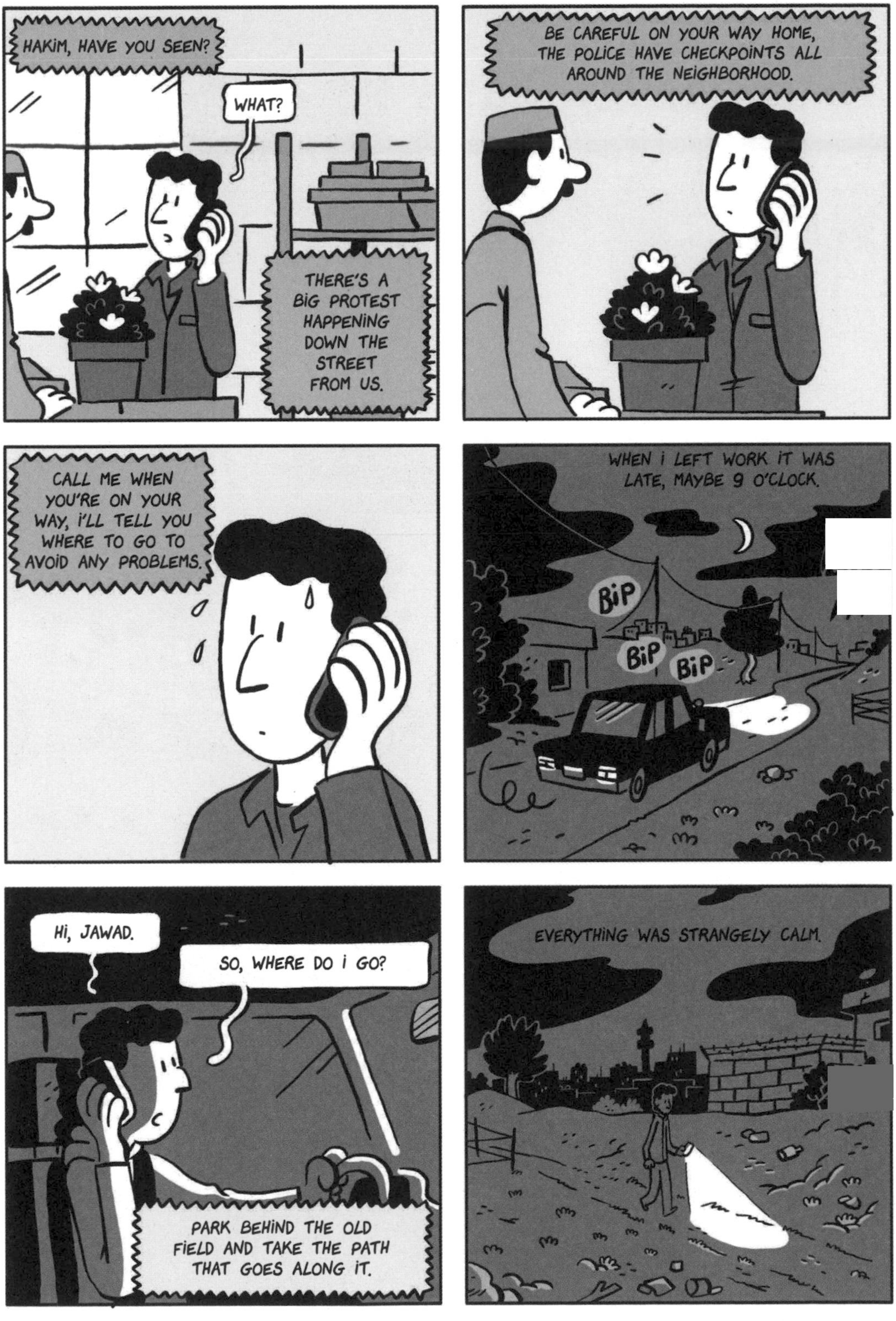
HAKIM, HAVE YOU SEEN?
WHAT?
THERE'S A BIG PROTEST HAPPENING DOWN THE STREET FROM US.
BE CAREFUL ON YOUR WAY HOME, THE POLICE HAVE CHECKPOINTS ALL AROUND THE NEIGHBORHOOD.
CALL ME WHEN YOU'RE ON YOUR WAY, I'LL TELL YOU WHERE TO GO TO AVOID ANY PROBLEMS.
WHEN I LEFT WORK IT WAS LATE, MAYBE 9 O'CLOCK.
BIP
BIP
BIP
HI, JAWAD.
SO, WHERE DO I GO?
PARK BEHIND THE OLD FIELD AND TAKE THE PATH THAT GOES ALONG IT.
EVERYTHING WAS STRANGELY CALM.

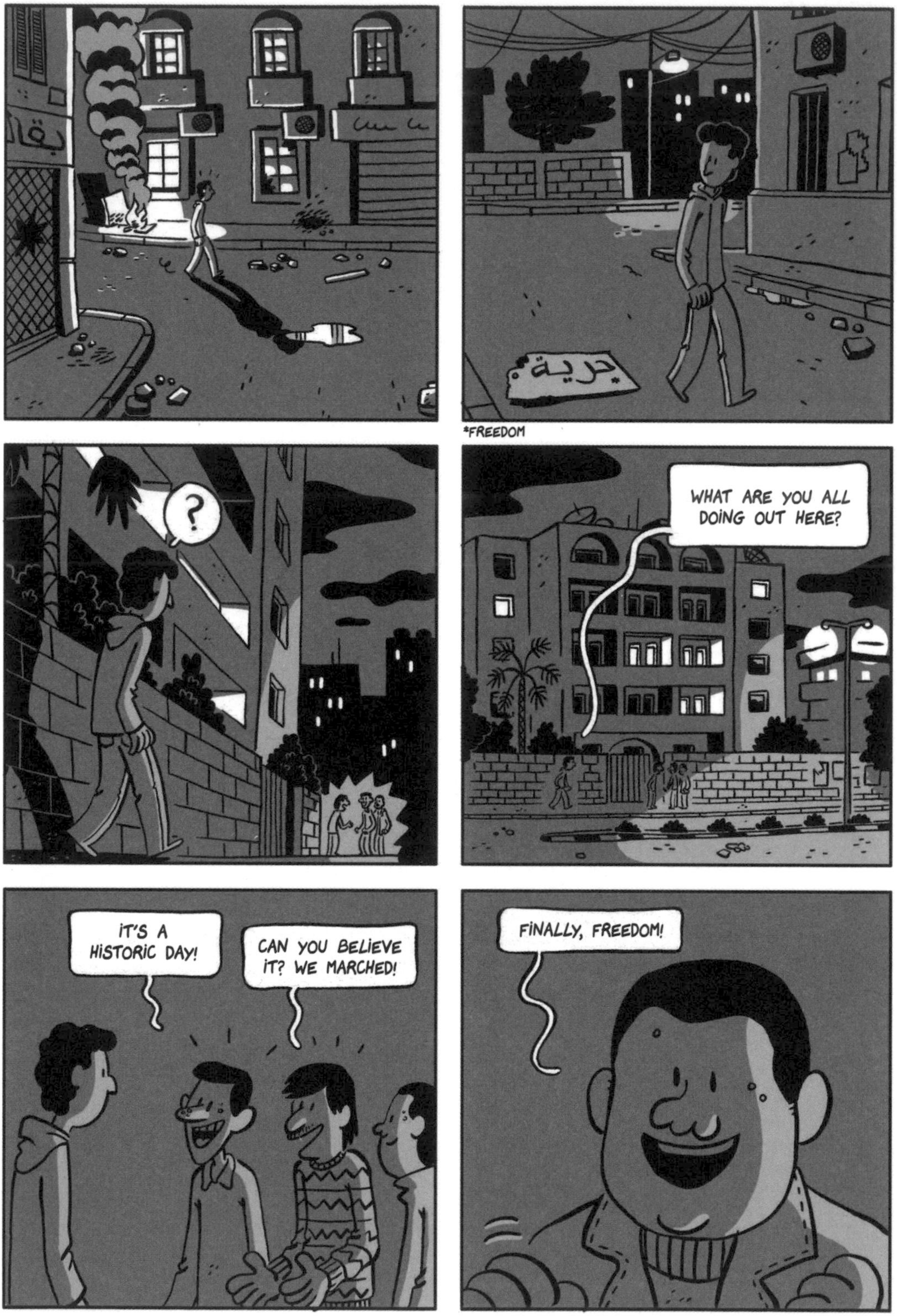
حرية
*FREEDOM
?
WHAT ARE YOU ALL DOING OUT HERE?
IT'S A HISTORIC DAY!
CAN YOU BELIEVE IT? WE MARCHED!
FINALLY, FREEDOM!

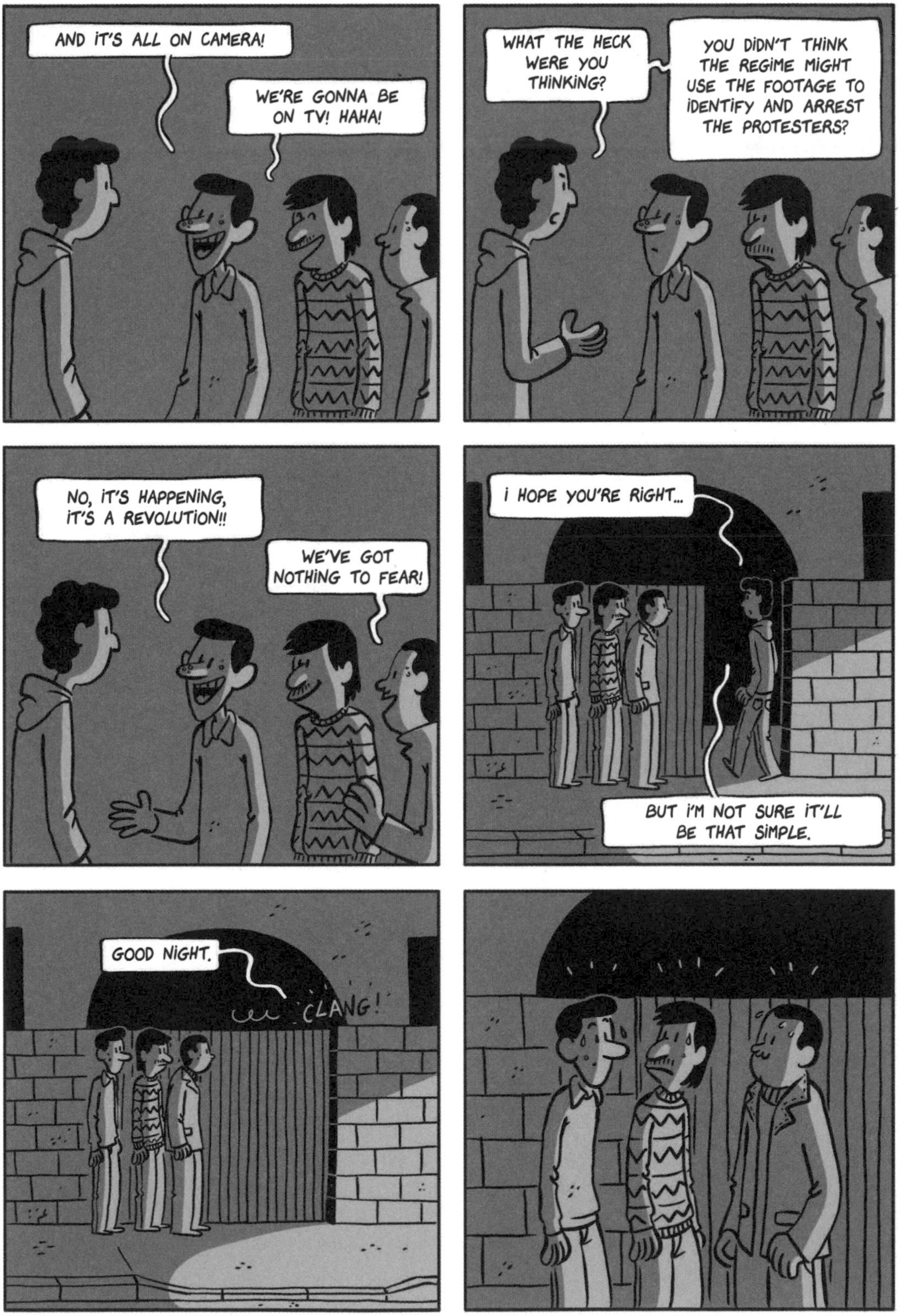
AND IT'S ALL ON CAMERA!
WE'RE GONNA BE ON TV! HAHA!
WHAT THE HECK WERE YOU THINKING?
YOU DIDN'T THINK THE REGIME MIGHT USE THE FOOTAGE TO IDENTIFY AND ARREST THE PROTESTERS?
NO, IT'S HAPPENING, IT'S A REVOLUTION!!
WE'VE GOT NOTHING TO FEAR!
I HOPE YOU'RE RIGHT...
BUT I'M NOT SURE IT'LL BE THAT SIMPLE.
GOOD NIGHT.
CLANG!

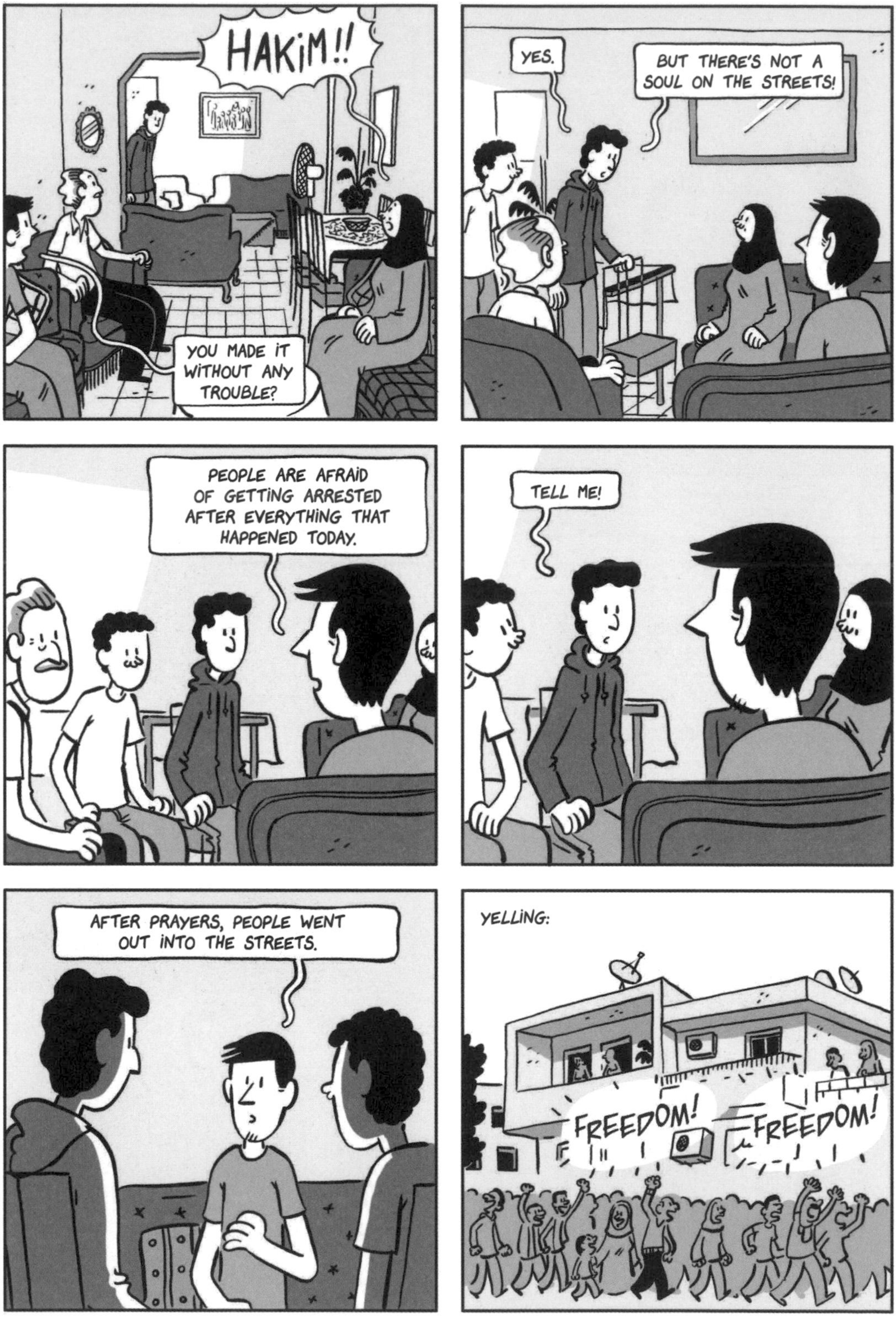
HAKIM!!
YOU MADE IT WITHOUT ANY TROUBLE?
YES.
BUT THERE'S NOT A SOUL ON THE STREETS!
PEOPLE ARE AFRAID OF GETTING ARRESTED AFTER EVERYTHING THAT HAPPENED TODAY.
TELL ME!
AFTER PRAYERS, PEOPLE WENT OUT INTO THE STREETS.
YELLING:
FREEDOM!
FREEDOM!

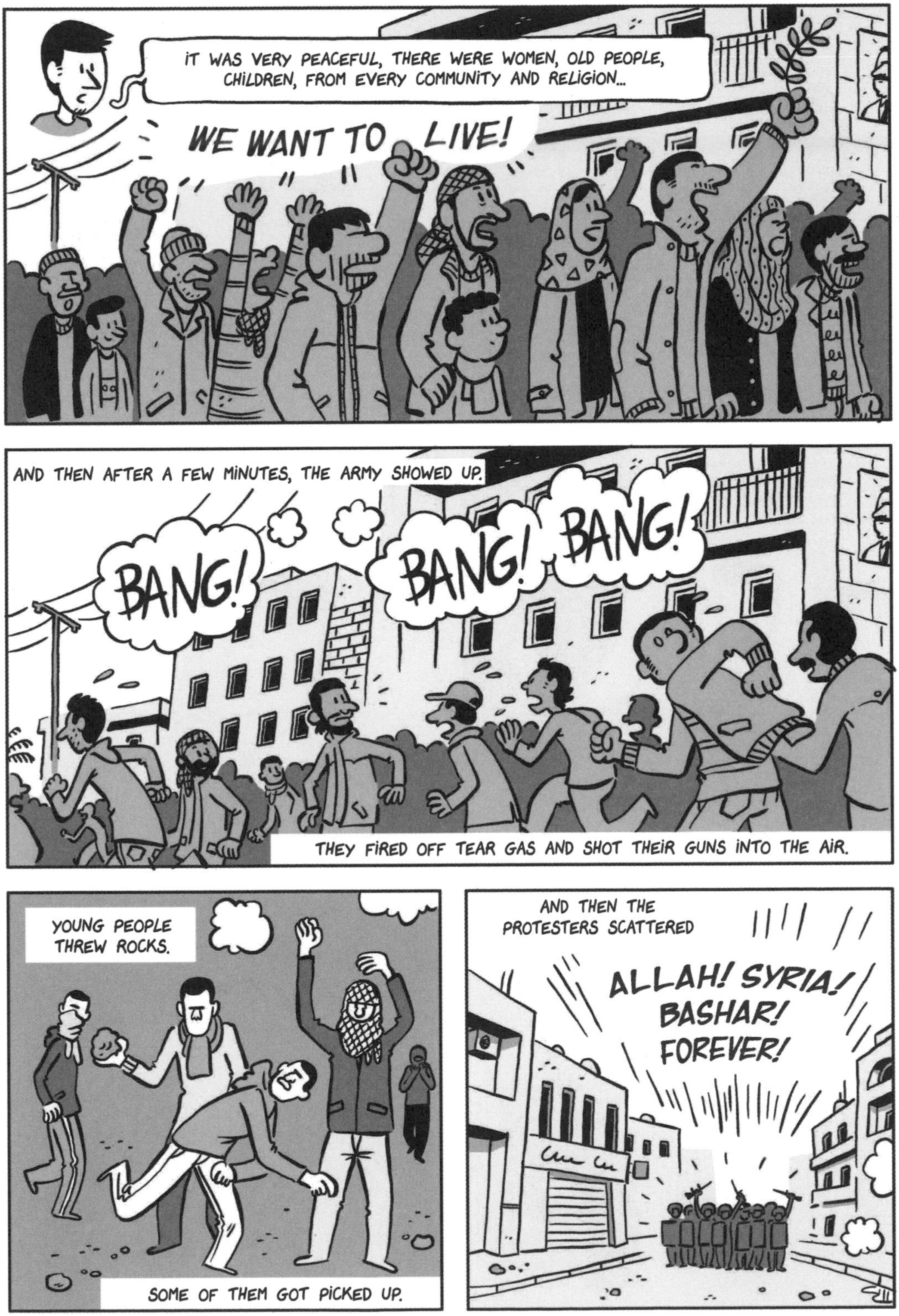
IT WAS VERY PEACEFUL, THERE WERE WOMEN, OLD PEOPLE, CHILDREN, FROM EVERY COMMUNITY AND RELIGION...
WE WANT TO LIVE!
AND THEN AFTER A FEW MINUTES, THE ARMY SHOWED UP.
BANG!
BANG! BANG!
THEY FIRED OFF TEAR GAS AND SHOT THEIR GUNS INTO THE AIR.
YOUNG PEOPLE THREW ROCKS.
SOME OF THEM GOT PICKED UP.
AND THEN THE PROTESTERS SCATTERED
ALLAH! SYRIA! BASHAR! FOREVER!

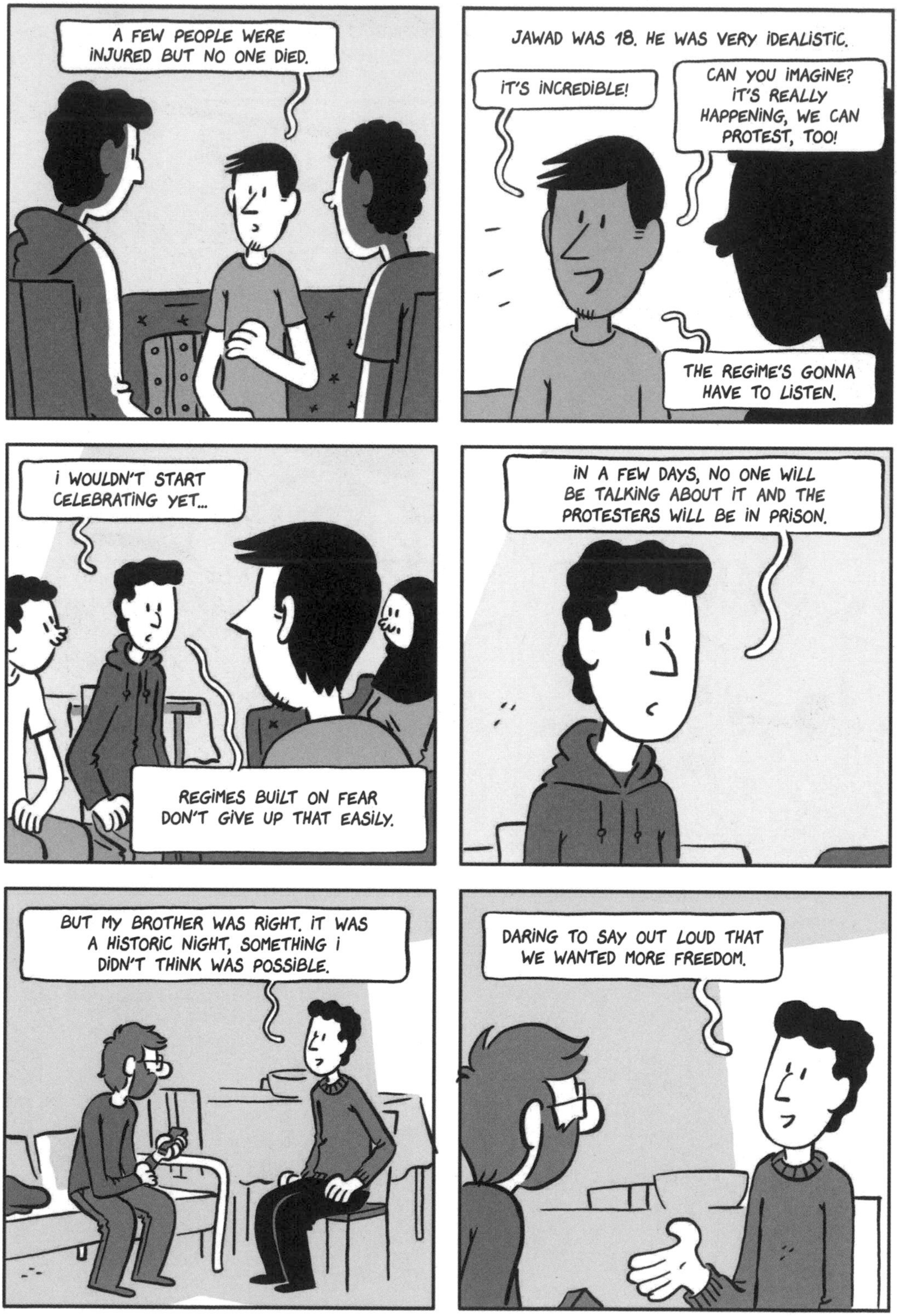
A FEW PEOPLE WERE INJURED BUT NO ONE DIED.
JAWAD WAS 18. HE WAS VERY IDEALISTIC.
IT'S INCREDIBLE!
CAN YOU IMAGINE? IT'S REALLY HAPPENING, WE CAN PROTEST, TOO!
THE REGIME'S GONNA HAVE TO LISTEN.
I WOULDN'T START CELEBRATING YET...
REGIMES BUILT ON FEAR DON'T GIVE UP THAT EASILY.
IN A FEW DAYS, NO ONE WILL BE TALKING ABOUT IT AND THE PROTESTERS WILL BE IN PRISON.
BUT MY BROTHER WAS RIGHT. IT WAS A HISTORIC NIGHT, SOMETHING I DIDN'T THINK WAS POSSIBLE.
DARING TO SAY OUT LOUD THAT WE WANTED MORE FREEDOM.

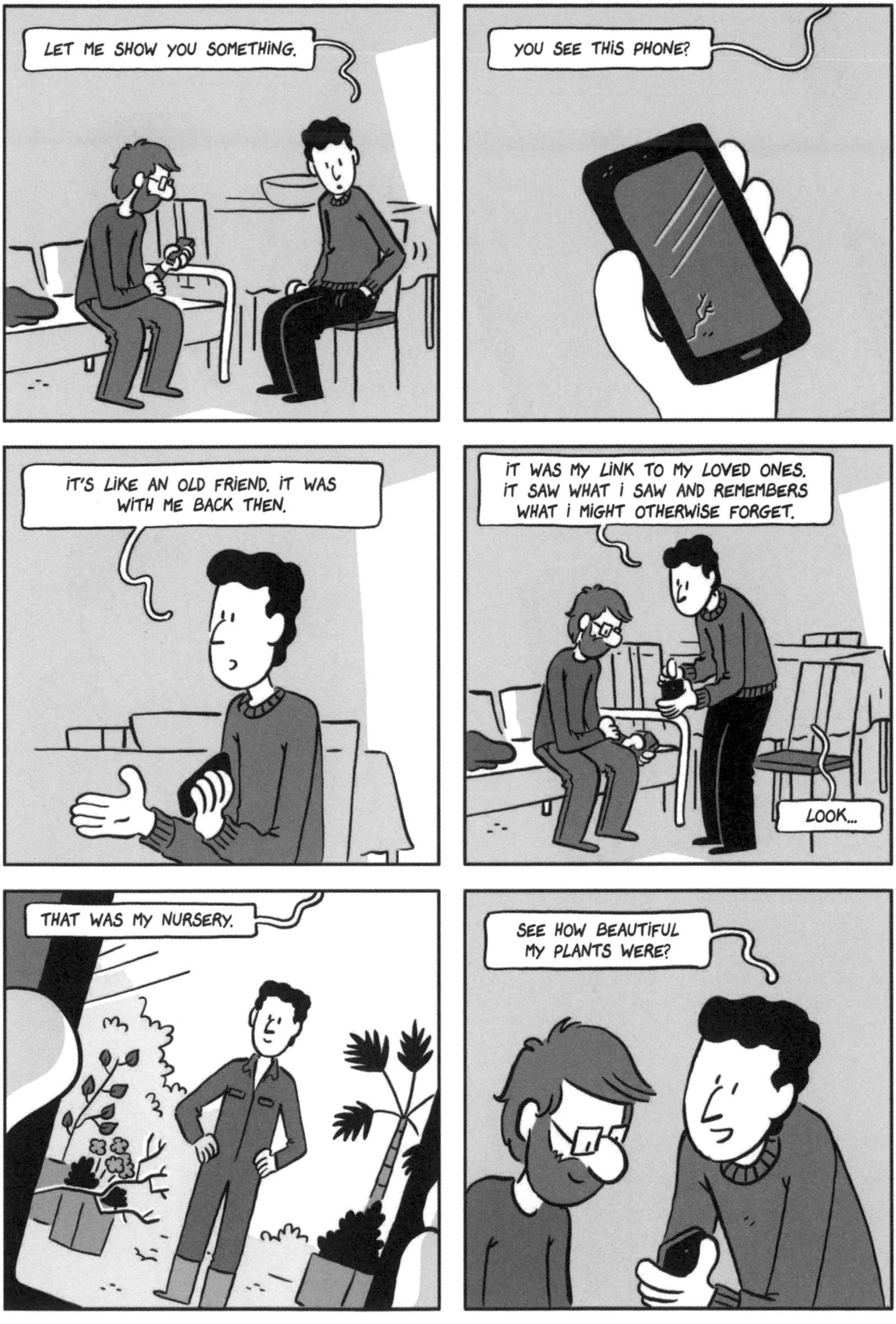
LET ME SHOW YOU SOMETHING.
YOU SEE THIS PHONE?
IT'S LIKE AN OLD FRIEND. IT WAS WITH ME BACK THEN.
IT WAS MY LINK TO MY LOVED ONES. IT SAW WHAT I SAW AND REMEMBERS WHAT I MIGHT OTHERWISE FORGET.
LOOK...
THAT WAS MY NURSERY.
SEE HOW BEAUTIFUL MY PLANTS WERE?

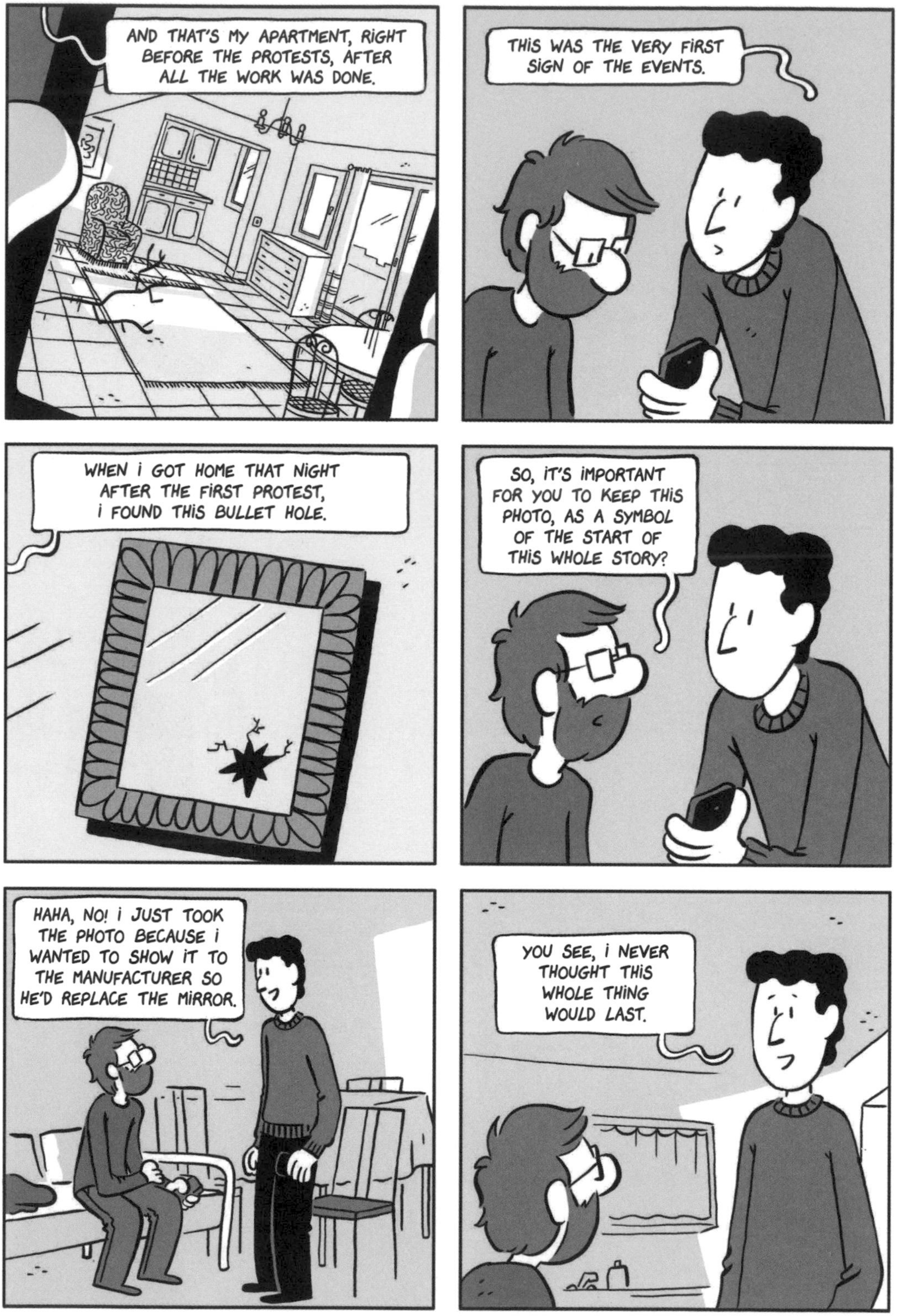
AND THAT'S MY APARTMENT, RIGHT BEFORE THE PROTESTS, AFTER ALL THE WORK WAS DONE.
THIS WAS THE VERY FIRST SIGN OF THE EVENTS.
WHEN I GOT HOME THAT NIGHT AFTER THE FIRST PROTEST, I FOUND THIS BULLET HOLE.
SO, IT'S IMPORTANT FOR YOU TO KEEP THIS PHOTO, AS A SYMBOL OF THE START OF THIS WHOLE STORY?
HAHA, NO! I JUST TOOK THE PHOTO BECAUSE I WANTED TO SHOW IT TO THE MANUFACTURER SO HE'D REPLACE THE MIRROR.
YOU SEE, I NEVER THOUGHT THIS WHOLE THING WOULD LAST.

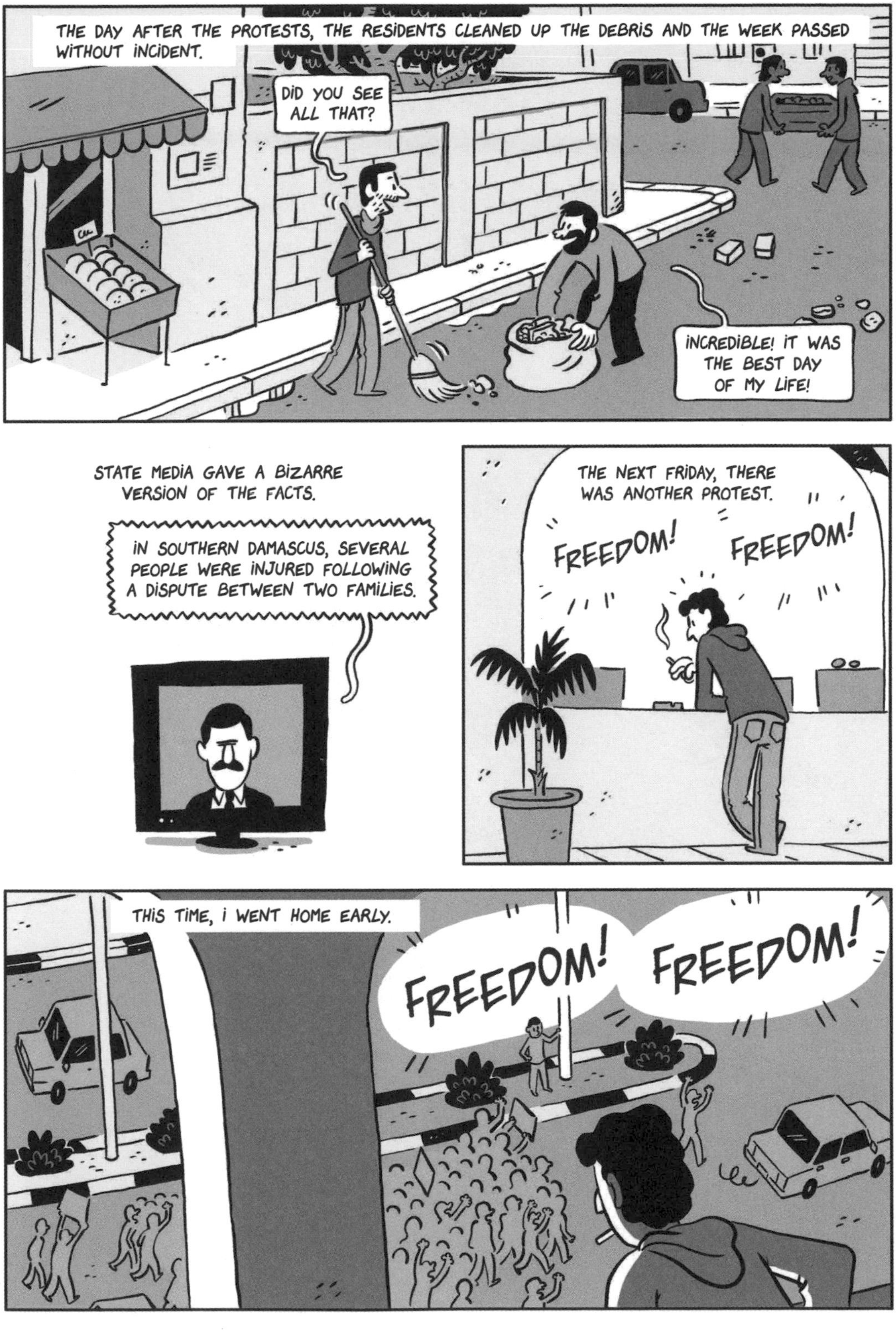
THE DAY AFTER THE PROTESTS, THE RESIDENTS CLEANED UP THE DEBRIS AND THE WEEK PASSED WITHOUT INCIDENT.
DID YOU SEE ALL THAT?
INCREDIBLE! IT WAS THE BEST DAY OF MY LIFE!
STATE MEDIA GAVE A BIZARRE VERSION OF THE FACTS.
IN SOUTHERN DAMASCUS, SEVERAL PEOPLE WERE INJURED FOLLOWING A DISPUTE BETWEEN TWO FAMILIES.
THE NEXT FRIDAY, THERE WAS ANOTHER PROTEST.
FREEDOM!
FREEDOM!
THIS TIME, I WENT HOME EARLY.
FREEDOM!
FREEDOM!

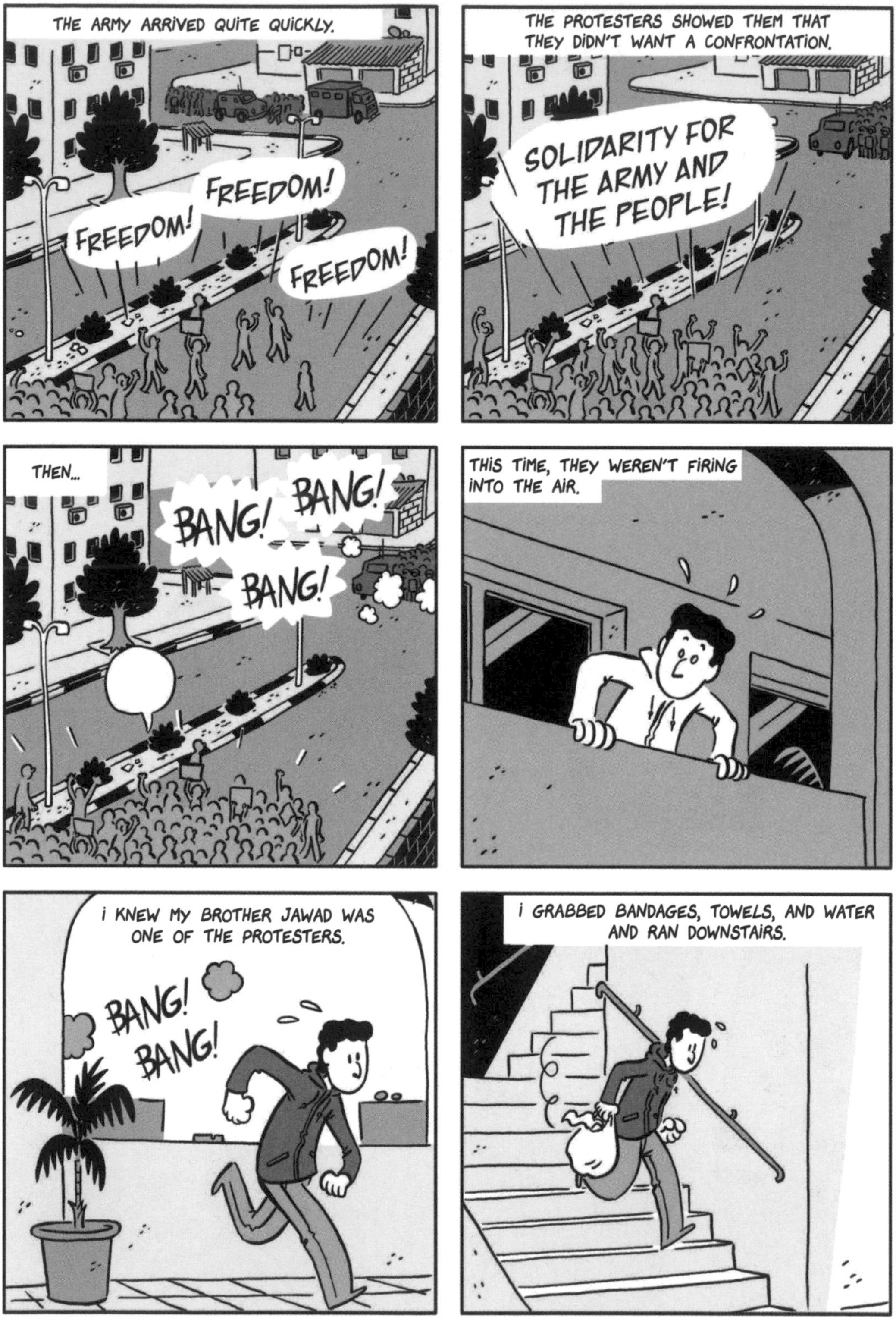
THE ARMY ARRIVED QUICKLY.
FREEDOM!
FREEDOM!
FREEDOM!
THE PROTESTERS SHOWED THEM THAT THEY DIDN'T WANT A CONFRONTATION.
SOLIDARITY FOR THE ARMY AND THE PEOPLE!
THEN...
BANG!
BANG!
BANG!
THIS TIME, THEY WEREN'T FIRING INTO THE AIR.
I KNEW MY BROTHER JAWAD WAS ONE OF THE PROTESTERS.
BANG!
BANG!
I GRABBED BANDAGES, TOWELS, AND WATER AND RAN DOWNSTAIRS.

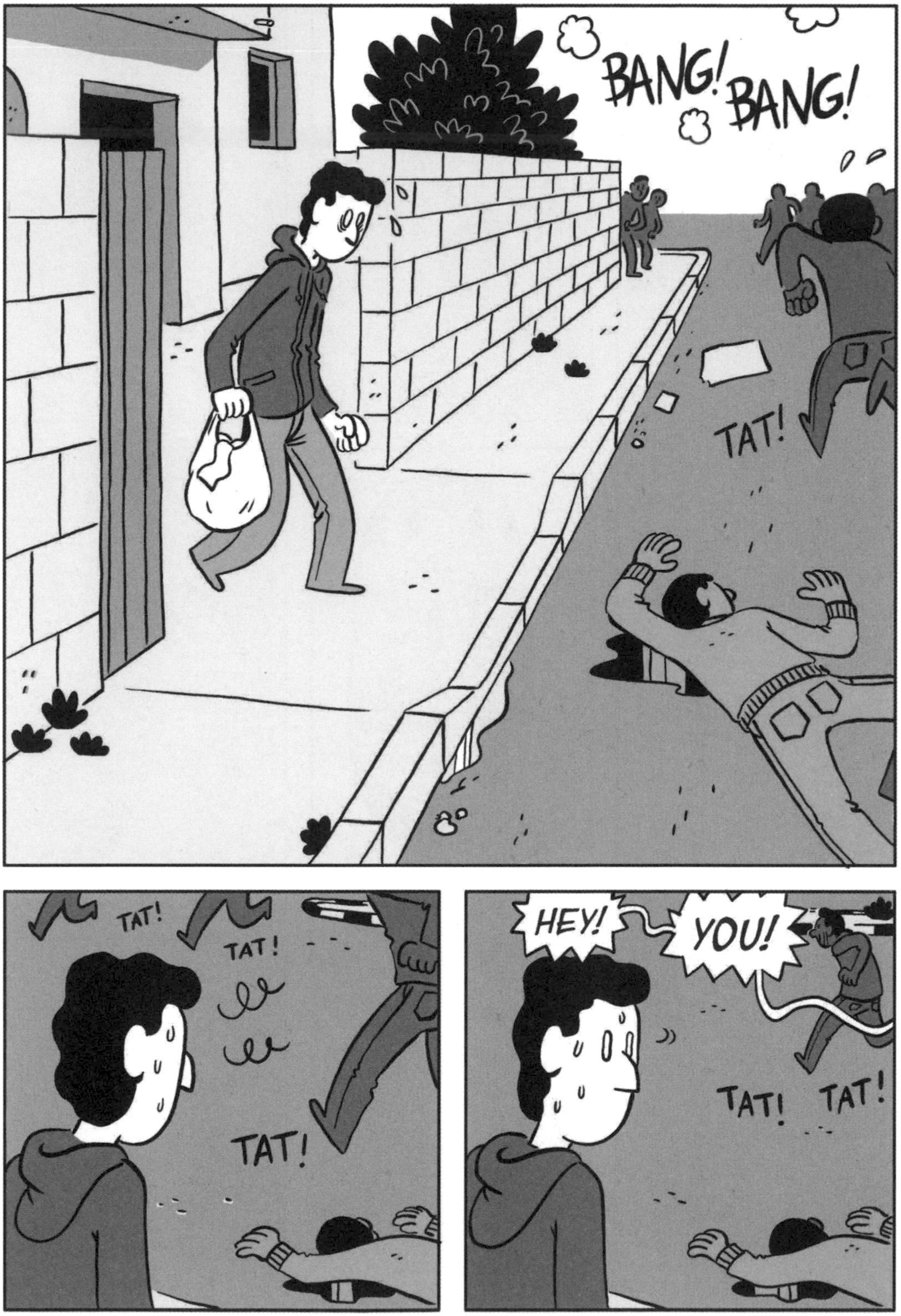
BANG! BANG!
TAT!
TAT!
TAT!
TAT!
HEY!
YOU!
TAT! TAT!

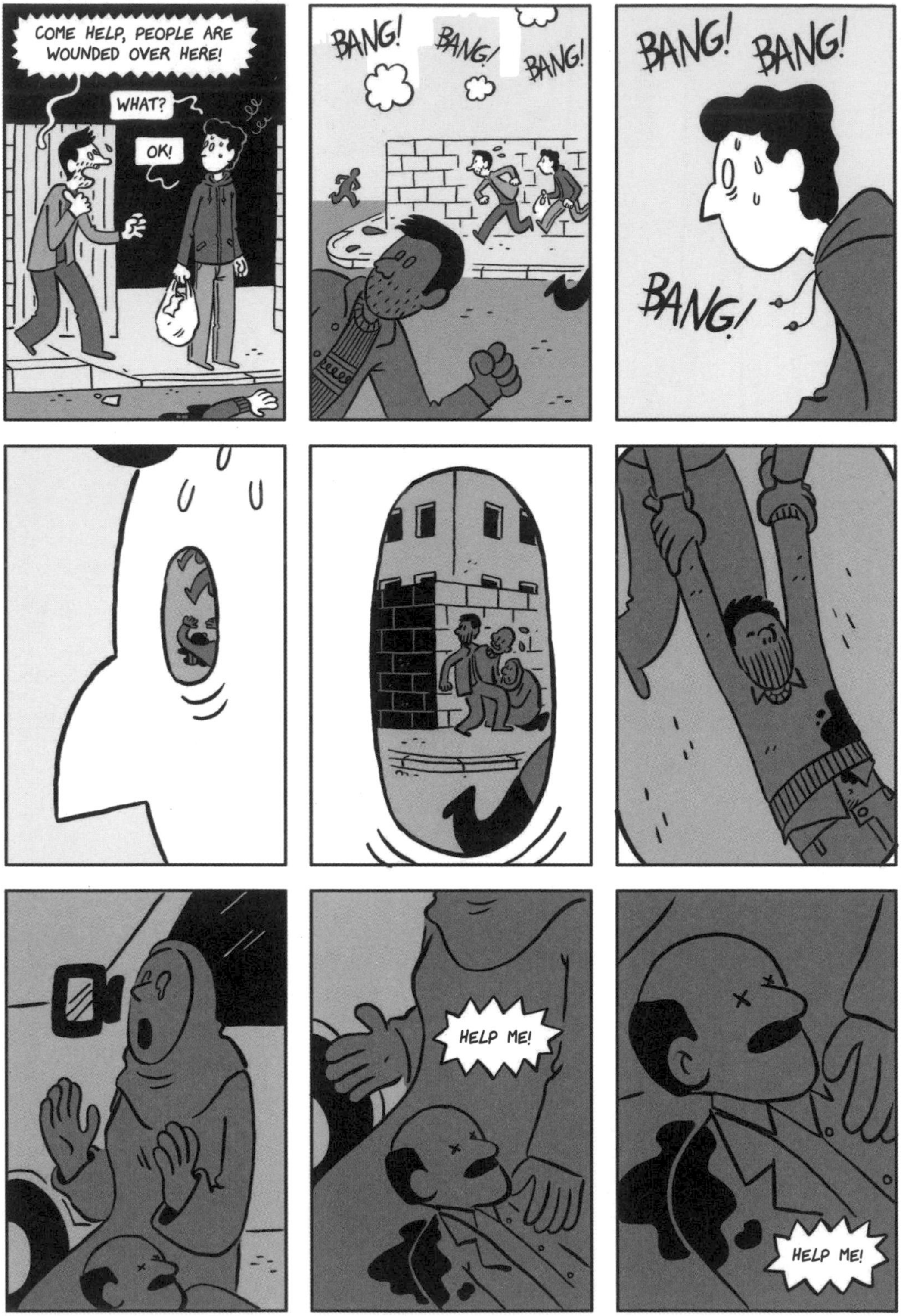
COME HELP, PEOPLE ARE WOUNDED OVER HERE!
WHAT?
OK!
BANG!
BANG!
BANG!
BANG!
BANG!
BANG!
HELP ME!
HELP ME!

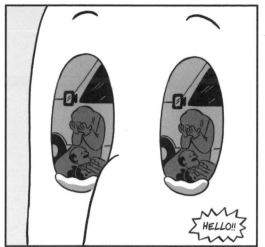

HELLO!!

BANG! HUH? BANG!

HELP ME, I SAID!

GRAB HIS LEGS, WE'LL GET HIM SOMEWHERE SAFE!

BANG! BANG! HAKIM!

JAWAD!

YOU'RE ALRIGHT? NOT HURT?

I'M OK...

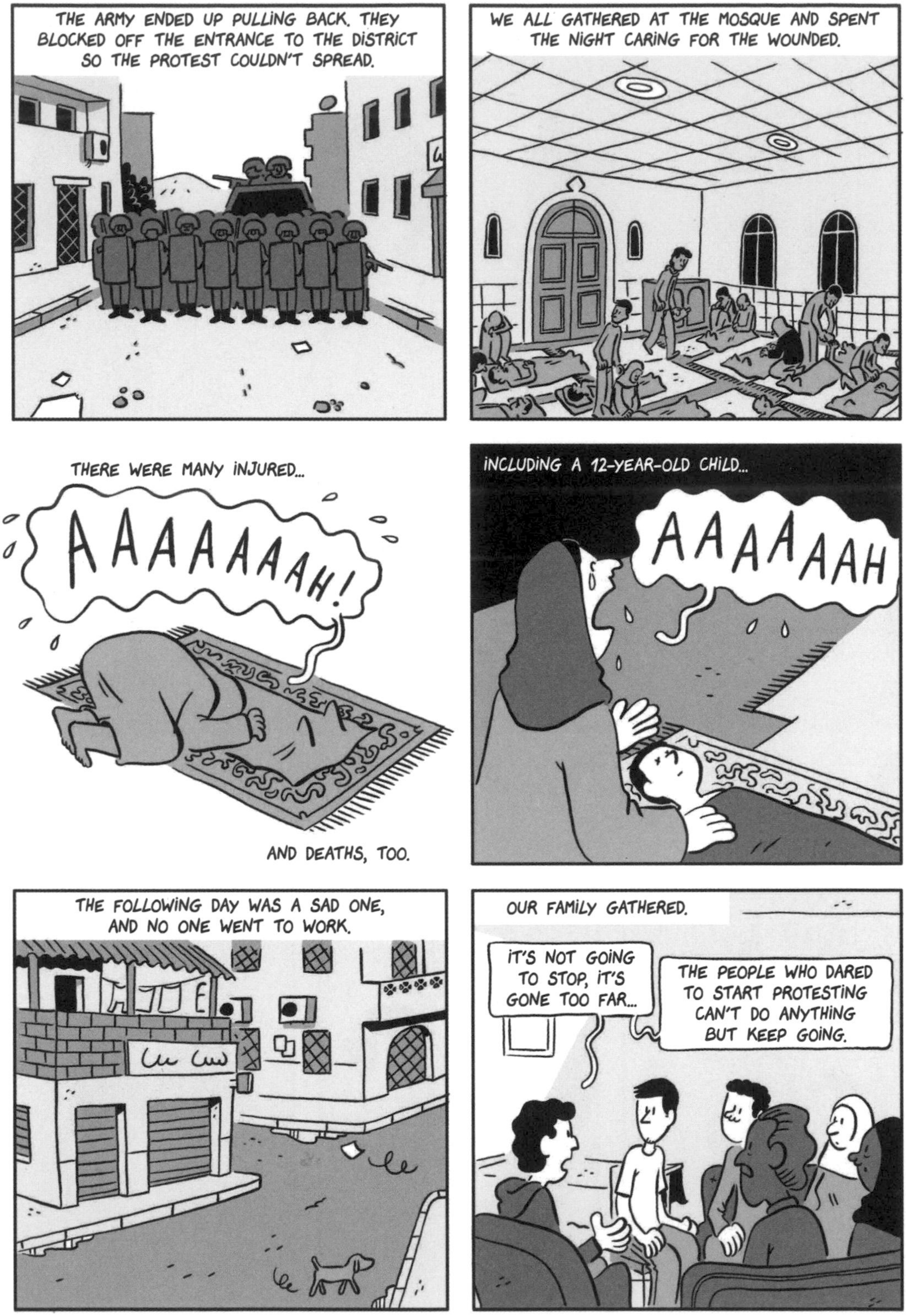
THE ARMY ENDED UP PULLING BACK. THEY BLOCKED OFF THE ENTRANCE TO THE DISTRICT SO THE PROTEST COULDN'T SPREAD.
WE ALL GATHERED AT THE MOSQUE AND SPENT THE NIGHT CARING FOR THE WOUNDED.
THERE WERE MANY INJURED...
AAAAAAAAH!
AND DEATHS, TOO.
INCLUDING A 12-YEAR-OLD CHILD...
AAAAAAH
THE FOLLOWING DAY WAS A SAD ONE, AND NO ONE WENT TO WORK.
OUR FAMILY GATHERED.
IT'S NOT GOING TO STOP, IT'S GONE TOO FAR...
THE PEOPLE WHO DARED TO START PROTESTING CAN'T DO ANYTHING BUT KEEP GOING.

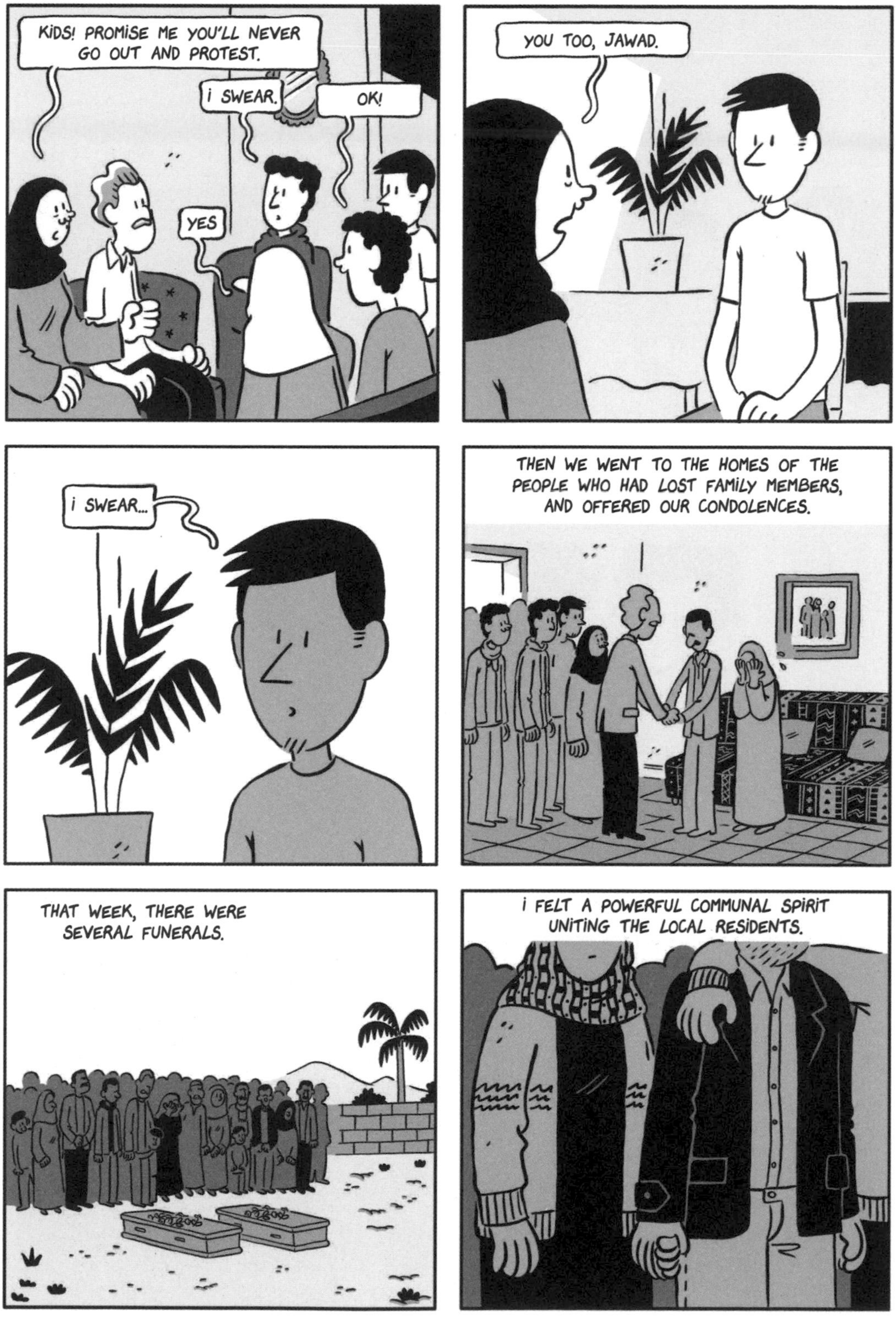
KIDS! PROMISE ME YOU'LL NEVER GO OUT AND PROTEST.
I SWEAR.
OK!
YES
YOU TOO, JAWAD.
I SWEAR...
THEN WE WENT TO THE HOMES OF THE PEOPLE WHO HAD LOST FAMILY MEMBERS, AND OFFERED OUR CONDOLENCES.
THAT WEEK, THERE WERE SEVERAL FUNERALS.
I FELT A POWERFUL COMMUNAL SPIRIT UNITING THE LOCAL RESIDENTS.

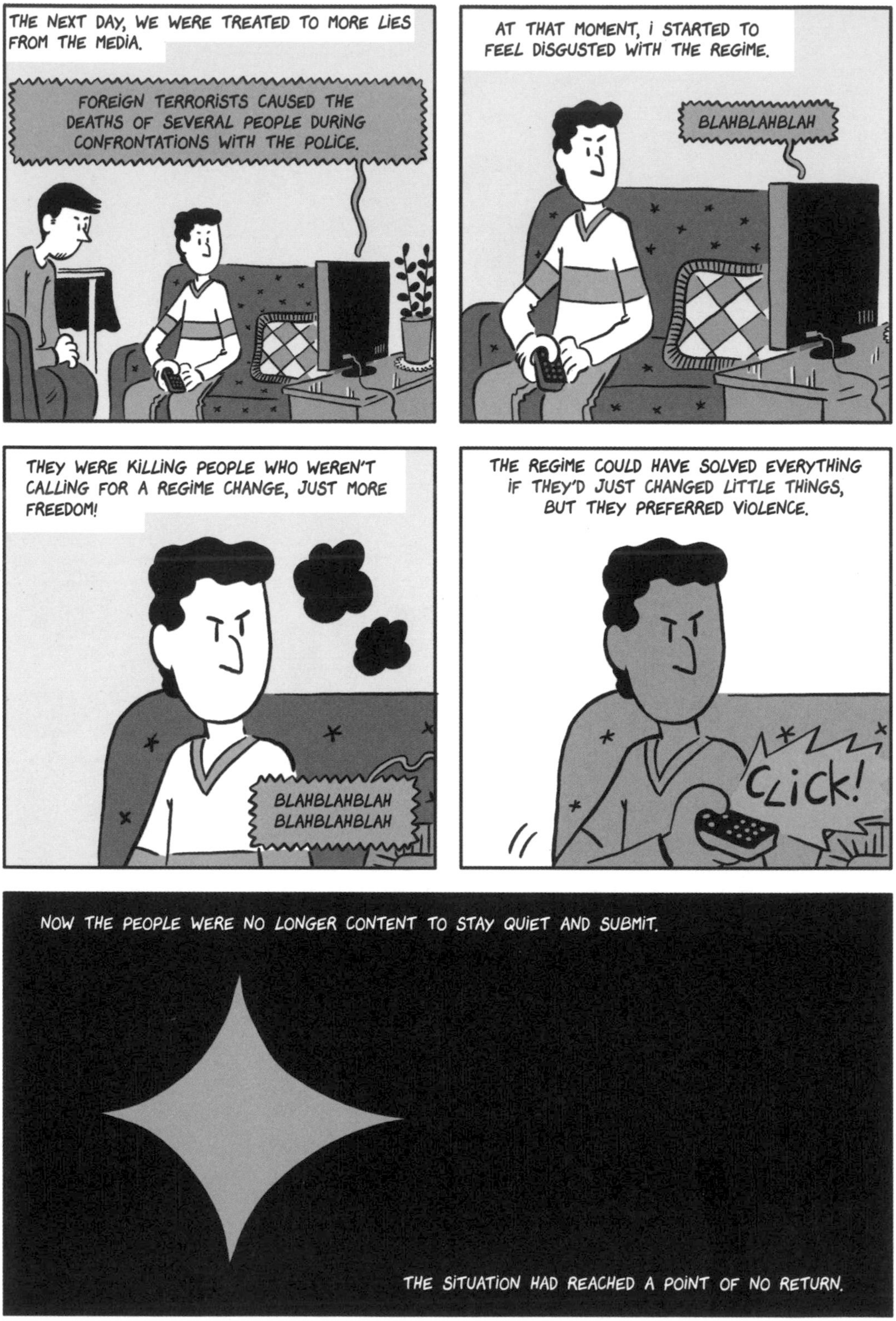
THE NEXT DAY, WE WERE TREATED TO MORE LIES FROM THE MEDIA.
FOREIGN TERRORISTS CAUSED THE DEATHS OF SEVERAL PEOPLE DURING CONFRONTATIONS WITH THE POLICE.
AT THAT MOMENT, I STARTED TO FEEL DISGUSTED WITH THE REGIME.
BLAHBLAHBLAH
THEY WERE KILLING PEOPLE WHO WEREN'T CALLING FOR A REGIME CHANGE, JUST MORE FREEDOM!
BLAHBLAHBLAH BLAHBLAHBLAH
THE REGIME COULD HAVE SOLVED EVERYTHING IF THEY'D JUST CHANGED LITTLE THINGS, BUT THEY PREFERRED VIOLENCE.
CLICK!
NOW THE PEOPLE WERE NO LONGER CONTENT TO STAY QUIET AND SUBMIT.
THE SITUATION HAD REACHED A POINT OF NO RETURN.

Chapter 3:
Escalating Violence

"HOW CAN ASSAD DO THIS TO HIS OWN PEOPLE?"

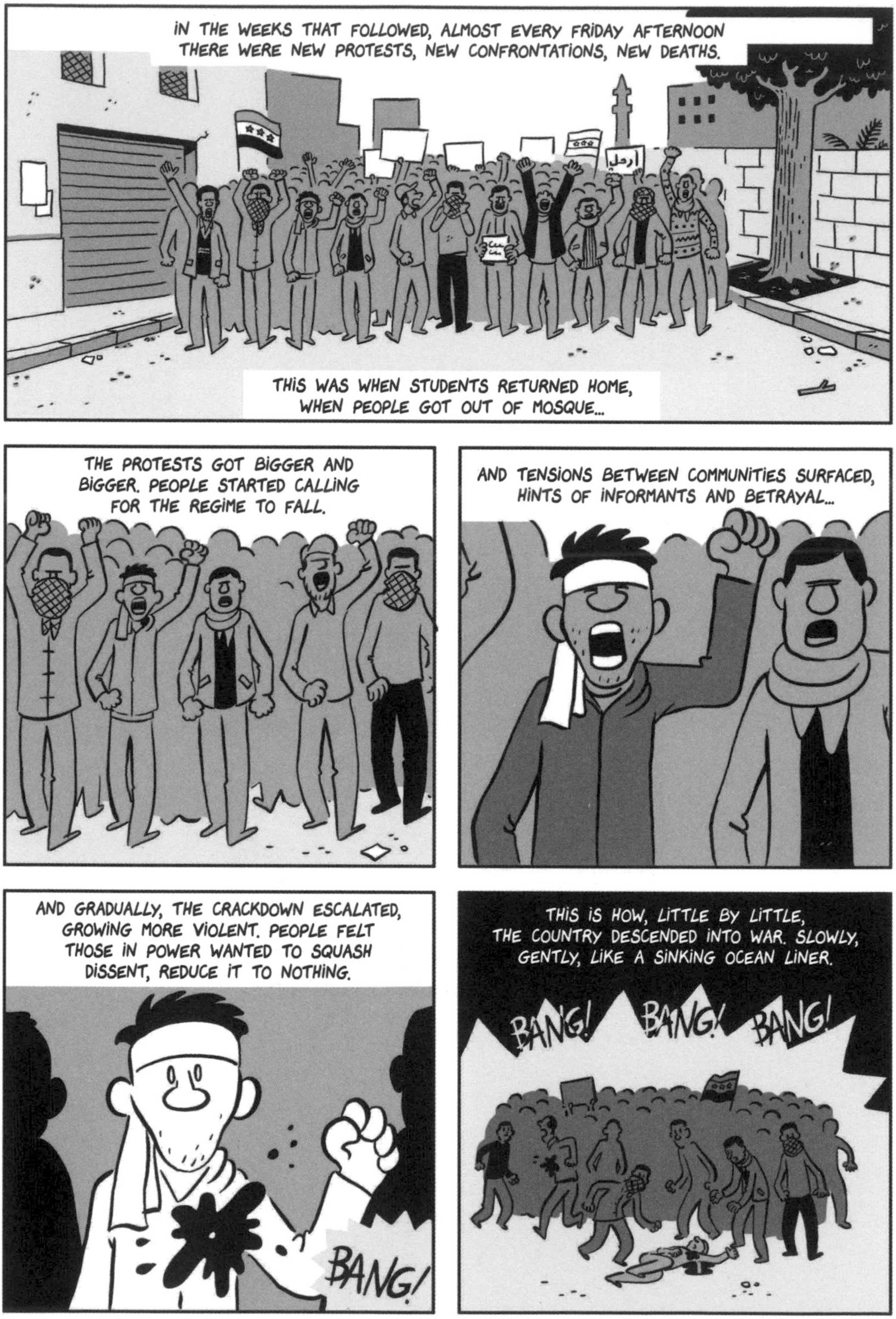
IN THE WEEKS THAT FOLLOWED, ALMOST EVERY FRIDAY AFTERNOON THERE WERE NEW PROTESTS, NEW CONFRONTATIONS, NEW DEATHS.
THIS WAS WHEN STUDENTS RETURNED HOME, WHEN PEOPLE GOT OUT OF MOSQUE...
THE PROTESTS GOT BIGGER AND BIGGER. PEOPLE STARTED CALLING FOR THE REGIME TO FALL.
AND TENSIONS BETWEEN COMMUNITIES SURFACED, HINTS OF INFORMANTS AND BETRAYAL...
AND GRADUALLY, THE CRACKDOWN ESCALATED, GROWING MORE VIOLENT. PEOPLE FELT THOSE IN POWER WANTED TO SQUASH DISSENT, REDUCE IT TO NOTHING.
BANG!
THIS IS HOW, LITTLE BY LITTLE, THE COUNTRY DESCENDED INTO WAR. SLOWLY, GENTLY, LIKE A SINKING OCEAN LINER.
BANG! BANG! BANG!

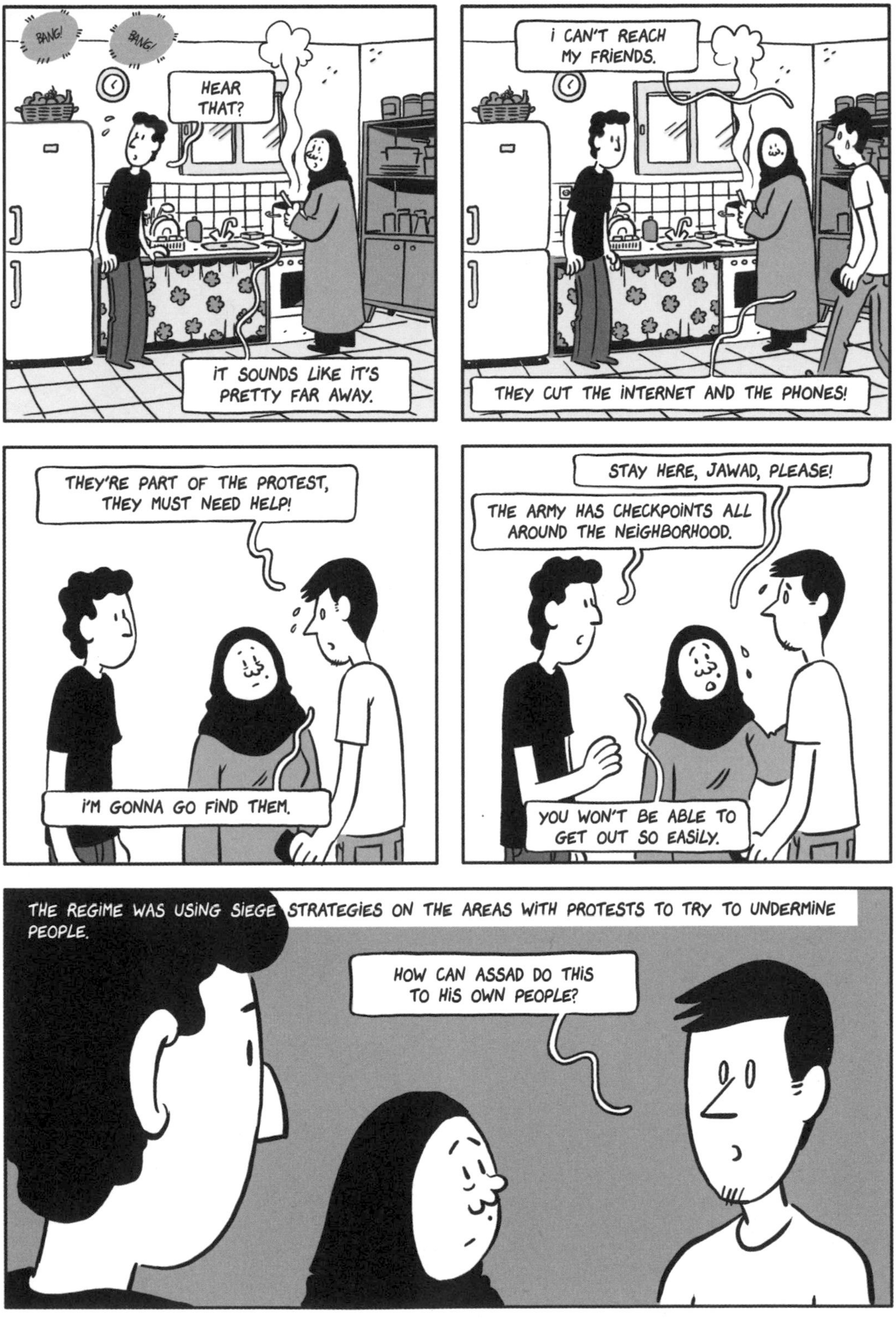
BANG!
BANG!
HEAR THAT?
IT SOUNDS LIKE IT'S PRETTY FAR AWAY.
I CAN'T REACH MY FRIENDS.
THEY CUT THE INTERNET AND THE PHONES!
THEY'RE PART OF THE PROTEST, THEY MUST NEED HELP!
I'M GONNA GO FIND THEM.
STAY HERE, JAWAD, PLEASE!
THE ARMY HAS CHECKPOINTS ALL AROUND THE NEIGHBORHOOD.
YOU WON'T BE ABLE TO GET OUT SO EASILY.
THE REGIME WAS USING SIEGE STRATEGIES ON THE AREAS WITH PROTESTS TO TRY TO UNDERMINE PEOPLE.
HOW CAN ASSAD DO THIS TO HIS OWN PEOPLE?

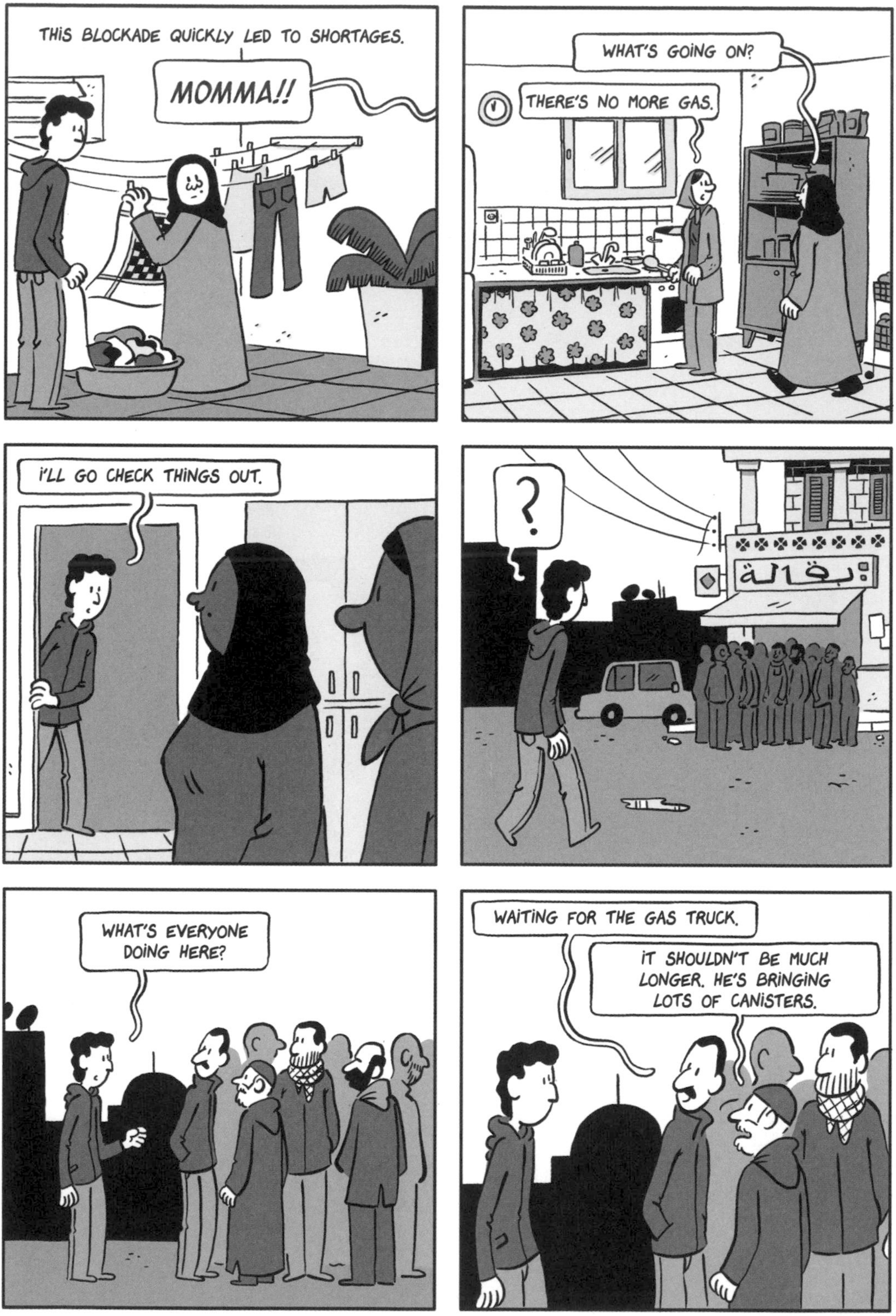
THIS BLOCKADE QUICKLY LED TO SHORTAGES.
MOMMA!!
WHAT'S GOING ON?
THERE'S NO MORE GAS.
I'LL GO CHECK THINGS OUT.
?
بقالة
WHAT'S EVERYONE DOING HERE?
WAITING FOR THE GAS TRUCK.
IT SHOULDN'T BE MUCH LONGER. HE'S BRINGING LOTS OF CANISTERS.

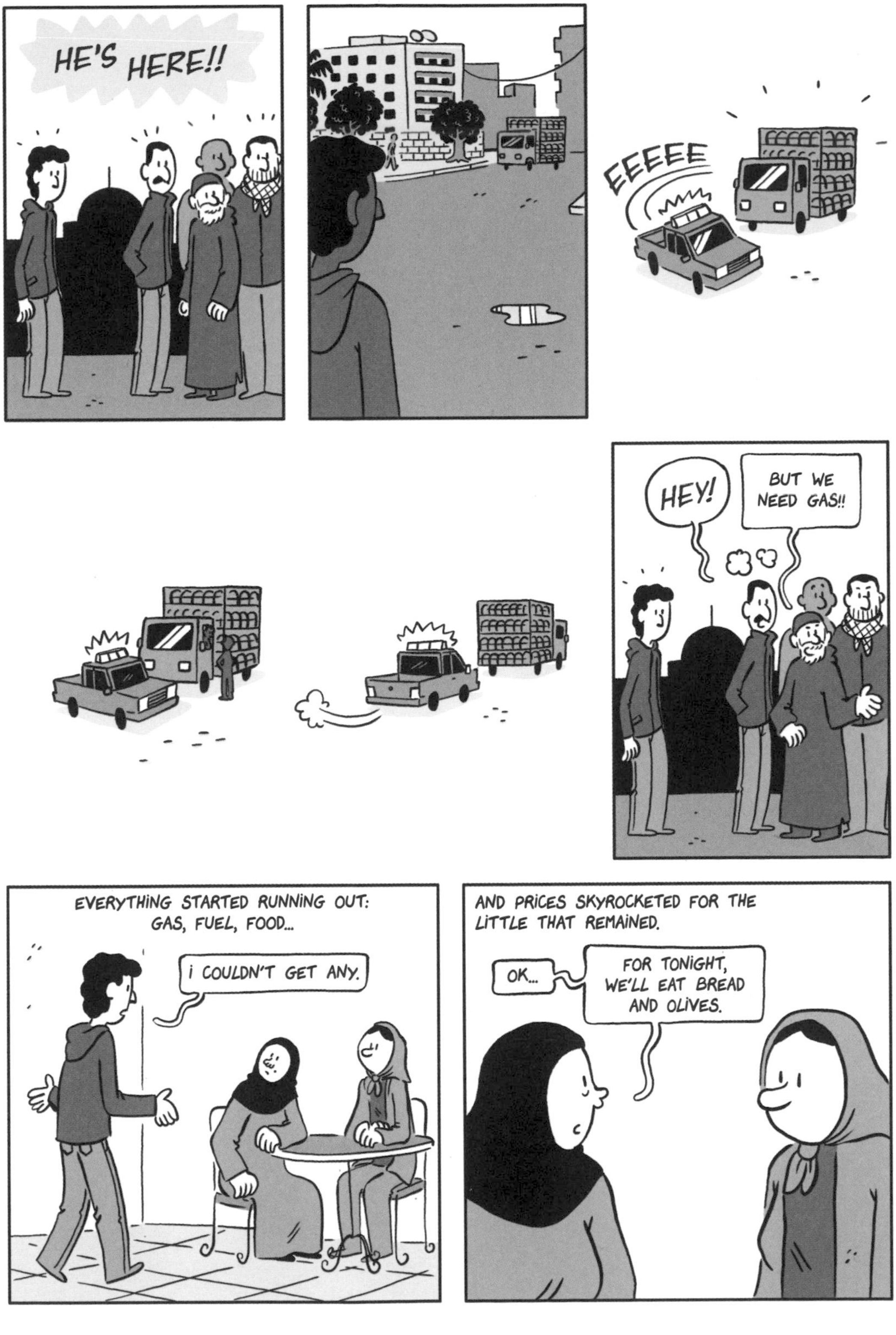
HE'S HERE!!
EEEEE
HEY!
BUT WE NEED GAS!!
EVERYTHING STARTED RUNNING OUT: GAS, FUEL, FOOD...
I COULDN'T GET ANY.
AND PRICES SKYROCKETED FOR THE LITTLE THAT REMAINED.
OK...
FOR TONIGHT, WE'LL EAT BREAD AND OLIVES.

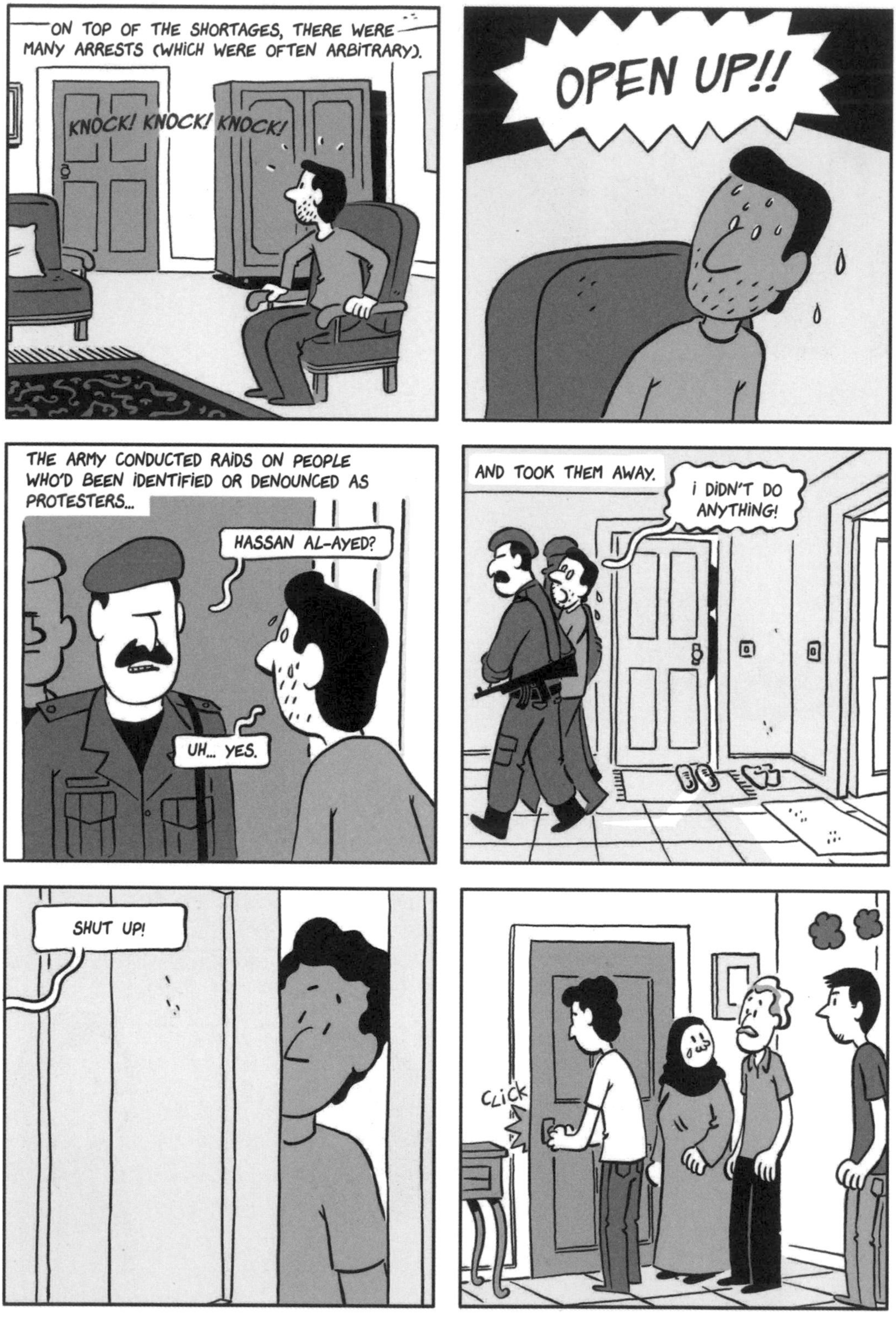

ON TOP OF THE SHORTAGES, THERE WERE MANY ARRESTS (WHICH WERE OFTEN ARBITRARY).
KNOCK! KNOCK! KNOCK!
OPEN UP!!
THE ARMY CONDUCTED RAIDS ON PEOPLE WHO'D BEEN IDENTIFIED OR DENOUNCED AS PROTESTERS...
HASSAN AL-AYED?
UH... YES.
AND TOOK THEM AWAY.
I DIDN'T DO ANYTHING!
SHUT UP!
CLICK

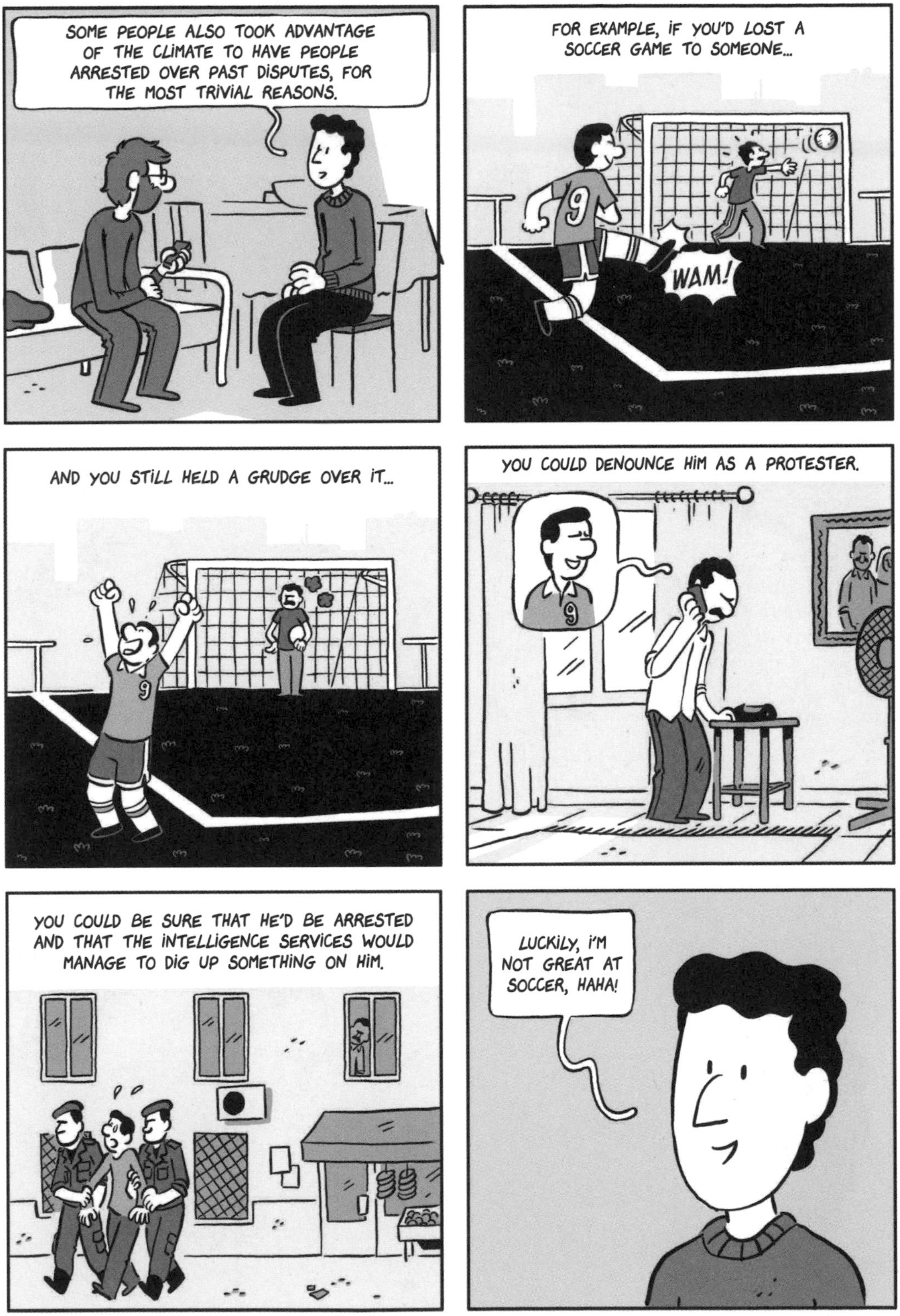
SOME PEOPLE ALSO TOOK ADVANTAGE OF THE CLIMATE TO HAVE PEOPLE ARRESTED OVER PAST DISPUTES, FOR THE MOST TRIVIAL REASONS.
FOR EXAMPLE, IF YOU'D LOST A SOCCER GAME TO SOMEONE...
WAM!
AND YOU STILL HELD A GRUDGE OVER IT...
YOU COULD DENOUNCE HIM AS A PROTESTER.
YOU COULD BE SURE THAT HE'D BE ARRESTED AND THAT THE INTELLIGENCE SERVICES WOULD MANAGE TO DIG UP SOMETHING ON HIM.
LUCKILY, I'M NOT GREAT AT SOCCER, HAHA!

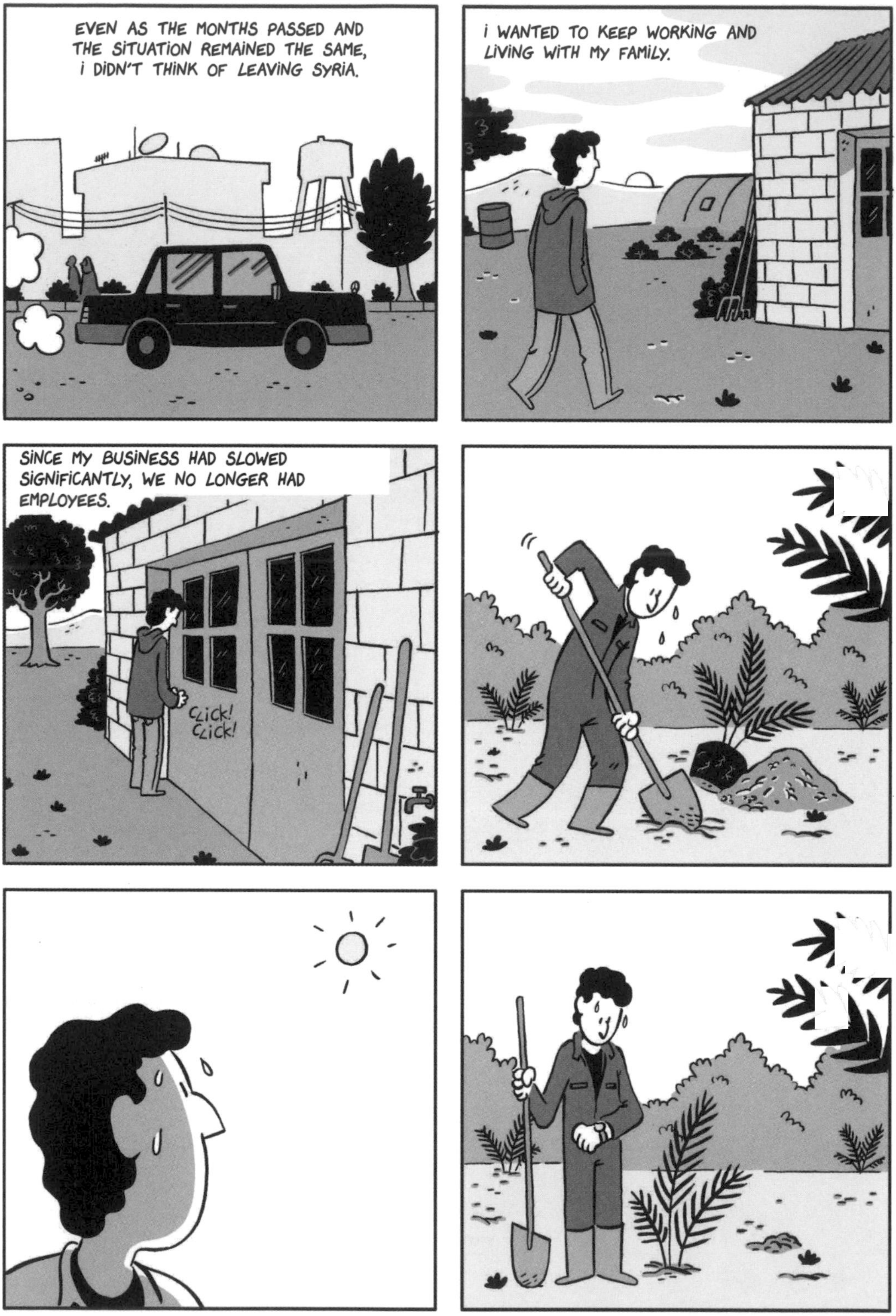

EVEN AS THE MONTHS PASSED AND THE SITUATION REMAINED THE SAME, I DIDN'T THINK OF LEAVING SYRIA.
I WANTED TO KEEP WORKING AND LIVING WITH MY FAMILY.
SINCE MY BUSINESS HAD SLOWED SIGNIFICANTLY, WE NO LONGER HAD EMPLOYEES.
CLICK! CLICK!

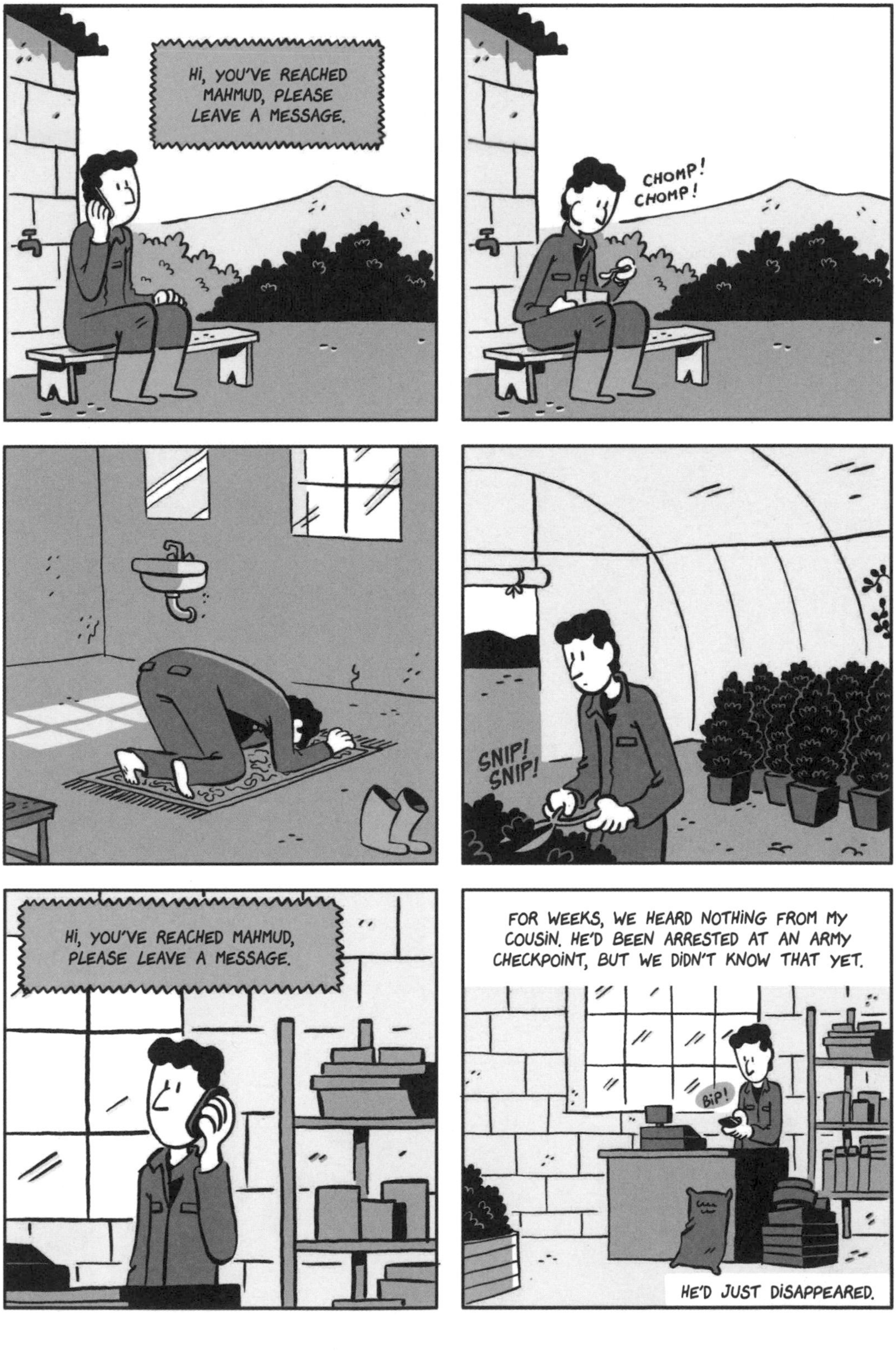
HI, YOU'VE REACHED MAHMUD, PLEASE LEAVE A MESSAGE.
CHOMP! CHOMP!
SNIP! SNIP!
HI, YOU'VE REACHED MAHMUD, PLEASE LEAVE A MESSAGE.
FOR WEEKS, WE HEARD NOTHING FROM MY COUSIN. HE'D BEEN ARRESTED AT AN ARMY CHECKPOINT, BUT WE DIDN'T KNOW THAT YET.
BIP!
HE'D JUST DISAPPEARED.

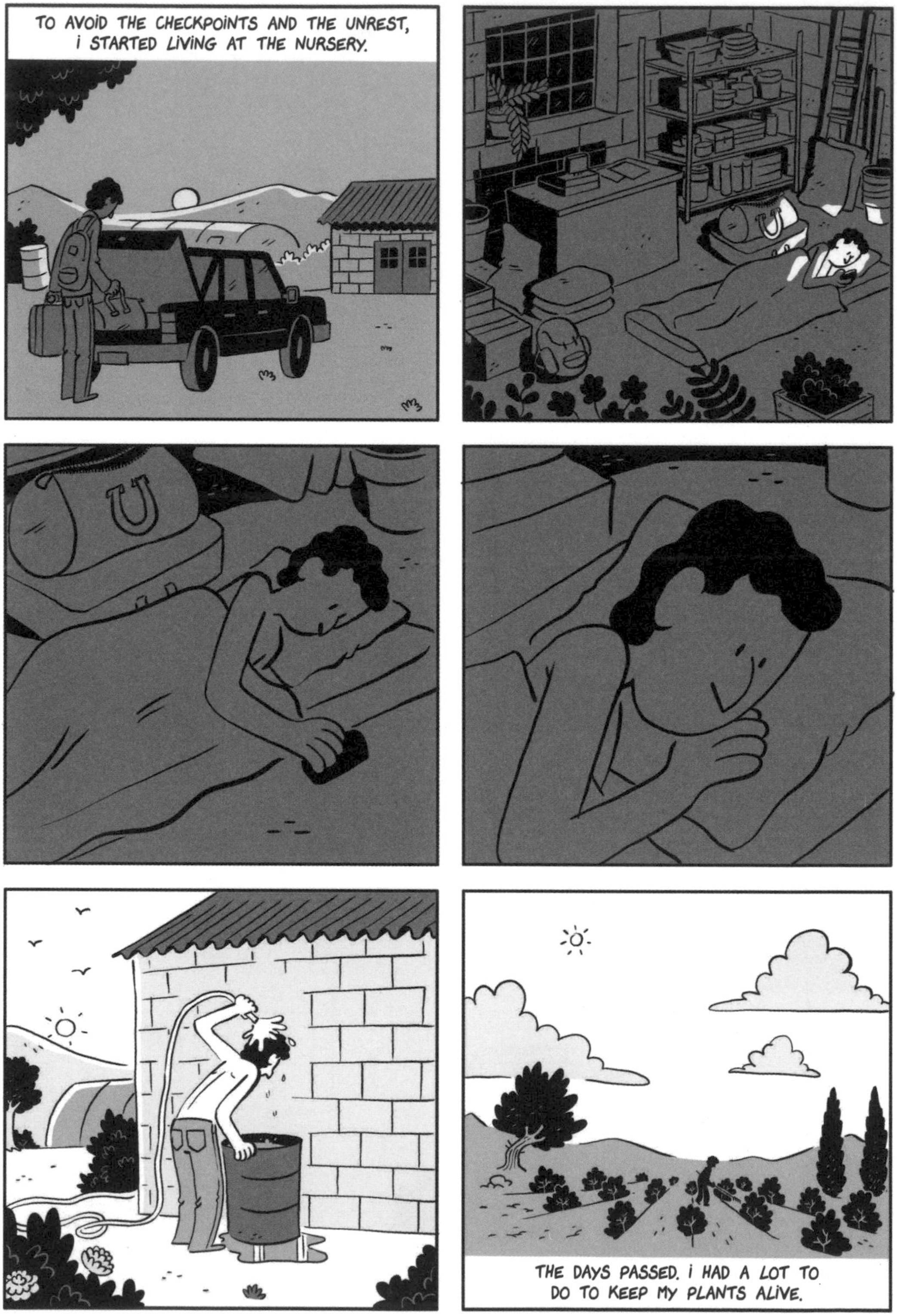
TO AVOID THE CHECKPOINTS AND THE UNREST, I STARTED LIVING AT THE NURSERY.
THE DAYS PASSED. I HAD A LOT TO DO TO KEEP MY PLANTS ALIVE.

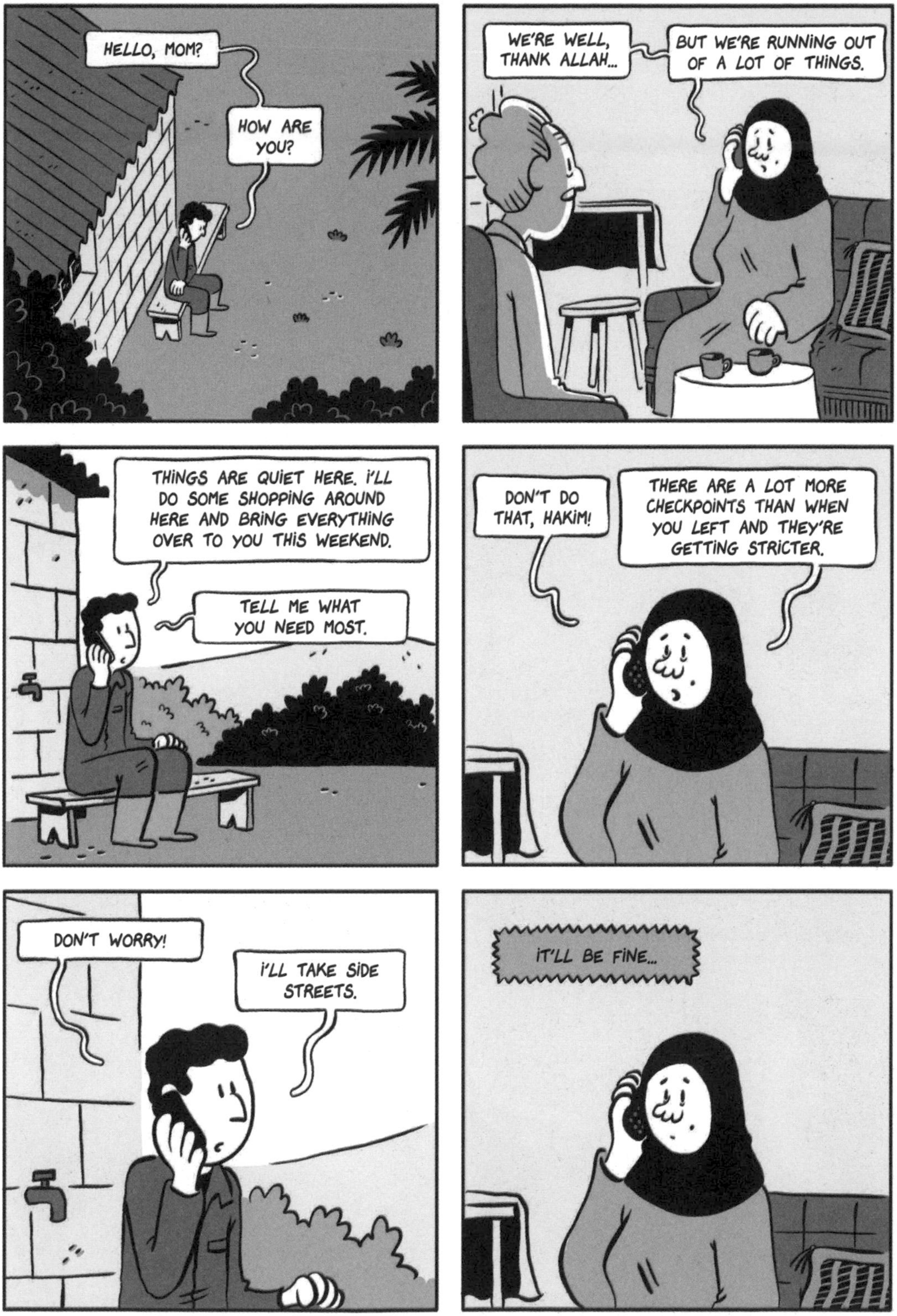
HELLO, MOM?
HOW ARE YOU?
WE'RE WELL, THANK ALLAH...
BUT WE'RE RUNNING OUT OF A LOT OF THINGS.
THINGS ARE QUIET HERE. I'LL DO SOME SHOPPING AROUND HERE AND BRING EVERYTHING OVER TO YOU THIS WEEKEND.
TELL ME WHAT YOU NEED MOST.
DON'T DO THAT, HAKIM!
THERE ARE A LOT MORE CHECKPOINTS THAN WHEN YOU LEFT AND THEY'RE GETTING STRICTER.
DON'T WORRY!
I'LL TAKE SIDE STREETS.
IT'LL BE FINE...

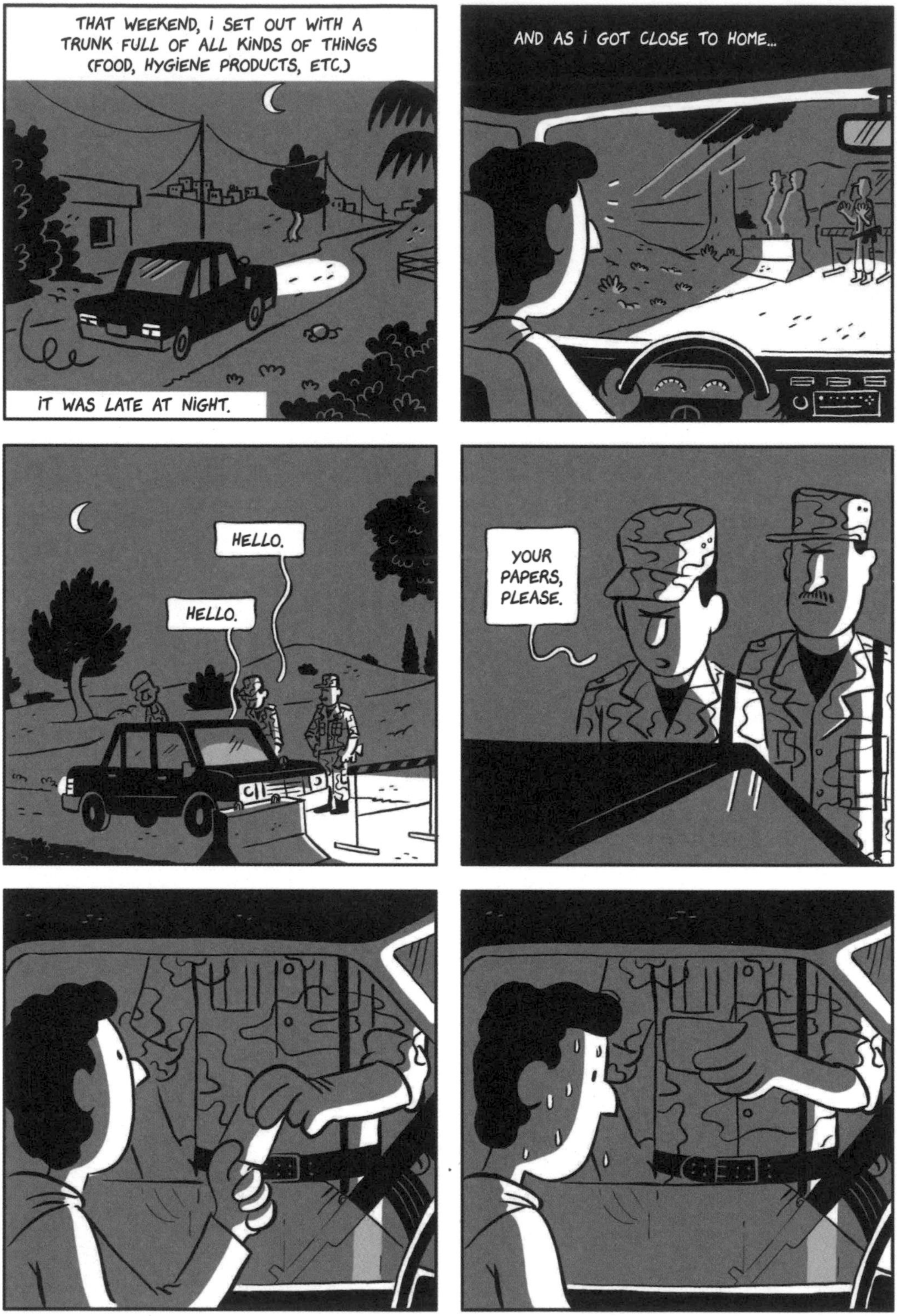
THAT WEEKEND, i SET OUT WiTH A TRUNK FULL OF ALL KiNDS OF THiNGS (FOOD, HYGiENE PRODUCTS, ETC.)
iT WAS LATE AT NiGHT.
AND AS i GOT CLOSE TO HOME...
HELLO.
HELLO.
YOUR PAPERS, PLEASE.

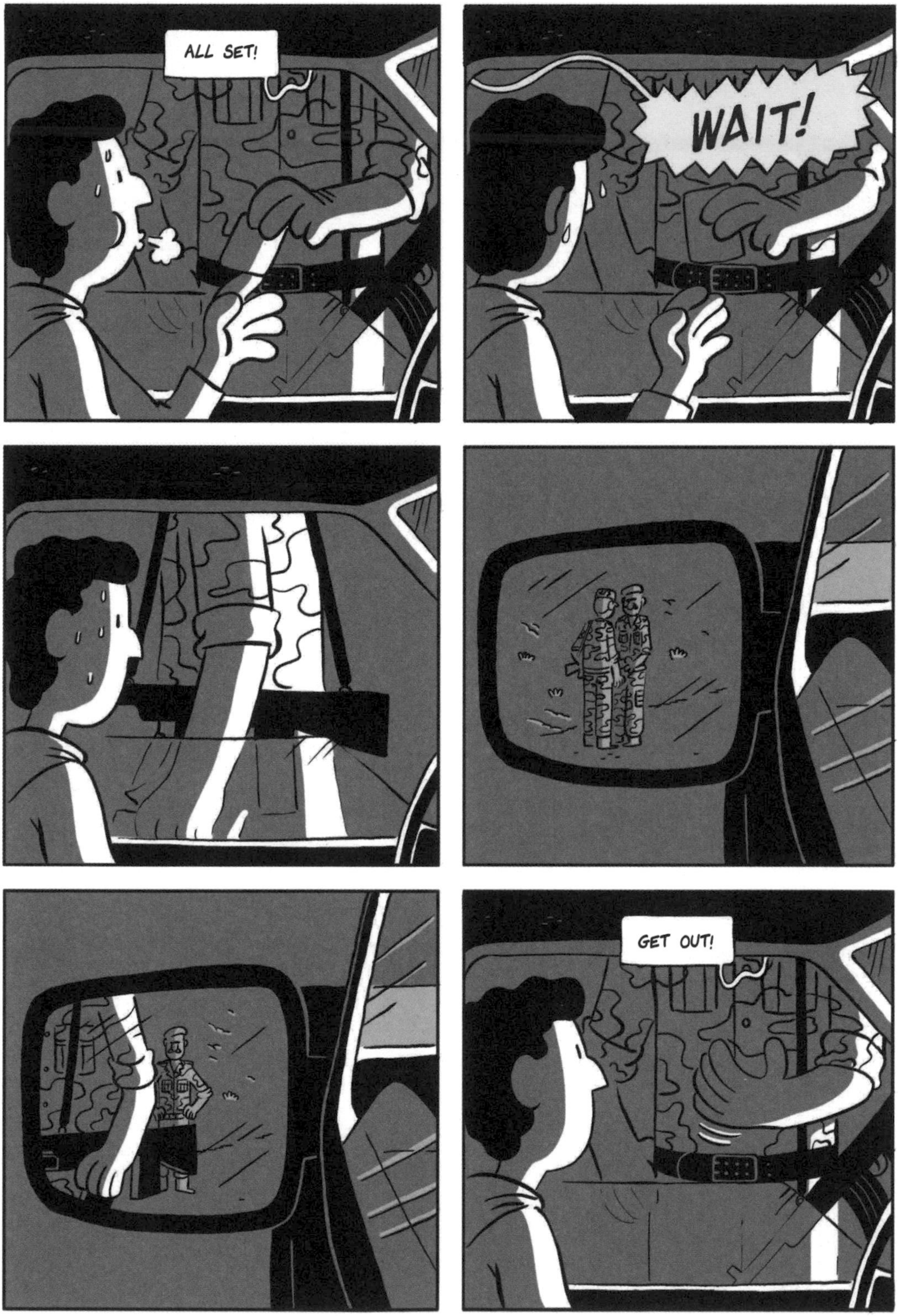
ALL SET!
WAIT!
GET OUT!

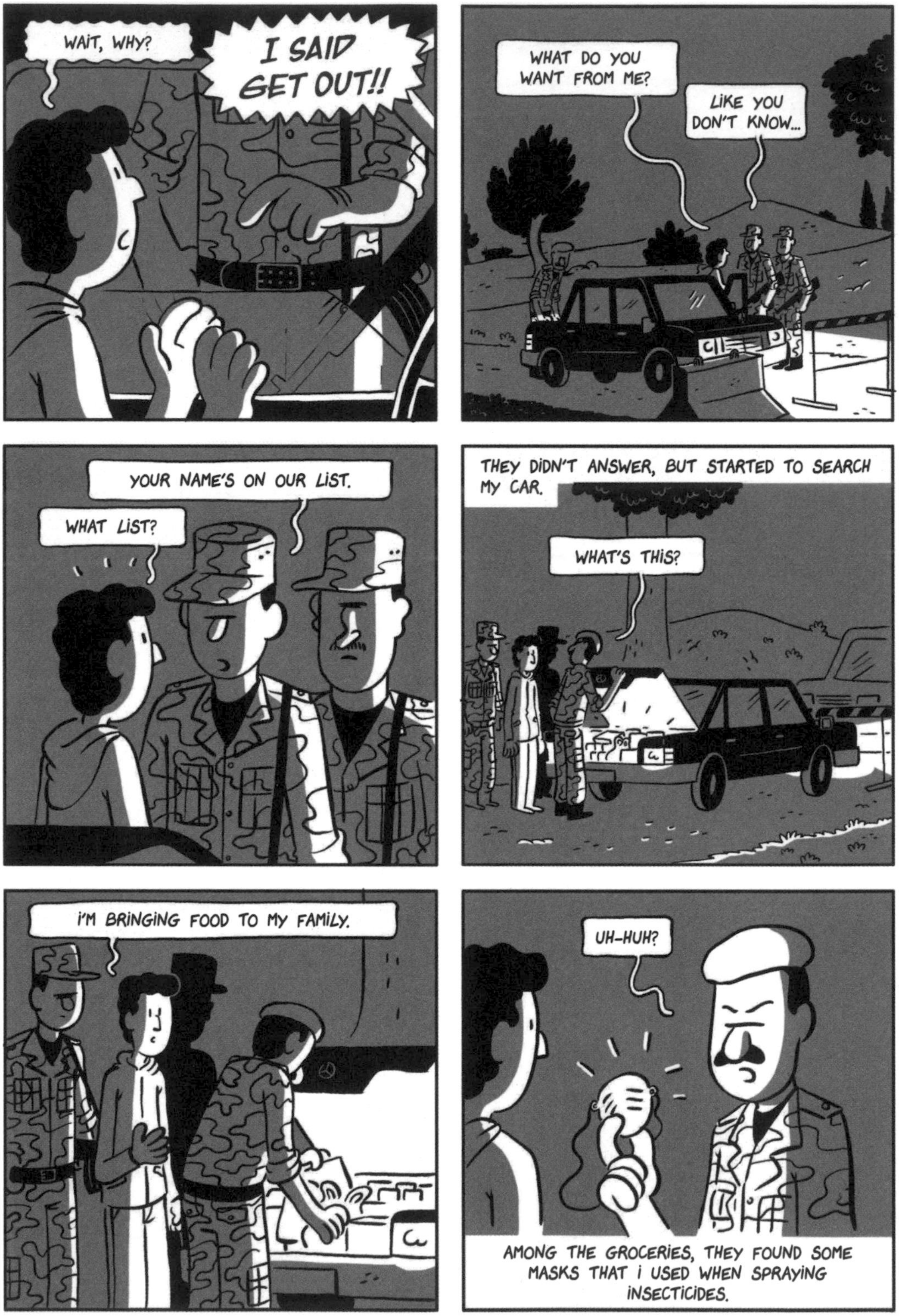
WAIT, WHY?
I SAID GET OUT!!
WHAT DO YOU WANT FROM ME?
LIKE YOU DON'T KNOW...
YOUR NAME'S ON OUR LIST.
WHAT LIST?
THEY DIDN'T ANSWER, BUT STARTED TO SEARCH MY CAR.
WHAT'S THIS?
I'M BRINGING FOOD TO MY FAMILY.
UH-HUH?
AMONG THE GROCERIES, THEY FOUND SOME MASKS THAT I USED WHEN SPRAYING INSECTICIDES.

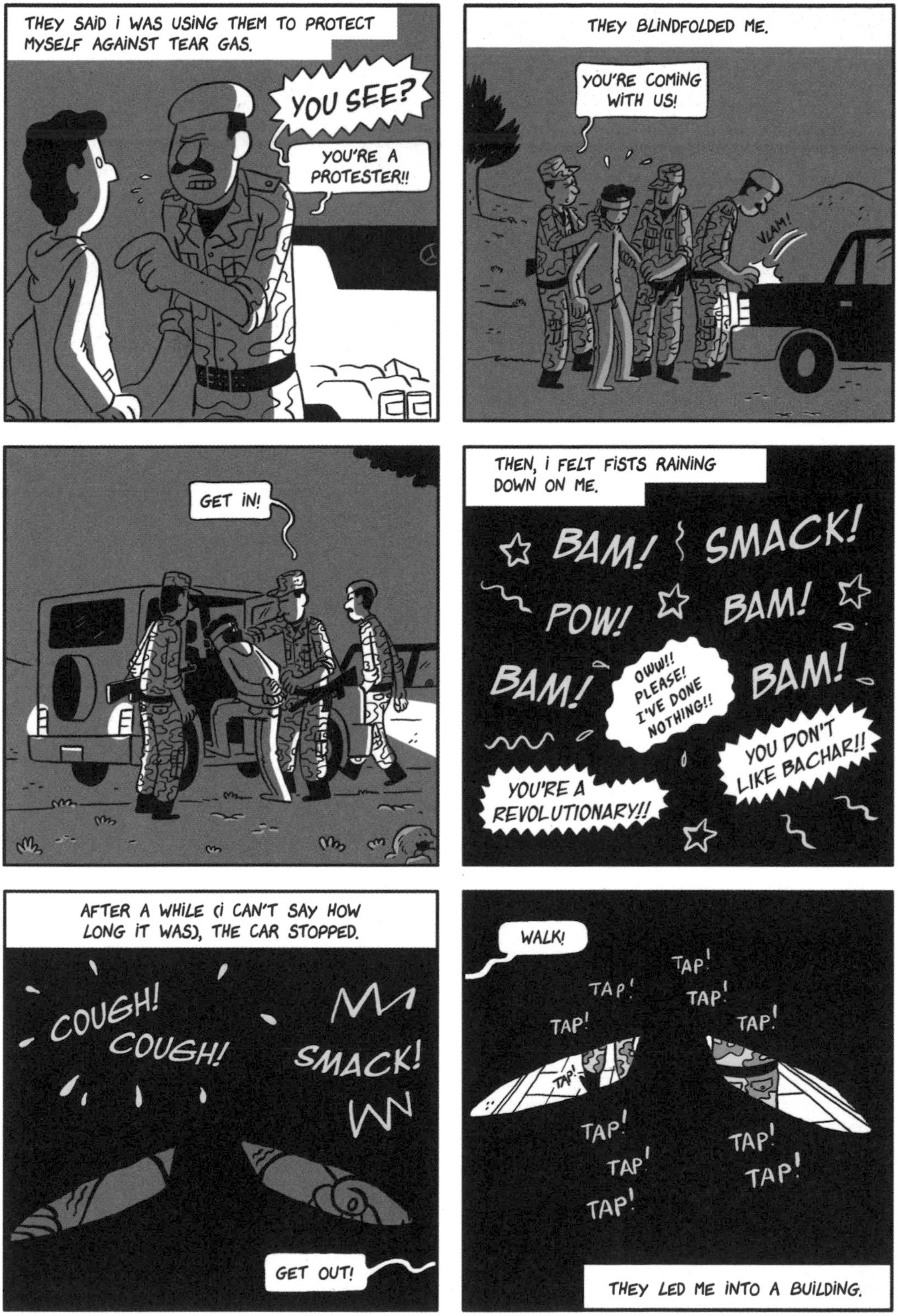
THEY SAID I WAS USING THEM TO PROTECT MYSELF AGAINST TEAR GAS.
YOU SEE?
YOU'RE A PROTESTER!!
THEY BLINDFOLDED ME.
YOU'RE COMING WITH US!
VLAM!
GET IN!
THEN, I FELT FISTS RAINING DOWN ON ME.
BAM! SMACK!
POW! BAM!
BAM!
OWW!! PLEASE! I'VE DONE NOTHING!!
BAM!
YOU DON'T LIKE BACHAR!!
YOU'RE A REVOLUTIONARY!!
AFTER A WHILE (I CAN'T SAY HOW LONG IT WAS), THE CAR STOPPED.
COUGH! COUGH!
SMACK!
GET OUT!
WALK!
TAP! TAP! TAP! TAP! TAP! TAP!
TAP! TAP! TAP! TAP! TAP!
THEY LED ME INTO A BUILDING.

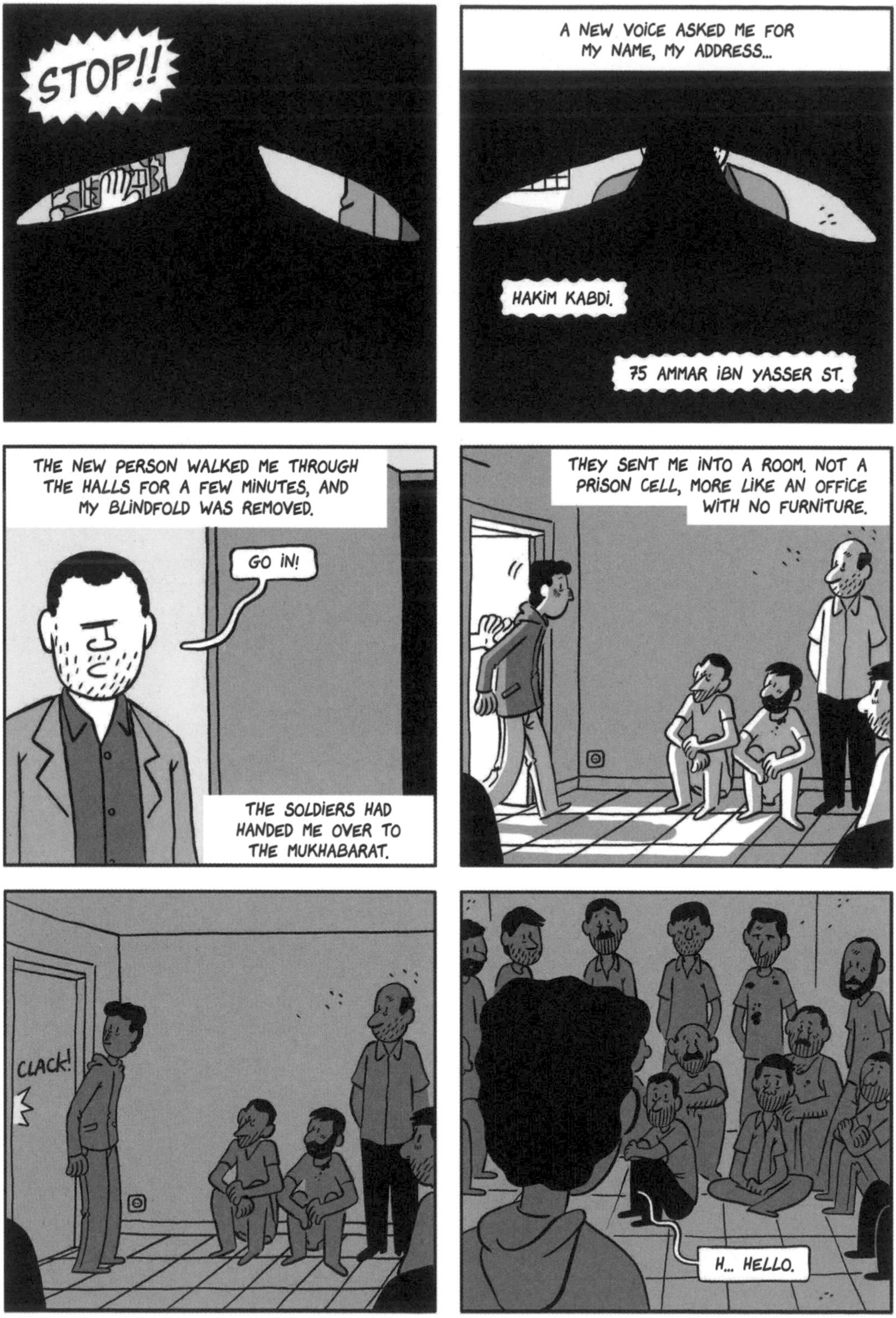
STOP!!
A NEW VOICE ASKED ME FOR MY NAME, MY ADDRESS...
HAKIM KABDI.
75 AMMAR IBN YASSER ST.
THE NEW PERSON WALKED ME THROUGH THE HALLS FOR A FEW MINUTES, AND MY BLINDFOLD WAS REMOVED.
GO IN!
THE SOLDIERS HAD HANDED ME OVER TO THE MUKHABARAT.
THEY SENT ME INTO A ROOM. NOT A PRISON CELL, MORE LIKE AN OFFICE WITH NO FURNITURE.
CLACK!
H... HELLO.

Chapter 4: Prison

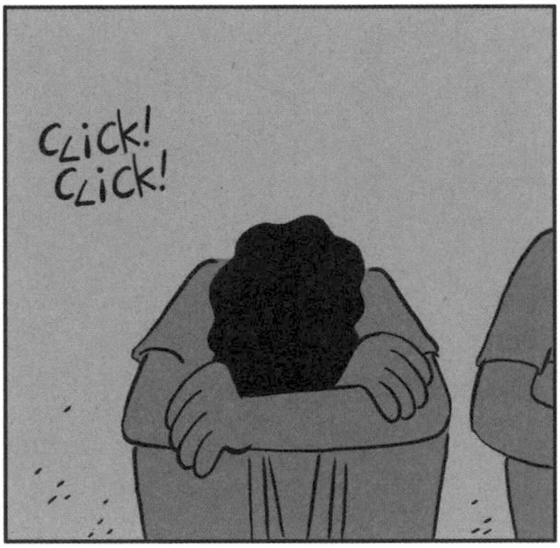
CLICK!
CLICK!

"YOU'RE A REVOLUTIONARY, TOO."

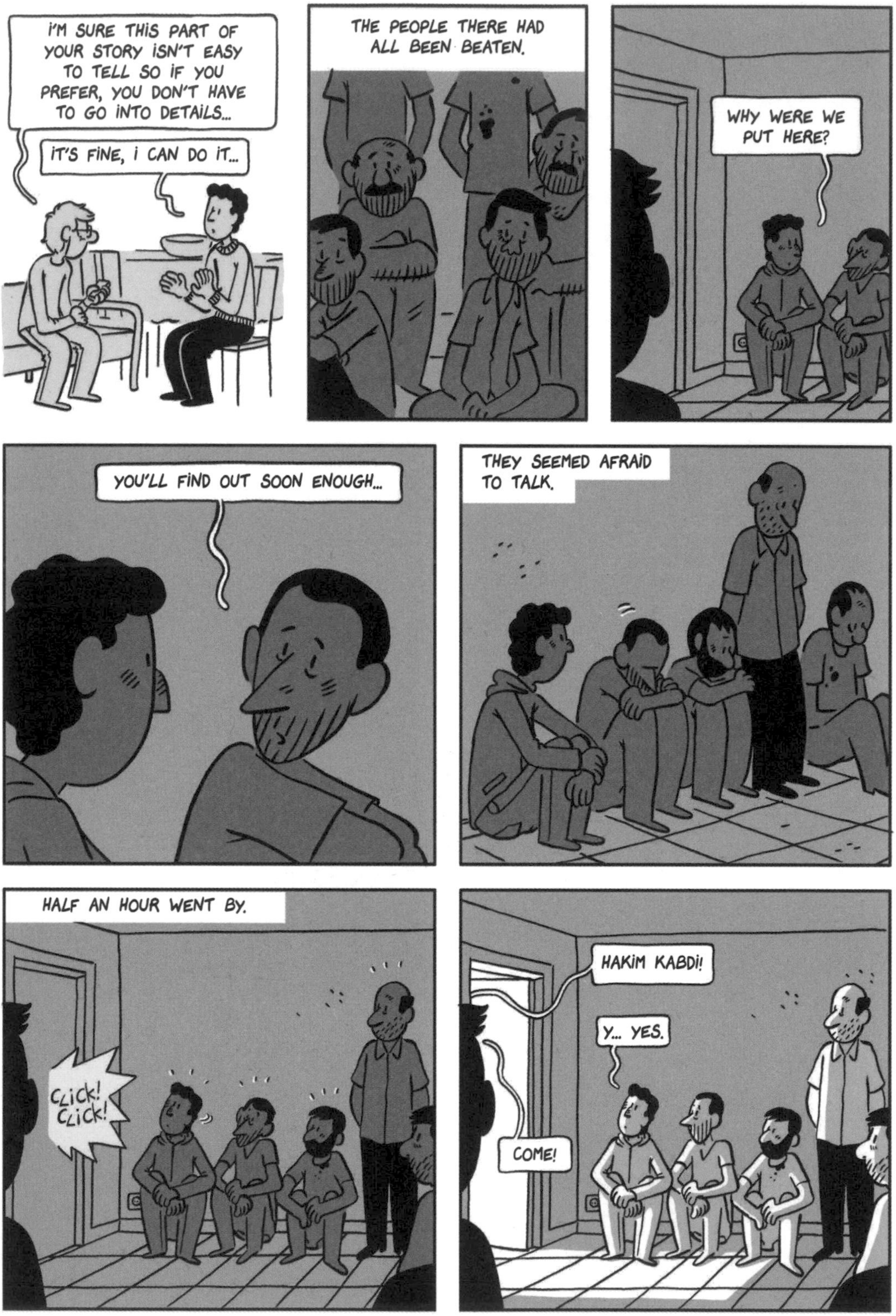
I'M SURE THIS PART OF YOUR STORY ISN'T EASY TO TELL SO IF YOU PREFER, YOU DON'T HAVE TO GO INTO DETAILS...
IT'S FINE, I CAN DO IT...
THE PEOPLE THERE HAD ALL BEEN BEATEN.
WHY WERE WE PUT HERE?
YOU'LL FIND OUT SOON ENOUGH...
THEY SEEMED AFRAID TO TALK.
HALF AN HOUR WENT BY.
CLICK! CLICK!
HAKIM KABDI!
Y... YES.
COME!

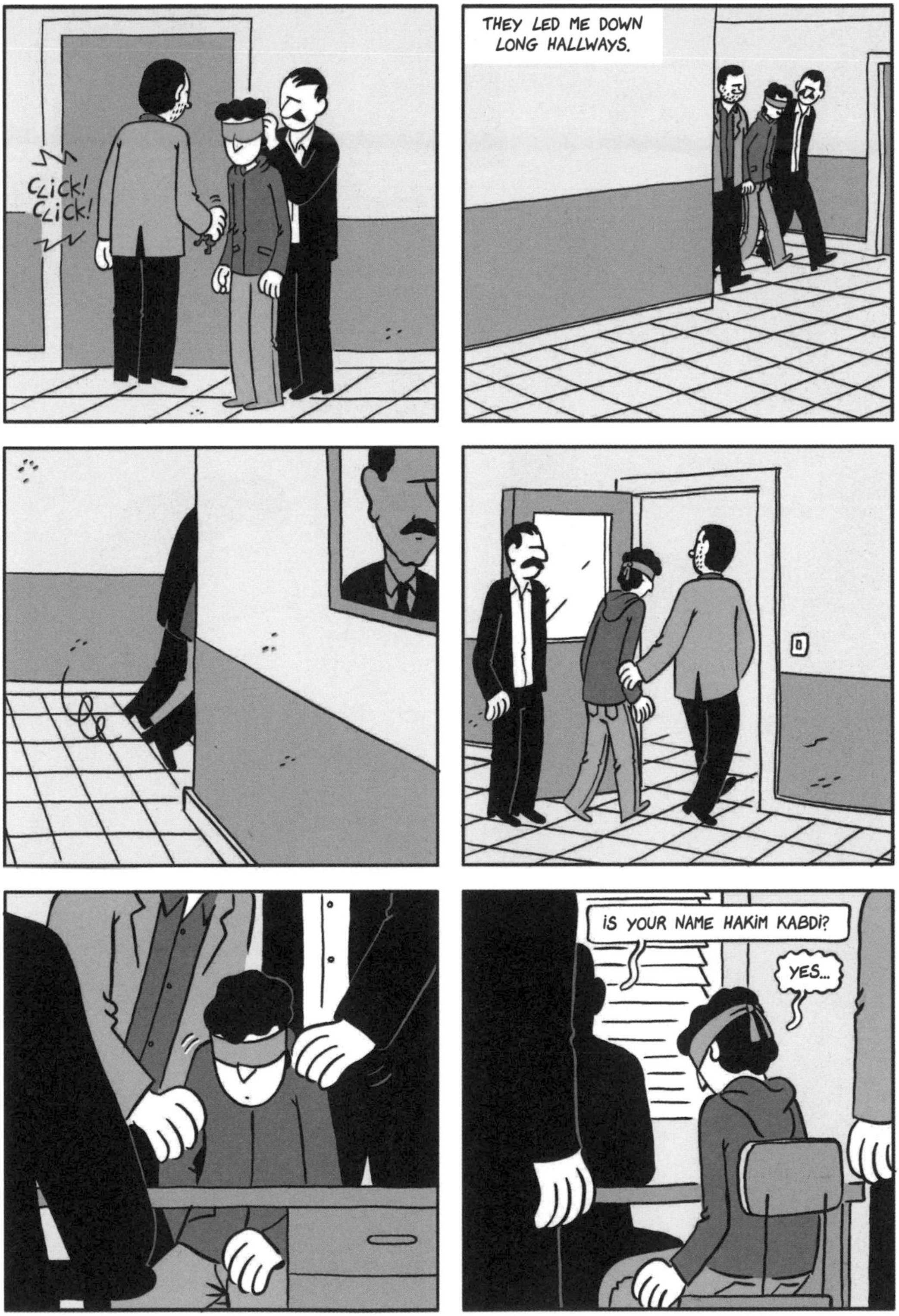
CLICK! CLICK!
THEY LED ME DOWN LONG HALLWAYS.
IS YOUR NAME HAKIM KABDI?
YES...

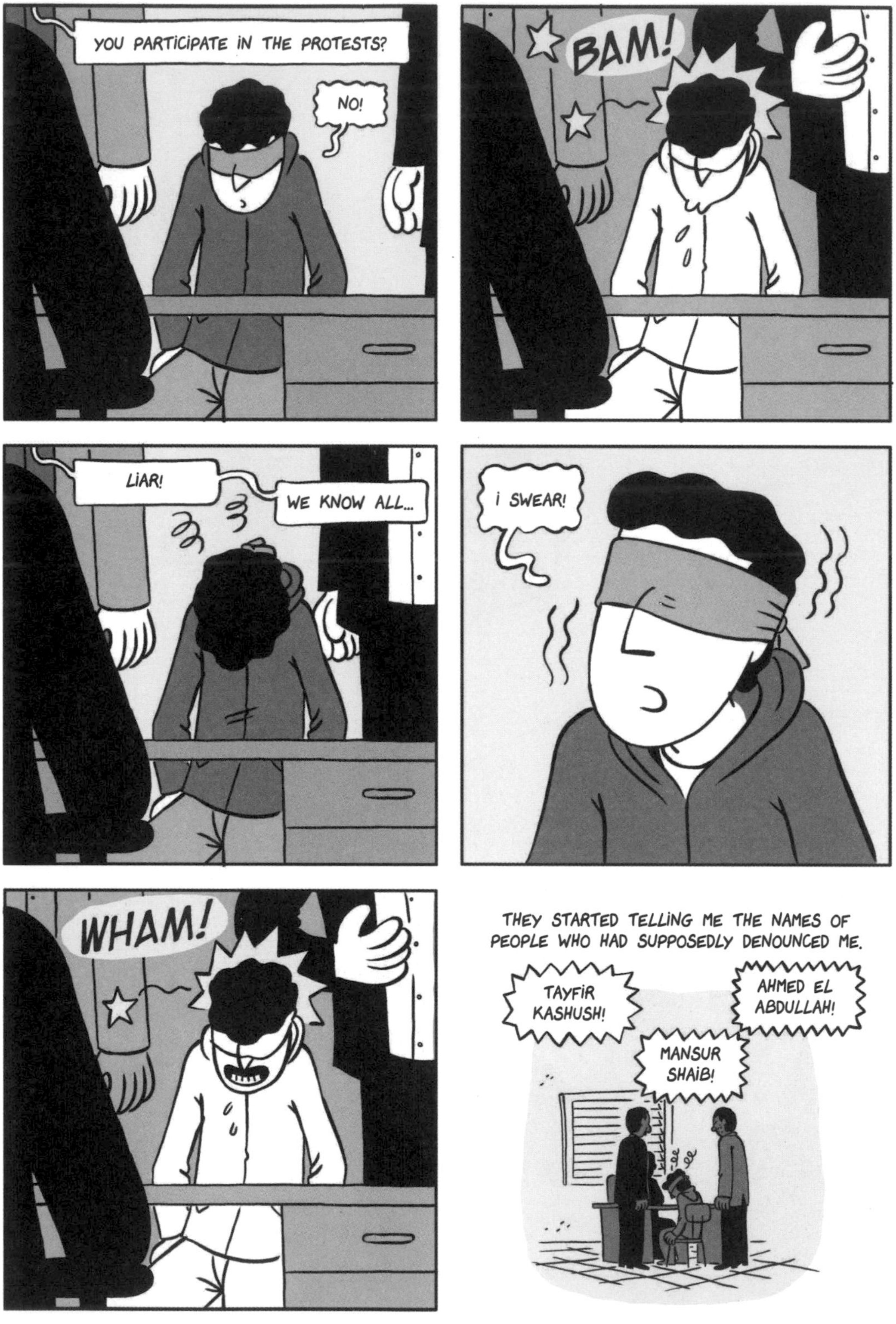
YOU PARTICIPATE IN THE PROTESTS?
NO!
BAM!
LIAR!
WE KNOW ALL...
I SWEAR!
WHAM!
THEY STARTED TELLING ME THE NAMES OF PEOPLE WHO HAD SUPPOSEDLY DENOUNCED ME.
TAYFIR KASHUSH!
AHMED EL ABDULLAH!
MANSUR SHAIB!

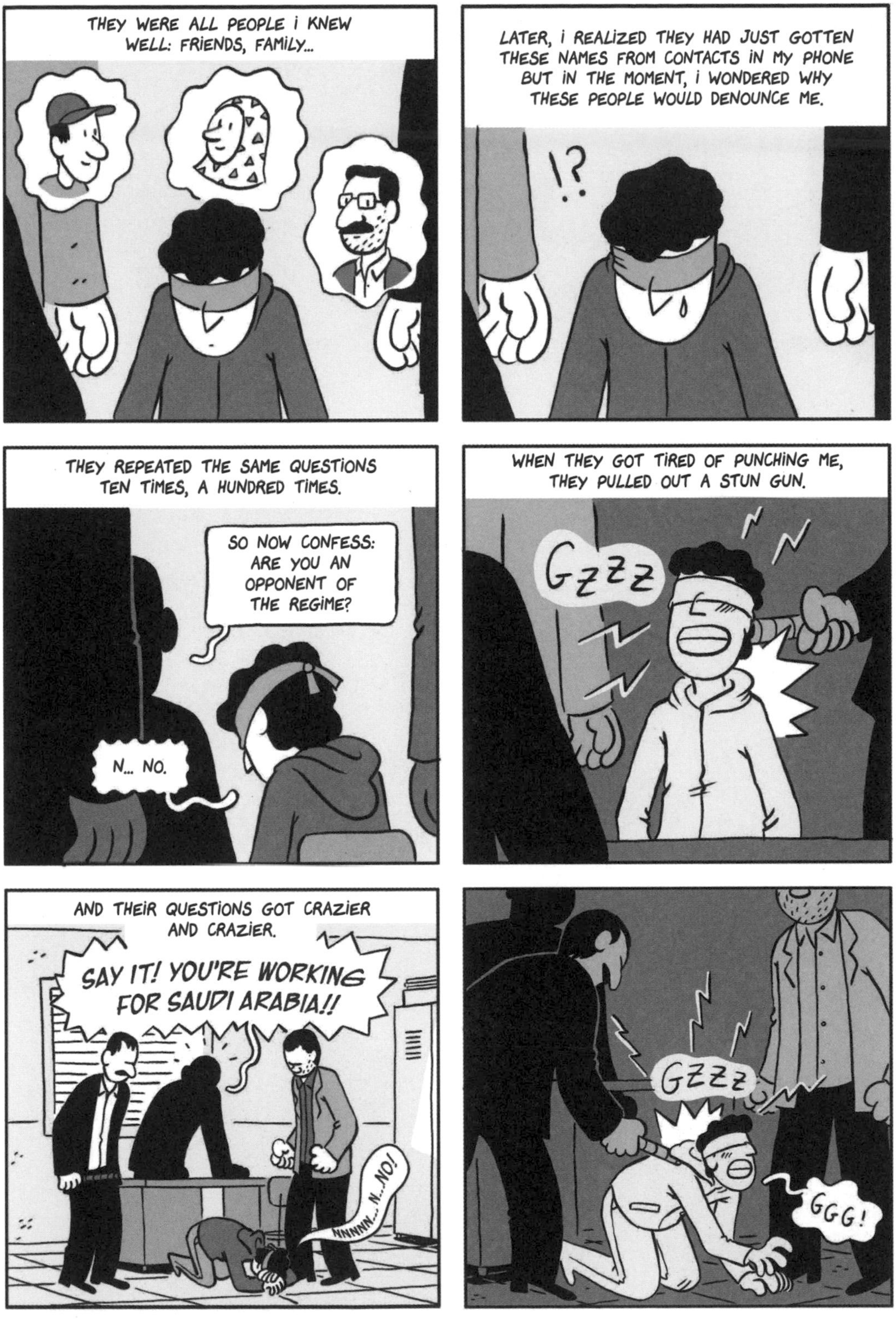
THEY WERE ALL PEOPLE i KNEW WELL: FRIENDS, FAMiLY...
LATER, i REALiZED THEY HAD JUST GOTTEN THESE NAMES FROM CONTACTS iN MY PHONE BUT iN THE MOMENT, i WONDERED WHY THESE PEOPLE WOULD DENOUNCE ME.
!?
THEY REPEATED THE SAME QUESTiONS TEN TiMES, A HUNDRED TiMES.
SO NOW CONFESS: ARE YOU AN OPPONENT OF THE REGiME?
N... NO.
WHEN THEY GOT TiRED OF PUNCHiNG ME, THEY PULLED OUT A STUN GUN.
GZZZ
AND THEiR QUESTiONS GOT CRAZiER AND CRAZiER.
SAY IT! YOU'RE WORKING FOR SAUDI ARABIA!!
NNNNN... N...NO!
GZZZ
GGG!

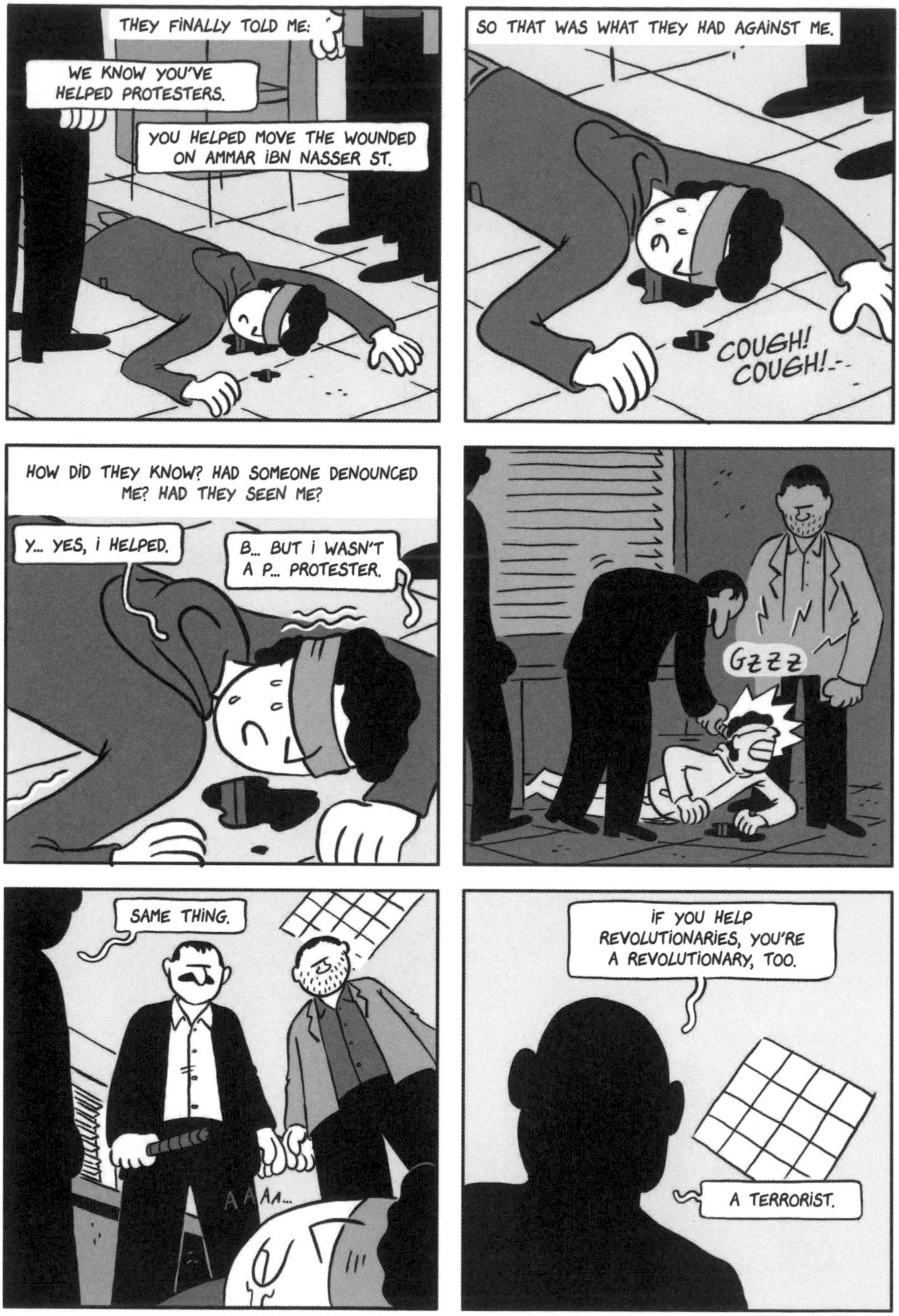
THEY FINALLY TOLD ME:
WE KNOW YOU'VE HELPED PROTESTERS.
YOU HELPED MOVE THE WOUNDED ON AMMAR IBN NASSER ST.
SO THAT WAS WHAT THEY HAD AGAINST ME.
COUGH! COUGH!
HOW DID THEY KNOW? HAD SOMEONE DENOUNCED ME? HAD THEY SEEN ME?
Y... YES, I HELPED.
B... BUT I WASN'T A P... PROTESTER.
GZZZ
SAME THING.
AAAA...
IF YOU HELP REVOLUTIONARIES, YOU'RE A REVOLUTIONARY, TOO.
A TERRORIST.

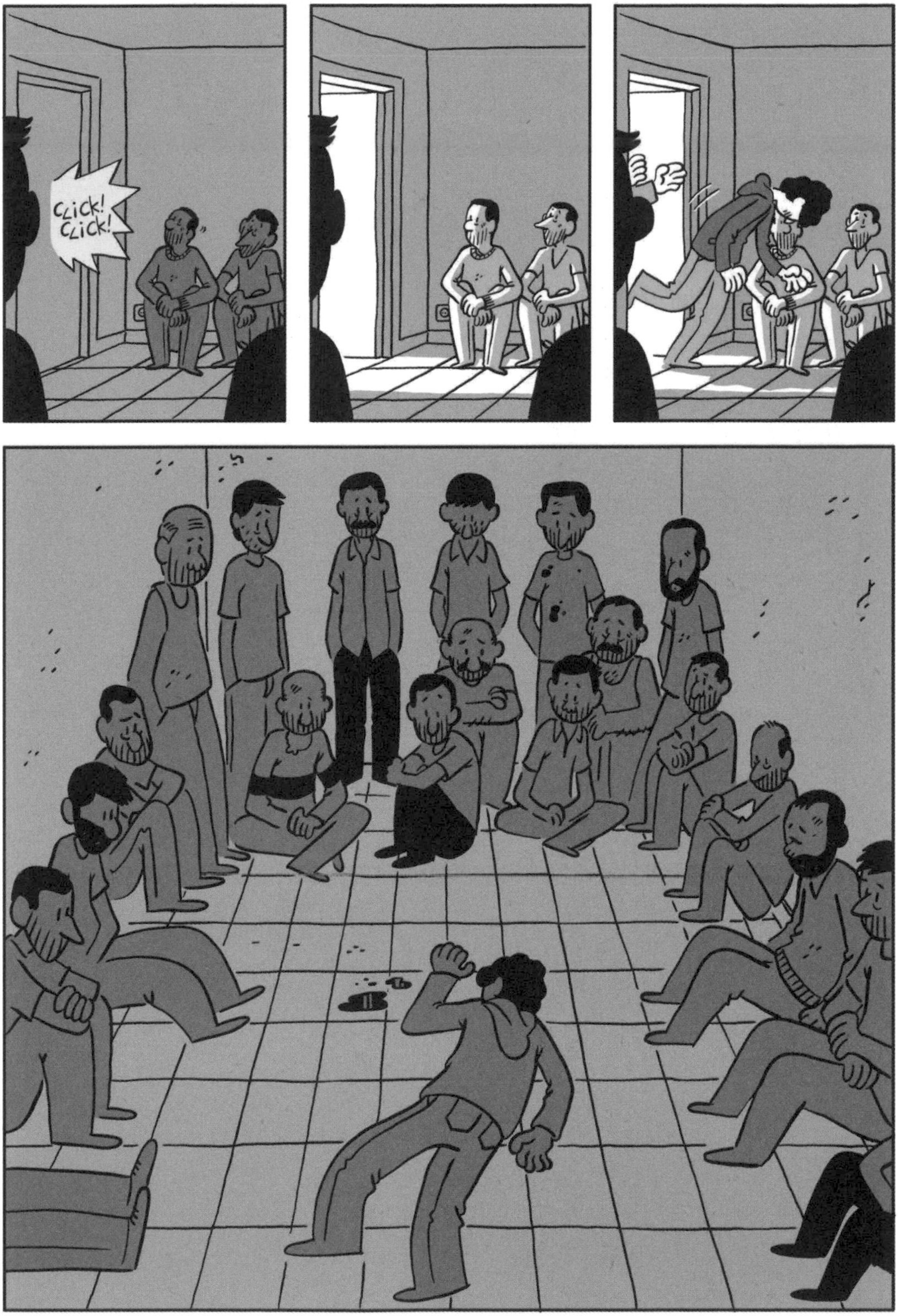
CLICK! CLICK!

THIS TREATMENT WENT ON FOR A WEEK THAT SEEMED TO LAST FOR MONTHS.

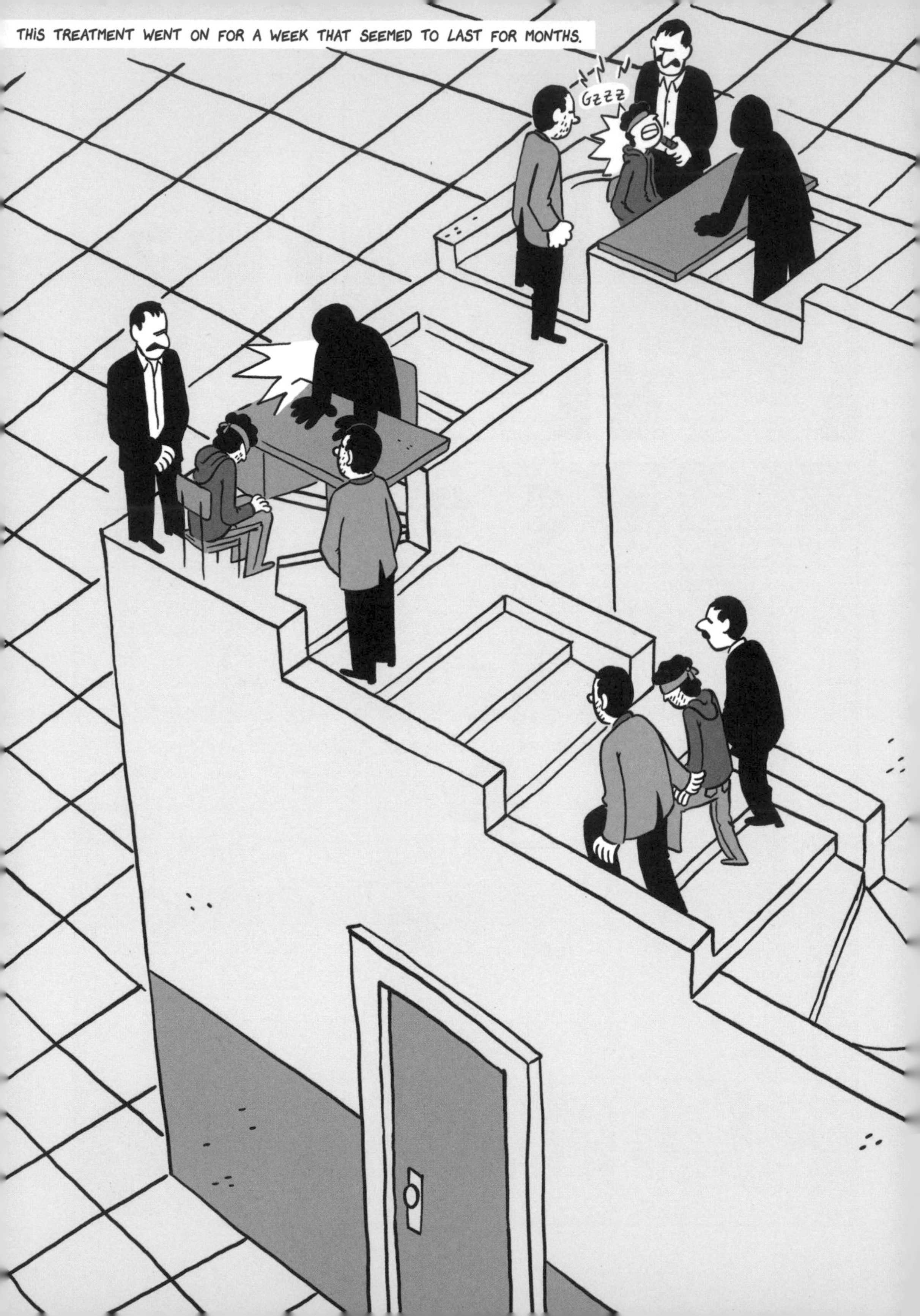
GZZZ

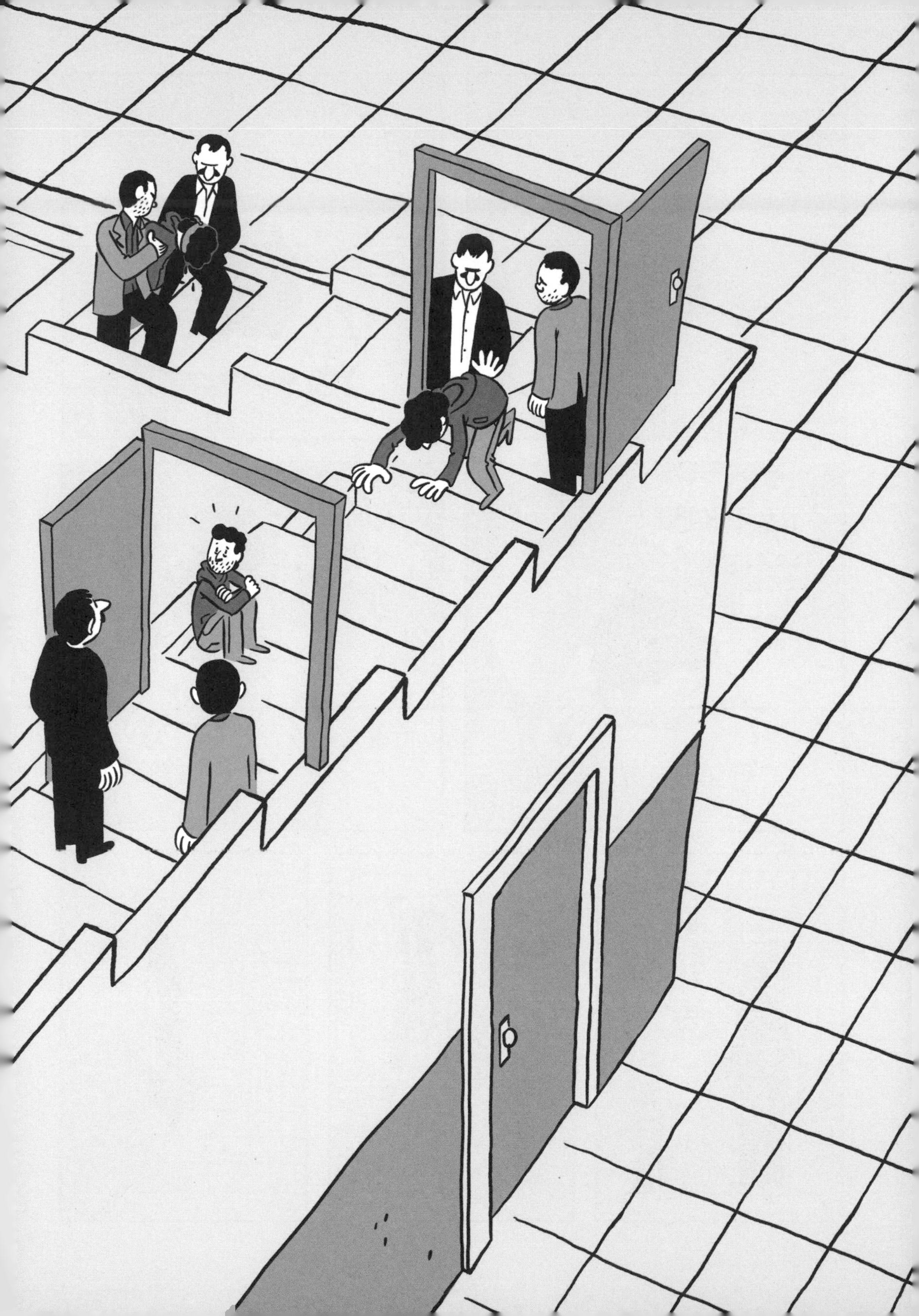

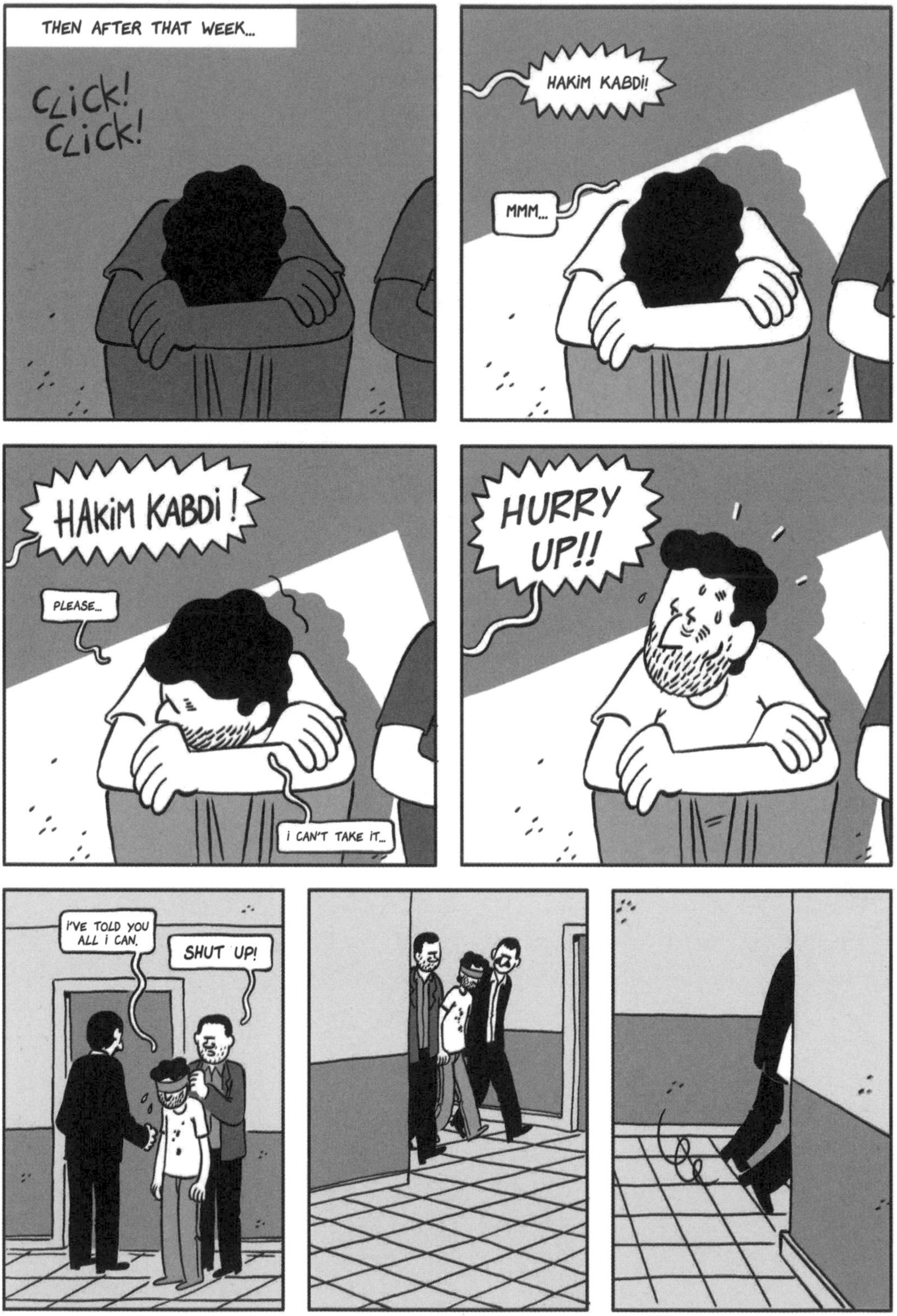
THEN AFTER THAT WEEK...
CLICK! CLICK!
HAKIM KABDI!
MMM...
HAKIM KABDI!
PLEASE...
I CAN'T TAKE IT...
HURRY UP!!
I'VE TOLD YOU ALL I CAN.
SHUT UP!

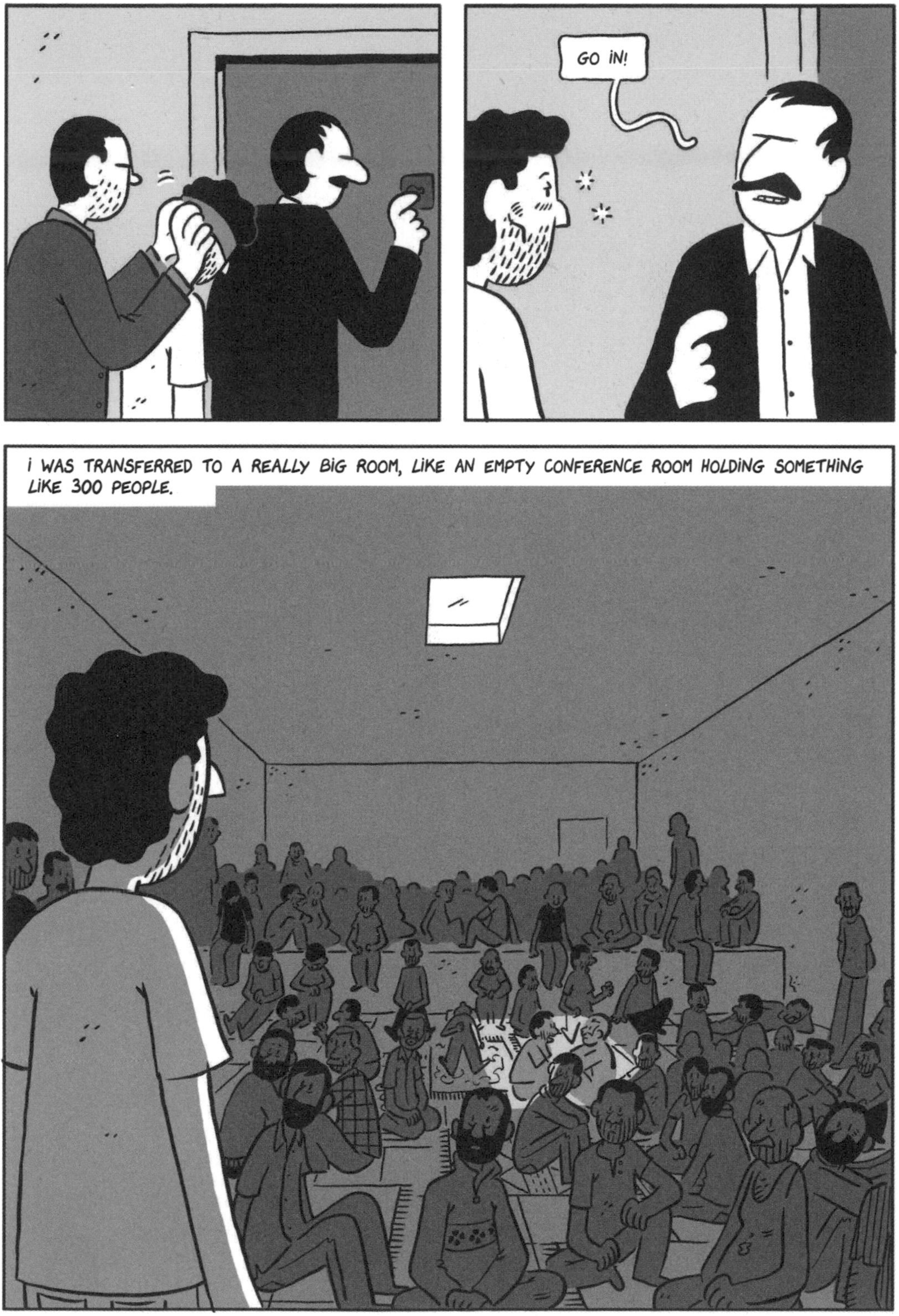
GO IN!
I WAS TRANSFERRED TO A REALLY BIG ROOM, LIKE AN EMPTY CONFERENCE ROOM HOLDING SOMETHING LIKE 300 PEOPLE.

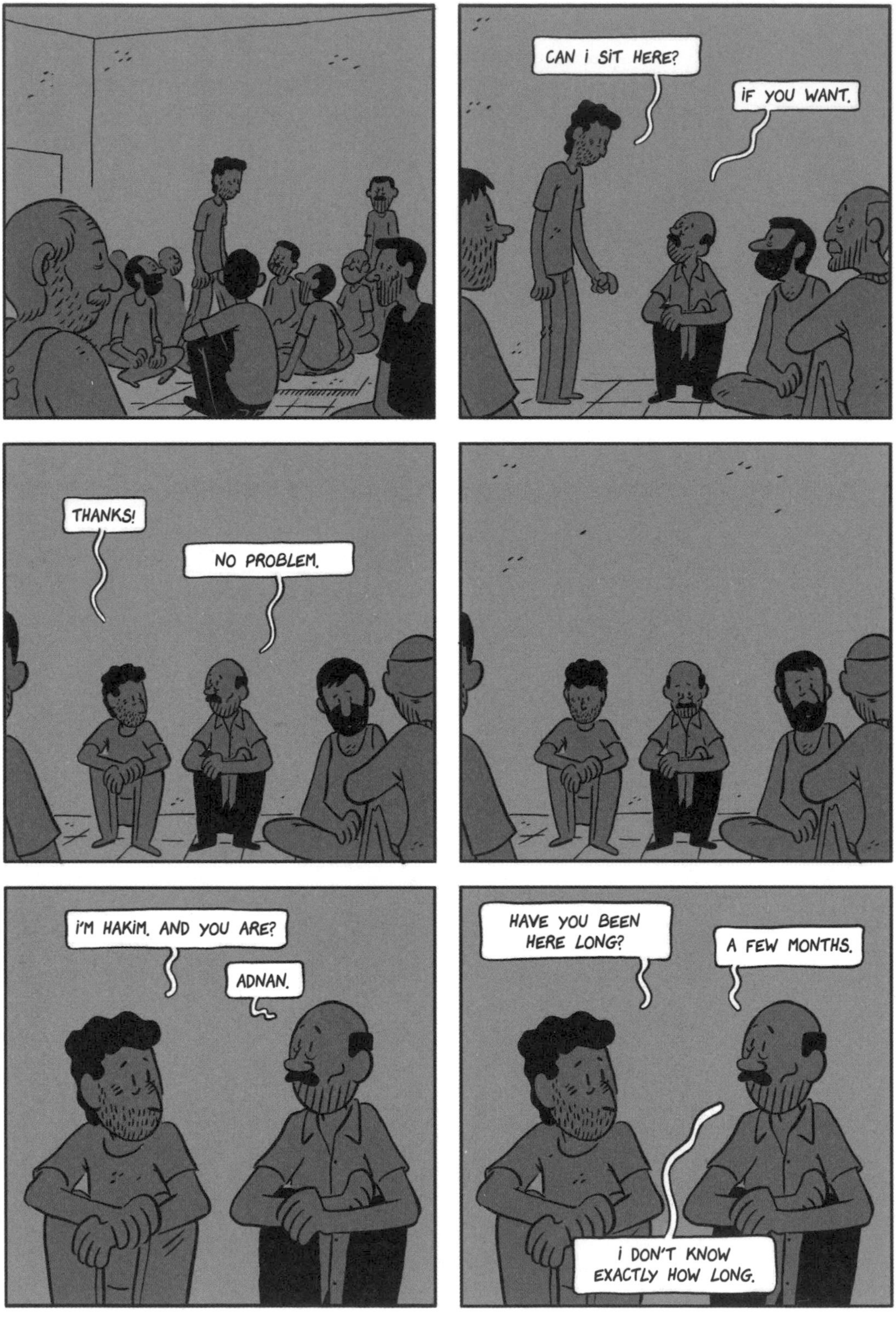
CAN I SIT HERE?
IF YOU WANT.
THANKS!
NO PROBLEM.
I'M HAKIM. AND YOU ARE?
ADNAN.
HAVE YOU BEEN HERE LONG?
A FEW MONTHS.
I DON'T KNOW EXACTLY HOW LONG.

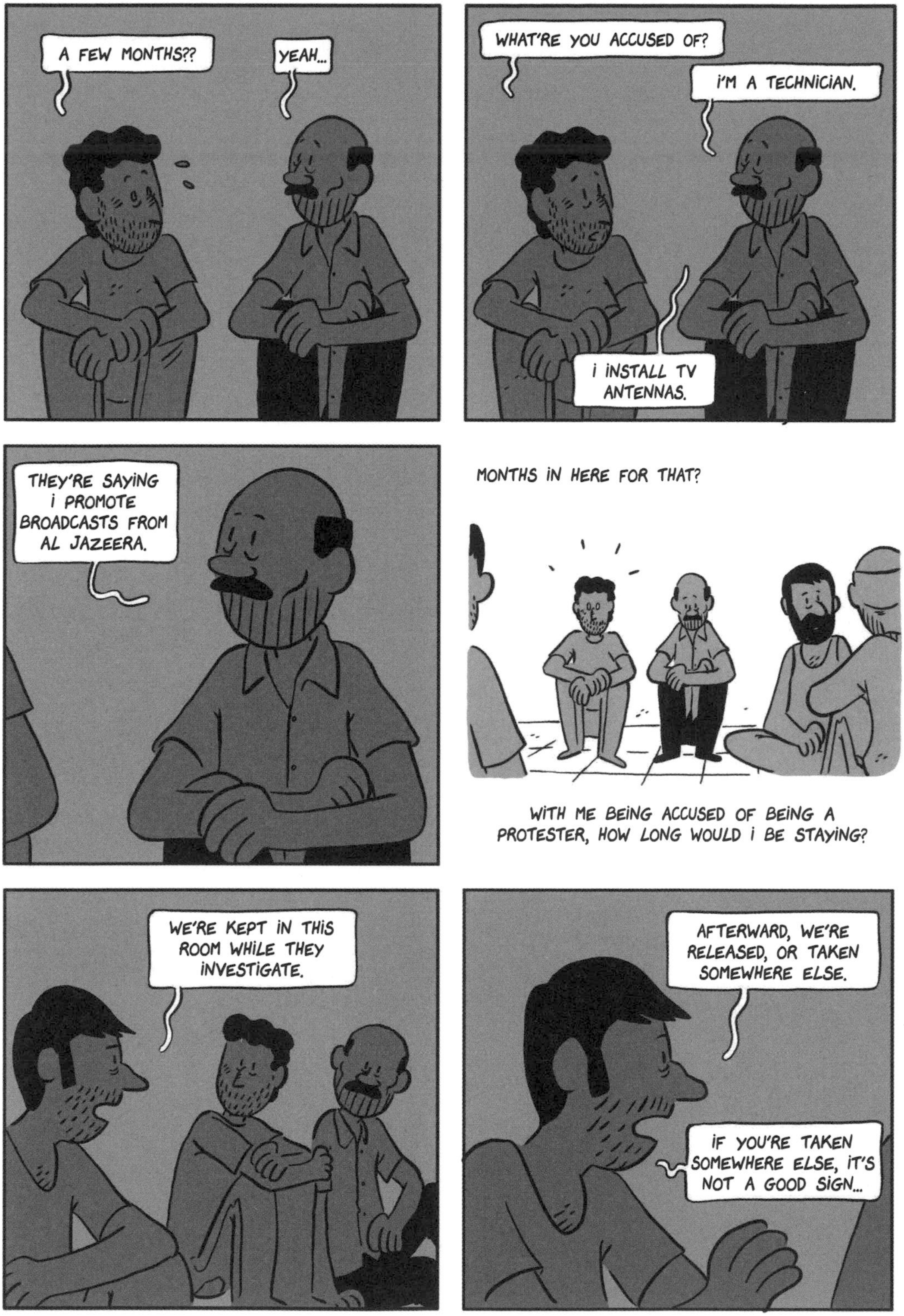
A FEW MONTHS??
YEAH...
WHAT'RE YOU ACCUSED OF?
I'M A TECHNICIAN.
I INSTALL TV ANTENNAS.
THEY'RE SAYING I PROMOTE BROADCASTS FROM AL JAZEERA.
MONTHS IN HERE FOR THAT?
WITH ME BEING ACCUSED OF BEING A PROTESTER, HOW LONG WOULD I BE STAYING?
WE'RE KEPT IN THIS ROOM WHILE THEY INVESTIGATE.
AFTERWARD, WE'RE RELEASED, OR TAKEN SOMEWHERE ELSE.
IF YOU'RE TAKEN SOMEWHERE ELSE, IT'S NOT A GOOD SIGN...

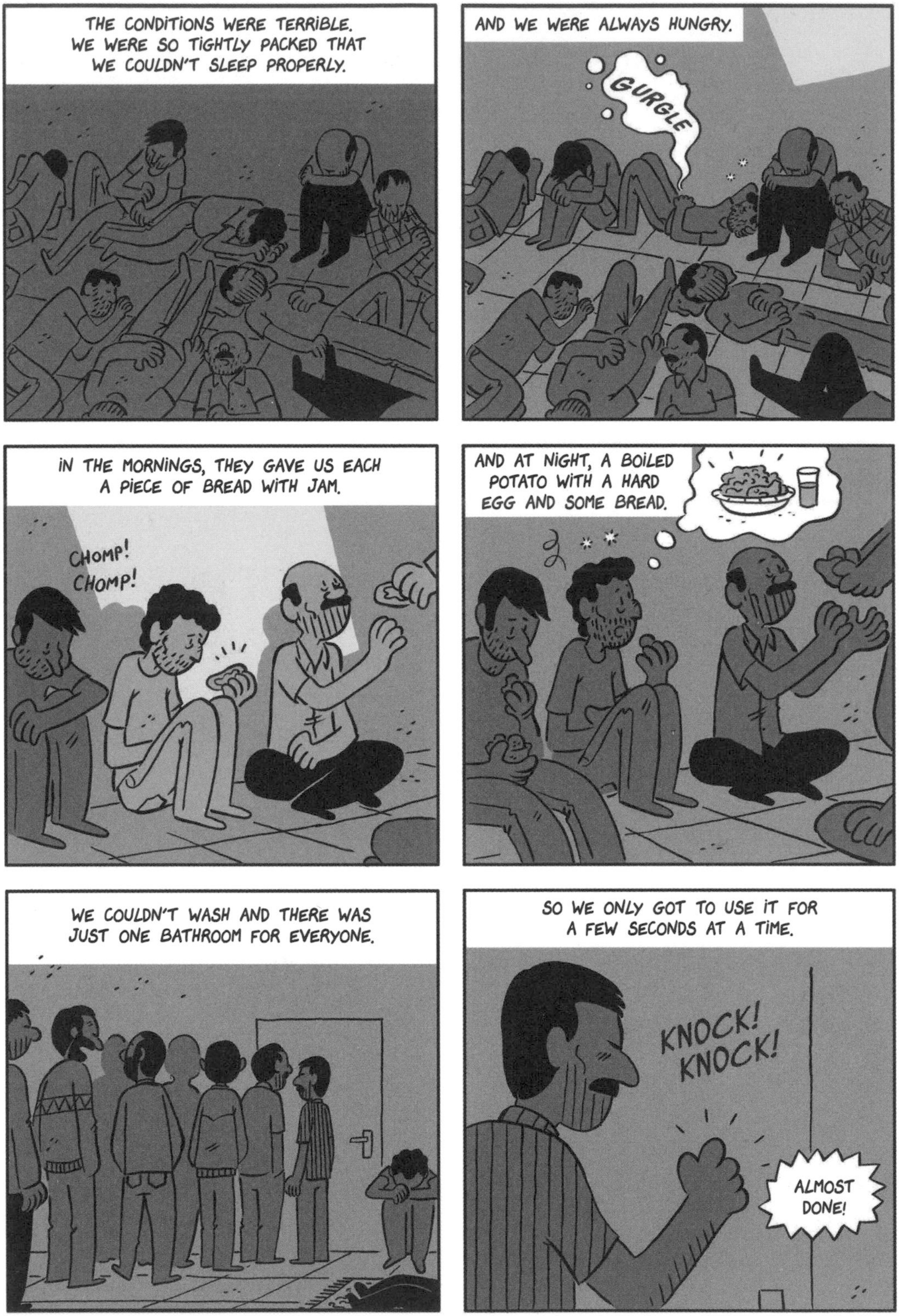
THE CONDITIONS WERE TERRIBLE. WE WERE SO TIGHTLY PACKED THAT WE COULDN'T SLEEP PROPERLY.
AND WE WERE ALWAYS HUNGRY.
GURGLE
IN THE MORNINGS, THEY GAVE US EACH A PIECE OF BREAD WITH JAM.
CHOMP! CHOMP!
AND AT NIGHT, A BOILED POTATO WITH A HARD EGG AND SOME BREAD.
WE COULDN'T WASH AND THERE WAS JUST ONE BATHROOM FOR EVERYONE.
SO WE ONLY GOT TO USE IT FOR A FEW SECONDS AT A TIME.
KNOCK! KNOCK!
ALMOST DONE!

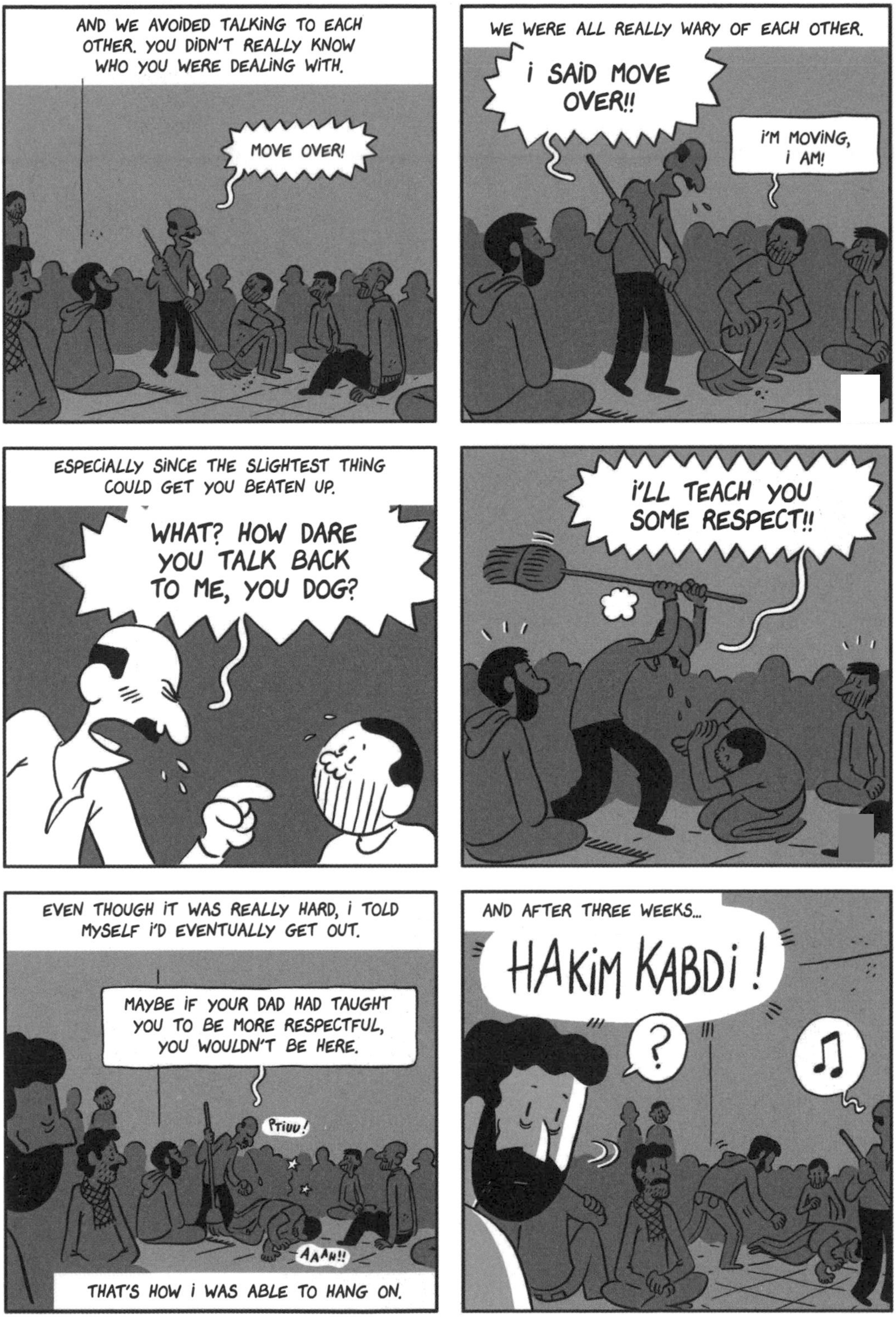

AND WE AVOIDED TALKING TO EACH OTHER. YOU DIDN'T REALLY KNOW WHO YOU WERE DEALING WITH.
MOVE OVER!
WE WERE ALL REALLY WARY OF EACH OTHER.
I SAID MOVE OVER!!
I'M MOVING, I AM!
ESPECIALLY SINCE THE SLIGHTEST THING COULD GET YOU BEATEN UP.
WHAT? HOW DARE YOU TALK BACK TO ME, YOU DOG?
I'LL TEACH YOU SOME RESPECT!!
EVEN THOUGH IT WAS REALLY HARD, I TOLD MYSELF I'D EVENTUALLY GET OUT.
MAYBE IF YOUR DAD HAD TAUGHT YOU TO BE MORE RESPECTFUL, YOU WOULDN'T BE HERE.
PTIUU!
AAAH!!
THAT'S HOW I WAS ABLE TO HANG ON.
AND AFTER THREE WEEKS...
HAKIM KABDI!
?

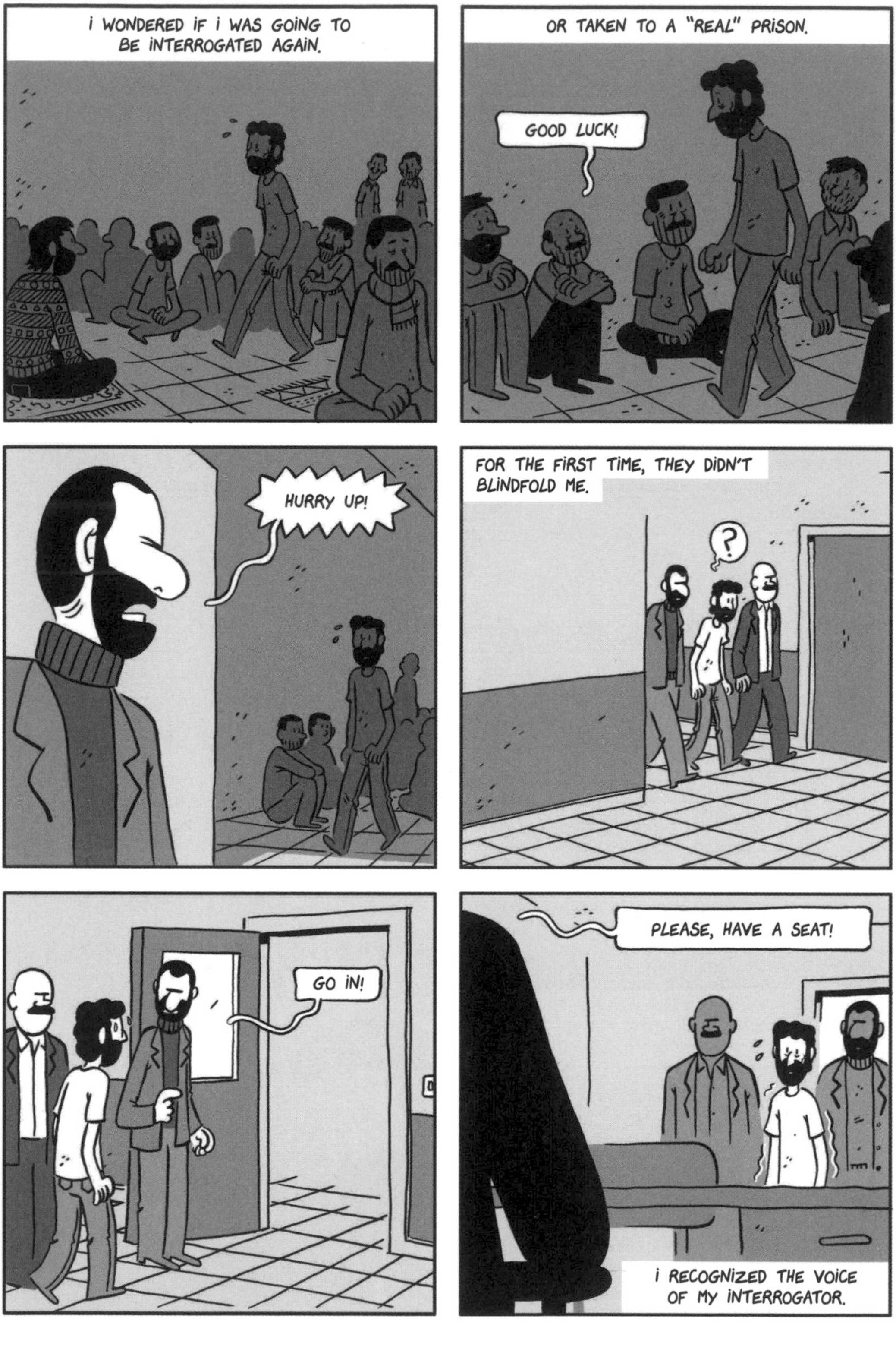
I WONDERED IF I WAS GOING TO BE INTERROGATED AGAIN.
OR TAKEN TO A "REAL" PRISON.
GOOD LUCK!
HURRY UP!
FOR THE FIRST TIME, THEY DIDN'T BLINDFOLD ME.
?
GO IN!
PLEASE, HAVE A SEAT!
I RECOGNIZED THE VOICE OF MY INTERROGATOR.

THIS NEW POLITENESS WAS SO STRANGE.

SIGN HERE!

?

WHAT IS IT?

YOUR DEPOSITION.

CAN I READ IT?

NO.

JUST SIGN IT.

MY MIND WAS RACING.

I THOUGHT THEY MIGHT BE HAVING ME SIGN A FALSE CONFESSION SO THEY COULD PUT ME IN PRISON, OR WORSE, EXECUTE ME.

I GLANCED AT ONE OF THE PAPERS AND SAW:

blablablablablablablablabla
blablablablablablablablablabl
blablablablablablablablablab
blablablablablablablablablab
We confused this Hakim Kabdi
for another Hakim Kabdi. blab
blablablablablablablablabla
blablablablablablablablabla
blablablablablablablablabl
blablablablablablablabla
blablablablablablab
blablablablab

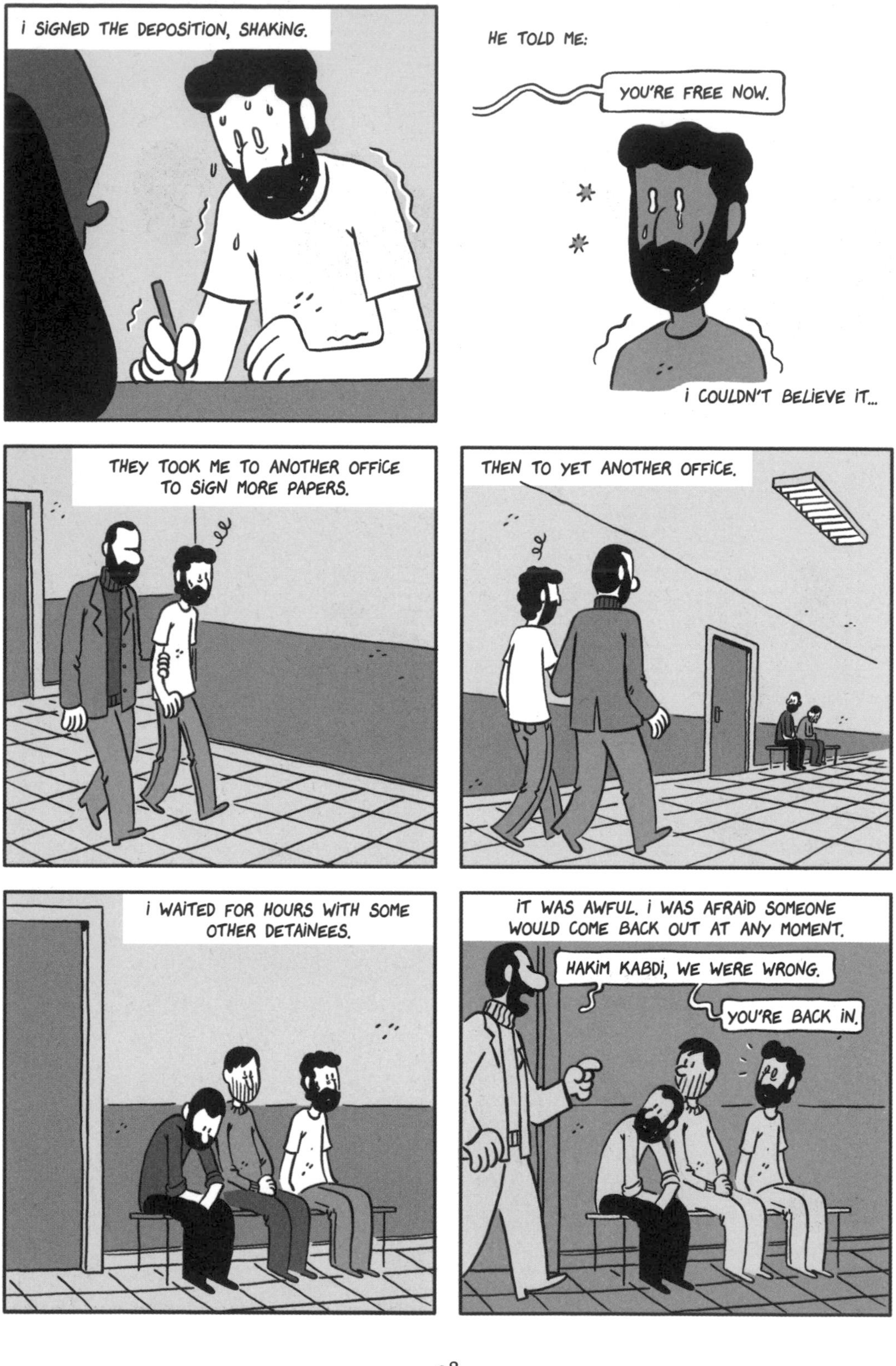
I SIGNED THE DEPOSITION, SHAKING.
HE TOLD ME:
YOU'RE FREE NOW.
I COULDN'T BELIEVE IT...
THEY TOOK ME TO ANOTHER OFFICE TO SIGN MORE PAPERS.
THEN TO YET ANOTHER OFFICE.
I WAITED FOR HOURS WITH SOME OTHER DETAINEES.
IT WAS AWFUL. I WAS AFRAID SOMEONE WOULD COME BACK OUT AT ANY MOMENT.
HAKIM KABDI, WE WERE WRONG.
YOU'RE BACK IN.

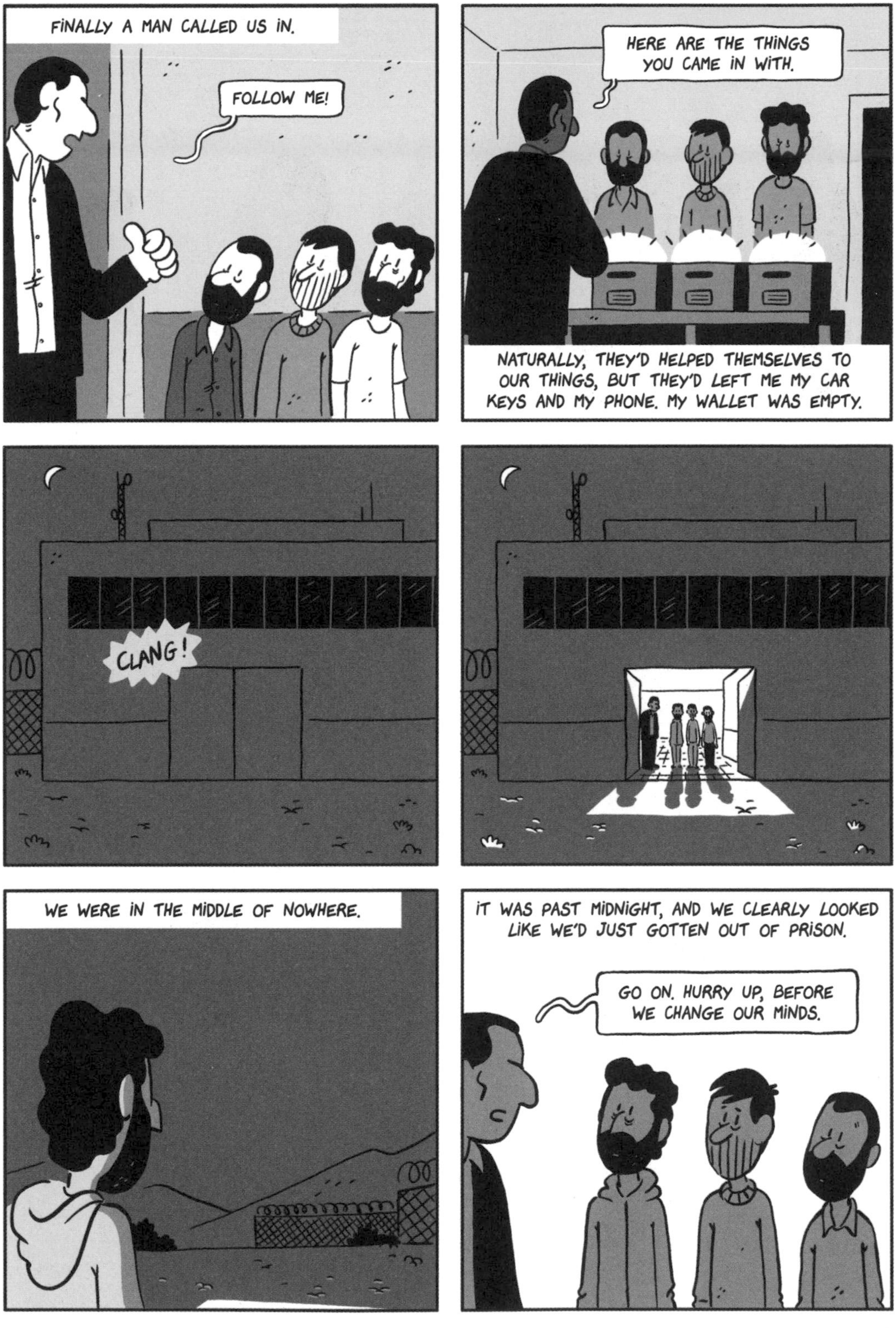

FINALLY A MAN CALLED US IN.
FOLLOW ME!
HERE ARE THE THINGS YOU CAME IN WITH.
NATURALLY, THEY'D HELPED THEMSELVES TO OUR THINGS, BUT THEY'D LEFT ME MY CAR KEYS AND MY PHONE. MY WALLET WAS EMPTY.
CLANG!
WE WERE IN THE MIDDLE OF NOWHERE.
IT WAS PAST MIDNIGHT, AND WE CLEARLY LOOKED LIKE WE'D JUST GOTTEN OUT OF PRISON.
GO ON. HURRY UP, BEFORE WE CHANGE OUR MINDS.

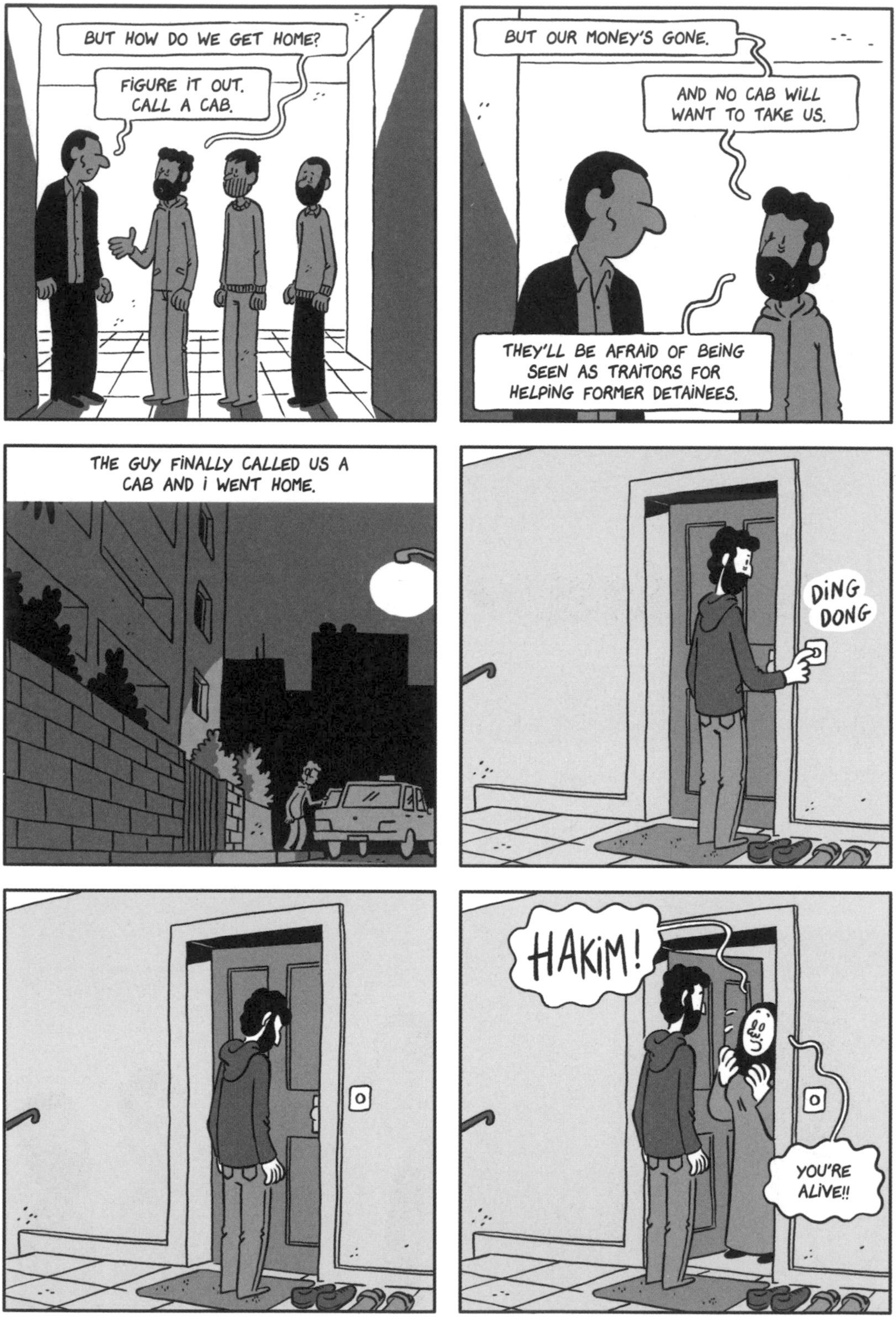
BUT HOW DO WE GET HOME?
FIGURE IT OUT. CALL A CAB.
BUT OUR MONEY'S GONE.
AND NO CAB WILL WANT TO TAKE US.
THEY'LL BE AFRAID OF BEING SEEN AS TRAITORS FOR HELPING FORMER DETAINEES.
THE GUY FINALLY CALLED US A CAB AND I WENT HOME.
DING DONG
HAKIM!
YOU'RE ALIVE!!

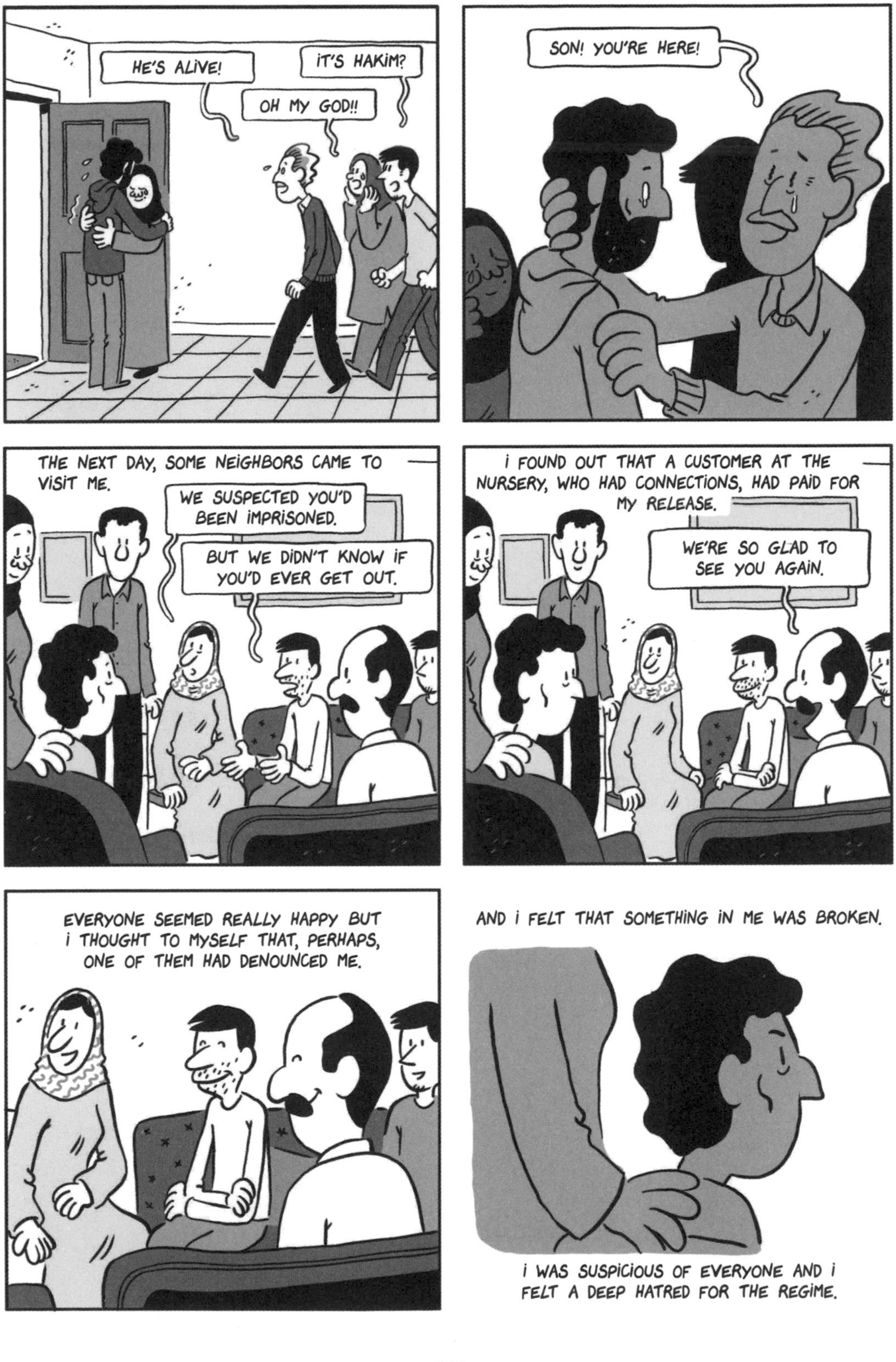
HE'S ALIVE!
IT'S HAKIM?
OH MY GOD!!
SON! YOU'RE HERE!
THE NEXT DAY, SOME NEIGHBORS CAME TO VISIT ME.
WE SUSPECTED YOU'D BEEN IMPRISONED.
BUT WE DIDN'T KNOW IF YOU'D EVER GET OUT.
I FOUND OUT THAT A CUSTOMER AT THE NURSERY, WHO HAD CONNECTIONS, HAD PAID FOR MY RELEASE.
WE'RE SO GLAD TO SEE YOU AGAIN.
EVERYONE SEEMED REALLY HAPPY BUT I THOUGHT TO MYSELF THAT, PERHAPS, ONE OF THEM HAD DENOUNCED ME.
AND I FELT THAT SOMETHING IN ME WAS BROKEN.
I WAS SUSPICIOUS OF EVERYONE AND I FELT A DEEP HATRED FOR THE REGIME.

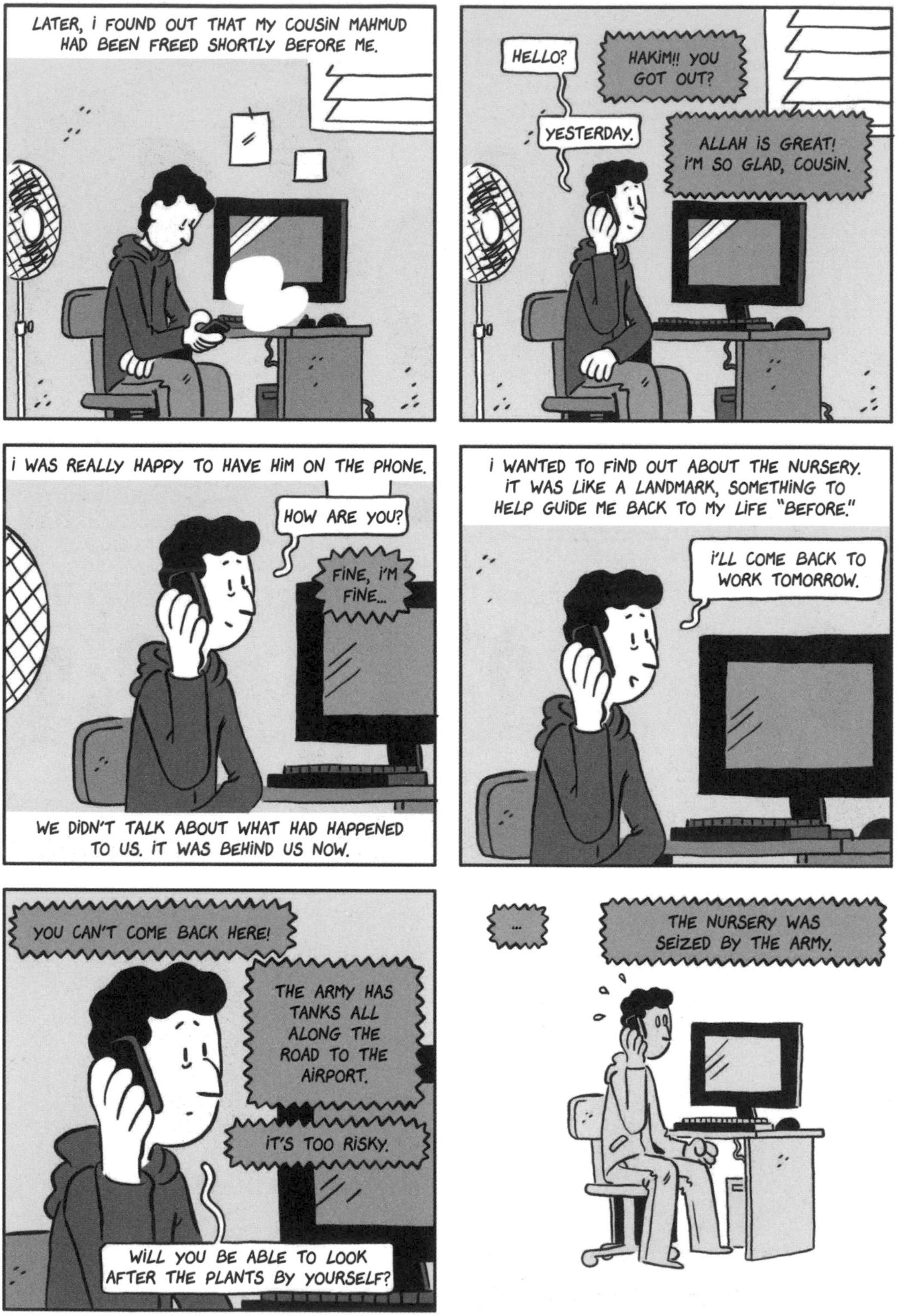
LATER, I FOUND OUT THAT MY COUSIN MAHMUD HAD BEEN FREED SHORTLY BEFORE ME.
HELLO?
HAKIM!! YOU GOT OUT?
YESTERDAY.
ALLAH IS GREAT! I'M SO GLAD, COUSIN.
I WAS REALLY HAPPY TO HAVE HIM ON THE PHONE.
HOW ARE YOU?
FINE, I'M FINE...
WE DIDN'T TALK ABOUT WHAT HAD HAPPENED TO US. IT WAS BEHIND US NOW.
I WANTED TO FIND OUT ABOUT THE NURSERY. IT WAS LIKE A LANDMARK, SOMETHING TO HELP GUIDE ME BACK TO MY LIFE "BEFORE."
I'LL COME BACK TO WORK TOMORROW.
YOU CAN'T COME BACK HERE!
THE ARMY HAS TANKS ALL ALONG THE ROAD TO THE AIRPORT.
IT'S TOO RISKY.
WILL YOU BE ABLE TO LOOK AFTER THE PLANTS BY YOURSELF?
...
THE NURSERY WAS SEIZED BY THE ARMY.

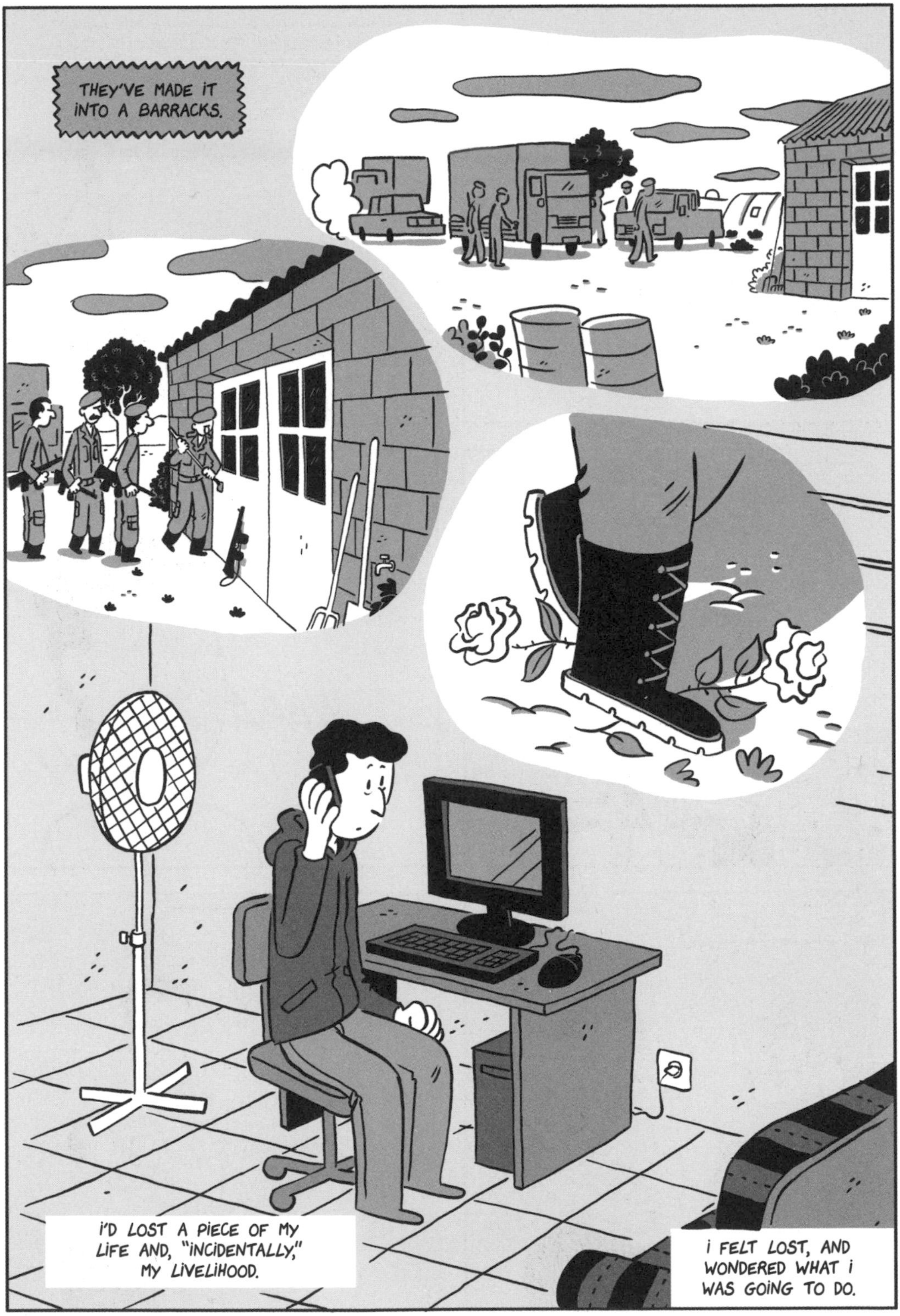
THEY'VE MADE IT INTO A BARRACKS.
I'D LOST A PIECE OF MY LIFE AND, "INCIDENTALLY," MY LIVELIHOOD.
I FELT LOST, AND WONDERED WHAT I WAS GOING TO DO.

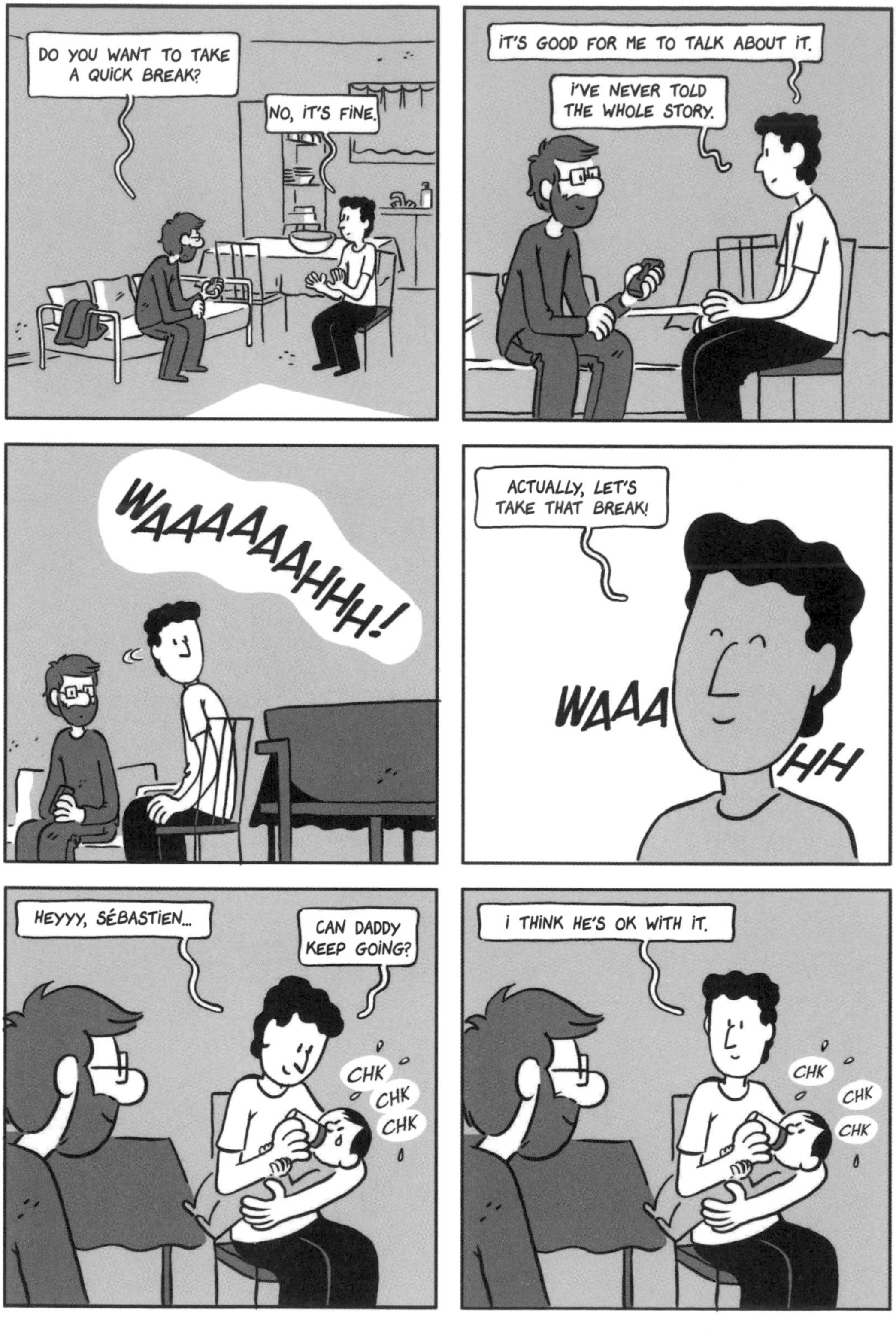
DO YOU WANT TO TAKE A QUICK BREAK?
NO, IT'S FINE.
IT'S GOOD FOR ME TO TALK ABOUT IT.
I'VE NEVER TOLD THE WHOLE STORY.
WAAAAAAAHHHH!
ACTUALLY, LET'S TAKE THAT BREAK!
WAAA HH
HEYYY, SÉBASTIEN...
CAN DADDY KEEP GOING?
CHK
CHK
CHK
I THINK HE'S OK WITH IT.
CHK
CHK
CHK

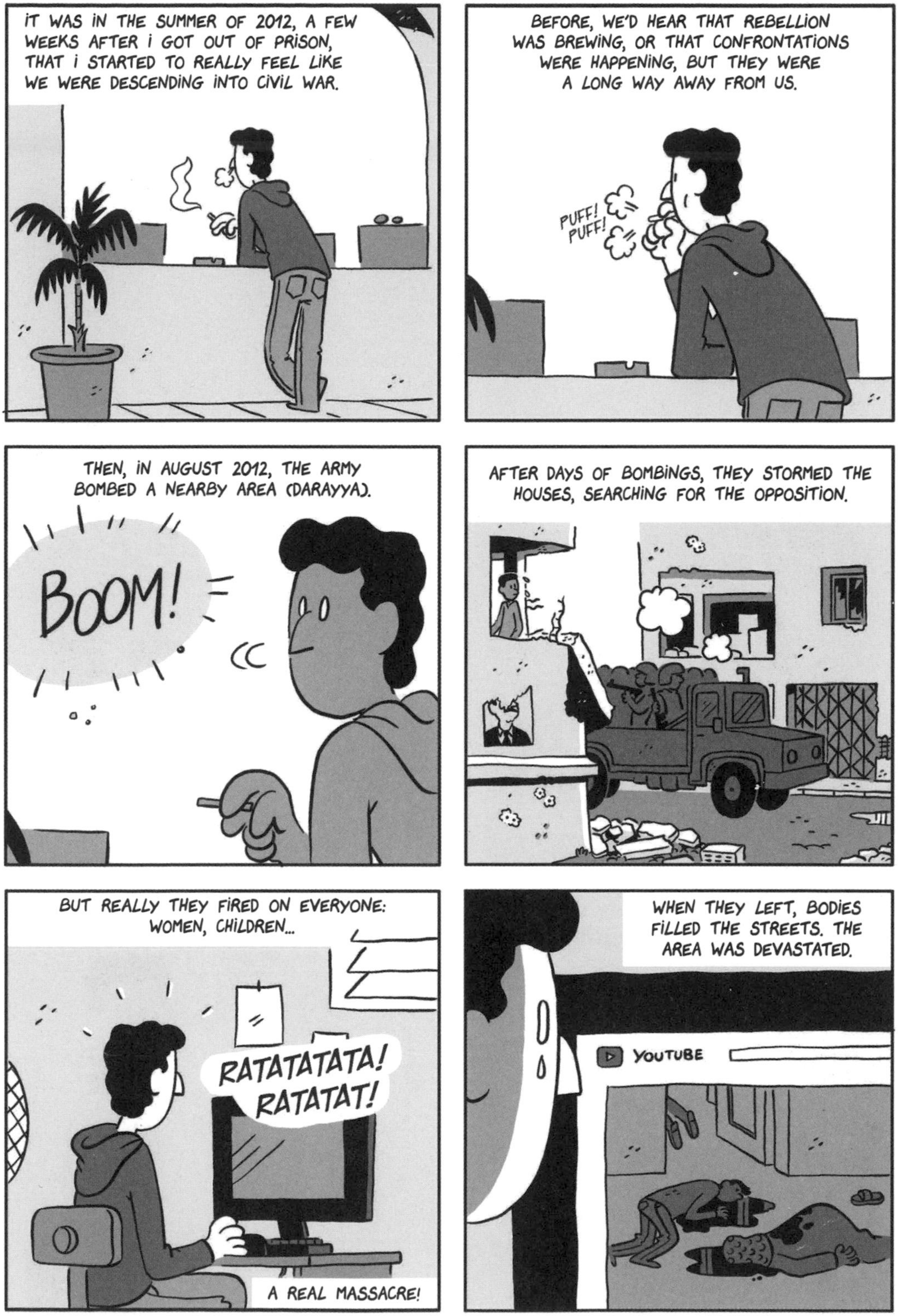
IT WAS IN THE SUMMER OF 2012, A FEW WEEKS AFTER I GOT OUT OF PRISON, THAT I STARTED TO REALLY FEEL LIKE WE WERE DESCENDING INTO CIVIL WAR.
BEFORE, WE'D HEAR THAT REBELLION WAS BREWING, OR THAT CONFRONTATIONS WERE HAPPENING, BUT THEY WERE A LONG WAY AWAY FROM US.
PUFF! PUFF!
THEN, IN AUGUST 2012, THE ARMY BOMBED A NEARBY AREA (DARAYYA).
BOOM!
AFTER DAYS OF BOMBINGS, THEY STORMED THE HOUSES, SEARCHING FOR THE OPPOSITION.
BUT REALLY THEY FIRED ON EVERYONE: WOMEN, CHILDREN...
RATATATATA! RATATAT!
A REAL MASSACRE!
WHEN THEY LEFT, BODIES FILLED THE STREETS. THE AREA WAS DEVASTATED.
YOUTUBE

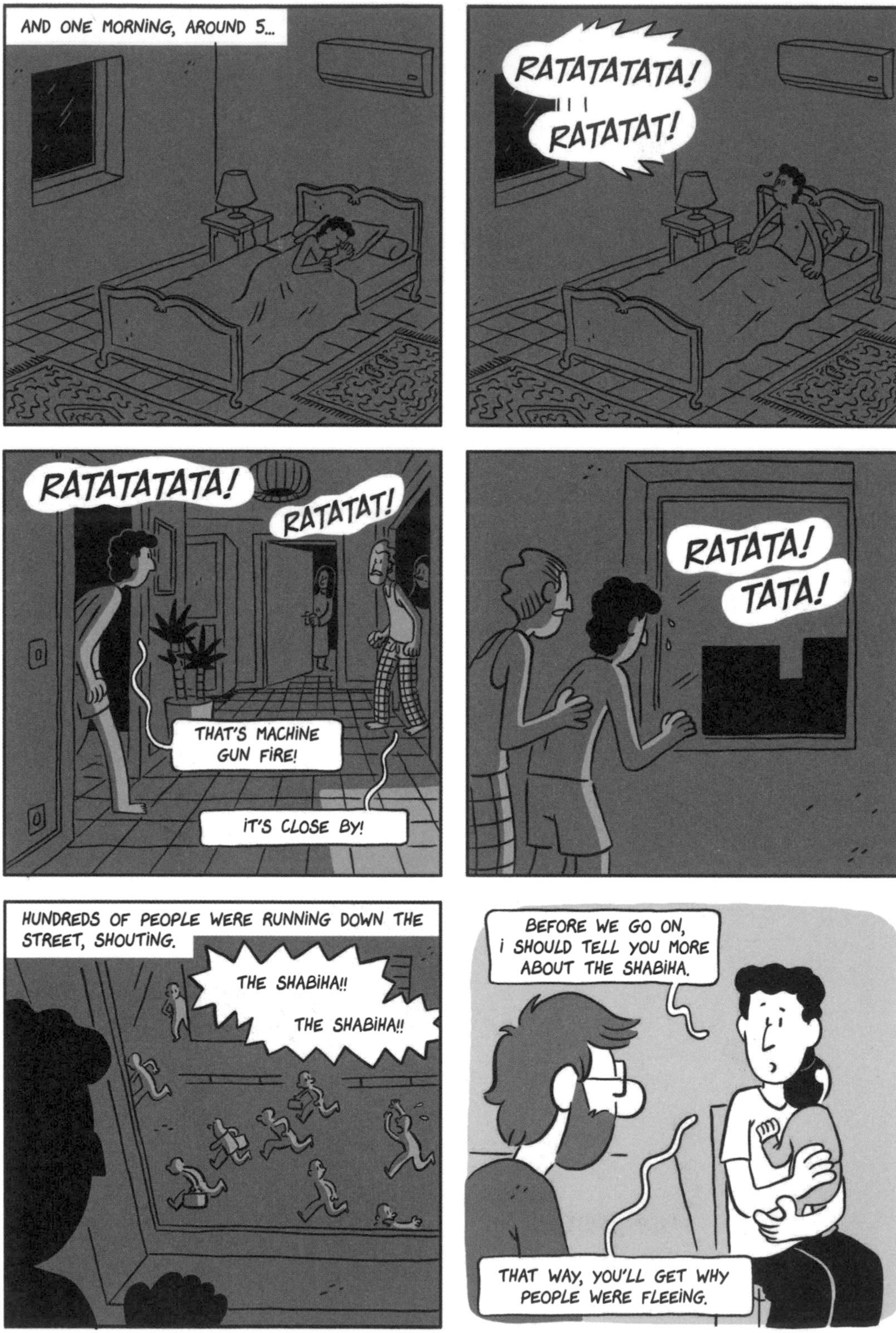
AND ONE MORNING, AROUND 5...
RATATATATA!
RATATAT!
RATATATATA!
RATATAT!
THAT'S MACHINE GUN FIRE!
IT'S CLOSE BY!
RATATA!
TATA!
HUNDREDS OF PEOPLE WERE RUNNING DOWN THE STREET, SHOUTING.
THE SHABIHA!!
THE SHABIHA!!
BEFORE WE GO ON, I SHOULD TELL YOU MORE ABOUT THE SHABIHA.
THAT WAY, YOU'LL GET WHY PEOPLE WERE FLEEING.

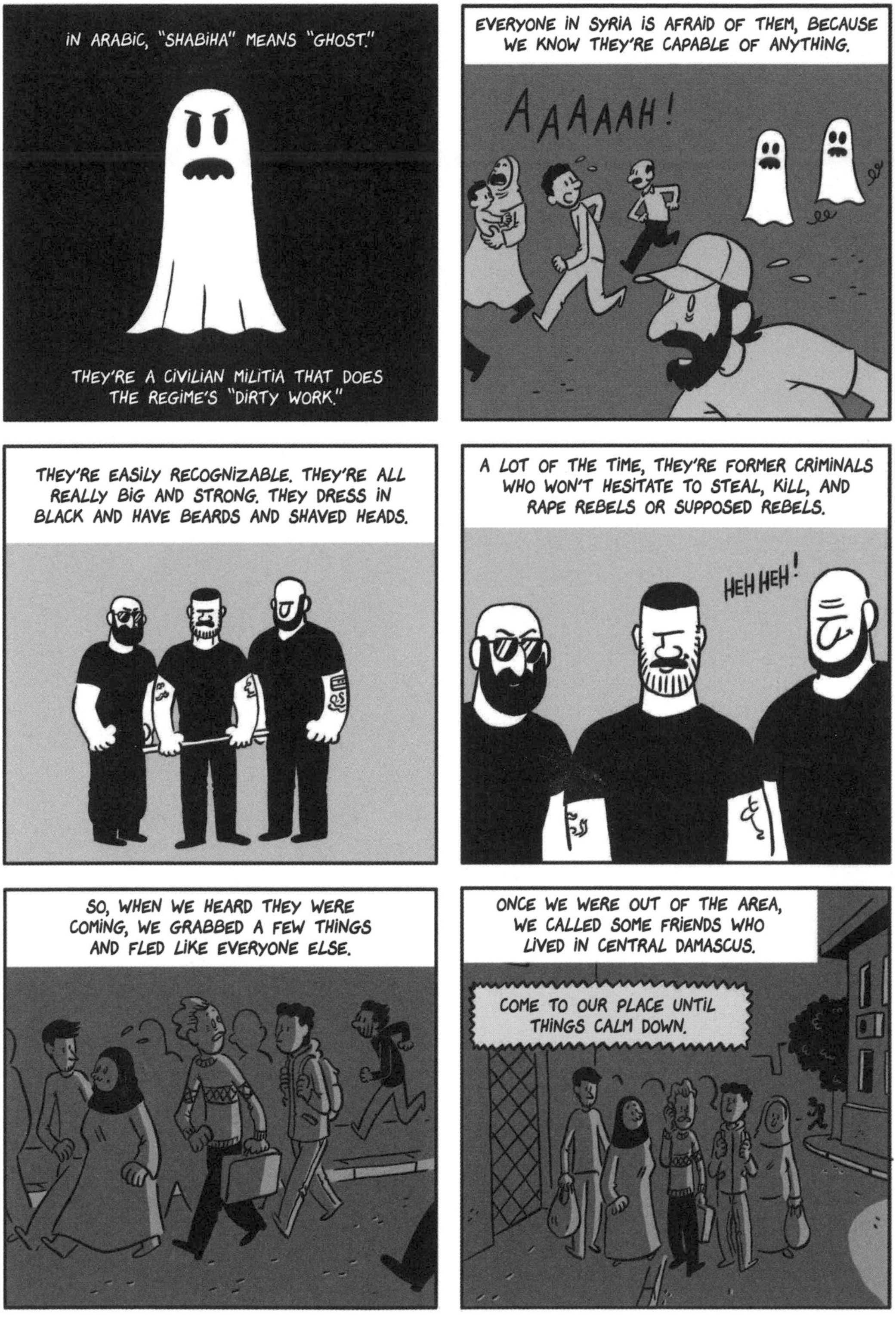
IN ARABIC, "SHABIHA" MEANS "GHOST."
THEY'RE A CIVILIAN MILITIA THAT DOES THE REGIME'S "DIRTY WORK."
EVERYONE IN SYRIA IS AFRAID OF THEM, BECAUSE WE KNOW THEY'RE CAPABLE OF ANYTHING.
AAAAAH!
THEY'RE EASILY RECOGNIZABLE. THEY'RE ALL REALLY BIG AND STRONG. THEY DRESS IN BLACK AND HAVE BEARDS AND SHAVED HEADS.
A LOT OF THE TIME, THEY'RE FORMER CRIMINALS WHO WON'T HESITATE TO STEAL, KILL, AND RAPE REBELS OR SUPPOSED REBELS.
HEH HEH!
SO, WHEN WE HEARD THEY WERE COMING, WE GRABBED A FEW THINGS AND FLED LIKE EVERYONE ELSE.
ONCE WE WERE OUT OF THE AREA, WE CALLED SOME FRIENDS WHO LIVED IN CENTRAL DAMASCUS.
COME TO OUR PLACE UNTIL THINGS CALM DOWN.

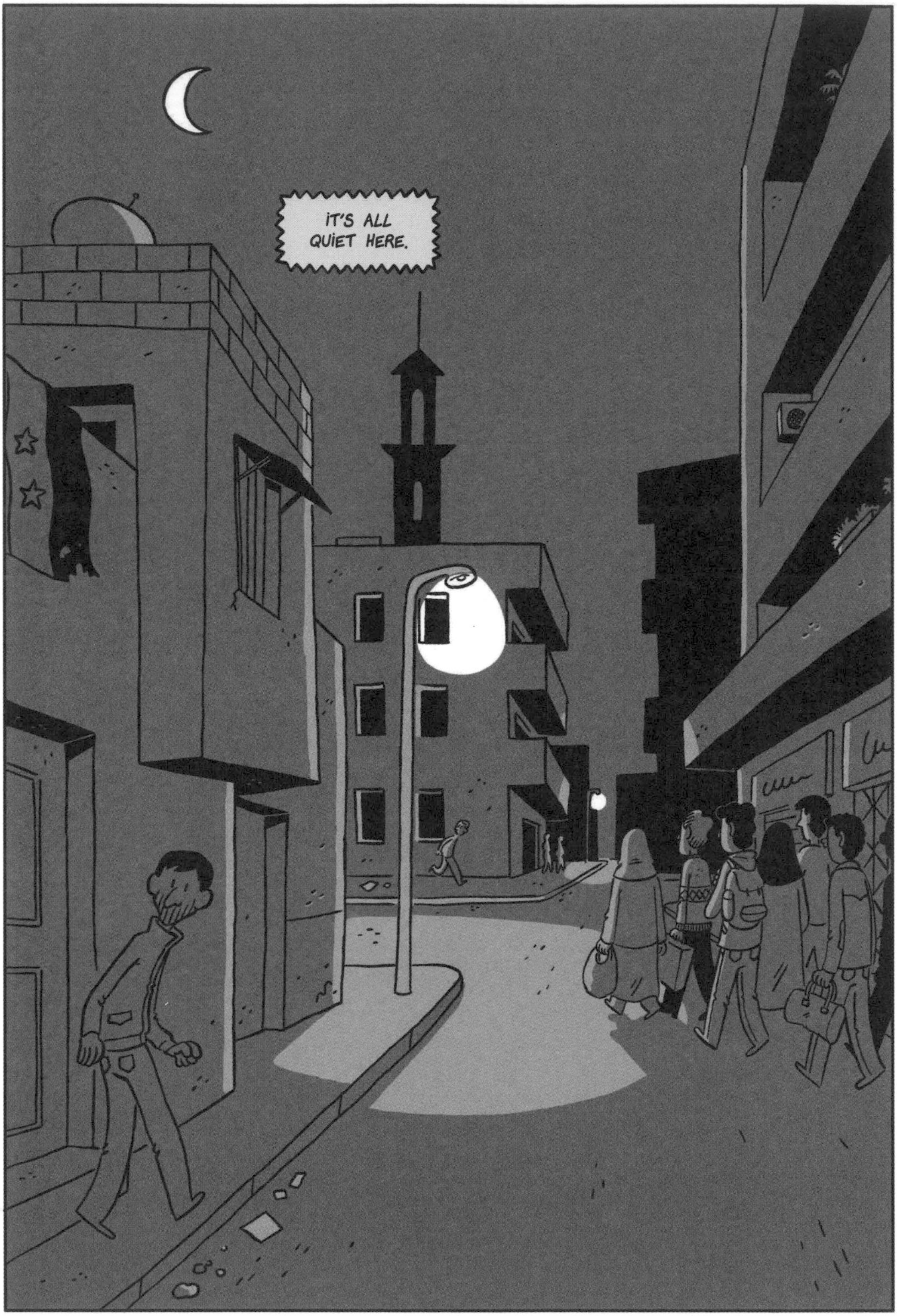
IT'S ALL QUIET HERE.

Chapter 5:
Damascus
(December 2012)

"YOU'VE SEEN IT, THINGS ARE SAFE THERE."

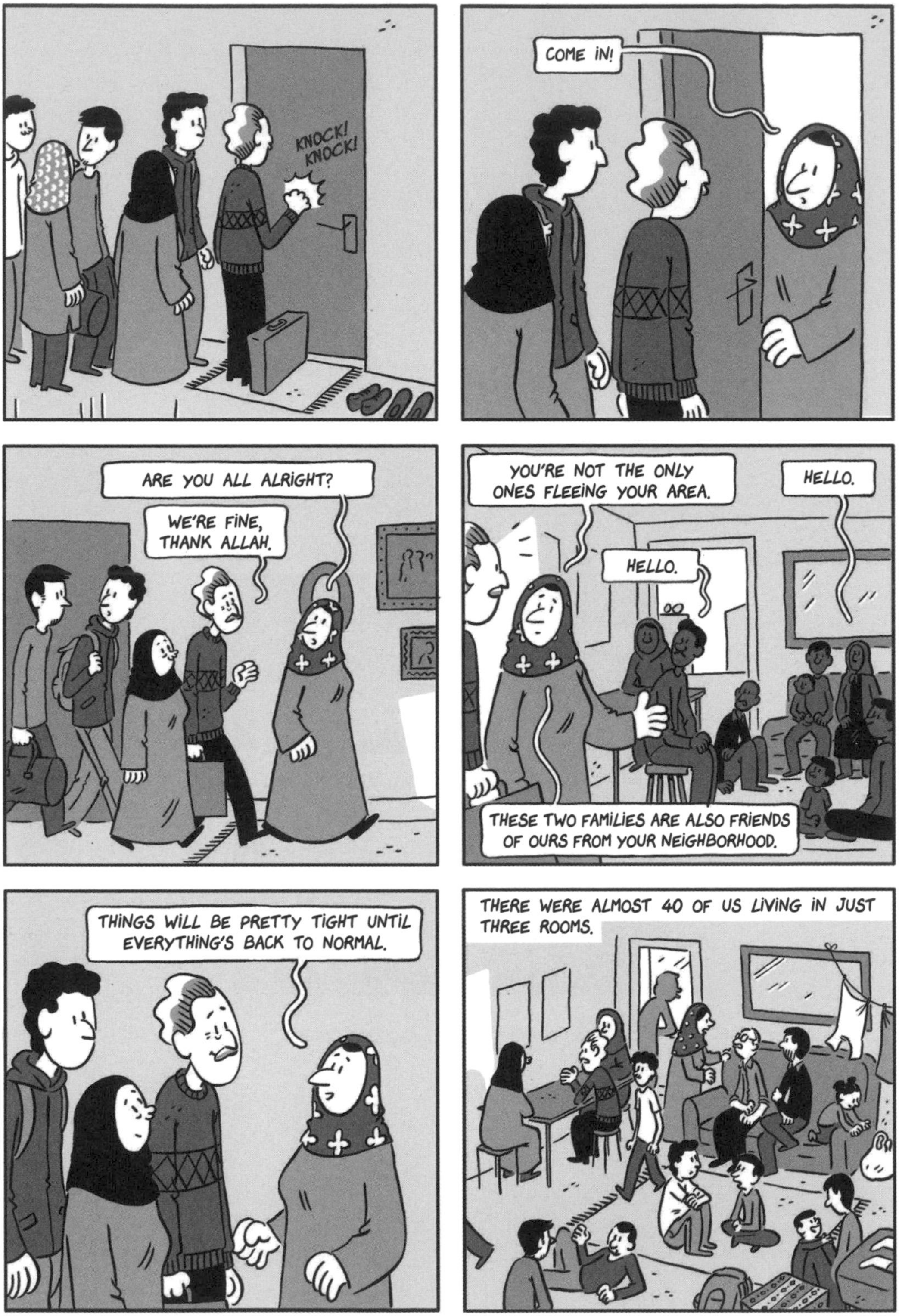
KNOCK! KNOCK!
COME IN!
ARE YOU ALL ALRIGHT?
WE'RE FINE, THANK ALLAH.
YOU'RE NOT THE ONLY ONES FLEEING YOUR AREA.
HELLO.
HELLO.
THESE TWO FAMILIES ARE ALSO FRIENDS OF OURS FROM YOUR NEIGHBORHOOD.
THINGS WILL BE PRETTY TIGHT UNTIL EVERYTHING'S BACK TO NORMAL.
THERE WERE ALMOST 40 OF US LIVING IN JUST THREE ROOMS.

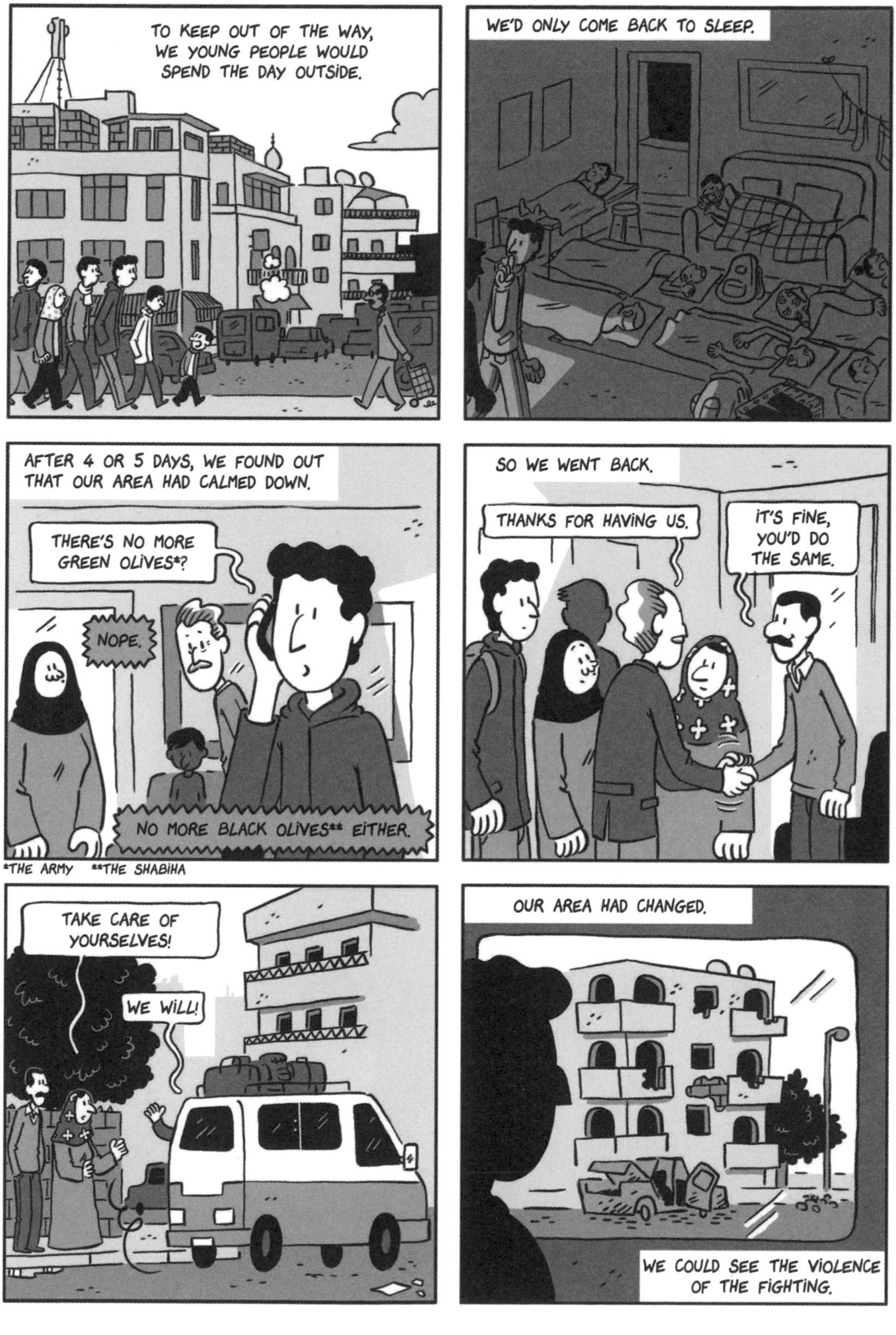
TO KEEP OUT OF THE WAY, WE YOUNG PEOPLE WOULD SPEND THE DAY OUTSIDE.
WE'D ONLY COME BACK TO SLEEP.
AFTER 4 OR 5 DAYS, WE FOUND OUT THAT OUR AREA HAD CALMED DOWN.
THERE'S NO MORE GREEN OLIVES*?
NOPE.
NO MORE BLACK OLIVES** EITHER.
*THE ARMY **THE SHABIHA
SO WE WENT BACK.
THANKS FOR HAVING US.
IT'S FINE, YOU'D DO THE SAME.
TAKE CARE OF YOURSELVES!
WE WILL!
OUR AREA HAD CHANGED.
WE COULD SEE THE VIOLENCE OF THE FIGHTING.

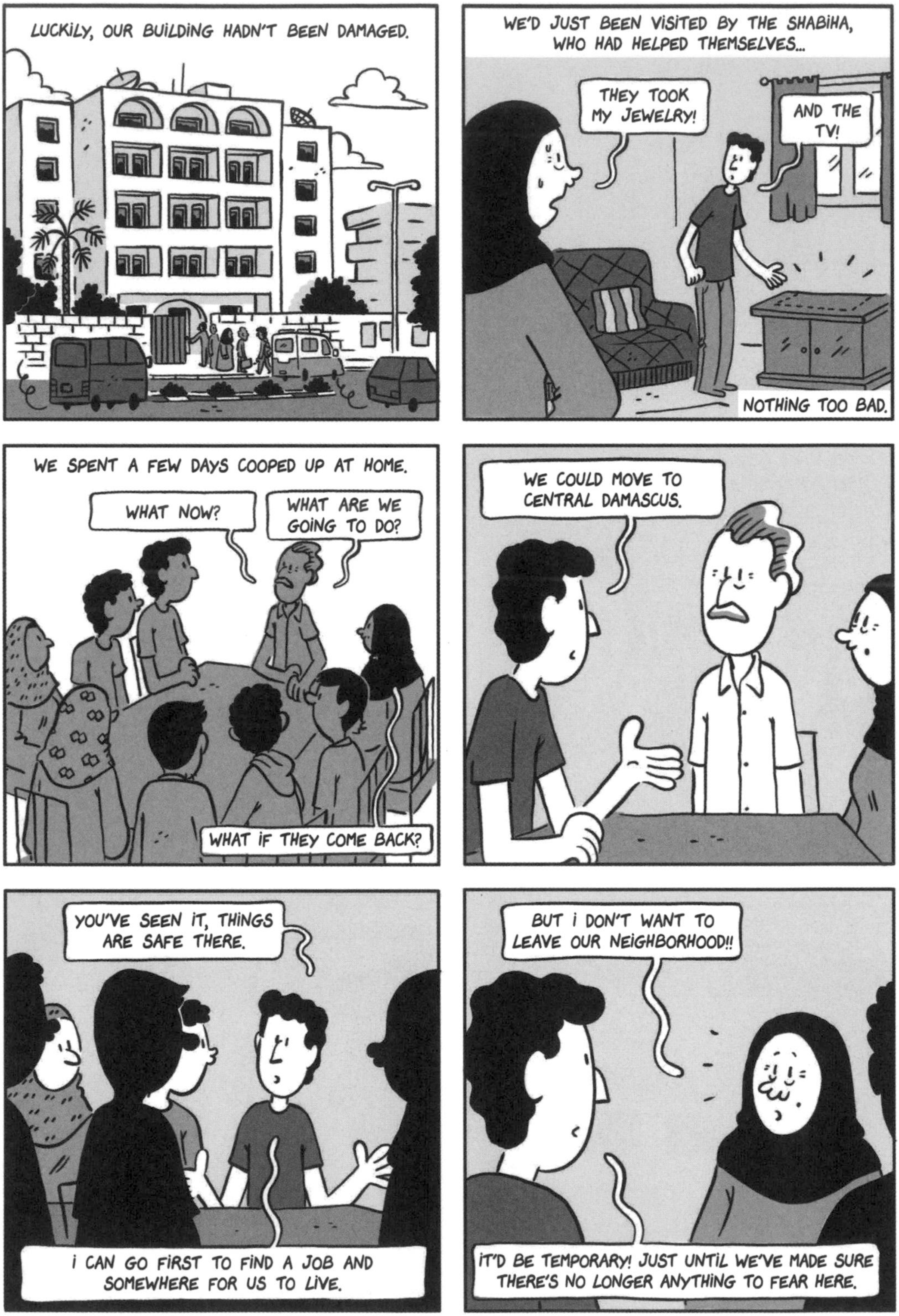
LUCKILY, OUR BUILDING HADN'T BEEN DAMAGED.
WE'D JUST BEEN VISITED BY THE SHABIHA, WHO HAD HELPED THEMSELVES...
THEY TOOK MY JEWELRY!
AND THE TV!
NOTHING TOO BAD.
WE SPENT A FEW DAYS COOPED UP AT HOME.
WHAT NOW?
WHAT ARE WE GOING TO DO?
WHAT IF THEY COME BACK?
WE COULD MOVE TO CENTRAL DAMASCUS.
YOU'VE SEEN IT, THINGS ARE SAFE THERE.
I CAN GO FIRST TO FIND A JOB AND SOMEWHERE FOR US TO LIVE.
BUT I DON'T WANT TO LEAVE OUR NEIGHBORHOOD!!
IT'D BE TEMPORARY! JUST UNTIL WE'VE MADE SURE THERE'S NO LONGER ANYTHING TO FEAR HERE.

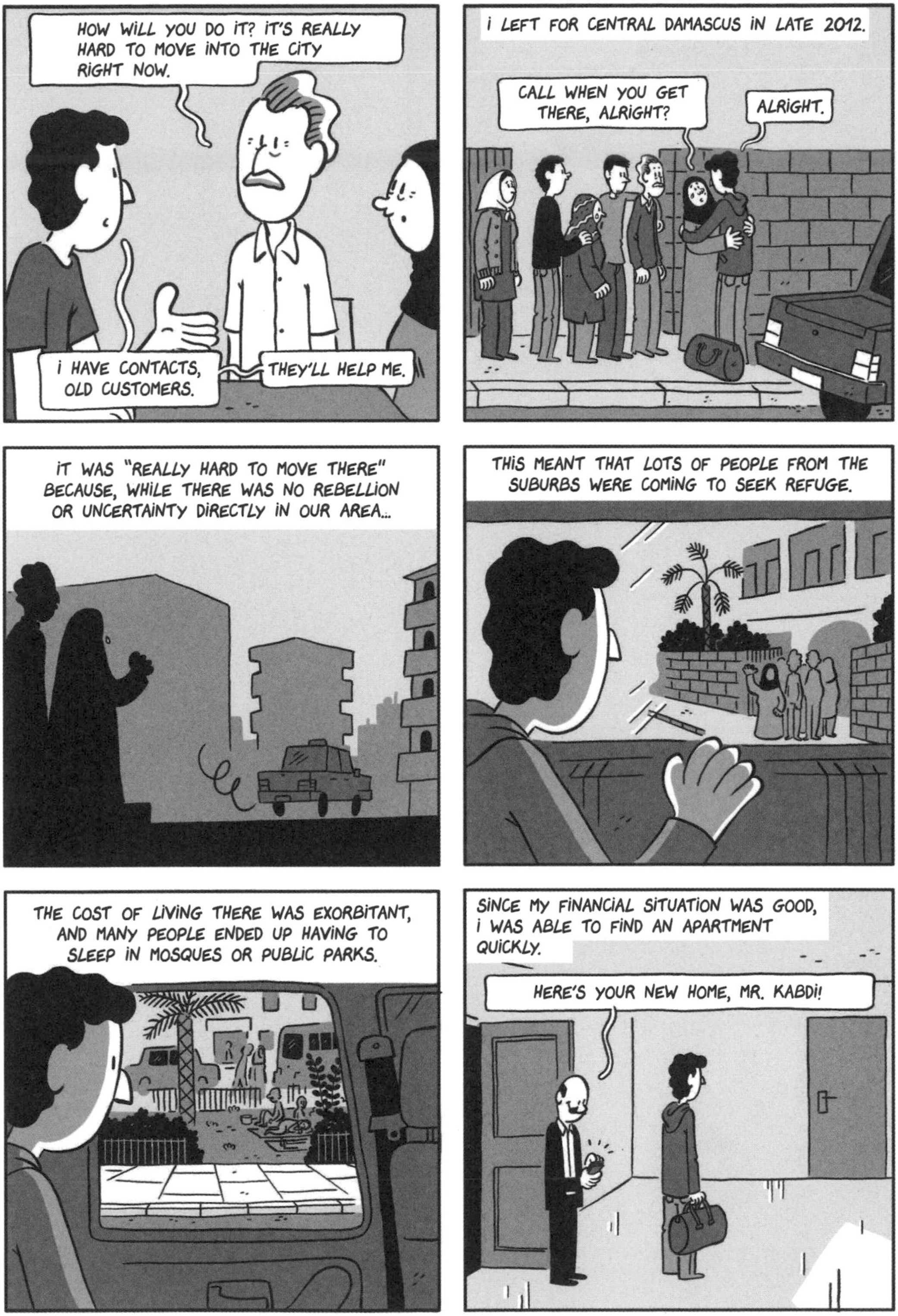
HOW WILL YOU DO IT? IT'S REALLY HARD TO MOVE INTO THE CITY RIGHT NOW.
I HAVE CONTACTS, OLD CUSTOMERS.
THEY'LL HELP ME.
I LEFT FOR CENTRAL DAMASCUS IN LATE 2012.
CALL WHEN YOU GET THERE, ALRIGHT?
ALRIGHT.
IT WAS "REALLY HARD TO MOVE THERE" BECAUSE, WHILE THERE WAS NO REBELLION OR UNCERTAINTY DIRECTLY IN OUR AREA...
THIS MEANT THAT LOTS OF PEOPLE FROM THE SUBURBS WERE COMING TO SEEK REFUGE.
THE COST OF LIVING THERE WAS EXORBITANT, AND MANY PEOPLE ENDED UP HAVING TO SLEEP IN MOSQUES OR PUBLIC PARKS.
SINCE MY FINANCIAL SITUATION WAS GOOD, I WAS ABLE TO FIND AN APARTMENT QUICKLY.
HERE'S YOUR NEW HOME, MR. KABDI!

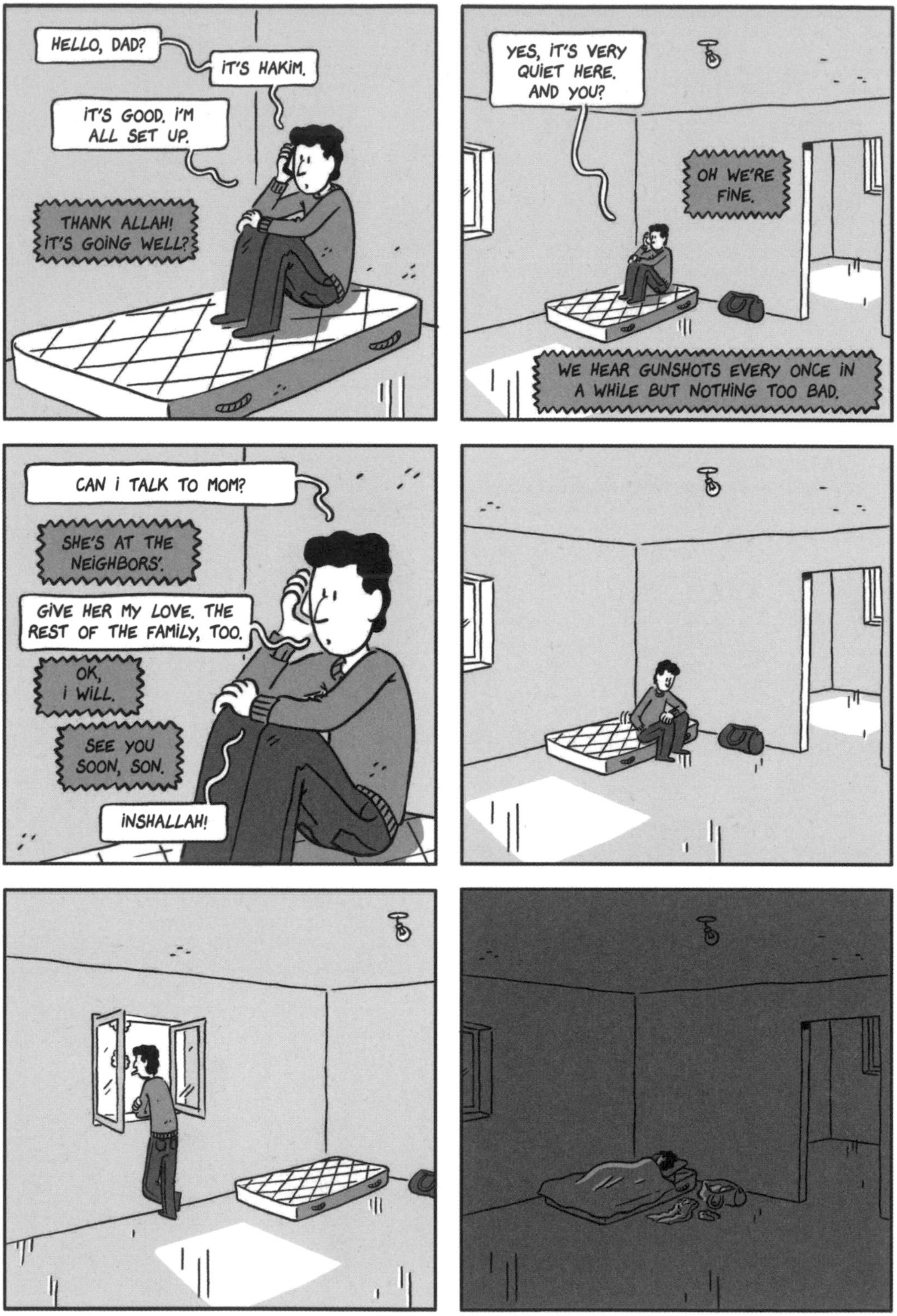

HELLO, DAD?
IT'S HAKIM.
IT'S GOOD. I'M ALL SET UP.
THANK ALLAH! IT'S GOING WELL?
YES, IT'S VERY QUIET HERE. AND YOU?
OH WE'RE FINE.
WE HEAR GUNSHOTS EVERY ONCE IN A WHILE BUT NOTHING TOO BAD.
CAN I TALK TO MOM?
SHE'S AT THE NEIGHBORS'.
GIVE HER MY LOVE. THE REST OF THE FAMILY, TOO.
OK, I WILL.
SEE YOU SOON, SON.
INSHALLAH!

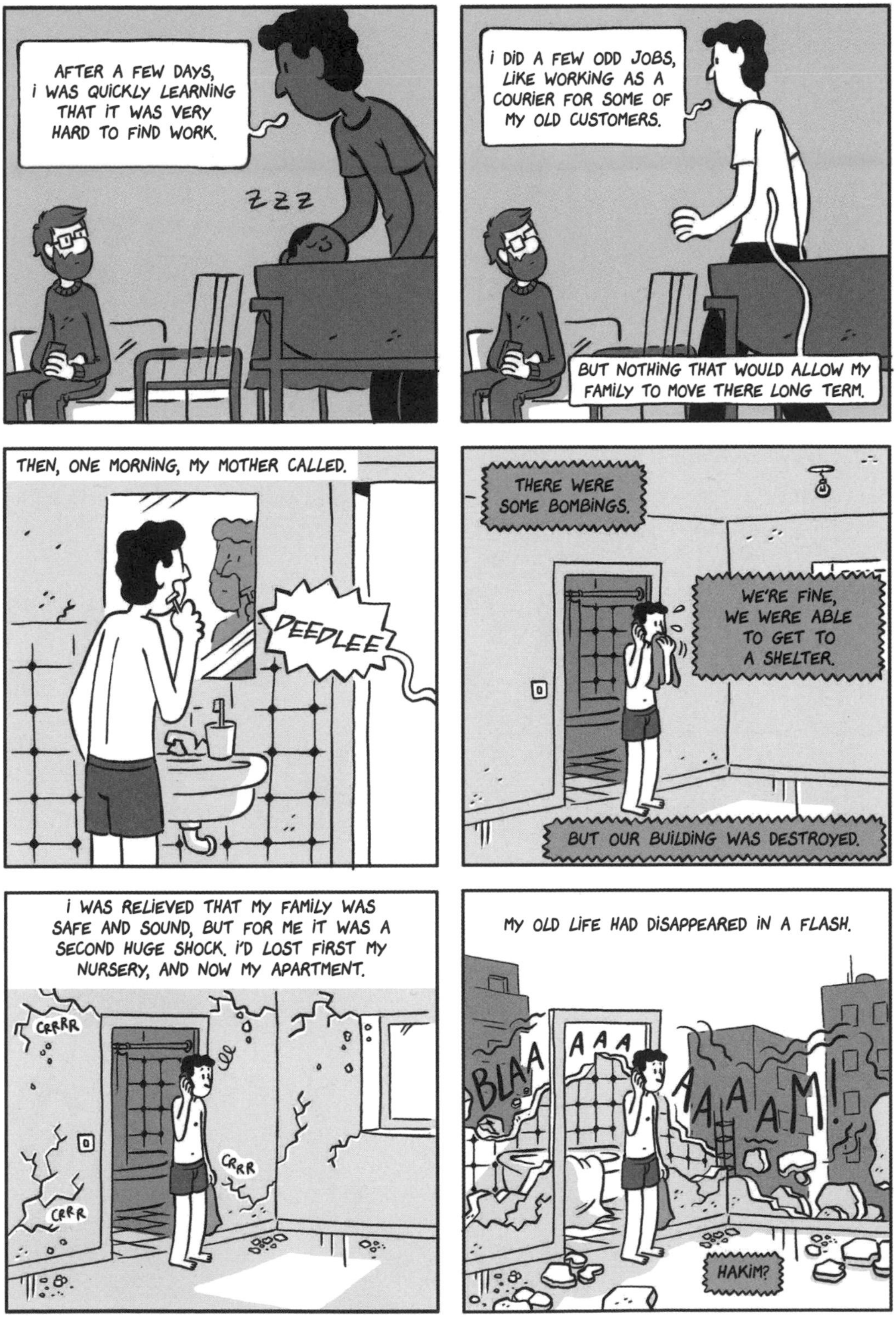

AFTER A FEW DAYS, i WAS QUICKLY LEARNING THAT iT WAS VERY HARD TO FiND WORK.
Z Z Z
i DiD A FEW ODD JOBS, LiKE WORKiNG AS A COURiER FOR SOME OF MY OLD CUSTOMERS.
BUT NOTHiNG THAT WOULD ALLOW MY FAMiLY TO MOVE THERE LONG TERM.
THEN, ONE MORNiNG, MY MOTHER CALLED.
DEEDLEE
THERE WERE SOME BOMBiNGS.
WE'RE FiNE, WE WERE ABLE TO GET TO A SHELTER.
BUT OUR BUiLDiNG WAS DESTROYED.
i WAS RELiEVED THAT MY FAMiLY WAS SAFE AND SOUND, BUT FOR ME iT WAS A SECOND HUGE SHOCK. i'D LOST FiRST MY NURSERY, AND NOW MY APARTMENT.
CRRRR
CRRR
CRRR
MY OLD LiFE HAD DiSAPPEARED iN A FLASH.
BLAAAAAAAAAM!
HAKiM?

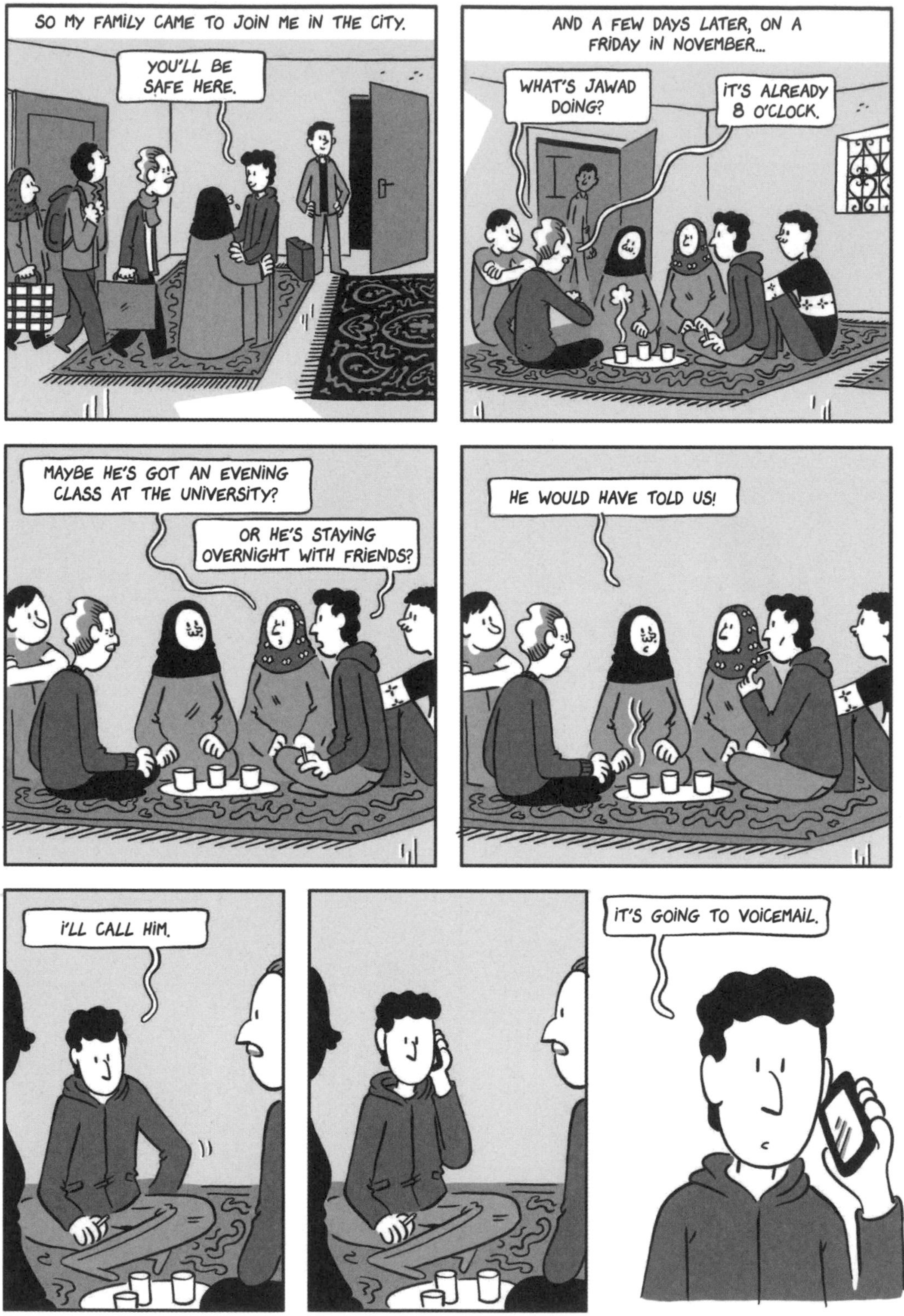
SO MY FAMILY CAME TO JOIN ME IN THE CITY.
YOU'LL BE SAFE HERE.
AND A FEW DAYS LATER, ON A FRIDAY IN NOVEMBER...
WHAT'S JAWAD DOING?
IT'S ALREADY 8 O'CLOCK.
MAYBE HE'S GOT AN EVENING CLASS AT THE UNIVERSITY?
OR HE'S STAYING OVERNIGHT WITH FRIENDS?
HE WOULD HAVE TOLD US!
I'LL CALL HIM.
IT'S GOING TO VOICEMAIL.

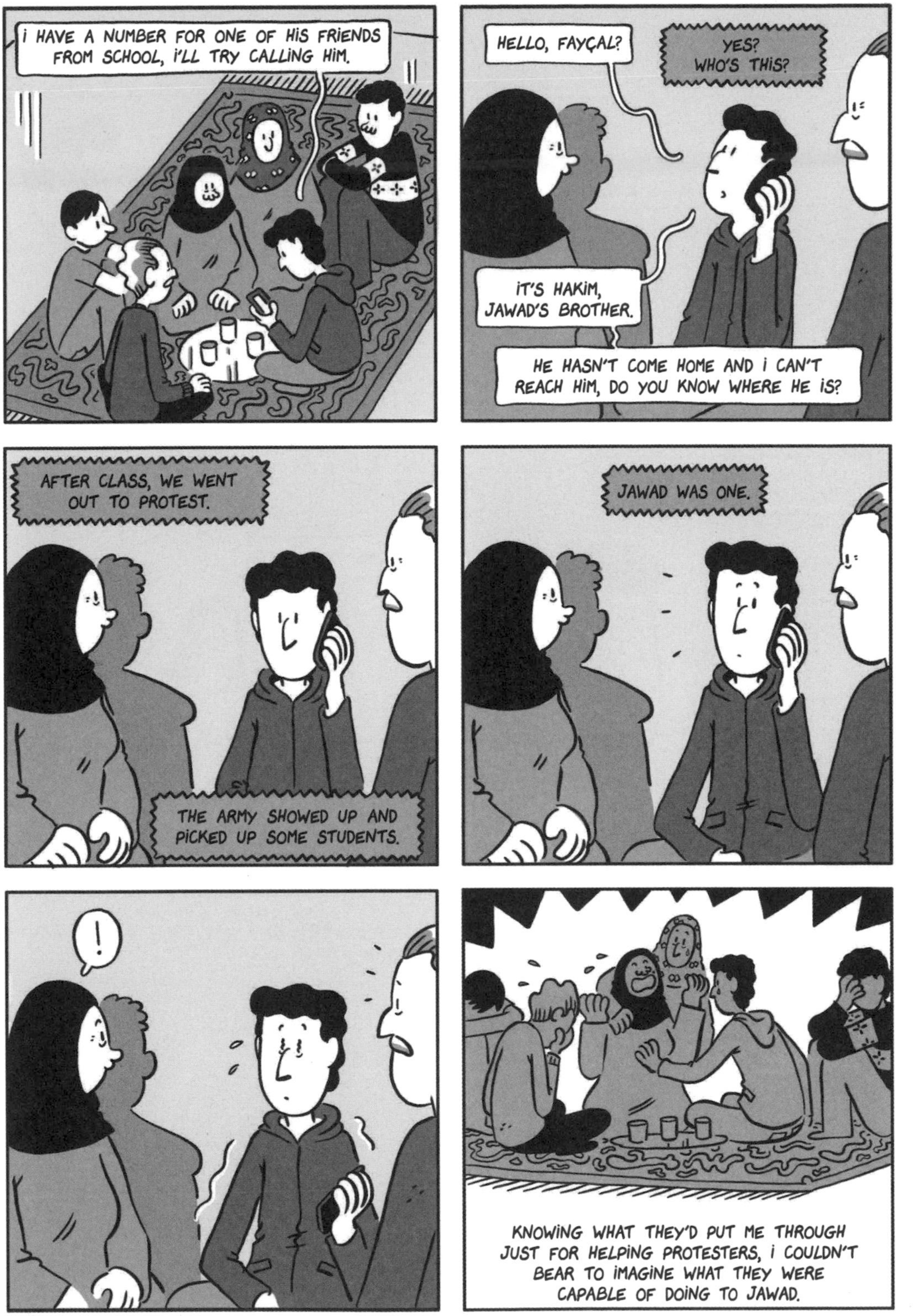
I HAVE A NUMBER FOR ONE OF HIS FRIENDS FROM SCHOOL, I'LL TRY CALLING HIM.
HELLO, FAYÇAL?
YES? WHO'S THIS?
IT'S HAKIM, JAWAD'S BROTHER.
HE HASN'T COME HOME AND I CAN'T REACH HIM, DO YOU KNOW WHERE HE IS?
AFTER CLASS, WE WENT OUT TO PROTEST.
THE ARMY SHOWED UP AND PICKED UP SOME STUDENTS.
JAWAD WAS ONE.
!
KNOWING WHAT THEY'D PUT ME THROUGH JUST FOR HELPING PROTESTERS, I COULDN'T BEAR TO IMAGINE WHAT THEY WERE CAPABLE OF DOING TO JAWAD.

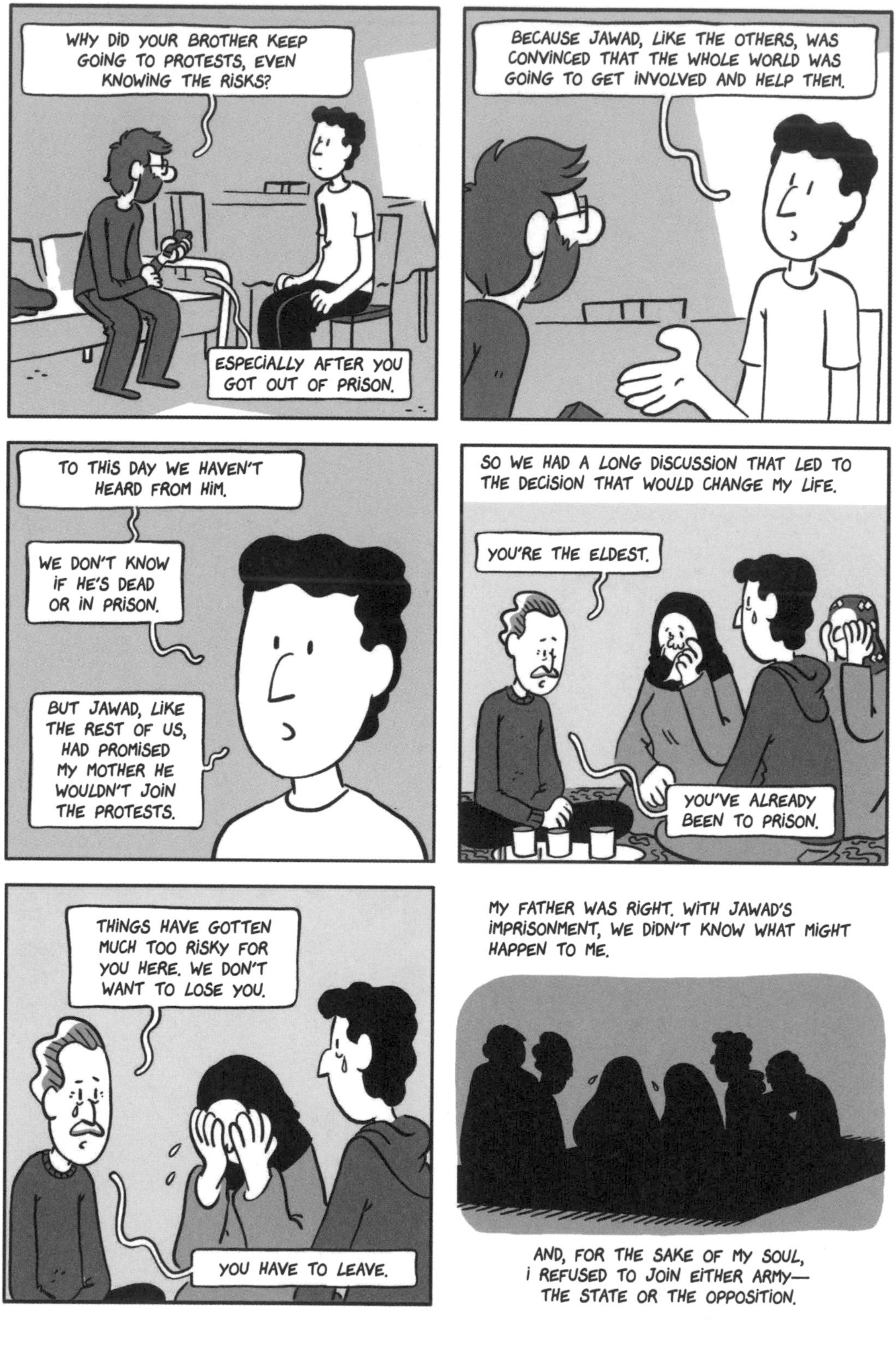
WHY DID YOUR BROTHER KEEP GOING TO PROTESTS, EVEN KNOWING THE RISKS?
ESPECIALLY AFTER YOU GOT OUT OF PRISON.
BECAUSE JAWAD, LIKE THE OTHERS, WAS CONVINCED THAT THE WHOLE WORLD WAS GOING TO GET INVOLVED AND HELP THEM.
TO THIS DAY WE HAVEN'T HEARD FROM HIM.
WE DON'T KNOW IF HE'S DEAD OR IN PRISON.
BUT JAWAD, LIKE THE REST OF US, HAD PROMISED MY MOTHER HE WOULDN'T JOIN THE PROTESTS.
SO WE HAD A LONG DISCUSSION THAT LED TO THE DECISION THAT WOULD CHANGE MY LIFE.
YOU'RE THE ELDEST.
YOU'VE ALREADY BEEN TO PRISON.
THINGS HAVE GOTTEN MUCH TOO RISKY FOR YOU HERE. WE DON'T WANT TO LOSE YOU.
YOU HAVE TO LEAVE.
MY FATHER WAS RIGHT. WITH JAWAD'S IMPRISONMENT, WE DIDN'T KNOW WHAT MIGHT HAPPEN TO ME.
AND, FOR THE SAKE OF MY SOUL, I REFUSED TO JOIN EITHER ARMY— THE STATE OR THE OPPOSITION.

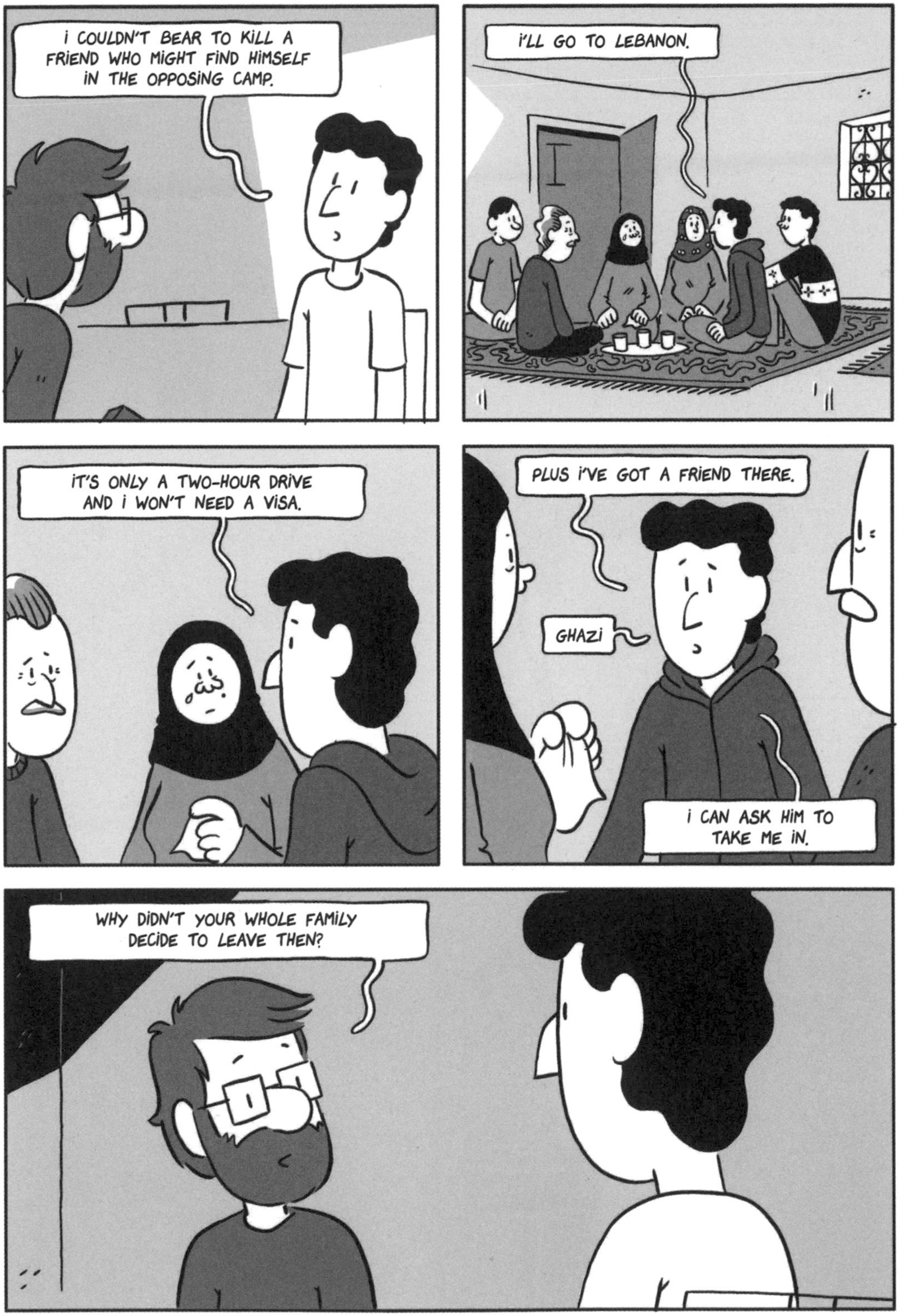
I COULDN'T BEAR TO KILL A FRIEND WHO MIGHT FIND HIMSELF IN THE OPPOSING CAMP.
I'LL GO TO LEBANON.
IT'S ONLY A TWO-HOUR DRIVE AND I WON'T NEED A VISA.
PLUS I'VE GOT A FRIEND THERE.
GHAZI
I CAN ASK HIM TO TAKE ME IN.
WHY DIDN'T YOUR WHOLE FAMILY DECIDE TO LEAVE THEN?

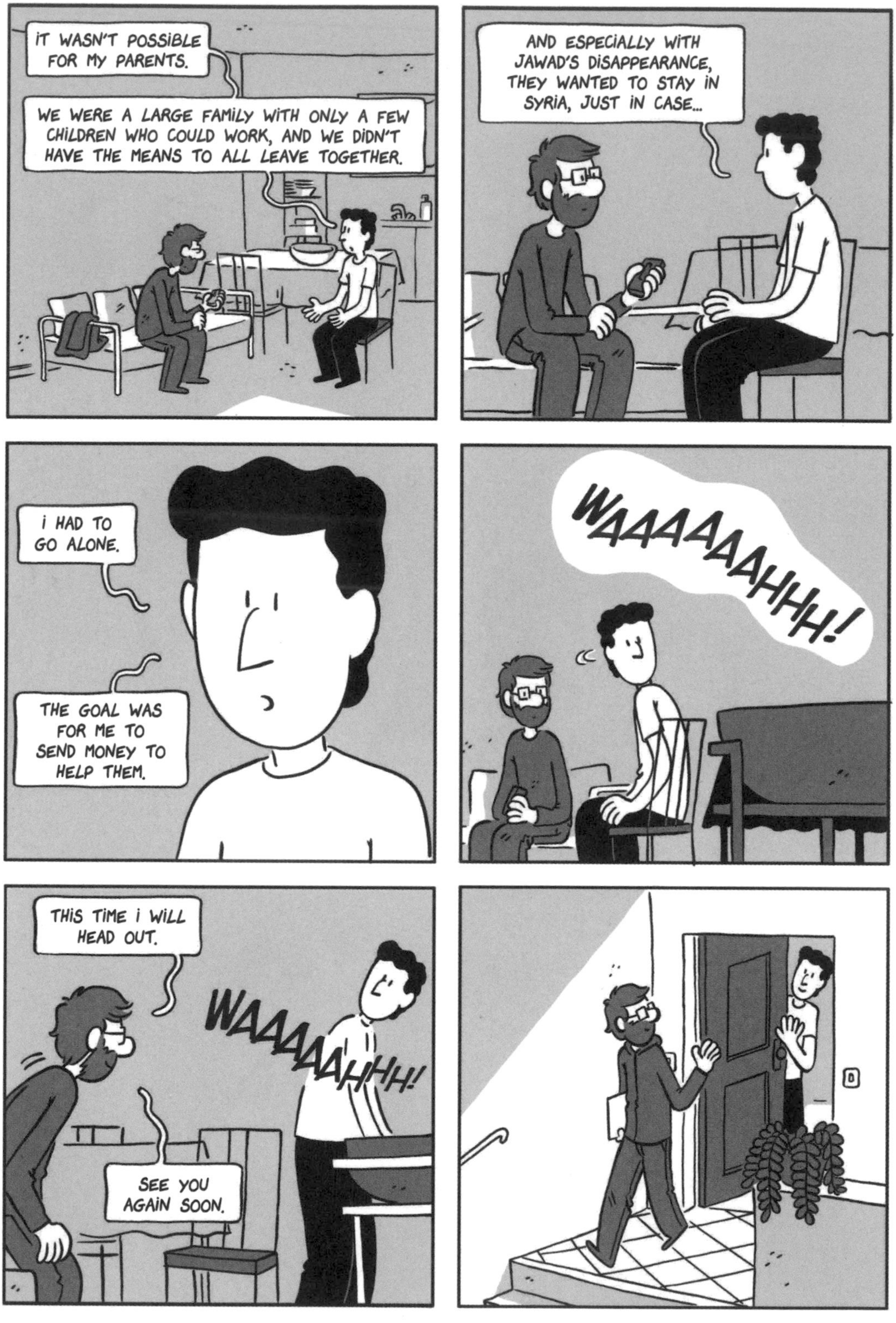

IT WASN'T POSSIBLE FOR MY PARENTS.
WE WERE A LARGE FAMILY WITH ONLY A FEW CHILDREN WHO COULD WORK, AND WE DIDN'T HAVE THE MEANS TO ALL LEAVE TOGETHER.
AND ESPECIALLY WITH JAWAD'S DISAPPEARANCE, THEY WANTED TO STAY IN SYRIA, JUST IN CASE...
I HAD TO GO ALONE.
THE GOAL WAS FOR ME TO SEND MONEY TO HELP THEM.
WAAAAAAHHHH!
THIS TIME I WILL HEAD OUT.
WAAAAAAHHHH!
SEE YOU AGAIN SOON.

Chapter 6: Beirut (January 2013)

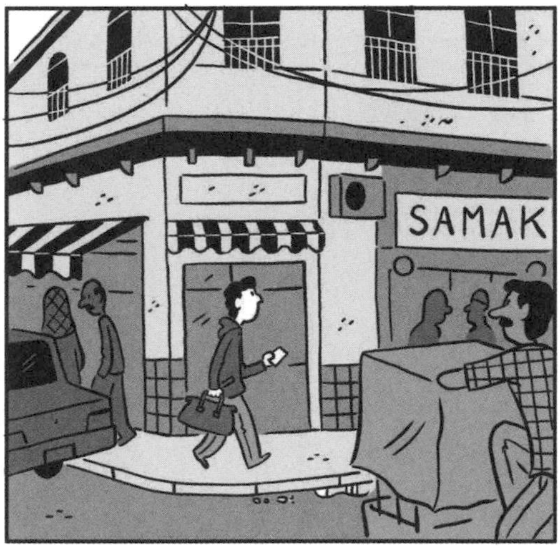
SAMAK

"AS SOON AS THINGS CALM DOWN A BIT, I'LL COME BACK."

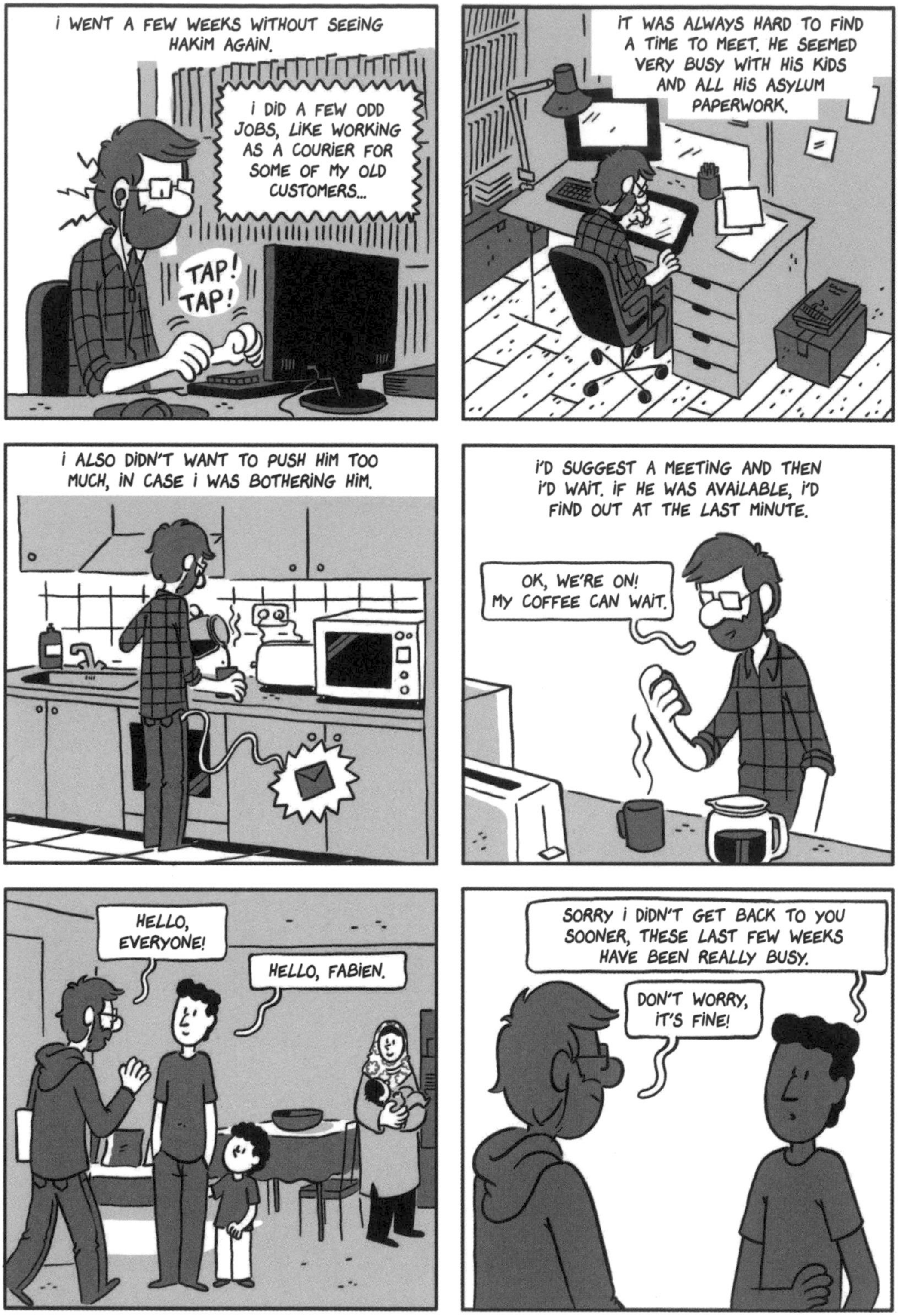
I WENT A FEW WEEKS WITHOUT SEEING HAKIM AGAIN.
I DID A FEW ODD JOBS, LIKE WORKING AS A COURIER FOR SOME OF MY OLD CUSTOMERS...
TAP! TAP!
IT WAS ALWAYS HARD TO FIND A TIME TO MEET. HE SEEMED VERY BUSY WITH HIS KIDS AND ALL HIS ASYLUM PAPERWORK.
I ALSO DIDN'T WANT TO PUSH HIM TOO MUCH, IN CASE I WAS BOTHERING HIM.
I'D SUGGEST A MEETING AND THEN I'D WAIT. IF HE WAS AVAILABLE, I'D FIND OUT AT THE LAST MINUTE.
OK, WE'RE ON! MY COFFEE CAN WAIT.
HELLO, EVERYONE!
HELLO, FABIEN.
SORRY I DIDN'T GET BACK TO YOU SOONER, THESE LAST FEW WEEKS HAVE BEEN REALLY BUSY.
DON'T WORRY, IT'S FINE!

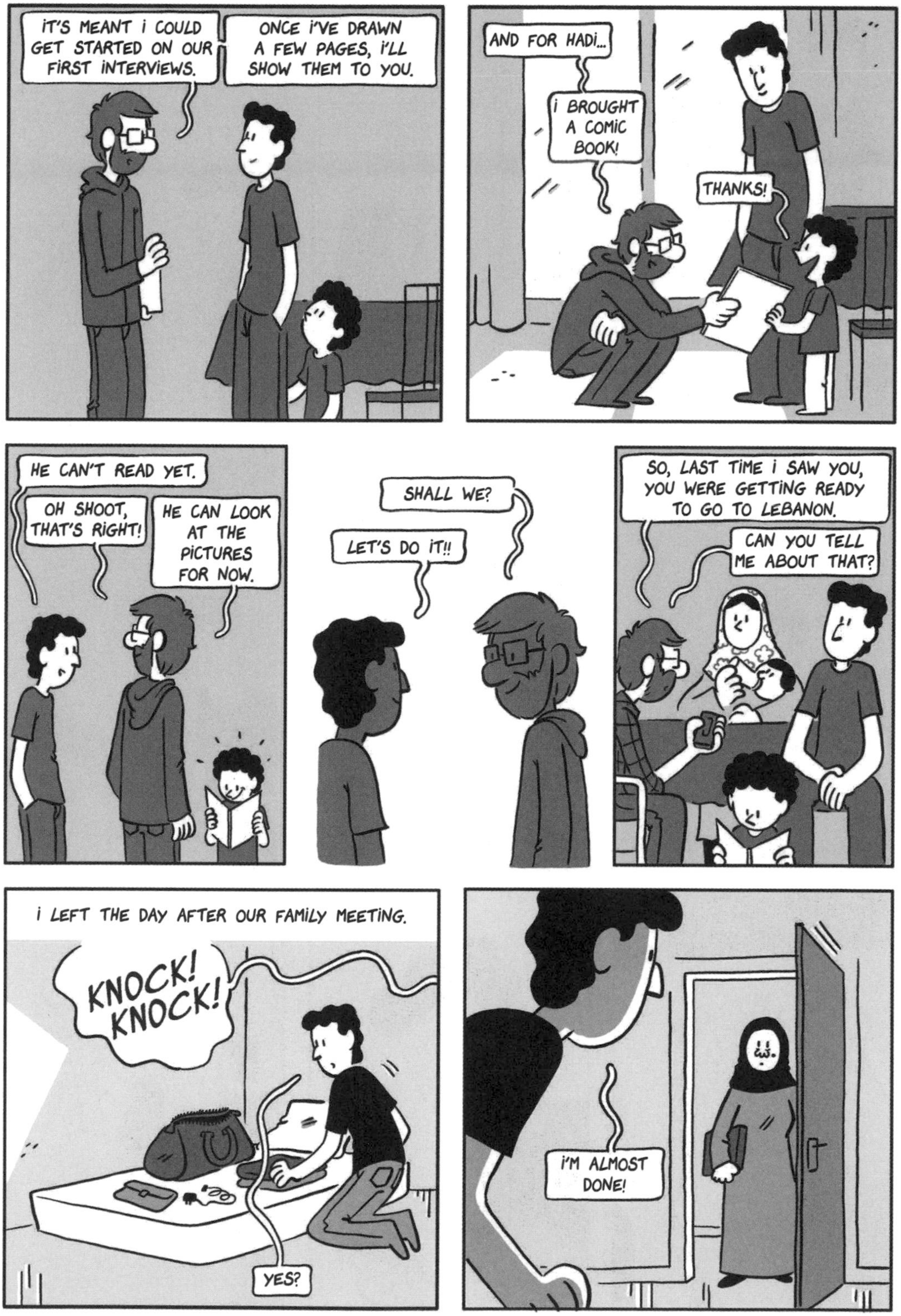
IT'S MEANT I COULD GET STARTED ON OUR FIRST INTERVIEWS.
ONCE I'VE DRAWN A FEW PAGES, I'LL SHOW THEM TO YOU.
AND FOR HADI...
I BROUGHT A COMIC BOOK!
THANKS!
HE CAN'T READ YET.
OH SHOOT, THAT'S RIGHT!
HE CAN LOOK AT THE PICTURES FOR NOW.
SHALL WE?
LET'S DO IT!!
SO, LAST TIME I SAW YOU, YOU WERE GETTING READY TO GO TO LEBANON.
CAN YOU TELL ME ABOUT THAT?
I LEFT THE DAY AFTER OUR FAMILY MEETING.
KNOCK! KNOCK!
YES?
I'M ALMOST DONE!

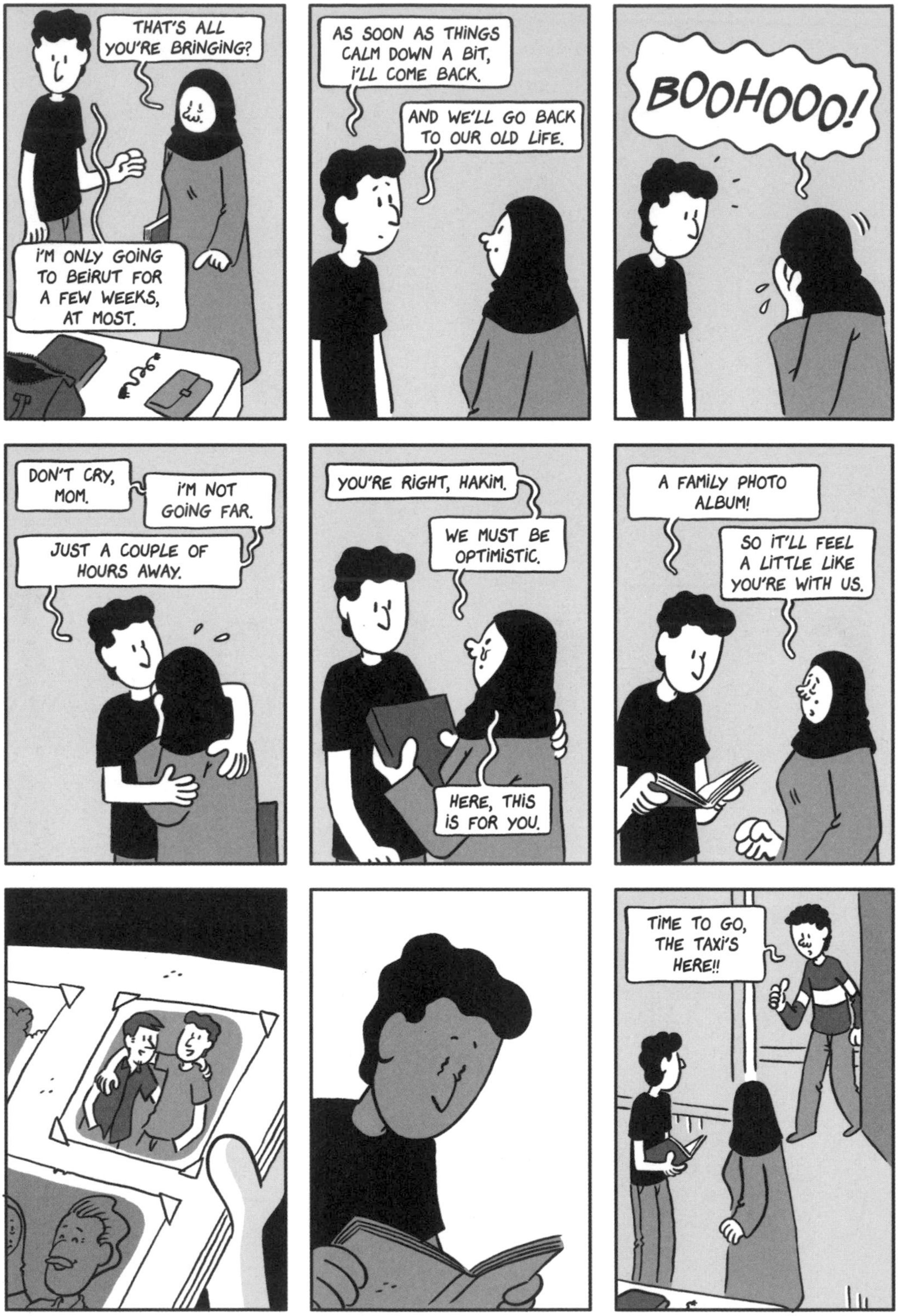
THAT'S ALL YOU'RE BRINGING?
I'M ONLY GOING TO BEIRUT FOR A FEW WEEKS, AT MOST.
AS SOON AS THINGS CALM DOWN A BIT, I'LL COME BACK.
AND WE'LL GO BACK TO OUR OLD LIFE.
BOOHOOO!
DON'T CRY, MOM.
I'M NOT GOING FAR.
JUST A COUPLE OF HOURS AWAY.
YOU'RE RIGHT, HAKIM.
WE MUST BE OPTIMISTIC.
HERE, THIS IS FOR YOU.
A FAMILY PHOTO ALBUM!
SO IT'LL FEEL A LITTLE LIKE YOU'RE WITH US.
TIME TO GO, THE TAXI'S HERE!!

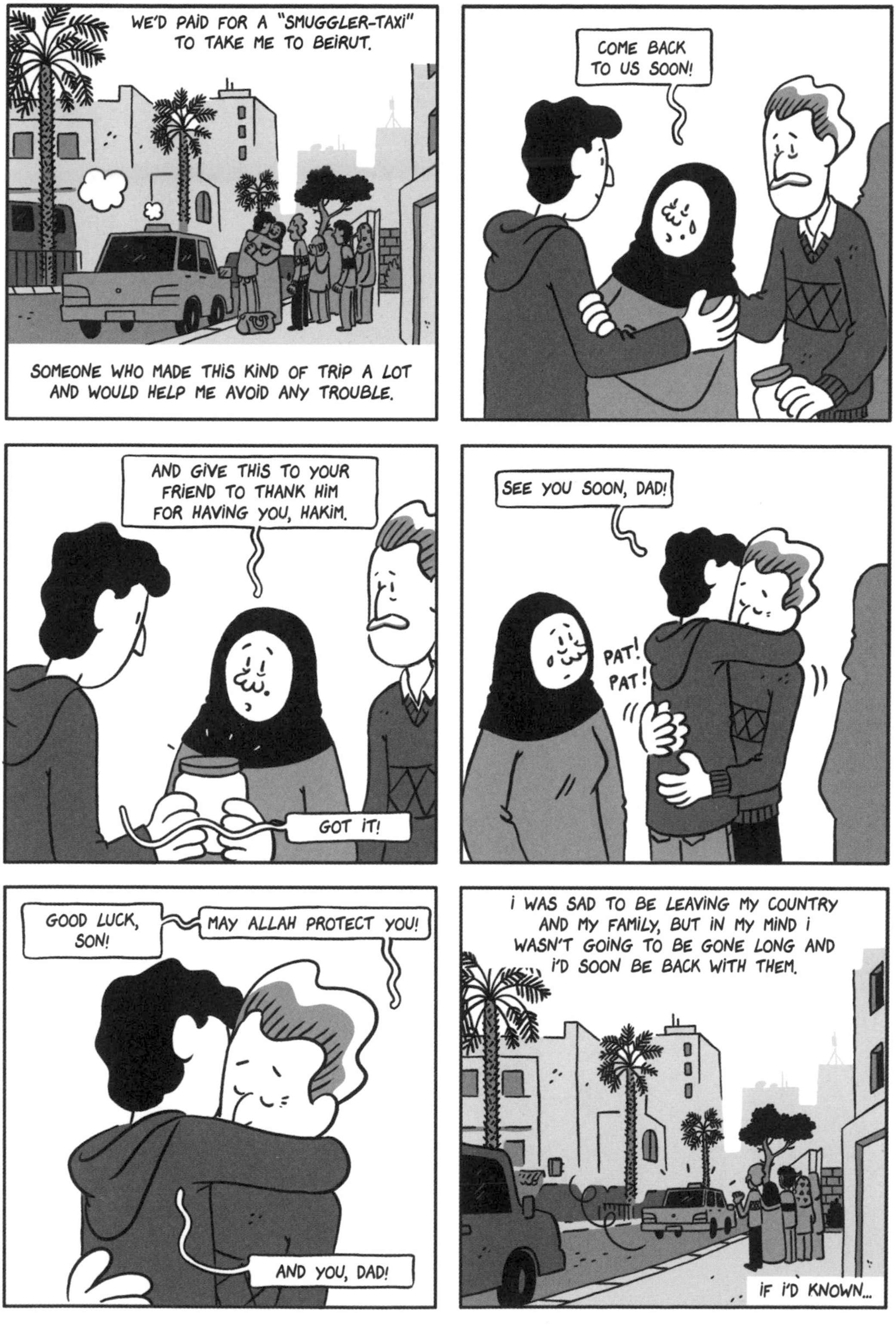
WE'D PAID FOR A "SMUGGLER-TAXI" TO TAKE ME TO BEIRUT.
SOMEONE WHO MADE THIS KIND OF TRIP A LOT AND WOULD HELP ME AVOID ANY TROUBLE.
COME BACK TO US SOON!
AND GIVE THIS TO YOUR FRIEND TO THANK HIM FOR HAVING YOU, HAKIM.
GOT IT!
SEE YOU SOON, DAD!
PAT! PAT!
GOOD LUCK, SON!
MAY ALLAH PROTECT YOU!
AND YOU, DAD!
I WAS SAD TO BE LEAVING MY COUNTRY AND MY FAMILY, BUT IN MY MIND I WASN'T GOING TO BE GONE LONG AND I'D SOON BE BACK WITH THEM.
IF I'D KNOWN...

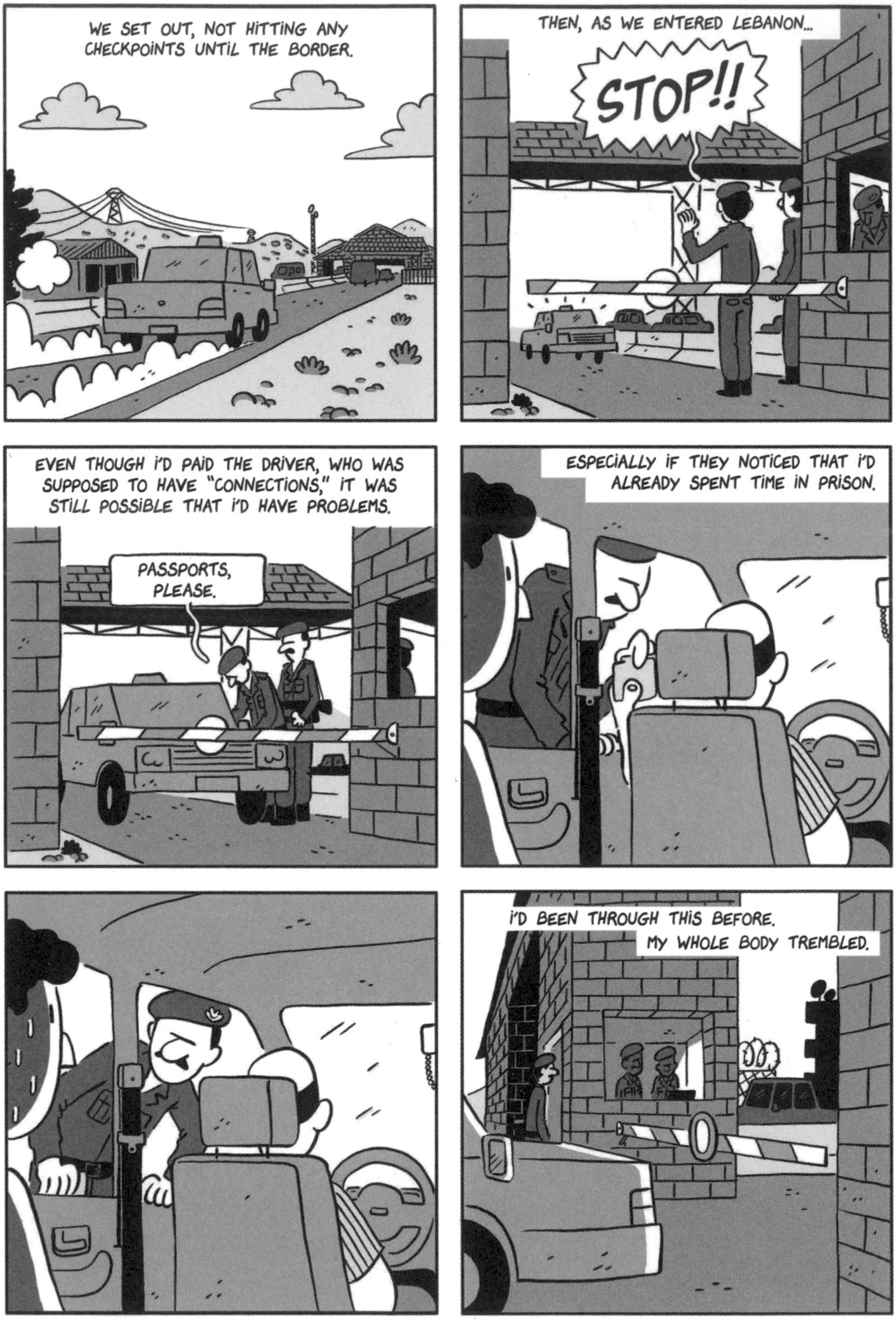
WE SET OUT, NOT HITTING ANY CHECKPOINTS UNTIL THE BORDER.
THEN, AS WE ENTERED LEBANON...
STOP!!
EVEN THOUGH I'D PAID THE DRIVER, WHO WAS SUPPOSED TO HAVE "CONNECTIONS," IT WAS STILL POSSIBLE THAT I'D HAVE PROBLEMS.
PASSPORTS, PLEASE.
ESPECIALLY IF THEY NOTICED THAT I'D ALREADY SPENT TIME IN PRISON.
I'D BEEN THROUGH THIS BEFORE.
MY WHOLE BODY TREMBLED.

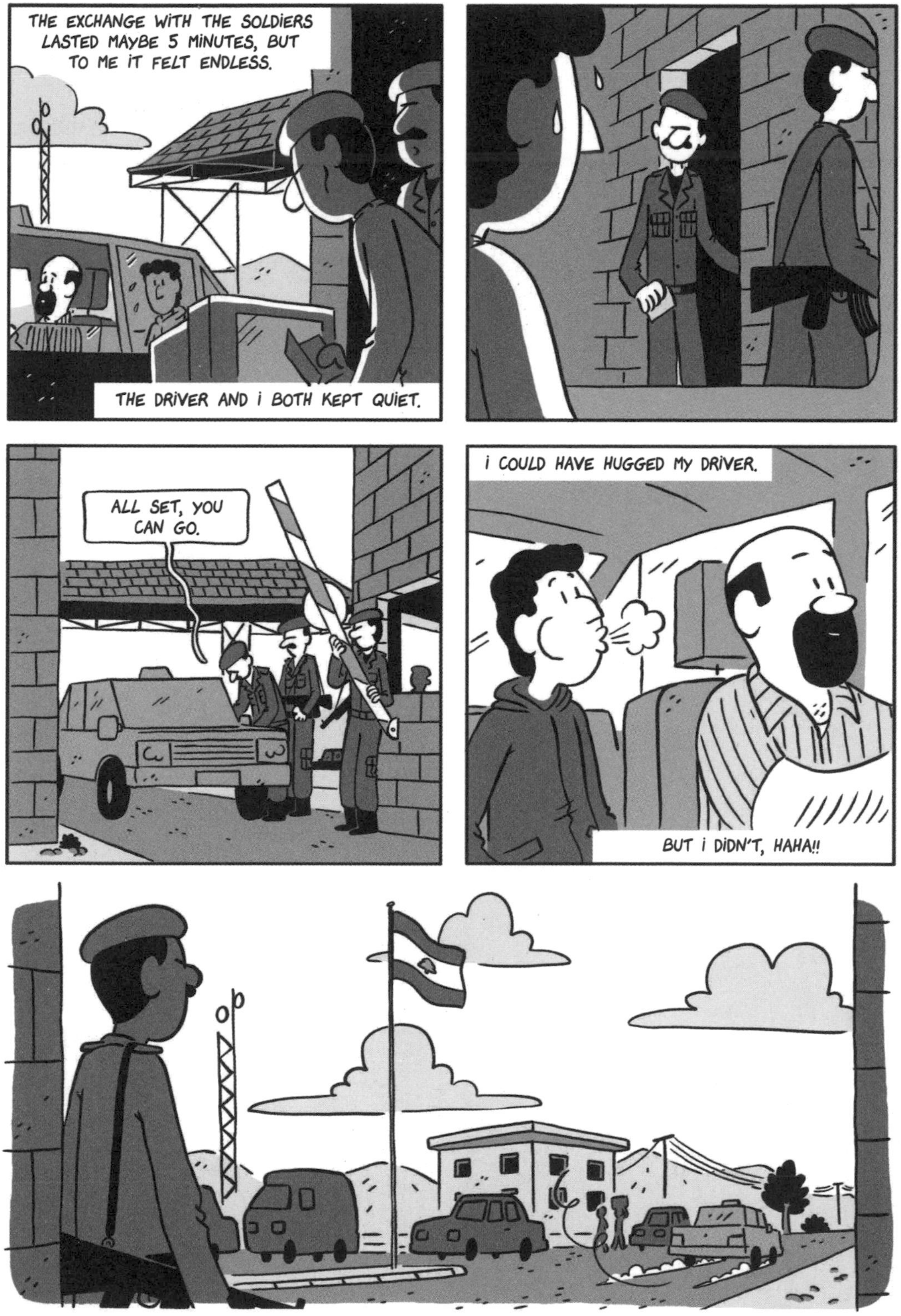
THE EXCHANGE WITH THE SOLDIERS LASTED MAYBE 5 MINUTES, BUT TO ME IT FELT ENDLESS.
THE DRIVER AND I BOTH KEPT QUIET.
ALL SET, YOU CAN GO.
I COULD HAVE HUGGED MY DRIVER.
BUT I DIDN'T, HAHA!!

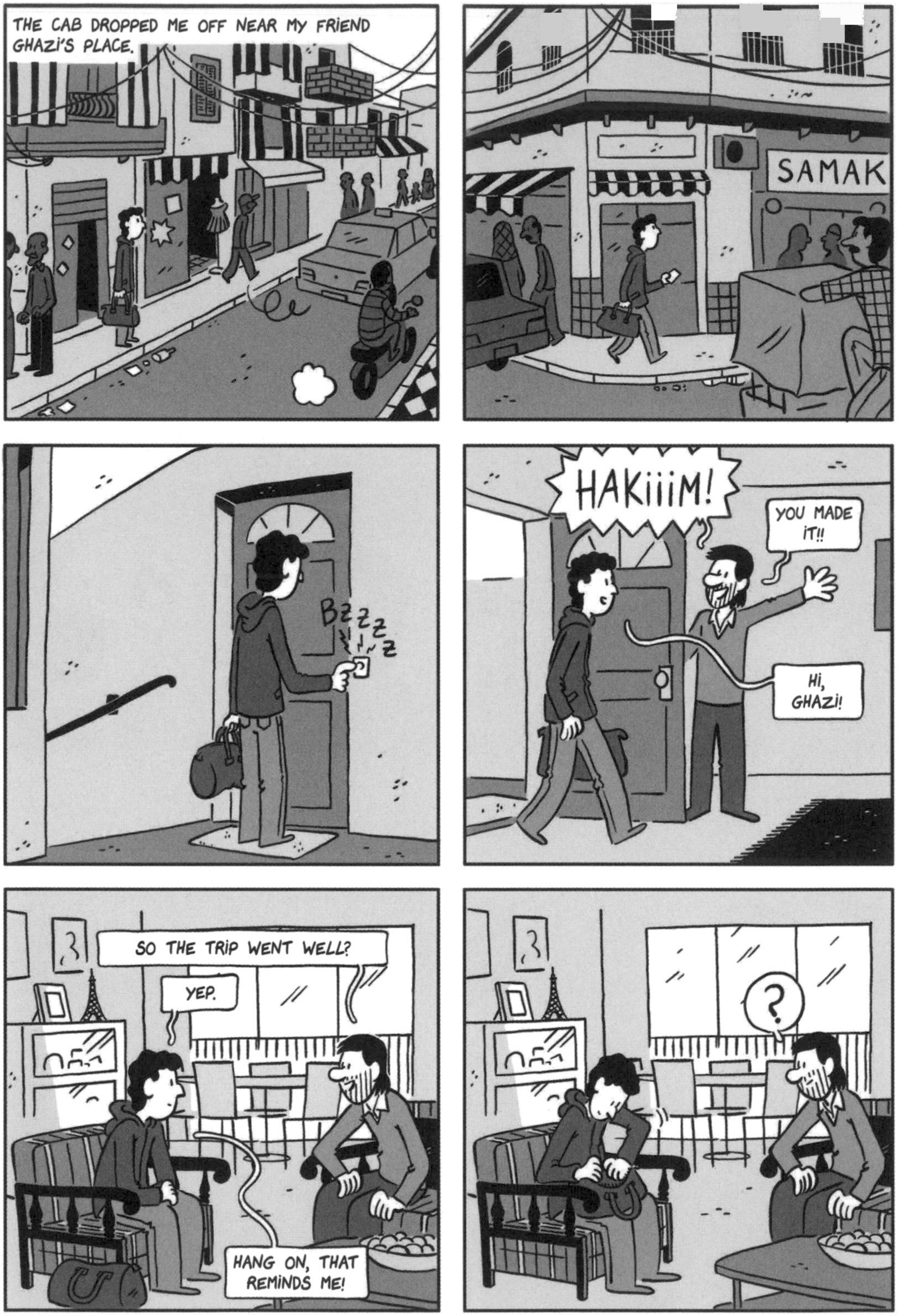
THE CAB DROPPED ME OFF NEAR MY FRIEND GHAZI'S PLACE.
SAMAK
BZZZZ
HAKiiiM!
YOU MADE iT!!
Hi, GHAZI!
SO THE TRiP WENT WELL?
YEP.
HANG ON, THAT REMiNDS ME!
?

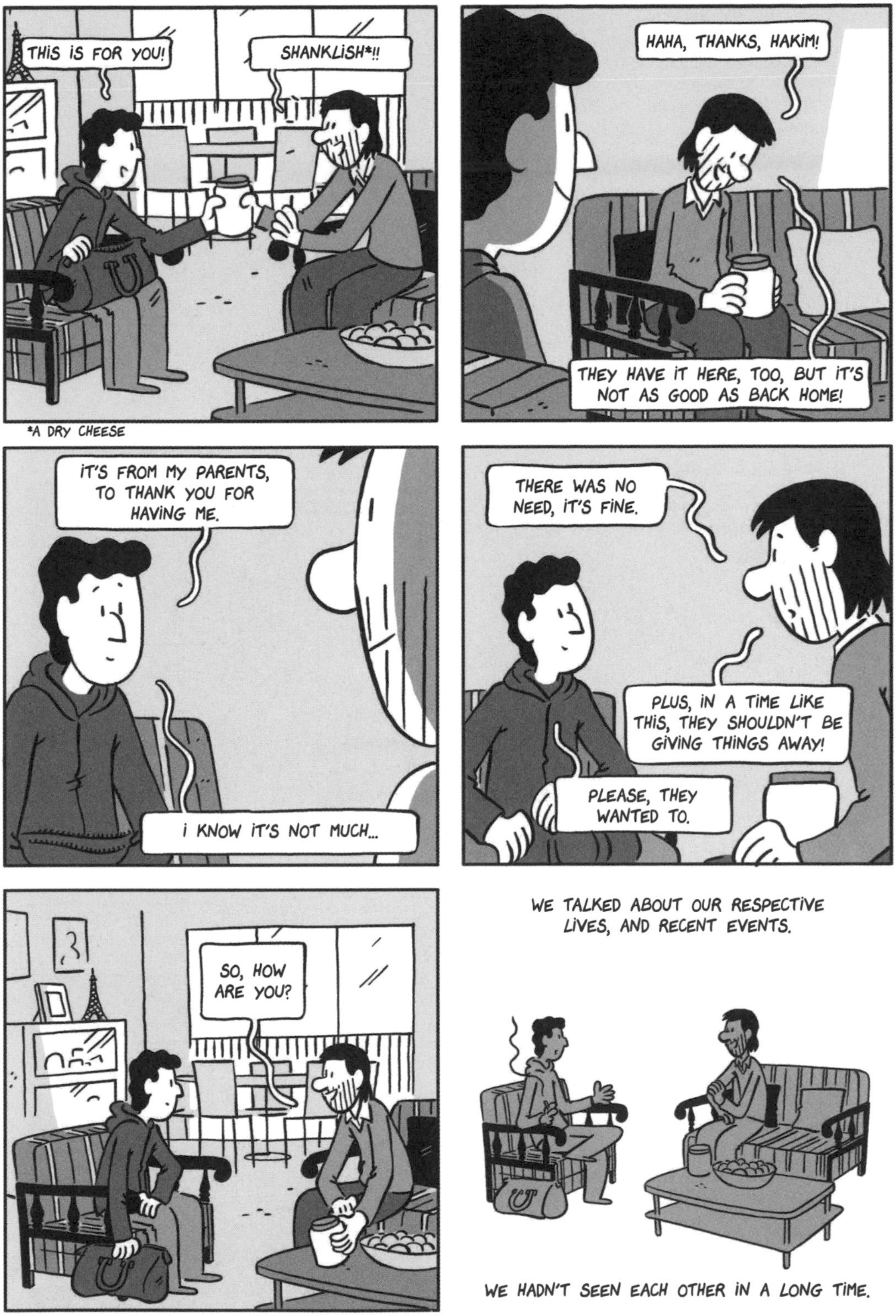
THIS IS FOR YOU!
SHANKLISH*!!
*A DRY CHEESE
HAHA, THANKS, HAKIM!
THEY HAVE IT HERE, TOO, BUT IT'S NOT AS GOOD AS BACK HOME!
IT'S FROM MY PARENTS, TO THANK YOU FOR HAVING ME.
I KNOW IT'S NOT MUCH...
THERE WAS NO NEED, IT'S FINE.
PLUS, IN A TIME LIKE THIS, THEY SHOULDN'T BE GIVING THINGS AWAY!
PLEASE, THEY WANTED TO.
SO, HOW ARE YOU?
WE TALKED ABOUT OUR RESPECTIVE LIVES, AND RECENT EVENTS.
WE HADN'T SEEN EACH OTHER IN A LONG TIME.

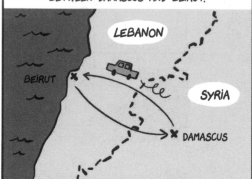

GHAZI WAS A FRIEND FROM HIGH SCHOOL. HE WORKED IN THE CLOTHING INDUSTRY AND SOLD HIS PRODUCTS TO LEBANESE SHOPS. HE OFTEN WENT BACK AND FORTH BETWEEN DAMASCUS AND BEIRUT.

LEBANON

BEIRUT

SYRIA

DAMASCUS

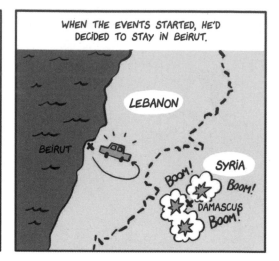

WHEN THE EVENTS STARTED, HE'D DECIDED TO STAY IN BEIRUT.

LEBANON

BEIRUT

SYRIA

BOOM! BOOM!

DAMASCUS

BOOM!

I'M SURE YOU'RE TIRED.

YOUR ROOM IS READY.

I HAVE A BEDROOM TO MYSELF?

THAT'S NOT NECESSARY!

IT'S NO PROBLEM, I HAVE TWO.

YOU'LL SEE, IT'LL BE COMFORTABLE.

GOOD NIGHT, HAKIM!

STAY AS LONG AS YOU LIKE. CONSIDER THIS YOUR HOME.

THANKS!

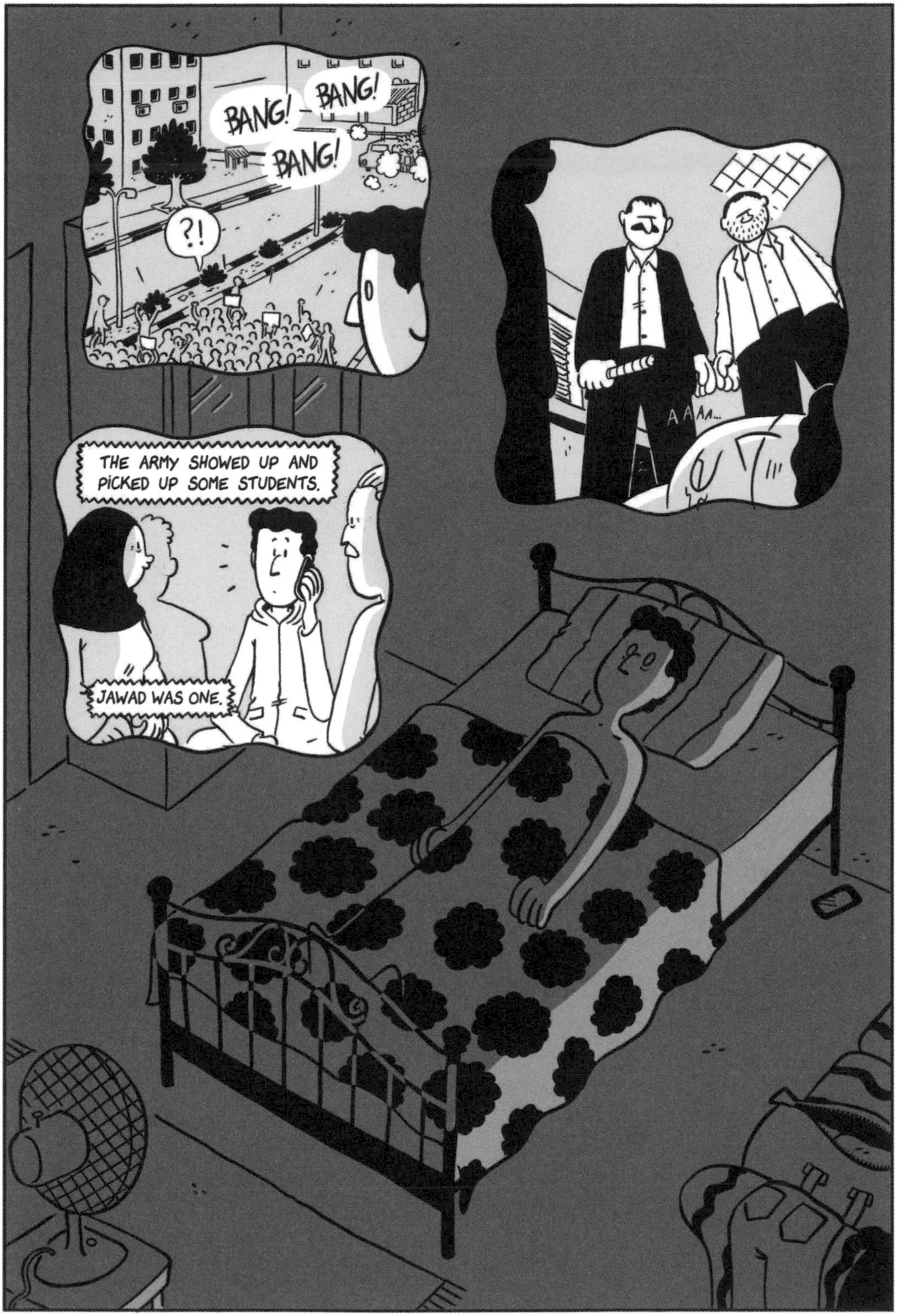
BANG!
BANG!
BANG!
?!
AAAA...
THE ARMY SHOWED UP AND PICKED UP SOME STUDENTS.
JAWAD WAS ONE.

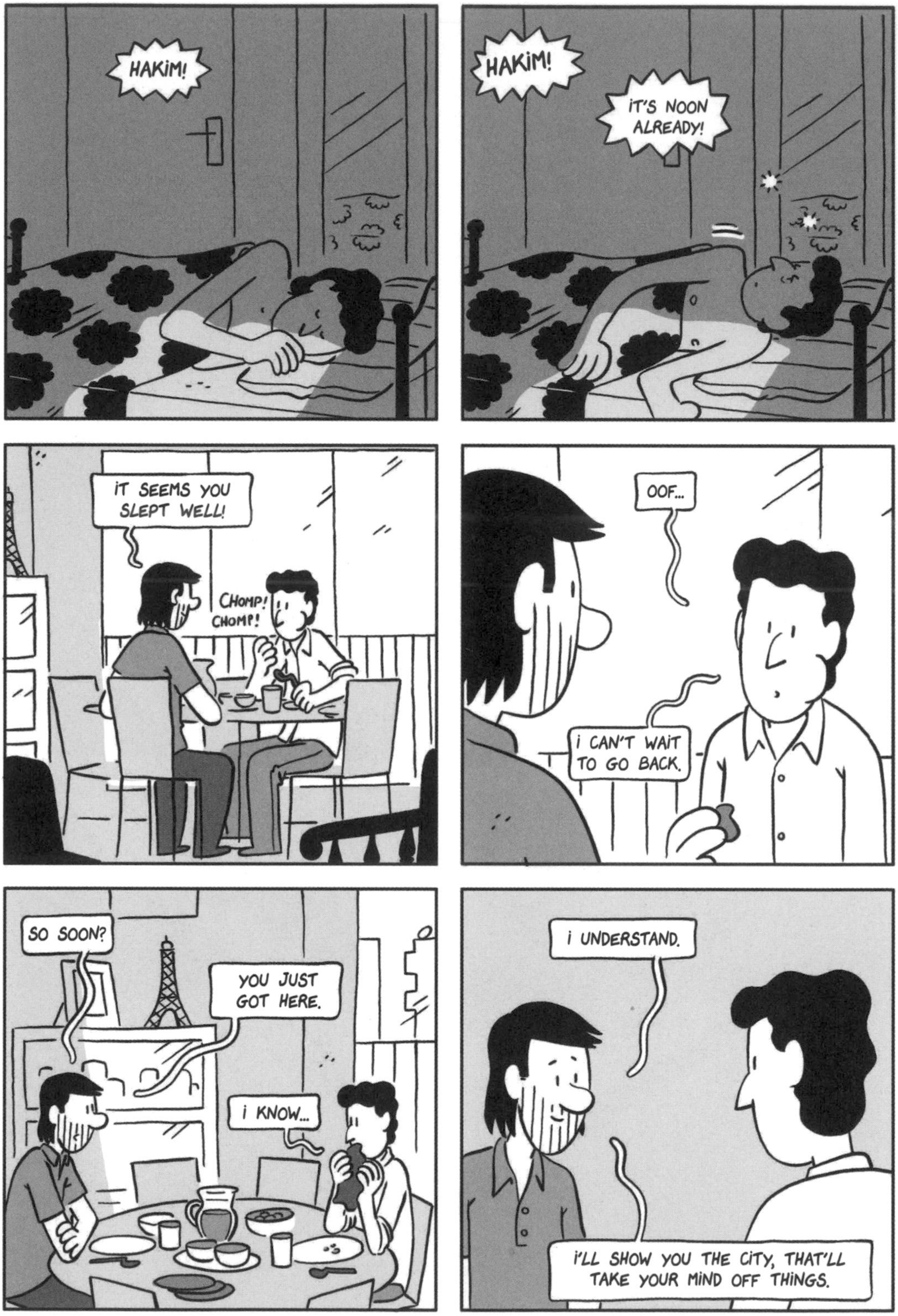
HAKIM!
HAKIM!
IT'S NOON ALREADY!
IT SEEMS YOU SLEPT WELL!
CHOMP! CHOMP!
OOF...
I CAN'T WAIT TO GO BACK.
SO SOON?
YOU JUST GOT HERE.
I KNOW...
I UNDERSTAND.
I'LL SHOW YOU THE CITY, THAT'LL TAKE YOUR MIND OFF THINGS.

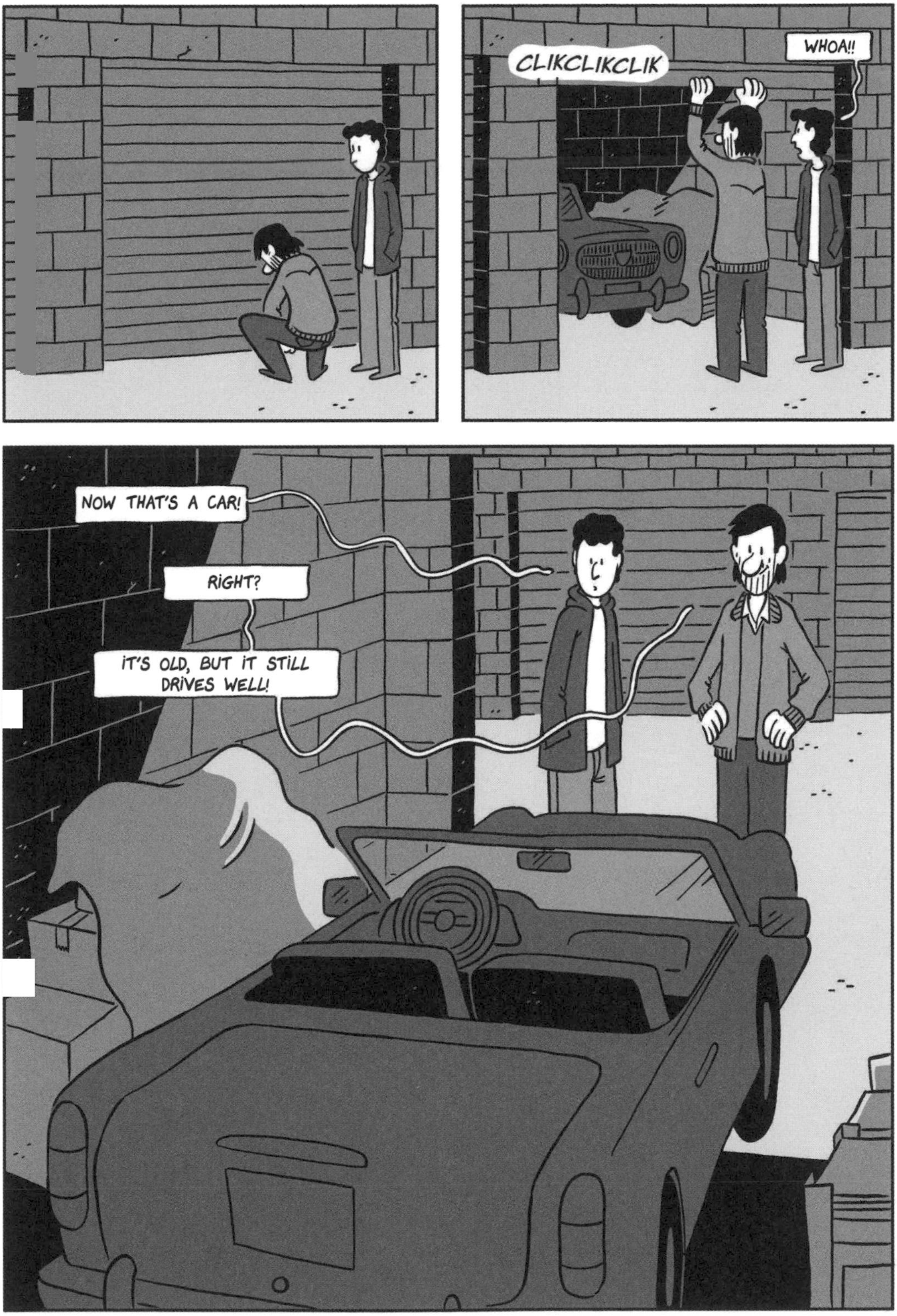
CLIKCLIKCLIK
WHOA!!
NOW THAT'S A CAR!
RIGHT?
IT'S OLD, BUT IT STILL DRIVES WELL!

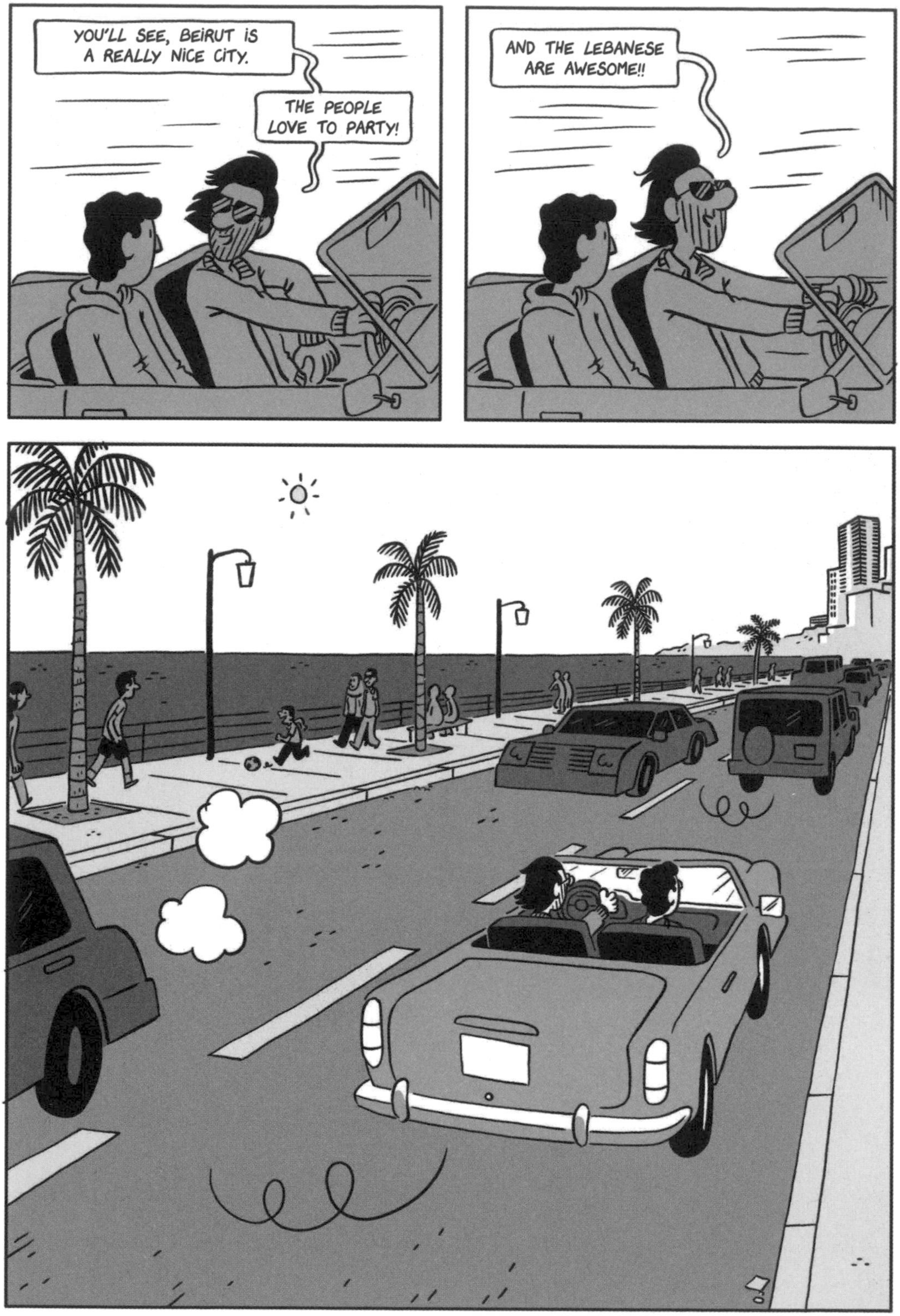
YOU'LL SEE, BEIRUT IS A REALLY NICE CITY.
THE PEOPLE LOVE TO PARTY!
AND THE LEBANESE ARE AWESOME!!

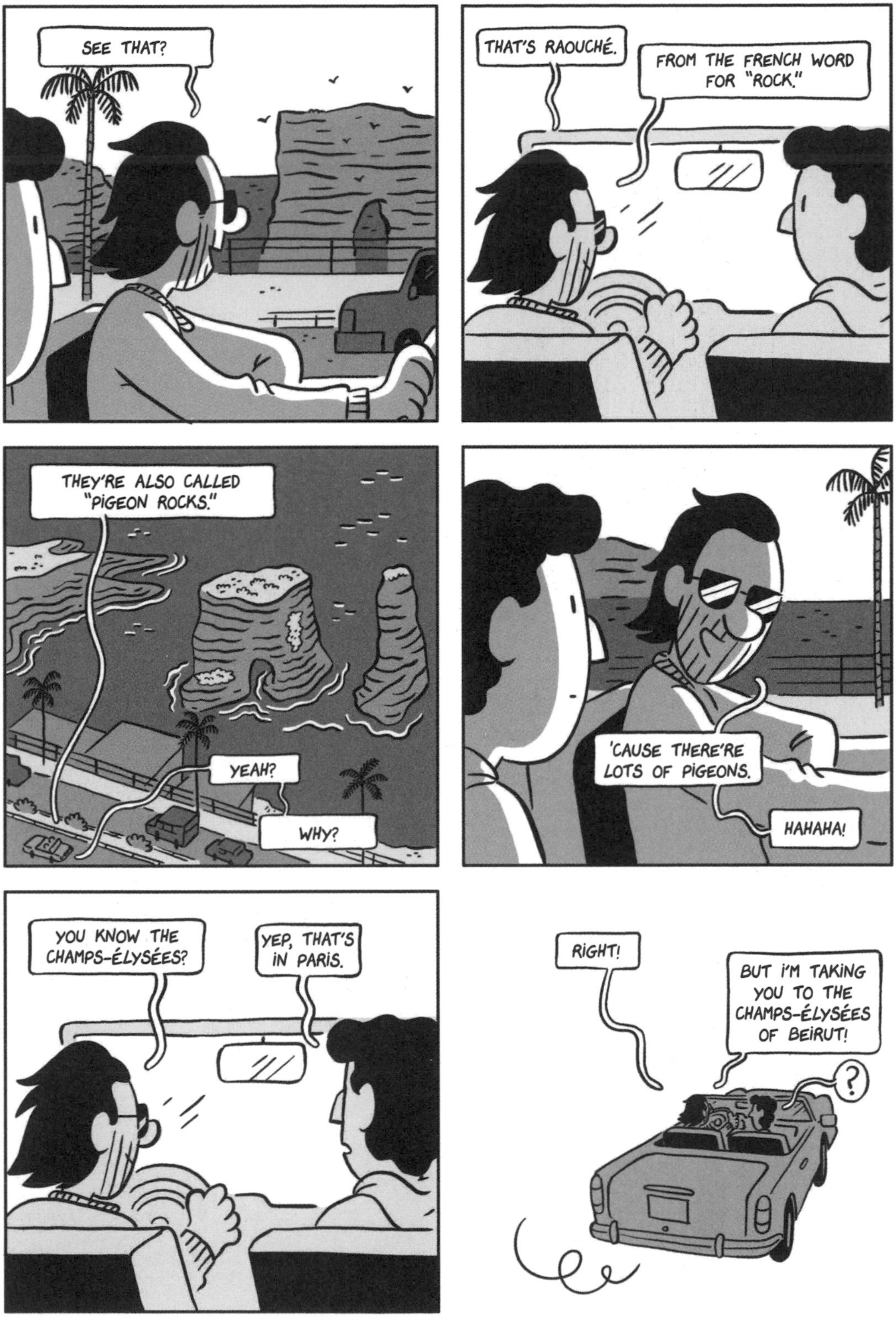
SEE THAT?
THAT'S RAOUCHÉ.
FROM THE FRENCH WORD FOR "ROCK."
THEY'RE ALSO CALLED "PIGEON ROCKS."
YEAH?
WHY?
'CAUSE THERE'RE LOTS OF PIGEONS.
HAHAHA!
YOU KNOW THE CHAMPS-ÉLYSÉES?
YEP, THAT'S IN PARIS.
RIGHT!
BUT I'M TAKING YOU TO THE CHAMPS-ÉLYSÉES OF BEIRUT!
?

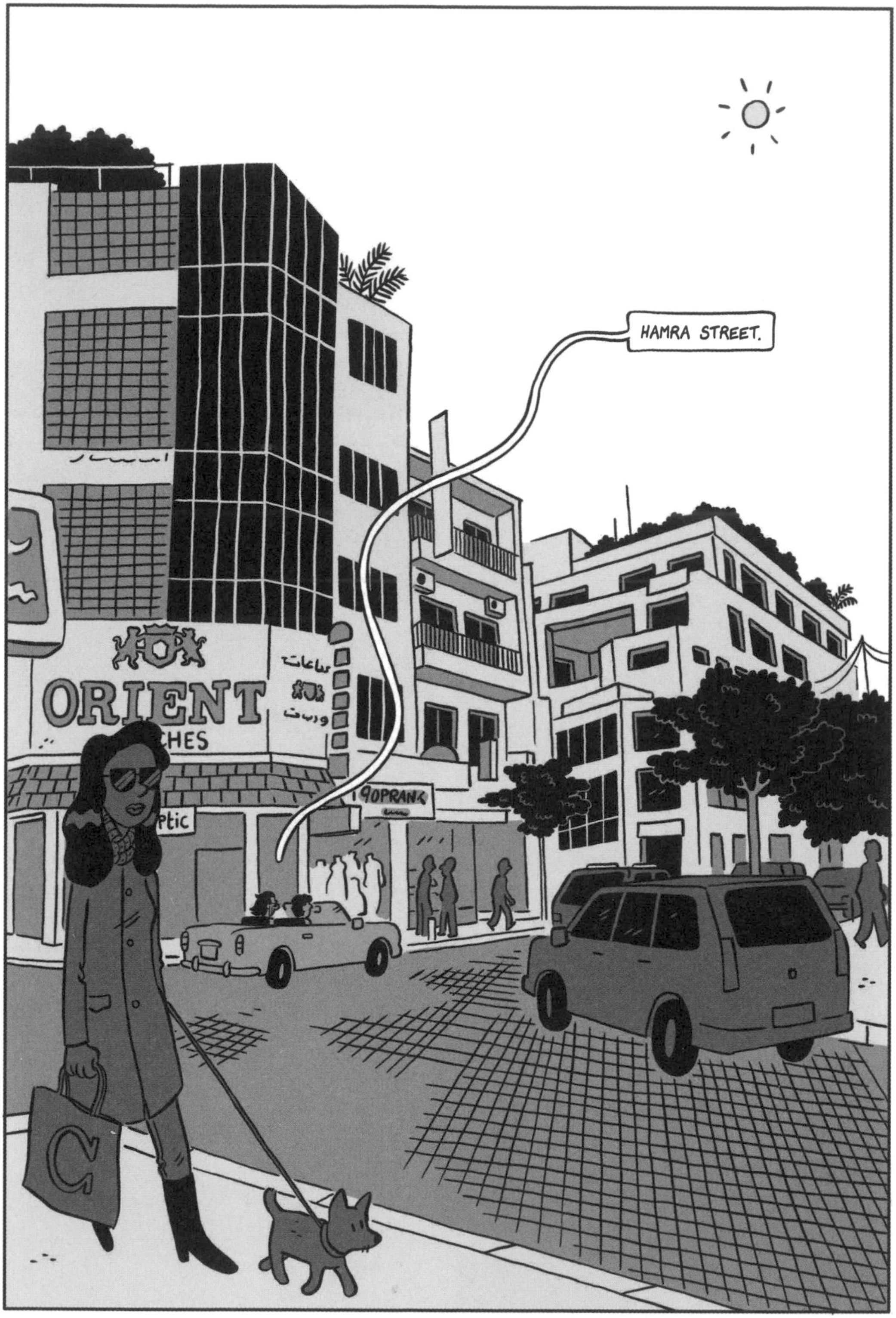
HAMRA STREET.
ORIENT
CHES
ptic

IT'S NICE, HUH?

YEAH.

SPA 500

IT'S GREAT FOR GOING OUT!

WE CAN GO ONE NIGHT, IF YOU WANT.

MONNOT STREET IS NICE, TOO.

IT'S GOT LOTS OF BARS AND CLUBS.

café HAMRA

YOU STILL LIKE GOING TO CLUBS?

YEAH.

BUT I'M NOT SURE I'M IN THE MOOD FOR IT.

IT'LL BE GOOD FOR YOU, YOU'LL SEE.

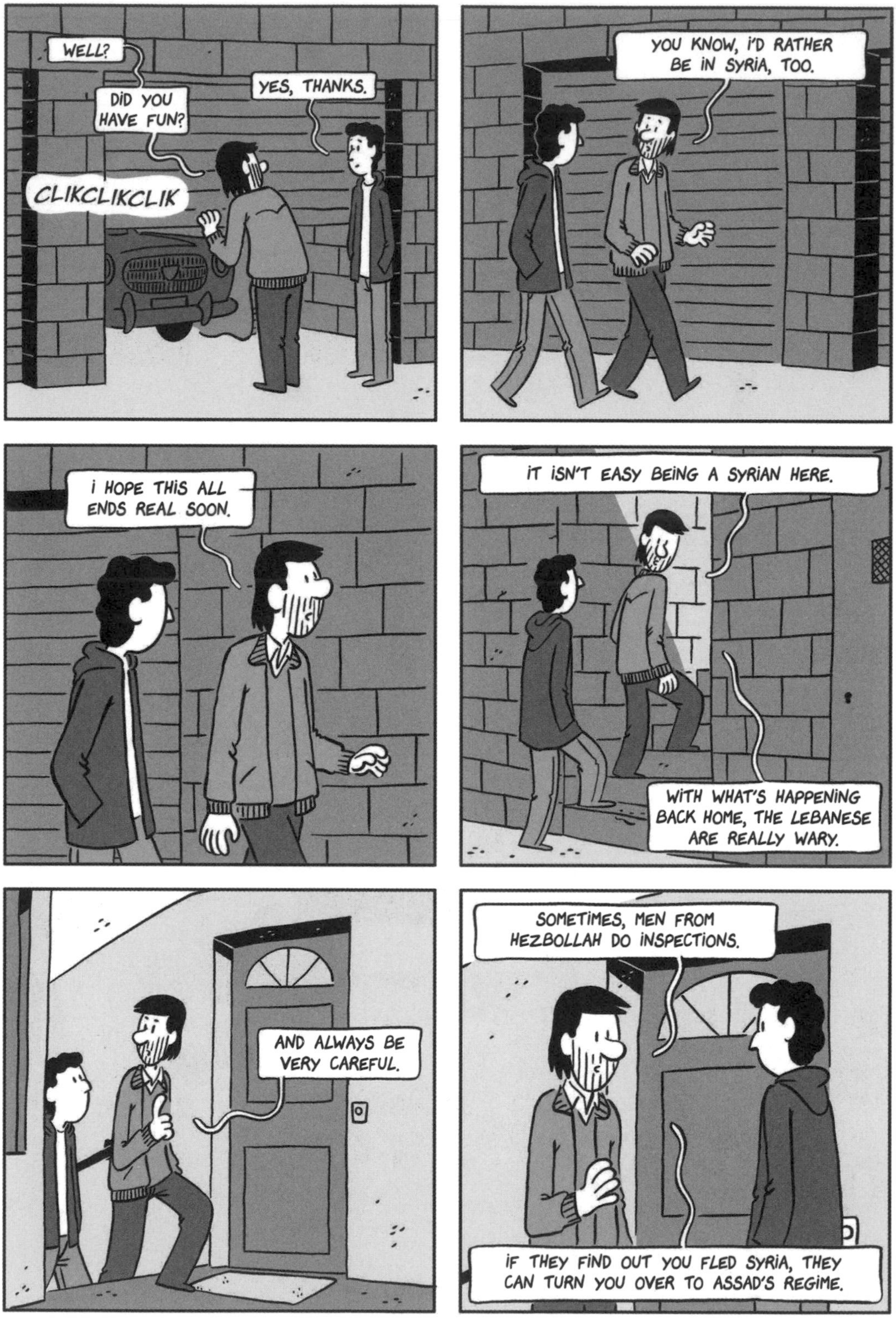
WELL?
DID YOU HAVE FUN?
CLIKCLIKCLIK
YES, THANKS.
YOU KNOW, I'D RATHER BE IN SYRIA, TOO.
I HOPE THIS ALL ENDS REAL SOON.
IT ISN'T EASY BEING A SYRIAN HERE.
WITH WHAT'S HAPPENING BACK HOME, THE LEBANESE ARE REALLY WARY.
AND ALWAYS BE VERY CAREFUL.
SOMETIMES, MEN FROM HEZBOLLAH DO INSPECTIONS.
IF THEY FIND OUT YOU FLED SYRIA, THEY CAN TURN YOU OVER TO ASSAD'S REGIME.

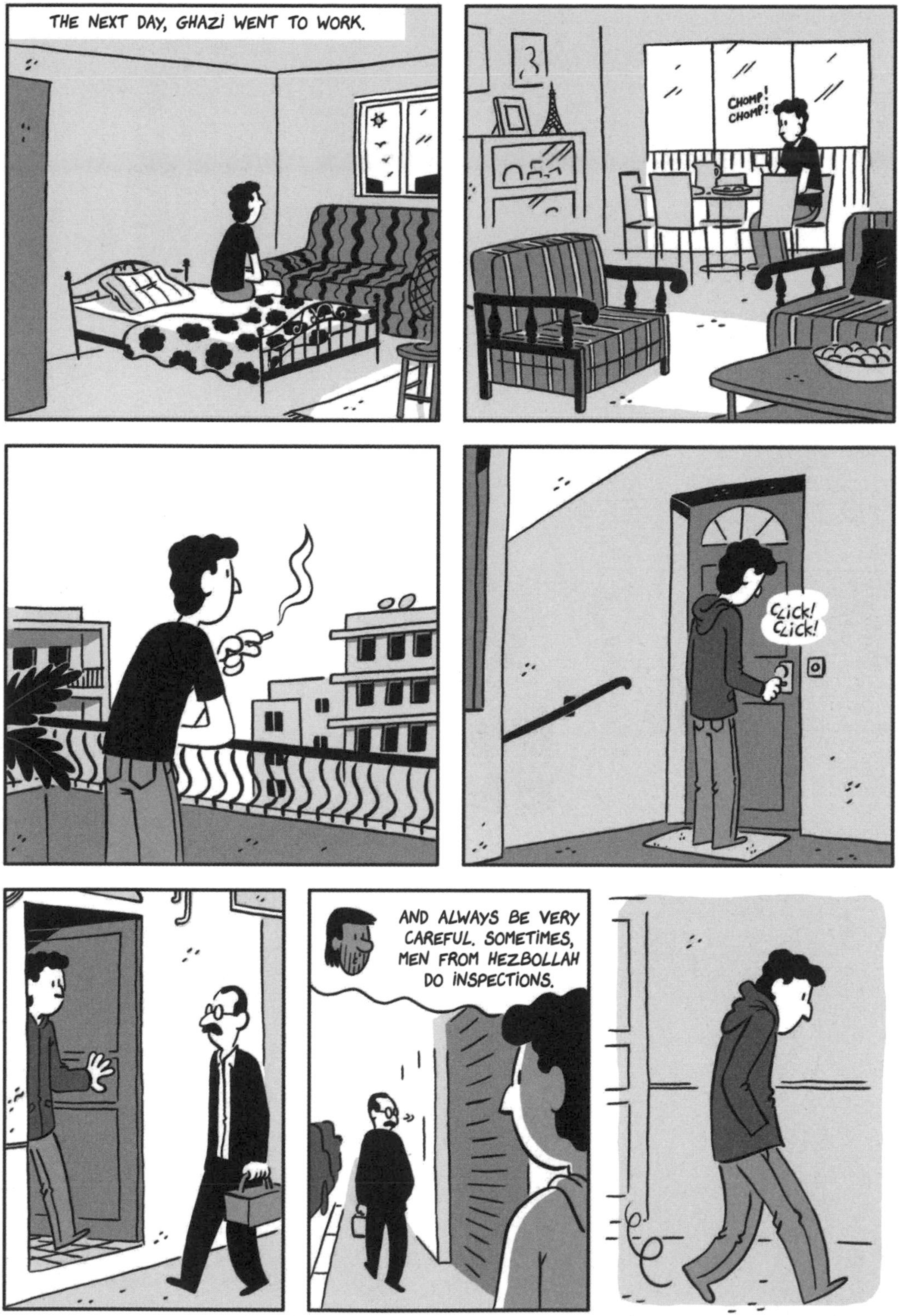
THE NEXT DAY, GHAZI WENT TO WORK.
CHOMP! CHOMP!
CLICK! CLICK!
AND ALWAYS BE VERY CAREFUL. SOMETIMES, MEN FROM HEZBOLLAH DO INSPECTIONS.

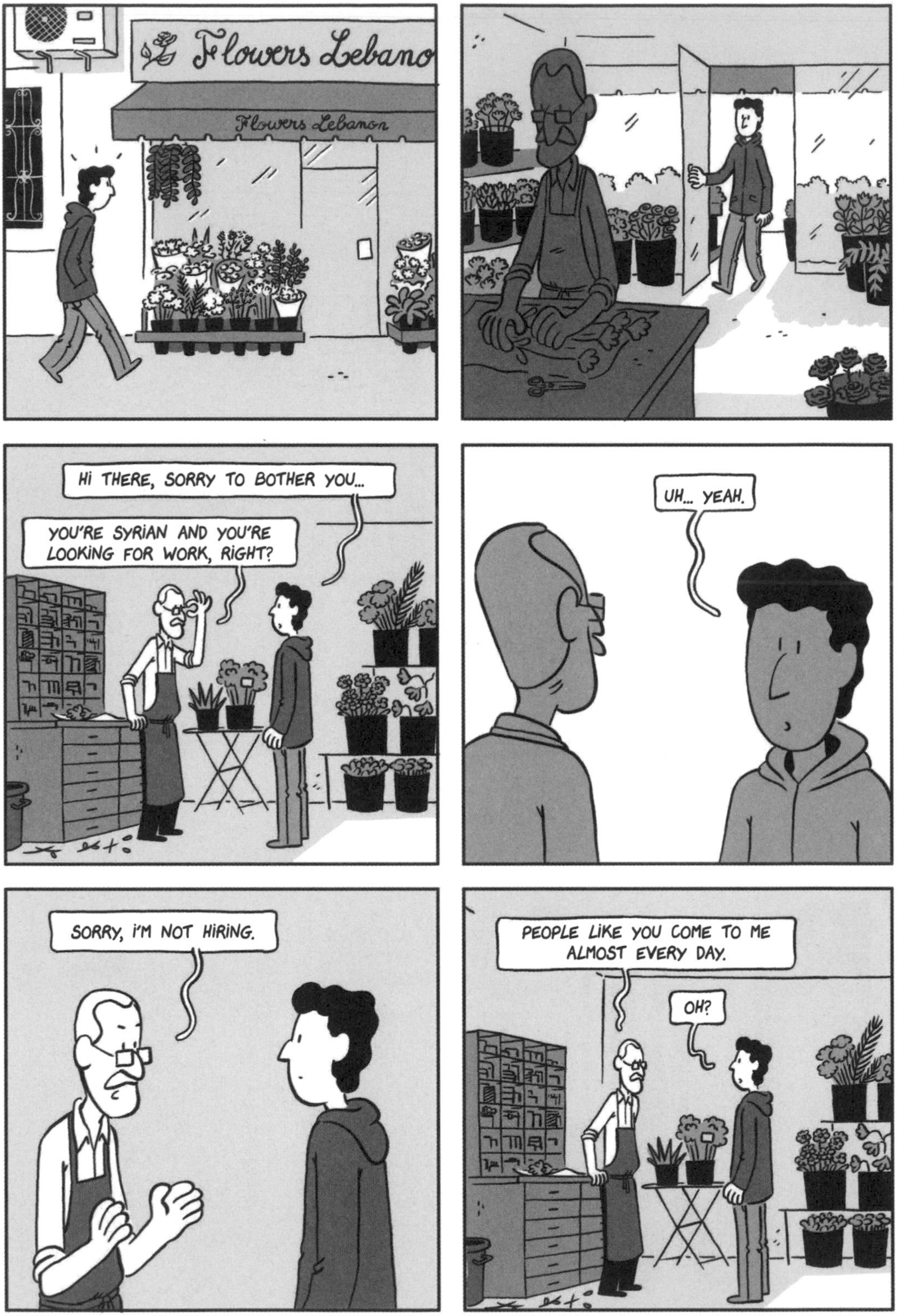
Flowers Lebano
Flowers Lebanon
Hi THERE, SORRY TO BOTHER YOU...
YOU'RE SYRiAN AND YOU'RE LOOKiNG FOR WORK, RiGHT?
UH... YEAH.
SORRY, i'M NOT HiRiNG.
PEOPLE LiKE YOU COME TO ME ALMOST EVERY DAY.
OH?

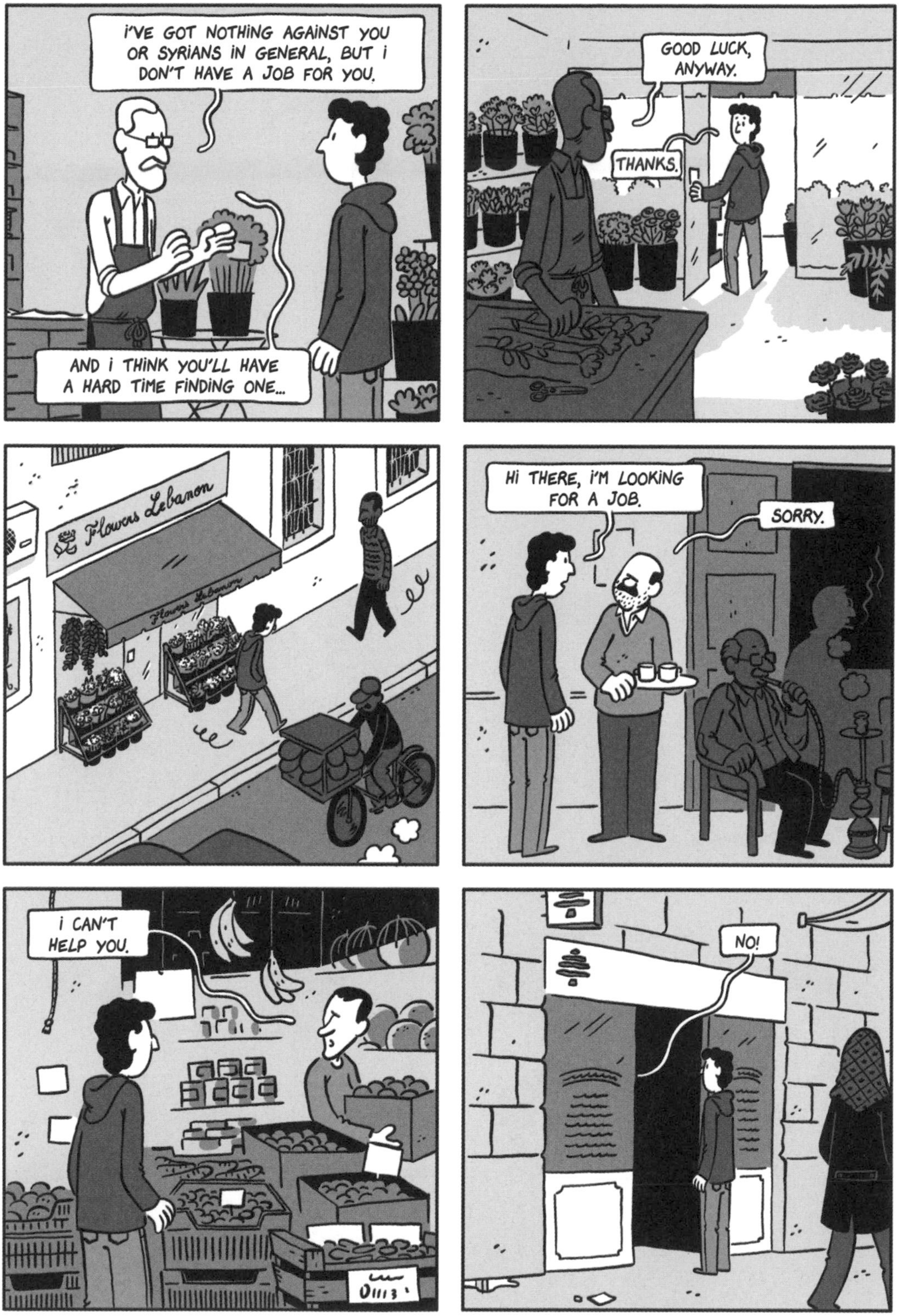
I'VE GOT NOTHING AGAINST YOU OR SYRIANS IN GENERAL, BUT I DON'T HAVE A JOB FOR YOU.
AND I THINK YOU'LL HAVE A HARD TIME FINDING ONE...
GOOD LUCK, ANYWAY.
THANKS.
Flowers Lebanon
HI THERE, I'M LOOKING FOR A JOB.
SORRY.
I CAN'T HELP YOU.
NO!

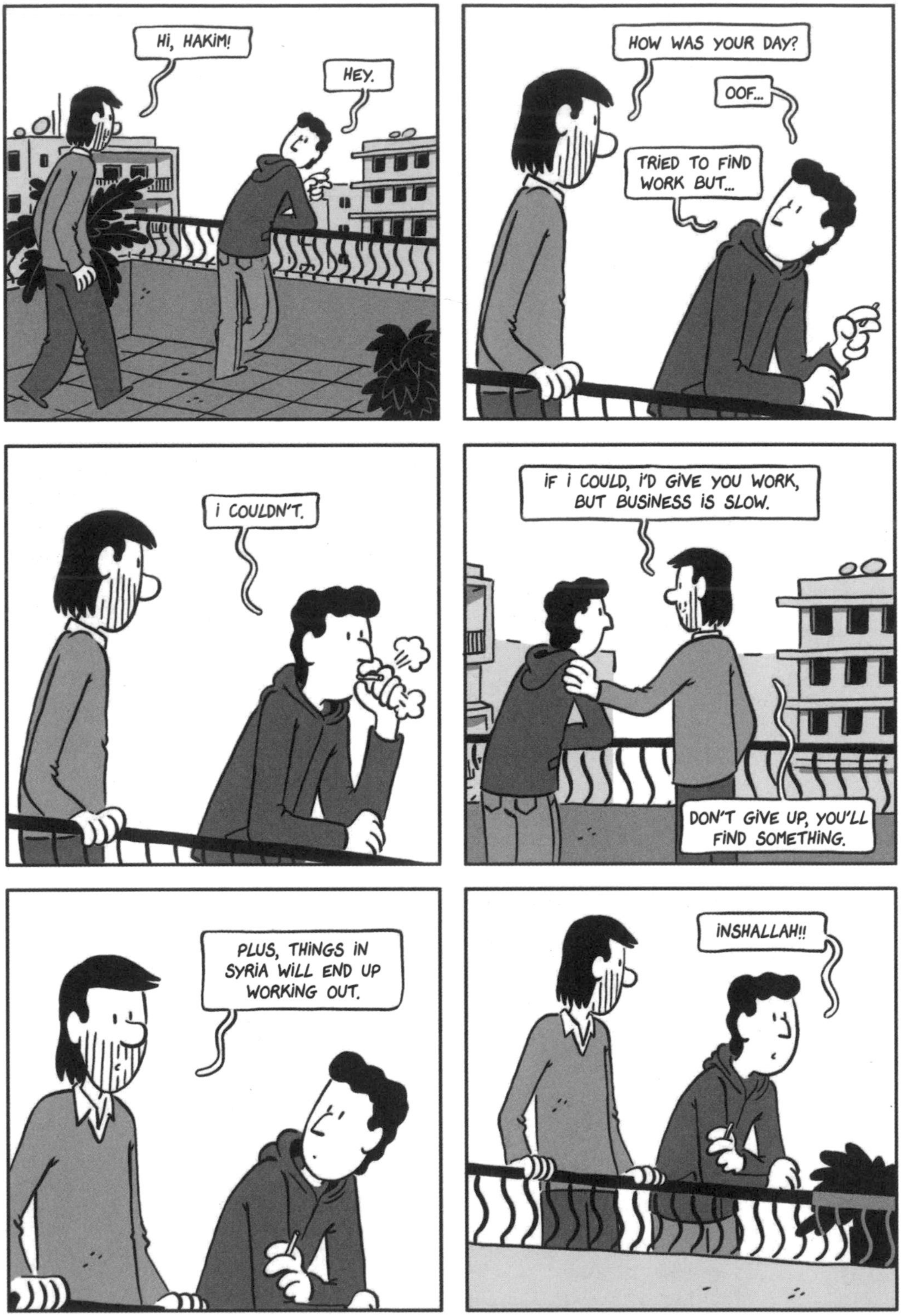

HI, HAKIM!
HEY.
HOW WAS YOUR DAY?
OOF...
TRIED TO FIND WORK BUT...
I COULDN'T.
IF I COULD, I'D GIVE YOU WORK, BUT BUSINESS IS SLOW.
DON'T GIVE UP, YOU'LL FIND SOMETHING.
PLUS, THINGS IN SYRIA WILL END UP WORKING OUT.
INSHALLAH!!

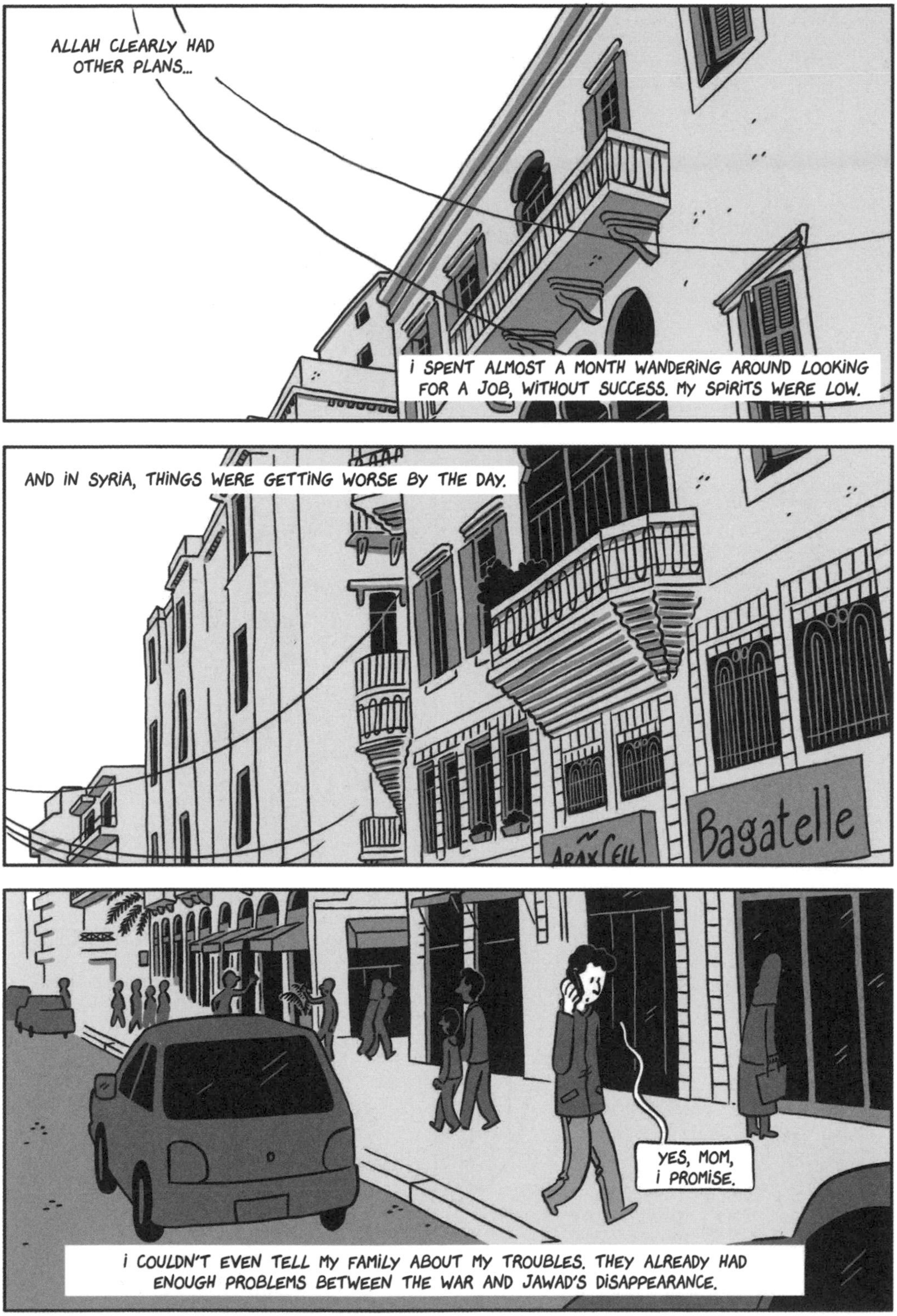
ALLAH CLEARLY HAD OTHER PLANS...
I SPENT ALMOST A MONTH WANDERING AROUND LOOKING FOR A JOB, WITHOUT SUCCESS. MY SPIRITS WERE LOW.
AND IN SYRIA, THINGS WERE GETTING WORSE BY THE DAY.
Bagatelle
YES, MOM, I PROMISE.
I COULDN'T EVEN TELL MY FAMILY ABOUT MY TROUBLES. THEY ALREADY HAD ENOUGH PROBLEMS BETWEEN THE WAR AND JAWAD'S DISAPPEARANCE.

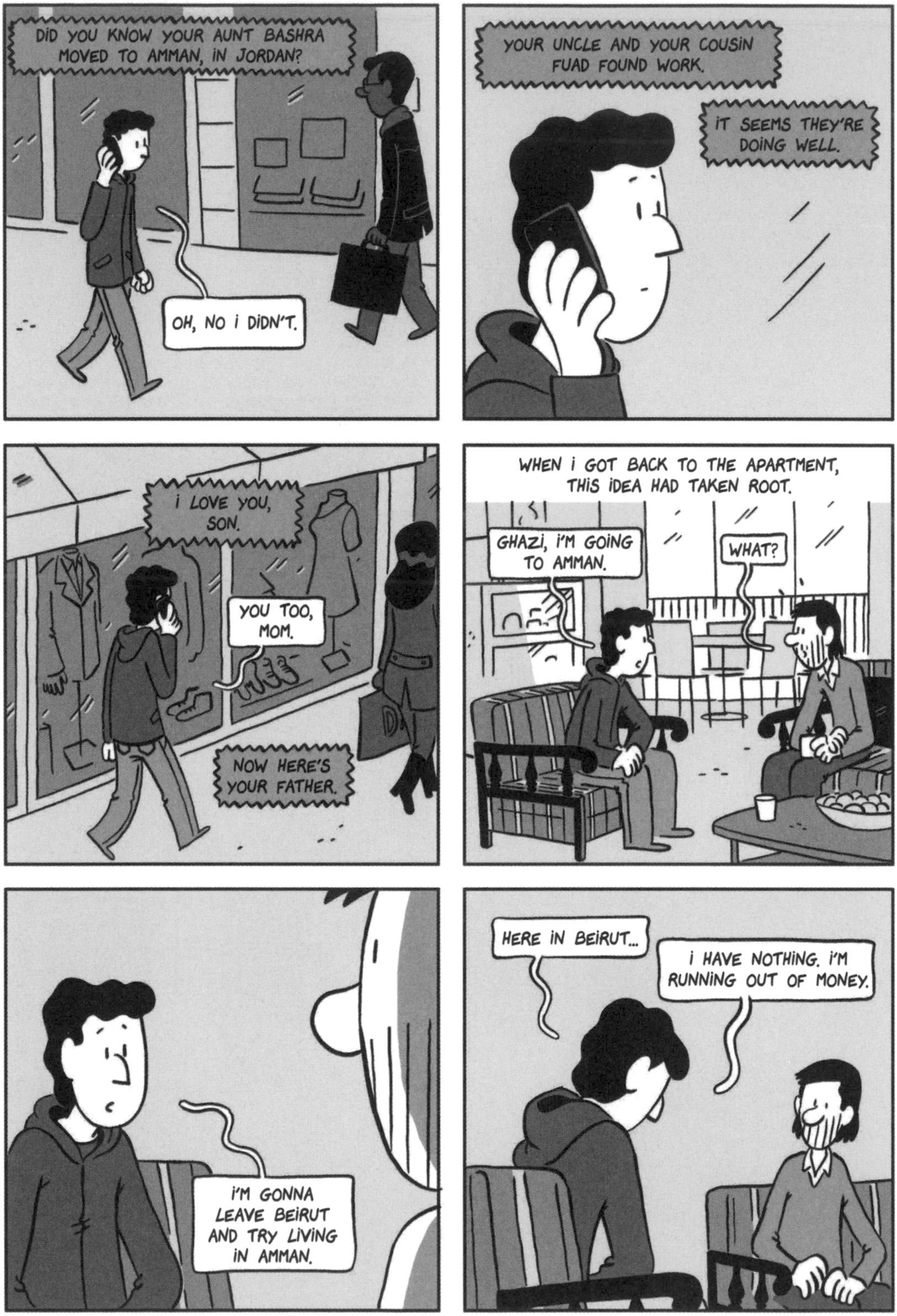
DID YOU KNOW YOUR AUNT BASHRA MOVED TO AMMAN, IN JORDAN?
OH, NO I DIDN'T.
YOUR UNCLE AND YOUR COUSIN FUAD FOUND WORK.
IT SEEMS THEY'RE DOING WELL.
I LOVE YOU, SON.
YOU TOO, MOM.
NOW HERE'S YOUR FATHER.
WHEN I GOT BACK TO THE APARTMENT, THIS IDEA HAD TAKEN ROOT.
GHAZI, I'M GOING TO AMMAN.
WHAT?
I'M GONNA LEAVE BEIRUT AND TRY LIVING IN AMMAN.
HERE IN BEIRUT...
I HAVE NOTHING. I'M RUNNING OUT OF MONEY.

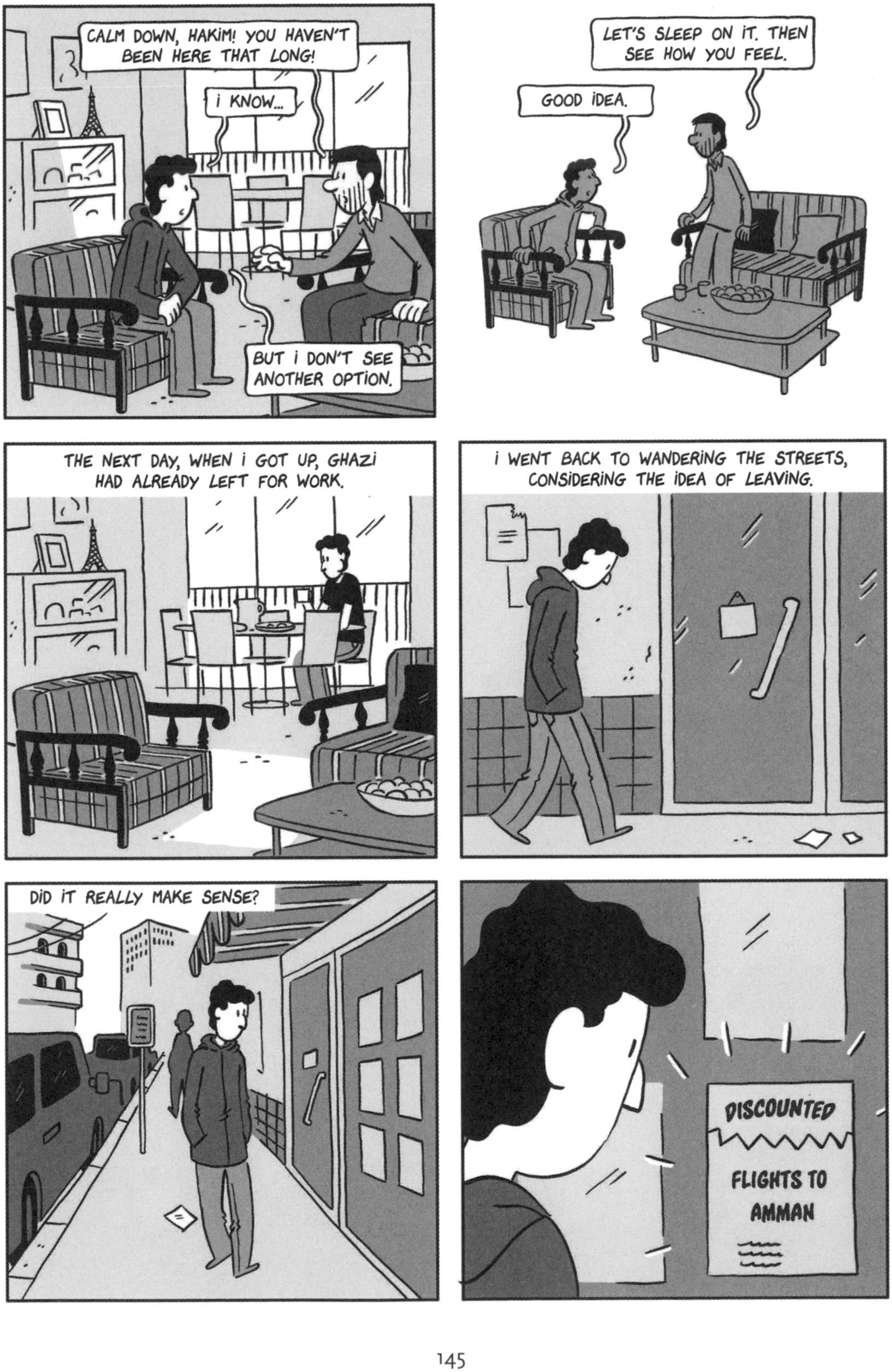
CALM DOWN, HAKIM! YOU HAVEN'T BEEN HERE THAT LONG!
I KNOW...
BUT I DON'T SEE ANOTHER OPTION.
LET'S SLEEP ON IT. THEN SEE HOW YOU FEEL.
GOOD IDEA.
THE NEXT DAY, WHEN I GOT UP, GHAZI HAD ALREADY LEFT FOR WORK.
I WENT BACK TO WANDERING THE STREETS, CONSIDERING THE IDEA OF LEAVING.
DID IT REALLY MAKE SENSE?
DISCOUNTED
FLIGHTS TO AMMAN

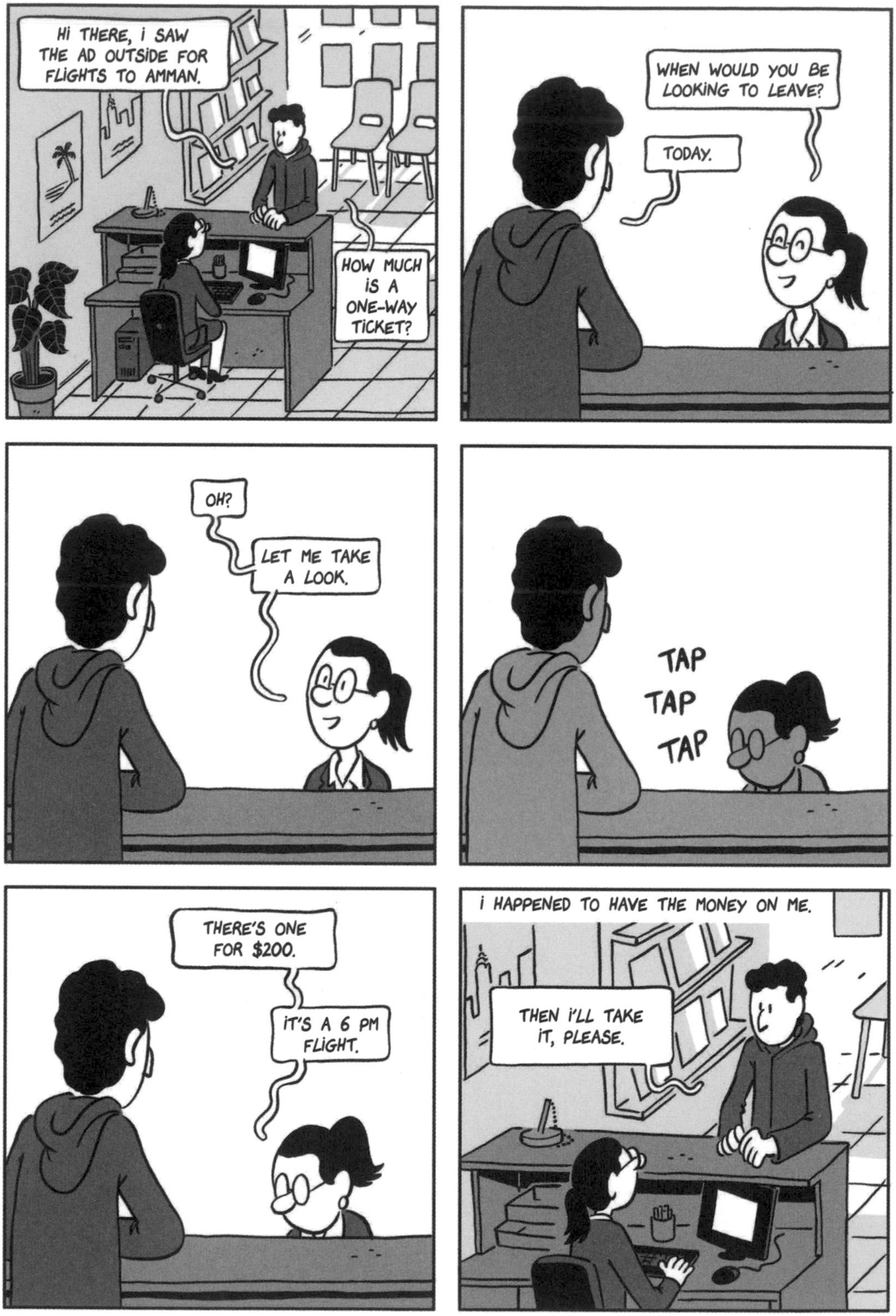
HI THERE, I SAW THE AD OUTSIDE FOR FLIGHTS TO AMMAN.
HOW MUCH IS A ONE-WAY TICKET?
WHEN WOULD YOU BE LOOKING TO LEAVE?
TODAY.
OH?
LET ME TAKE A LOOK.
TAP
TAP
TAP
THERE'S ONE FOR $200.
IT'S A 6 PM FLIGHT.
I HAPPENED TO HAVE THE MONEY ON ME.
THEN I'LL TAKE IT, PLEASE.

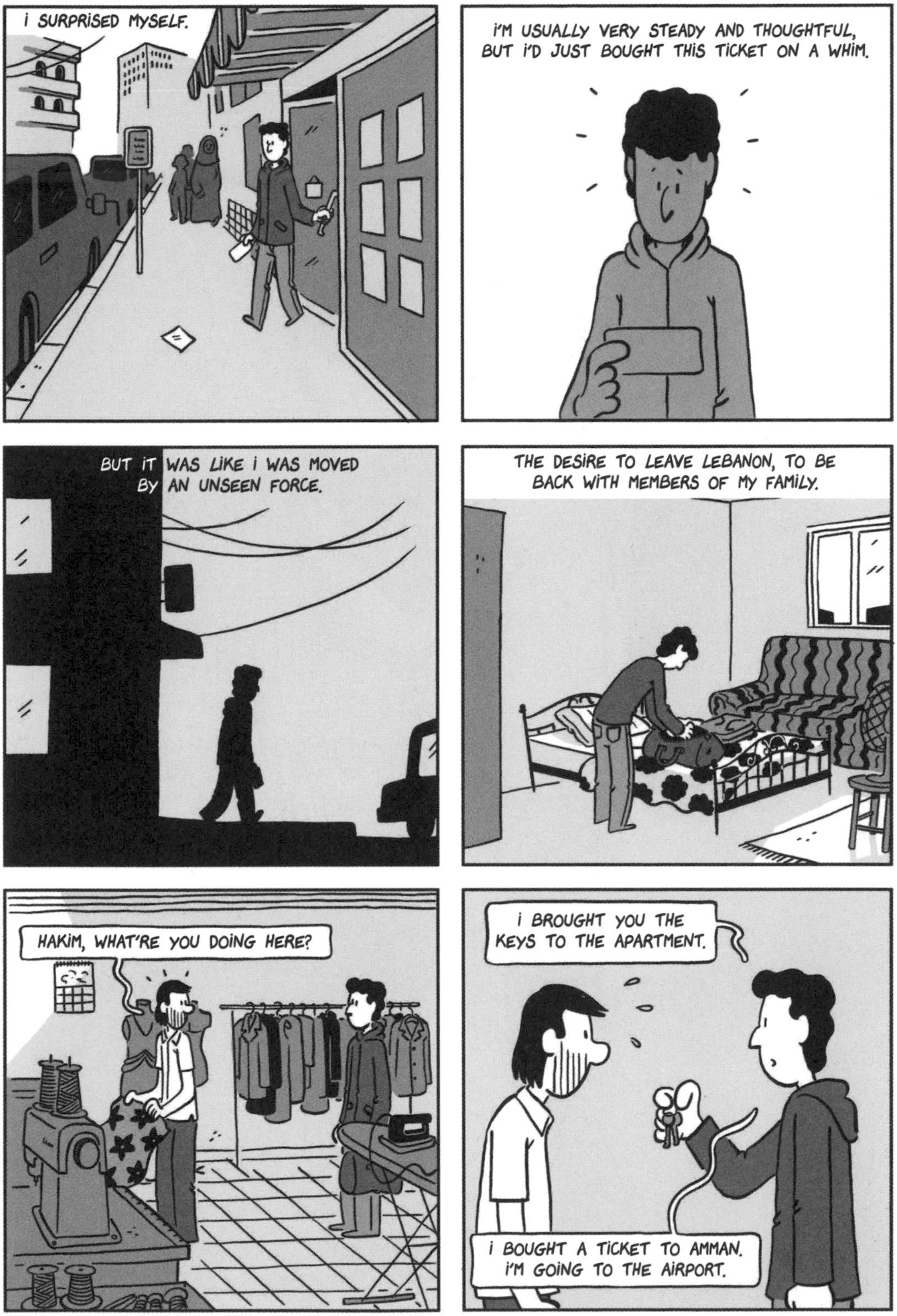
i SURPRISED MYSELF.
i'M USUALLY VERY STEADY AND THOUGHTFUL, BUT i'D JUST BOUGHT THIS TICKET ON A WHiM.
BUT iT WAS LiKE i WAS MOVED BY AN UNSEEN FORCE.
THE DESiRE TO LEAVE LEBANON, TO BE BACK WiTH MEMBERS OF MY FAMiLY.
HAKiM, WHAT'RE YOU DOiNG HERE?
i BROUGHT YOU THE KEYS TO THE APARTMENT.
i BOUGHT A TiCKET TO AMMAN. i'M GOiNG TO THE AiRPORT.

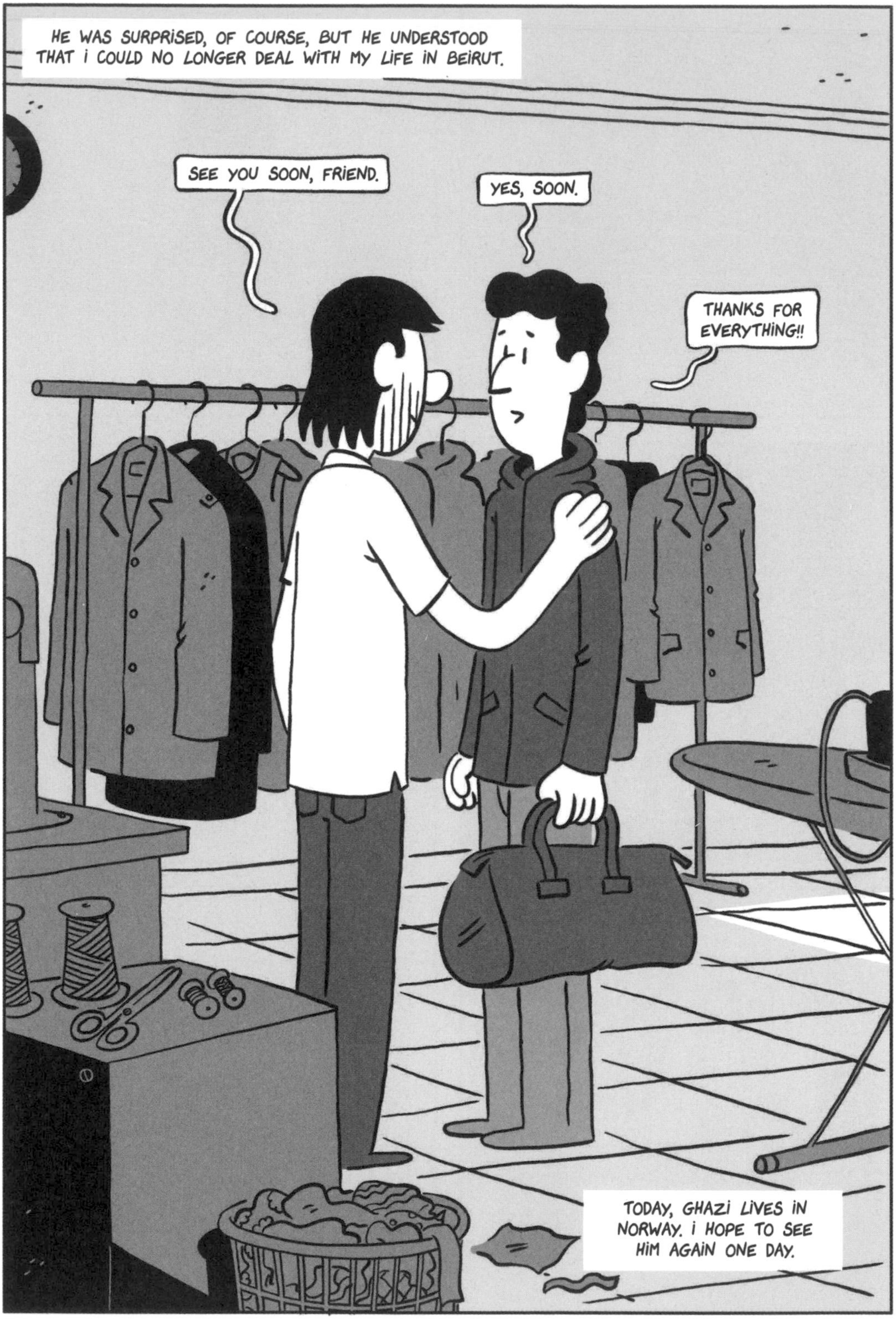
HE WAS SURPRISED, OF COURSE, BUT HE UNDERSTOOD THAT I COULD NO LONGER DEAL WITH MY LIFE IN BEIRUT.
SEE YOU SOON, FRIEND.
YES, SOON.
THANKS FOR EVERYTHING!!
TODAY, GHAZI LIVES IN NORWAY. I HOPE TO SEE HIM AGAIN ONE DAY.

Chapter 7:
Amman
(Late January 2013)

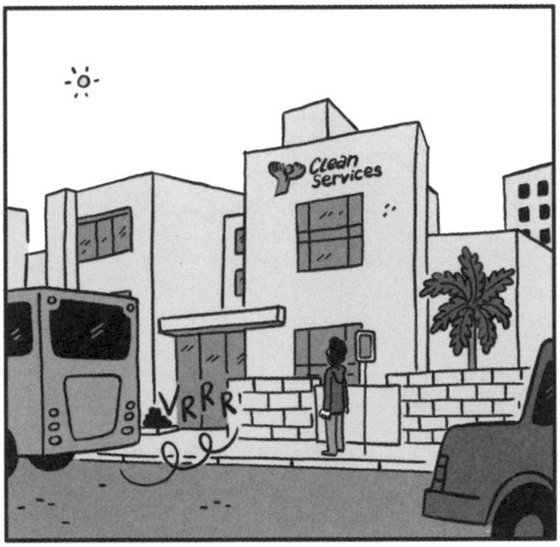
Clean Services
VRRR

"IF YOU'RE GOOD, YOU'LL MOVE UP IN THE COMPANY."

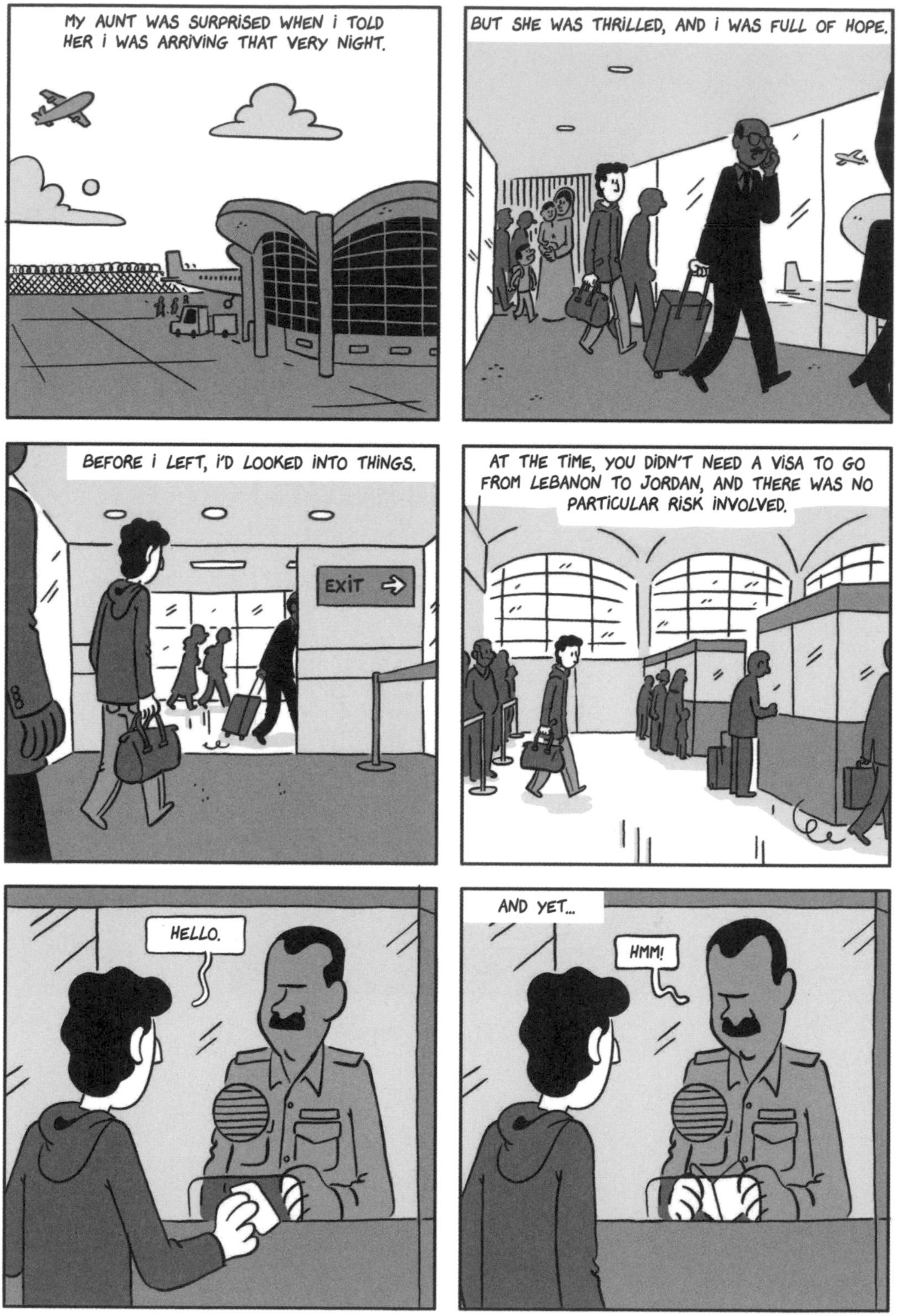
MY AUNT WAS SURPRISED WHEN I TOLD HER I WAS ARRIVING THAT VERY NIGHT.
BUT SHE WAS THRILLED, AND I WAS FULL OF HOPE.
BEFORE I LEFT, I'D LOOKED INTO THINGS.
EXIT
AT THE TIME, YOU DIDN'T NEED A VISA TO GO FROM LEBANON TO JORDAN, AND THERE WAS NO PARTICULAR RISK INVOLVED.
HELLO.
AND YET...
HMM!

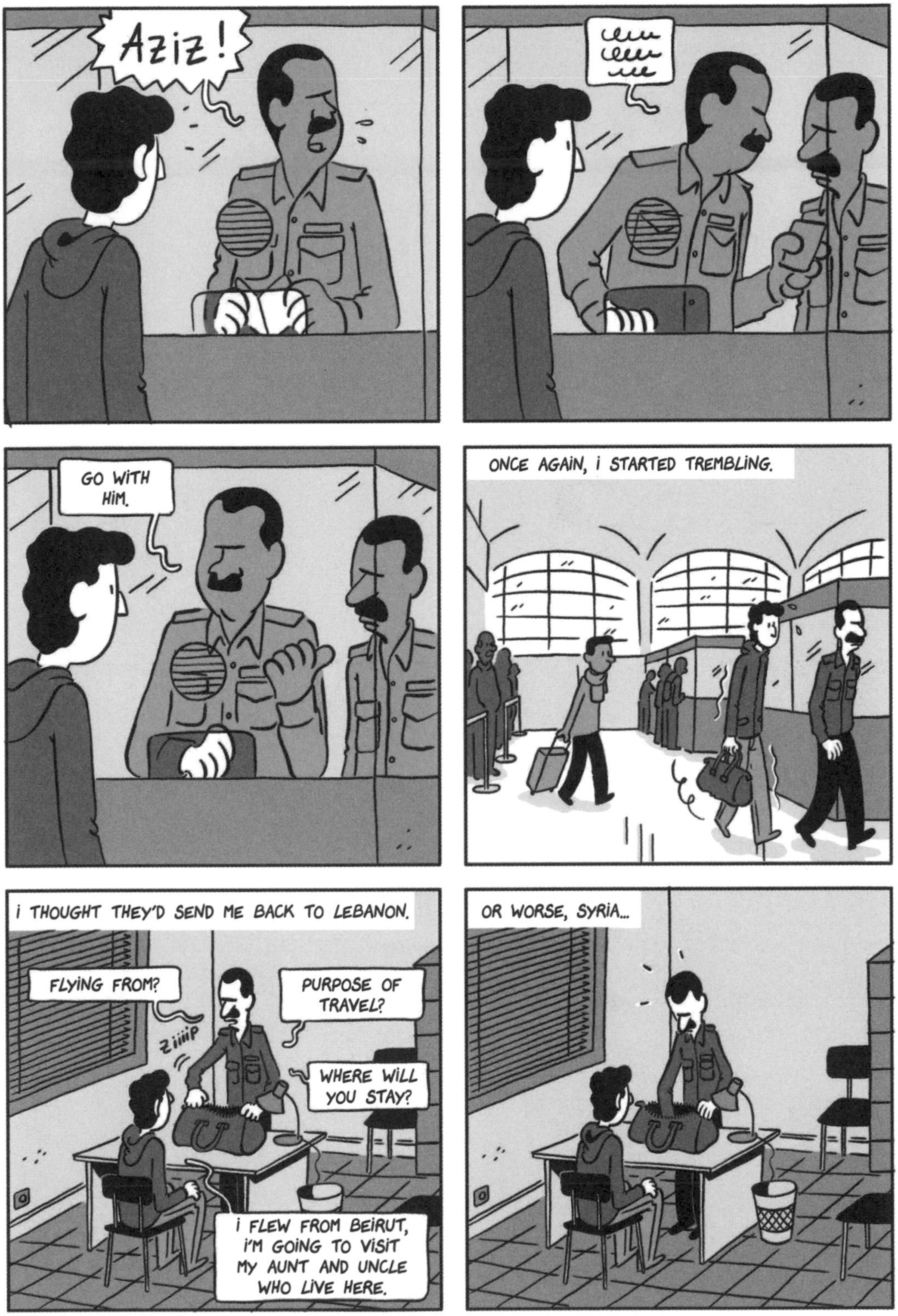
Aziz!
GO WITH HIM.
ONCE AGAIN, i STARTED TREMBLING.
i THOUGHT THEY'D SEND ME BACK TO LEBANON.
FLYING FROM?
PURPOSE OF TRAVEL?
ziiiip
WHERE WiLL YOU STAY?
i FLEW FROM BEIRUT, i'M GOING TO ViSiT MY AUNT AND UNCLE WHO LiVE HERE.
OR WORSE, SYRiA...

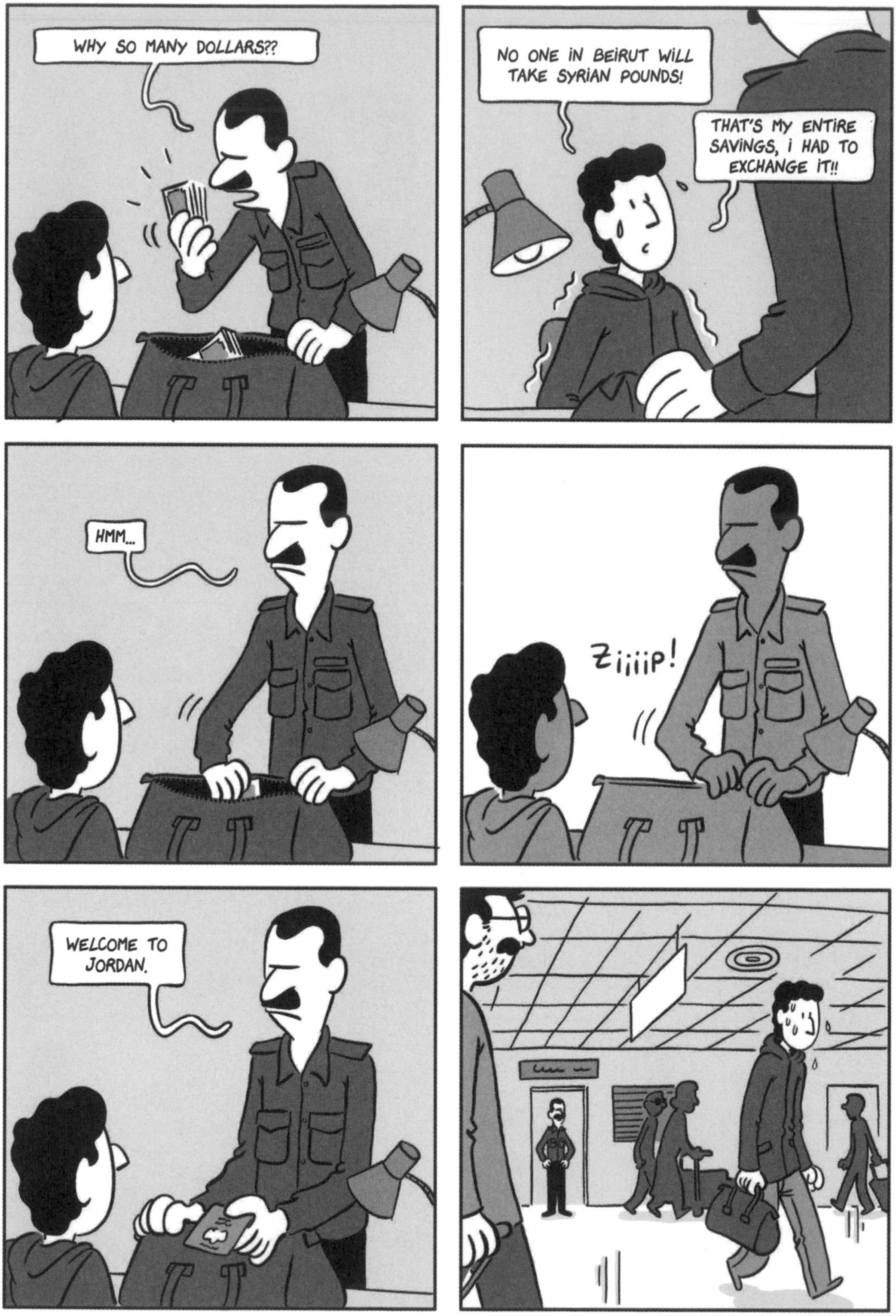
WHY SO MANY DOLLARS??
NO ONE IN BEIRUT WILL TAKE SYRIAN POUNDS!
THAT'S MY ENTIRE SAVINGS, I HAD TO EXCHANGE IT!!
HMM...
ZiiiiP!
WELCOME TO JORDAN.

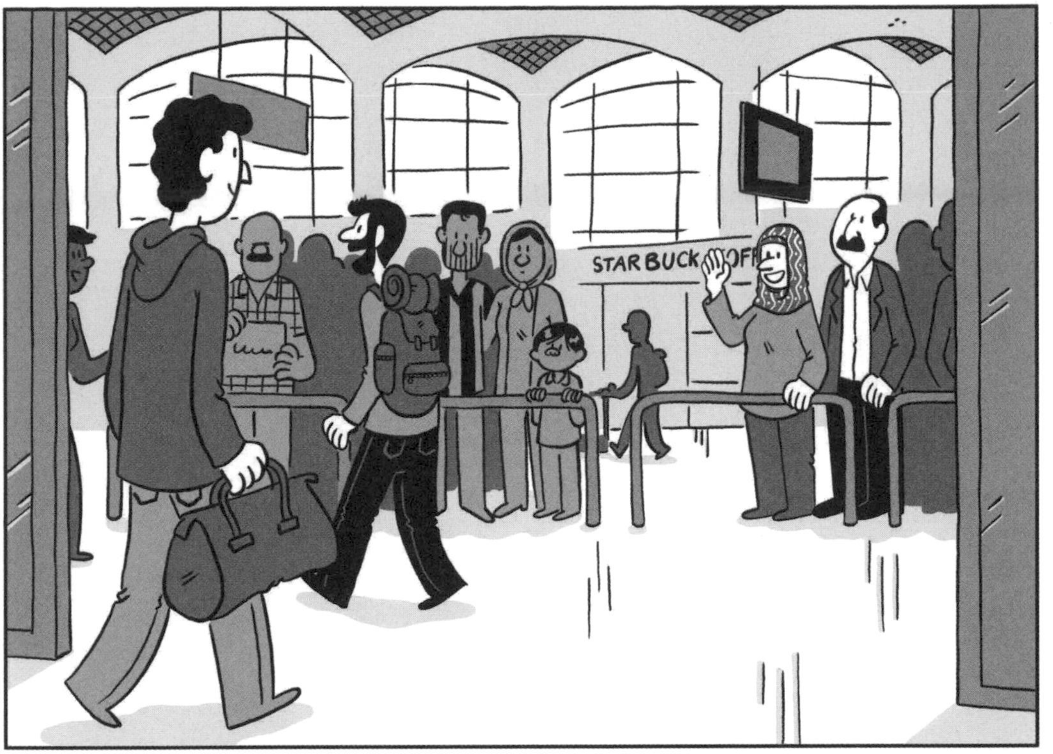
STAR BUCK

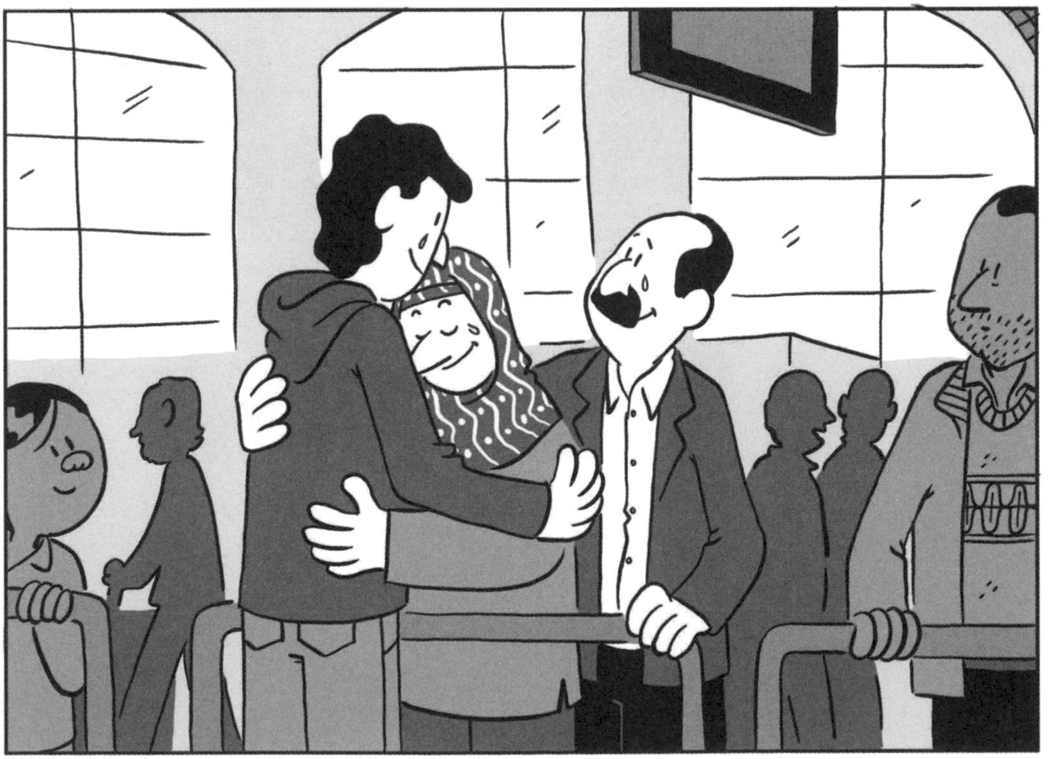

MY AUNT'S FAMILY LIVED IN A SYRIAN NEIGHBORHOOD IN AMMAN.

THEY LIVED IN A NICE, BIG HOUSE.

WELCOME TO YOUR NEW HOME!

OF COURSE THERE WERE A LOT OF PEOPLE LIVING THERE: MY UNCLE, MY AUNT, MY COUSIN FUAD, HIS WIFE AND THEIR SON, PLUS FOUR OTHER COUSINS I DIDN'T KNOW AS WELL.

HEY, HAKIM!

HEY, FUAD!

HI, EVERYONE!

MOM TOLD ME ABOUT YOUR HARD TIMES IN LEBANON.

REST ASSURED, THERE'S MORE WORK HERE.

YOU'LL EASILY FIND SOMETHING.

I WORK IN A CAFÉ.

AND FATIMA FOUND A JOB AS A HAIRDRESSER WITHIN A FEW DAYS.

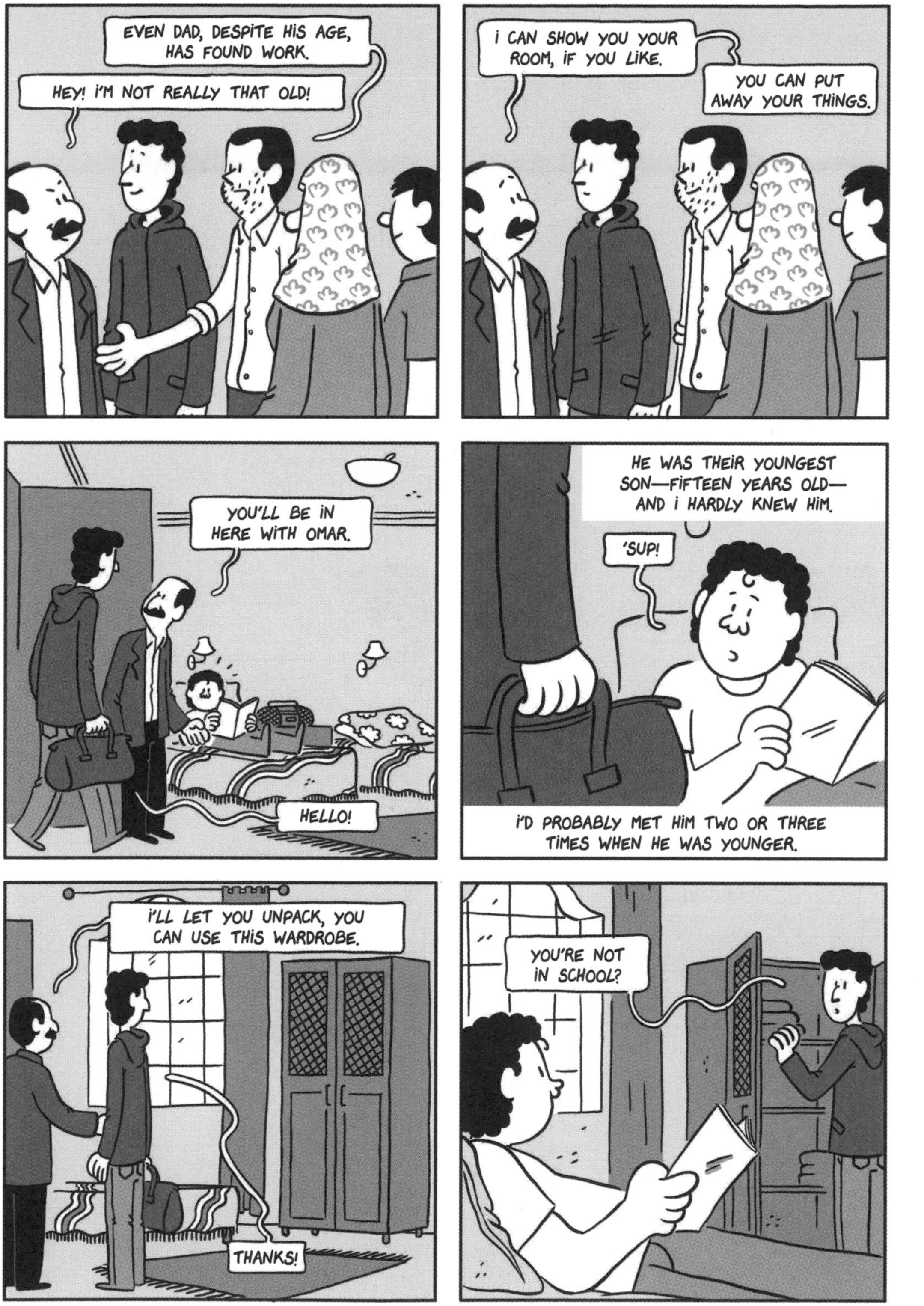
EVEN DAD, DESPITE HIS AGE, HAS FOUND WORK.
HEY! I'M NOT REALLY THAT OLD!
I CAN SHOW YOU YOUR ROOM, IF YOU LIKE.
YOU CAN PUT AWAY YOUR THINGS.
YOU'LL BE IN HERE WITH OMAR.
HELLO!
HE WAS THEIR YOUNGEST SON—FIFTEEN YEARS OLD—AND I HARDLY KNEW HIM.
'SUP!
I'D PROBABLY MET HIM TWO OR THREE TIMES WHEN HE WAS YOUNGER.
I'LL LET YOU UNPACK, YOU CAN USE THIS WARDROBE.
THANKS!
YOU'RE NOT IN SCHOOL?

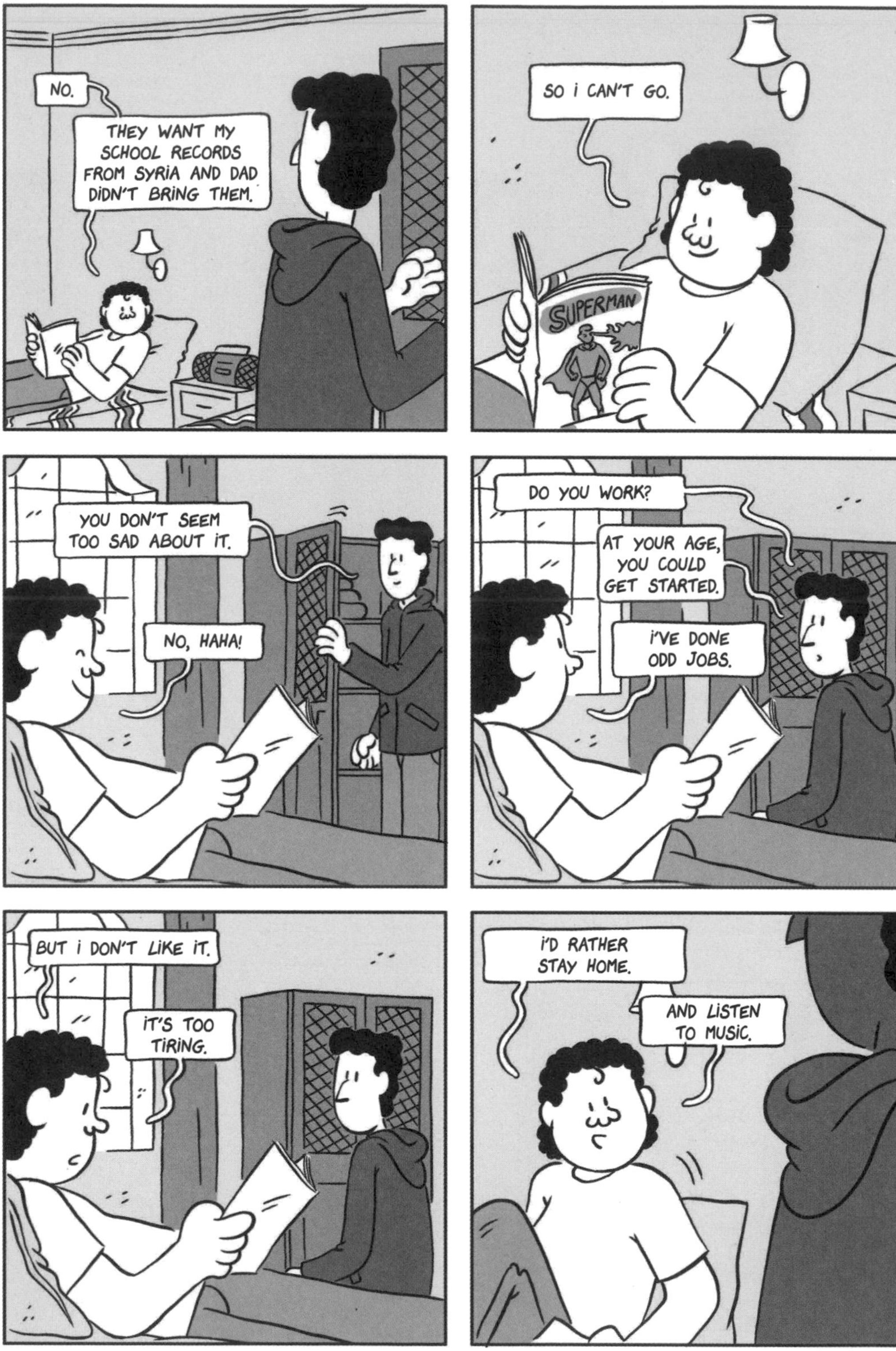
NO.
THEY WANT MY SCHOOL RECORDS FROM SYRIA AND DAD DIDN'T BRING THEM.
SO I CAN'T GO.
SUPERMAN
YOU DON'T SEEM TOO SAD ABOUT IT.
NO, HAHA!
DO YOU WORK?
AT YOUR AGE, YOU COULD GET STARTED.
I'VE DONE ODD JOBS.
BUT I DON'T LIKE IT.
IT'S TOO TIRING.
I'D RATHER STAY HOME.
AND LISTEN TO MUSIC.

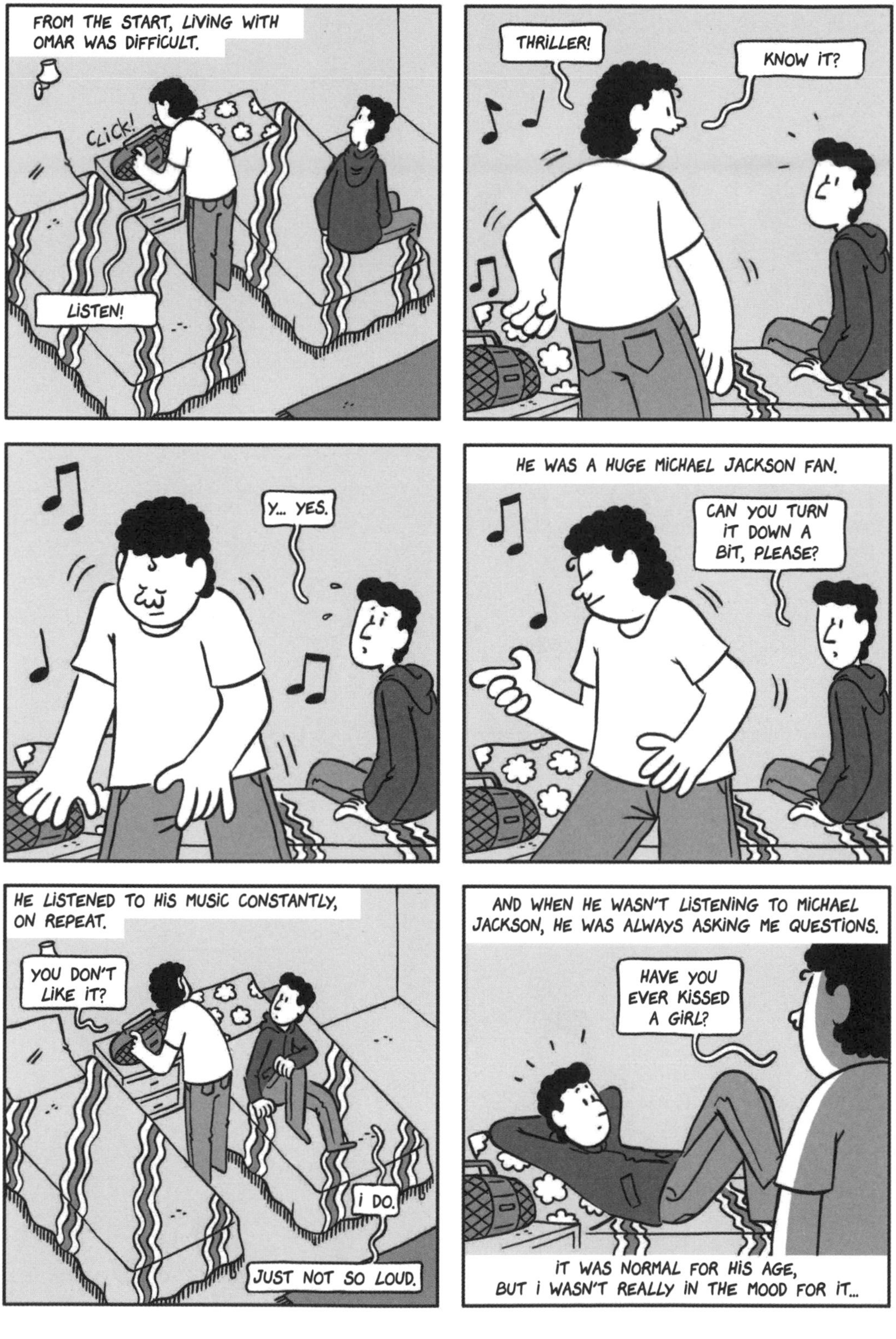
FROM THE START, LIVING WITH OMAR WAS DIFFICULT.
CLICK!
LISTEN!
THRILLER!
KNOW IT?
Y... YES.
HE WAS A HUGE MICHAEL JACKSON FAN.
CAN YOU TURN IT DOWN A BIT, PLEASE?
HE LISTENED TO HIS MUSIC CONSTANTLY, ON REPEAT.
YOU DON'T LIKE IT?
I DO.
JUST NOT SO LOUD.
AND WHEN HE WASN'T LISTENING TO MICHAEL JACKSON, HE WAS ALWAYS ASKING ME QUESTIONS.
HAVE YOU EVER KISSED A GIRL?
IT WAS NORMAL FOR HIS AGE, BUT I WASN'T REALLY IN THE MOOD FOR IT...

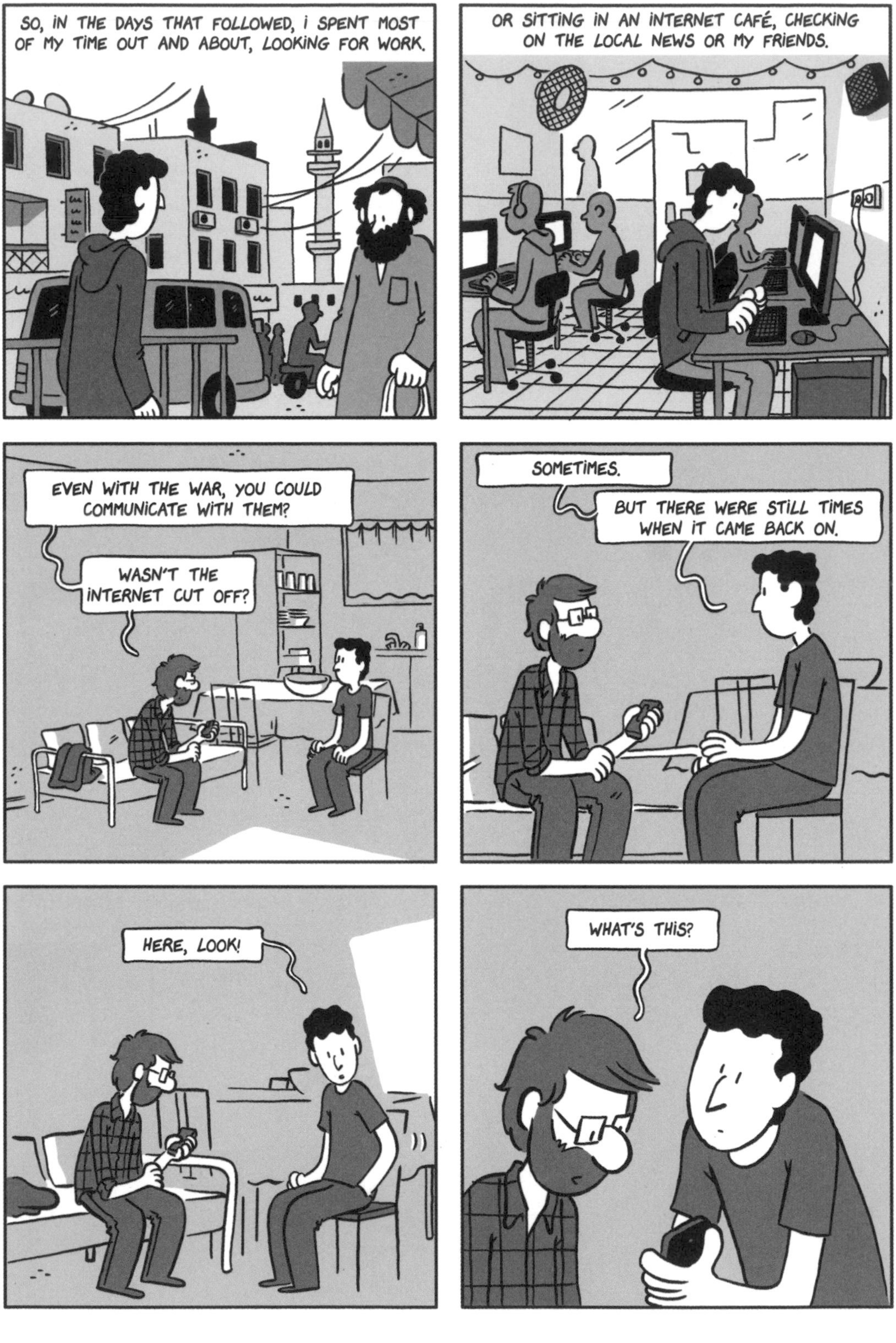
SO, IN THE DAYS THAT FOLLOWED, I SPENT MOST OF MY TIME OUT AND ABOUT, LOOKING FOR WORK.
OR SITTING IN AN INTERNET CAFÉ, CHECKING ON THE LOCAL NEWS OR MY FRIENDS.
EVEN WITH THE WAR, YOU COULD COMMUNICATE WITH THEM?
WASN'T THE INTERNET CUT OFF?
SOMETIMES.
BUT THERE WERE STILL TIMES WHEN IT CAME BACK ON.
HERE, LOOK!
WHAT'S THIS?

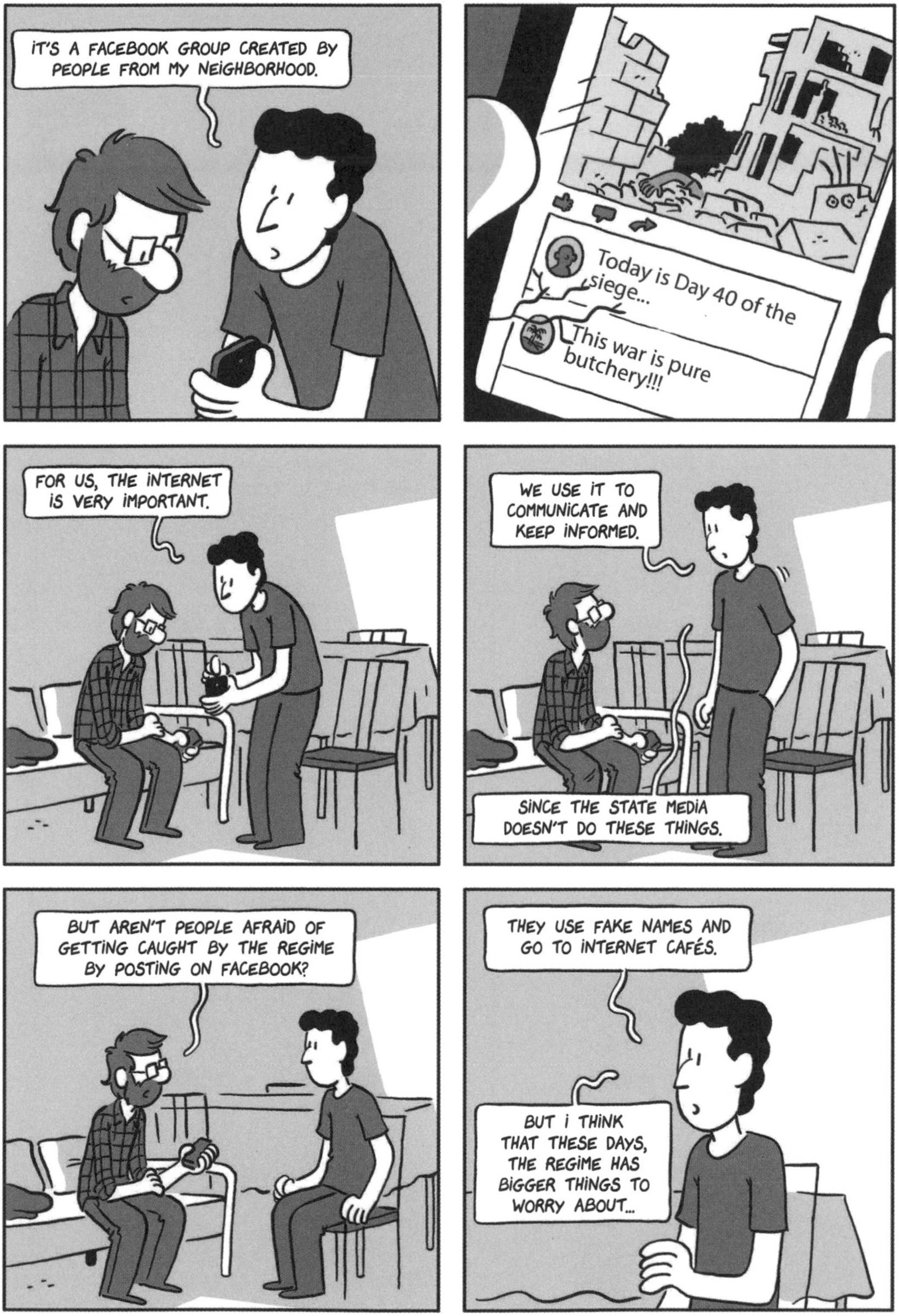
IT'S A FACEBOOK GROUP CREATED BY PEOPLE FROM MY NEIGHBORHOOD.
Today is Day 40 of the siege...
This war is pure butchery!!!
FOR US, THE INTERNET IS VERY IMPORTANT.
WE USE IT TO COMMUNICATE AND KEEP INFORMED.
SINCE THE STATE MEDIA DOESN'T DO THESE THINGS.
BUT AREN'T PEOPLE AFRAID OF GETTING CAUGHT BY THE REGIME BY POSTING ON FACEBOOK?
THEY USE FAKE NAMES AND GO TO INTERNET CAFÉS.
BUT I THINK THAT THESE DAYS, THE REGIME HAS BIGGER THINGS TO WORRY ABOUT...

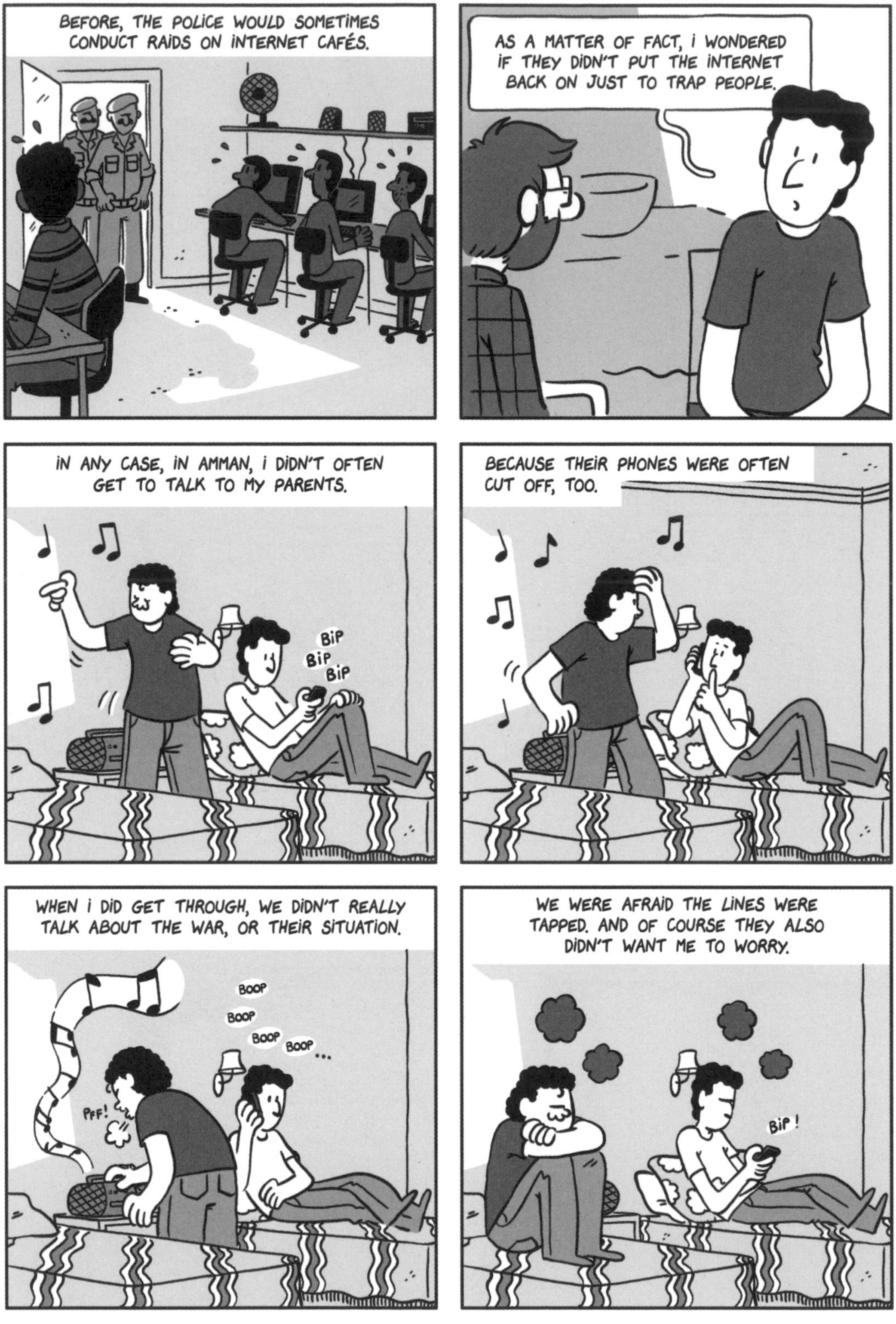
BEFORE, THE POLICE WOULD SOMETIMES CONDUCT RAIDS ON INTERNET CAFÉS.
AS A MATTER OF FACT, I WONDERED IF THEY DIDN'T PUT THE INTERNET BACK ON JUST TO TRAP PEOPLE.
IN ANY CASE, IN AMMAN, I DIDN'T OFTEN GET TO TALK TO MY PARENTS.
BIP
BIP
BIP
BECAUSE THEIR PHONES WERE OFTEN CUT OFF, TOO.
WHEN I DID GET THROUGH, WE DIDN'T REALLY TALK ABOUT THE WAR, OR THEIR SITUATION.
BOOP
BOOP
BOOP
BOOP...
PFF!
WE WERE AFRAID THE LINES WERE TAPPED. AND OF COURSE THEY ALSO DIDN'T WANT ME TO WORRY.
BIP!

HAKIM, JOIN US FOR SOME TEA?

NO THANKS, I'M GOING FOR A WALK.

IT'LL BE GOOD FOR ME...

CLACK!

TAP!

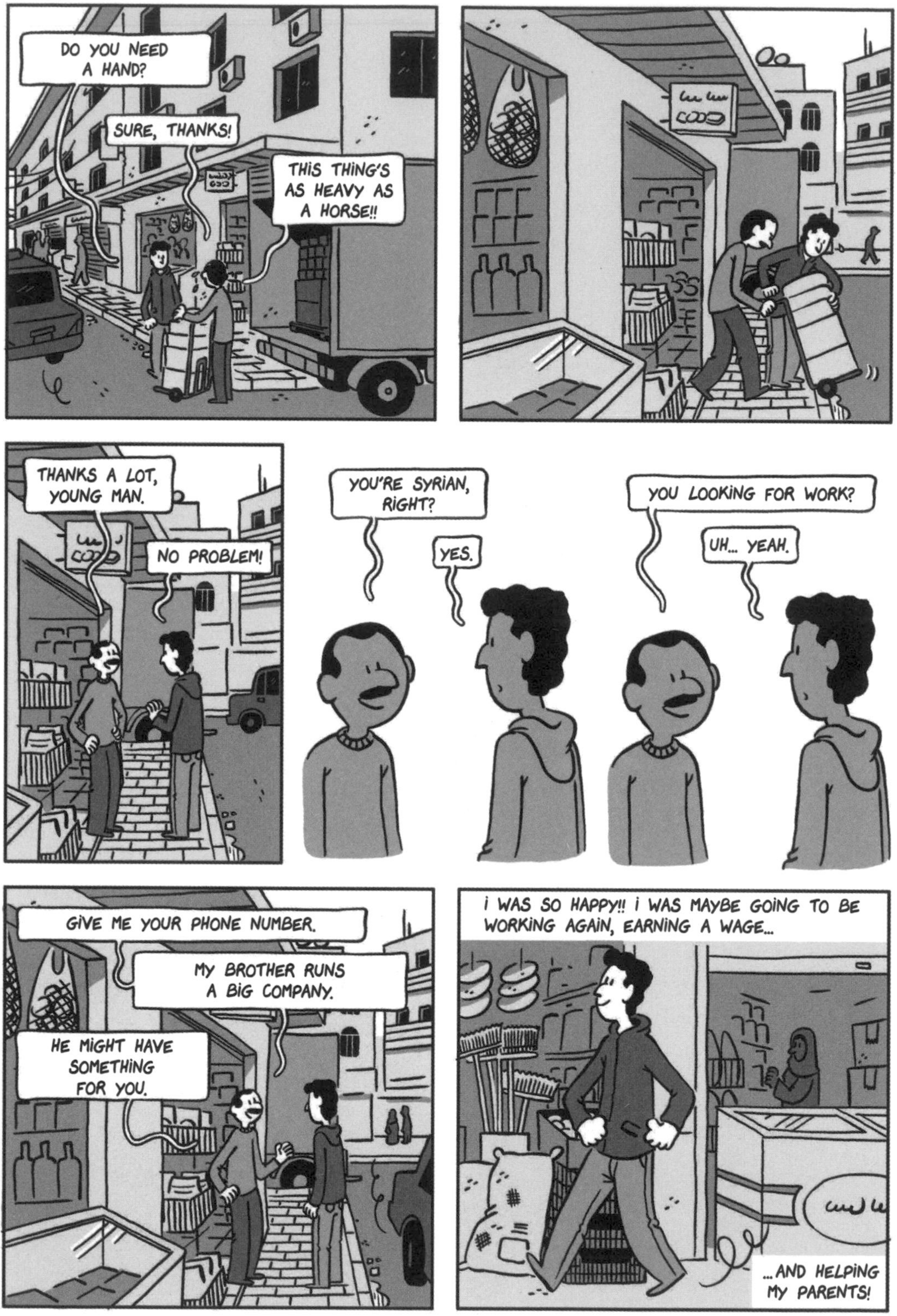
DO YOU NEED A HAND?
SURE, THANKS!
THIS THING'S AS HEAVY AS A HORSE!!
THANKS A LOT, YOUNG MAN.
NO PROBLEM!
YOU'RE SYRIAN, RIGHT?
YES.
YOU LOOKING FOR WORK?
UH... YEAH.
GIVE ME YOUR PHONE NUMBER.
MY BROTHER RUNS A BIG COMPANY.
HE MIGHT HAVE SOMETHING FOR YOU.
I WAS SO HAPPY!! I WAS MAYBE GOING TO BE WORKING AGAIN, EARNING A WAGE...
...AND HELPING MY PARENTS!

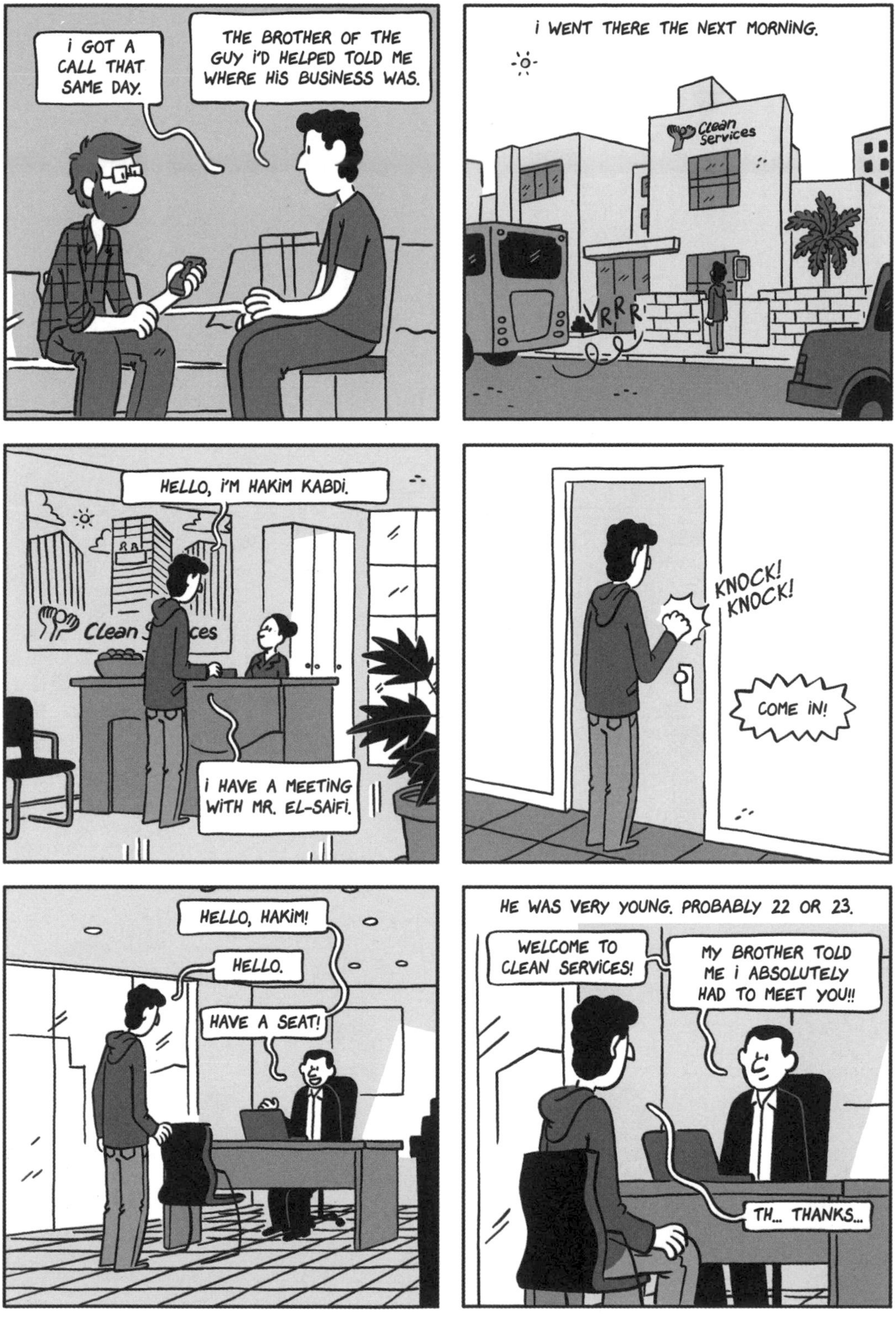
I GOT A CALL THAT SAME DAY.
THE BROTHER OF THE GUY I'D HELPED TOLD ME WHERE HIS BUSINESS WAS.
I WENT THERE THE NEXT MORNING.
Clean Services
VRRR
HELLO, I'M HAKIM KABDI.
Clean Services
I HAVE A MEETING WITH MR. EL-SAIFI.
KNOCK! KNOCK!
COME IN!
HELLO, HAKIM!
HELLO.
HAVE A SEAT!
HE WAS VERY YOUNG. PROBABLY 22 OR 23.
WELCOME TO CLEAN SERVICES!
MY BROTHER TOLD ME I ABSOLUTELY HAD TO MEET YOU!!
TH... THANKS...

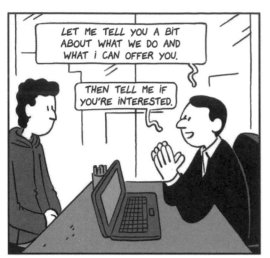

LET ME TELL YOU A BIT ABOUT WHAT WE DO AND WHAT I CAN OFFER YOU.
THEN TELL ME IF YOU'RE INTERESTED.
CLEAN SERVICES IS A HUNDRED-PERSON COMPANY.
WE PERFORM CLEANING SERVICES FOR VARIOUS CLIENTS.
Clean Services
FOR COMPANIES, AND INDIVIDUALS...
BUSINESS IS BOOMING!!
Clean Services
AND I'M ALWAYS LOOKING FOR GOOD PEOPLE TO JOIN OUR TEAM.
WELL?
WHAT DO YOU SAY?
YES, I'M INTERESTED.
I'VE NEVER DONE THIS TYPE OF WORK BEFORE, THOUGH.

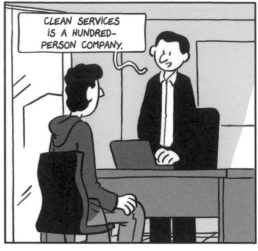

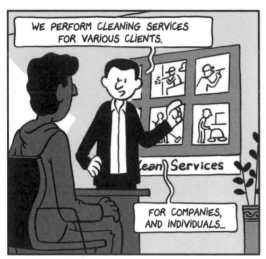

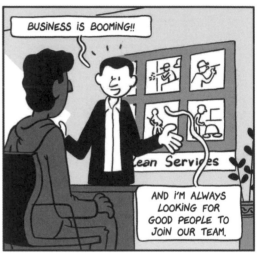

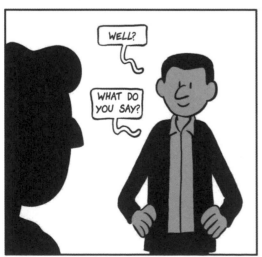

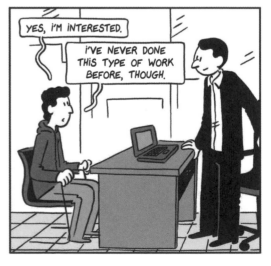

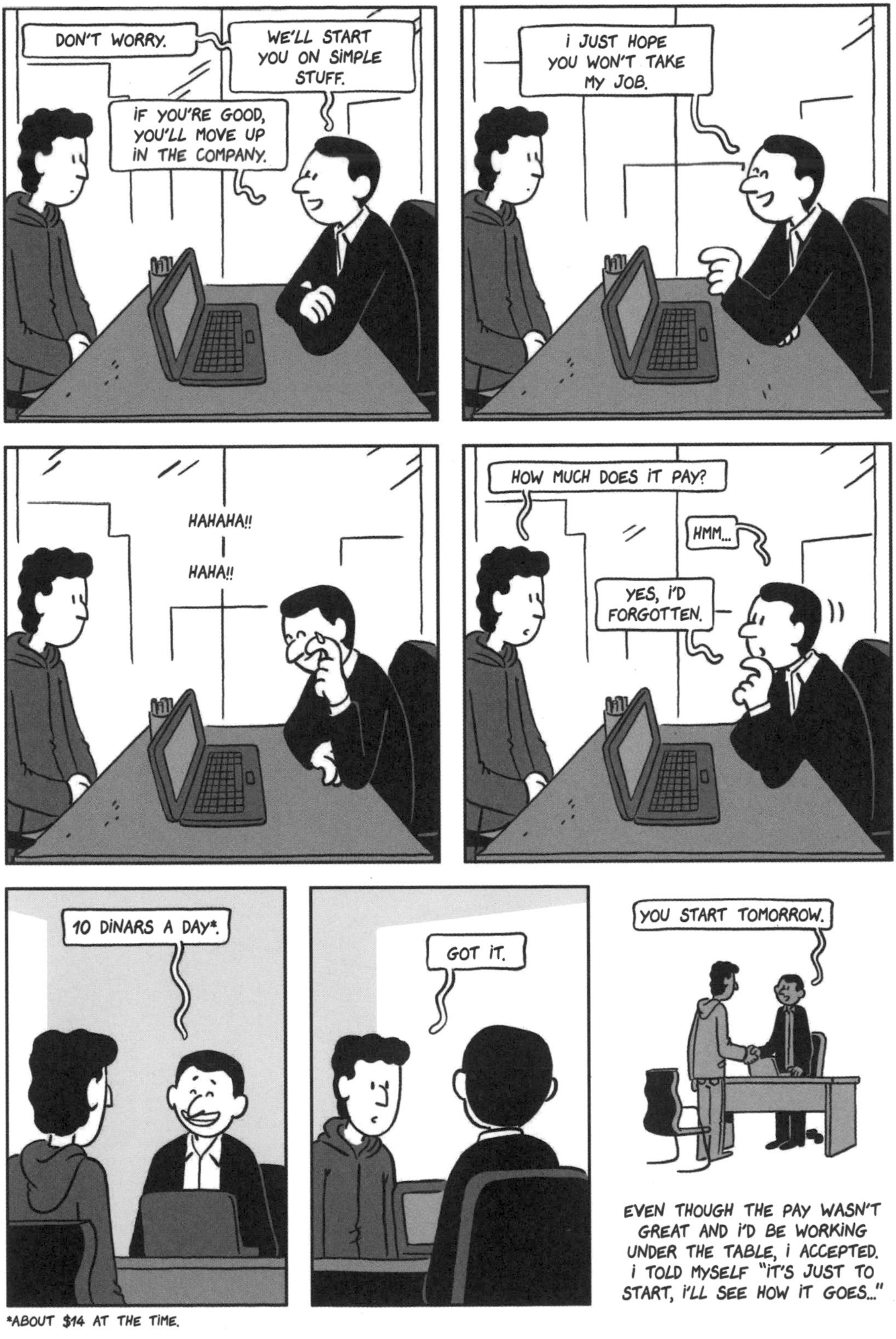
DON'T WORRY.
WE'LL START YOU ON SIMPLE STUFF.
IF YOU'RE GOOD, YOU'LL MOVE UP IN THE COMPANY.
I JUST HOPE YOU WON'T TAKE MY JOB.
HAHAHA!!
HAHA!!
HOW MUCH DOES IT PAY?
HMM...
YES, I'D FORGOTTEN.
10 DINARS A DAY*.
GOT IT.
YOU START TOMORROW.
EVEN THOUGH THE PAY WASN'T GREAT AND I'D BE WORKING UNDER THE TABLE, I ACCEPTED. I TOLD MYSELF "IT'S JUST TO START, I'LL SEE HOW IT GOES..."
*ABOUT $14 AT THE TIME.

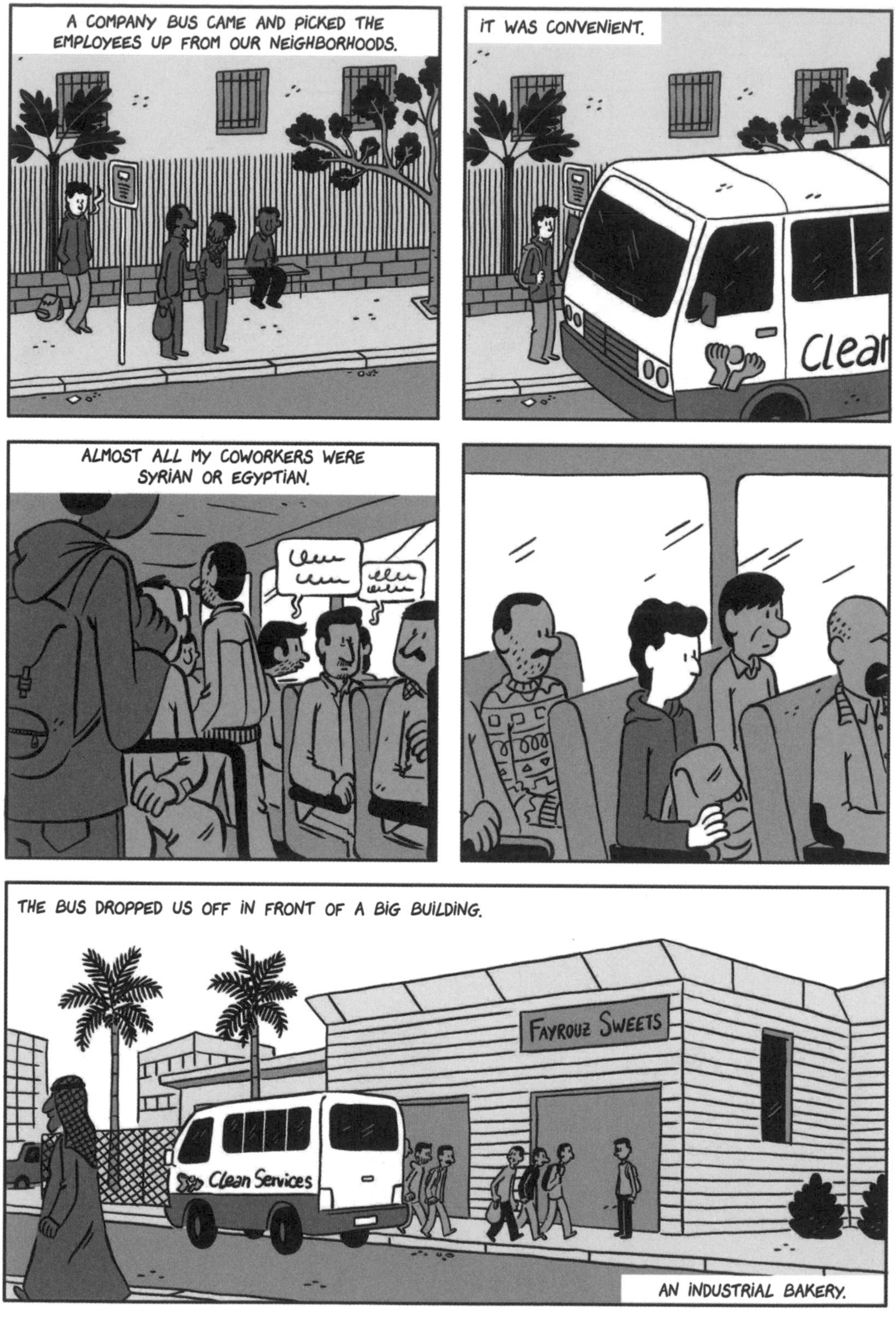
A COMPANY BUS CAME AND PICKED THE EMPLOYEES UP FROM OUR NEIGHBORHOODS.
IT WAS CONVENIENT.
Clean
ALMOST ALL MY COWORKERS WERE SYRIAN OR EGYPTIAN.
THE BUS DROPPED US OFF IN FRONT OF A BIG BUILDING.
FAYROUZ SWEETS
Clean Services
AN INDUSTRIAL BAKERY.

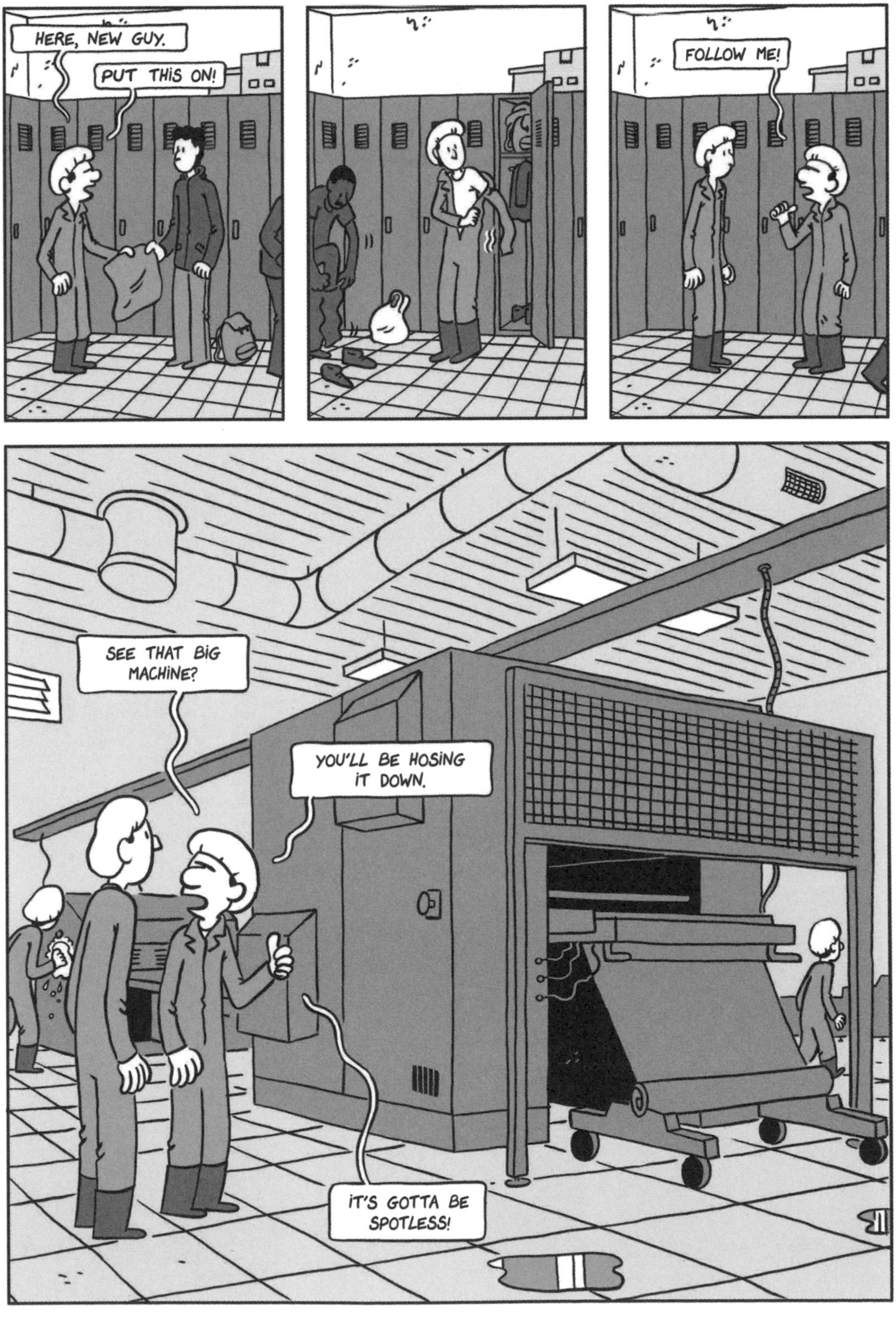
HERE, NEW GUY.
PUT THIS ON!
FOLLOW ME!
SEE THAT BIG MACHINE?
YOU'LL BE HOSING IT DOWN.
IT'S GOTTA BE SPOTLESS!

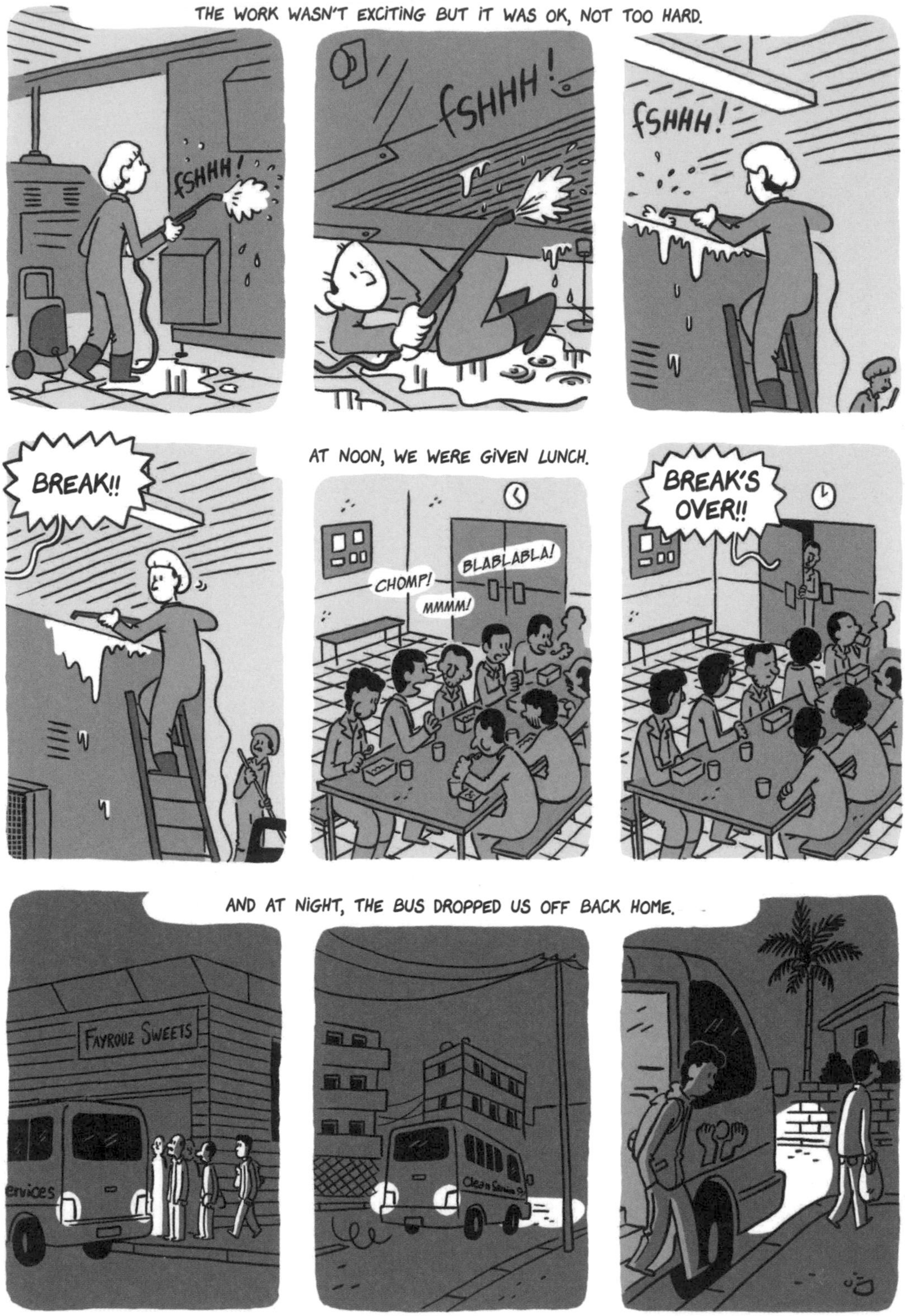
THE WORK WASN'T EXCITING BUT IT WAS OK, NOT TOO HARD.
FSHHH!
FSHHH!
FSHHH!
BREAK!!
AT NOON, WE WERE GIVEN LUNCH.
CHOMP!
BLABLABLA!
MMMM!
BREAK'S OVER!!
AND AT NIGHT, THE BUS DROPPED US OFF BACK HOME.
FAYROUZ SWEETS
ervices
Clean Service

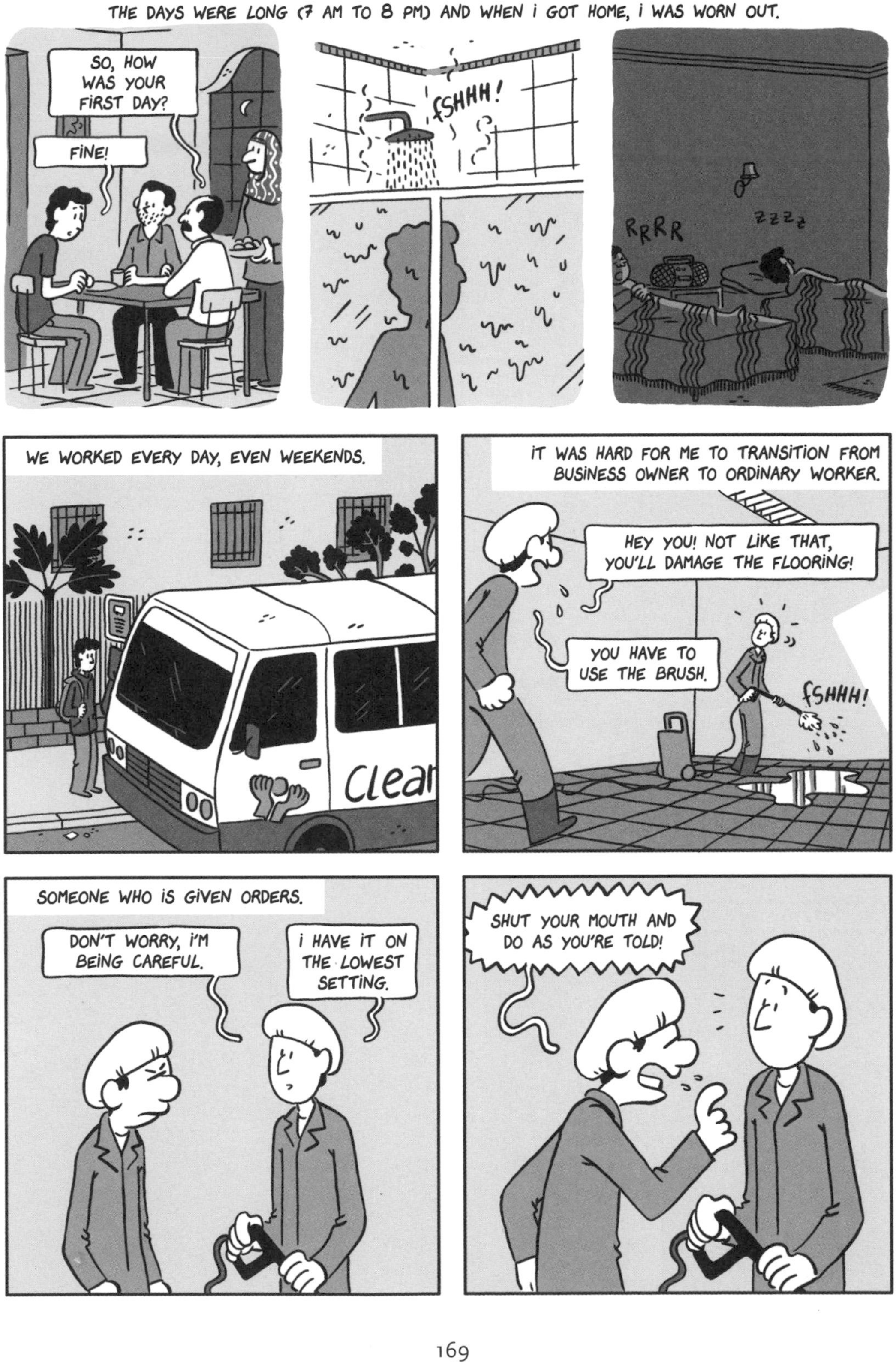
THE DAYS WERE LONG (7 AM TO 8 PM) AND WHEN I GOT HOME, I WAS WORN OUT.
SO, HOW WAS YOUR FIRST DAY?
FINE!
FSHHH!
RRRR
ZZZZ
WE WORKED EVERY DAY, EVEN WEEKENDS.
Clear
IT WAS HARD FOR ME TO TRANSITION FROM BUSINESS OWNER TO ORDINARY WORKER.
HEY YOU! NOT LIKE THAT, YOU'LL DAMAGE THE FLOORING!
YOU HAVE TO USE THE BRUSH.
FSHHH!
SOMEONE WHO IS GIVEN ORDERS.
DON'T WORRY, I'M BEING CAREFUL.
I HAVE IT ON THE LOWEST SETTING.
SHUT YOUR MOUTH AND DO AS YOU'RE TOLD!

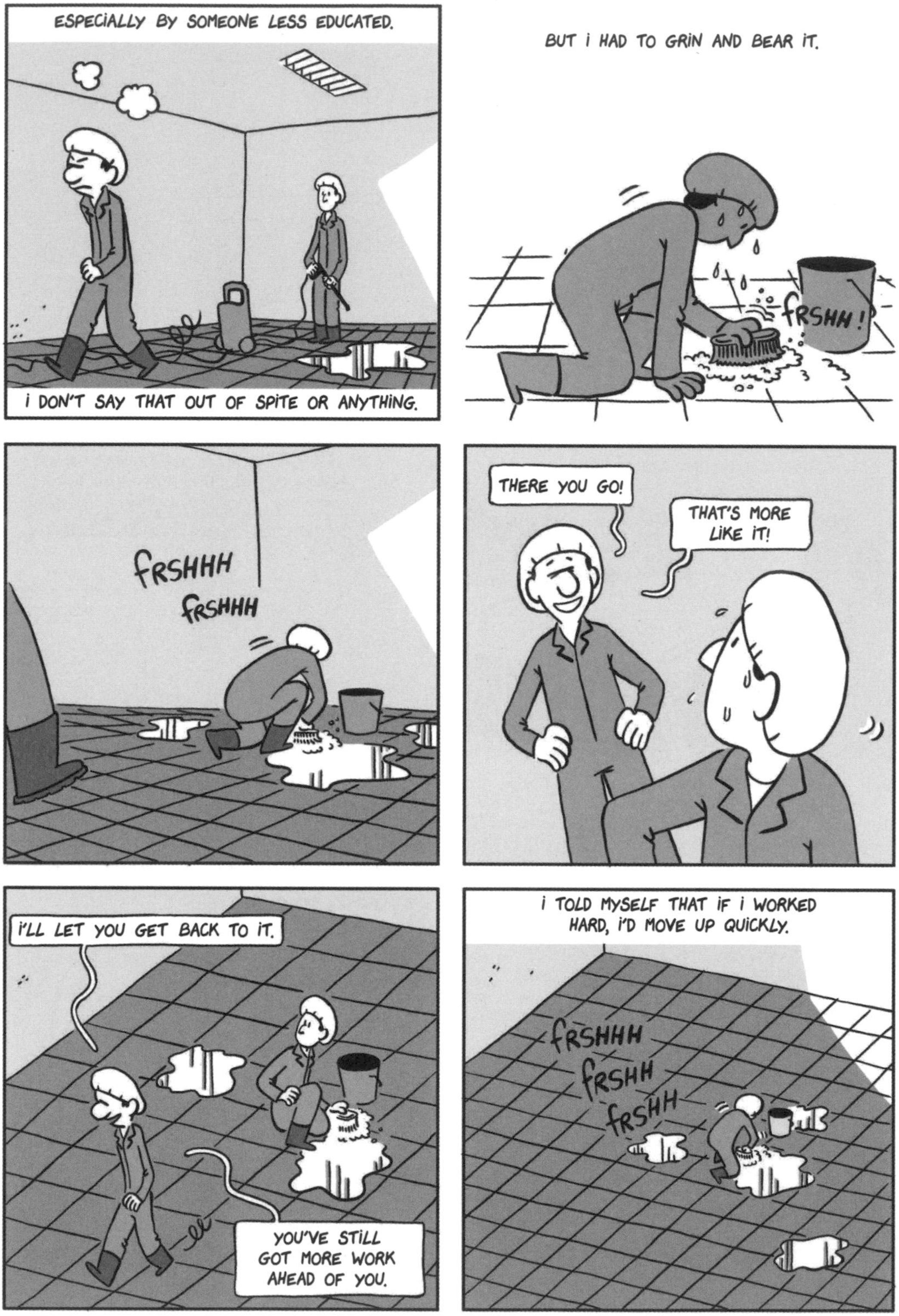
ESPECIALLY BY SOMEONE LESS EDUCATED.
I DON'T SAY THAT OUT OF SPITE OR ANYTHING.
BUT I HAD TO GRIN AND BEAR IT.
FRSHH!
FRSHHH
FRSHHH
THERE YOU GO!
THAT'S MORE LIKE IT!
I'LL LET YOU GET BACK TO IT.
YOU'VE STILL GOT MORE WORK AHEAD OF YOU.
I TOLD MYSELF THAT IF I WORKED HARD, I'D MOVE UP QUICKLY.
FRSHHH
FRSHH
FRSHH

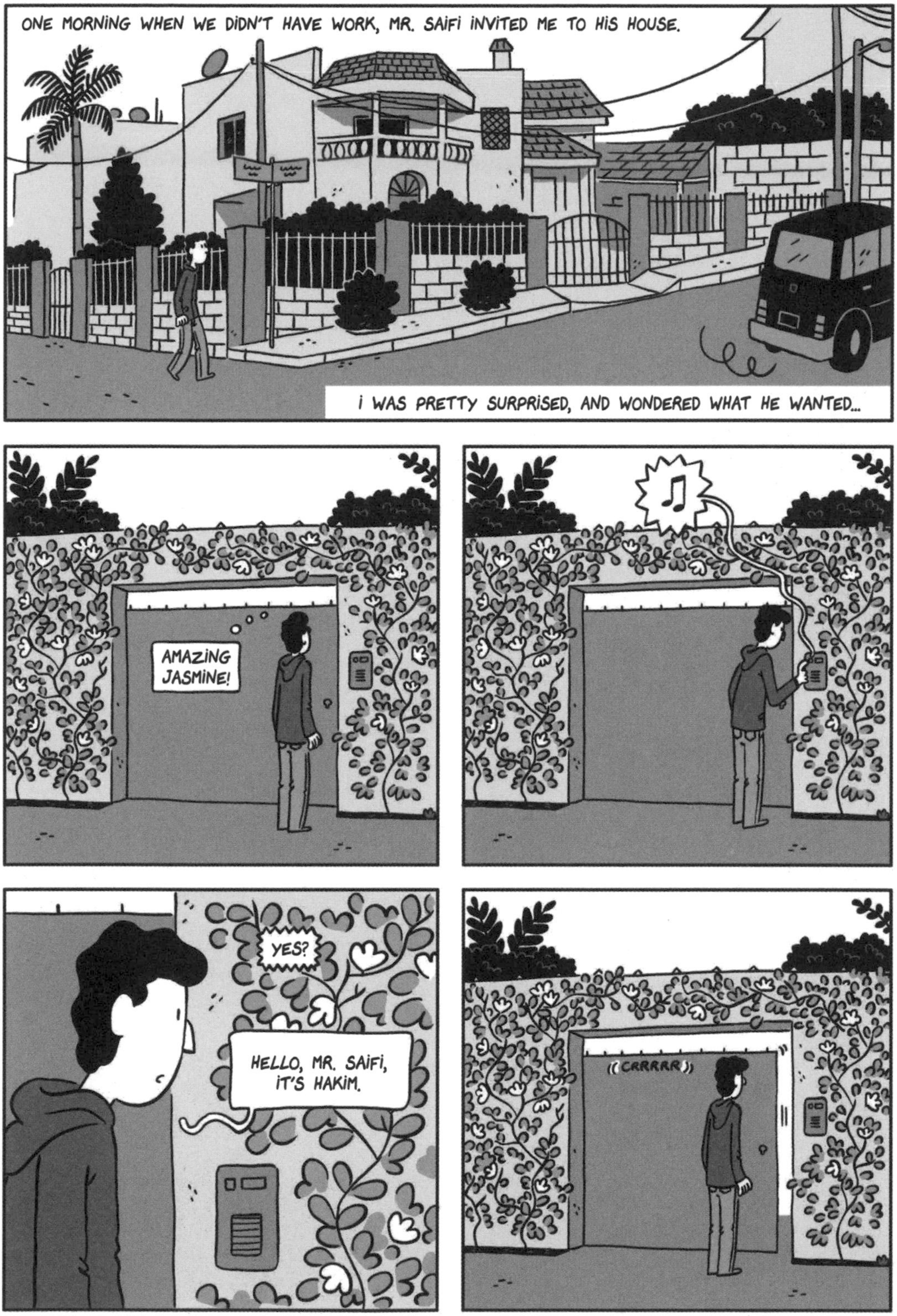
ONE MORNING WHEN WE DIDN'T HAVE WORK, MR. SAIFI INVITED ME TO HIS HOUSE.
I WAS PRETTY SURPRISED, AND WONDERED WHAT HE WANTED...
AMAZING JASMINE!
YES?
HELLO, MR. SAIFI, IT'S HAKIM.
CRRRRR

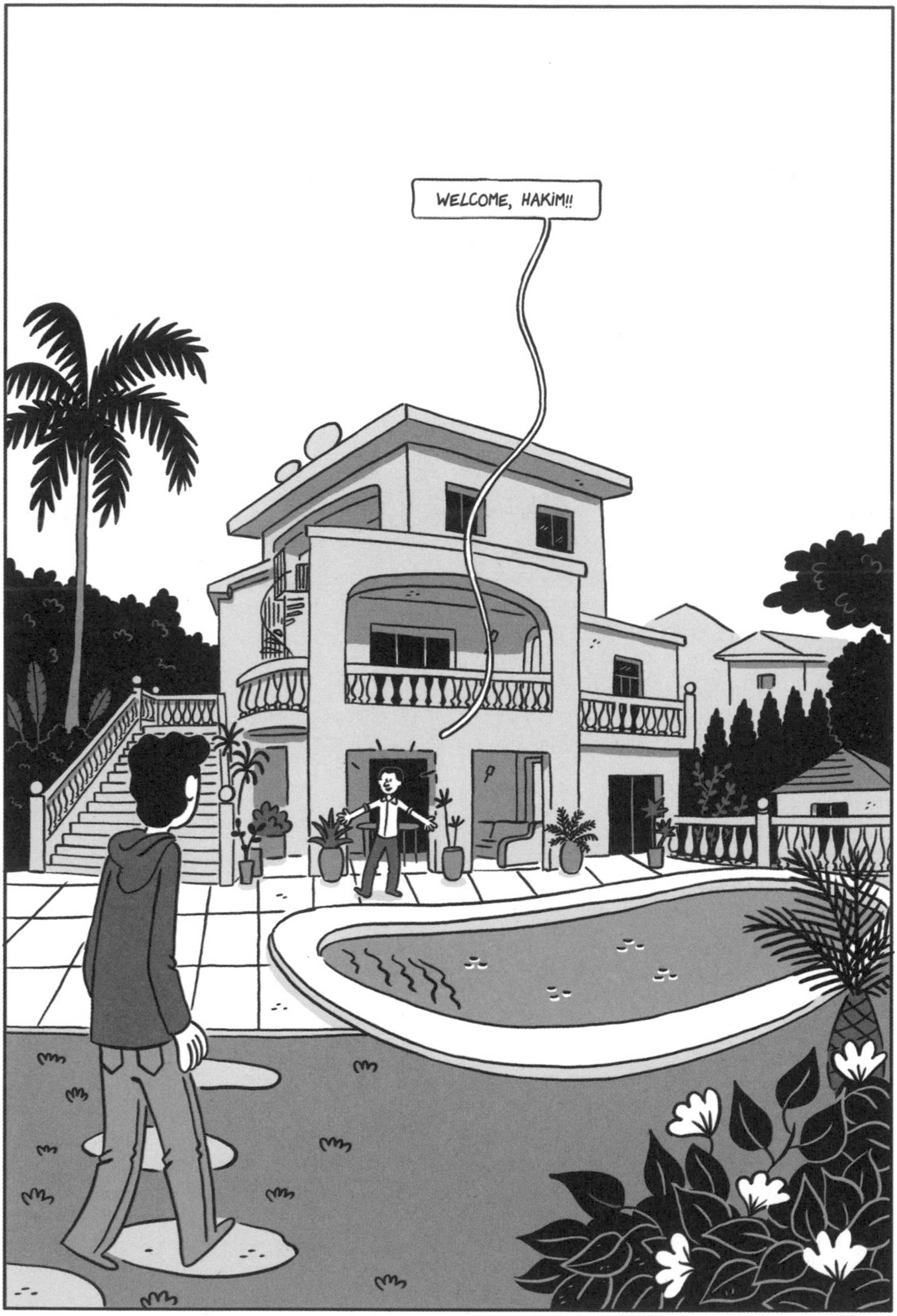
WELCOME, HAKIM!!

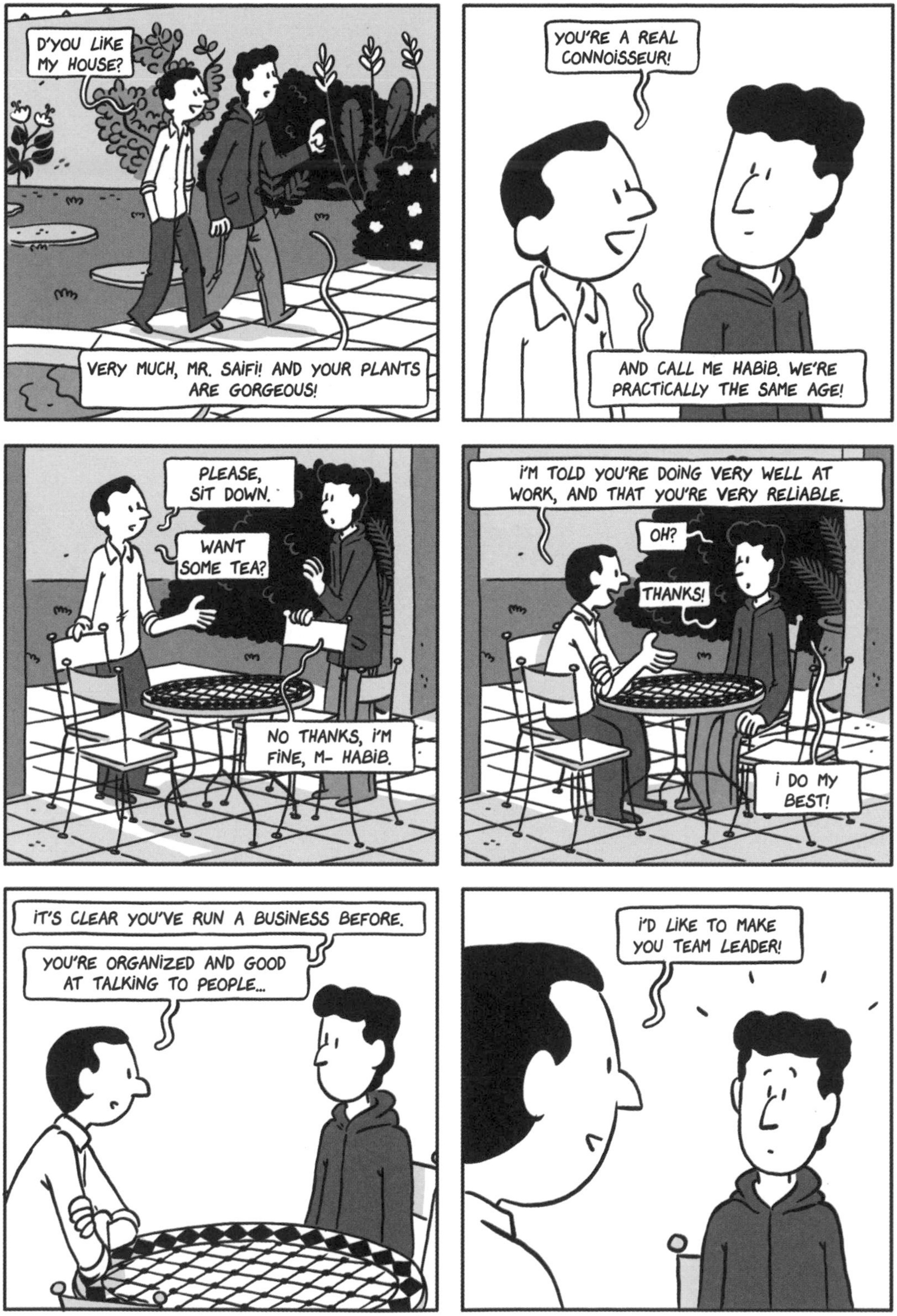
D'YOU LIKE MY HOUSE?
VERY MUCH, MR. SAIFI! AND YOUR PLANTS ARE GORGEOUS!
YOU'RE A REAL CONNOISSEUR!
AND CALL ME HABIB. WE'RE PRACTICALLY THE SAME AGE!
PLEASE, SIT DOWN.
WANT SOME TEA?
NO THANKS, I'M FINE, M– HABIB.
I'M TOLD YOU'RE DOING VERY WELL AT WORK, AND THAT YOU'RE VERY RELIABLE.
OH?
THANKS!
I DO MY BEST!
IT'S CLEAR YOU'VE RUN A BUSINESS BEFORE.
YOU'RE ORGANIZED AND GOOD AT TALKING TO PEOPLE...
I'D LIKE TO MAKE YOU TEAM LEADER!

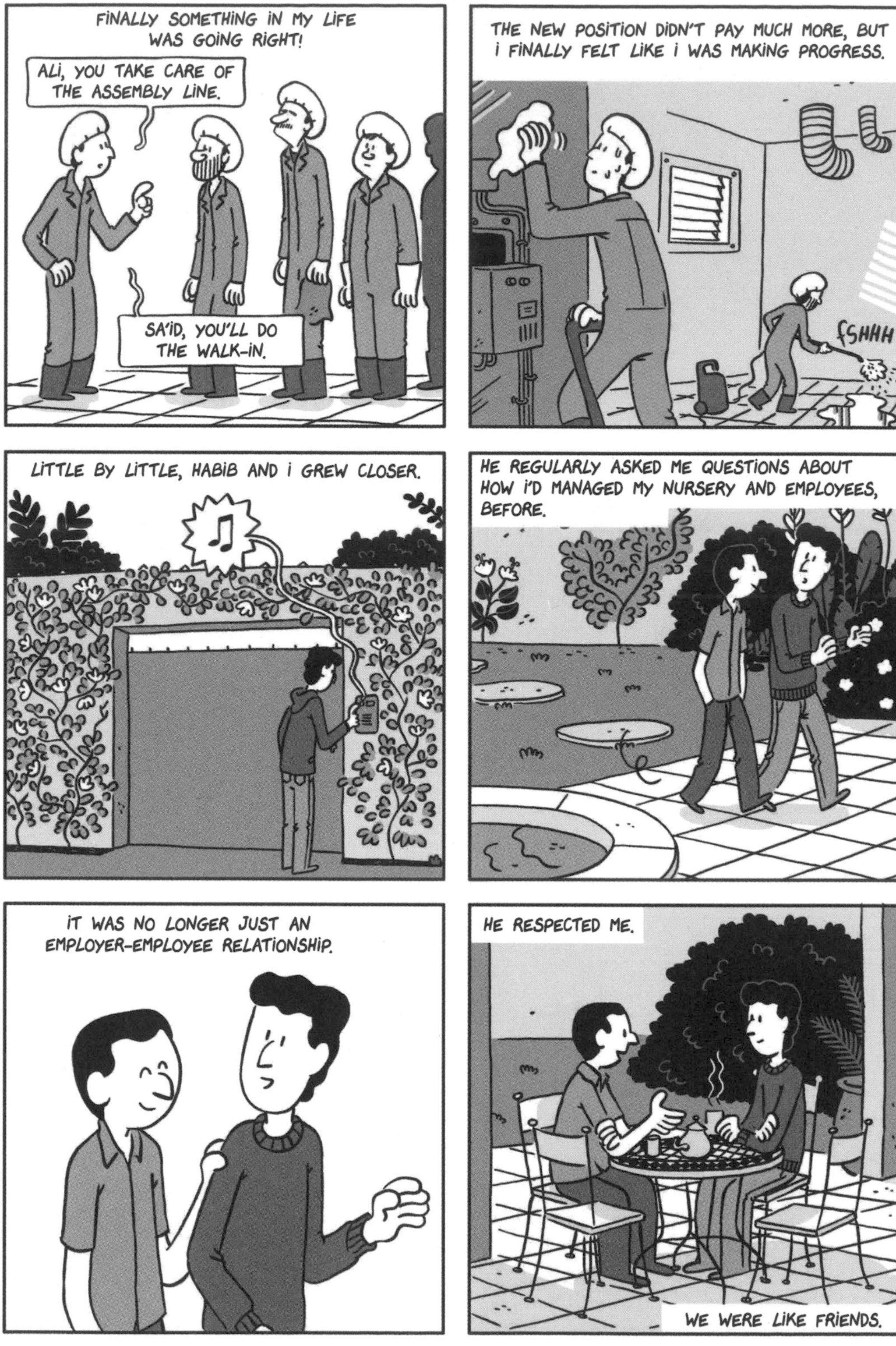
FINALLY SOMETHING IN MY LIFE WAS GOING RIGHT!
ALI, YOU TAKE CARE OF THE ASSEMBLY LINE.
SA'ID, YOU'LL DO THE WALK-IN.
THE NEW POSITION DIDN'T PAY MUCH MORE, BUT I FINALLY FELT LIKE I WAS MAKING PROGRESS.
FSHHH
LITTLE BY LITTLE, HABIB AND I GREW CLOSER.
HE REGULARLY ASKED ME QUESTIONS ABOUT HOW I'D MANAGED MY NURSERY AND EMPLOYEES, BEFORE.
IT WAS NO LONGER JUST AN EMPLOYER-EMPLOYEE RELATIONSHIP.
HE RESPECTED ME.
WE WERE LIKE FRIENDS.

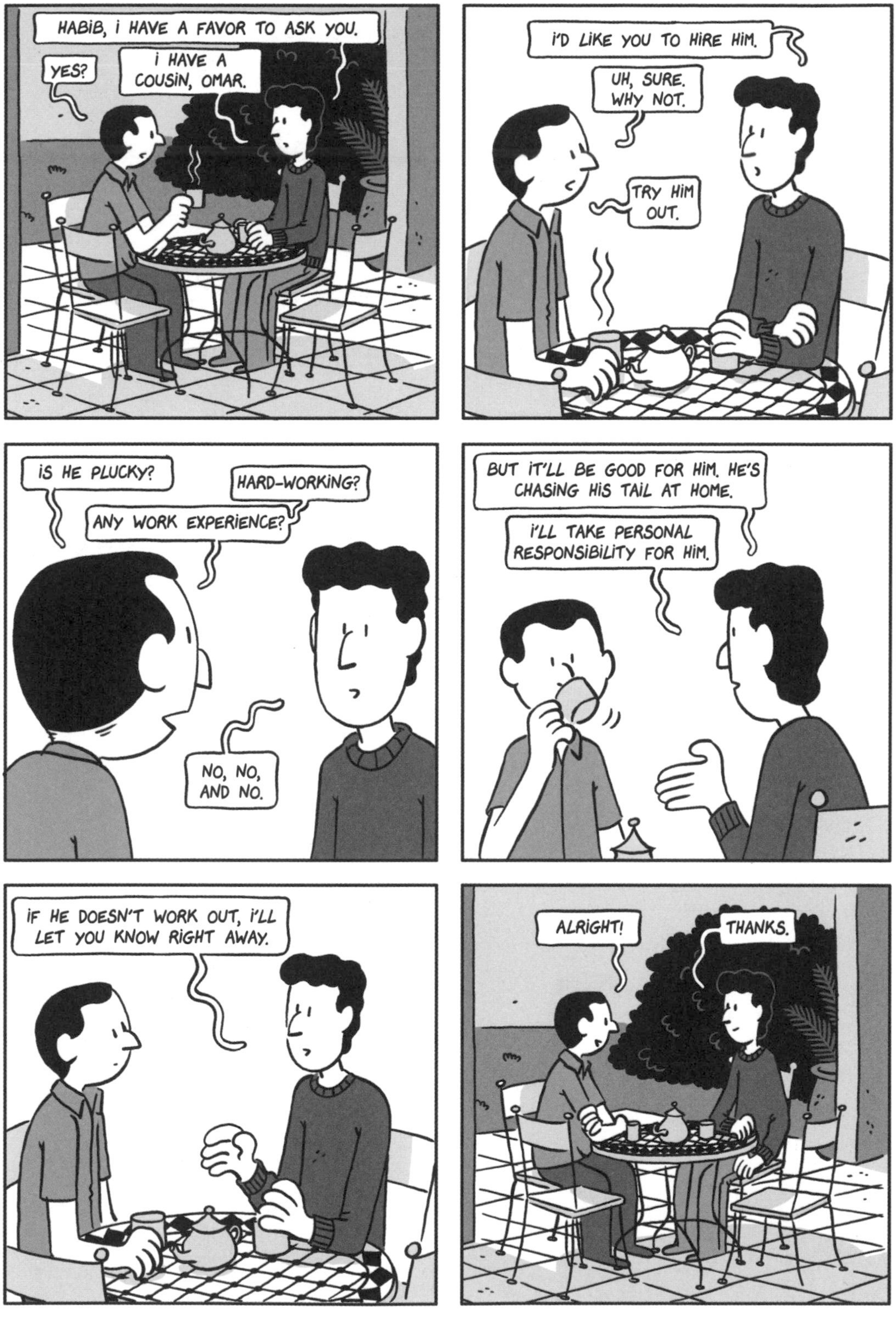
HABIB, I HAVE A FAVOR TO ASK YOU.
YES?
I HAVE A COUSIN, OMAR.
I'D LIKE YOU TO HIRE HIM.
UH, SURE. WHY NOT.
TRY HIM OUT.
IS HE PLUCKY?
HARD-WORKING?
ANY WORK EXPERIENCE?
NO, NO, AND NO.
BUT IT'LL BE GOOD FOR HIM. HE'S CHASING HIS TAIL AT HOME.
I'LL TAKE PERSONAL RESPONSIBILITY FOR HIM.
IF HE DOESN'T WORK OUT, I'LL LET YOU KNOW RIGHT AWAY.
ALRIGHT!
THANKS.

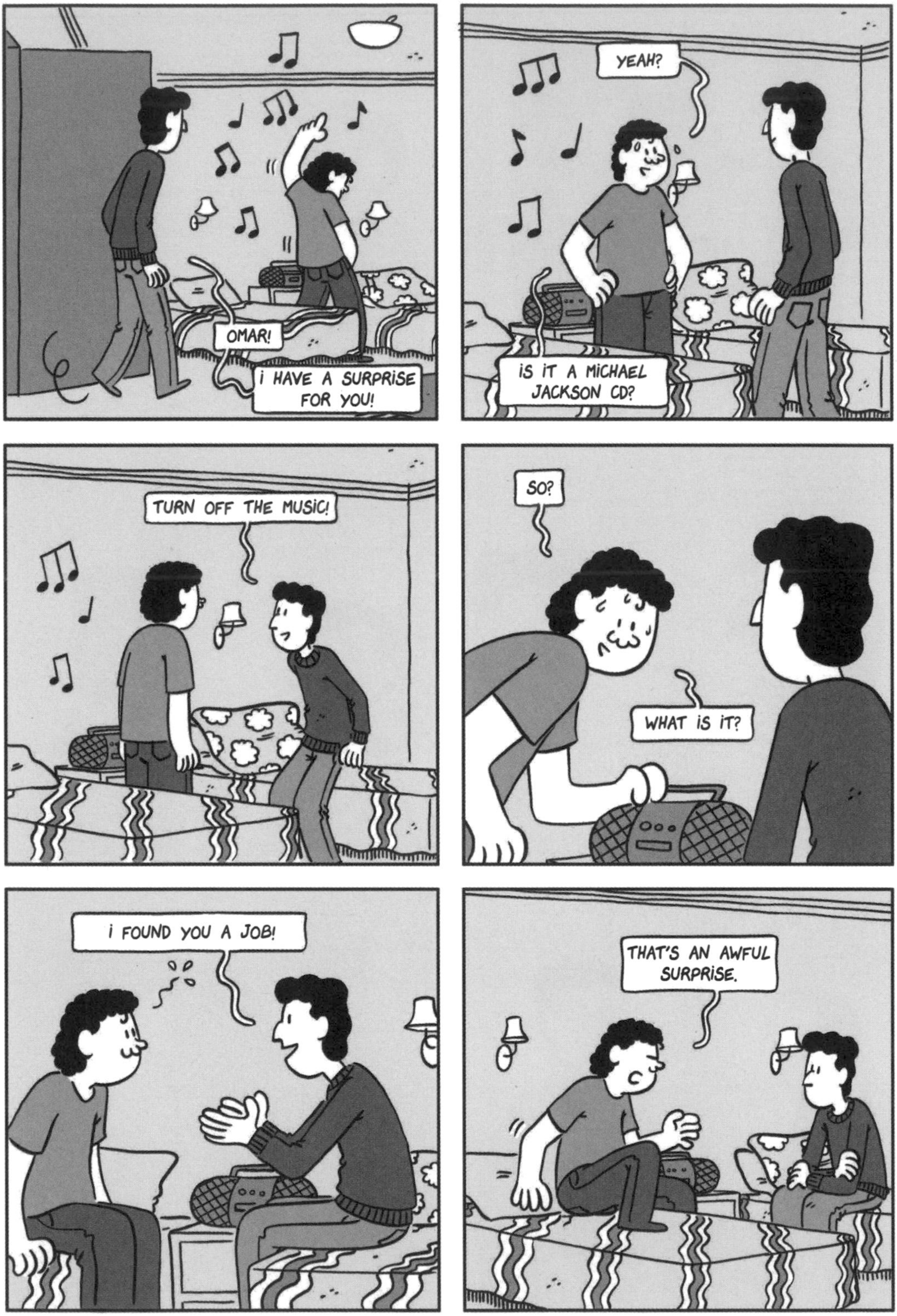
OMAR!
I HAVE A SURPRISE FOR YOU!
YEAH?
IS IT A MICHAEL JACKSON CD?
TURN OFF THE MUSIC!
SO?
WHAT IS IT?
I FOUND YOU A JOB!
THAT'S AN AWFUL SURPRISE.

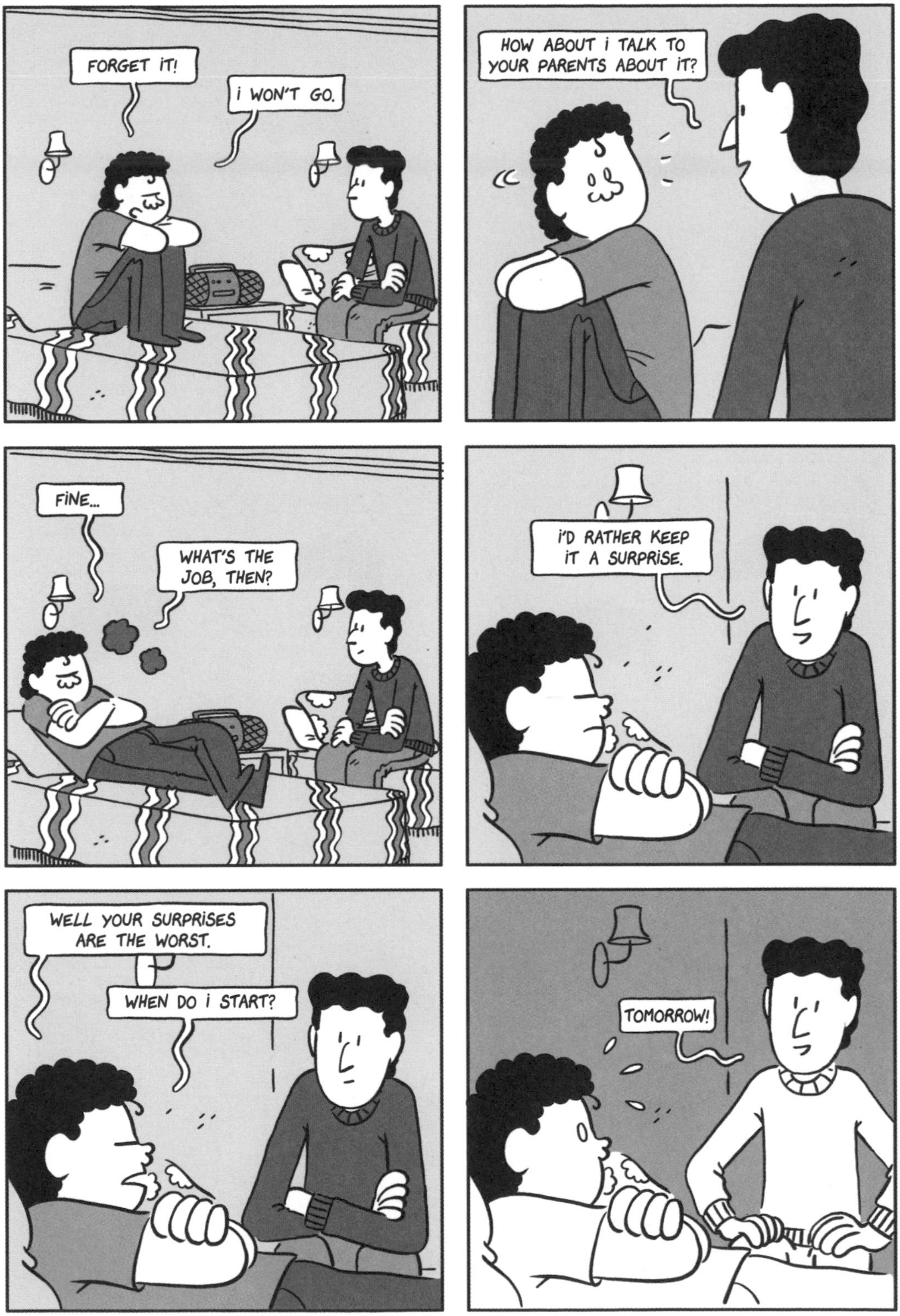
FORGET iT!
i WON'T GO.
HOW ABOUT i TALK TO YOUR PARENTS ABOUT iT?
FiNE...
WHAT'S THE JOB, THEN?
i'D RATHER KEEP iT A SURPRiSE.
WELL YOUR SURPRiSES ARE THE WORST.
WHEN DO i START?
TOMORROW!

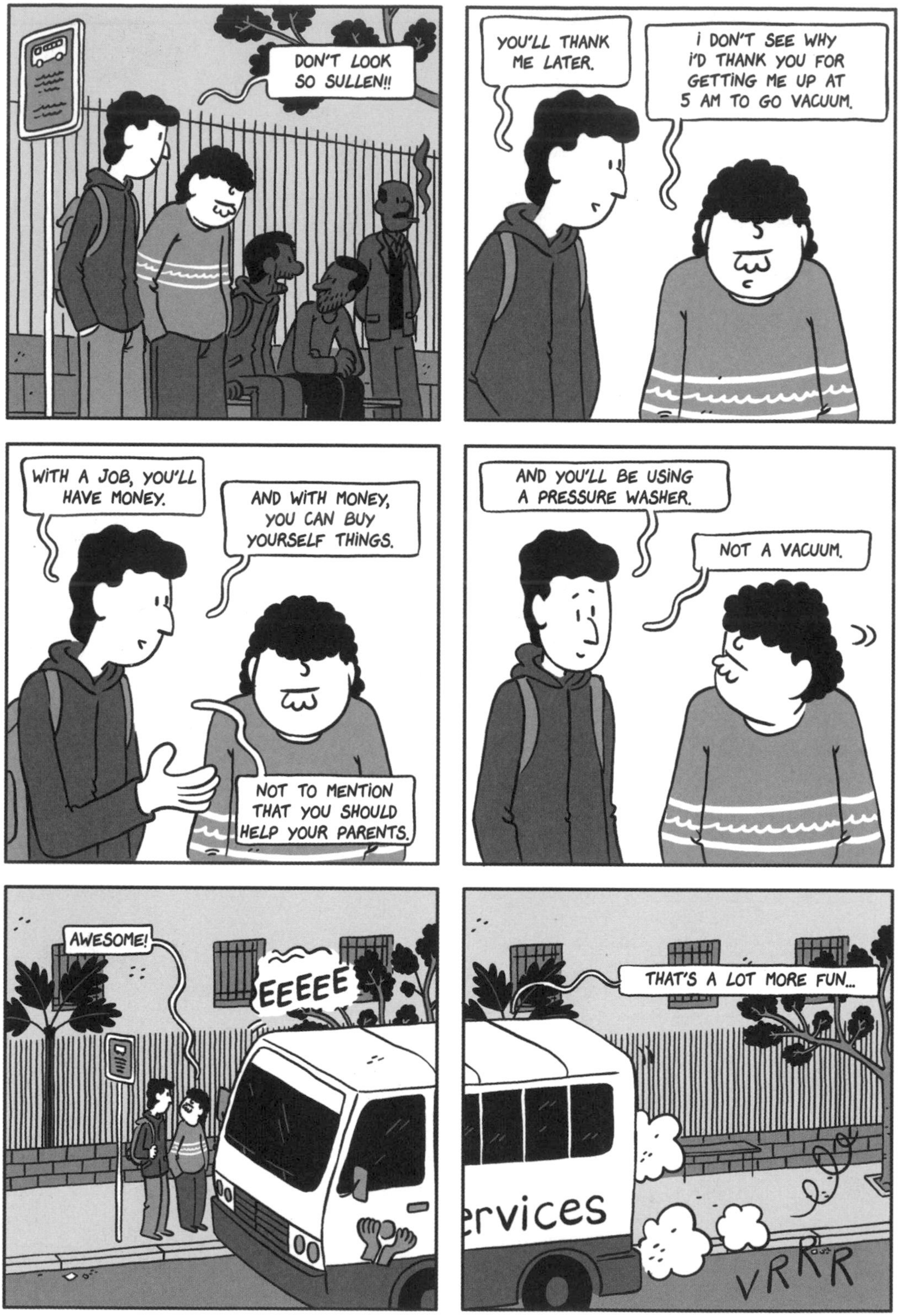
DON'T LOOK SO SULLEN!!
YOU'LL THANK ME LATER.
I DON'T SEE WHY I'D THANK YOU FOR GETTING ME UP AT 5 AM TO GO VACUUM.
WITH A JOB, YOU'LL HAVE MONEY.
AND WITH MONEY, YOU CAN BUY YOURSELF THINGS.
NOT TO MENTION THAT YOU SHOULD HELP YOUR PARENTS.
AND YOU'LL BE USING A PRESSURE WASHER.
NOT A VACUUM.
AWESOME!
EEEEE
THAT'S A LOT MORE FUN...
ervices
VRRR

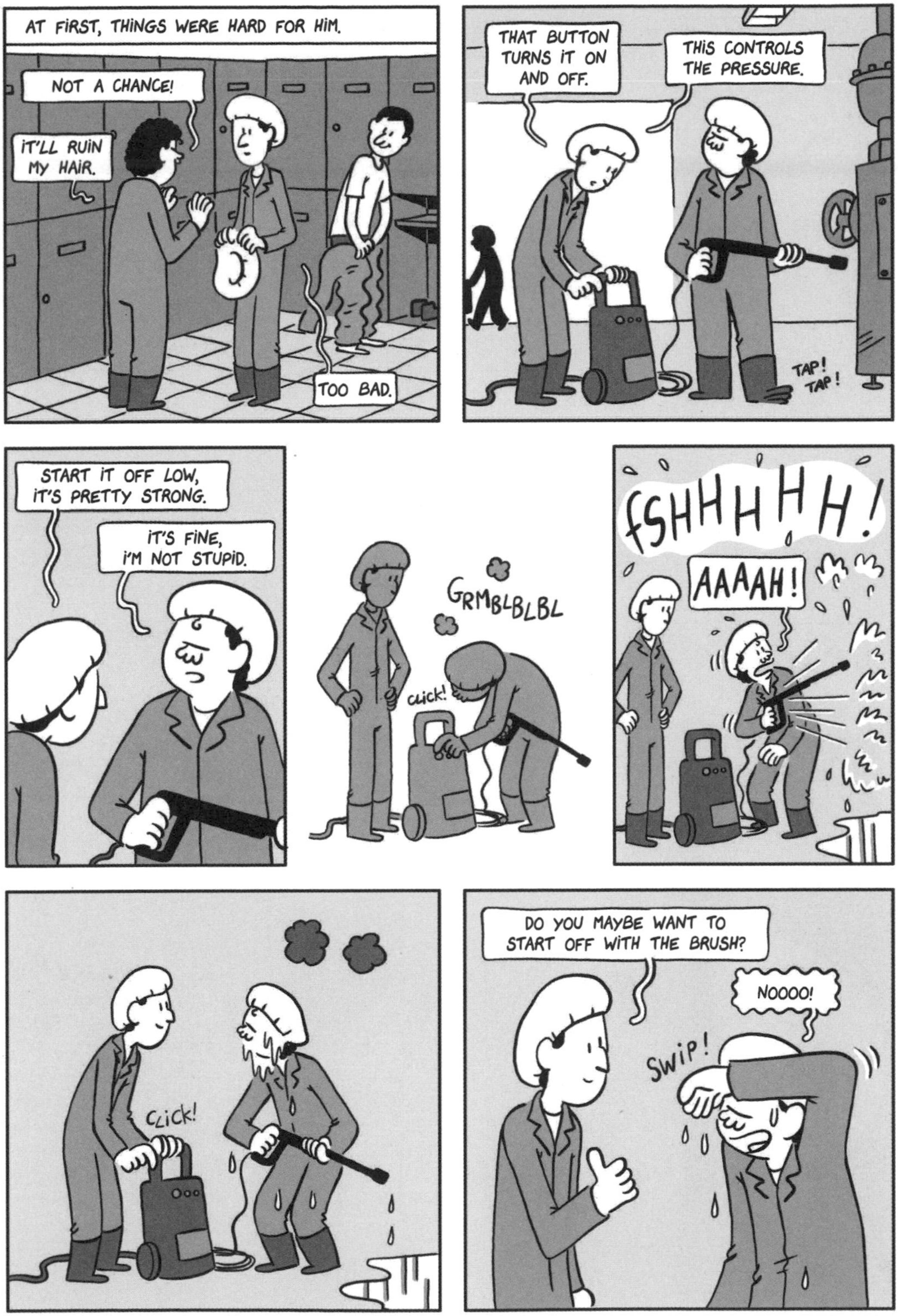
AT FIRST, THINGS WERE HARD FOR HIM.
NOT A CHANCE!
IT'LL RUIN MY HAIR.
TOO BAD.
THAT BUTTON TURNS IT ON AND OFF.
THIS CONTROLS THE PRESSURE.
TAP! TAP!
START IT OFF LOW, IT'S PRETTY STRONG.
IT'S FINE, I'M NOT STUPID.
GRMBLBLBL
CLICK!
FSHHHHHH!
AAAAH!
CLICK!
DO YOU MAYBE WANT TO START OFF WITH THE BRUSH?
NOOOO!
SWIP!

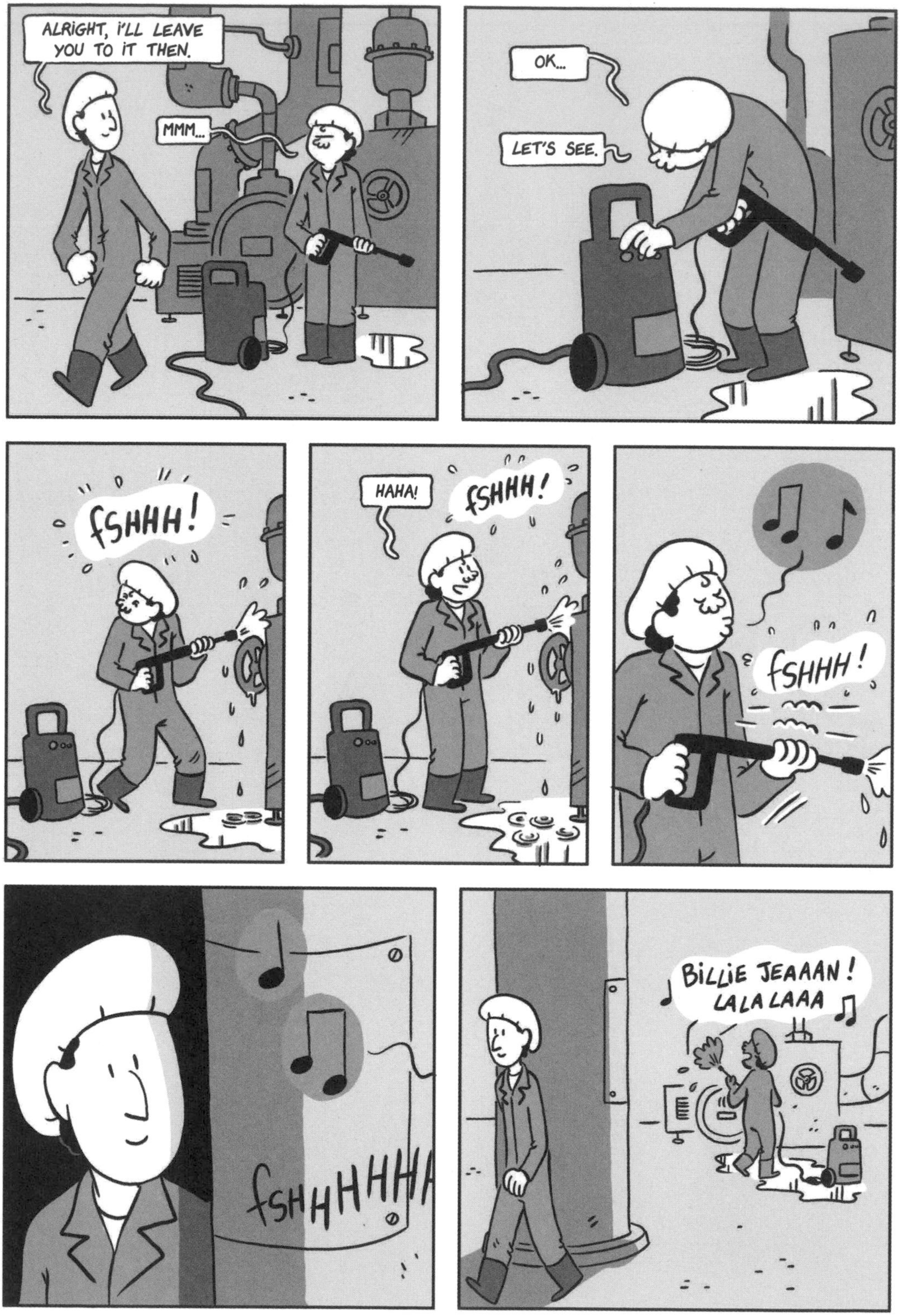
ALRIGHT, I'LL LEAVE YOU TO IT THEN.
MMM...
OK...
LET'S SEE.
fSHHH!
HAHA!
fSHHH!
fSHHH!
fSHHHHHH
BILLIE JEAAAN! LALA LAAA

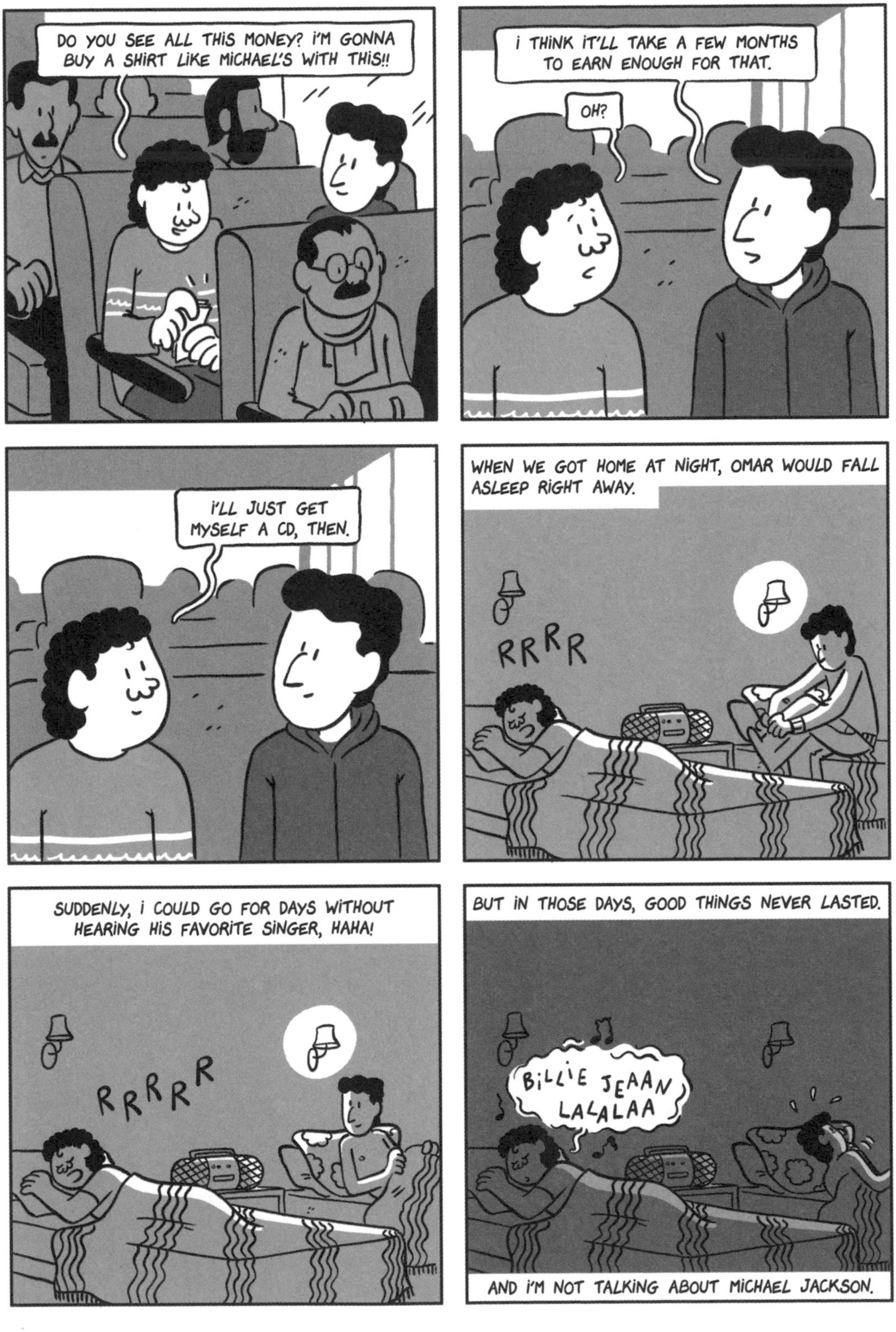
DO YOU SEE ALL THIS MONEY? I'M GONNA BUY A SHIRT LIKE MICHAEL'S WITH THIS!!
I THINK IT'LL TAKE A FEW MONTHS TO EARN ENOUGH FOR THAT.
OH?
I'LL JUST GET MYSELF A CD, THEN.
WHEN WE GOT HOME AT NIGHT, OMAR WOULD FALL ASLEEP RIGHT AWAY.
RRRR
SUDDENLY, I COULD GO FOR DAYS WITHOUT HEARING HIS FAVORITE SINGER, HAHA!
RRRRR
BUT IN THOSE DAYS, GOOD THINGS NEVER LASTED.
BILLIE JEAAN LALALAA
AND I'M NOT TALKING ABOUT MICHAEL JACKSON.

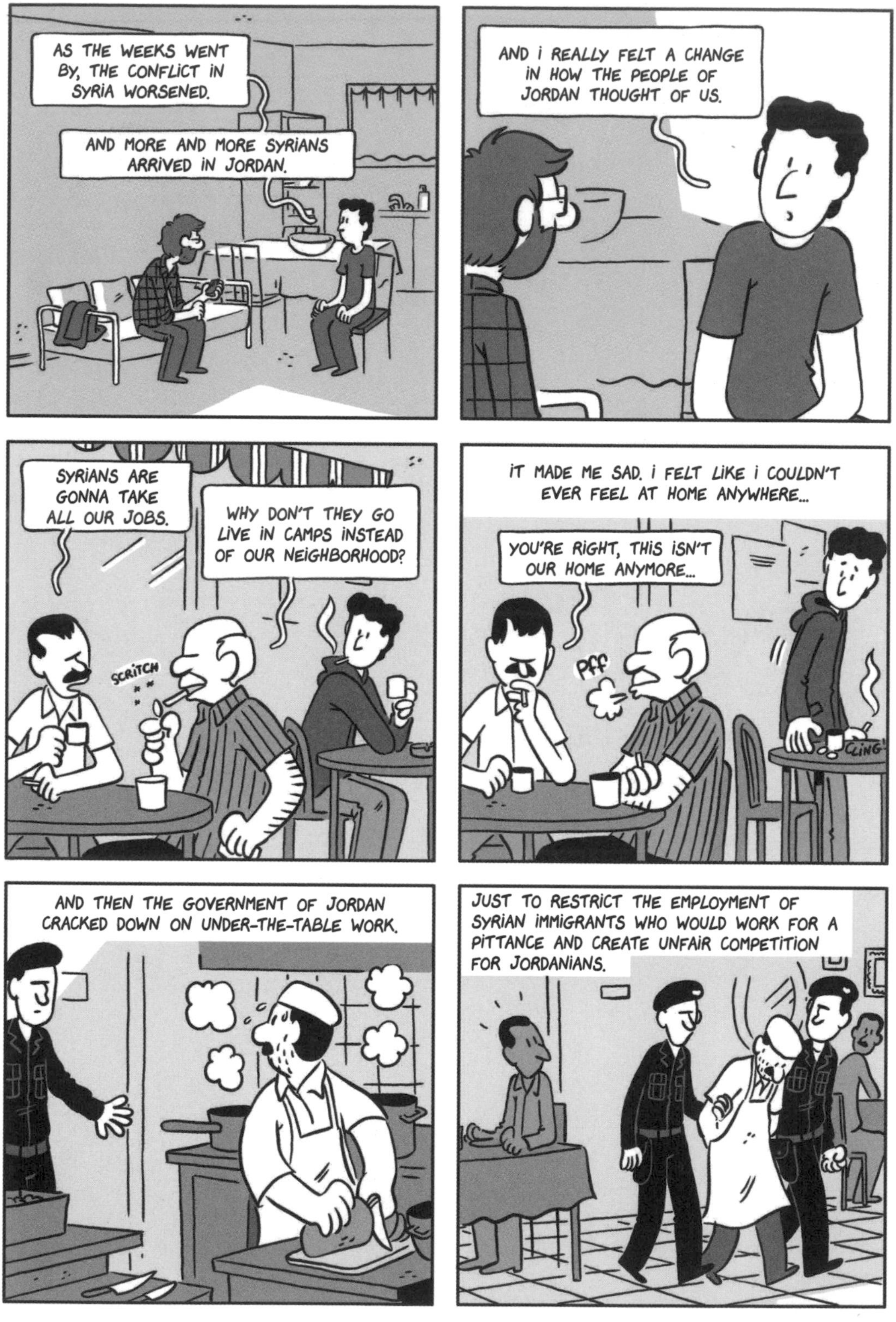
AS THE WEEKS WENT BY, THE CONFLICT IN SYRIA WORSENED.
AND MORE AND MORE SYRIANS ARRIVED IN JORDAN.
AND I REALLY FELT A CHANGE IN HOW THE PEOPLE OF JORDAN THOUGHT OF US.
SYRIANS ARE GONNA TAKE ALL OUR JOBS.
WHY DON'T THEY GO LIVE IN CAMPS INSTEAD OF OUR NEIGHBORHOOD?
SCRITCH
IT MADE ME SAD. I FELT LIKE I COULDN'T EVER FEEL AT HOME ANYWHERE...
YOU'RE RIGHT, THIS ISN'T OUR HOME ANYMORE...
PFF
CLING
AND THEN THE GOVERNMENT OF JORDAN CRACKED DOWN ON UNDER-THE-TABLE WORK.
JUST TO RESTRICT THE EMPLOYMENT OF SYRIAN IMMIGRANTS WHO WOULD WORK FOR A PITTANCE AND CREATE UNFAIR COMPETITION FOR JORDANIANS.

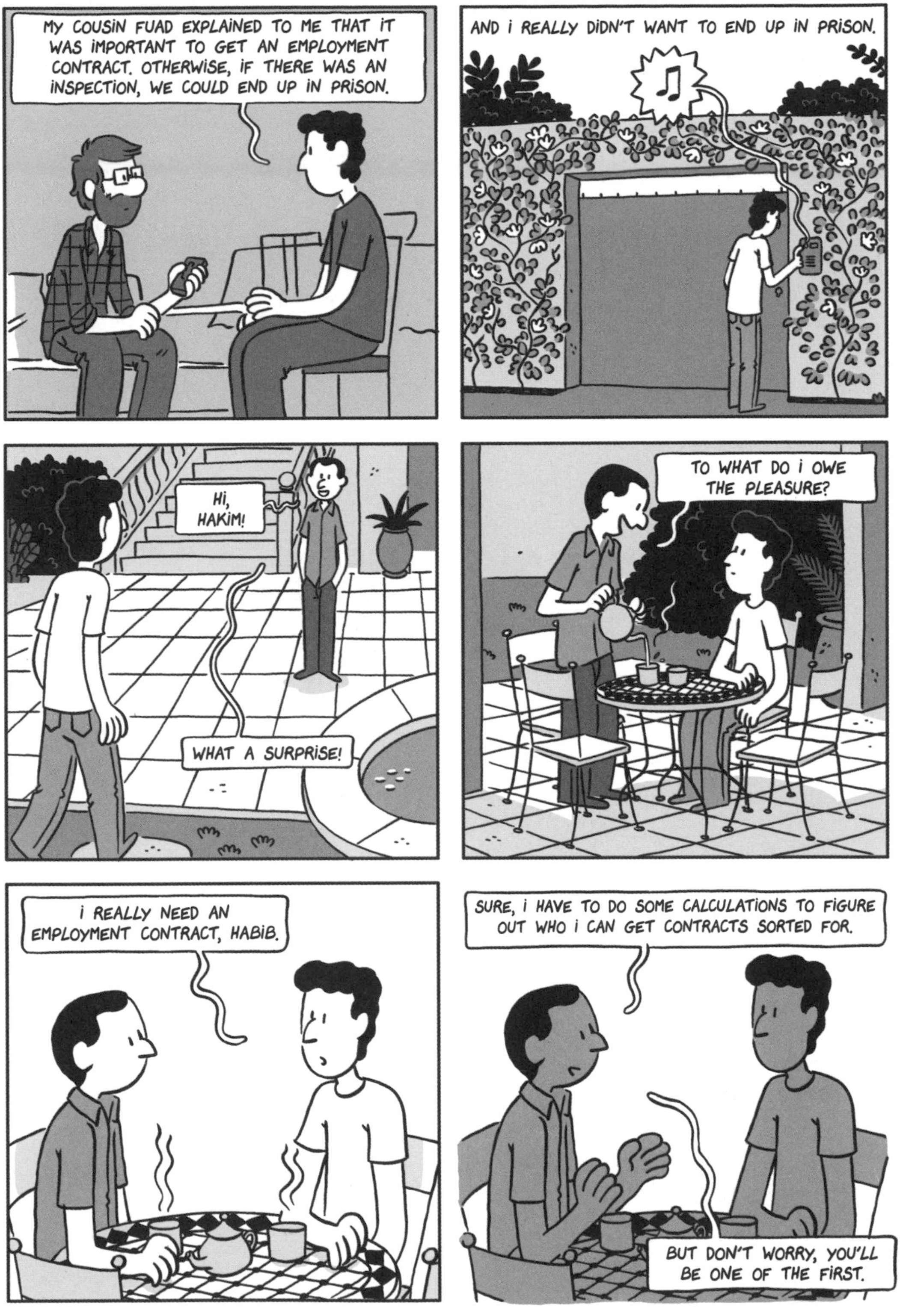
MY COUSIN FUAD EXPLAINED TO ME THAT IT WAS IMPORTANT TO GET AN EMPLOYMENT CONTRACT. OTHERWISE, IF THERE WAS AN INSPECTION, WE COULD END UP IN PRISON.
AND I REALLY DIDN'T WANT TO END UP IN PRISON.
HI, HAKIM!
WHAT A SURPRISE!
TO WHAT DO I OWE THE PLEASURE?
I REALLY NEED AN EMPLOYMENT CONTRACT, HABIB.
SURE, I HAVE TO DO SOME CALCULATIONS TO FIGURE OUT WHO I CAN GET CONTRACTS SORTED FOR.
BUT DON'T WORRY, YOU'LL BE ONE OF THE FIRST.

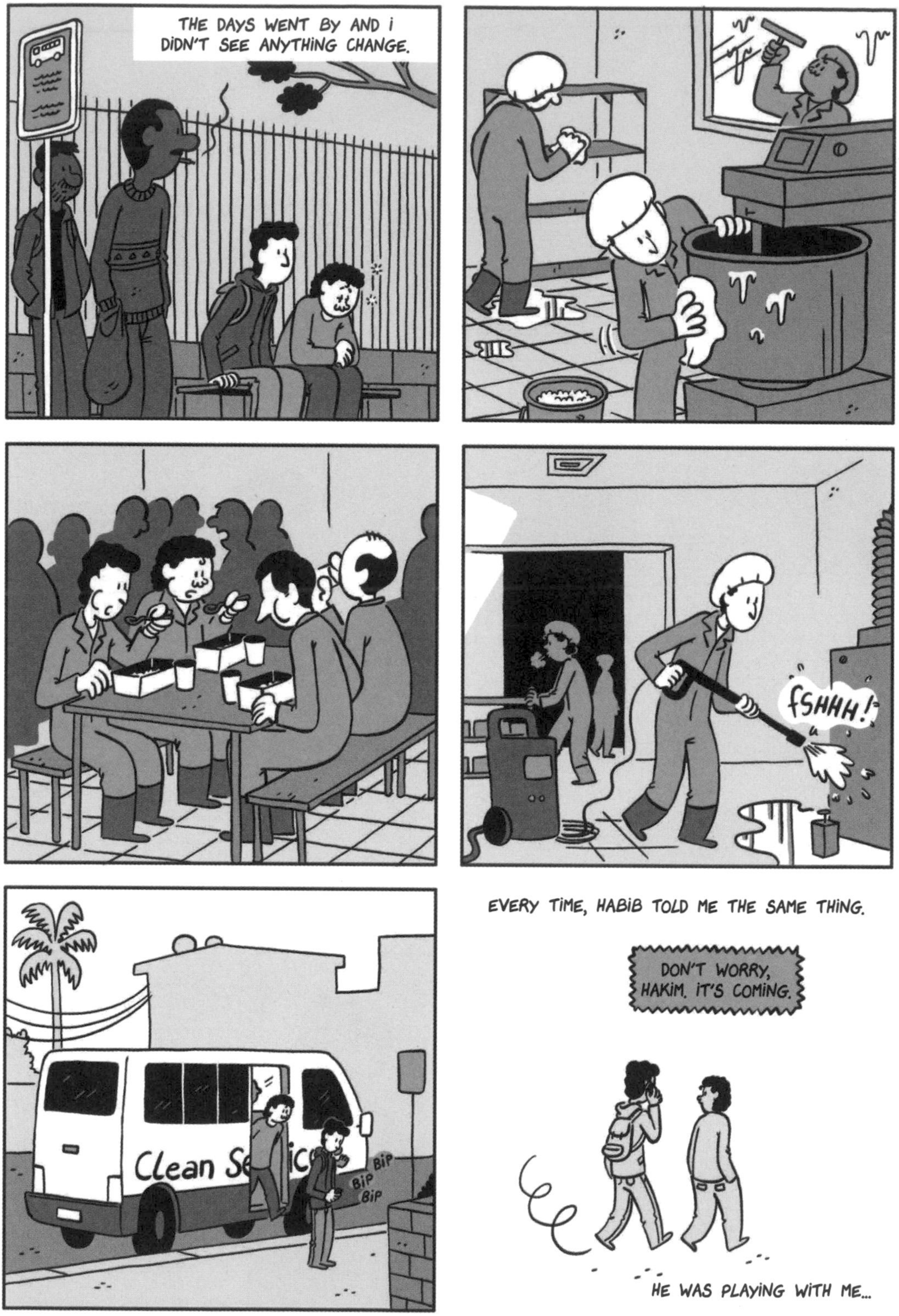
THE DAYS WENT BY AND I DIDN'T SEE ANYTHING CHANGE.
FSHHH!
BIP
BIP
BIP
EVERY TIME, HABIB TOLD ME THE SAME THING.
DON'T WORRY, HAKIM. IT'S COMING.
HE WAS PLAYING WITH ME...

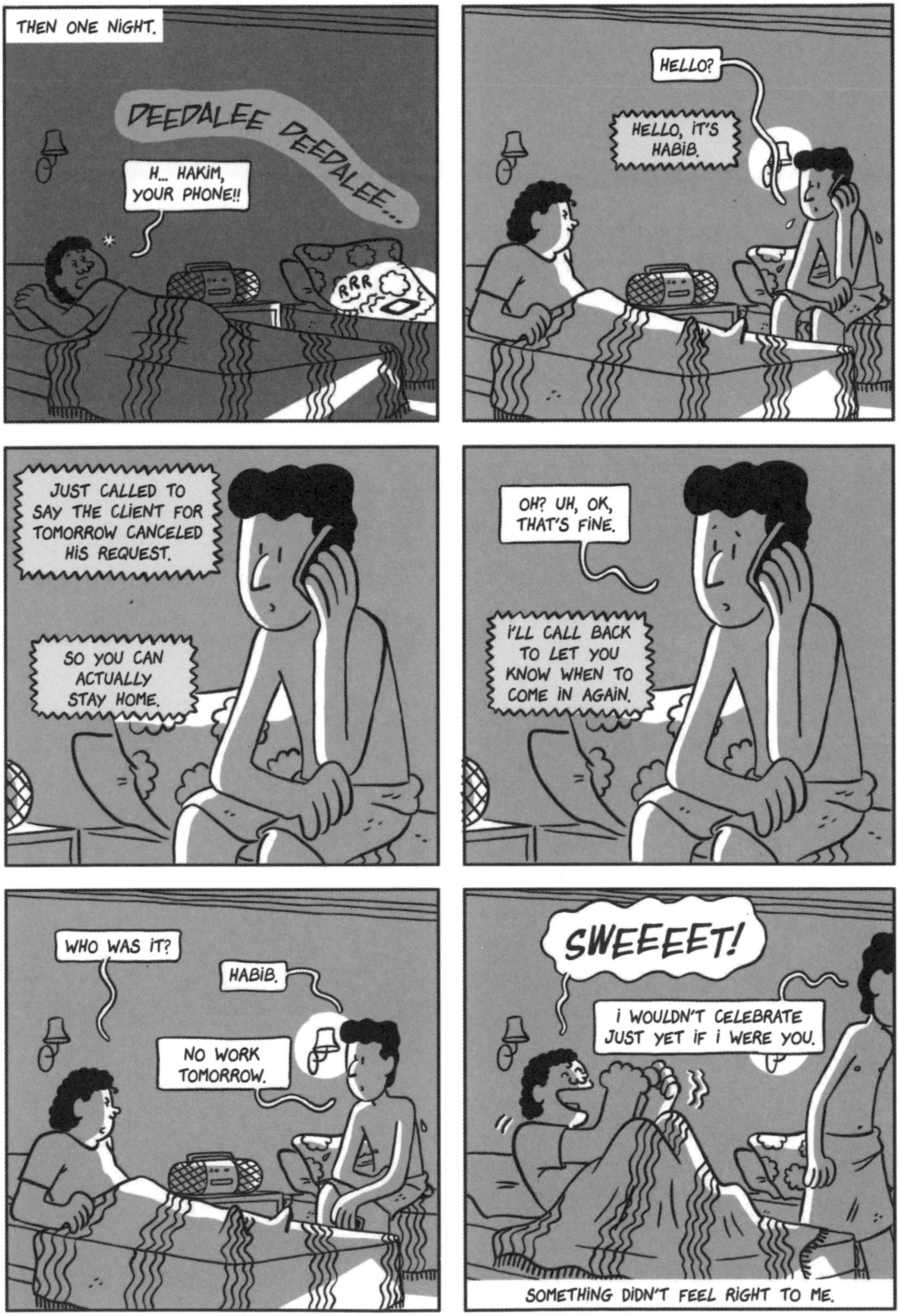
THEN ONE NIGHT.
DEEDALEE DEEDALEE DEEDALEE...
H... HAKIM, YOUR PHONE!!
RRR
HELLO?
HELLO, IT'S HABIB.
JUST CALLED TO SAY THE CLIENT FOR TOMORROW CANCELED HIS REQUEST.
SO YOU CAN ACTUALLY STAY HOME.
OH? UH, OK, THAT'S FINE.
I'LL CALL BACK TO LET YOU KNOW WHEN TO COME IN AGAIN.
WHO WAS IT?
HABIB.
NO WORK TOMORROW.
SWEEEET!
I WOULDN'T CELEBRATE JUST YET IF I WERE YOU.
SOMETHING DIDN'T FEEL RIGHT TO ME.

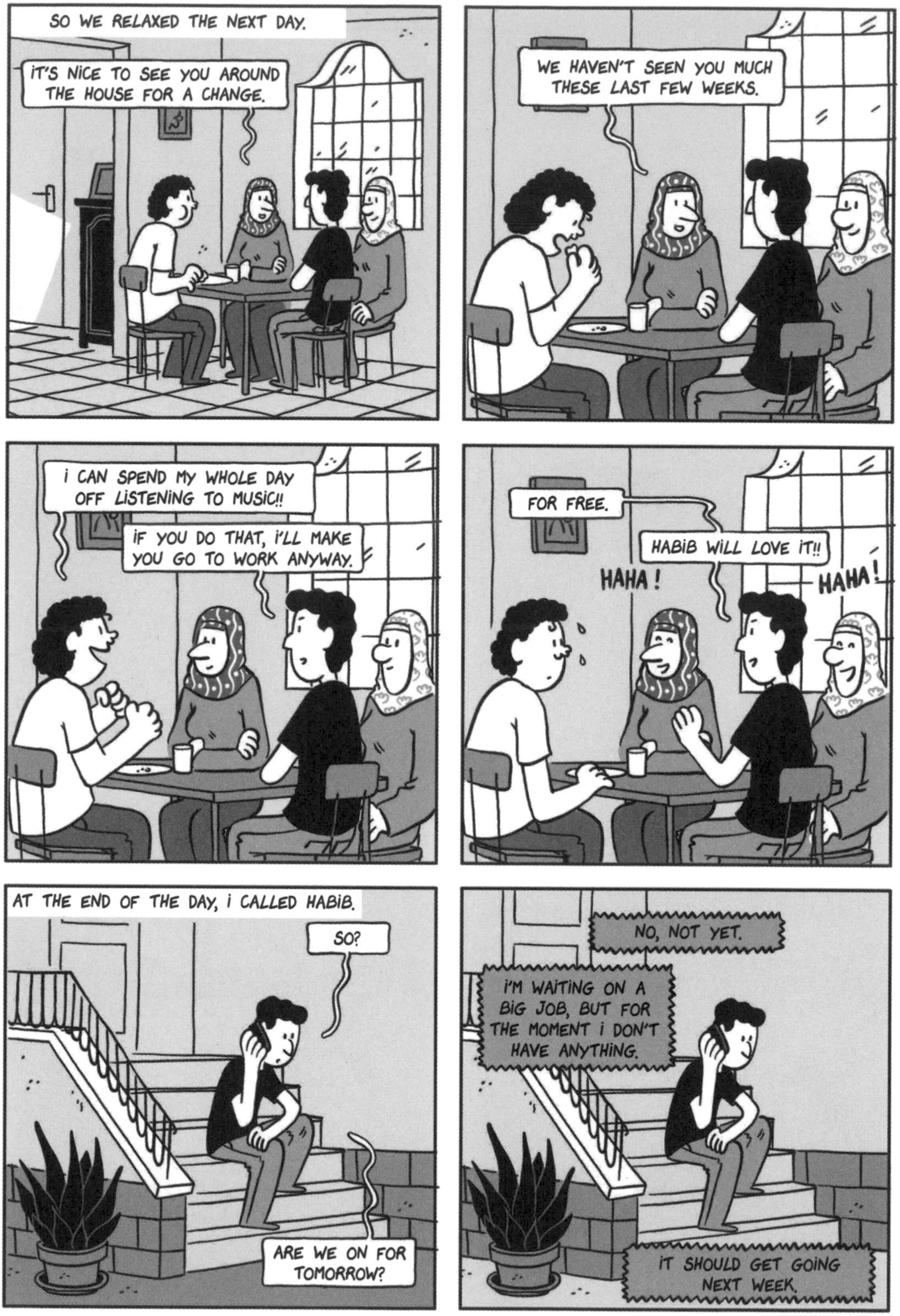
SO WE RELAXED THE NEXT DAY.
IT'S NICE TO SEE YOU AROUND THE HOUSE FOR A CHANGE.
WE HAVEN'T SEEN YOU MUCH THESE LAST FEW WEEKS.
I CAN SPEND MY WHOLE DAY OFF LISTENING TO MUSIC!!
IF YOU DO THAT, I'LL MAKE YOU GO TO WORK ANYWAY.
FOR FREE.
HABIB WILL LOVE IT!!
HAHA!
HAHA!
AT THE END OF THE DAY, I CALLED HABIB.
SO?
ARE WE ON FOR TOMORROW?
NO, NOT YET.
I'M WAITING ON A BIG JOB, BUT FOR THE MOMENT I DON'T HAVE ANYTHING.
IT SHOULD GET GOING NEXT WEEK.

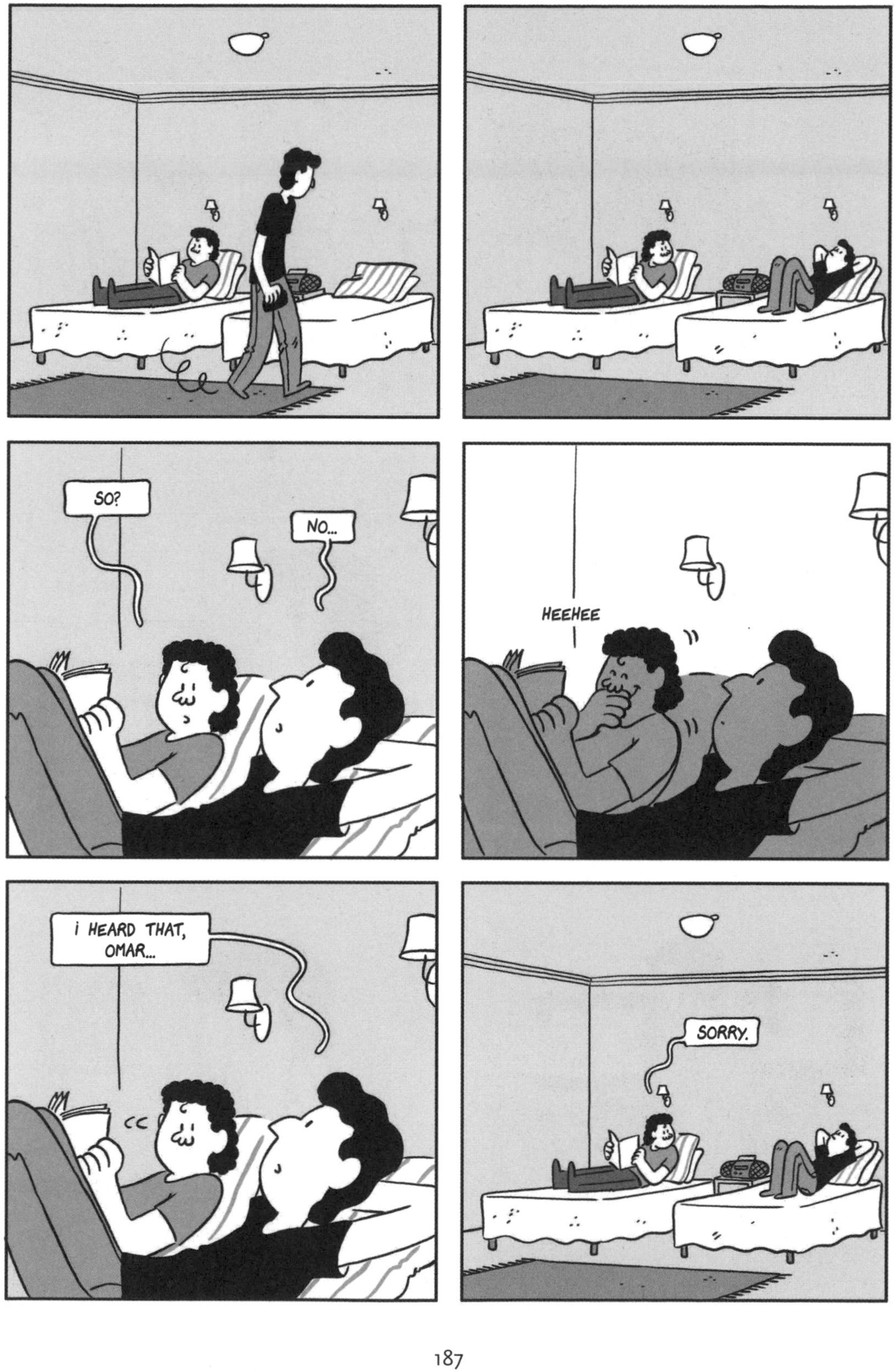
SO?
NO...
HEEHEE
I HEARD THAT, OMAR...
SORRY.

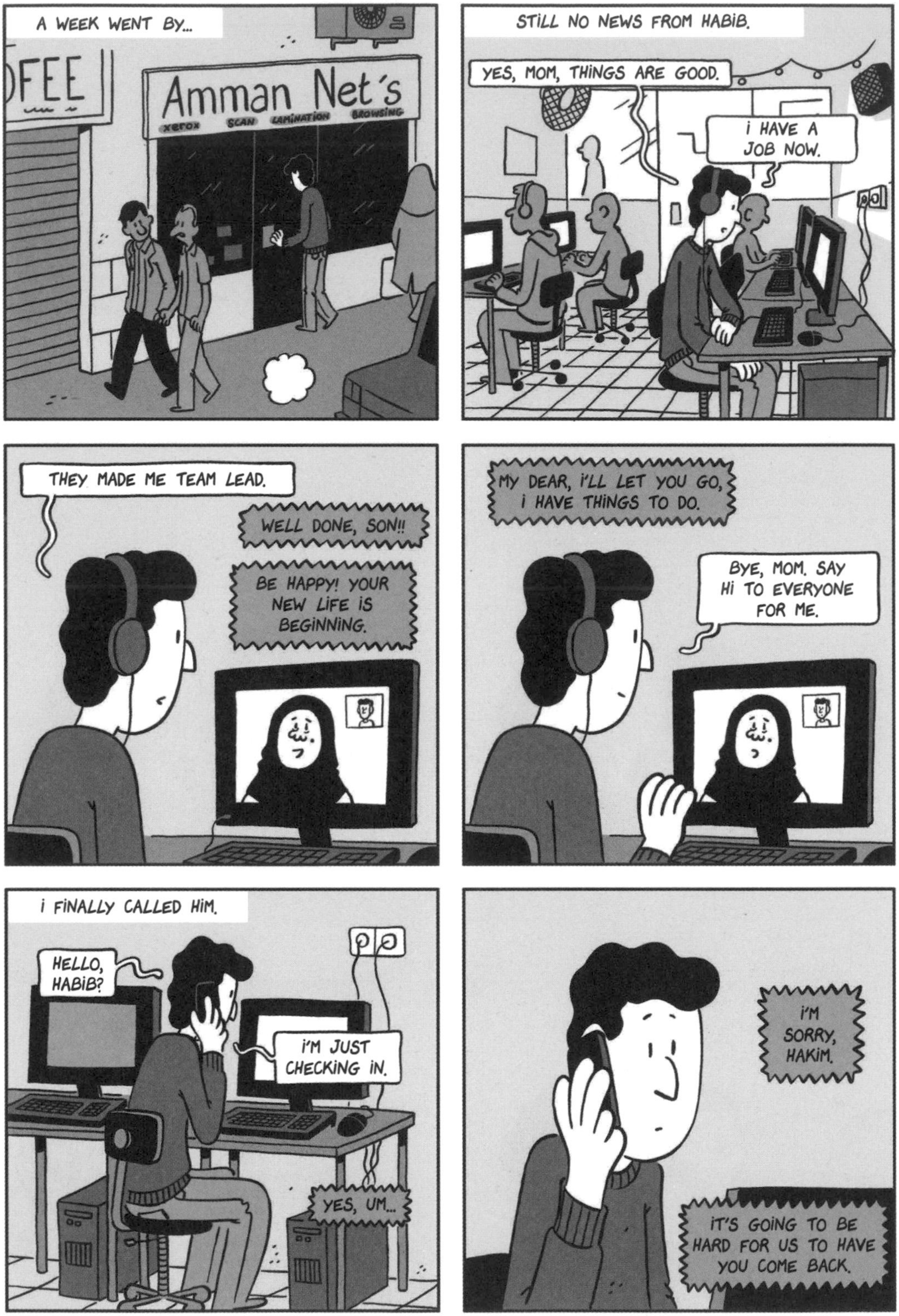
A WEEK WENT BY...
OFEE
Amman Net´s
xerox SCAN LAMINATION BROWSING
STILL NO NEWS FROM HABIB.
YES, MOM, THINGS ARE GOOD.
I HAVE A JOB NOW.
THEY MADE ME TEAM LEAD.
WELL DONE, SON!!
BE HAPPY! YOUR NEW LIFE IS BEGINNING.
MY DEAR, I'LL LET YOU GO, I HAVE THINGS TO DO.
BYE, MOM. SAY HI TO EVERYONE FOR ME.
I FINALLY CALLED HIM.
HELLO, HABIB?
I'M JUST CHECKING IN.
YES, UM...
I'M SORRY, HAKIM.
IT'S GOING TO BE HARD FOR US TO HAVE YOU COME BACK.

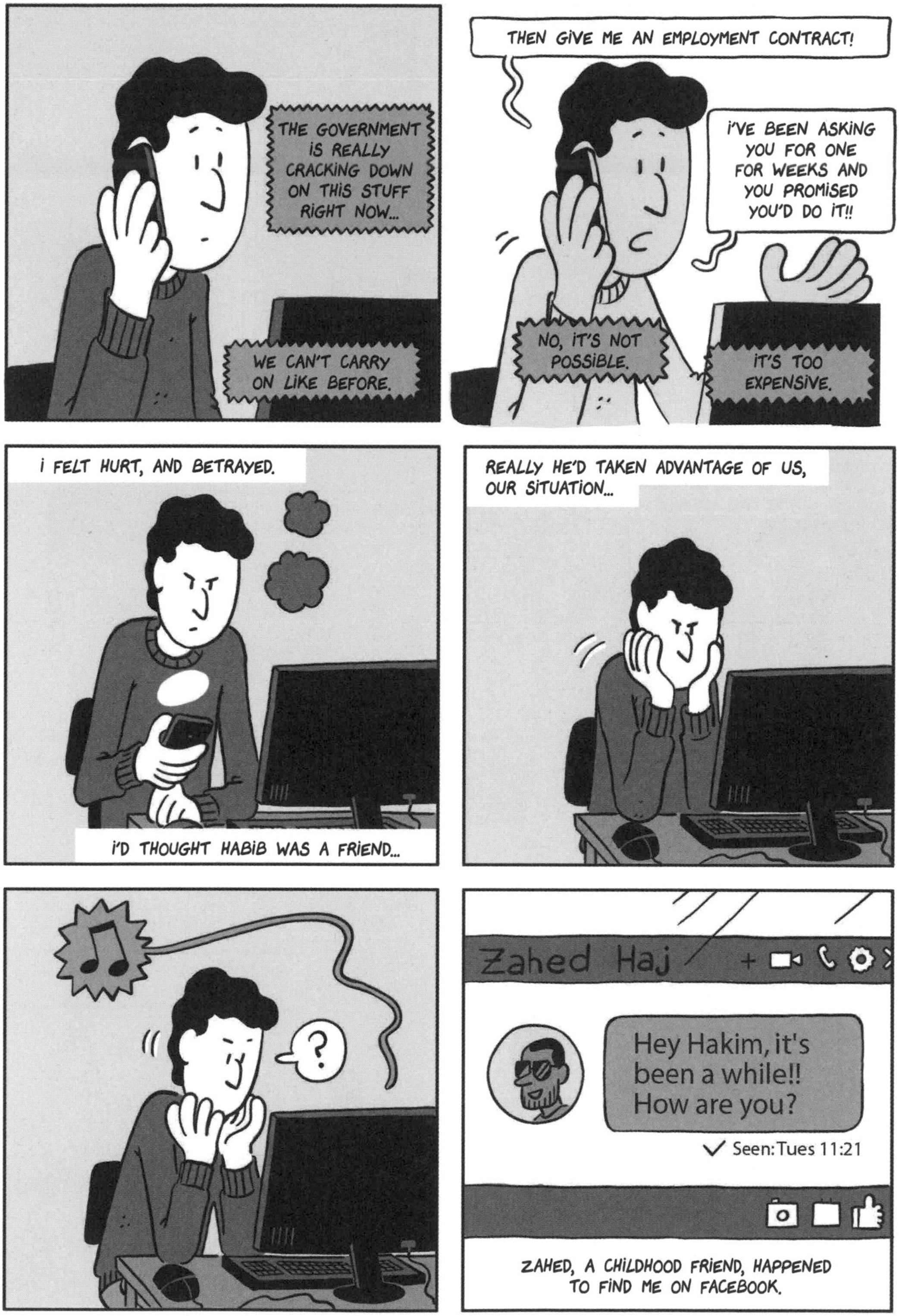
THE GOVERNMENT IS REALLY CRACKING DOWN ON THIS STUFF RIGHT NOW...
WE CAN'T CARRY ON LIKE BEFORE.
THEN GIVE ME AN EMPLOYMENT CONTRACT!
I'VE BEEN ASKING YOU FOR ONE FOR WEEKS AND YOU PROMISED YOU'D DO IT!!
NO, IT'S NOT POSSIBLE.
IT'S TOO EXPENSIVE.
I FELT HURT, AND BETRAYED.
I'D THOUGHT HABIB WAS A FRIEND...
REALLY HE'D TAKEN ADVANTAGE OF US, OUR SITUATION...
?
Zahed Haj
Hey Hakim, it's been a while!! How are you?
Seen:Tues 11:21
ZAHED, A CHILDHOOD FRIEND, HAPPENED TO FIND ME ON FACEBOOK.

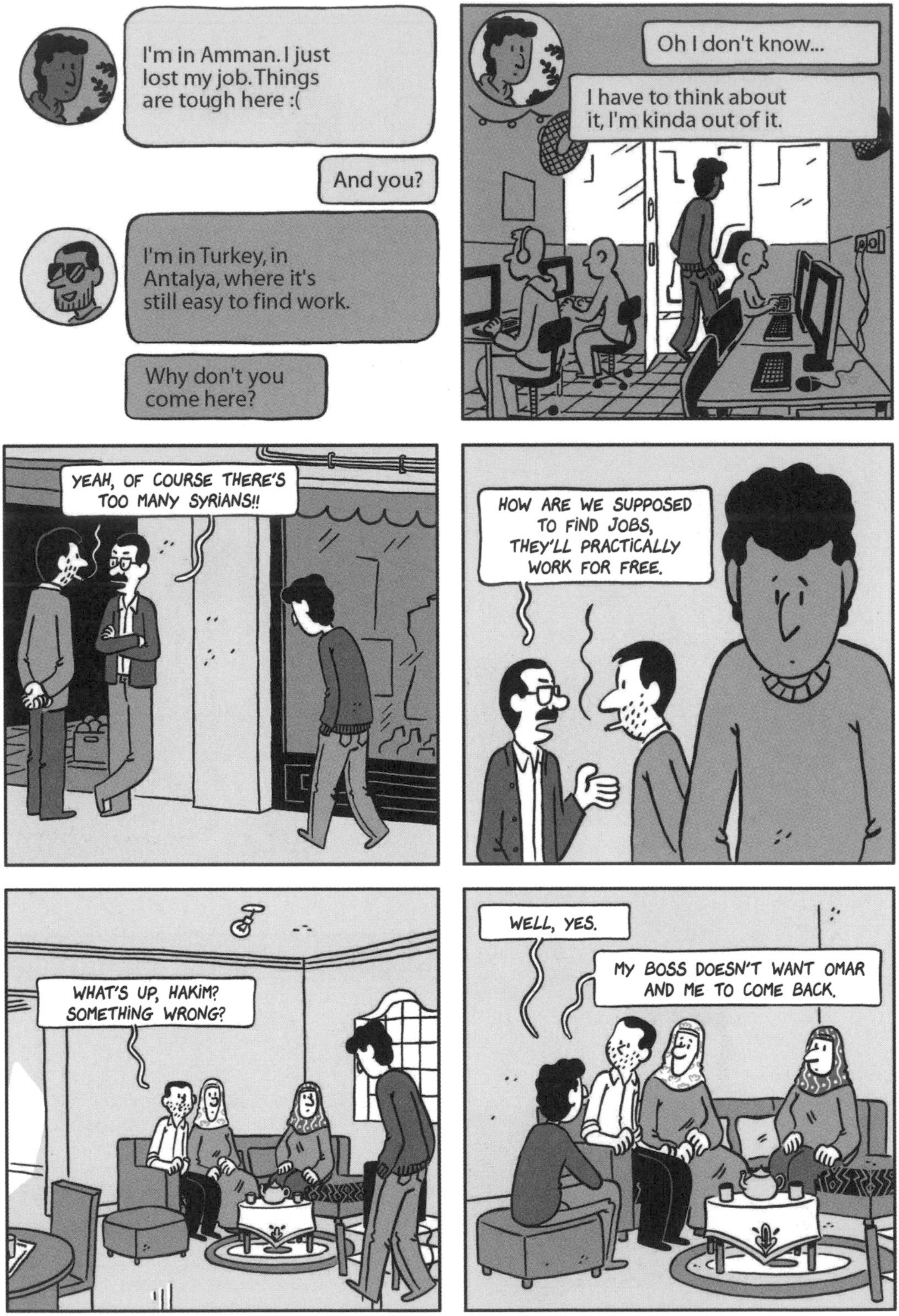
I'm in Amman. I just lost my job. Things are tough here :(
And you?
I'm in Turkey, in Antalya, where it's still easy to find work.
Why don't you come here?
Oh I don't know...
I have to think about it, I'm kinda out of it.
YEAH, OF COURSE THERE'S TOO MANY SYRIANS!!
HOW ARE WE SUPPOSED TO FIND JOBS, THEY'LL PRACTICALLY WORK FOR FREE.
WHAT'S UP, HAKIM? SOMETHING WRONG?
WELL, YES.
MY BOSS DOESN'T WANT OMAR AND ME TO COME BACK.

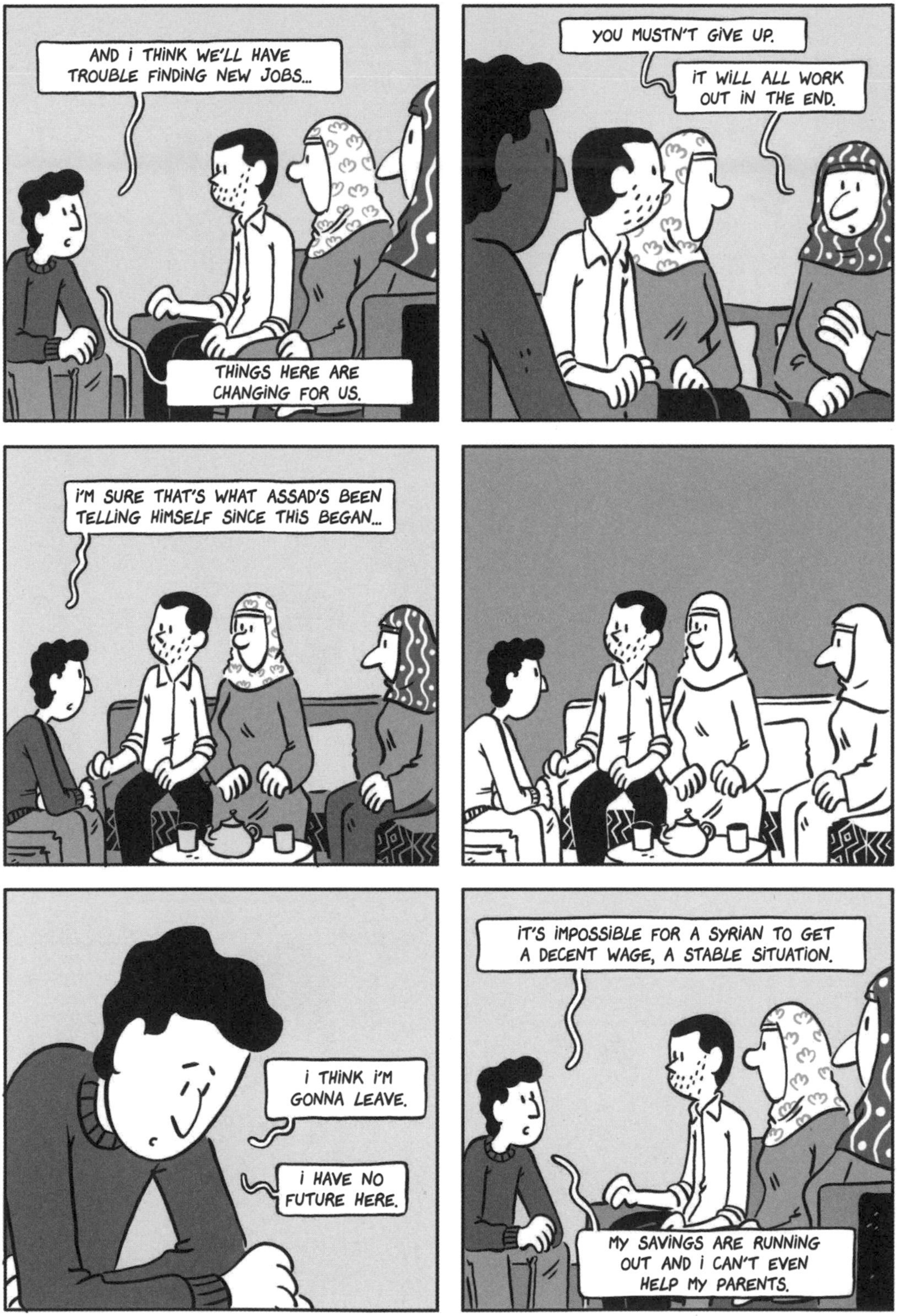
AND I THINK WE'LL HAVE TROUBLE FINDING NEW JOBS...
THINGS HERE ARE CHANGING FOR US.
YOU MUSTN'T GIVE UP.
IT WILL ALL WORK OUT IN THE END.
I'M SURE THAT'S WHAT ASSAD'S BEEN TELLING HIMSELF SINCE THIS BEGAN...
I THINK I'M GONNA LEAVE.
I HAVE NO FUTURE HERE.
IT'S IMPOSSIBLE FOR A SYRIAN TO GET A DECENT WAGE, A STABLE SITUATION.
MY SAVINGS ARE RUNNING OUT AND I CAN'T EVEN HELP MY PARENTS.

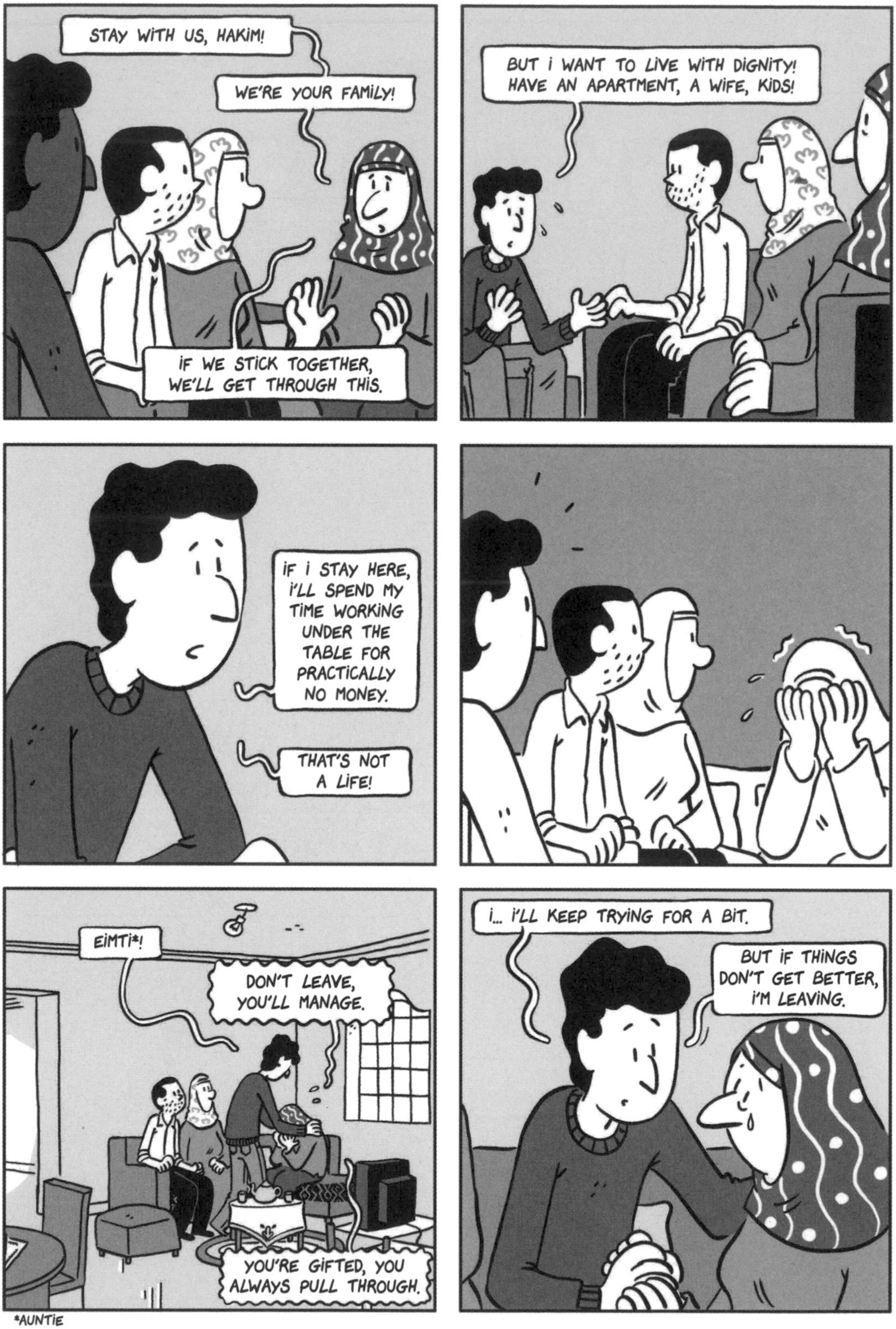
STAY WITH US, HAKIM!
WE'RE YOUR FAMILY!
IF WE STICK TOGETHER, WE'LL GET THROUGH THIS.
BUT I WANT TO LIVE WITH DIGNITY! HAVE AN APARTMENT, A WIFE, KIDS!
IF I STAY HERE, I'LL SPEND MY TIME WORKING UNDER THE TABLE FOR PRACTICALLY NO MONEY.
THAT'S NOT A LIFE!
EIMTI*!
DON'T LEAVE, YOU'LL MANAGE.
YOU'RE GIFTED, YOU ALWAYS PULL THROUGH.
I... I'LL KEEP TRYING FOR A BIT.
BUT IF THINGS DON'T GET BETTER, I'M LEAVING.

*AUNTIE

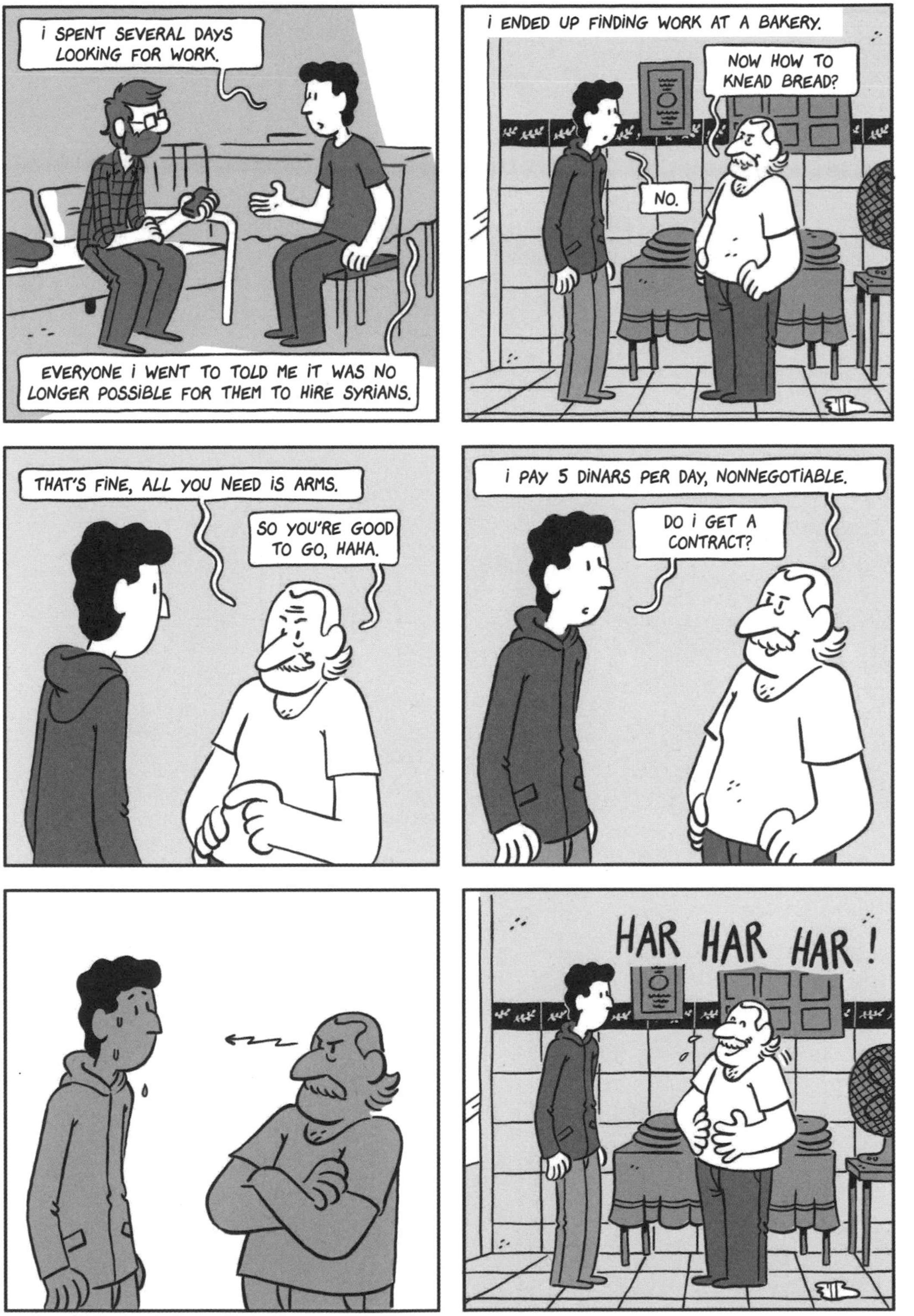
I SPENT SEVERAL DAYS LOOKING FOR WORK.
EVERYONE I WENT TO TOLD ME IT WAS NO LONGER POSSIBLE FOR THEM TO HIRE SYRIANS.
I ENDED UP FINDING WORK AT A BAKERY.
NOW HOW TO KNEAD BREAD?
NO.
THAT'S FINE, ALL YOU NEED IS ARMS.
SO YOU'RE GOOD TO GO, HAHA.
I PAY 5 DINARS PER DAY, NONNEGOTIABLE.
DO I GET A CONTRACT?
HAR HAR HAR!

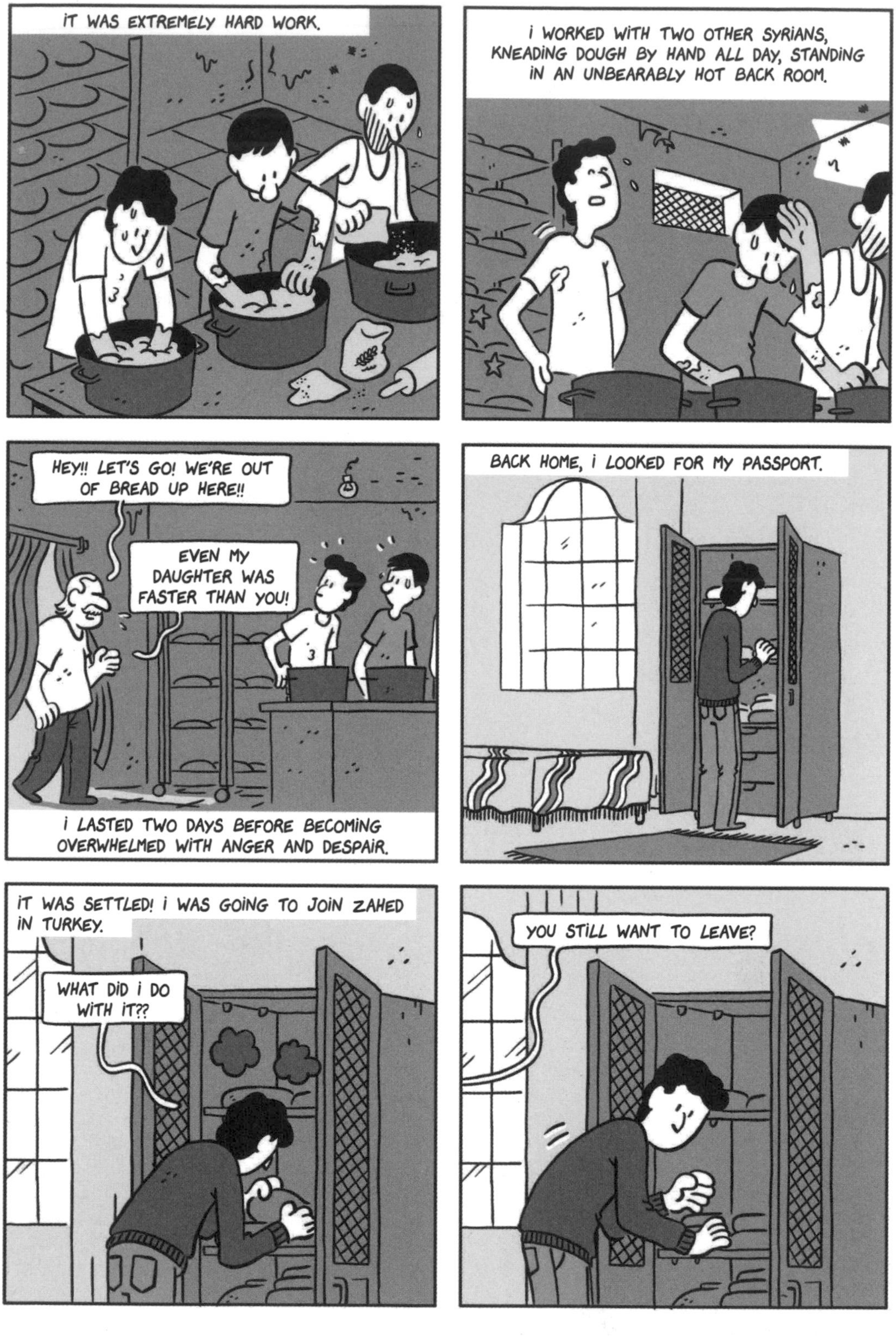
IT WAS EXTREMELY HARD WORK.
I WORKED WITH TWO OTHER SYRIANS, KNEADING DOUGH BY HAND ALL DAY, STANDING IN AN UNBEARABLY HOT BACK ROOM.
HEY!! LET'S GO! WE'RE OUT OF BREAD UP HERE!!
EVEN MY DAUGHTER WAS FASTER THAN YOU!
I LASTED TWO DAYS BEFORE BECOMING OVERWHELMED WITH ANGER AND DESPAIR.
BACK HOME, I LOOKED FOR MY PASSPORT.
IT WAS SETTLED! I WAS GOING TO JOIN ZAHED IN TURKEY.
WHAT DID I DO WITH IT??
YOU STILL WANT TO LEAVE?

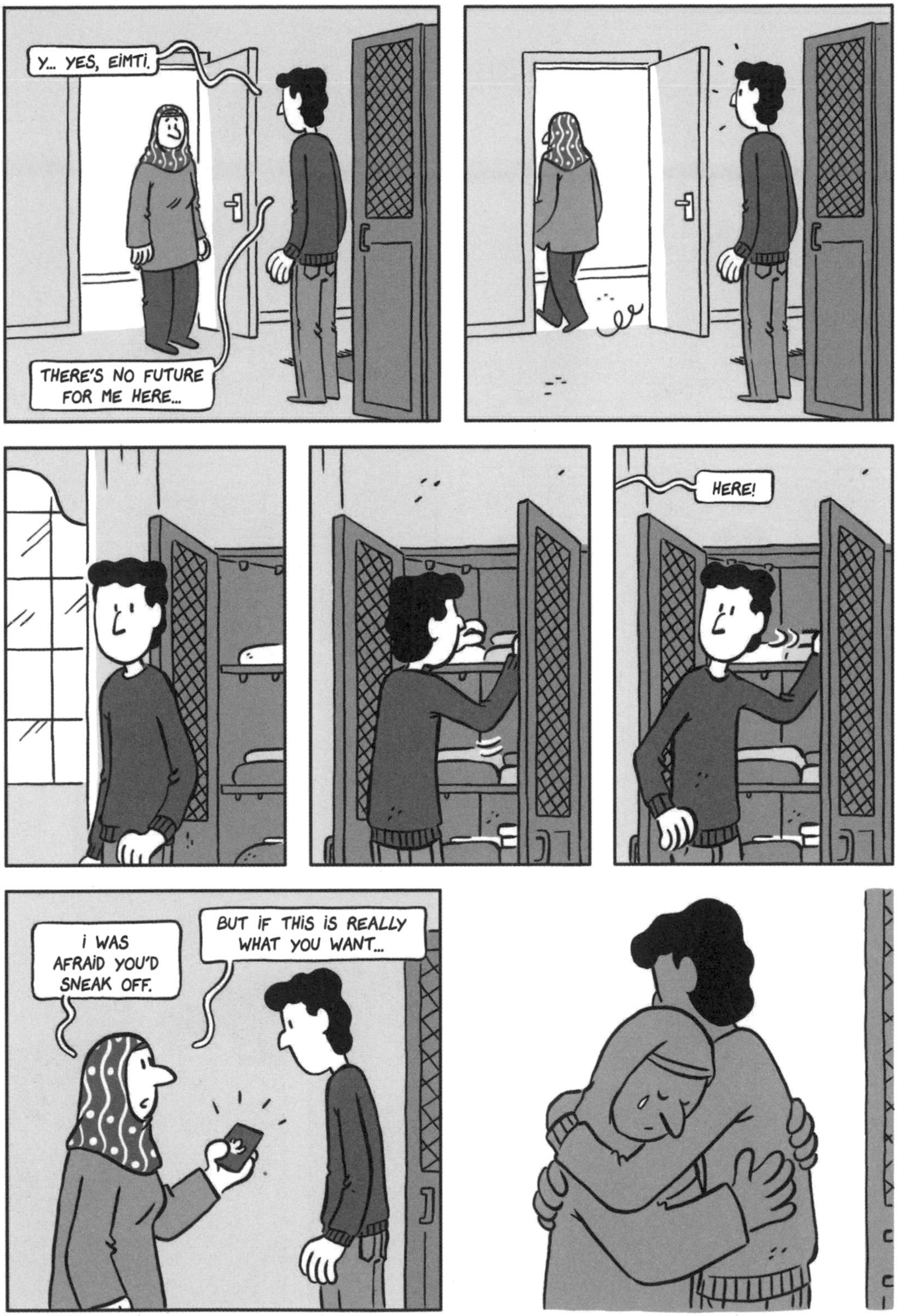
Y... YES, EIMTI.
THERE'S NO FUTURE FOR ME HERE...
HERE!
I WAS AFRAID YOU'D SNEAK OFF.
BUT IF THIS IS REALLY WHAT YOU WANT...

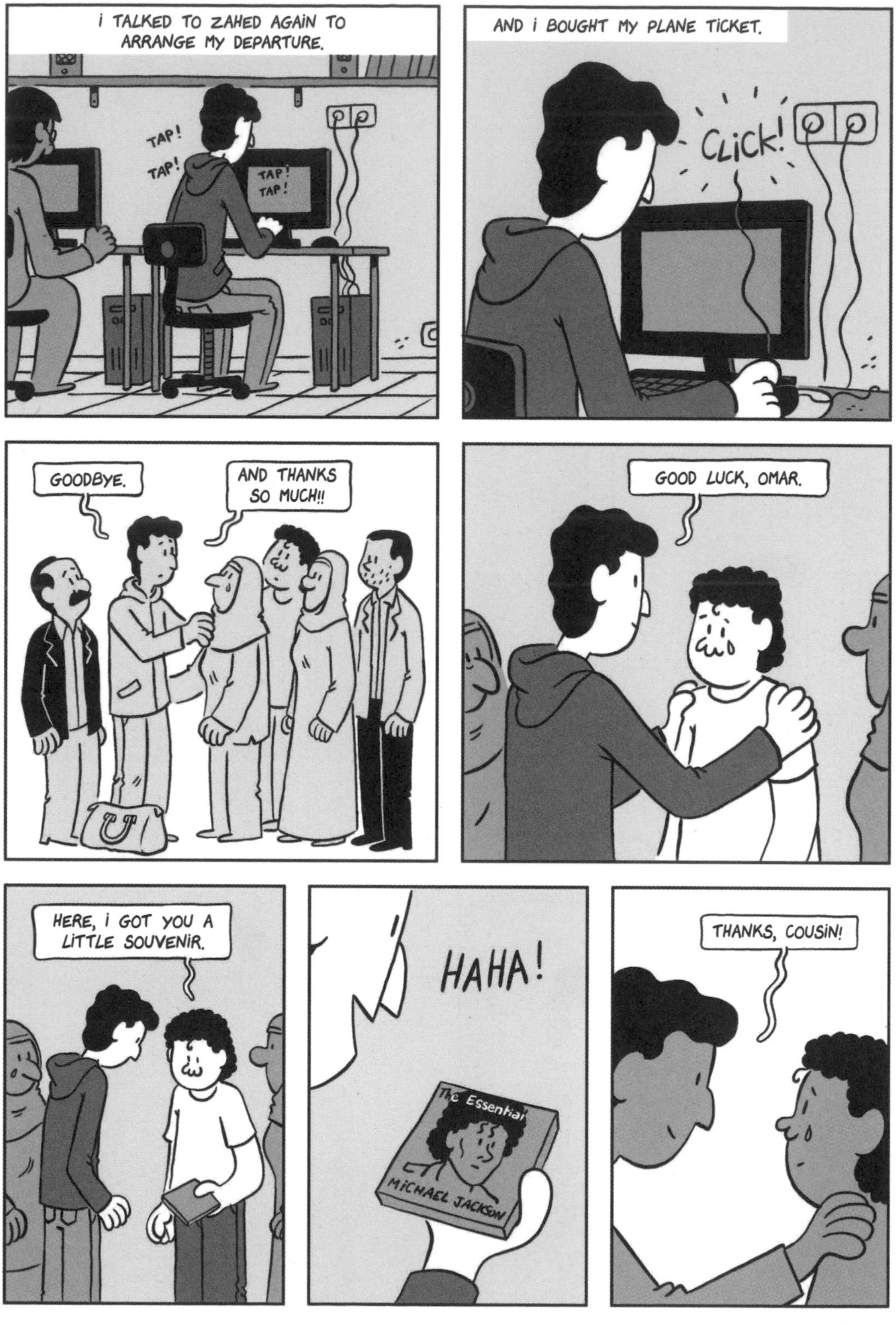
I TALKED TO ZAHED AGAIN TO ARRANGE MY DEPARTURE.
TAP! TAP!
TAP! TAP!
AND I BOUGHT MY PLANE TICKET.
CLICK!
GOODBYE.
AND THANKS SO MUCH!!
GOOD LUCK, OMAR.
HERE, I GOT YOU A LITTLE SOUVENIR.
HAHA!
The Essential
MICHAEL JACKSON
THANKS, COUSIN!

Chapter 8:
Antalya
(March 2013)

"DON'T WORRY, IT'S DIFFERENT HERE."

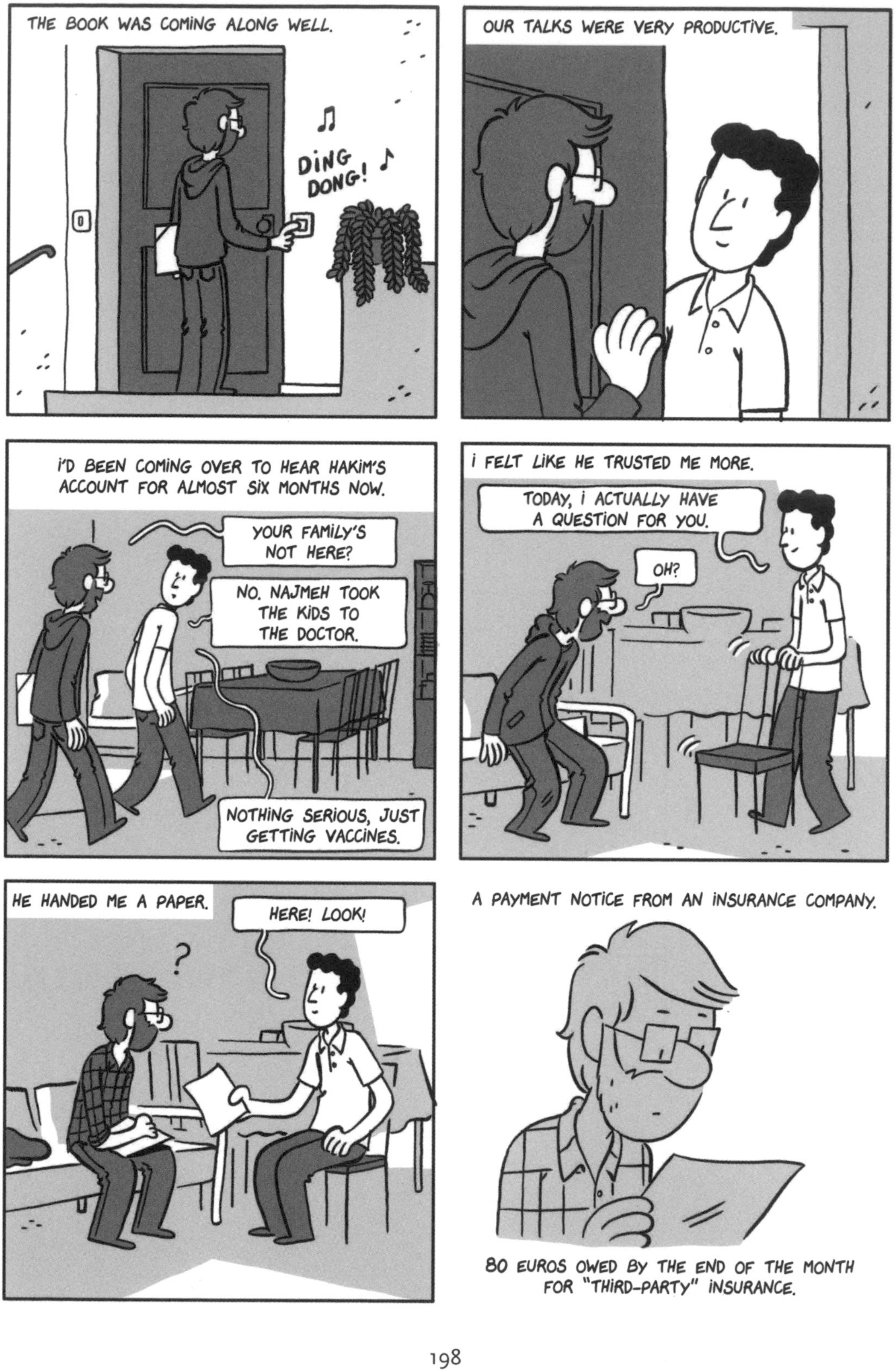
THE BOOK WAS COMING ALONG WELL.
DING DONG!
OUR TALKS WERE VERY PRODUCTIVE.
I'D BEEN COMING OVER TO HEAR HAKIM'S ACCOUNT FOR ALMOST SIX MONTHS NOW.
YOUR FAMILY'S NOT HERE?
NO. NAJMEH TOOK THE KIDS TO THE DOCTOR.
NOTHING SERIOUS, JUST GETTING VACCINES.
I FELT LIKE HE TRUSTED ME MORE.
TODAY, I ACTUALLY HAVE A QUESTION FOR YOU.
OH?
HE HANDED ME A PAPER.
HERE! LOOK!
?
A PAYMENT NOTICE FROM AN INSURANCE COMPANY.
80 EUROS OWED BY THE END OF THE MONTH FOR "THIRD-PARTY" INSURANCE.

WHAT DO THEY MEAN BY "THIRD-PARTY"?

CLEARLY HE'D BEEN TOLD TO TAKE OUT A POLICY, BUT HADN'T BEEN TOLD WHY.

WELL, IT'S TO PAY FOR POTENTIAL DAMAGE THAT YOU COULD DO TO SOMEONE.

FOR EXAMPLE, IF YOU KNOCK SOMEONE OVER AND THEY BREAK THEIR GLASSES, YOUR INSURANCE WILL COVER THE GLASSES.

OH! THAT'S GOOD, THEN.

I HOPE BASHAR AL-ASSAD HAS GOOD THIRD-PARTY INSURANCE FOR ALL THE DAMAGE HE'S CAUSED THE SYRIAN PEOPLE.

NOT SURE...

BUT HOW DO I PAY THIS?

YOU SIGN THE DOCUMENTARY COLLECTION AND SEND IT IN WITH A BBAN.

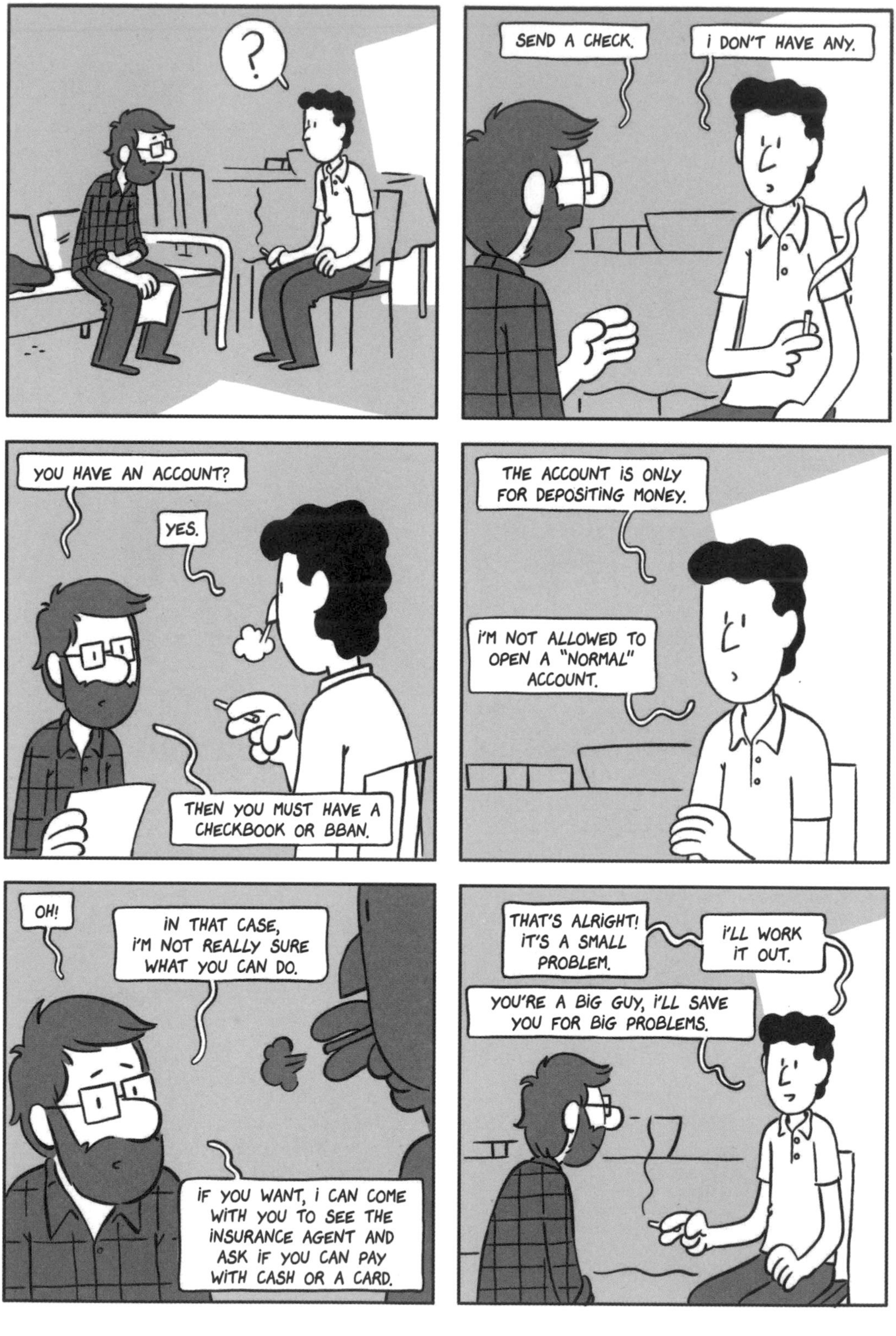
?
SEND A CHECK.
i DON'T HAVE ANY.
YOU HAVE AN ACCOUNT?
YES.
THEN YOU MUST HAVE A CHECKBOOK OR BBAN.
THE ACCOUNT iS ONLY FOR DEPOSiTiNG MONEY.
i'M NOT ALLOWED TO OPEN A "NORMAL" ACCOUNT.
OH!
iN THAT CASE, i'M NOT REALLY SURE WHAT YOU CAN DO.
iF YOU WANT, i CAN COME WiTH YOU TO SEE THE iNSURANCE AGENT AND ASK iF YOU CAN PAY WiTH CASH OR A CARD.
THAT'S ALRiGHT! iT'S A SMALL PROBLEM.
i'LL WORK iT OUT.
YOU'RE A BiG GUY, i'LL SAVE YOU FOR BiG PROBLEMS.

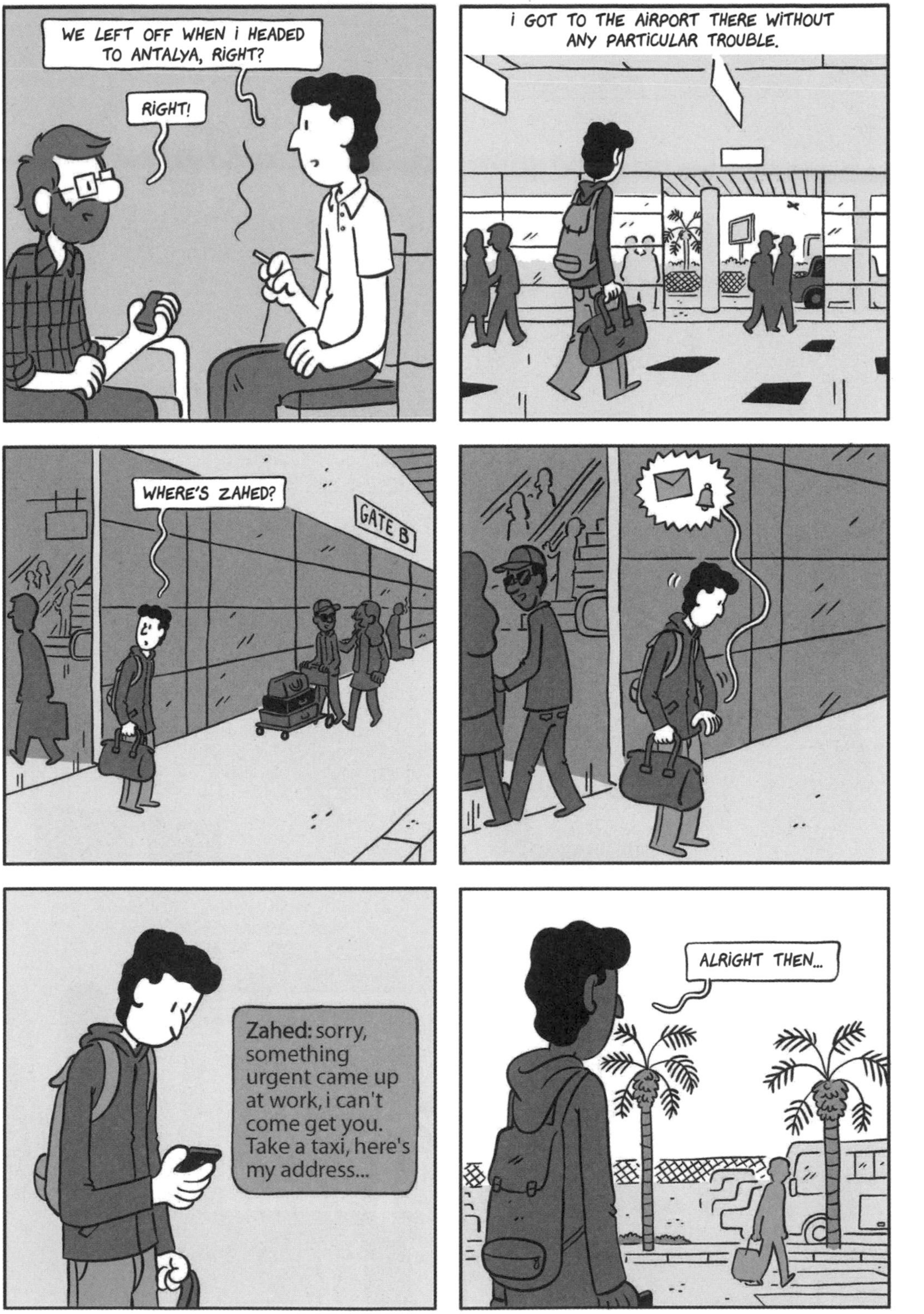
WE LEFT OFF WHEN I HEADED TO ANTALYA, RIGHT?
RIGHT!
I GOT TO THE AIRPORT THERE WITHOUT ANY PARTICULAR TROUBLE.
WHERE'S ZAHED?
GATE B
Zahed: sorry, something urgent came up at work, i can't come get you. Take a taxi, here's my address...
ALRIGHT THEN...

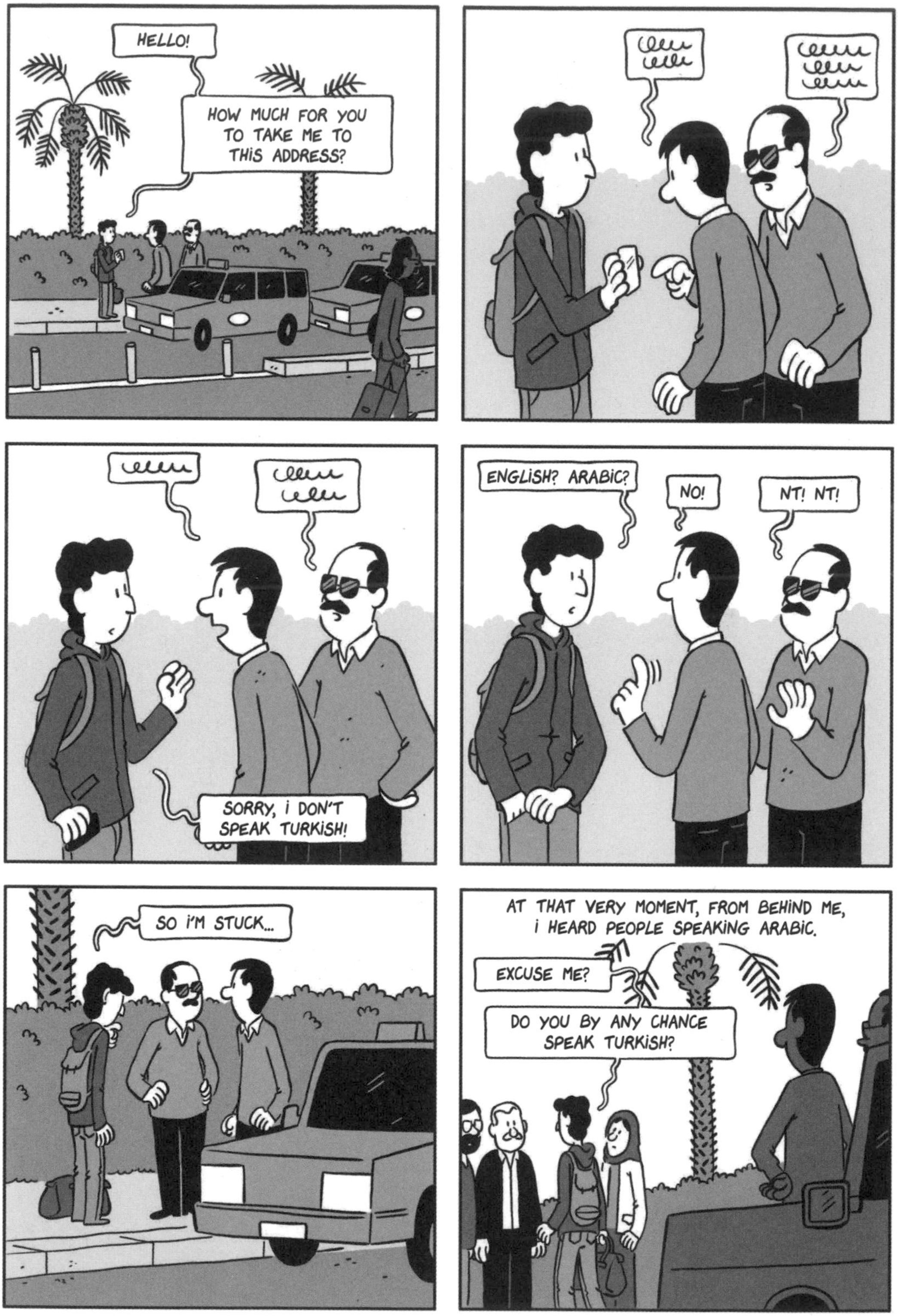
HELLO!
HOW MUCH FOR YOU TO TAKE ME TO THIS ADDRESS?
SORRY, I DON'T SPEAK TURKISH!
ENGLISH? ARABIC?
NO!
NT! NT!
SO I'M STUCK...
AT THAT VERY MOMENT, FROM BEHIND ME, I HEARD PEOPLE SPEAKING ARABIC.
EXCUSE ME?
DO YOU BY ANY CHANCE SPEAK TURKISH?

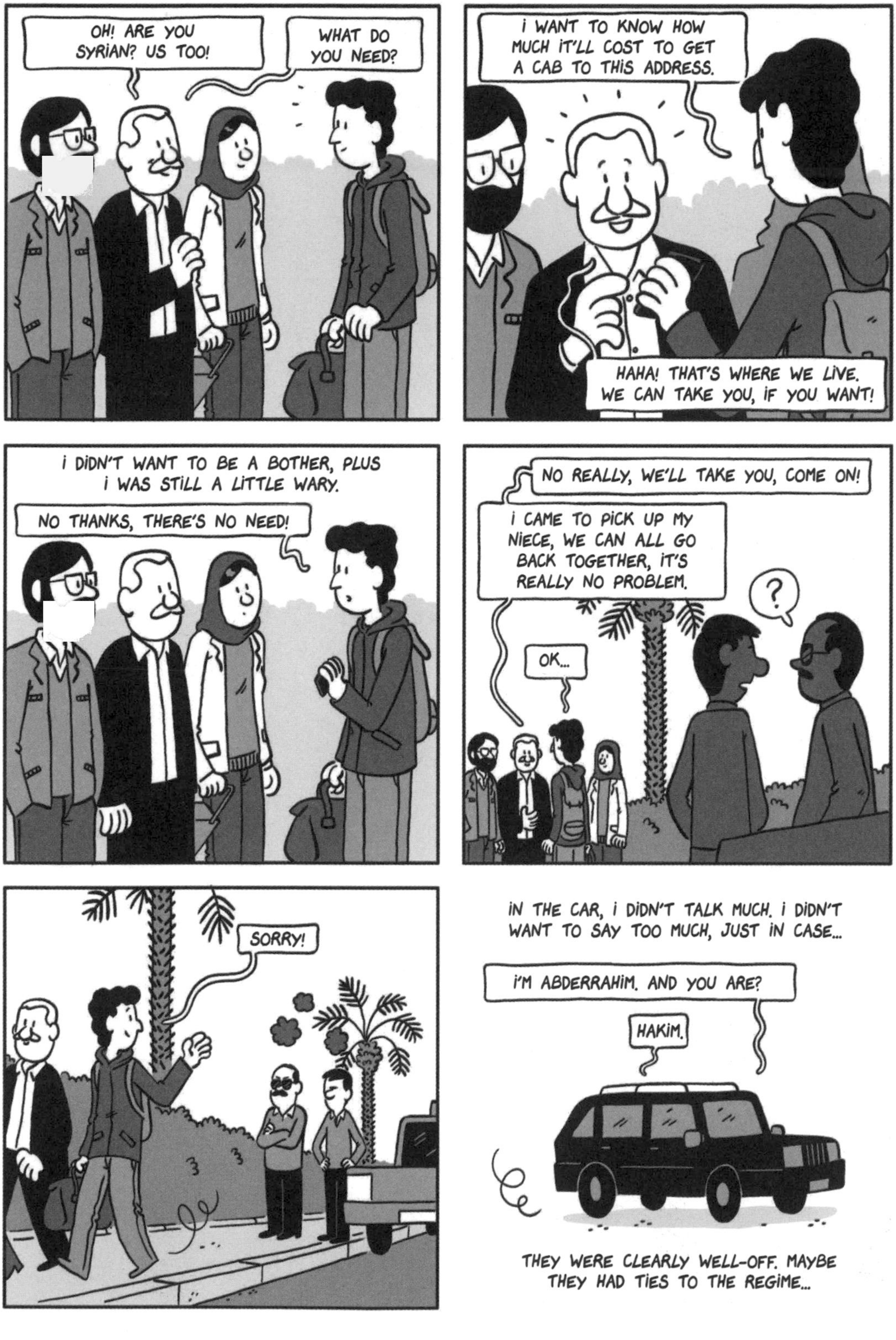
OH! ARE YOU SYRIAN? US TOO!
WHAT DO YOU NEED?
I WANT TO KNOW HOW MUCH IT'LL COST TO GET A CAB TO THIS ADDRESS.
HAHA! THAT'S WHERE WE LIVE. WE CAN TAKE YOU, IF YOU WANT!
I DIDN'T WANT TO BE A BOTHER, PLUS I WAS STILL A LITTLE WARY.
NO THANKS, THERE'S NO NEED!
NO REALLY, WE'LL TAKE YOU, COME ON!
I CAME TO PICK UP MY NIECE, WE CAN ALL GO BACK TOGETHER, IT'S REALLY NO PROBLEM.
?
OK...
SORRY!
IN THE CAR, I DIDN'T TALK MUCH. I DIDN'T WANT TO SAY TOO MUCH, JUST IN CASE...
I'M ABDERRAHIM. AND YOU ARE?
HAKIM.
THEY WERE CLEARLY WELL-OFF. MAYBE THEY HAD TIES TO THE REGIME...

i MAINLY LOOKED AT THE SCENERY, THE CITY.

AHMET SABOĞLU
ERKEK ÖĞLENCE

iT WAS VERY CLEAN AND MODERN.

ARE YOU HERE VISITING FAMILY?

NO, JUST A FRIEND.

HIS NAME'S ZAHED.

SOMETHING CAME UP, HE COULDN'T COME GET ME.

OH YES, i KNOW HIM.

AT LEAST, WE SAY HELLO.

IN OUR BUILDING, THERE ARE QUITE A FEW SYRIANS.

WITH WHAT'S HAPPENING BACK HOME...

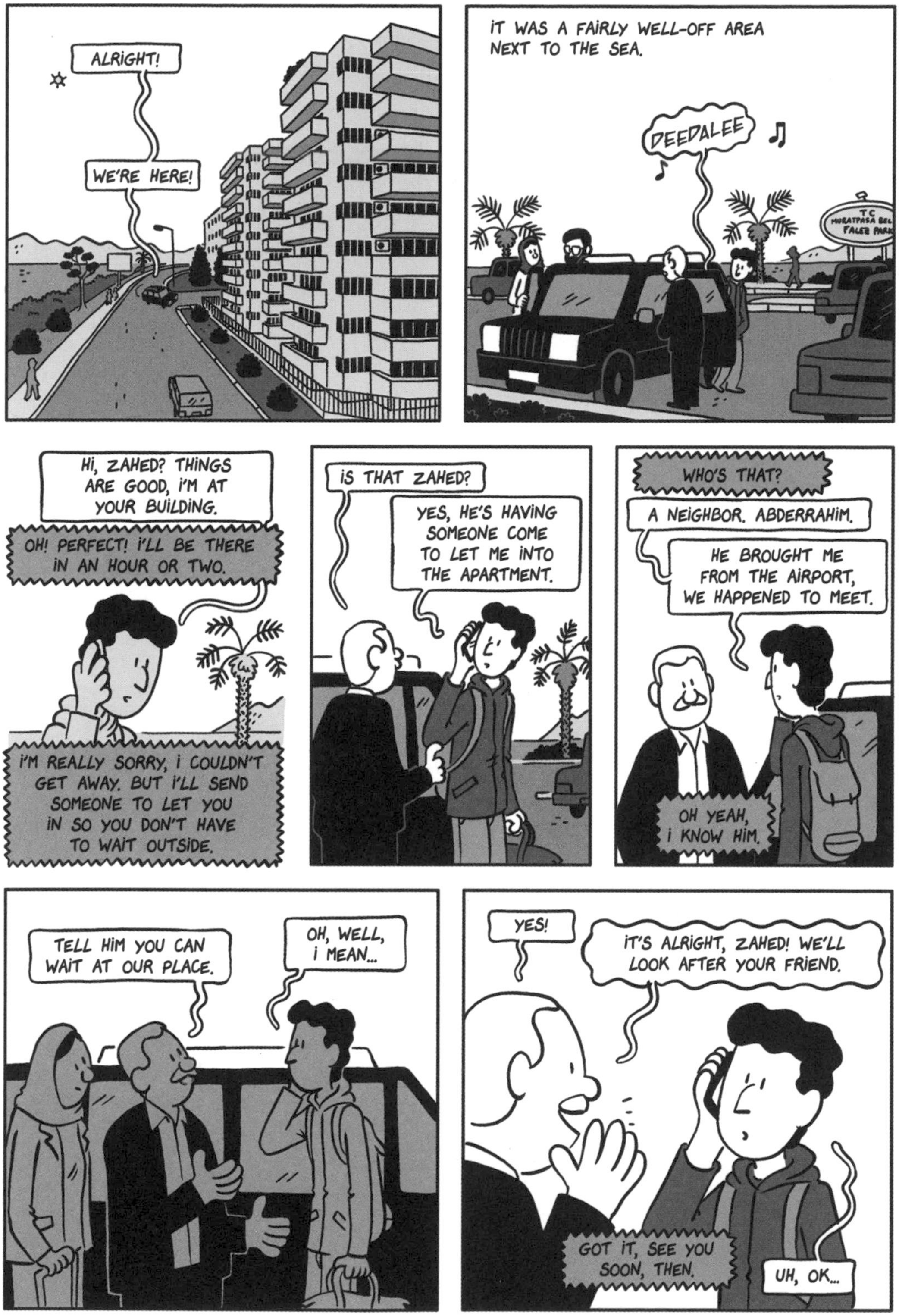
ALRIGHT!
WE'RE HERE!
IT WAS A FAIRLY WELL-OFF AREA NEXT TO THE SEA.
DEEDALEE
HI, ZAHED? THINGS ARE GOOD, I'M AT YOUR BUILDING.
OH! PERFECT! I'LL BE THERE IN AN HOUR OR TWO.
I'M REALLY SORRY, I COULDN'T GET AWAY. BUT I'LL SEND SOMEONE TO LET YOU IN SO YOU DON'T HAVE TO WAIT OUTSIDE.
IS THAT ZAHED?
YES, HE'S HAVING SOMEONE COME TO LET ME INTO THE APARTMENT.
WHO'S THAT?
A NEIGHBOR. ABDERRAHIM.
HE BROUGHT ME FROM THE AIRPORT, WE HAPPENED TO MEET.
OH YEAH, I KNOW HIM.
TELL HIM YOU CAN WAIT AT OUR PLACE.
OH, WELL, I MEAN...
YES!
IT'S ALRIGHT, ZAHED! WE'LL LOOK AFTER YOUR FRIEND.
GOT IT, SEE YOU SOON, THEN.
UH, OK...

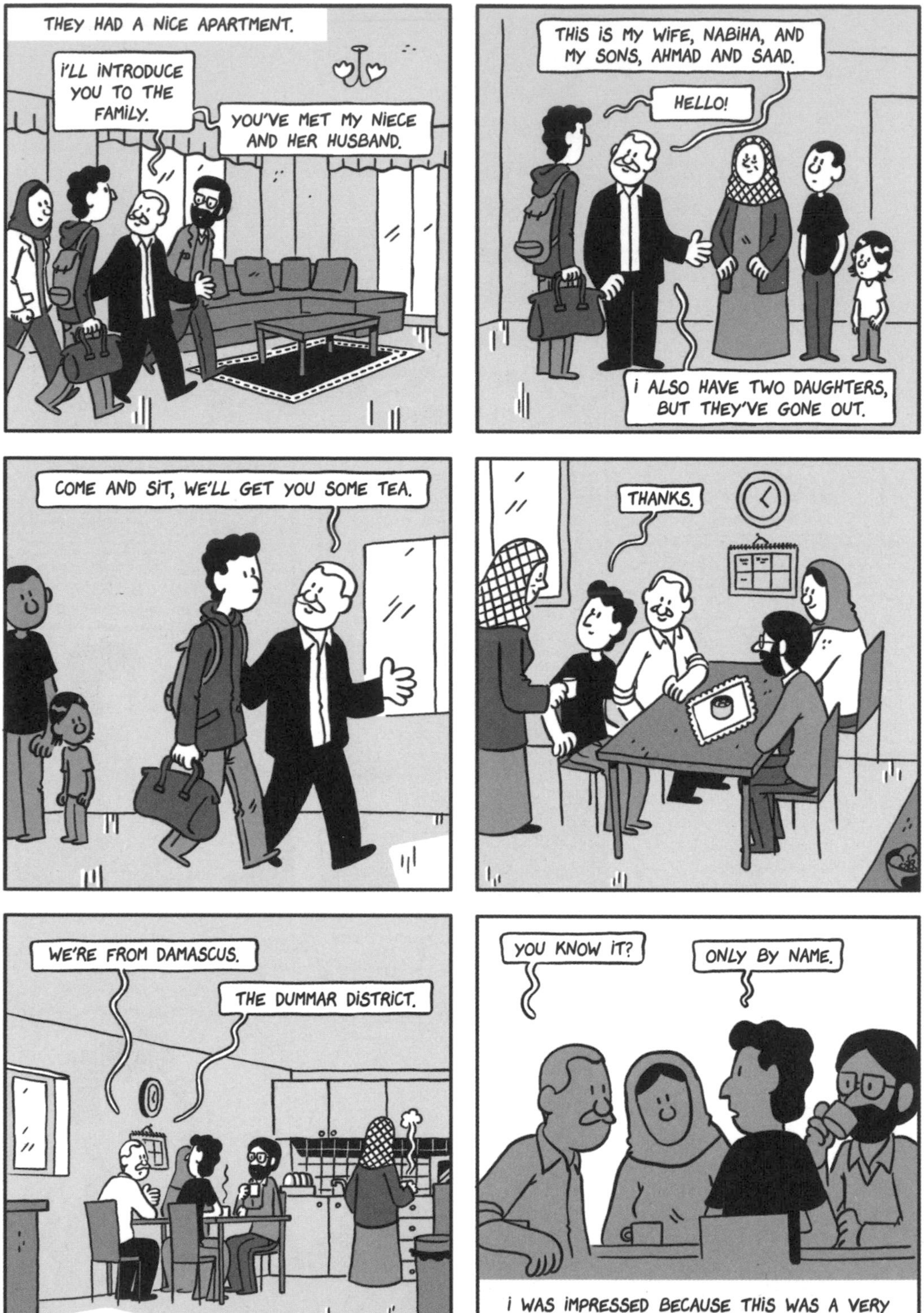
THEY HAD A NICE APARTMENT.
I'LL INTRODUCE YOU TO THE FAMILY.
YOU'VE MET MY NIECE AND HER HUSBAND.
THIS IS MY WIFE, NABIHA, AND MY SONS, AHMAD AND SAAD.
HELLO!
I ALSO HAVE TWO DAUGHTERS, BUT THEY'VE GONE OUT.
COME AND SIT, WE'LL GET YOU SOME TEA.
THANKS.
WE'RE FROM DAMASCUS.
THE DUMMAR DISTRICT.
YOU KNOW IT?
ONLY BY NAME.
I WAS IMPRESSED BECAUSE THIS WAS A VERY NICE AREA NEAR THE PRESIDENTIAL PALACE.

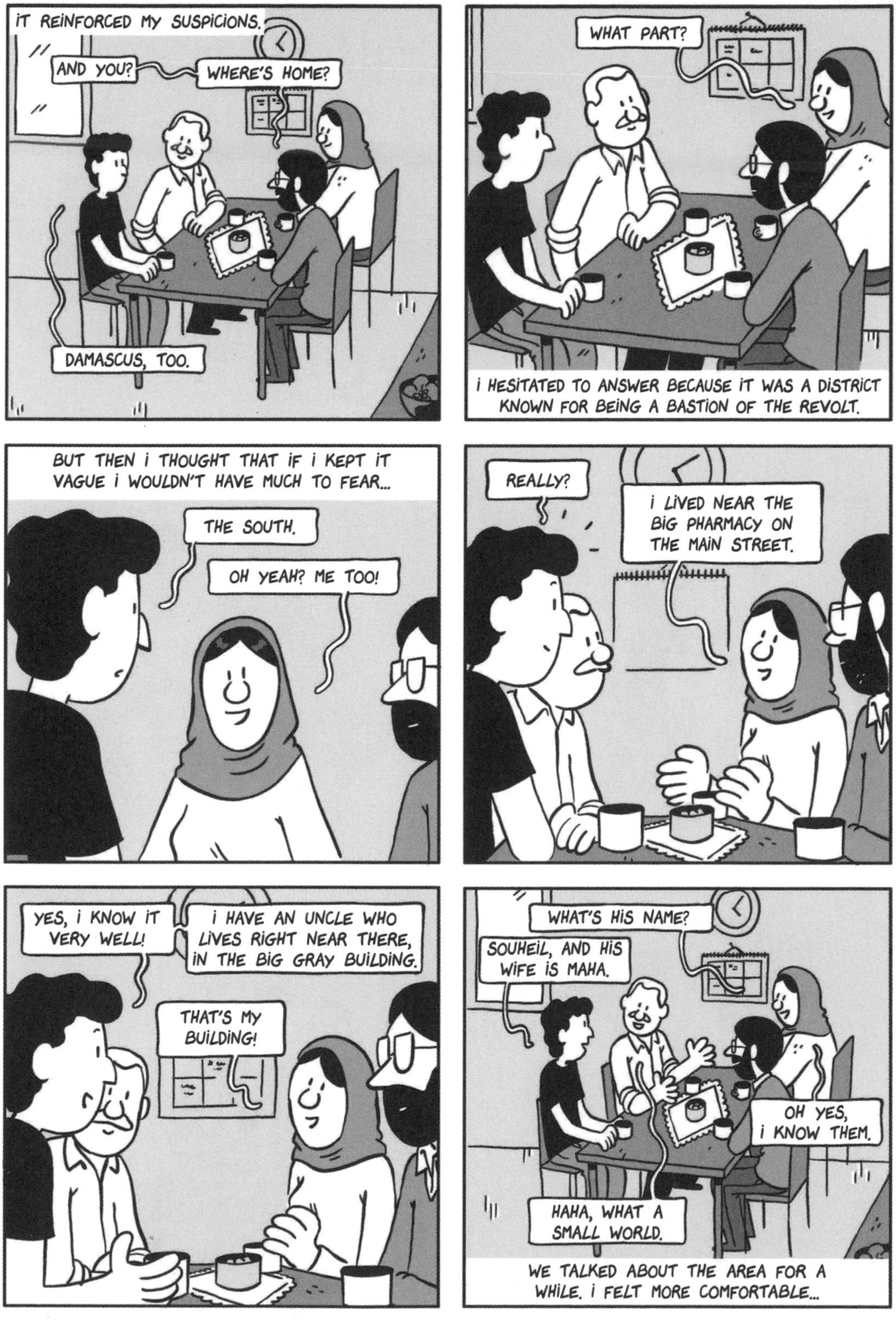

IT REINFORCED MY SUSPICIONS.
AND YOU?
WHERE'S HOME?
DAMASCUS, TOO.
WHAT PART?
I HESITATED TO ANSWER BECAUSE IT WAS A DISTRICT KNOWN FOR BEING A BASTION OF THE REVOLT.
BUT THEN I THOUGHT THAT IF I KEPT IT VAGUE I WOULDN'T HAVE MUCH TO FEAR...
THE SOUTH.
OH YEAH? ME TOO!
REALLY?
I LIVED NEAR THE BIG PHARMACY ON THE MAIN STREET.
YES, I KNOW IT VERY WELL!
I HAVE AN UNCLE WHO LIVES RIGHT NEAR THERE, IN THE BIG GRAY BUILDING.
THAT'S MY BUILDING!
WHAT'S HIS NAME?
SOUHEIL, AND HIS WIFE IS MAHA.
OH YES, I KNOW THEM.
HAHA, WHAT A SMALL WORLD.
WE TALKED ABOUT THE AREA FOR A WHILE. I FELT MORE COMFORTABLE...

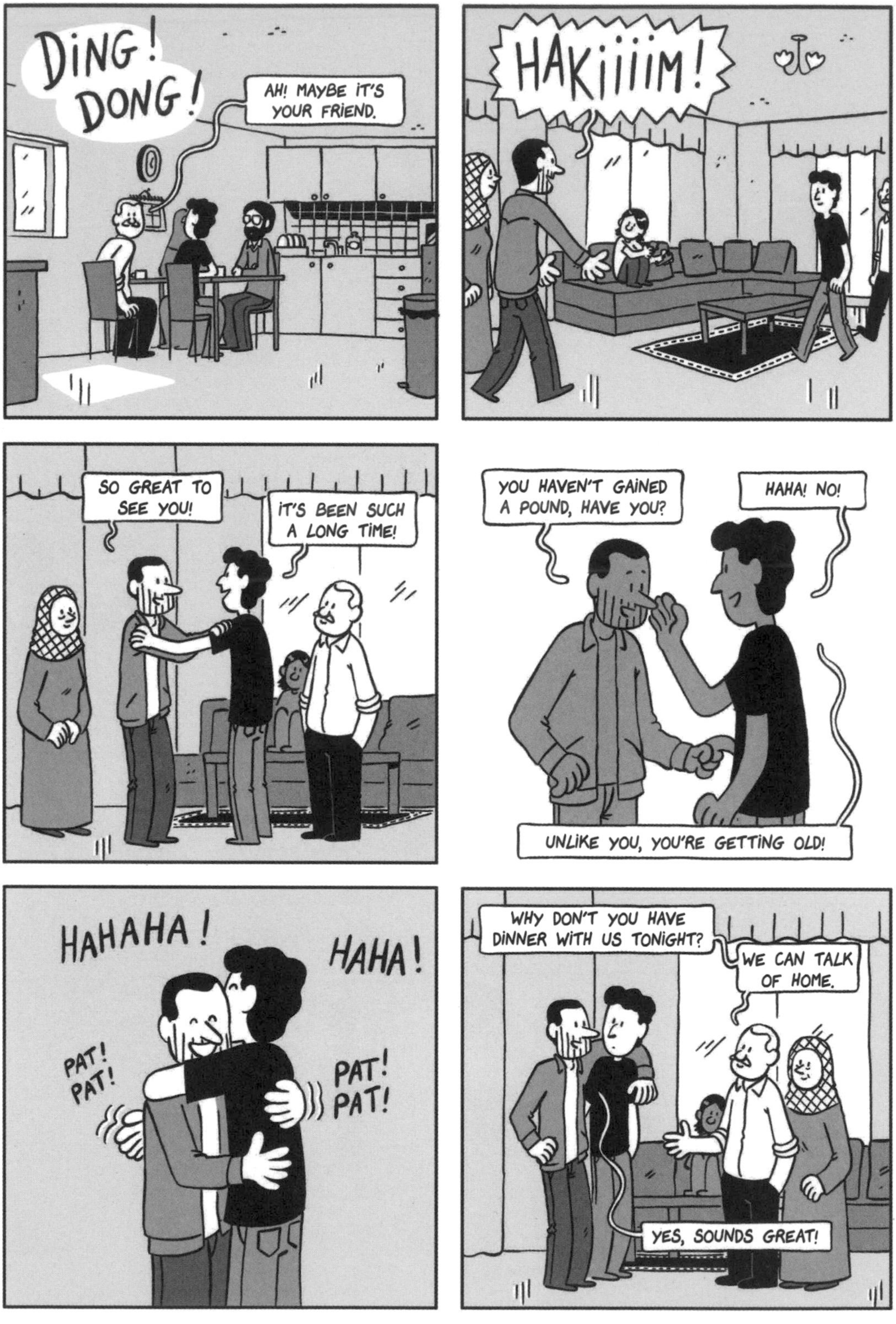
DING! DONG!
AH! MAYBE IT'S YOUR FRIEND.
HAKiiiiM!
SO GREAT TO SEE YOU!
IT'S BEEN SUCH A LONG TIME!
YOU HAVEN'T GAINED A POUND, HAVE YOU?
HAHA! NO!
UNLIKE YOU, YOU'RE GETTING OLD!
HAHAHA!
HAHA!
PAT! PAT!
PAT! PAT!
WHY DON'T YOU HAVE DINNER WITH US TONIGHT?
WE CAN TALK OF HOME.
YES, SOUNDS GREAT!

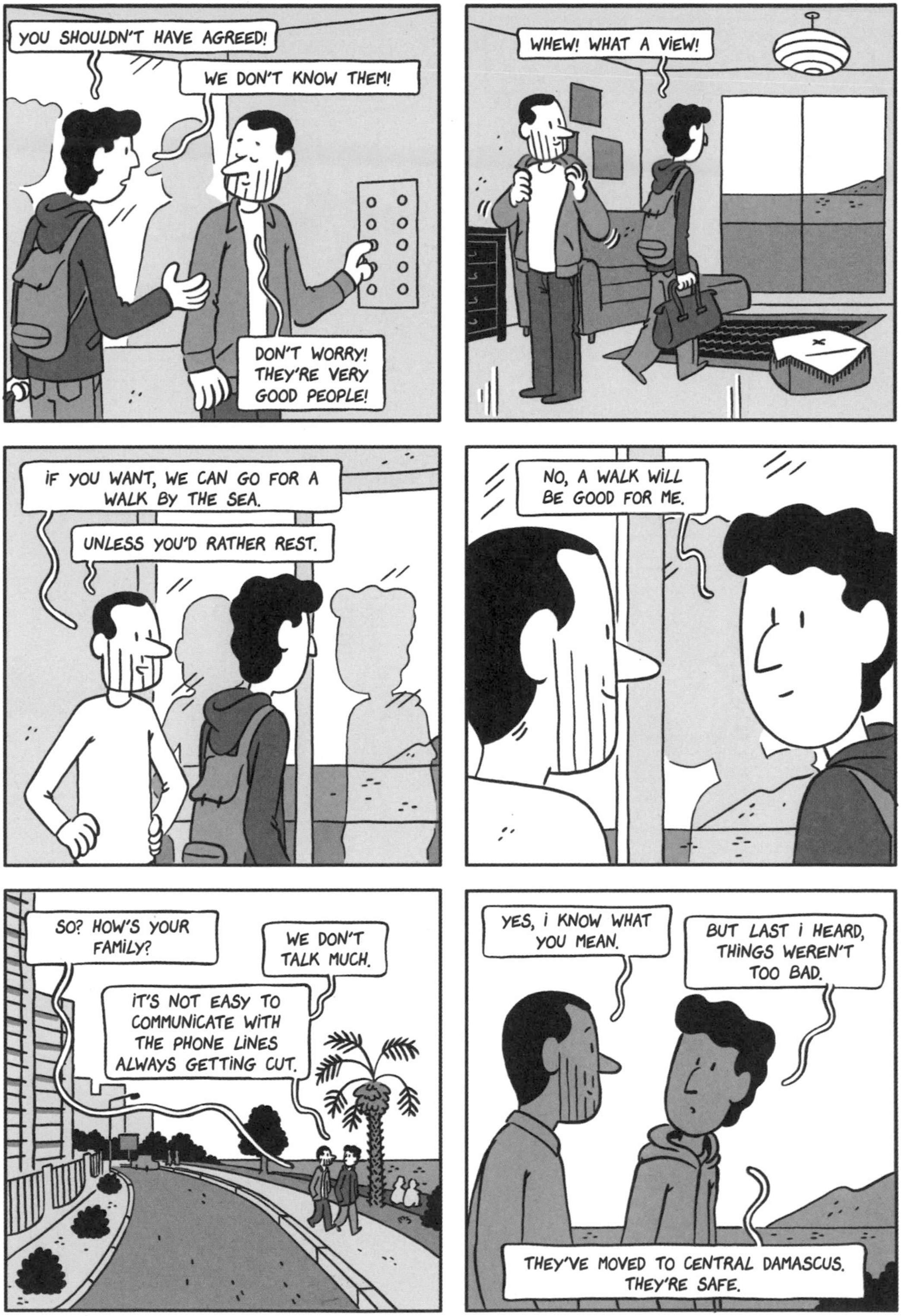
YOU SHOULDN'T HAVE AGREED!
WE DON'T KNOW THEM!
DON'T WORRY! THEY'RE VERY GOOD PEOPLE!
WHEW! WHAT A VIEW!
IF YOU WANT, WE CAN GO FOR A WALK BY THE SEA.
UNLESS YOU'D RATHER REST.
NO, A WALK WILL BE GOOD FOR ME.
SO? HOW'S YOUR FAMILY?
WE DON'T TALK MUCH.
IT'S NOT EASY TO COMMUNICATE WITH THE PHONE LINES ALWAYS GETTING CUT.
YES, I KNOW WHAT YOU MEAN.
BUT LAST I HEARD, THINGS WEREN'T TOO BAD.
THEY'VE MOVED TO CENTRAL DAMASCUS. THEY'RE SAFE.

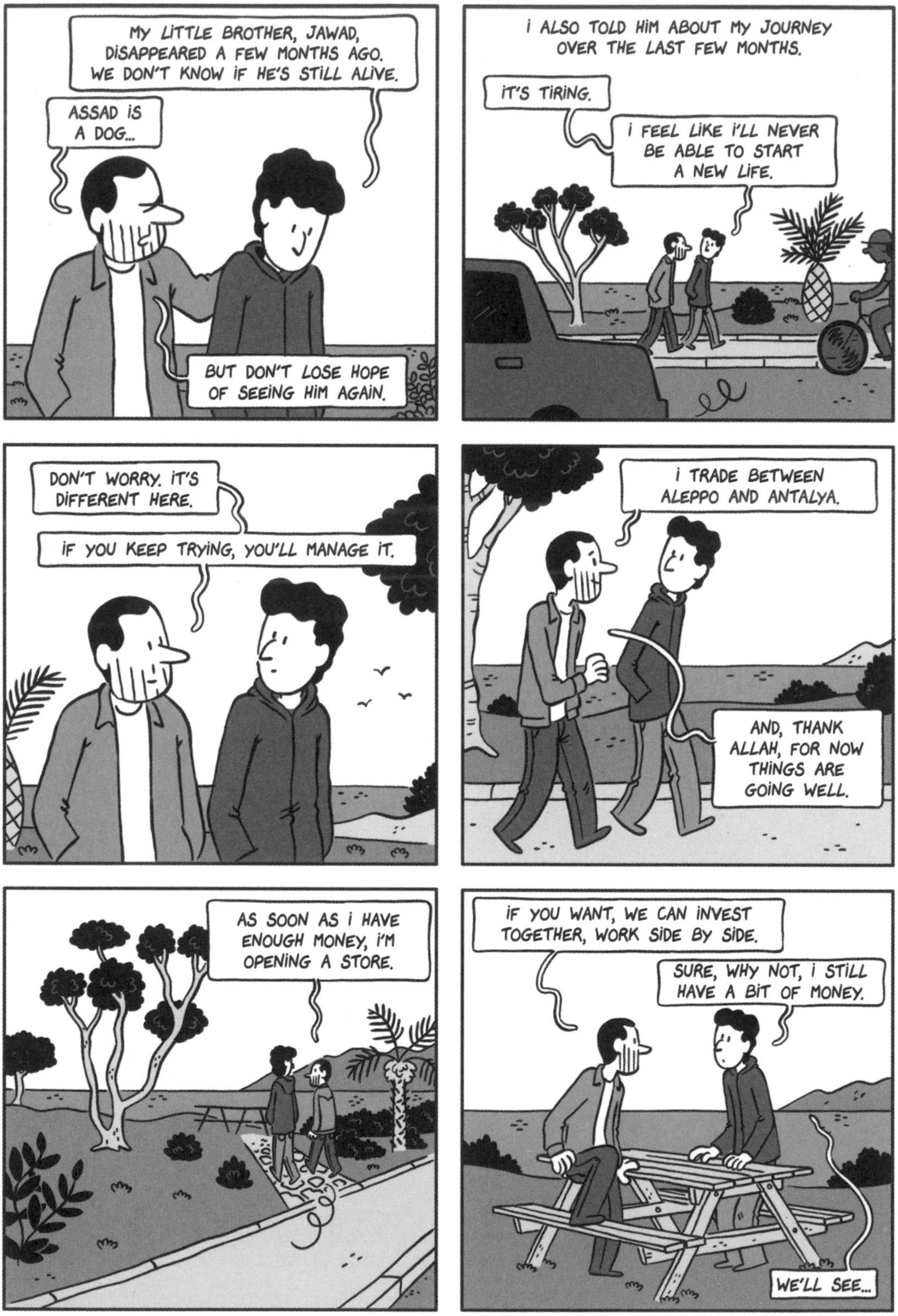
MY LITTLE BROTHER, JAWAD, DISAPPEARED A FEW MONTHS AGO. WE DON'T KNOW IF HE'S STILL ALIVE.
ASSAD IS A DOG...
BUT DON'T LOSE HOPE OF SEEING HIM AGAIN.
I ALSO TOLD HIM ABOUT MY JOURNEY OVER THE LAST FEW MONTHS.
IT'S TIRING.
I FEEL LIKE I'LL NEVER BE ABLE TO START A NEW LIFE.
DON'T WORRY. IT'S DIFFERENT HERE.
IF YOU KEEP TRYING, YOU'LL MANAGE IT.
I TRADE BETWEEN ALEPPO AND ANTALYA.
AND, THANK ALLAH, FOR NOW THINGS ARE GOING WELL.
AS SOON AS I HAVE ENOUGH MONEY, I'M OPENING A STORE.
IF YOU WANT, WE CAN INVEST TOGETHER, WORK SIDE BY SIDE.
SURE, WHY NOT, I STILL HAVE A BIT OF MONEY.
WE'LL SEE...

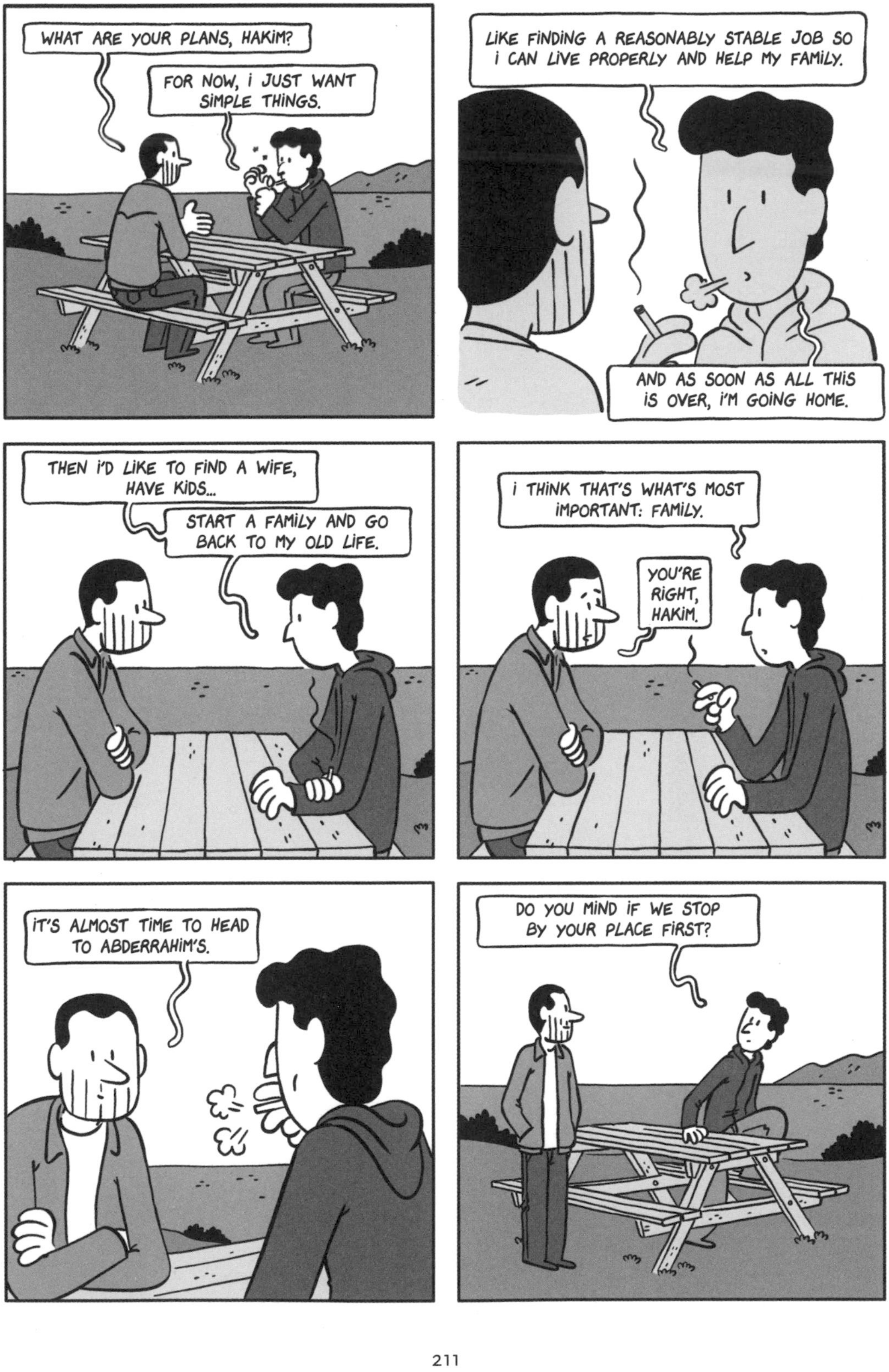
WHAT ARE YOUR PLANS, HAKIM?
FOR NOW, I JUST WANT SIMPLE THINGS.
LIKE FINDING A REASONABLY STABLE JOB SO I CAN LIVE PROPERLY AND HELP MY FAMILY.
AND AS SOON AS ALL THIS IS OVER, I'M GOING HOME.
THEN I'D LIKE TO FIND A WIFE, HAVE KIDS...
START A FAMILY AND GO BACK TO MY OLD LIFE.
I THINK THAT'S WHAT'S MOST IMPORTANT: FAMILY.
YOU'RE RIGHT, HAKIM.
IT'S ALMOST TIME TO HEAD TO ABDERRAHIM'S.
DO YOU MIND IF WE STOP BY YOUR PLACE FIRST?

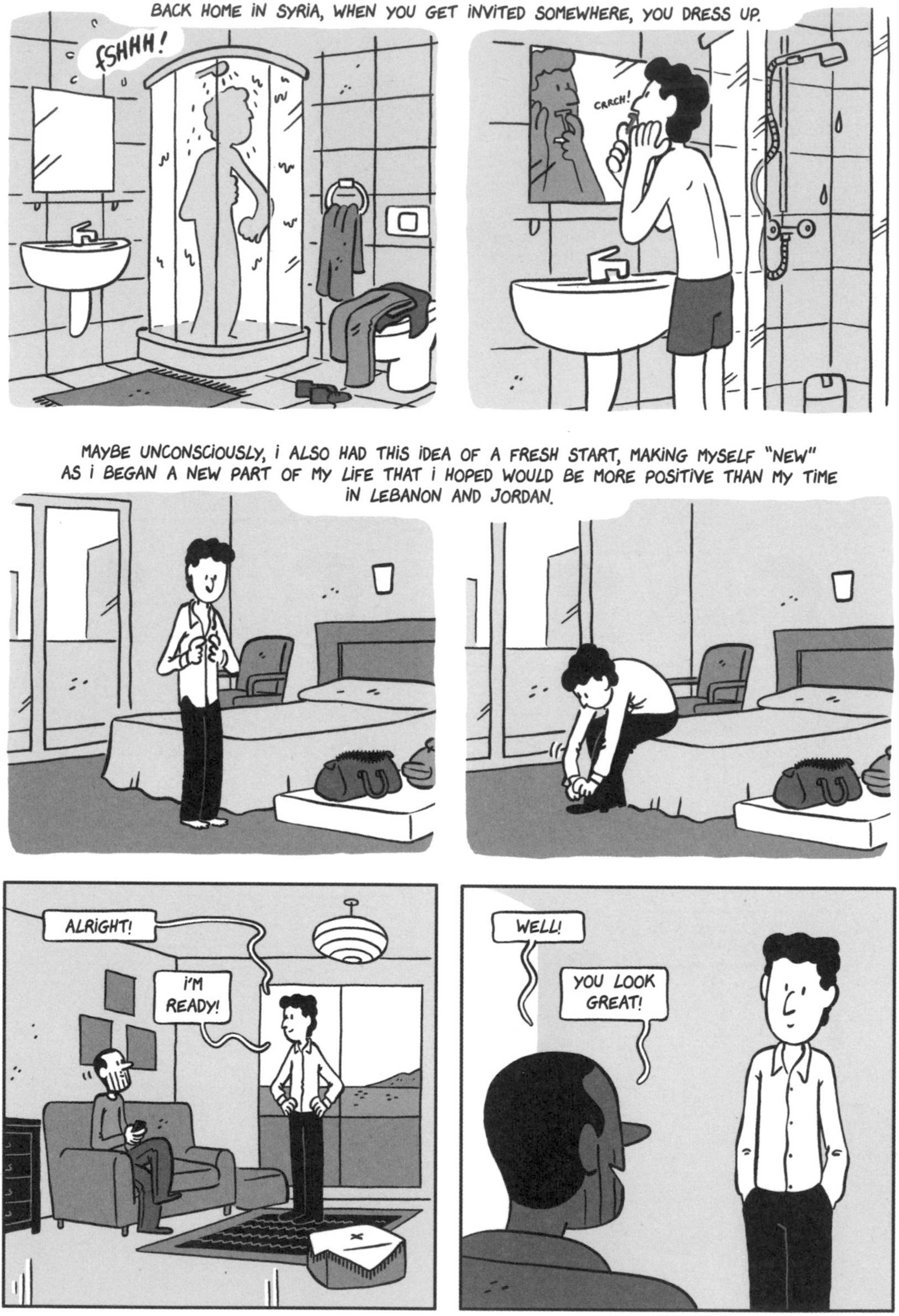
BACK HOME IN SYRIA, WHEN YOU GET INVITED SOMEWHERE, YOU DRESS UP.
FSHHH!
CRRCH!
MAYBE UNCONSCIOUSLY, I ALSO HAD THIS IDEA OF A FRESH START, MAKING MYSELF "NEW" AS I BEGAN A NEW PART OF MY LIFE THAT I HOPED WOULD BE MORE POSITIVE THAN MY TIME IN LEBANON AND JORDAN.
ALRIGHT!
I'M READY!
WELL!
YOU LOOK GREAT!

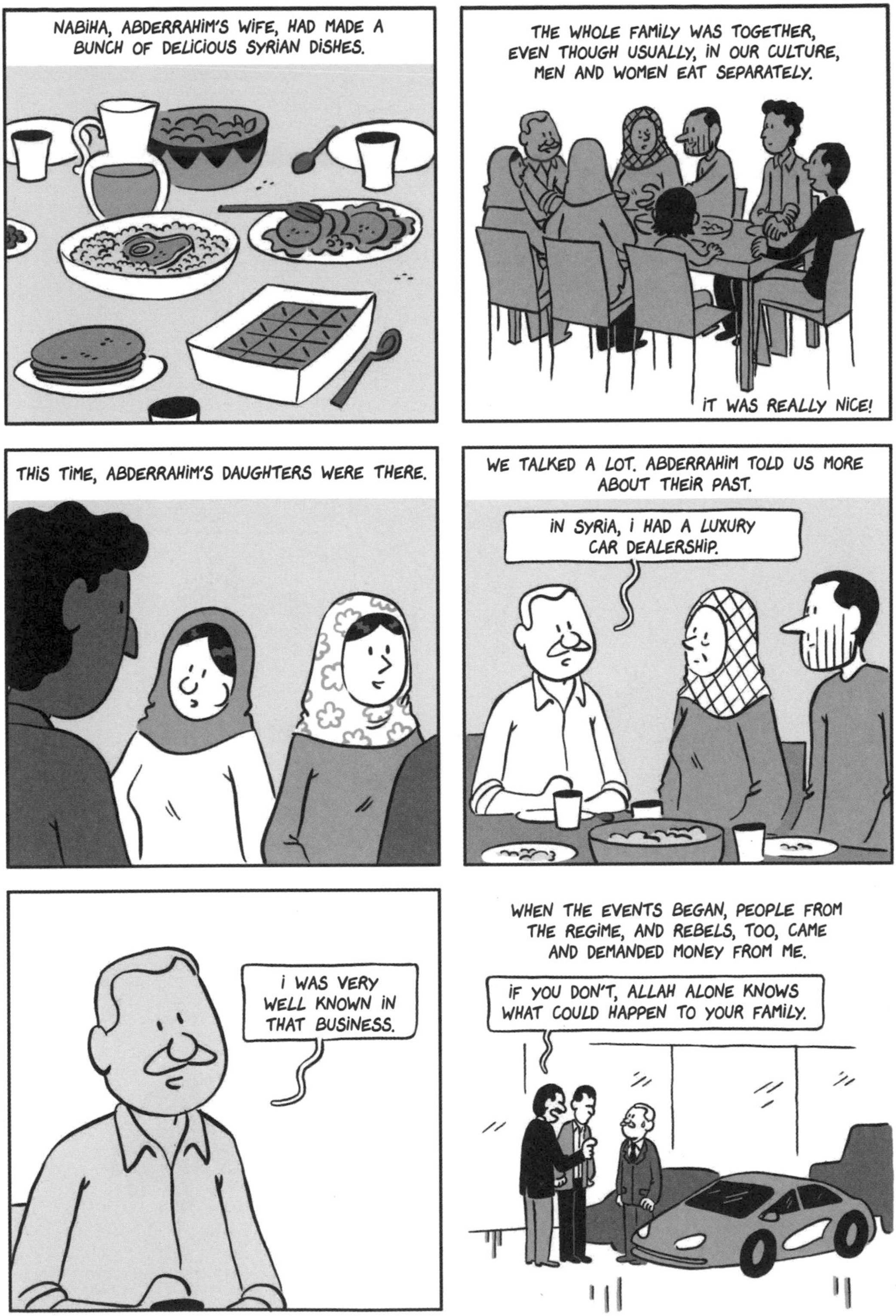
NABIHA, ABDERRAHIM'S WIFE, HAD MADE A BUNCH OF DELICIOUS SYRIAN DISHES.
THE WHOLE FAMILY WAS TOGETHER, EVEN THOUGH USUALLY, IN OUR CULTURE, MEN AND WOMEN EAT SEPARATELY.
IT WAS REALLY NICE!
THIS TIME, ABDERRAHIM'S DAUGHTERS WERE THERE.
WE TALKED A LOT. ABDERRAHIM TOLD US MORE ABOUT THEIR PAST.
IN SYRIA, I HAD A LUXURY CAR DEALERSHIP.
I WAS VERY WELL KNOWN IN THAT BUSINESS.
WHEN THE EVENTS BEGAN, PEOPLE FROM THE REGIME, AND REBELS, TOO, CAME AND DEMANDED MONEY FROM ME.
IF YOU DON'T, ALLAH ALONE KNOWS WHAT COULD HAPPEN TO YOUR FAMILY.

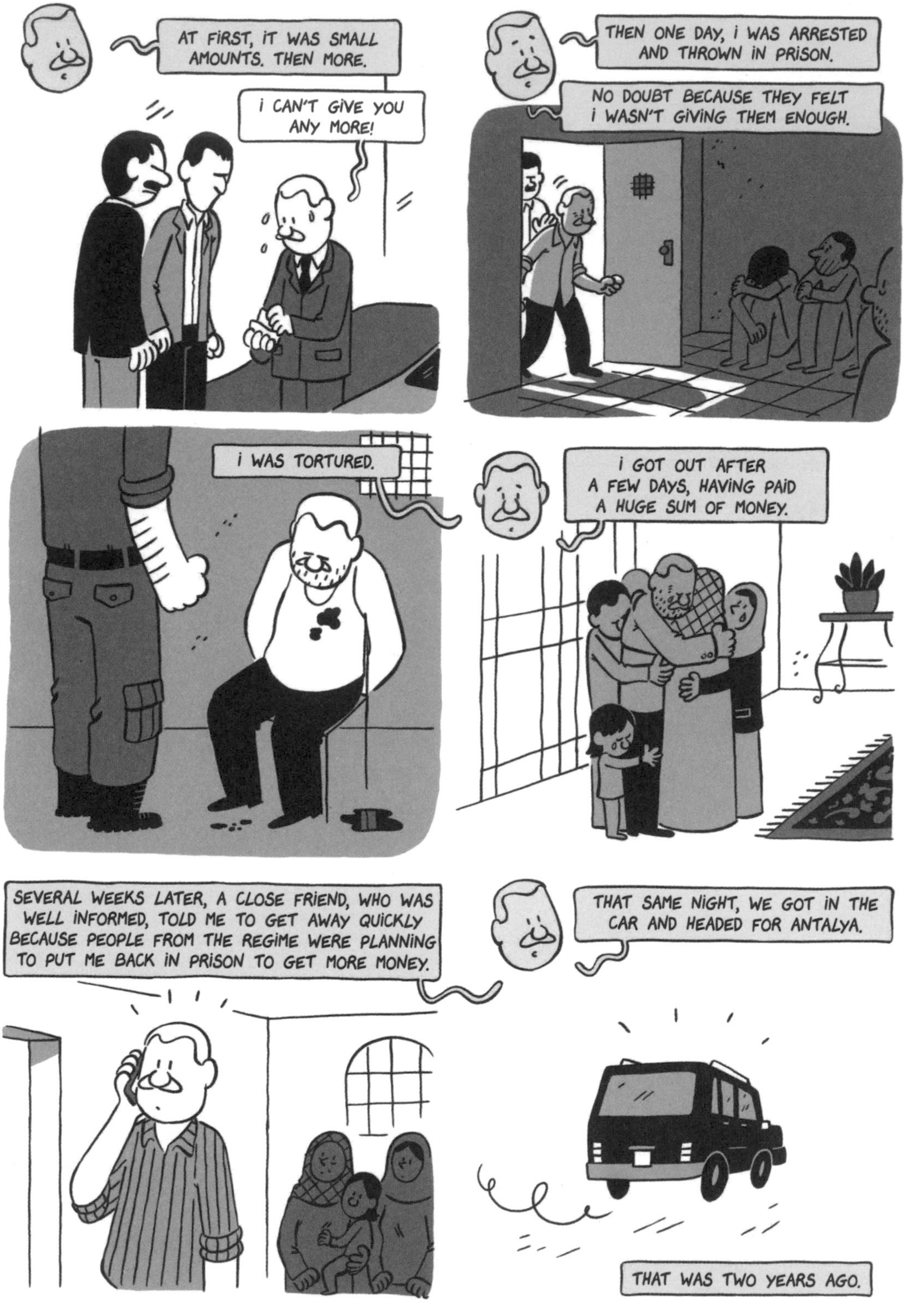
AT FIRST, IT WAS SMALL AMOUNTS. THEN MORE.
I CAN'T GIVE YOU ANY MORE!
THEN ONE DAY, I WAS ARRESTED AND THROWN IN PRISON.
NO DOUBT BECAUSE THEY FELT I WASN'T GIVING THEM ENOUGH.
I WAS TORTURED.
I GOT OUT AFTER A FEW DAYS, HAVING PAID A HUGE SUM OF MONEY.
SEVERAL WEEKS LATER, A CLOSE FRIEND, WHO WAS WELL INFORMED, TOLD ME TO GET AWAY QUICKLY BECAUSE PEOPLE FROM THE REGIME WERE PLANNING TO PUT ME BACK IN PRISON TO GET MORE MONEY.
THAT SAME NIGHT, WE GOT IN THE CAR AND HEADED FOR ANTALYA.
THAT WAS TWO YEARS AGO.

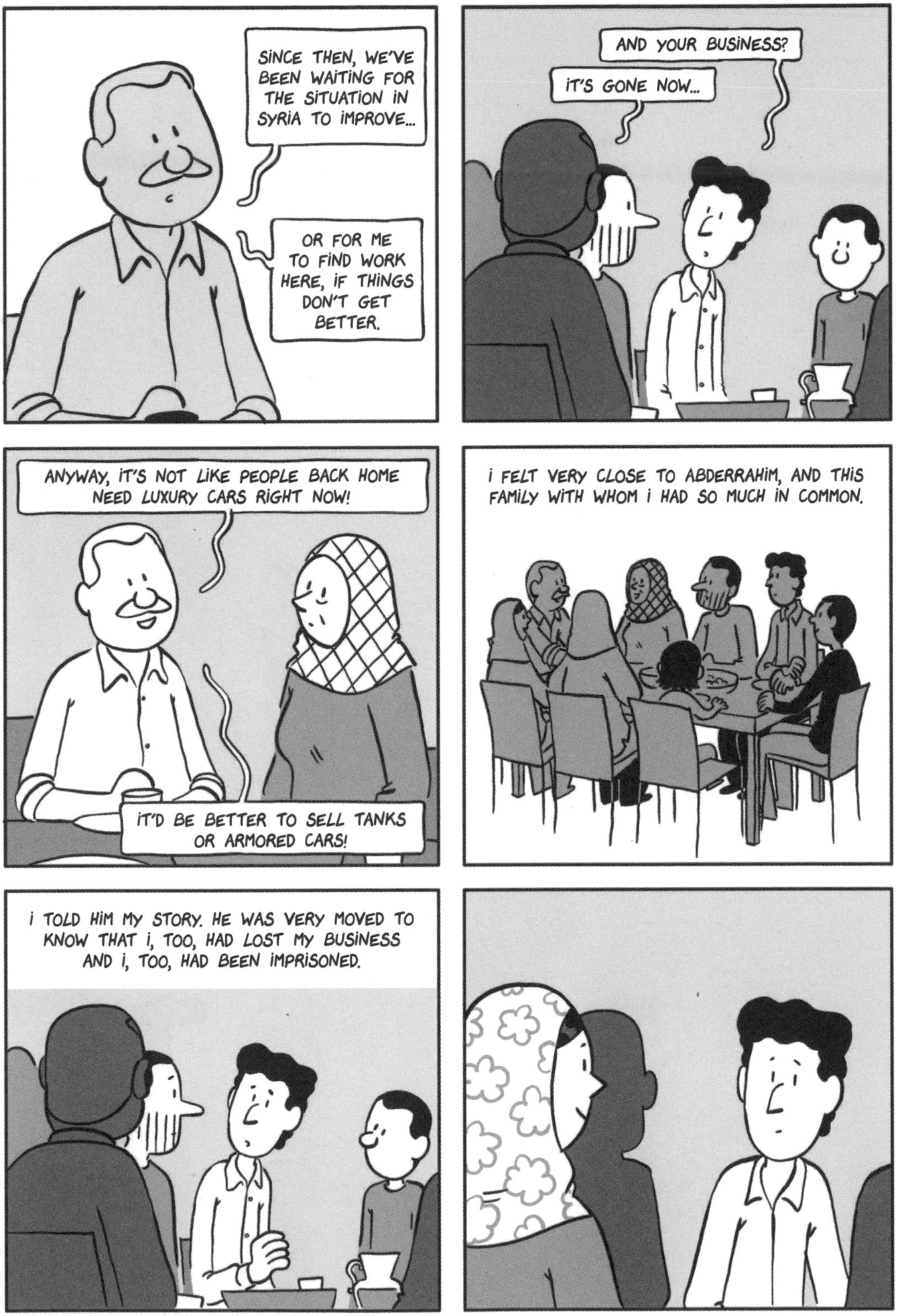
SINCE THEN, WE'VE BEEN WAITING FOR THE SITUATION IN SYRIA TO IMPROVE...
OR FOR ME TO FIND WORK HERE, IF THINGS DON'T GET BETTER.
AND YOUR BUSINESS?
IT'S GONE NOW...
ANYWAY, IT'S NOT LIKE PEOPLE BACK HOME NEED LUXURY CARS RIGHT NOW!
IT'D BE BETTER TO SELL TANKS OR ARMORED CARS!
I FELT VERY CLOSE TO ABDERRAHIM, AND THIS FAMILY WITH WHOM I HAD SO MUCH IN COMMON.
I TOLD HIM MY STORY. HE WAS VERY MOVED TO KNOW THAT I, TOO, HAD LOST MY BUSINESS AND I, TOO, HAD BEEN IMPRISONED.

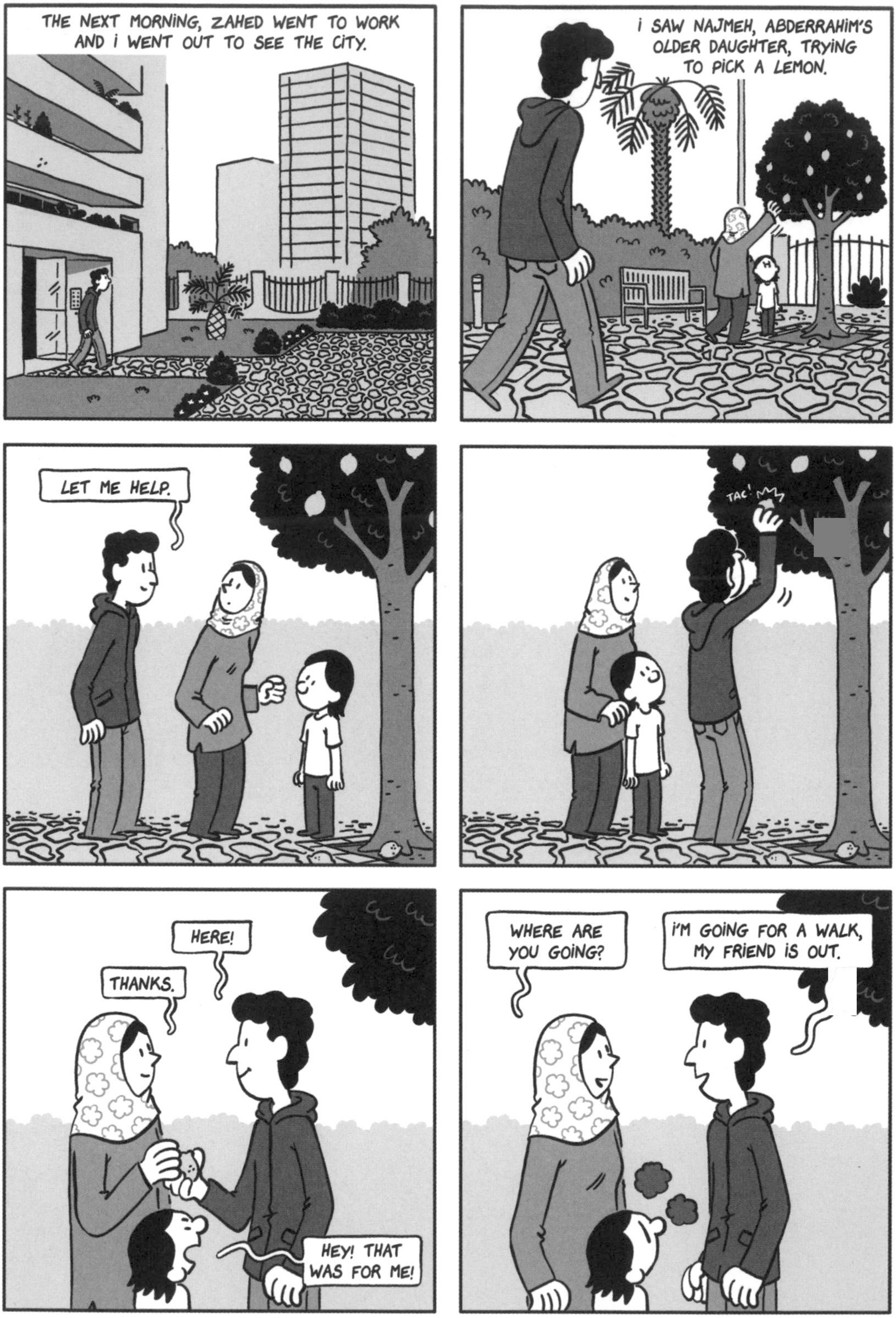
THE NEXT MORNING, ZAHED WENT TO WORK AND I WENT OUT TO SEE THE CITY.
I SAW NAJMEH, ABDERRAHIM'S OLDER DAUGHTER, TRYING TO PICK A LEMON.
LET ME HELP.
TAC!
THANKS.
HERE!
HEY! THAT WAS FOR ME!
WHERE ARE YOU GOING?
I'M GOING FOR A WALK, MY FRIEND IS OUT.

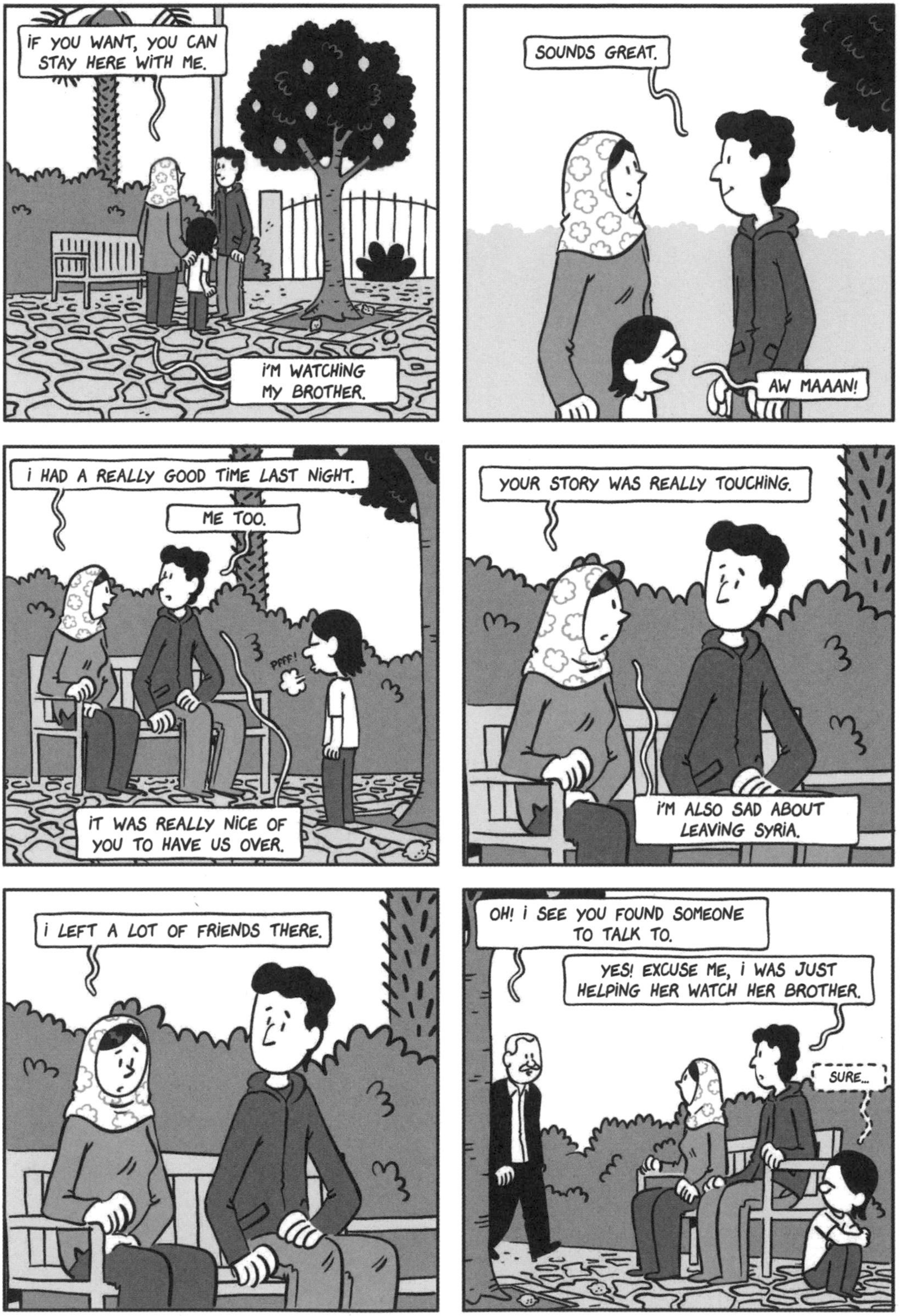
IF YOU WANT, YOU CAN STAY HERE WITH ME.
I'M WATCHING MY BROTHER.
SOUNDS GREAT.
AW MAAAN!
I HAD A REALLY GOOD TIME LAST NIGHT.
ME TOO.
PFFF!
IT WAS REALLY NICE OF YOU TO HAVE US OVER.
YOUR STORY WAS REALLY TOUCHING.
I'M ALSO SAD ABOUT LEAVING SYRIA.
I LEFT A LOT OF FRIENDS THERE.
OH! I SEE YOU FOUND SOMEONE TO TALK TO.
YES! EXCUSE ME, I WAS JUST HELPING HER WATCH HER BROTHER.
SURE...

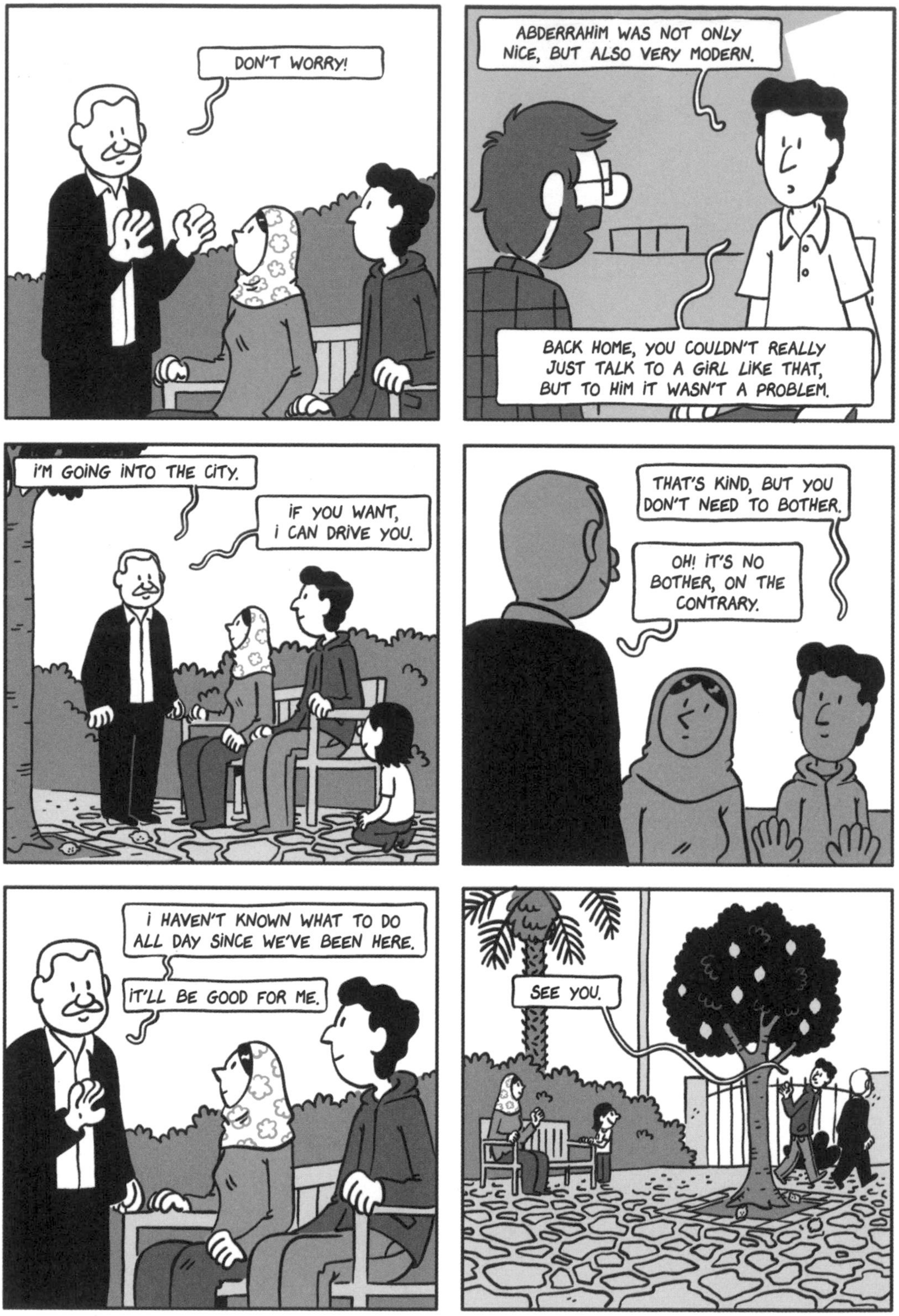
DON'T WORRY!
ABDERRAHIM WAS NOT ONLY NICE, BUT ALSO VERY MODERN.
BACK HOME, YOU COULDN'T REALLY JUST TALK TO A GIRL LIKE THAT, BUT TO HIM IT WASN'T A PROBLEM.
I'M GOING INTO THE CITY.
IF YOU WANT, I CAN DRIVE YOU.
THAT'S KIND, BUT YOU DON'T NEED TO BOTHER.
OH! IT'S NO BOTHER, ON THE CONTRARY.
I HAVEN'T KNOWN WHAT TO DO ALL DAY SINCE WE'VE BEEN HERE.
IT'LL BE GOOD FOR ME.
SEE YOU.

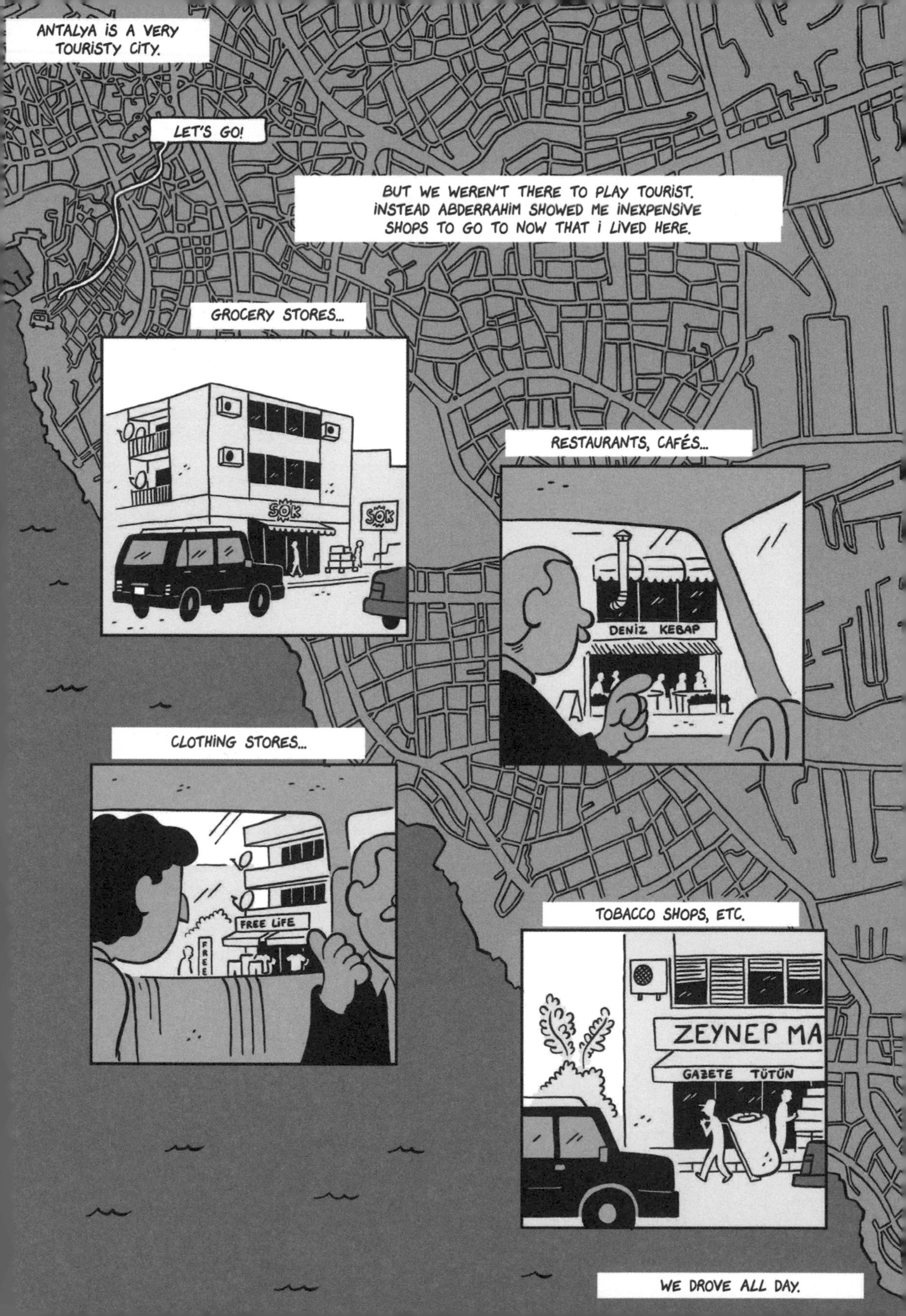
ANTALYA IS A VERY TOURISTY CITY.
LET'S GO!
BUT WE WEREN'T THERE TO PLAY TOURIST. INSTEAD ABDERRAHIM SHOWED ME INEXPENSIVE SHOPS TO GO TO NOW THAT I LIVED HERE.
GROCERY STORES...
ŞOK
ŞOK
RESTAURANTS, CAFÉS...
DENIZ KEBAP
CLOTHING STORES...
FREE LIFE
FREE
TOBACCO SHOPS, ETC.
ZEYNEP MA
GAZETE TÜTÜN
WE DROVE ALL DAY.

ABDERRAHIM DIDN'T SEEM VERY HAPPY IN THIS CITY.

TURKEY IS NOT AN EASY COUNTRY.

ZAHED TOLD ME I'D BE ABLE TO FIND WORK EASILY.

YOU'RE YOUNG!

IF YOU'RE NOT PICKY, YOU'LL FIND SOMETHING.

BUT FOR AN OLD MAN LIKE ME...

PLUS IT'S DIFFICULT TO FIT IN.

OFTEN, PEOPLE SPEAK ONLY TURKISH AND DON'T INTERMINGLE MUCH.

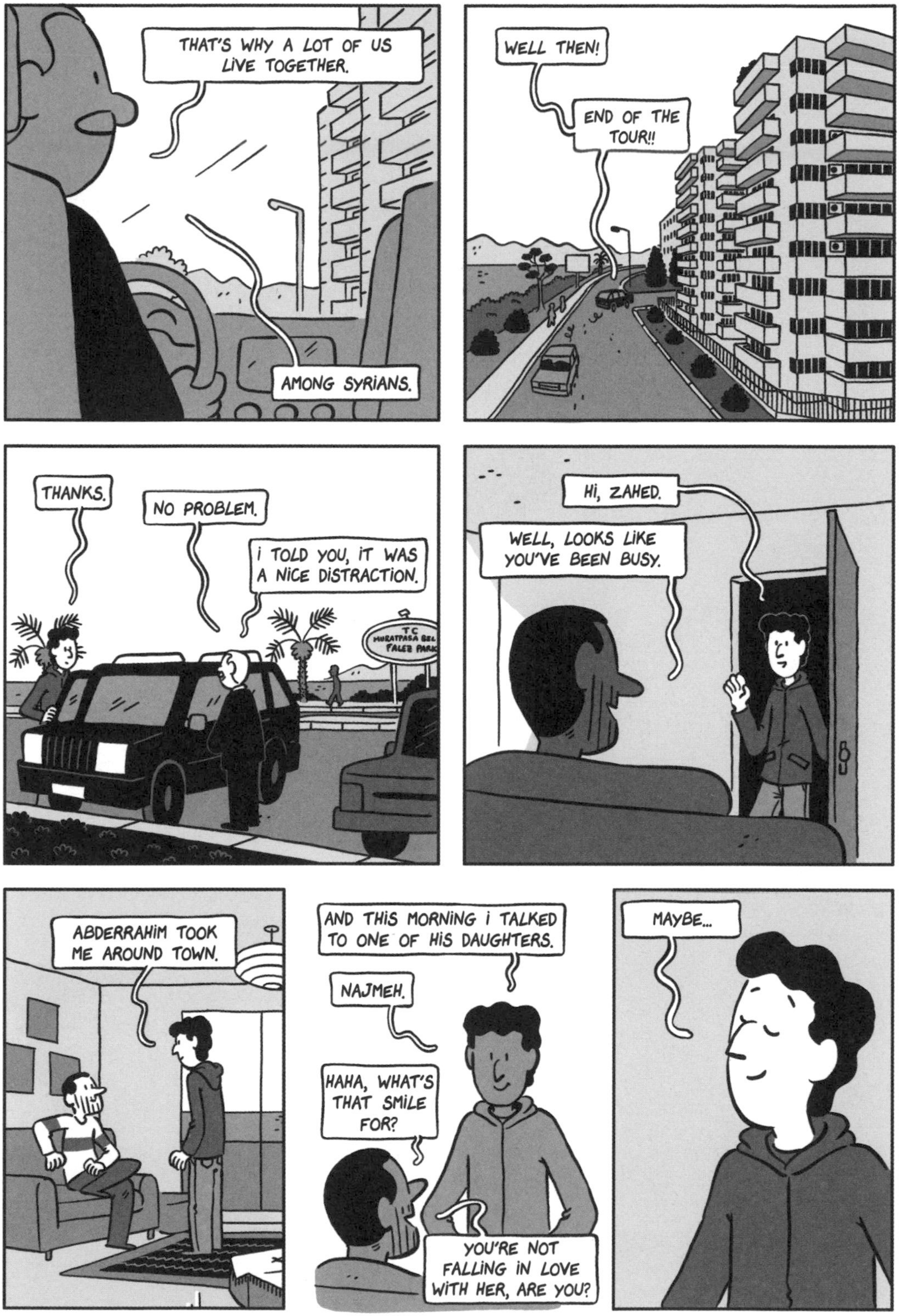
THAT'S WHY A LOT OF US LIVE TOGETHER.
AMONG SYRIANS.
WELL THEN!
END OF THE TOUR!!
THANKS.
NO PROBLEM.
I TOLD YOU, IT WAS A NICE DISTRACTION.
T.C. MURATPAŞA BEL. FALEZ PARK
HI, ZAHED.
WELL, LOOKS LIKE YOU'VE BEEN BUSY.
ABDERRAHIM TOOK ME AROUND TOWN.
AND THIS MORNING I TALKED TO ONE OF HIS DAUGHTERS.
NAJMEH.
HAHA, WHAT'S THAT SMILE FOR?
YOU'RE NOT FALLING IN LOVE WITH HER, ARE YOU?
MAYBE...

THE NEXT MORNING, AT THE SAME TIME, I WENT DOWN INTO THE YARD HOPING TO FIND HER.

AND SHE WAS THERE...

VRRR

HI, CAN I SIT HERE?

YES!

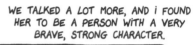
WE TALKED A LOT MORE, AND I FOUND HER TO BE A PERSON WITH A VERY BRAVE, STRONG CHARACTER.

AS SOON AS I'M OLD ENOUGH TO WORK, I'M GOING TO HELP MY FAMILY.

I DON'T WANT TO STAY AT HOME AND DO THE HOUSEWORK AND COOKING.

IT BECAME A KIND OF RITUAL. EVERY MORNING, I'D GO DOWN AND TALK WITH NAJMEH.

AGAIN?

WE KNEW WE LIKED EACH OTHER BUT DIDN'T SAY IT.

222

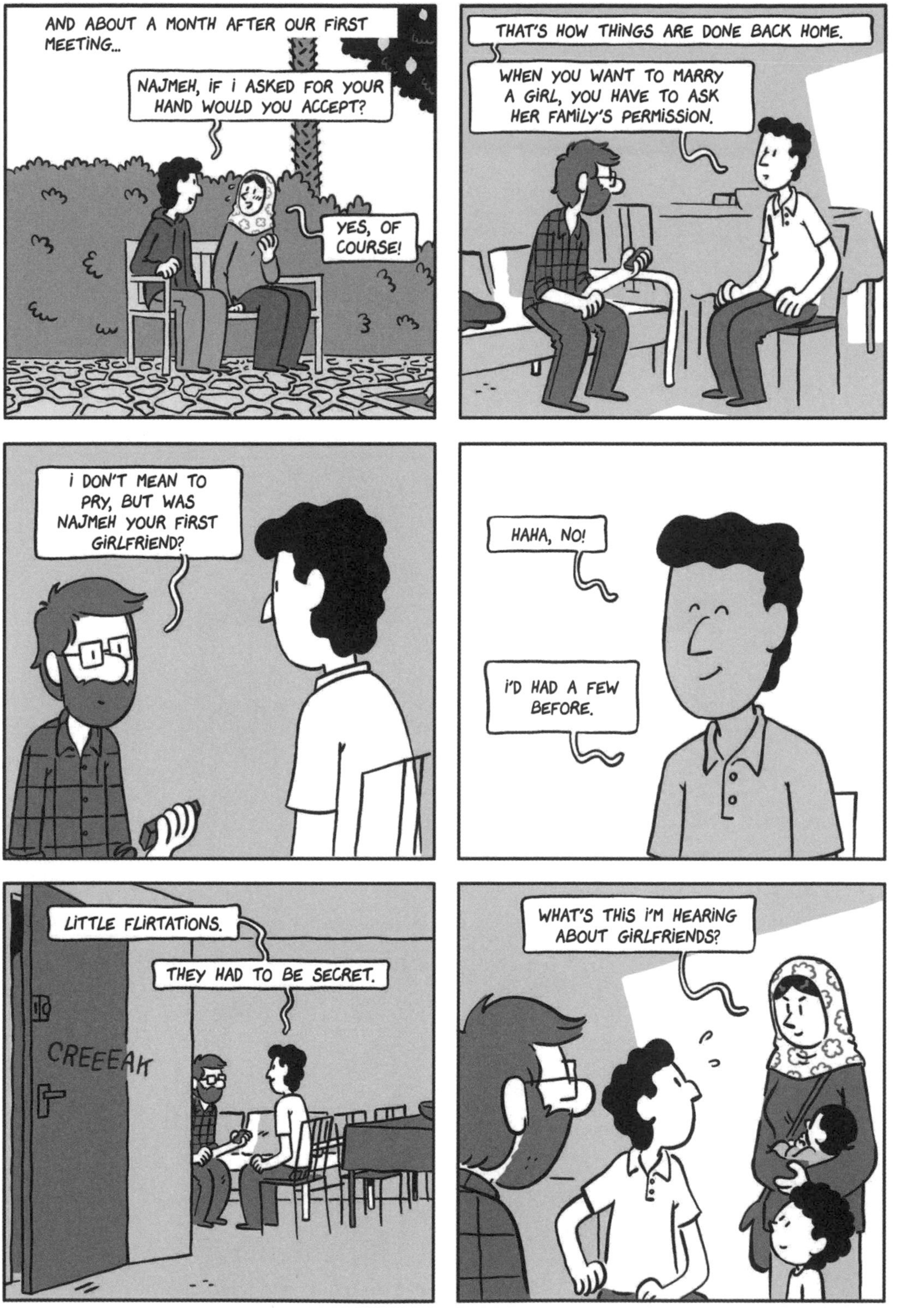
AND ABOUT A MONTH AFTER OUR FIRST MEETING...
NAJMEH, IF I ASKED FOR YOUR HAND WOULD YOU ACCEPT?
YES, OF COURSE!
THAT'S HOW THINGS ARE DONE BACK HOME.
WHEN YOU WANT TO MARRY A GIRL, YOU HAVE TO ASK HER FAMILY'S PERMISSION.
I DON'T MEAN TO PRY, BUT WAS NAJMEH YOUR FIRST GIRLFRIEND?
HAHA, NO!
I'D HAD A FEW BEFORE.
LITTLE FLIRTATIONS.
THEY HAD TO BE SECRET.
CREEEAK
WHAT'S THIS I'M HEARING ABOUT GIRLFRIENDS?

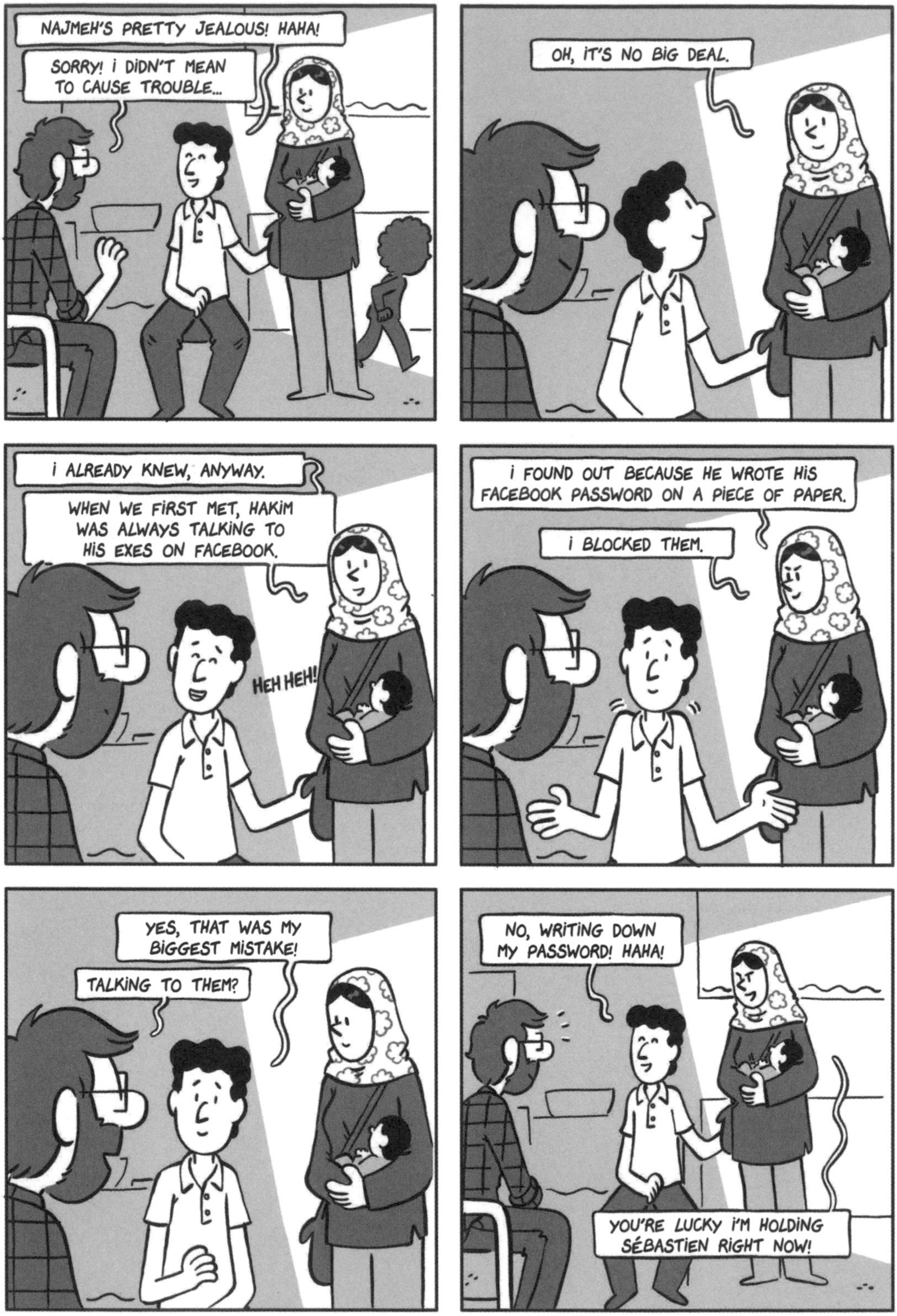
NAJMEH'S PRETTY JEALOUS! HAHA!
SORRY! i DIDN'T MEAN TO CAUSE TROUBLE...
OH, iT'S NO BiG DEAL.
i ALREADY KNEW, ANYWAY.
WHEN WE FiRST MET, HAKiM WAS ALWAYS TALKiNG TO HiS EXES ON FACEBOOK.
HEH HEH!
i FOUND OUT BECAUSE HE WROTE HiS FACEBOOK PASSWORD ON A PiECE OF PAPER.
i BLOCKED THEM.
TALKiNG TO THEM?
YES, THAT WAS MY BiGGEST MiSTAKE!
NO, WRiTiNG DOWN MY PASSWORD! HAHA!
YOU'RE LUCKY i'M HOLDiNG SÉBASTiEN RiGHT NOW!

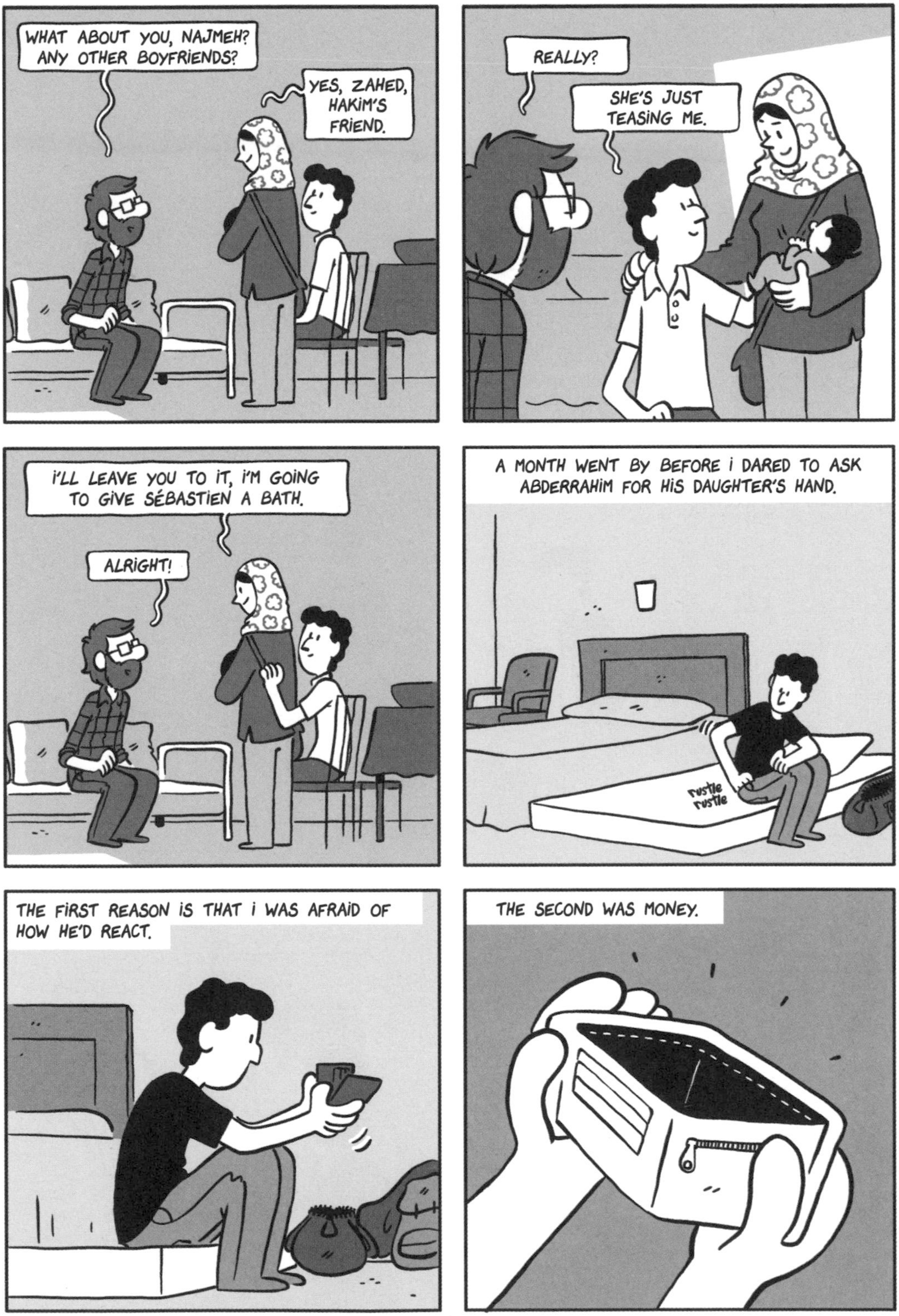

WHAT ABOUT YOU, NAJMEH? ANY OTHER BOYFRIENDS?
YES, ZAHED, HAKIM'S FRIEND.
REALLY?
SHE'S JUST TEASING ME.
I'LL LEAVE YOU TO IT, I'M GOING TO GIVE SÉBASTIEN A BATH.
ALRIGHT!
A MONTH WENT BY BEFORE I DARED TO ASK ABDERRAHIM FOR HIS DAUGHTER'S HAND.
rustle rustle
THE FIRST REASON IS THAT I WAS AFRAID OF HOW HE'D REACT.
THE SECOND WAS MONEY.

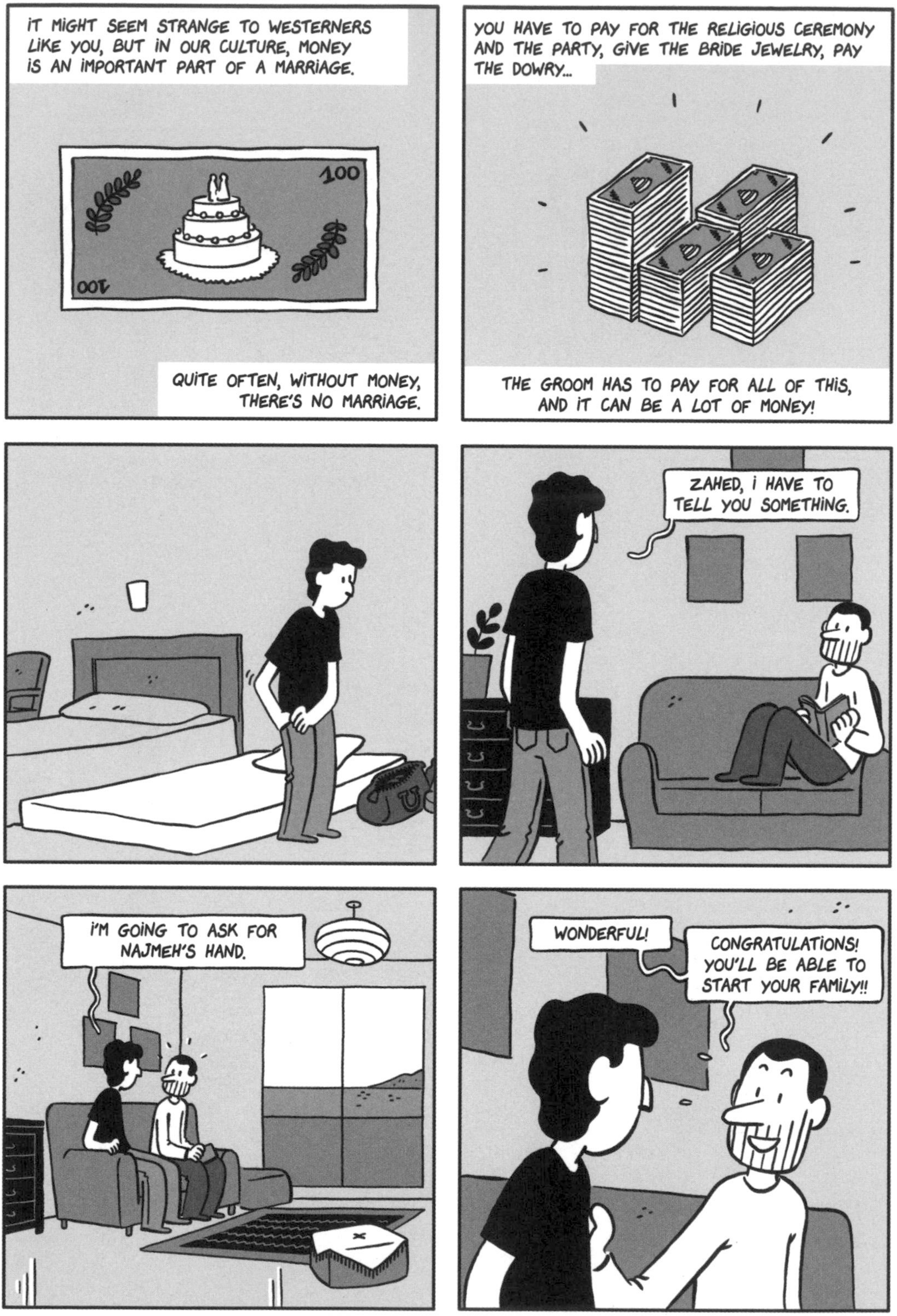
IT MIGHT SEEM STRANGE TO WESTERNERS LIKE YOU, BUT IN OUR CULTURE, MONEY IS AN IMPORTANT PART OF A MARRIAGE.
100
100
QUITE OFTEN, WITHOUT MONEY, THERE'S NO MARRIAGE.
YOU HAVE TO PAY FOR THE RELIGIOUS CEREMONY AND THE PARTY, GIVE THE BRIDE JEWELRY, PAY THE DOWRY...
THE GROOM HAS TO PAY FOR ALL OF THIS, AND IT CAN BE A LOT OF MONEY!
ZAHED, I HAVE TO TELL YOU SOMETHING.
I'M GOING TO ASK FOR NAJMEH'S HAND.
WONDERFUL!
CONGRATULATIONS! YOU'LL BE ABLE TO START YOUR FAMILY!!

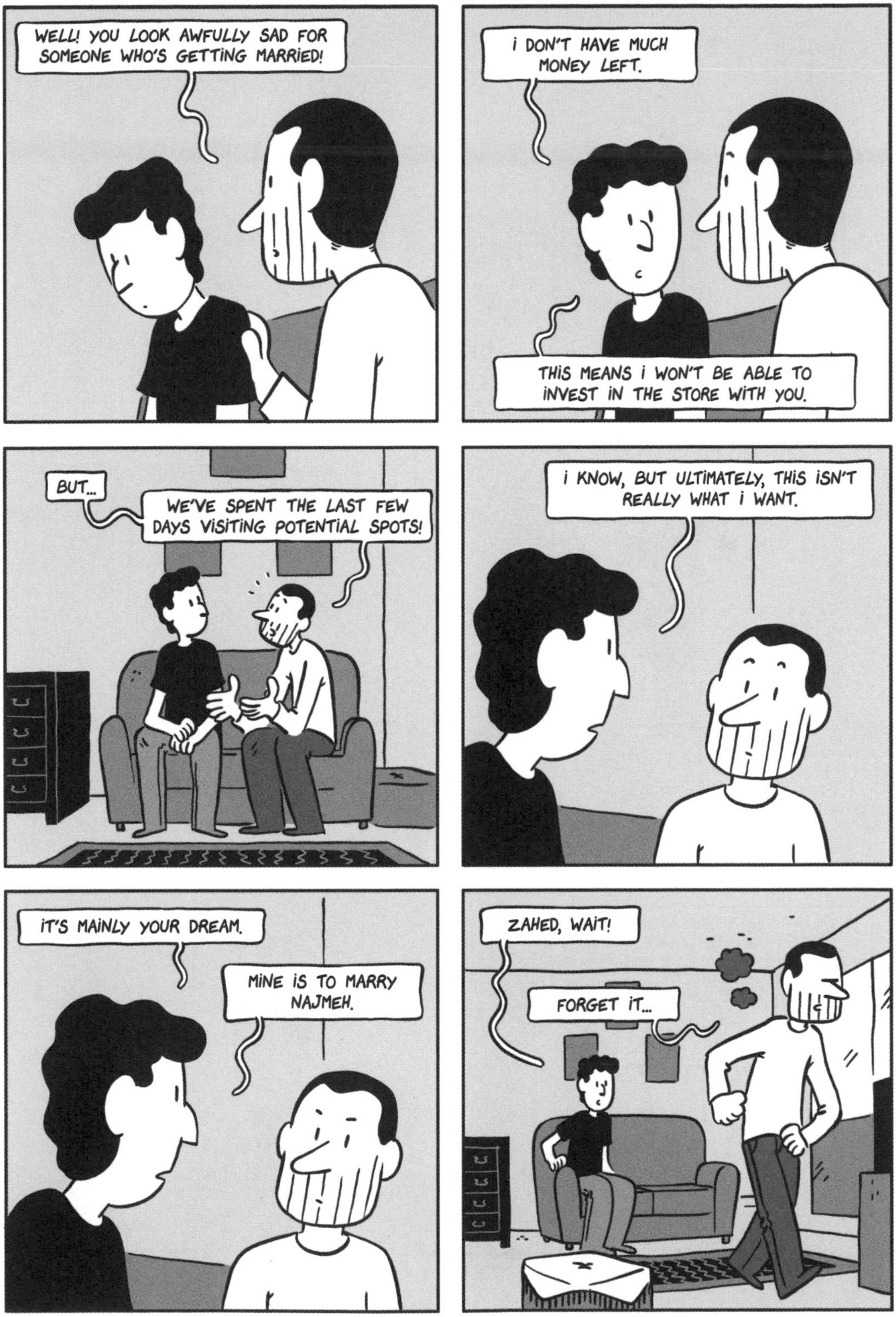
WELL! YOU LOOK AWFULLY SAD FOR SOMEONE WHO'S GETTING MARRIED!
I DON'T HAVE MUCH MONEY LEFT.
THIS MEANS I WON'T BE ABLE TO INVEST IN THE STORE WITH YOU.
BUT...
WE'VE SPENT THE LAST FEW DAYS VISITING POTENTIAL SPOTS!
I KNOW, BUT ULTIMATELY, THIS ISN'T REALLY WHAT I WANT.
IT'S MAINLY YOUR DREAM.
MINE IS TO MARRY NAJMEH.
ZAHED, WAIT!
FORGET IT...

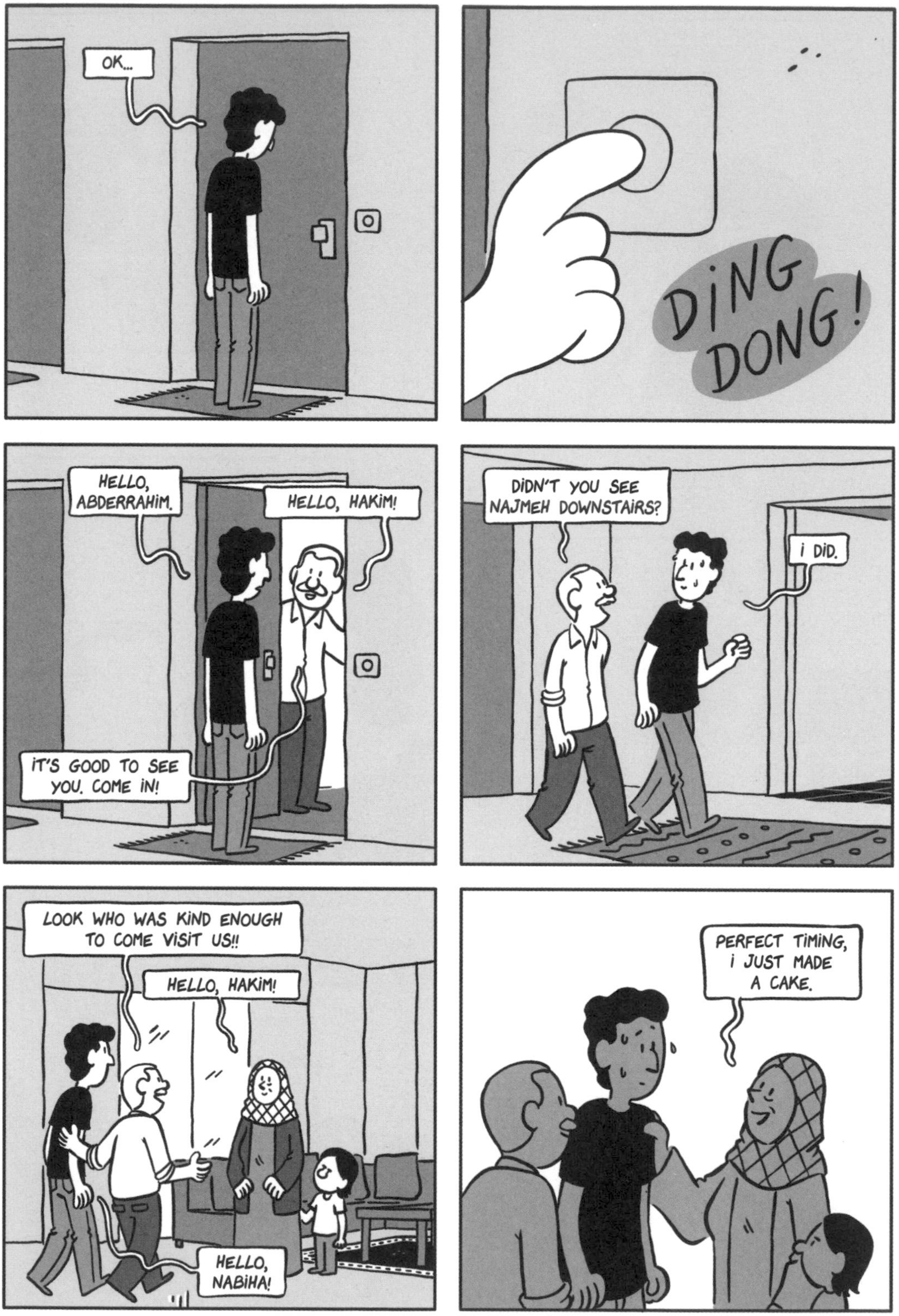
OK...
DING DONG!
HELLO, ABDERRAHIM.
HELLO, HAKIM!
IT'S GOOD TO SEE YOU. COME IN!
DIDN'T YOU SEE NAJMEH DOWNSTAIRS?
I DID.
LOOK WHO WAS KIND ENOUGH TO COME VISIT US!!
HELLO, HAKIM!
HELLO, NABIHA!
PERFECT TIMING, I JUST MADE A CAKE.

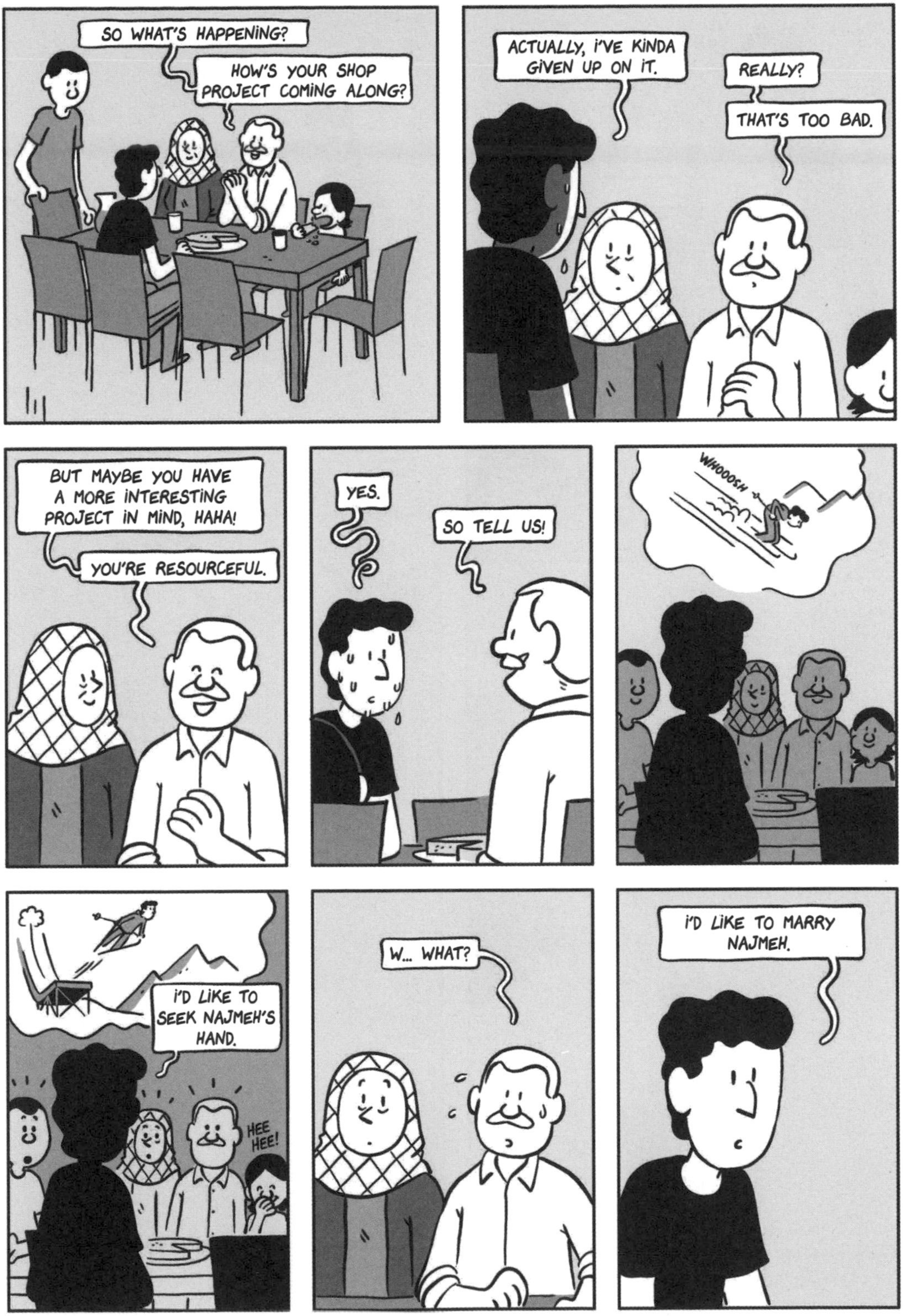
SO WHAT'S HAPPENING?
HOW'S YOUR SHOP PROJECT COMING ALONG?
ACTUALLY, I'VE KINDA GIVEN UP ON IT.
REALLY?
THAT'S TOO BAD.
BUT MAYBE YOU HAVE A MORE INTERESTING PROJECT IN MIND, HAHA!
YOU'RE RESOURCEFUL.
YES.
SO TELL US!
WHOOOSH
I'D LIKE TO SEEK NAJMEH'S HAND.
HEE HEE!
W... WHAT?
I'D LIKE TO MARRY NAJMEH.

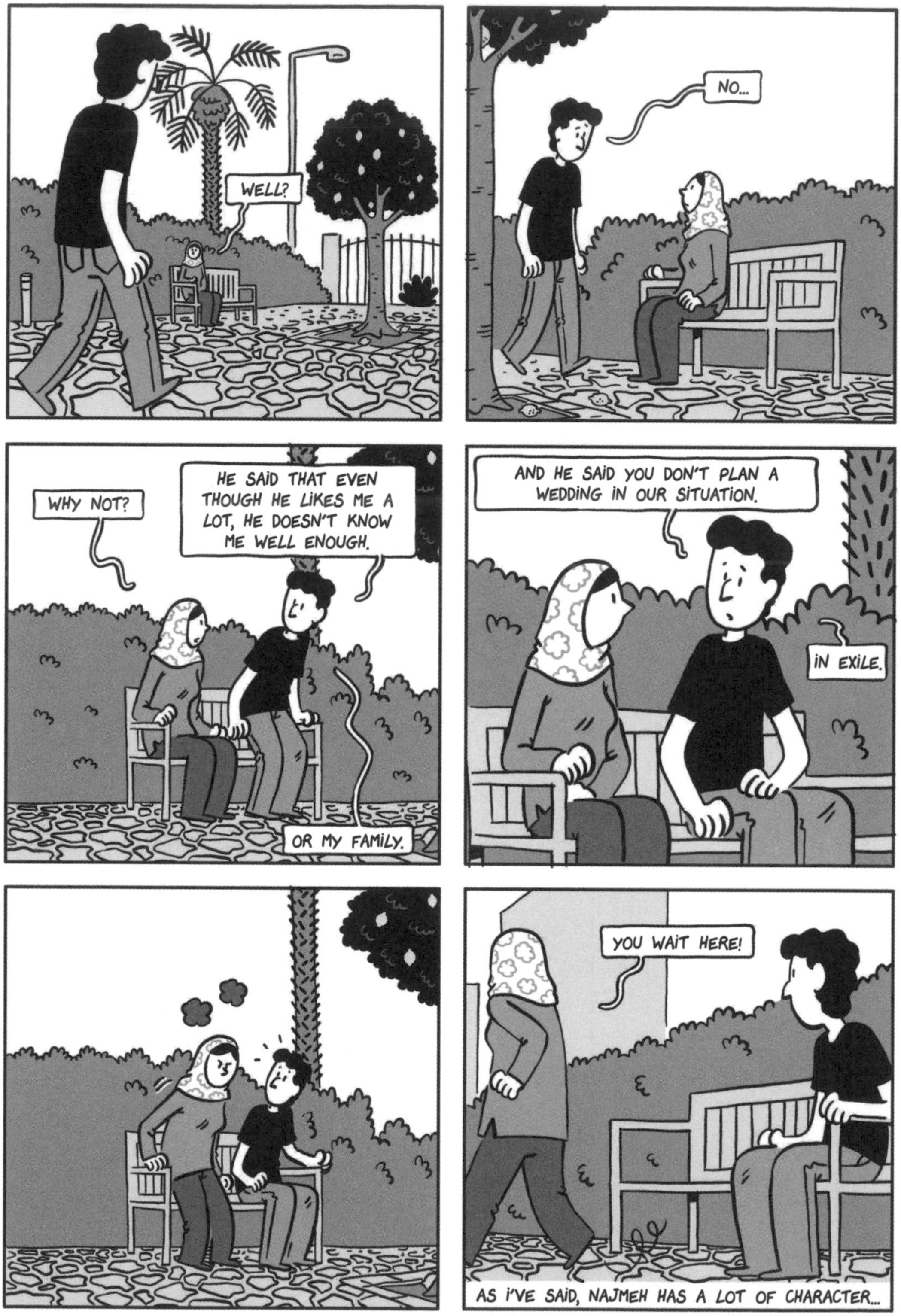
WELL?
NO...
WHY NOT?
HE SAID THAT EVEN THOUGH HE LIKES ME A LOT, HE DOESN'T KNOW ME WELL ENOUGH.
OR MY FAMILY.
AND HE SAID YOU DON'T PLAN A WEDDING IN OUR SITUATION.
IN EXILE.
YOU WAIT HERE!
AS I'VE SAID, NAJMEH HAS A LOT OF CHARACTER...

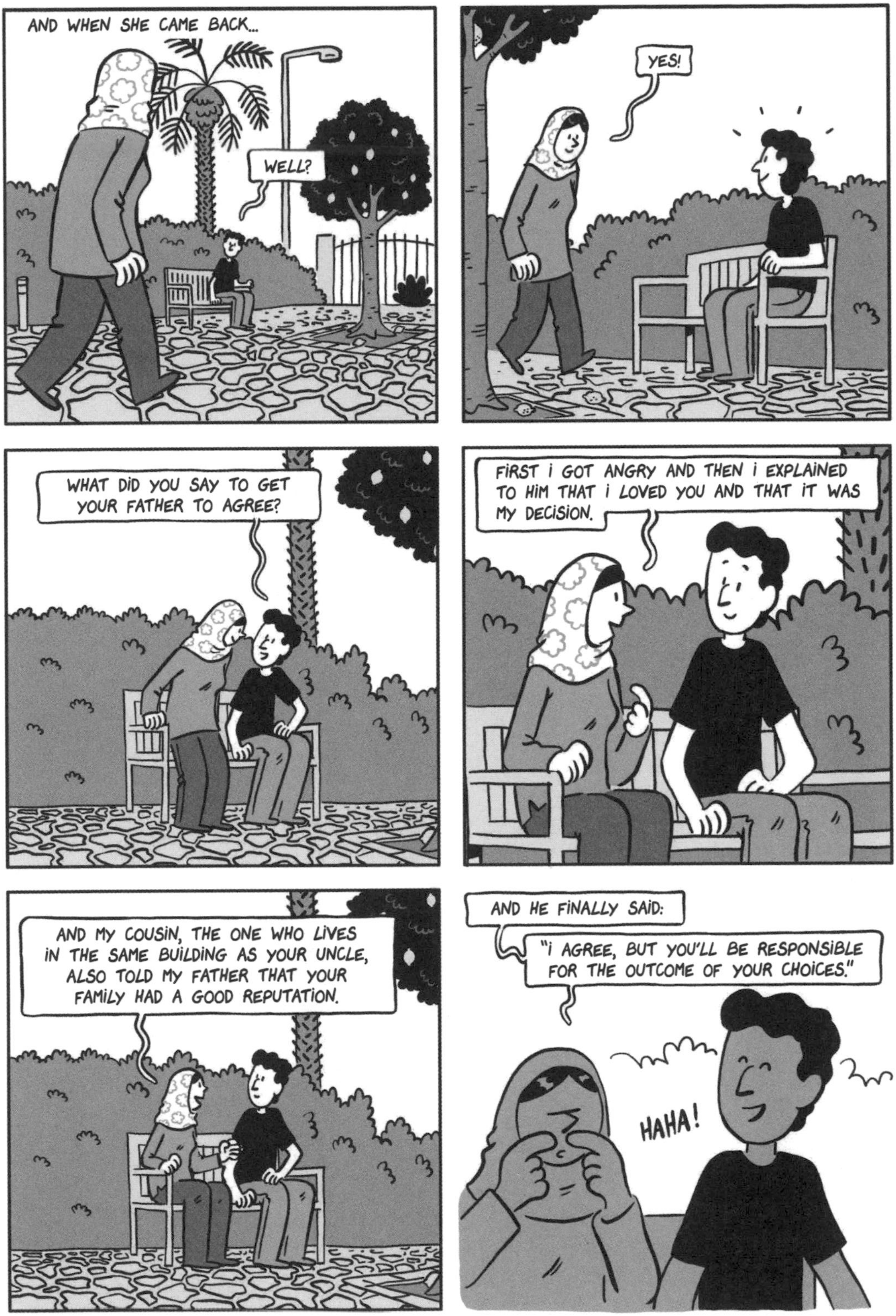

AND WHEN SHE CAME BACK...
WELL?
YES!
WHAT DID YOU SAY TO GET YOUR FATHER TO AGREE?
FIRST I GOT ANGRY AND THEN I EXPLAINED TO HIM THAT I LOVED YOU AND THAT IT WAS MY DECISION.
AND MY COUSIN, THE ONE WHO LIVES IN THE SAME BUILDING AS YOUR UNCLE, ALSO TOLD MY FATHER THAT YOUR FAMILY HAD A GOOD REPUTATION.
AND HE FINALLY SAID:
"I AGREE, BUT YOU'LL BE RESPONSIBLE FOR THE OUTCOME OF YOUR CHOICES."
HAHA!

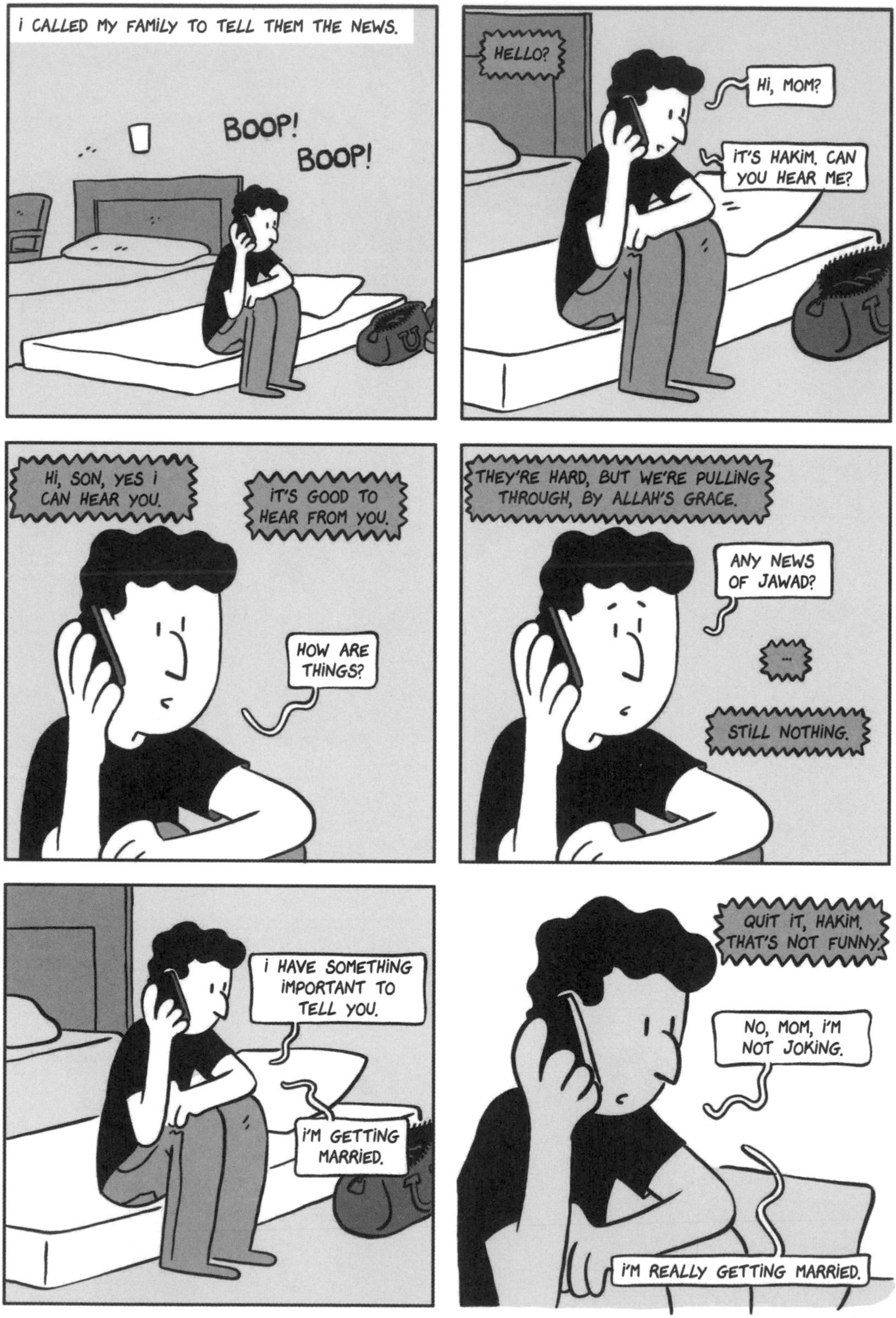
I CALLED MY FAMILY TO TELL THEM THE NEWS.
BOOP!
BOOP!
HELLO?
HI, MOM?
IT'S HAKIM. CAN YOU HEAR ME?
HI, SON, YES I CAN HEAR YOU.
IT'S GOOD TO HEAR FROM YOU.
HOW ARE THINGS?
THEY'RE HARD, BUT WE'RE PULLING THROUGH, BY ALLAH'S GRACE.
ANY NEWS OF JAWAD?
...
STILL NOTHING.
I HAVE SOMETHING IMPORTANT TO TELL YOU.
I'M GETTING MARRIED.
QUIT IT, HAKIM. THAT'S NOT FUNNY.
NO, MOM, I'M NOT JOKING.
I'M REALLY GETTING MARRIED.

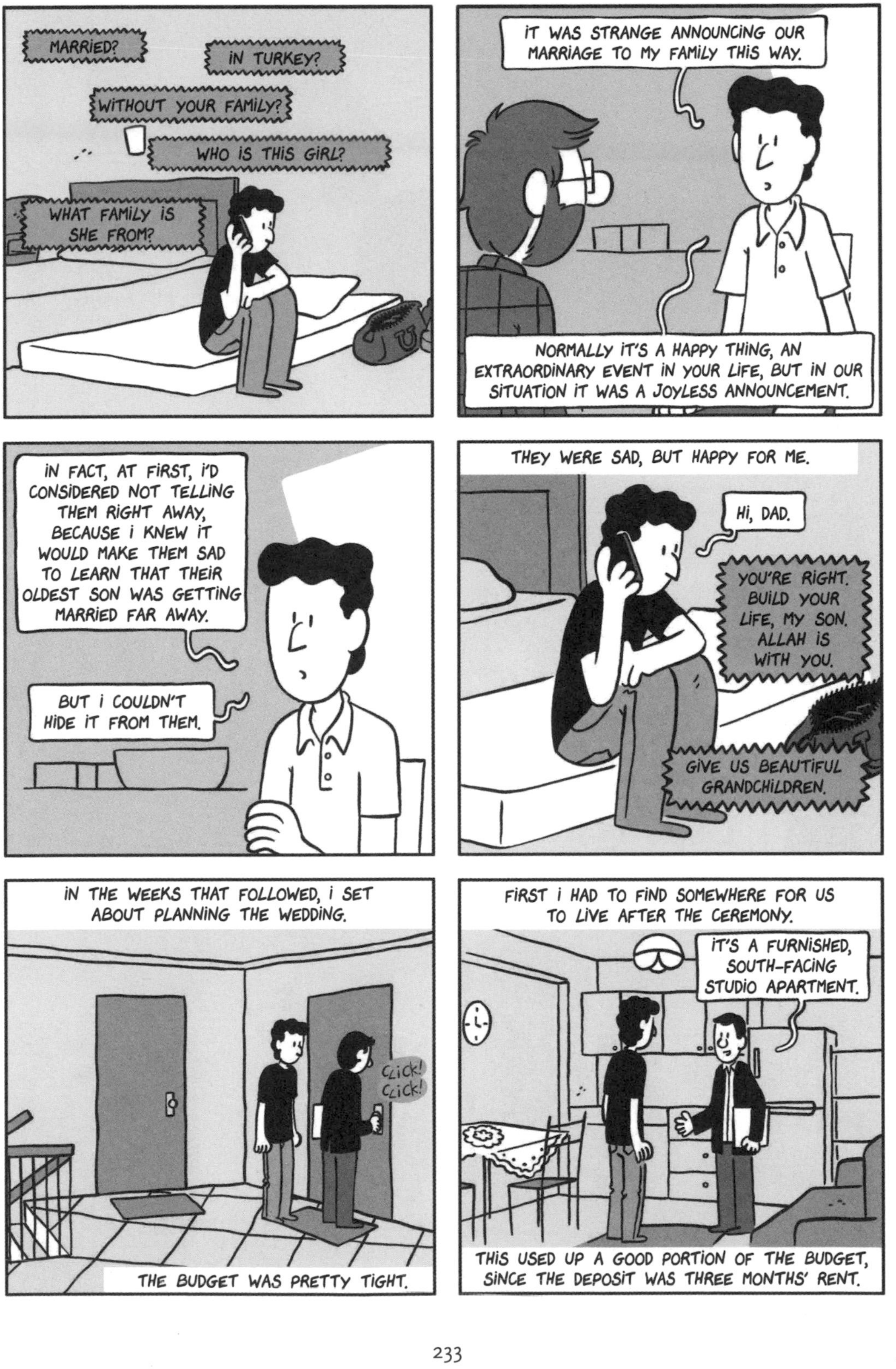
MARRIED?
IN TURKEY?
WITHOUT YOUR FAMILY?
WHO IS THIS GIRL?
WHAT FAMILY IS SHE FROM?
IT WAS STRANGE ANNOUNCING OUR MARRIAGE TO MY FAMILY THIS WAY.
NORMALLY IT'S A HAPPY THING, AN EXTRAORDINARY EVENT IN YOUR LIFE, BUT IN OUR SITUATION IT WAS A JOYLESS ANNOUNCEMENT.
IN FACT, AT FIRST, I'D CONSIDERED NOT TELLING THEM RIGHT AWAY, BECAUSE I KNEW IT WOULD MAKE THEM SAD TO LEARN THAT THEIR OLDEST SON WAS GETTING MARRIED FAR AWAY.
BUT I COULDN'T HIDE IT FROM THEM.
THEY WERE SAD, BUT HAPPY FOR ME.
HI, DAD.
YOU'RE RIGHT. BUILD YOUR LIFE, MY SON. ALLAH IS WITH YOU.
GIVE US BEAUTIFUL GRANDCHILDREN.
IN THE WEEKS THAT FOLLOWED, I SET ABOUT PLANNING THE WEDDING.
CLICK! CLICK!
THE BUDGET WAS PRETTY TIGHT.
FIRST I HAD TO FIND SOMEWHERE FOR US TO LIVE AFTER THE CEREMONY.
IT'S A FURNISHED, SOUTH-FACING STUDIO APARTMENT.
THIS USED UP A GOOD PORTION OF THE BUDGET, SINCE THE DEPOSIT WAS THREE MONTHS' RENT.

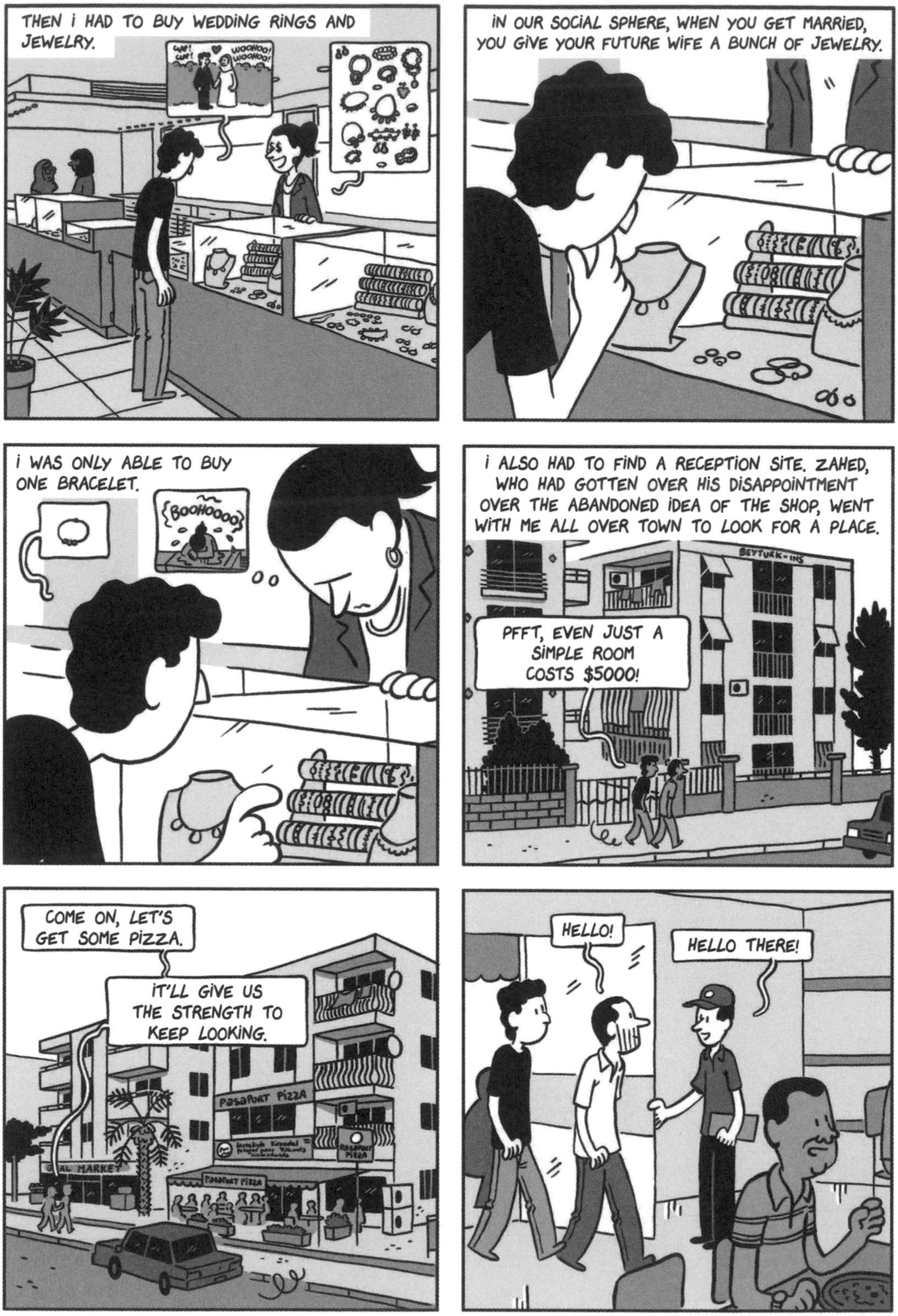

THEN I HAD TO BUY WEDDING RINGS AND JEWELRY.
IN OUR SOCIAL SPHERE, WHEN YOU GET MARRIED, YOU GIVE YOUR FUTURE WIFE A BUNCH OF JEWELRY.
I WAS ONLY ABLE TO BUY ONE BRACELET.
BOOHOOOO
I ALSO HAD TO FIND A RECEPTION SITE. ZAHED, WHO HAD GOTTEN OVER HIS DISAPPOINTMENT OVER THE ABANDONED IDEA OF THE SHOP, WENT WITH ME ALL OVER TOWN TO LOOK FOR A PLACE.
BEYTURK-INS
PFFT, EVEN JUST A SIMPLE ROOM COSTS $5000!
COME ON, LET'S GET SOME PIZZA.
IT'LL GIVE US THE STRENGTH TO KEEP LOOKING.
PASAPORT PIZZA
HELLO!
HELLO THERE!

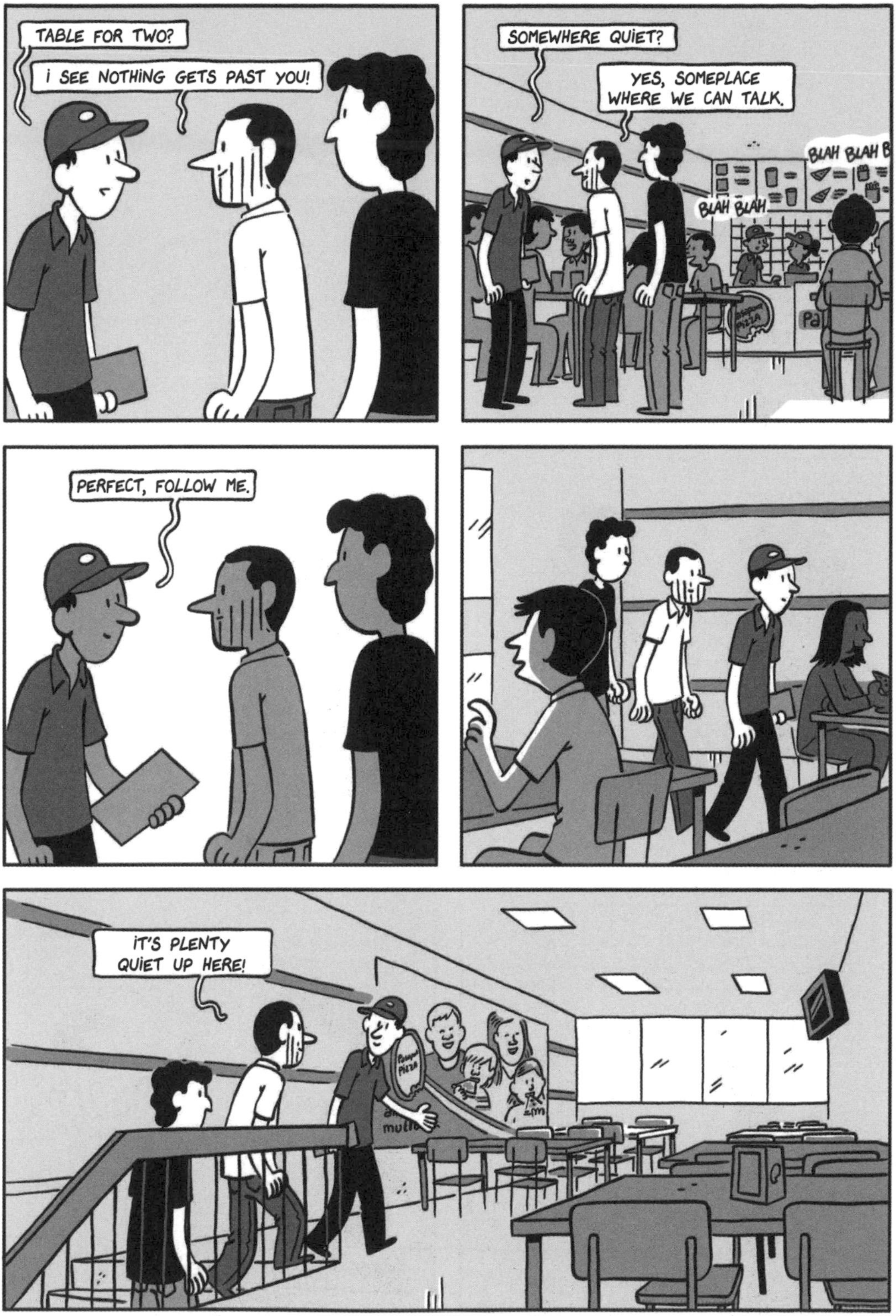
TABLE FOR TWO?
I SEE NOTHING GETS PAST YOU!
SOMEWHERE QUIET?
YES, SOMEPLACE WHERE WE CAN TALK.
BLAH BLAH
BLAH BLAH
PERFECT, FOLLOW ME.
IT'S PLENTY QUIET UP HERE!

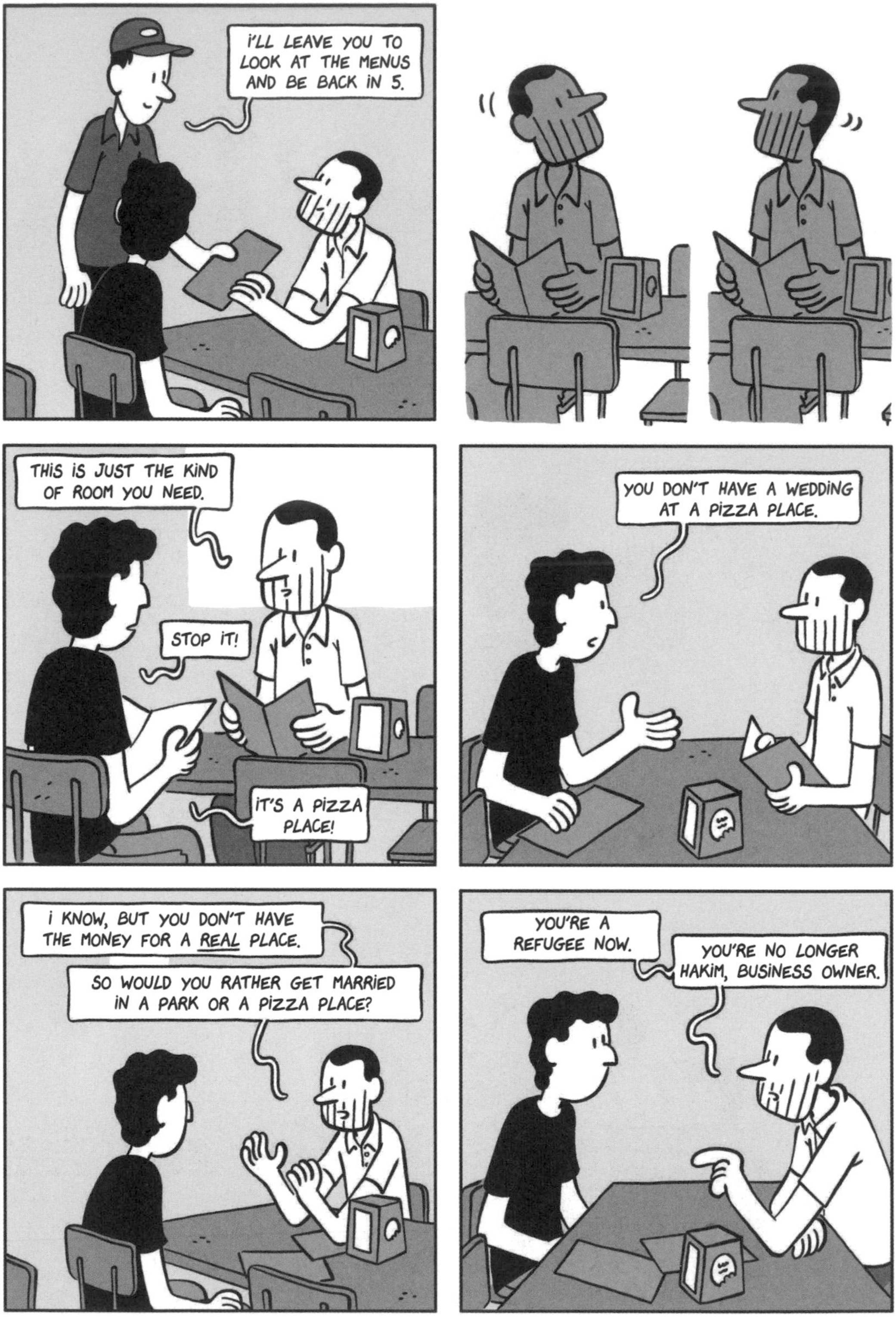
I'LL LEAVE YOU TO LOOK AT THE MENUS AND BE BACK IN 5.
THIS IS JUST THE KIND OF ROOM YOU NEED.
STOP IT!
IT'S A PIZZA PLACE!
YOU DON'T HAVE A WEDDING AT A PIZZA PLACE.
I KNOW, BUT YOU DON'T HAVE THE MONEY FOR A REAL PLACE.
SO WOULD YOU RATHER GET MARRIED IN A PARK OR A PIZZA PLACE?
YOU'RE A REFUGEE NOW.
YOU'RE NO LONGER HAKIM, BUSINESS OWNER.

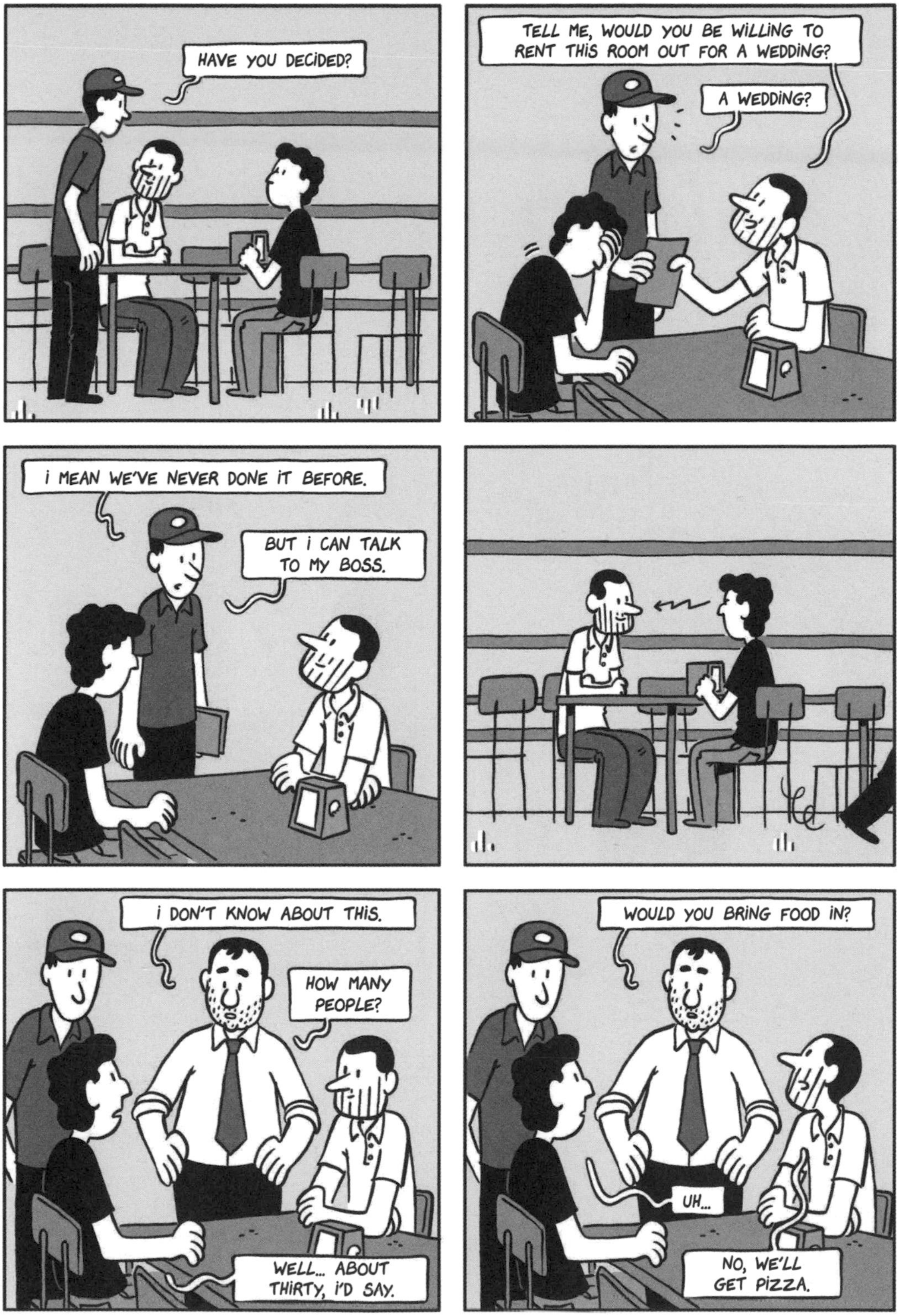
HAVE YOU DECIDED?
TELL ME, WOULD YOU BE WILLING TO RENT THIS ROOM OUT FOR A WEDDING?
A WEDDING?
I MEAN WE'VE NEVER DONE IT BEFORE.
BUT I CAN TALK TO MY BOSS.
I DON'T KNOW ABOUT THIS.
HOW MANY PEOPLE?
WELL... ABOUT THIRTY, I'D SAY.
WOULD YOU BRING FOOD IN?
UH...
NO, WE'LL GET PIZZA.

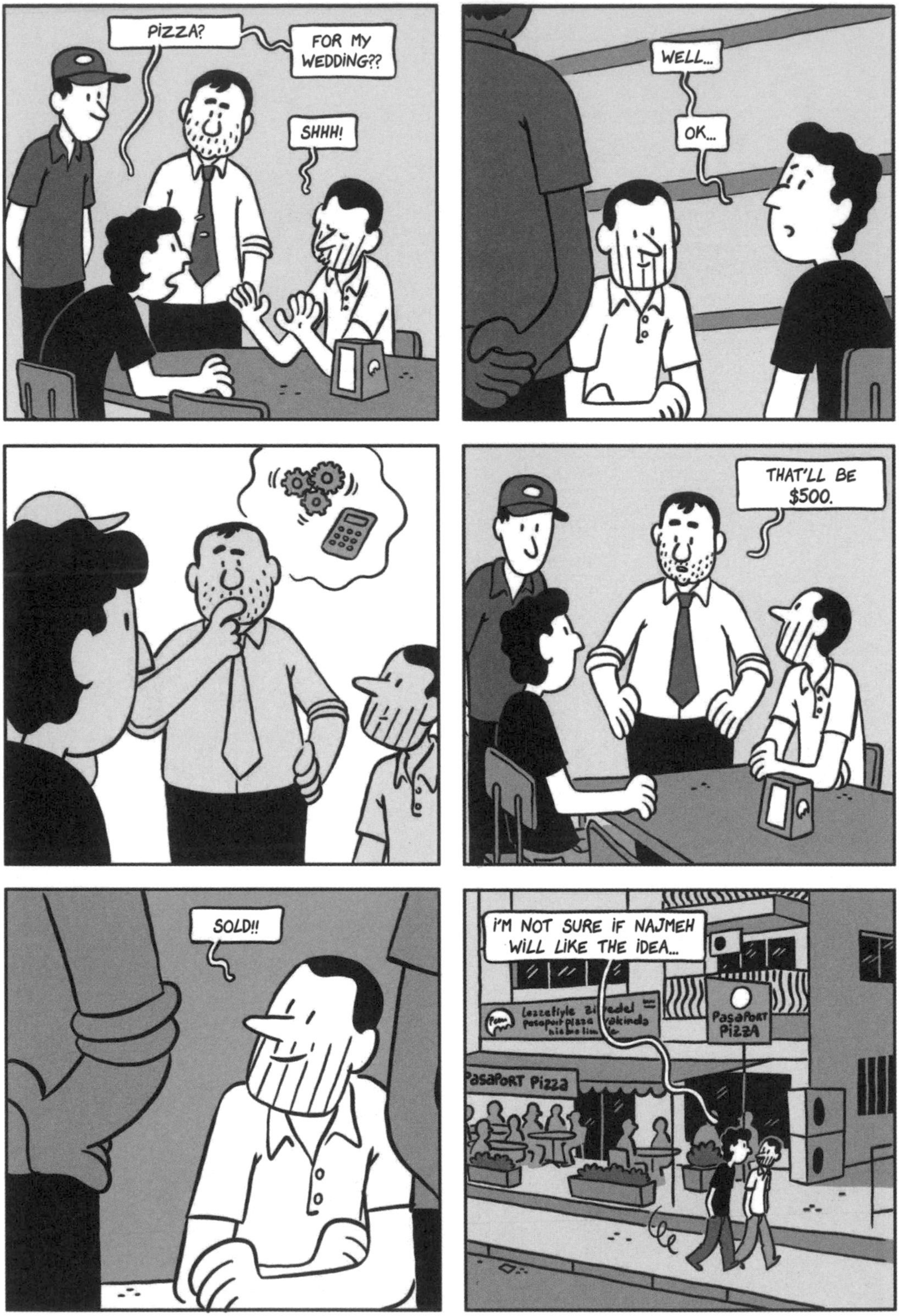
PiZZA?
FOR MY WEDDiNG??
SHHH!
WELL...
OK...
THAT'LL BE $500.
SOLD!!
i'M NOT SURE iF NAJMEH WiLL LiKE THE iDEA...
PaSaPORT PiZZA
PaSaPORT Pizza

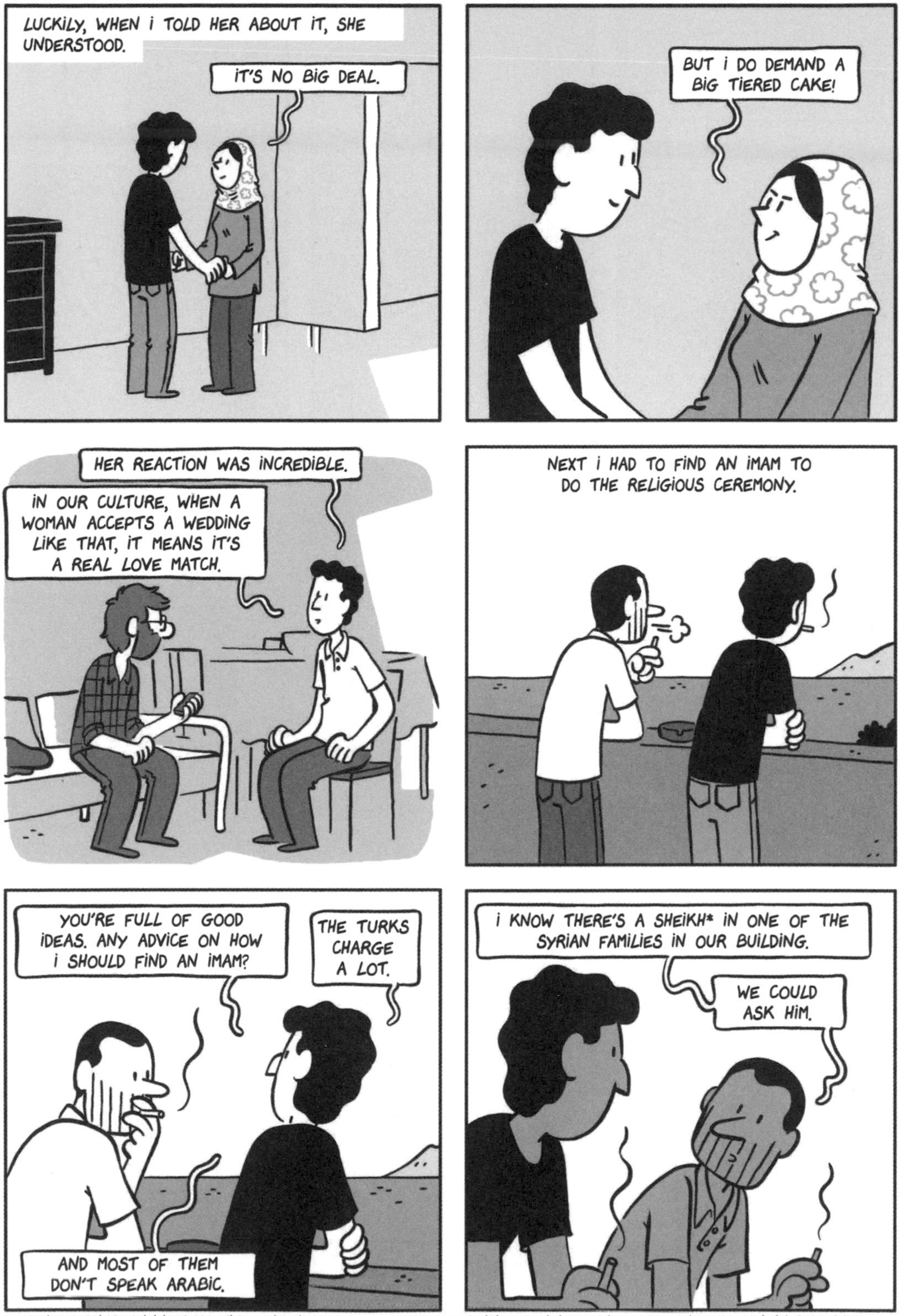
LUCKILY, WHEN I TOLD HER ABOUT IT, SHE UNDERSTOOD.
IT'S NO BIG DEAL.
BUT I DO DEMAND A BIG TIERED CAKE!
HER REACTION WAS INCREDIBLE.
IN OUR CULTURE, WHEN A WOMAN ACCEPTS A WEDDING LIKE THAT, IT MEANS IT'S A REAL LOVE MATCH.
NEXT I HAD TO FIND AN IMAM TO DO THE RELIGIOUS CEREMONY.
YOU'RE FULL OF GOOD IDEAS. ANY ADVICE ON HOW I SHOULD FIND AN IMAM?
THE TURKS CHARGE A LOT.
AND MOST OF THEM DON'T SPEAK ARABIC.
I KNOW THERE'S A SHEIKH* IN ONE OF THE SYRIAN FAMILIES IN OUR BUILDING.
WE COULD ASK HIM.

*AMONG MUSLIMS, AN INFORMAL TITLE GIVEN TO A MAN WHO HAS EXTENSIVE RELIGIOUS KNOWLEDGE AND WHO CAN, IN CERTAIN CEREMONIES, ACT AS A SUBSTITUTE FOR AN IMAM.

SO, GENTLEMEN, WHAT CAN I DO FOR YOU?

MY FRIEND, HAKIM, IS LOOKING FOR SOMEONE TO MARRY HIM.

AND WE WERE WONDERING IF YOU COULD DO IT?

...

YES, I CAN.

SHOULDN'T WE HAVE ASKED HIM HOW MUCH HE'D CHARGE?

HAHA, OF COURSE NOT, HAKIM! THAT KIND OF PERSON IS SELFLESS... HE'S DOING IT FOR THE LOVE OF PEOPLE AND ISLAM!

CLACK!

ANYWAY, THANKS, ZAHED!

WITHOUT YOU, THERE WOULD BE NO WEDDING.

THAT WOULD ALMOST BE BETTER FOR ME!

YOU'LL STILL MANAGE TO OPEN YOUR SHOP.

I'M SURE OF IT!

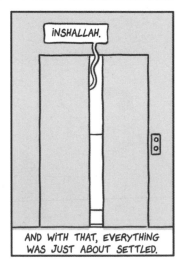

INSHALLAH.

AND WITH THAT, EVERYTHING WAS JUST ABOUT SETTLED.

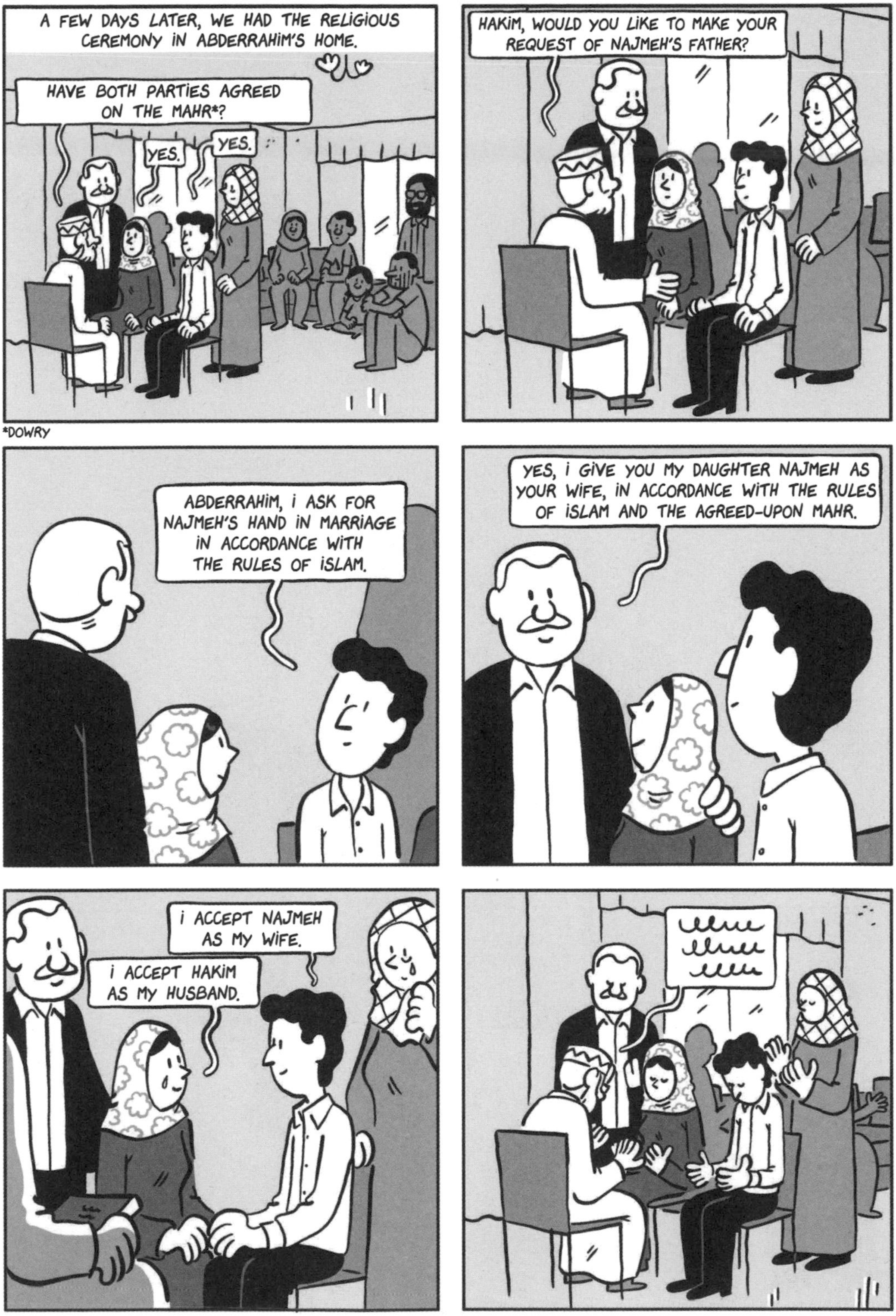
A FEW DAYS LATER, WE HAD THE RELIGIOUS CEREMONY IN ABDERRAHIM'S HOME.
HAVE BOTH PARTIES AGREED ON THE MAHR*?
YES.
YES.
HAKIM, WOULD YOU LIKE TO MAKE YOUR REQUEST OF NAJMEH'S FATHER?
ABDERRAHIM, I ASK FOR NAJMEH'S HAND IN MARRIAGE IN ACCORDANCE WITH THE RULES OF ISLAM.
YES, I GIVE YOU MY DAUGHTER NAJMEH AS YOUR WIFE, IN ACCORDANCE WITH THE RULES OF ISLAM AND THE AGREED-UPON MAHR.
I ACCEPT NAJMEH AS MY WIFE.
I ACCEPT HAKIM AS MY HUSBAND.

*DOWRY

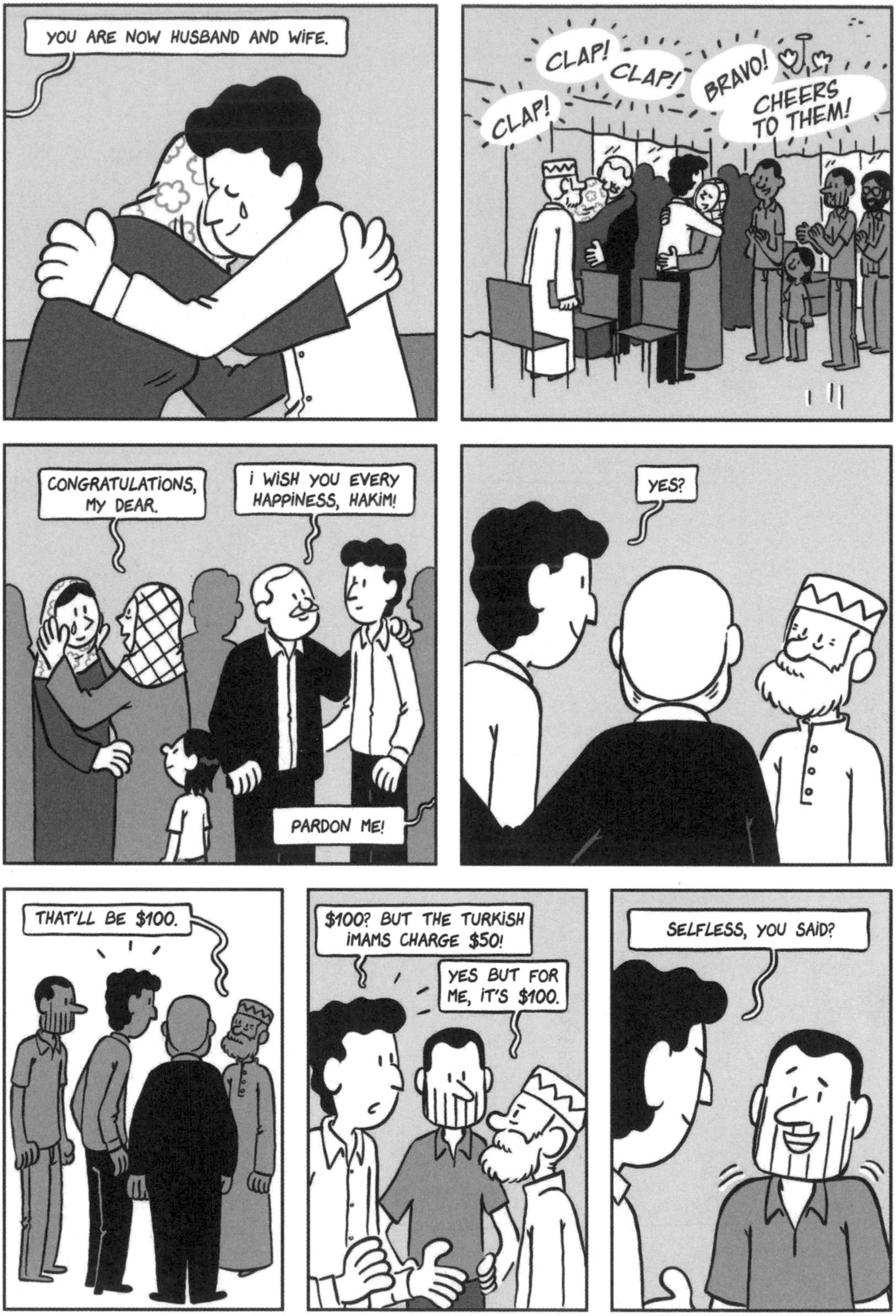
YOU ARE NOW HUSBAND AND WIFE.
CLAP!
CLAP!
CLAP!
BRAVO!
CHEERS TO THEM!
CONGRATULATIONS, MY DEAR.
I WISH YOU EVERY HAPPINESS, HAKIM!
PARDON ME!
YES?
THAT'LL BE $100.
$100? BUT THE TURKISH IMAMS CHARGE $50!
YES BUT FOR ME, IT'S $100.
SELFLESS, YOU SAID?

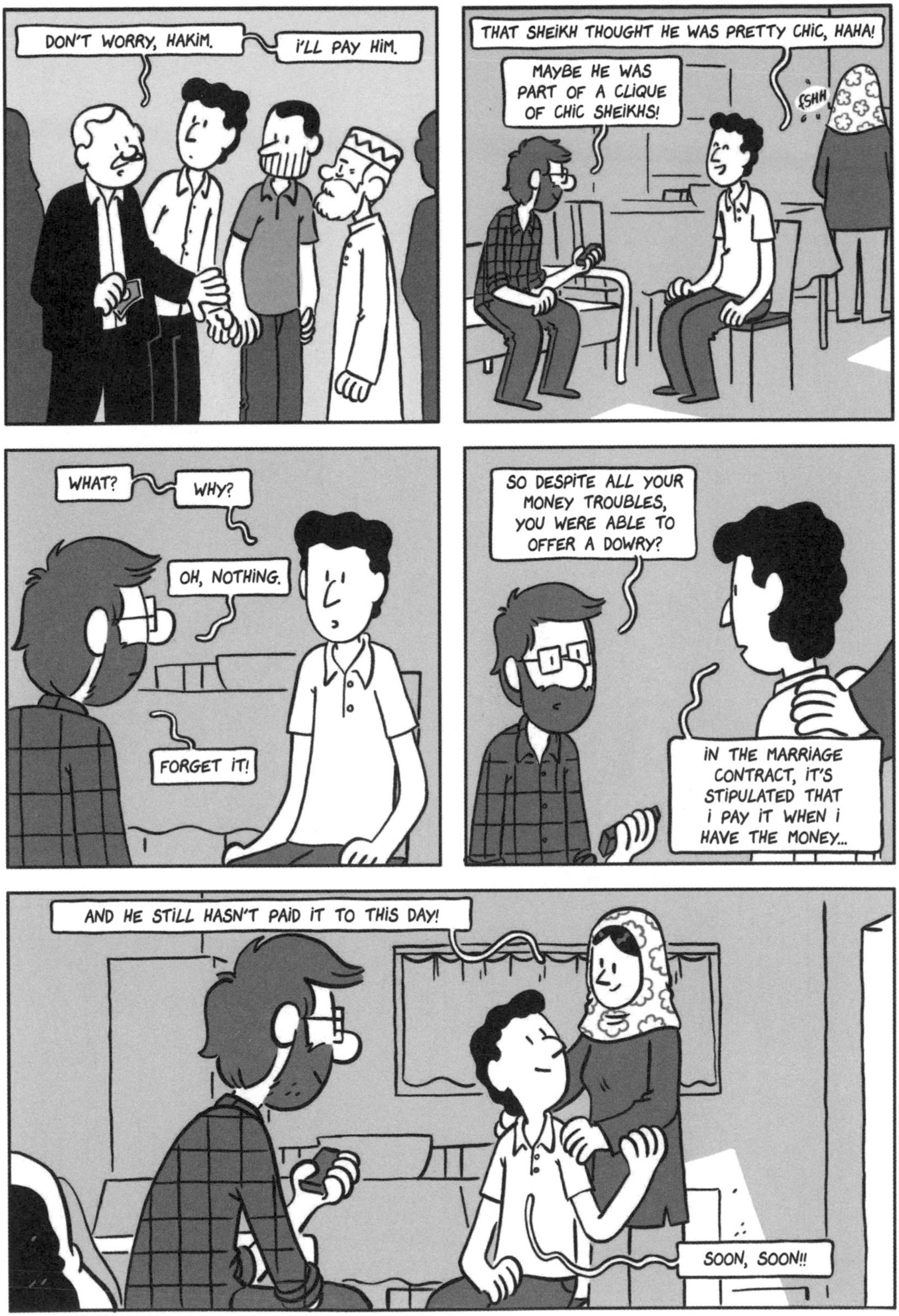
DON'T WORRY, HAKIM.
I'LL PAY HIM.
THAT SHEIKH THOUGHT HE WAS PRETTY CHIC, HAHA!
MAYBE HE WAS PART OF A CLIQUE OF CHIC SHEIKHS!
FSHH
WHAT?
WHY?
OH, NOTHING.
FORGET IT!
SO DESPITE ALL YOUR MONEY TROUBLES, YOU WERE ABLE TO OFFER A DOWRY?
IN THE MARRIAGE CONTRACT, IT'S STIPULATED THAT I PAY IT WHEN I HAVE THE MONEY...
AND HE STILL HASN'T PAID IT TO THIS DAY!
SOON, SOON!!

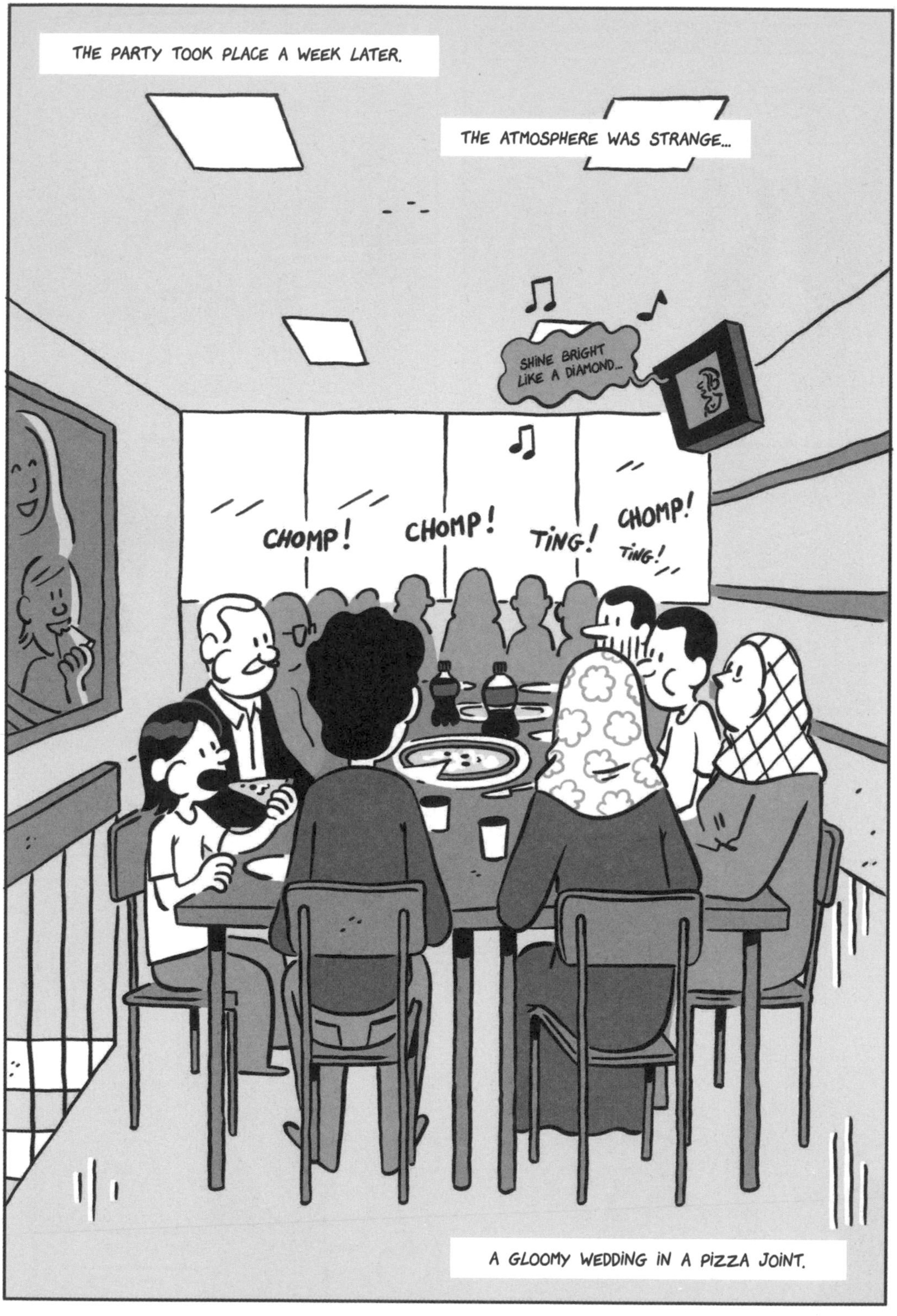
THE PARTY TOOK PLACE A WEEK LATER.
THE ATMOSPHERE WAS STRANGE...
SHINE BRIGHT LIKE A DIAMOND...
CHOMP!
CHOMP!
TING!
CHOMP!
TING!
A GLOOMY WEDDING IN A PIZZA JOINT.

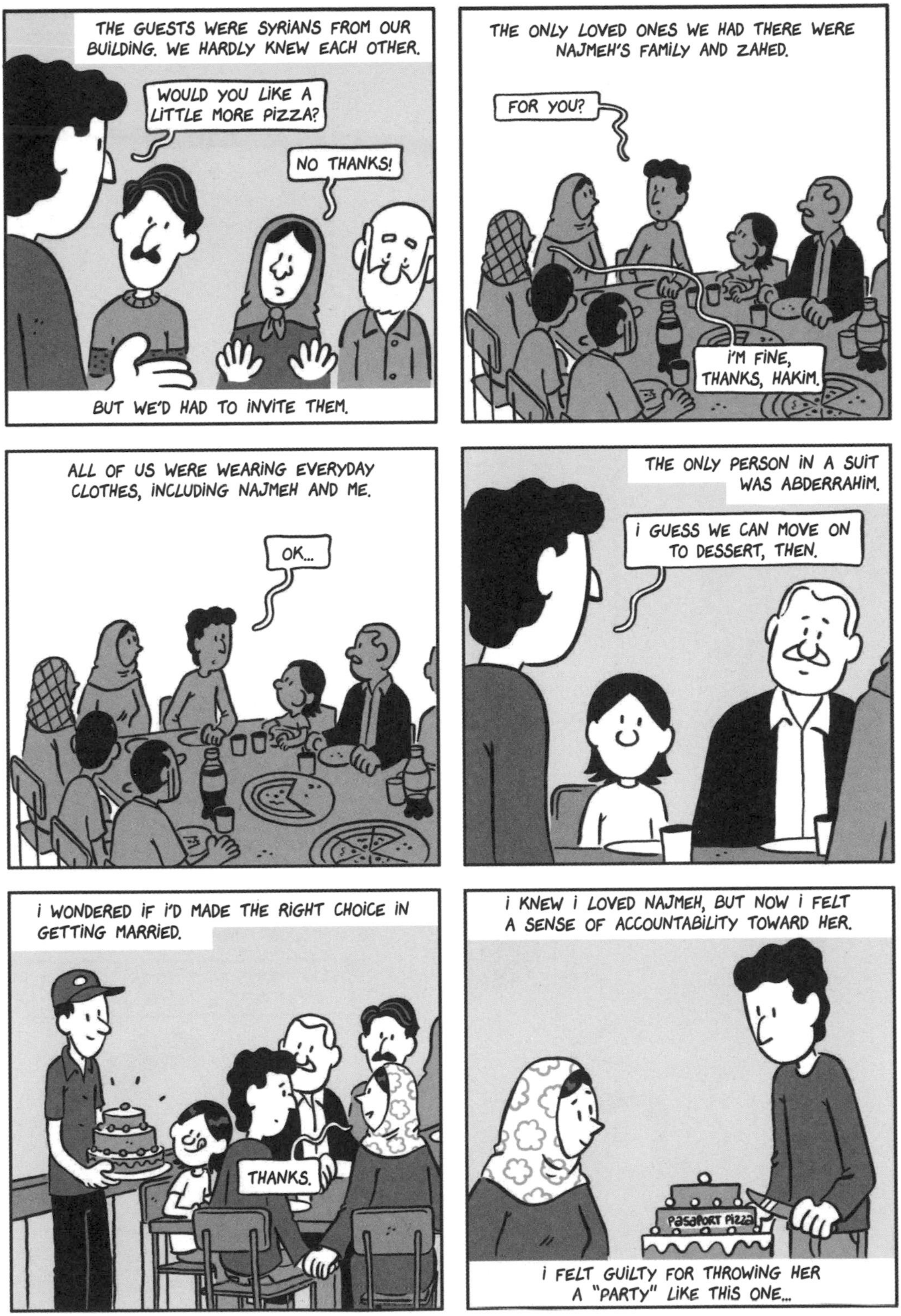
THE GUESTS WERE SYRIANS FROM OUR BUILDING. WE HARDLY KNEW EACH OTHER.
WOULD YOU LIKE A LITTLE MORE PIZZA?
NO THANKS!
BUT WE'D HAD TO INVITE THEM.
THE ONLY LOVED ONES WE HAD THERE WERE NAJMEH'S FAMILY AND ZAHED.
FOR YOU?
I'M FINE, THANKS, HAKIM.
ALL OF US WERE WEARING EVERYDAY CLOTHES, INCLUDING NAJMEH AND ME.
OK...
THE ONLY PERSON IN A SUIT WAS ABDERRAHIM.
I GUESS WE CAN MOVE ON TO DESSERT, THEN.
I WONDERED IF I'D MADE THE RIGHT CHOICE IN GETTING MARRIED.
THANKS.
I KNEW I LOVED NAJMEH, BUT NOW I FELT A SENSE OF ACCOUNTABILITY TOWARD HER.
PASAPORT PIZZA
I FELT GUILTY FOR THROWING HER A "PARTY" LIKE THIS ONE...

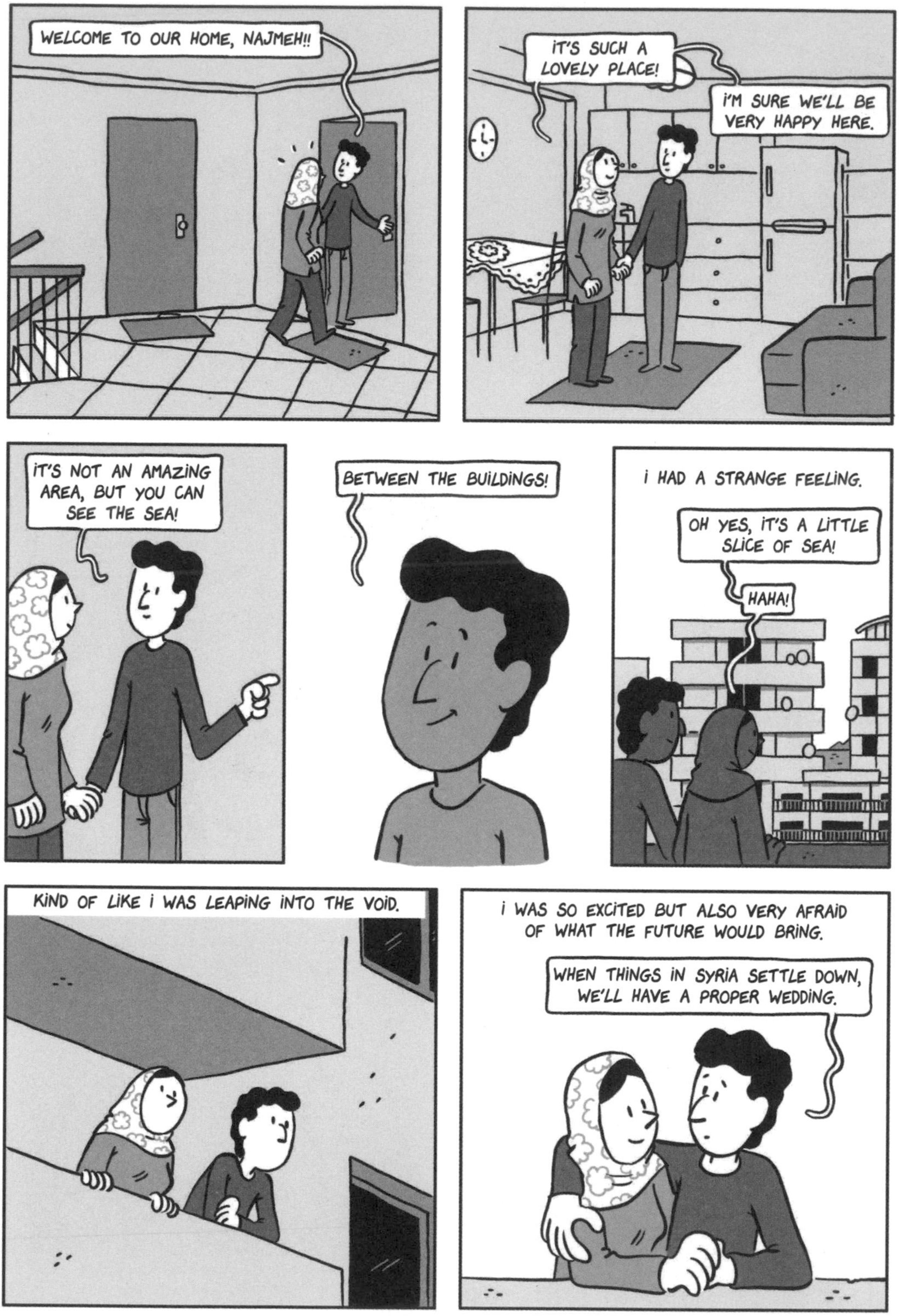
WELCOME TO OUR HOME, NAJMEH!!
IT'S SUCH A LOVELY PLACE!
I'M SURE WE'LL BE VERY HAPPY HERE.
IT'S NOT AN AMAZING AREA, BUT YOU CAN SEE THE SEA!
BETWEEN THE BUILDINGS!
I HAD A STRANGE FEELING.
OH YES, IT'S A LITTLE SLICE OF SEA!
HAHA!
KIND OF LIKE I WAS LEAPING INTO THE VOID.
I WAS SO EXCITED BUT ALSO VERY AFRAID OF WHAT THE FUTURE WOULD BRING.
WHEN THINGS IN SYRIA SETTLE DOWN, WE'LL HAVE A PROPER WEDDING.

IN THE DAYS THAT FOLLOWED, WE SPENT A LOT OF TIME TOGETHER, JUST THE TWO OF US. ABDERRAHIM LENT US HIS CAR AND WE WENT ALL OVER THE CITY.

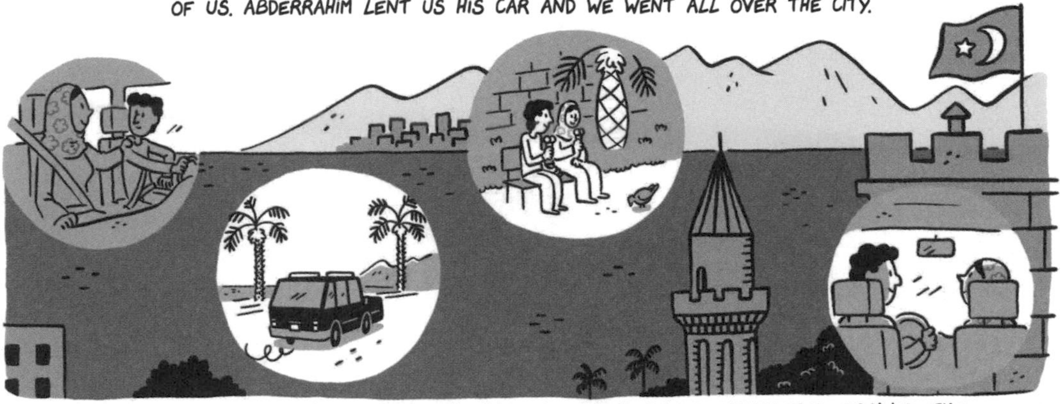

THIS WOULD BE OUR ONLY HONEYMOON, SINCE MY FINANCES WERE COMPLETELY DRAINED. THE WEDDING HAD USED UP ALL MY SAVINGS, AND IT WAS BECOMING URGENT THAT I FIND WORK.

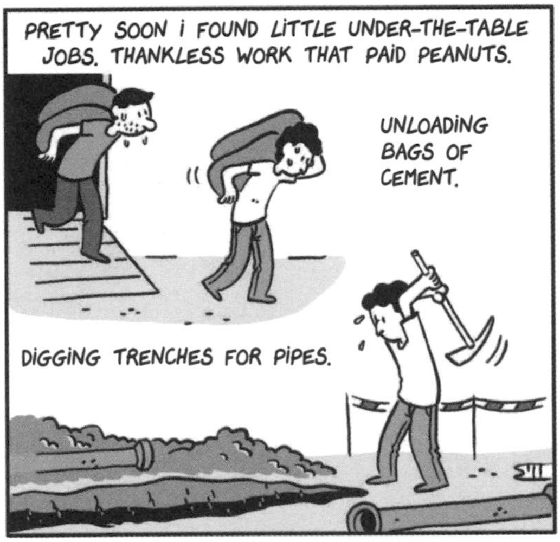
PRETTY SOON I FOUND LITTLE UNDER-THE-TABLE JOBS. THANKLESS WORK THAT PAID PEANUTS.
UNLOADING BAGS OF CEMENT.
DIGGING TRENCHES FOR PIPES.

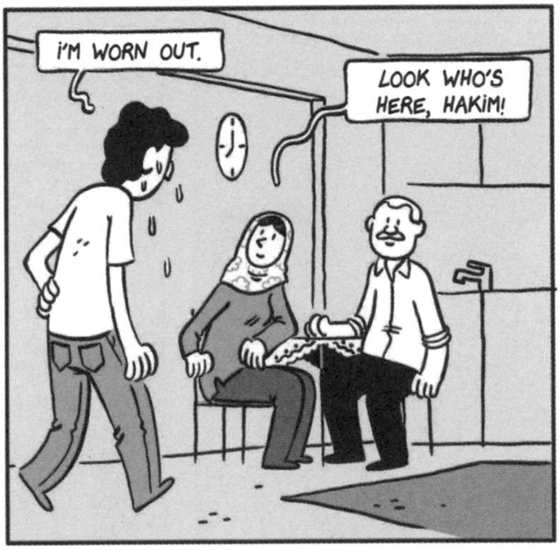
I'M WORN OUT.
LOOK WHO'S HERE, HAKIM!

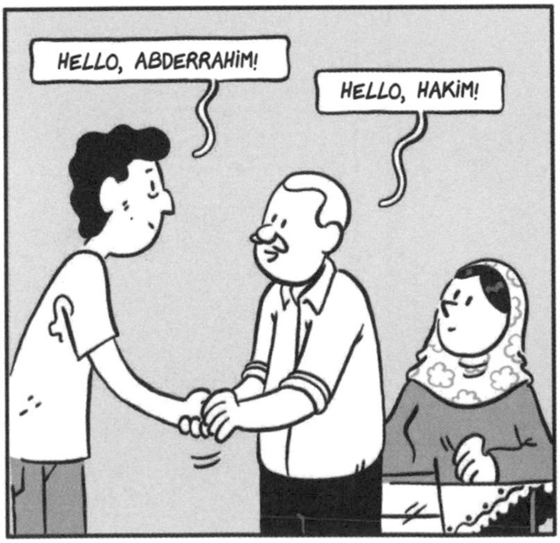
HELLO, ABDERRAHIM!
HELLO, HAKIM!

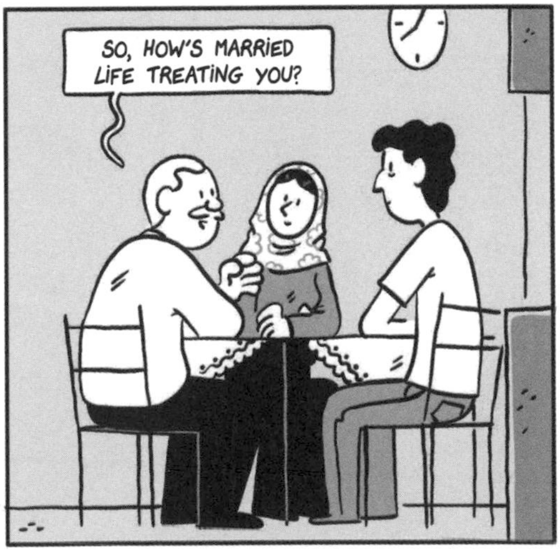
SO, HOW'S MARRIED LIFE TREATING YOU?

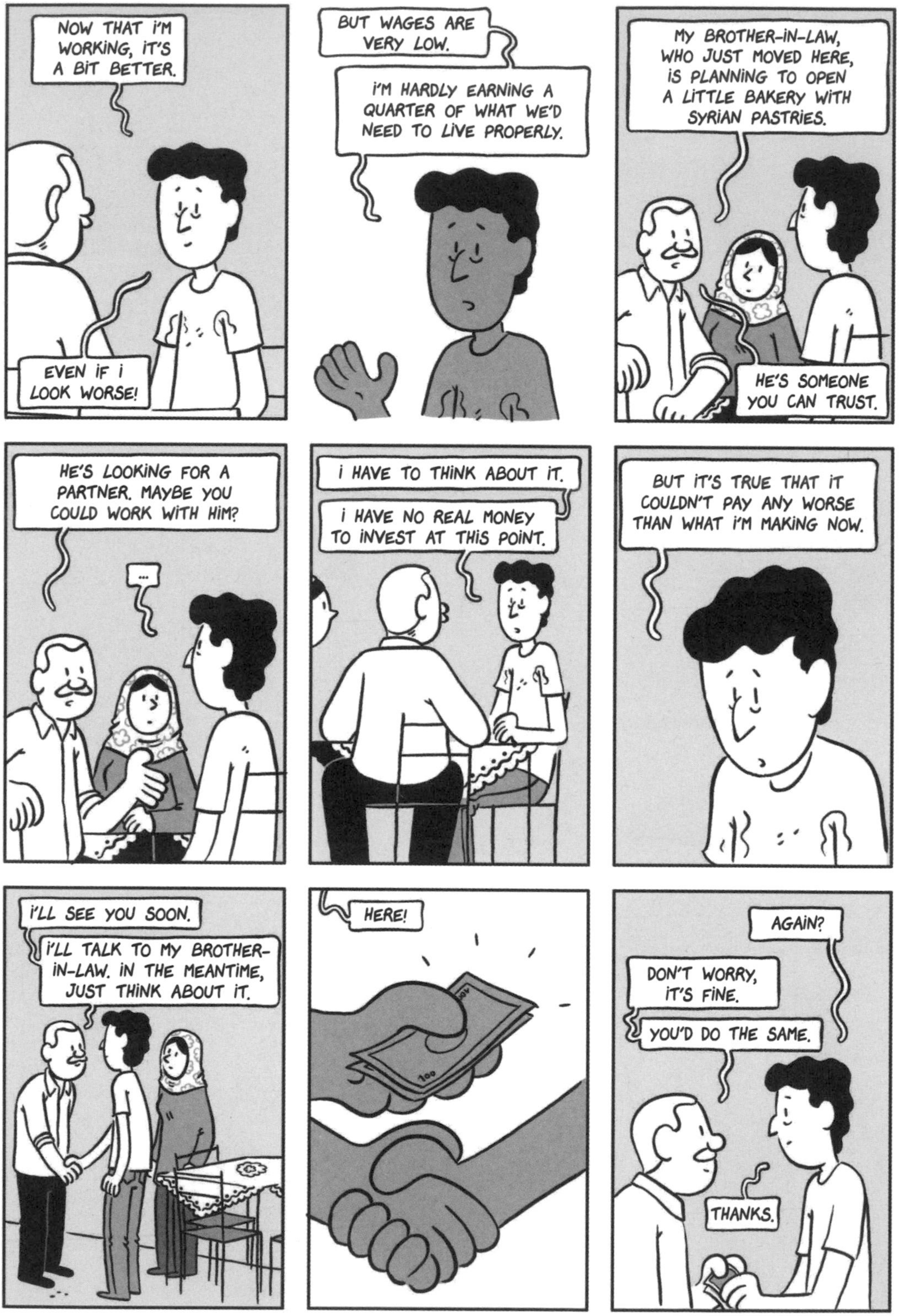
NOW THAT I'M WORKING, IT'S A BIT BETTER.
EVEN IF I LOOK WORSE!
BUT WAGES ARE VERY LOW.
I'M HARDLY EARNING A QUARTER OF WHAT WE'D NEED TO LIVE PROPERLY.
MY BROTHER-IN-LAW, WHO JUST MOVED HERE, IS PLANNING TO OPEN A LITTLE BAKERY WITH SYRIAN PASTRIES.
HE'S SOMEONE YOU CAN TRUST.
HE'S LOOKING FOR A PARTNER. MAYBE YOU COULD WORK WITH HIM?
...
I HAVE TO THINK ABOUT IT.
I HAVE NO REAL MONEY TO INVEST AT THIS POINT.
BUT IT'S TRUE THAT IT COULDN'T PAY ANY WORSE THAN WHAT I'M MAKING NOW.
I'LL SEE YOU SOON.
I'LL TALK TO MY BROTHER-IN-LAW. IN THE MEANTIME, JUST THINK ABOUT IT.
HERE!
AGAIN?
DON'T WORRY, IT'S FINE.
YOU'D DO THE SAME.
THANKS.

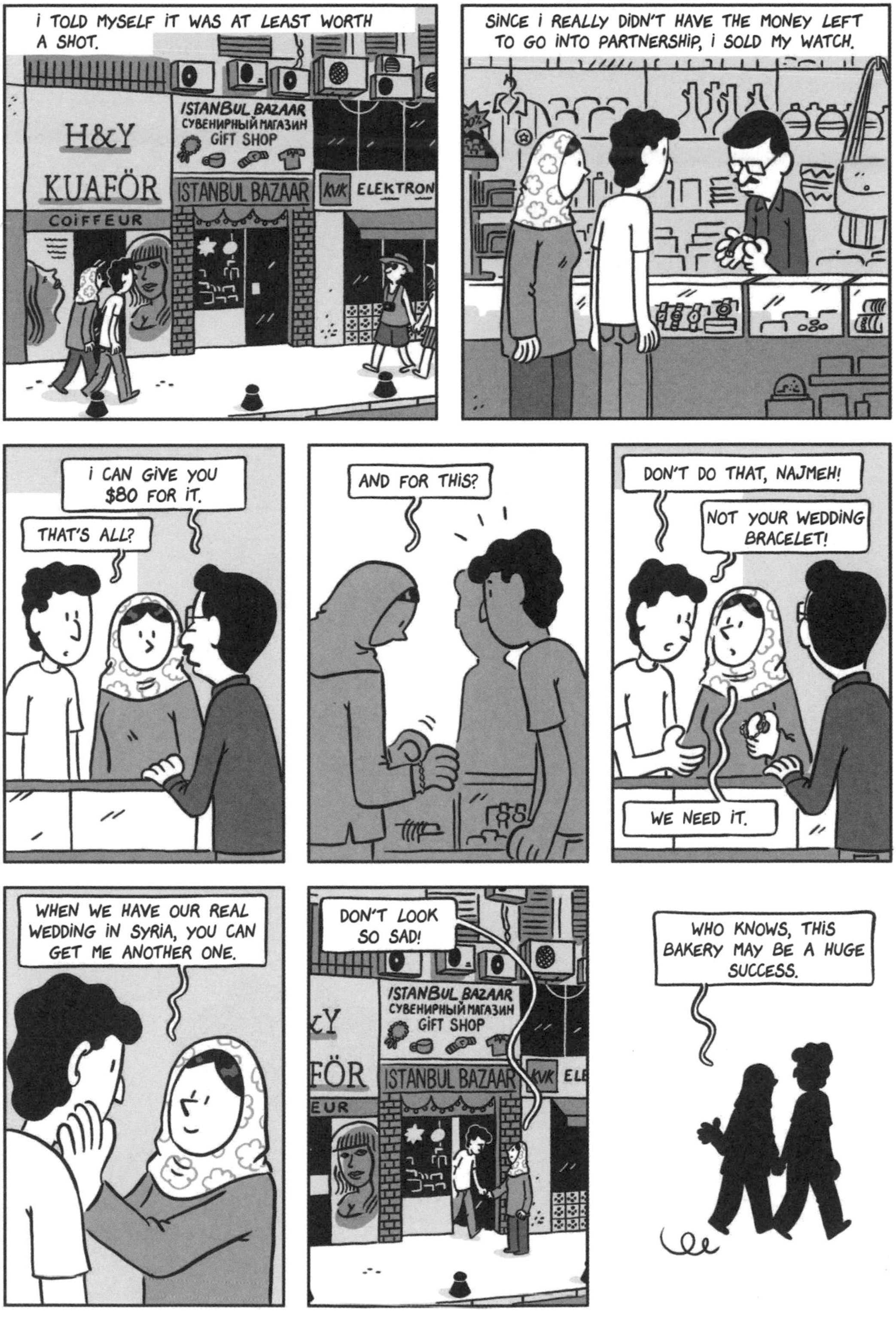
I TOLD MYSELF IT WAS AT LEAST WORTH A SHOT.
H&Y KUAFÖR
COIFFEUR
ISTANBUL BAZAAR
СУВЕНИРНЫЙ МАГАЗИН
GIFT SHOP
ISTANBUL BAZAAR
KVK ELEKTRON
SINCE I REALLY DIDN'T HAVE THE MONEY LEFT TO GO INTO PARTNERSHIP, I SOLD MY WATCH.
I CAN GIVE YOU $80 FOR IT.
THAT'S ALL?
AND FOR THIS?
DON'T DO THAT, NAJMEH!
NOT YOUR WEDDING BRACELET!
WE NEED IT.
WHEN WE HAVE OUR REAL WEDDING IN SYRIA, YOU CAN GET ME ANOTHER ONE.
DON'T LOOK SO SAD!
ISTANBUL BAZAAR
СУВЕНИРНЫЙ МАГАЗИН
GIFT SHOP
ISTANBUL BAZAAR
WHO KNOWS, THIS BAKERY MAY BE A HUGE SUCCESS.

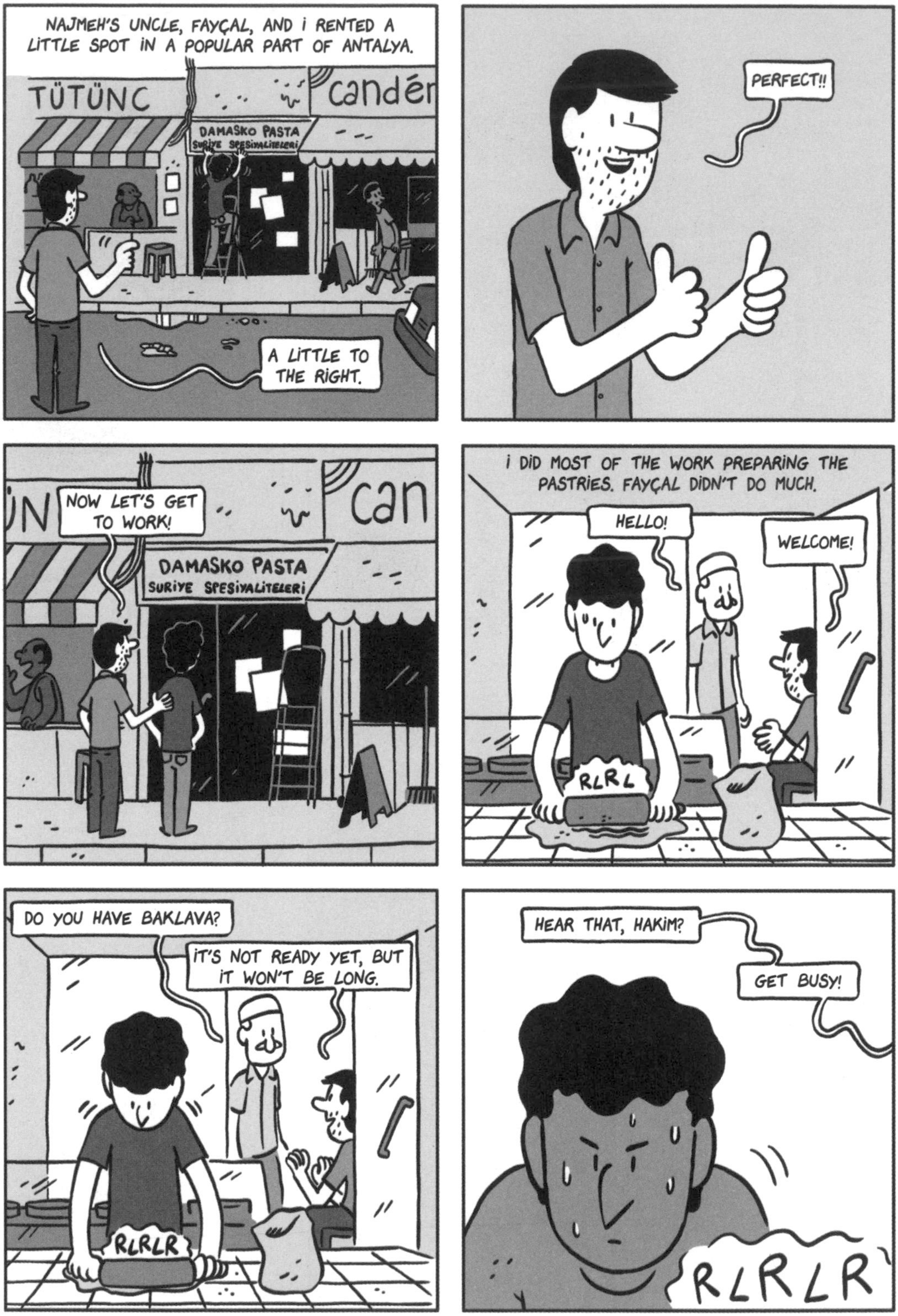
NAJMEH'S UNCLE, FAYÇAL, AND I RENTED A LITTLE SPOT IN A POPULAR PART OF ANTALYA.
TÜTÜNC
candér
DAMASKO PASTA
SURIYE SPESIYALITELERI
A LITTLE TO THE RIGHT.
PERFECT!!
NOW LET'S GET TO WORK!
DAMASKO PASTA
SURIYE SPESIYALITELERI
I DID MOST OF THE WORK PREPARING THE PASTRIES. FAYÇAL DIDN'T DO MUCH.
HELLO!
WELCOME!
RLRL
DO YOU HAVE BAKLAVA?
IT'S NOT READY YET, BUT IT WON'T BE LONG.
RLRLR
HEAR THAT, HAKIM?
GET BUSY!
RLRLR

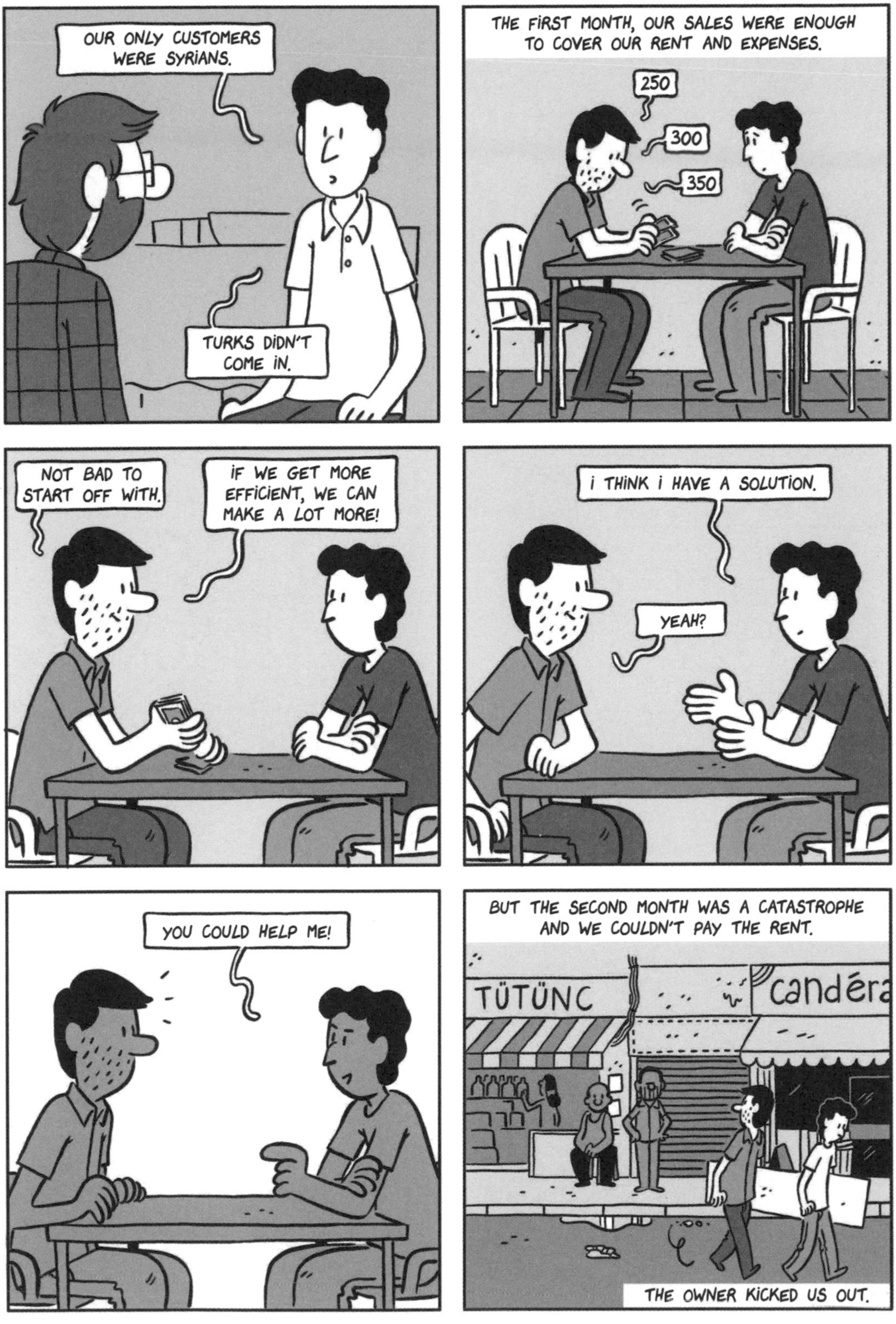
OUR ONLY CUSTOMERS WERE SYRIANS.
TURKS DIDN'T COME IN.
THE FIRST MONTH, OUR SALES WERE ENOUGH TO COVER OUR RENT AND EXPENSES.
250
300
350
NOT BAD TO START OFF WITH.
IF WE GET MORE EFFICIENT, WE CAN MAKE A LOT MORE!
I THINK I HAVE A SOLUTION.
YEAH?
YOU COULD HELP ME!
BUT THE SECOND MONTH WAS A CATASTROPHE AND WE COULDN'T PAY THE RENT.
TÜTÜNC
candéra
THE OWNER KICKED US OUT.

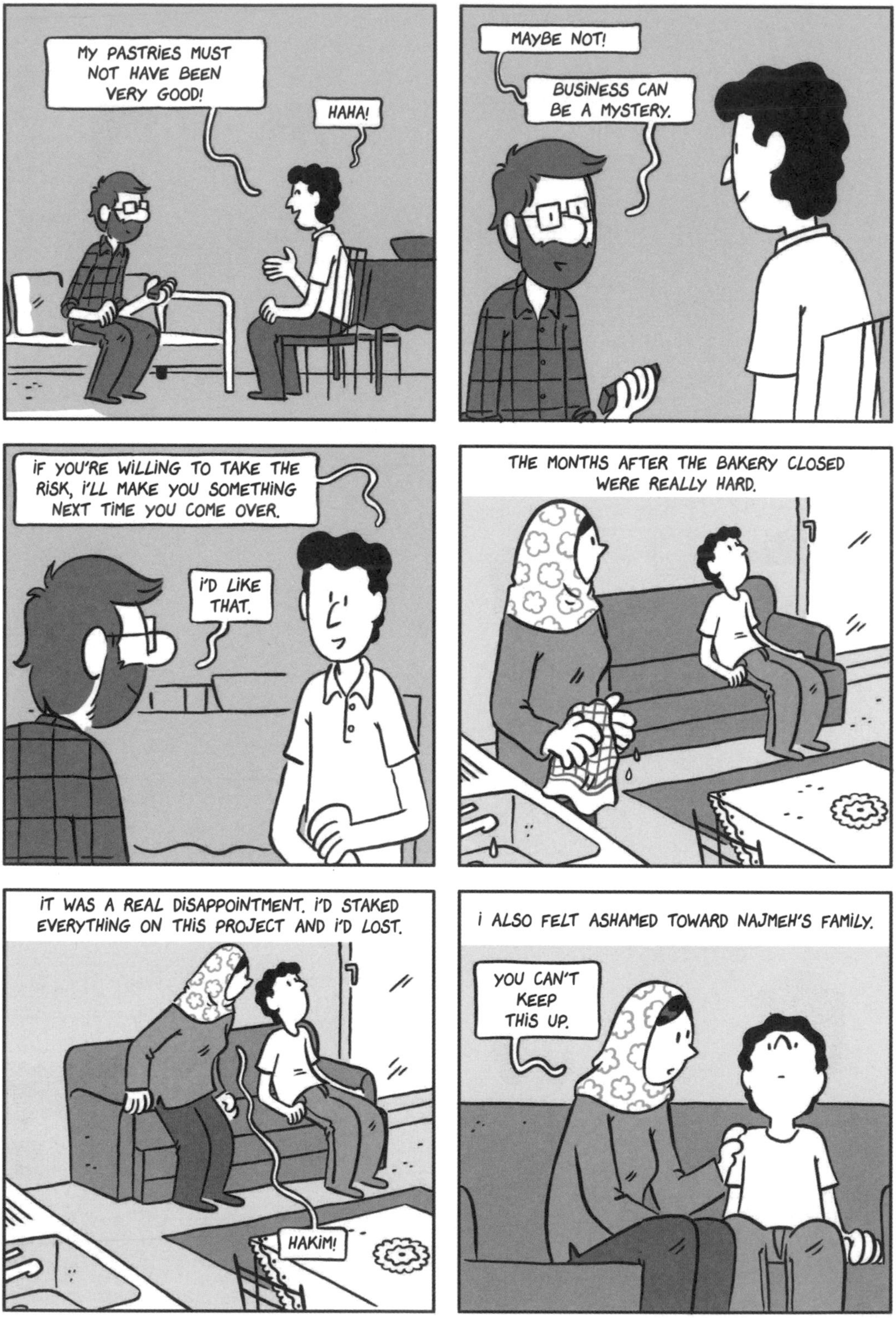
MY PASTRIES MUST NOT HAVE BEEN VERY GOOD!
HAHA!
MAYBE NOT!
BUSINESS CAN BE A MYSTERY.
IF YOU'RE WILLING TO TAKE THE RISK, I'LL MAKE YOU SOMETHING NEXT TIME YOU COME OVER.
I'D LIKE THAT.
THE MONTHS AFTER THE BAKERY CLOSED WERE REALLY HARD.
IT WAS A REAL DISAPPOINTMENT. I'D STAKED EVERYTHING ON THIS PROJECT AND I'D LOST.
HAKIM!
I ALSO FELT ASHAMED TOWARD NAJMEH'S FAMILY.
YOU CAN'T KEEP THIS UP.

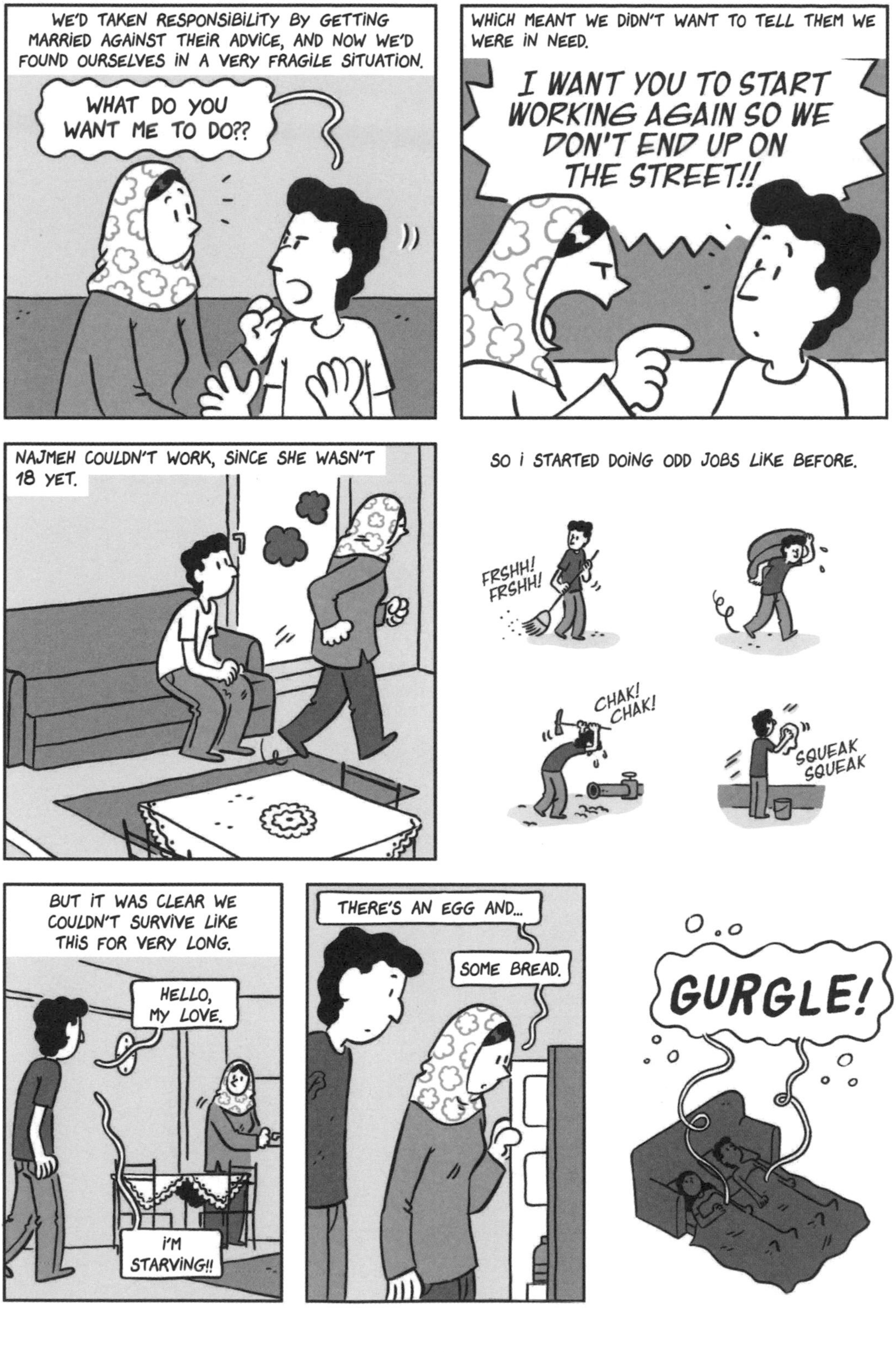
WE'D TAKEN RESPONSIBILITY BY GETTING MARRIED AGAINST THEIR ADVICE, AND NOW WE'D FOUND OURSELVES IN A VERY FRAGILE SITUATION.
WHAT DO YOU WANT ME TO DO??
WHICH MEANT WE DIDN'T WANT TO TELL THEM WE WERE IN NEED.
I WANT YOU TO START WORKING AGAIN SO WE DON'T END UP ON THE STREET!!
NAJMEH COULDN'T WORK, SINCE SHE WASN'T 18 YET.
SO I STARTED DOING ODD JOBS LIKE BEFORE.
FRSHH! FRSHH!
CHAK! CHAK!
SQUEAK SQUEAK
BUT IT WAS CLEAR WE COULDN'T SURVIVE LIKE THIS FOR VERY LONG.
HELLO, MY LOVE.
I'M STARVING!!
THERE'S AN EGG AND...
SOME BREAD.
GURGLE!

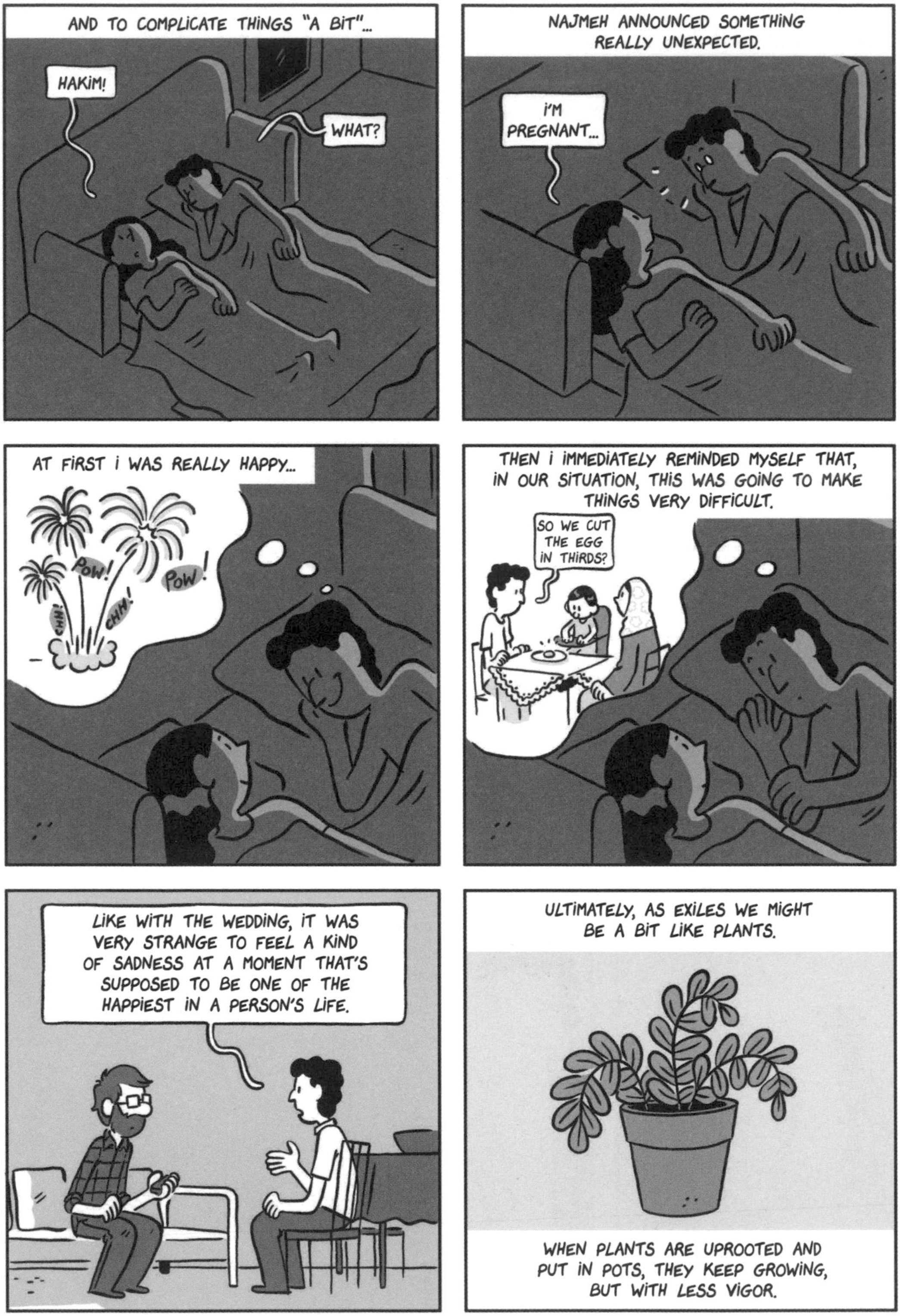
AND TO COMPLICATE THINGS "A BIT"...
HAKIM!
WHAT?
NAJMEH ANNOUNCED SOMETHING REALLY UNEXPECTED.
I'M PREGNANT...
AT FIRST I WAS REALLY HAPPY...
POW!
POW!
CHH!
CHH!
THEN I IMMEDIATELY REMINDED MYSELF THAT, IN OUR SITUATION, THIS WAS GOING TO MAKE THINGS VERY DIFFICULT.
SO WE CUT THE EGG IN THIRDS?
LIKE WITH THE WEDDING, IT WAS VERY STRANGE TO FEEL A KIND OF SADNESS AT A MOMENT THAT'S SUPPOSED TO BE ONE OF THE HAPPIEST IN A PERSON'S LIFE.
ULTIMATELY, AS EXILES WE MIGHT BE A BIT LIKE PLANTS.
WHEN PLANTS ARE UPROOTED AND PUT IN POTS, THEY KEEP GROWING, BUT WITH LESS VIGOR.

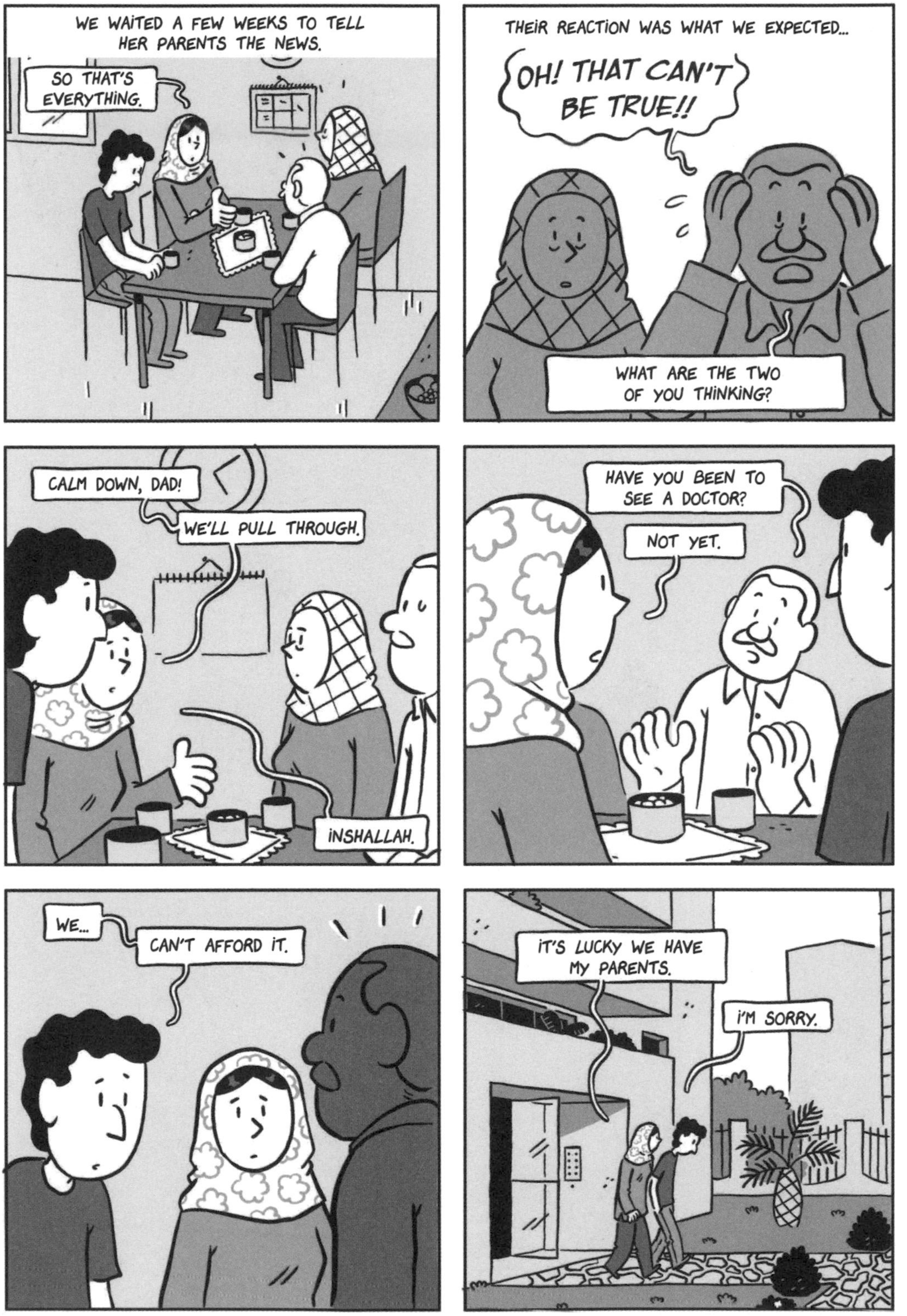
WE WAITED A FEW WEEKS TO TELL HER PARENTS THE NEWS.
SO THAT'S EVERYTHING.
THEIR REACTION WAS WHAT WE EXPECTED...
OH! THAT CAN'T BE TRUE!!
WHAT ARE THE TWO OF YOU THINKING?
CALM DOWN, DAD!
WE'LL PULL THROUGH.
INSHALLAH.
HAVE YOU BEEN TO SEE A DOCTOR?
NOT YET.
WE...
CAN'T AFFORD IT.
IT'S LUCKY WE HAVE MY PARENTS.
I'M SORRY.

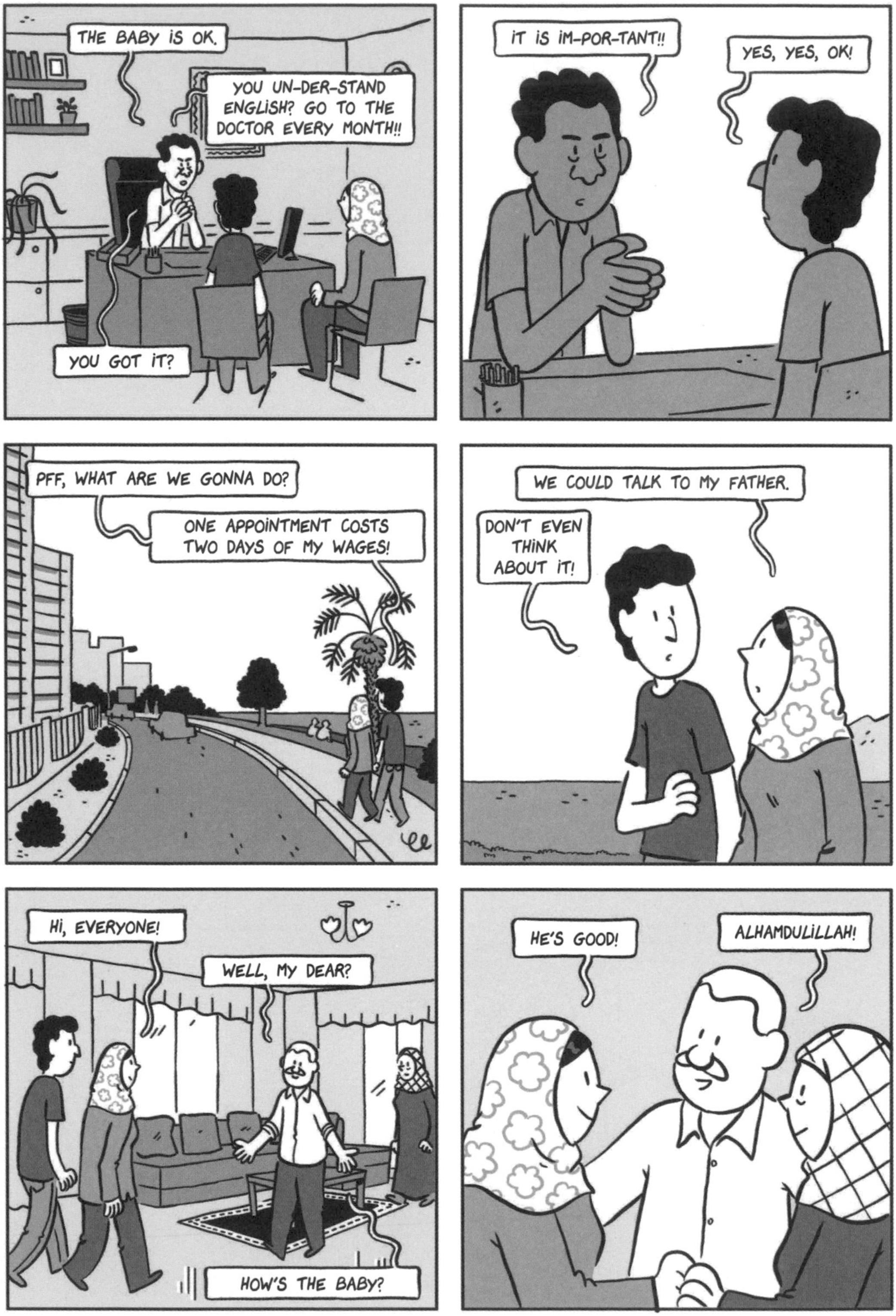
THE BABY IS OK.
YOU UN-DER-STAND ENGLISH? GO TO THE DOCTOR EVERY MONTH!!
YOU GOT IT?
IT IS IM-POR-TANT!!
YES, YES, OK!
PFF, WHAT ARE WE GONNA DO?
ONE APPOINTMENT COSTS TWO DAYS OF MY WAGES!
WE COULD TALK TO MY FATHER.
DON'T EVEN THINK ABOUT IT!
HI, EVERYONE!
WELL, MY DEAR?
HOW'S THE BABY?
HE'S GOOD!
ALHAMDULILLAH!

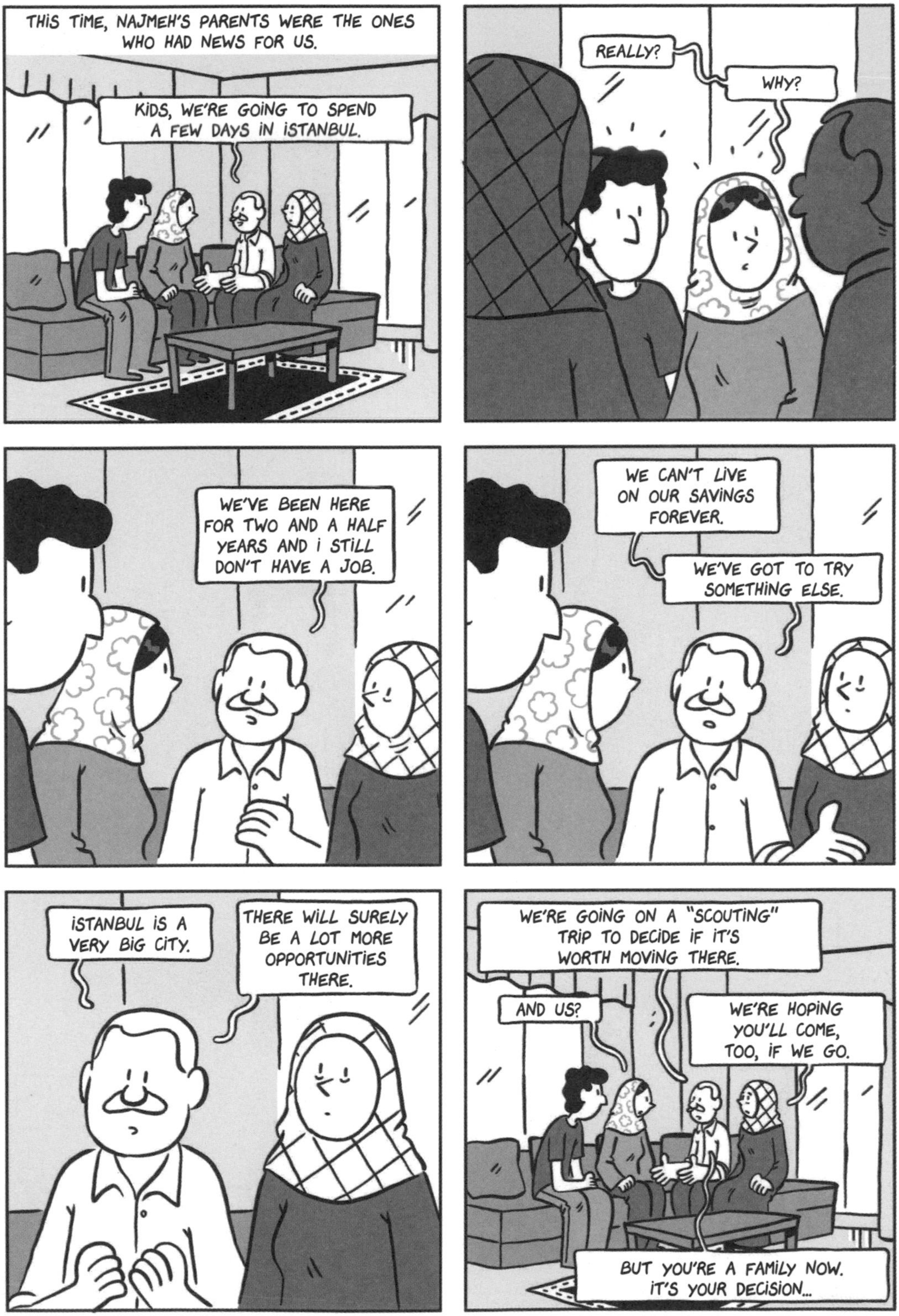
THIS TIME, NAJMEH'S PARENTS WERE THE ONES WHO HAD NEWS FOR US.
KIDS, WE'RE GOING TO SPEND A FEW DAYS IN ISTANBUL.
REALLY?
WHY?
WE'VE BEEN HERE FOR TWO AND A HALF YEARS AND I STILL DON'T HAVE A JOB.
WE CAN'T LIVE ON OUR SAVINGS FOREVER.
WE'VE GOT TO TRY SOMETHING ELSE.
ISTANBUL IS A VERY BIG CITY.
THERE WILL SURELY BE A LOT MORE OPPORTUNITIES THERE.
WE'RE GOING ON A "SCOUTING" TRIP TO DECIDE IF IT'S WORTH MOVING THERE.
AND US?
WE'RE HOPING YOU'LL COME, TOO, IF WE GO.
BUT YOU'RE A FAMILY NOW. IT'S YOUR DECISION...

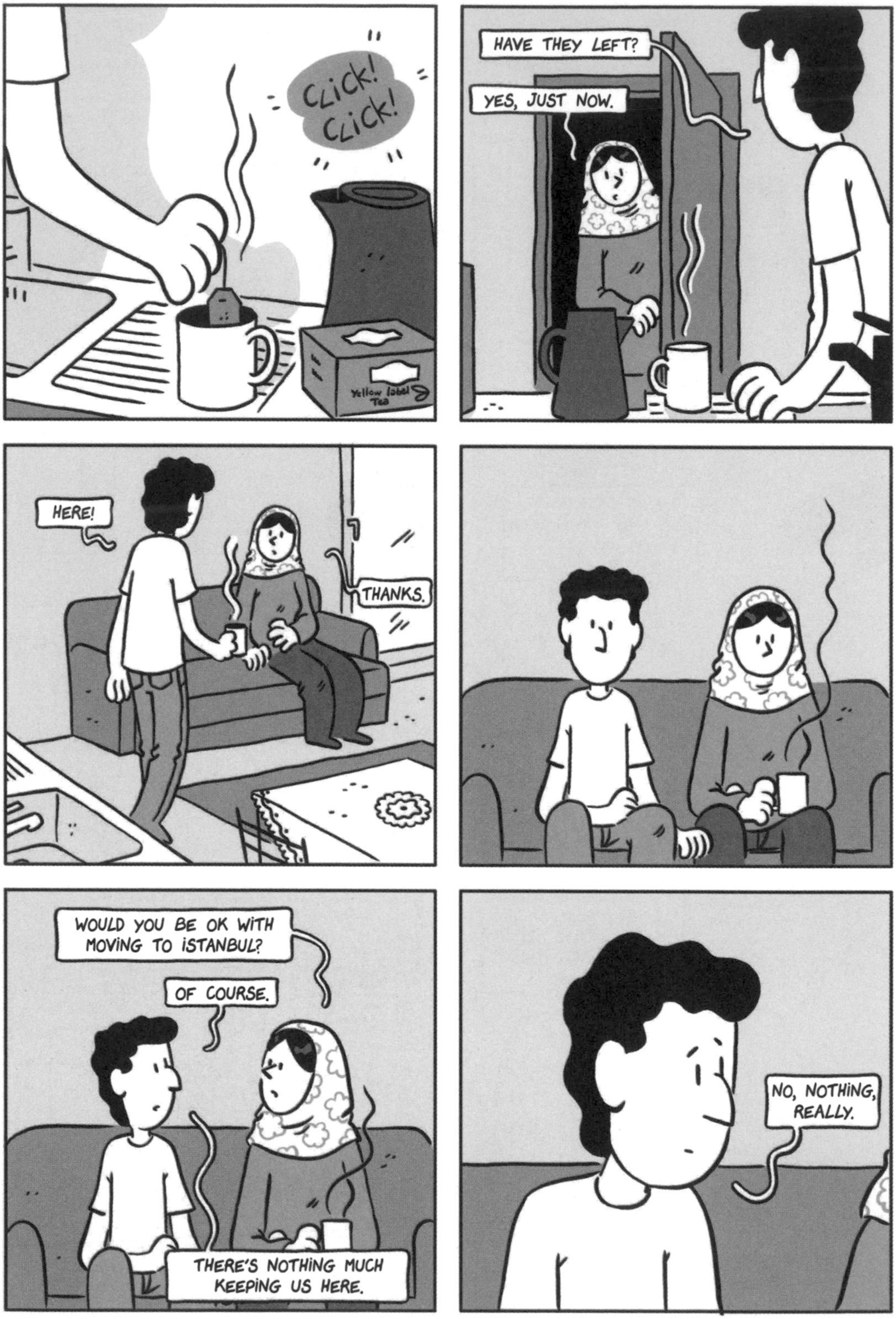
CLICK! CLICK!
Yellow label Tea
HAVE THEY LEFT?
YES, JUST NOW.
HERE!
THANKS.
WOULD YOU BE OK WITH MOVING TO İSTANBUL?
OF COURSE.
THERE'S NOTHING MUCH KEEPING US HERE.
NO, NOTHING, REALLY.

AND THIS WAY, OUR BABY WILL GROW UP WITH HIS GRANDPARENTS, HIS AUNTS AND UNCLES...

RIGHT, BABY?

DO YOU REALLY THINK WE'LL GET TO GO BACK TO SYRIA SOMEDAY?

i HOPE SO.

i HOPE OUR CHILD WILL KNOW MY FAMILY, MY FRIENDS, MY NEIGHBORHOOD.

i HOPE JAWAD WILL SHOW UP ONE DAY AND SAY:

i WAS LAYING LOW UNTIL THINGS CALMED DOWN.

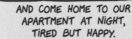

i HOPE i'LL SMELL THE FLOWERS AT MY NURSERY AGAIN.

AND COME HOME TO OUR APARTMENT AT NIGHT, TIRED BUT HAPPY.

DADDY!!

i HOPE.

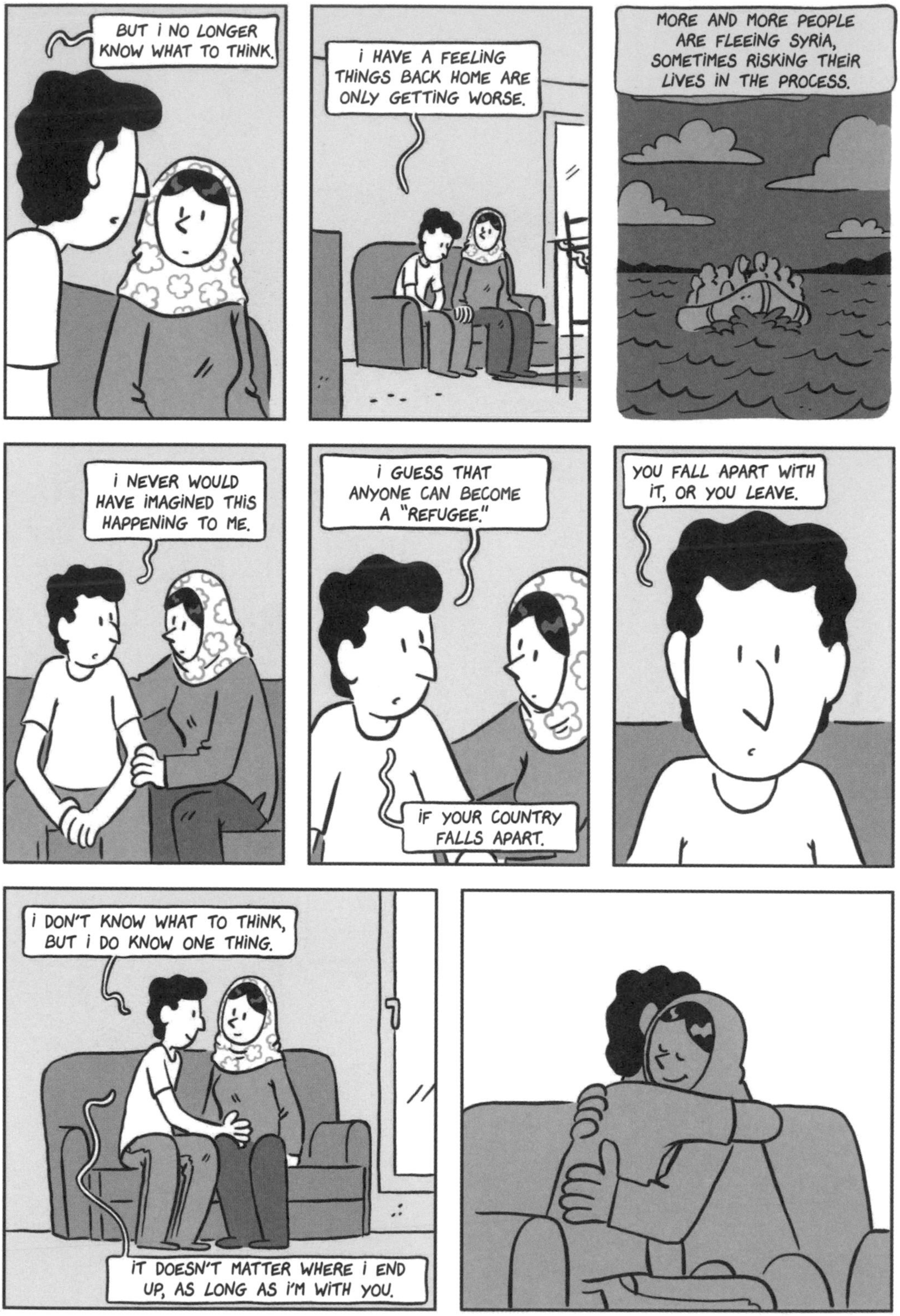

BUT i NO LONGER KNOW WHAT TO THiNK.
i HAVE A FEELiNG THiNGS BACK HOME ARE ONLY GETTiNG WORSE.
MORE AND MORE PEOPLE ARE FLEEiNG SYRiA, SOMETiMES RiSKiNG THEiR LiVES iN THE PROCESS.
i NEVER WOULD HAVE iMAGiNED THiS HAPPENiNG TO ME.
i GUESS THAT ANYONE CAN BECOME A "REFUGEE."
iF YOUR COUNTRY FALLS APART.
YOU FALL APART WiTH iT, OR YOU LEAVE.
i DON'T KNOW WHAT TO THiNK, BUT i DO KNOW ONE THiNG.
iT DOESN'T MATTER WHERE i END UP, AS LONG AS i'M WiTH YOU.

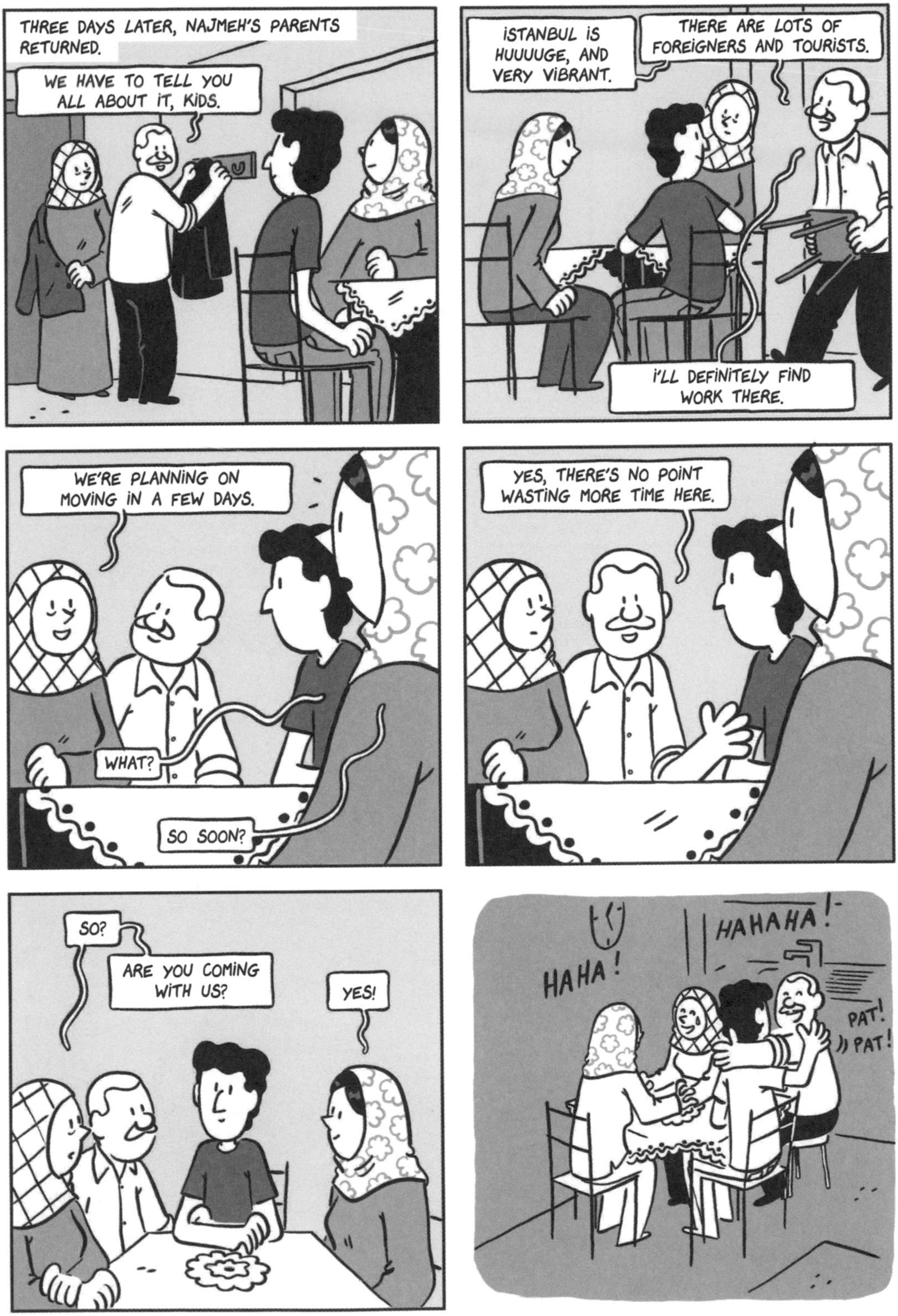
THREE DAYS LATER, NAJMEH'S PARENTS RETURNED.
WE HAVE TO TELL YOU ALL ABOUT IT, KIDS.
İSTANBUL İS HUUUUGE, AND VERY VİBRANT.
THERE ARE LOTS OF FOREİGNERS AND TOURİSTS.
İ'LL DEFİNİTELY FİND WORK THERE.
WE'RE PLANNİNG ON MOVİNG İN A FEW DAYS.
WHAT?
SO SOON?
YES, THERE'S NO POİNT WASTİNG MORE TİME HERE.
SO?
ARE YOU COMİNG WİTH US?
YES!
HAHA!
HAHAHA!
PAT! PAT!

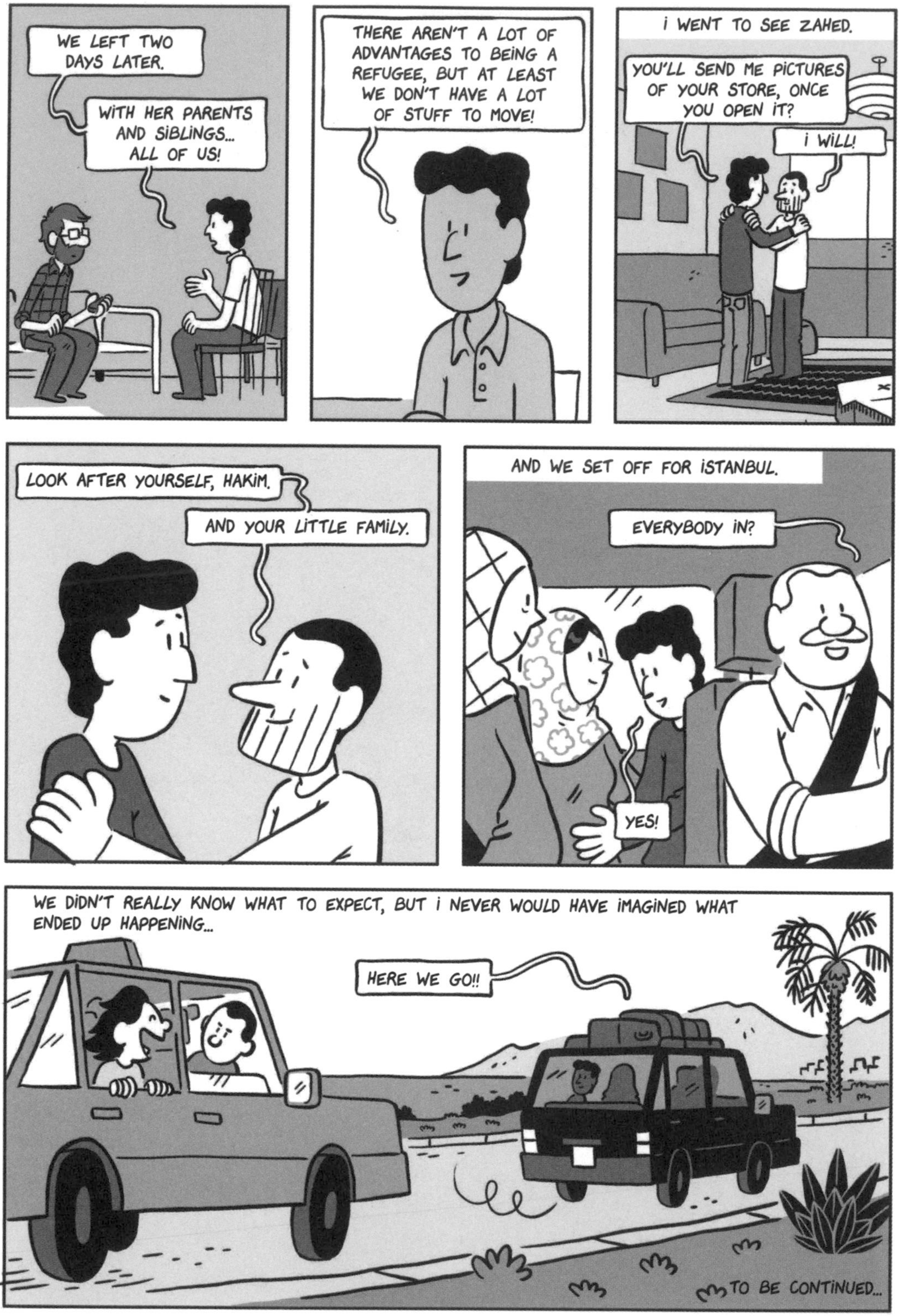
WE LEFT TWO DAYS LATER.
WITH HER PARENTS AND SIBLINGS... ALL OF US!
THERE AREN'T A LOT OF ADVANTAGES TO BEING A REFUGEE, BUT AT LEAST WE DON'T HAVE A LOT OF STUFF TO MOVE!
I WENT TO SEE ZAHED.
YOU'LL SEND ME PICTURES OF YOUR STORE, ONCE YOU OPEN IT?
I WILL!
LOOK AFTER YOURSELF, HAKIM.
AND YOUR LITTLE FAMILY.
AND WE SET OFF FOR ISTANBUL.
EVERYBODY IN?
YES!
WE DIDN'T REALLY KNOW WHAT TO EXPECT, BUT I NEVER WOULD HAVE IMAGINED WHAT ENDED UP HAPPENING...
HERE WE GO!!
TO BE CONTINUED...

Thanks to Yannick Lejeune, my editor, for his help and advice; to Patricia Haessig-Crevel and Laura Crevel-Floyd for connecting me with Hakim and for their help when the project ran into issues; to Manuel, Bouchra Petit, and Michel Nieto, the interpreters, for their indispensable aid; to Patricia Toulmé for her help with trimming as the deadline approached; to the teams at Delcourt (especially Leslie) who helped this book see the light of day; to the CNL for its support of this project; and my heartfelt thanks to Hakim, Najmeh, Hadi, and Sébastien for their patience and generosity.

Library of Congress Cataloging-in-Publication Data

Names: Toulmé, Fabien, 1980– author. | Chute, Hannah, 1992– translator.
Title: Hakim's odyssey / Fabien Toulmé ; translated by Hannah Chute.
Other titles: Odyssée d'Hakim. English
Description: University Park, Pennsylvania : Graphic Mundi, [2021]– | "Originally published as L'Odyssée d'Hakim, volume 1 by Fabien Toulmé, Editions Delcourt, 2018."—Book 1. | Contents: Book 1. From Syria to Turkey
Summary: "An account, in graphic novel format, of a young Syrian refugee and how war forced him to leave everything behind, including his family, his friends, his home, and his business. This narrative follows his travels from Syria, to Lebanon, Jordan, and Turkey"—Provided by publisher.
Identifiers: LCCN 2021017308 | ISBN 9781637790007 (hardback)
Subjects: LCSH: Refugees—Syria—Comic books, strips, etc. | Forced migration—Syria—Comic books, strips, etc. | Syria—History—Civil War, 2011—-Refugees—Comic books, strips, etc. | LCGFT: Graphic novels.
Classification: LCC PN6747.T68 03913 2021 | DDC 741.5/944—dc23
LC record available at https://lccn.loc.gov/2021017308

Printed in Lithuania
Published by The Pennsylvania State University Press,
University Park, PA 16802-1003

graphic mundi
drawing our worlds together

Graphic Mundi is an imprint of The Pennsylvania State University Press.

Translated by Hannah Chute
Additional lettering and art reconstruction by Zen

Originally published as *L'Odyssée d'Hakim*, volume 1
by Fabien Toulmé

The Pennsylvania State University Press is a member of the Association of University Presses.

It is the policy of The Pennsylvania State University Press to use acid-free paper. Publications on uncoated stock satisfy the minimum requirements of American National Standard for Information Sciences—Permanence of Paper for Printed Library Material, ANSI Z39.48–1992.